Brief Contents

Brief Contents

W9-BXN-161

Focus on
Writing
Paragraphs and Essays

Focus on
Writing
Paragraphs and Essays

Laurie G. Kirszner
University of the Sciences in Philadelphia

Stephen R. Mandell
Drexel University

with additional teaching tips and ESL tips by
Linda Mason Austin, McLennan Community College

Bedford/St. Martin's   Boston ◆ New York

For Bedford/St. Martin's

Developmental Editor: Joelle Hann
Senior Production Editor: Michael Weber
Senior Production Supervisor: Dennis J. Conroy
Marketing Manager: Casey Carroll
Art Director: Lucy Krikorian
Text Design: Claire Seng-Niemoeller
Copy Editor: Alice Vigliani
Photo Research: Melissa Cliver Photography
Cover Design: Donna Lee Dennison
Cover Photo: Veer Digital Vision Photography
Composition: Stratford/TexTech
Printing and Binding: R.R. Donnelley & Sons Company

President: Joan E. Feinberg
Editorial Director: Denise B. Wydra
Editor in Chief: Karen S. Henry
Director of Development: Erica T. Appel
Director of Marketing: Karen Melton Soeltz
Director of Editing, Design, and Production: Marcia Cohen
Managing Editor: Shuli Traub

Library of Congress Control Number: 2007939983

Manufactured in the United States of America.

2   1   0   9   8
f   e   d   c   b

For information, write: Bedford/St. Martin's, 75 Arlington Street, Boston, MA 02116
(617-399-4000)

ISBN-10: 0-312-44088-X   ISBN-13: 978-0-312-44088-6   (Instructor's Annotated Edition)
ISBN-10: 0-312-43423-5   ISBN-13: 978-0-312-43423-6   (Student Edition)

Acknowledgments

Acknowledgments and copyrights appear at the back of the book on page 681, which constitutes an extension of the copyright page.

Preface for Instructors

When we set out to write a new paragraph-to-essay developmental text, we knew what we wanted to accomplish. We wanted *Focus on Writing: Paragraphs and Essays* to reflect two of our central beliefs: first, that in college, writing comes first and second, that students learn writing and grammar skills best in the context of their own writing. We also knew that we had an opportunity to bring developmental textbooks to another level—to recognize who is taking basic writing classes today and to engage them in a new and different way. Our students may be basic writers, but they live in a world of images. We wanted to engage our students with a highly visual book and a contemporary design that reflected the most recent pedagogy about reaching basic writers. We conducted usability testing in classrooms to see how students responded to our books' designs and layouts. Consequently, the pages of *Focus on Writing* have clean, open margins, with the most important information moved directly into the body of the text, and an up-to-date look that takes the needs of today's basic writing students seriously. We also wanted this book to be accessible to all basic writers: the text explanations and instructions are clear and streamlined throughout to make them as transparent as possible.

Still, *Focus on Writing* is most importantly a writing text. For this reason, the book begins with thorough coverage of the writing process and includes extensive writing practice throughout the text. Most chapters open with a writing prompt that asks students to respond to an evocative and contemporary visual. Students practice not only by working through effective exercises but also by applying each chapter's concepts to their own original writing, giving them a sense of ownership of their work. We included lots of grammar support to help basic writers understand and apply the fundamentals of good writing, and our up-to-date exercise topics relate to students as citizens of the world beyond the college campus.

Further, because we know that the issues of the developmental classroom are not limited to writing, *Focus on Writing* offers other resources such

v

as help with college study skills, ESL usage, research skills, test-taking, and critical reading in a format that is flexible enough to support a variety of teaching styles and to meet the needs of individual students.

We wrote this book for our own interested, concerned, and hardworking students, and we tailored the book's approach and content to them. Instead of exercises that reinforce the idea that writing is a dull, pointless, and artificial activity, we chose fresh, contemporary examples (both student and professional) and worked hard to develop interesting exercises and writing assignments. Throughout *Focus on Writing*, we try to talk *to* students, not *at* or *down* to them. We try to be concise without being abrupt, thorough without being repetitive, direct without being rigid, specific without being prescriptive, and flexible without being inconsistent. Our most important goal is simple: to create an engaging text that motivates students to improve their writing and that gives them the tools to do so.

Organization

Focus on Writing: Paragraphs and Essays is divided into three general sections: "Writing Paragraphs and Essays," "Revising and Editing Your Writing," and "Becoming a Critical Reader." The first section is a comprehensive discussion of the writing process. The second section presents thorough coverage of sentence skills, grammar, punctuation, mechanics, and spelling. The third section introduces students to critical reading skills and includes thirteen professional essays and five sample student essays, each illustrating a particular pattern of development. Finally, three appendixes—Appendix A, "Strategies for College Success," Appendix B, "Using Research in Your Writing," and Appendix C, "Taking Standardized Assessment Tests"—provide help with skills that students will need in other courses and on standardized tests.

Features

With *Focus on Writing* we aimed to create a complete and contemporary paragraph-to-essay text for developmental writers in a format that students could relate to. Guided by our "student writing first" philosophy, we created the following innovative features designed to make students' writing practice meaningful, productive, and enjoyable.

The book's striking design is uncluttered and clear while the visual presentation of material helps students stay on track. Lively, eye-catching photographs in every chapter get students writing immediately. The open design uses color, call-out boxes, and highlighting to emphasize

- *Focus on Writing* **content for course management systems** is ready for use with Blackboard, WebCT, and other popular course management systems. For more information about Bedford/ St. Martin's course management offerings, visit **bedfordstmartins .com/cms**.

- *Adjunct Central* at bedfordstmartins.com/adjunctcentral offers a central place for adjuncts to find practical advice for the classroom and downloadable assignments that can be adapted as needed. The site also offers access to the Adjunct Advice blog, links to additional resources, and a free adjunct resource kit.

- *Just-in-Time Teaching* at bedfordstmartins.com/justintime is a library of classroom materials such as handouts, syllabi, tips for peer review exercises and teaching students with disabilities, and more. Perfect for last-minute class preparation, this site is searchable by activity and topic.

Student Resources:

- *The companion Web site* at bedfordstmartins.com/ focusonwriting offers helpful student and instructor resources including downloadable forms and annotated student paragraphs and essays that allow students to learn from strong, unified writing models in an interactive format. It also gives access to *Exercise Central*, the extensive online exercise collection, and to *Re:Writing Basics*.

- *Exercise Central* at **bedfordstmartins.com/focusonwriting** is the largest free collection of grammar and writing exercises available online. This comprehensive resource for skill development contains nearly 9,000 exercises, helping to identify students' strengths and weaknesses, recommend personalized study plans, and provides tutorials for common problems. *Exercise Central* also provides immediate feedback and allows instructors to monitor student progress.

*∗• The *Exercise Central to Go: Writing and Grammar Practices for Basic Writers* **CD-ROM** provides hundreds of practice items from the *Exercise Central* Web site to help students build their writing and editing skills. No Internet connection is necessary.

- *Re:Writing Basics* at **bedfordstmartins.com/rewritingbasics** is an easy-to-navigate Web site that offers the most popular and widely used free resources from Bedford/St. Martin's, including writing and grammar exercises, model documents, instructor resources, help with the writing process, tips on college success and more.

Print Resources

Instructor Resources:

- The *Instructor's Annotated Edition* contains answers to all the practice exercises, plus numerous ESL and teaching tips that offer ideas, reminders, and cross-references that are immediately helpful to teachers at any level.

- *Classroom Resources to Accompany Focus on Writing* offers advice for teaching developmental writing as well as chapter-by-chapter pointers for using *Focus on Writing* in the classroom. It contains answers to all of the book's practice exercises, sample syllabi, additional teaching materials, and full chapters on collaborative learning.

- *Diagnostic and Mastery Tests to Accompany Focus on Writing* offers diagnostic and mastery tests that complement the topics covered in *Focus on Writing*.

- *Transparency Masters to Accompany Focus on Writing* includes numerous models of student writing and is downloadable from the *Focus on Writing* Web site at **bedfordstmartins.com/focusonwriting**.

Student Resources:

- *Supplemental Exercises to Accompany Focus on Writing* provides students with even more practice on essential skills. Perforated pages are easy to copy and distribute.

- *The Bedford/St. Martin's ESL Workbook* includes a broad range of exercises covering grammatical issues for multilingual students of varying language skills and backgrounds. Answers are at the back.

- *From Practice to Mastery* is a study guide for the Florida Basic Skills Exit Tests in reading and writing that gives students all the resources they need to practice for—and pass—the test. It includes pre- and post-tests, abundant practices, and clear instruction on all the skills covered on the exam.

New Media Resources

Many resources are free. Starred titles are free when packaged with the book.

Instructor Resources:

- The *Testing Tool Kit: Writing and Grammar Test Bank* **CD-ROM** allows instructors to create secure, customized tests and quizzes from a pool of nearly 2,000 questions covering 47 topics. It also includes 10 prebuilt diagnostic tests.

annotation of *Teaching Developmental Writing: Background Readings* reflects her deep commitment to scholarship and teaching. We are very grateful for their contributions.

We thank Kristen Blanco, Stephanie Hopkins, Judith Lechner, Carolyn Lengel, Carol Sullivan, Jessica Carroll, Charlotte Gale, and Pamela Gerth for their contributions to the exercises and writing activities in the text, and Linda Stine for developing the PowerPoint presentation featured on the *Focus on Writing* Web site. Weena McKenzie, Kelly Lockmer, Lynette Ledoux, and Michelle McSweeney's work on the ancillary booklets was invaluable. Michael Dockray reviewed the ESL chapter and made helpful suggestions.

It almost goes without saying that *Focus on Writing* could not exist without our students, whose words appear on almost every page of the book, in sample sentences, paragraphs, and essays. We thank all of them, past and present, who allowed us to use their work.

Instructors throughout the country have contributed suggestions and encouragement at various stages of the book's development. For their collegial support we thank Sandra Albers, Leeward Community College; Elizabeth Altruda, Middlesex County College; Sheilagh Badanic, Douglas College; Craig Barto, Charleston Southern University; Kristina Beckman, University of Arizona; Michael Berndt, Normandale Community College; Lawrence Blasco, Wor-Wic Community College; Janet Brennar, Community College of Philadelphia; Jan Bromley, Douglas College; Alan Brownlie, Anne Arundel Community College; Elizabeth Butts, Delaware County Community College; Nancy Canavera, Charleston Southern University; Rita Coronado, Riverside Community College; Judy D. Covington, Trident Technical College; Jennifer Ferguson, Cazenovia College; Adam Fischer, Bowie State University; Tracy Gorrell, Robert Morris University; Gwen Graham, Holmes Community College; Jessica Grecco, Urban College of Boston; Beth Heelander, Lexington Community College; Elaine S. Herrick, Temple College; Linda Lora Hulbert, Wayne State University; Lonny Kaneko, Highline Community College; Cynthia Krause, Wilbur Wright College; Patsy Krech, University of Memphis; Jennifer Leamy, Wake Technical Community College; Marci MacGregor, Broward Community College; Tom Pierce, Central New Mexico Community College; Kelley Paystrup, Snow College; Janet Kay Porter, Leeward Community College; Melissa Rayborn, Valencia Community College; Melissa Renfrow, Maple Woods Community College; Sharisse Turner, Tallahassee Community College; Rhonda Wallace, Cuyahoga Community College; Michael T. Warren, Maple Woods Community College; George Wheelock, Anne Arundel Community College; Julie Yankanich, Camden County College.

At Bedford/St. Martin's, we thank founder and former president Chuck Christensen and president Joan Feinberg, who believed in this project and

Ordering Information

To order any of these ancillaries for *Focus on Writing*, contact your local Bedford/St. Martin's sales representative, send an email to sales_support@bfpub.com or visit our Web site at **bedfordstmartins .com/focusonwriting.**

Use these ISBNs when ordering the following supplements packaged with your students' book:

- *Focus on Writing* e-Book Access Card
  ISBN-10: 0-312-48093-8; ISBN-13: 978-0-312-48093-6
- *Supplemental Exercises*
  ISBN-10: 0-312-48083-0; ISBN-13: 978-0-312-48083-7
- *The Bedford/St. Martin's ESL Workbook*
  ISBN-10: 0-312-47395-8; ISBN-13: 978-0-312-47395-2
- *Exercise Central to Go* CD-ROM
  ISBN-10: 0-312-47396-6; ISBN-13: 978-0-312-47396-9
- *Make-a-Paragraph Kit* CD-ROM
  ISBN-10: 0-312-47364-8; ISBN-13: 978-0-312-47364-8
- *From Practice to Mastery*
  ISBN-10: 0-312-47394-X; ISBN-13: 978-0-312-47394-5

*● The *Make-a-Paragraph Kit* is a fun, interactive CD-ROM that includes "Extreme Paragraph Makeover" animation to teach students about paragraph development. It also contains exercises to help students build their own paragraphs, audiovisual tutorials on four of the most common serious errors for basic writers, and the content from *Exercise Central to Go: Writing and Grammar Practices for Basic Writers.*

Acknowledgments

In our work on *Focus on Writing*, we have benefited from the help of a great many people.

Franklin E. Horowitz of Teachers College, Columbia University, drafted an early version of Chapter 29, "Grammar and Usage for ESL Writers," and his linguist's insight continues to inform that chapter. Linda Stine and Linda Stengle of Lincoln University devoted energy and vision to the preparation of the helpful ancillary *Classroom Resources for Instructors Using* FOCUS ON WRITING. Linda Mason Austin of McLennan Community College drew on her extensive experience to contribute Teaching tips and ESL tips to the *Instructor's Annotated Edition*. Susan Bernstein's work on the compilation and

- **Checklists and mastery tests help reinforce new skills.** Review Checklists in the grammar chapters ask students to review key concepts before they move on. Chapter Reviews, and the five-paragraph, multi-error Unit Reviews, give students hands-on practice editing paragraphs and essays.

- **A full chapter on grammar and usage for ESL students addresses the concerns of nonnative speakers.** Chapter 29 addresses issues of special interest to nonnative speakers while marginal ESL tips throughout the Instructor's Annotated Edition help teachers support these students. The packagable ancillary, *Bedford/ St. Martin's ESL Workbook*, offers even more practice.

Focus on Writing *helps students make the connection between reading and writing.*   Chapter 35, "Reading for College," guides students through the process of critical reading and includes a sample annotated reading. Chapter 36, "Readings for Writers," contains eighteen professional and student essays that illustrate the major rhetorical patterns. End-of-reading questions check for comprehension, build vocabulary skills, and suggest topics for student writing.

Three full appendixes help students with research, test taking, and vocabulary development.   Appendix A, "Strategies for College Success," introduces students to practical strategies that they can use throughout their college careers. Appendix B, "Using Research in Your Writing," introduces students to the process of doing research for college, including finding print and Internet sources, and documenting sources using MLA style. Appendix C, "Taking Standardized Assessment Tests," orients students to important exit and assessment exams and offers them a spectrum of test-taking strategies. The marginal *Word Power* boxes throughout the book expand students' vocabularies as they work on their own writing.

The Focus on Writing *e-book offers an online version of the print text.*   The first of its kind developed for the developmental writing class, this online version of the print book includes interactive exercises and multimedia tutorials that let students do the work of the class—from responding to writing prompts to grammar exercises—right in the e-book. Additionally, instructors can create their own multipart lessons, pages, quizzes, discussion forums, and more while keeping track of student progress in an integrated gradebook.

Ancillaries

Focus on Writing is accompanied by comprehensive teaching support that includes the following items. Many resources are free. Starred titles are free when packaged with the book.

important information and new concepts with a minimum of distractions to keep basic writing students focused.

Clear, step-by-step coverage of every stage of the writing process helps students master drafting, revising, and editing.   Nine chapters on paragraph writing cover the patterns of development, supported by plenty of student-friendly examples and exercises. Models of student writing, one for each pattern of development, show every stage of the writing process, with a final, finished student paragraph annotated to show how it has been improved. Two more chapters on the writing process and two on essay writing cover the rhetorical skills students need to master.

"Writing-in-context" activities, a hallmark of our developmental books, get students writing immediately and help them practice rhetorical skills while revising and editing their own writing.   In each chapter, students respond in writing to a full-page photo or other visual. Then, a series of *Flashback* and *Revising and Editing* activities throughout the chapters ask students to return to their initial writing, apply new skills they are learning, and create a polished draft.

TEST provides a powerful tool to help students understand how paragraphs work and to revise their own writing.   Introduced early in the book, the easy-to-remember TEST acronym (topic sentence, evidence, summary statement, and transitions) helps students self-check their paragraphs for unity, support, and coherence. Clear and practical directions for applying TEST to their writing allow students to quickly see where their drafts need more work before they revise toward a final draft.

Better grammar coverage — with less jargon and clearer explanations — than any other basic writing text gives students lots of practice and lots of support.

- **Uncomplicated explanations of grammar topics help students master the essentials.** Clear instructions, basic definitions, and well-illustrated examples make fundamental grammar issues easy to grasp. "Grammar in Context" boxes in the paragraph chapters highlight issues particularly relevant to each rhetorical mode.
- **Hundreds of exercises offer abundant practice.** Exercises range from very basic to more challenging, with topics that developmental students find engaging. Additional practice is available at the nearly 9,000-item online database, *Exercise Central.*

gave us support and encouragement from the outset. We thank Erica Appel, Director of Development, for overseeing this edition, and Nancy Perry, our long-time friend and former Editor in Chief, for helping us to conceptualize the book. We also thank Laura King, associate editor, for her work in managing the revision of the book's ancillaries and coordinating the writing of exercises. We are also grateful to Robin Butterhof and Nina Gantcheva, editorial assistants, for helping with numerous tasks, big and small; and to Dennis Conroy, senior production supervisor; Irwin Zucker and Michael Weber, senior project editors; and Shuli Traub, managing editor, for guiding the book ably through production. Anna Palchik, senior art director, offered invaluable help at the initial stages of design, and Claire Seng-Niemoeller, book designer, created an extraordinary look for *Focus on Writing*, one that brings an entirely fresh perspective to the developmental writing text. Working with Claire was Melissa Cliver, whose photographs, photo research, and visual acuity produced the images that open each chapter. Lucy Krikorian, art director, oversaw the finalized design and art program. Thanks also go to Casey Carroll, marketing manager, and his team, to our outstanding copyeditor, Alice Vigliani, and to terrific proofreader, Martha Huelsman. And finally, we thank our editor, Joelle Hann, whose hard work and dedication kept the project moving along.

We are grateful for the continued support of our families — Mark, Adam, and Rebecca Kirszner; and Demi, David, and Sarah Mandell. Finally, we are grateful for the survival and growth of the writing partnership we entered into when we were graduate students. We had no idea then of the wonderful places our collaborative efforts would take us. Now, we know.

Laurie G. Kirszner
Stephen R. Mandell

Contents

Writing Paragraphs and Essays

Unit One   **Writing Paragraphs   1**

1 Understanding the Writing Process   2

Revising and Editing Your Writing

Unit Four   **Writing Sentences   205**

14   Writing Simple Sentences   206

15   Writing Compound Sentences   220

16   Writing Complex Sentences   238

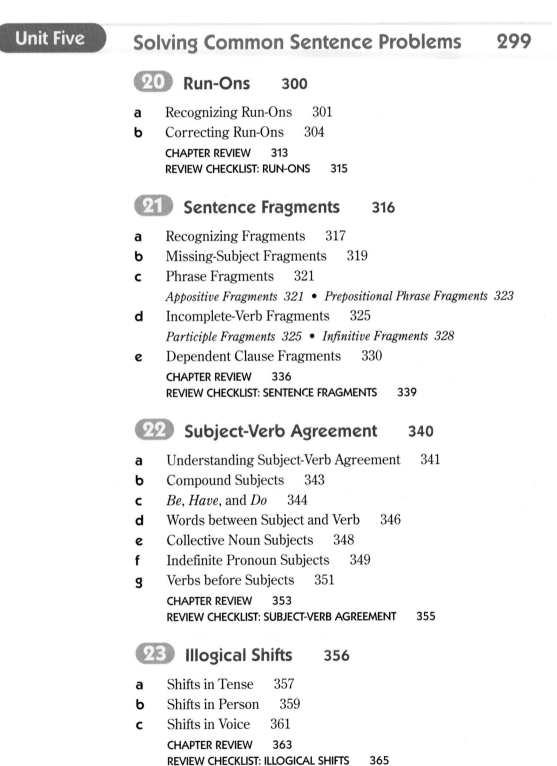

Unit Five   ## Solving Common Sentence Problems   299

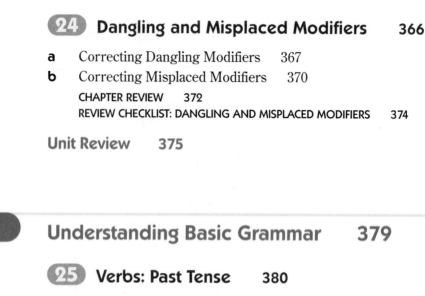

Unit Seven

Understanding Punctuation, Mechanics, and Spelling 485

30 Using Commas 486

31 Using Apostrophes 504

Becoming a Critical Reader

APPENDIX A. Strategies for College Success   625

APPENDIX B. Using Research in Your Writing   639

APPENDIX C. Taking Standardized Assessment Tests   659

A Student's Guide to Using *Focus on Writing*

What *Focus on Writing* Can Do for You

It's no secret that writing will be very important in most of the courses you take in college. Whether you write lab reports or English papers, midterms or final exams, your ability to organize your thoughts and express them in writing will help to determine how well you do. In other words, succeeding at writing is the first step toward succeeding in college. Perhaps even more important, writing is a key to success outside the classroom. On the job and in everyday life, if you can express yourself clearly and effectively, you will stand a better chance of achieving your goals and making a difference in the world.

Whether you write as a student, as an employee, as a parent, or as a concerned citizen, your writing almost always has a specific purpose. For example, when you write an essay, a memo, a letter, or a research paper, you are writing not just to complete an exercise but to give other people information or to tell them your ideas or opinions. That is why, in this book, we don't just ask you to do grammar exercises and fill in blanks; in each chapter, we also ask you to apply the skills you are learning to a writing assignment of your own.

As teachers—and as former students—we know how demanding college can be and how hard it is to juggle assignments with work and family responsibilities. We also know that you don't want to waste your time. That's why in *Focus on Writing* we make information easy to find and use and include many different features to help you become a better writer.

The following sections describe key features of *Focus on Writing*. If you take the time now to familiarize yourself with these elements of the book, you will be able to use the book more effectively later on.

How *Focus on Writing* Can Help You Become a Better Writer

Focus on Writing contains a lot of information that will be helpful to you in college and beyond. Review the book's tools and elements listed below so that you know how to locate important information and understand how the book is organized.

Highlight boxes   Throughout the book, blue boxes with a bright yellow outline highlight useful information, identify key points, and explain difficult concepts.

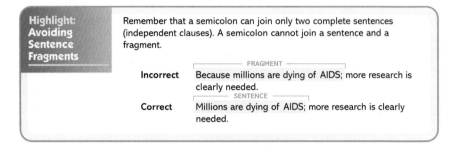

Grammar in Context boxes   In Chapters 3–11 you will find boxes that identify key grammar issues in the patterns of paragraph development. Use these boxes to increase your understanding of important issues in your writing.

Grammar in Context: Definition

A definition paragraph often includes a formal definition of the term or idea you are going to discuss. When you write a formal definition, be careful not to use the phrase *is where* or *is when.*

Happiness is ~~when you have~~ a feeling of contentment or joy.

Checklists   At the end of every chapter you will find a checklist that will help you review and apply the skills that you are learning.

- **Self-Assessment Checklists**   Chapters 1 and 12 include Self-Assessment Checklists that give you a handy way to review your understanding of basic paragraph and essay structure.

Self-Assessment Checklist: Editing Your Paragraph

☐ Are all your sentences complete and grammatically correct?
☐ Do all your subjects and verbs agree?
☐ Have you used the correct verb tenses?
☐ Are commas used where they are required?
☐ Have you used apostrophes correctly?
☐ Have you used other punctuation marks correctly?
☐ Have you used capital letters where they are required?
☐ Are all words spelled correctly?

For help with grammar, punctuation, mechanics, and spelling, see Units 6–7 of this text.

- **TEST Checklists**   Chapters 2–11 include TEST checklists that give you a helpful and easy-to-remember way to check drafts of your paragraphs before you revise and hand them in.

T E S Ting an Argument Paragraph

Topic Sentence Unifies Your Paragraph

☐ Do you have a clearly worded topic sentence that states your paragraphs main idea?

☐ Does your topic sentence state your position on a debatable topic?

☐ Do you need to revise your topic sentence to include new ideas?

Evidence Supports Your Paragraph's Topic Sentence

☐ Does all your evidence support your paragraph's main idea?

☐ Have you included enough evidence to support your points, or do you need to add more?

Summary Statement Reinforces Your Paragraph's Unity

☐ Does your paragraph end with a statement that summarizes your main idea?

Transitions Add Coherence to Your Paragraph

☐ Do you use transitional words and phrases to let readers know when you are moving from one point to another?

☐ Do you use transitional words and phrases to indicate when you are addressing opposing arguments?

☐ Do you need to add transitions to make your paragraph more coherent?

- **Review Checklists**   All grammar chapters and some of the writing chapters end with a summary of the most important information in the chapter. Use these checklists to review material for quizzes or to remind yourself of the main points.

Review Checklist: Writing Simple Sentences

☐ A sentence expresses a complete thought. The subject tells who or what is being talked about in the sentence. (See 14A.)

☐ A prepositional phrase consists of a preposition and its object (the noun or pronoun it introduces). The object of a preposition cannot be the subject of a sentence. (See 14B.)

☐ An action verb tells what the subject does, did, or will do. (See 14C.)

☐ A linking verb connects the subject to a word or words that describe or rename it. (See 14C.)

☐ Many verbs are made up of more than one word. The complete verb in a sentence includes the main verb plus any helping verbs. (See 14C.)

Answers to Odd-Numbered Exercise Items   Starting on page 669, you'll find answers for some of the Practice exercises in the book. When you need to study a topic independently, or when your instructor has you complete a Practice but not hand it in, you can consult these answers to see if you're on the right track.

WORD POWER

idol someone who is admired or adored

role model a person who serves as a model for other people to imitate

emulate to try to equal or excel

 On the Web
For more practice, visit Exercise Central *at* <bedfordstmartins.com/ focusonwriting>.

Notes in the margins   In the margins of *Focus on Writing*, you'll find two kinds of notes that highlight additional, important information. *Word Power* boxes define words that may be useful in working with a particular writing assignment or reading selection. Cross-references to *Exercise Central*, an online collection of more than 9,000 exercises, indicate where to find additional practice with specific skills.

How to Access Additional Exercises and Resources Online

Focus on Writing's companion Web site gives you free access to *Exercise Central*, a database of nearly 9,000 practice exercises where you can take a diagnostic test to see which skills you need help with and get a personalized study plan that will help you to practice and improve. Here, you will find access to *Re:Writing Basics*, a resource center with help for many issues you will encounter in the writing classroom and in college, like how to take good notes and how to avoid plagiarism.

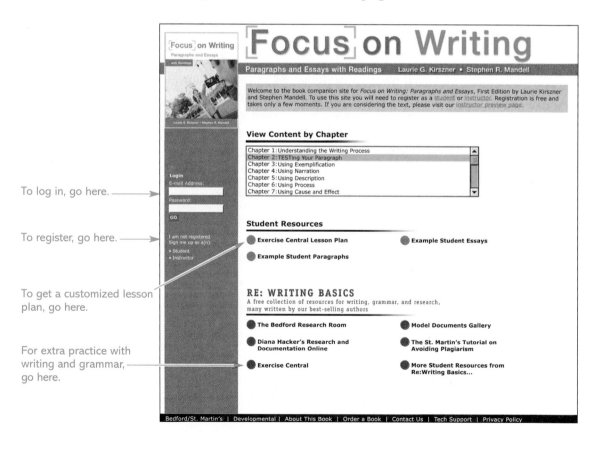

To log in, go here. ——→

To register, go here. ——→

To get a customized lesson plan, go here.

For extra practice with writing and grammar, go here.

Teaching Tip
To be sure students
do not misplace their
username and password,
have them write this
important information
directly into the book
as soon as they register
on the *Focus on Writing*
Web site.

Visit **bedfordstmartins.com/focusonwriting** to register. It's free and you will only have to register once. Keep a record of your username and password by writing them on the lines below so that you can easily sign in on future visits.

Username: _____

Password: _____

How *Focus on Writing* Can Help You Succeed in Other Courses

In a sense, this whole book is about succeeding in other courses. As we said earlier, writing is the key to success in college. But *Focus on Writing* also includes appendixes and other information at the end of the book that you may find especially useful in courses you take later on in college. We have designed these sections so you can use them either on your own or with your instructor's help.

Appendix A: Strategies for College Success   In this appendix you will find tips for making your semester (and your writing course) as successful as possible. Included are effective strategies for taking notes, completing homework assignments, doing well on exams, and managing your time efficiently.

Appendix B: Using Research in Your Writing   This appendix gives a short overview of the research process and shows how to document sources and create a list of works cited. A student research paper, complete with helpful marginal notes, is also included.

Appendix C: Taking Standardized Assessment Tests   This appendix gives an overview of important placement tests and exams, along with tips and strategies on how to prepare for them.

List of correction symbols   The chart on the last page of the book lists marks that many instructors use when evaluating and grading student papers. Become familiar with these symbols so that you can get the most out of your instructor's comments.

Review of the parts of speech   On the inside back cover you will find the eight major parts of speech defined with examples. Use it to review this essential information as often as you need.

Checklists for Writing Paragraphs and Essays

Units 1–3 of *Focus on Writing* include a number of checklists designed to help you check, revise, and fine-tune your paragraphs and essays. You can use these checklists both in your writing course and in other courses that include written assignments. The following list shows the page number for each checklist.

Unit One
Writing Paragraphs

Chapter 1

Understanding the Writing Process

In 2005, an estimated 600,000 students graduated from two-year colleges, while 2.3 million students graduated from four-year colleges.

Writing is not just something you do in school; writing is a life skill. If you can write clearly, you can express your ideas convincingly to others—in school, on the job, and in your community.

Writing takes many different forms. In college, you might write a single paragraph, an essay exam, a short paper, or a long research paper. At work, you might write a memo, a proposal, or a report. In your daily life as a citizen (or as a member of your community), you might write a letter or an email asking for information or explaining a problem that needs to be solved.

Writing is important. If you can write, you can communicate; if you can communicate effectively, you can succeed in school and beyond.

Highlight: The Writing Process

Writing is a **process**, a series of steps that begins when you get an assignment.

Step 1: Planning You start by thinking about what you want to say and finding ideas to write about. Then, you identify the main idea you want to get across.

Step 2: Organizing Once you have material to write about, you arrange your supporting points in an order that makes sense to you.

Step 3: Drafting When you have decided on an arrangement for your ideas, you write a first draft.

Step 4: Revising and Editing Finally, you revise and edit your draft until you are satisfied with it.

This chapter takes you through the process of writing a paragraph.

→ Focus on Writing

As the pictures on the opposite page show, students in college today may find themselves either in a traditional classroom or in a more career-oriented setting. What do you think is the primary purpose of college—to give students a general education or to prepare them for specific careers? Look at the pictures, and think about this question carefully as you read the pages that follow. This is the topic you will be writing about as you move through this chapter.

WORD POWER
primary most important
aspiration a strong desire for high achievement; an ambitious goal

STEP 1: PLANNING

1a   Understanding Paragraph Structure

Before you can begin the process of writing a paragraph, you need to have a basic understanding of paragraph structure. Because paragraphs are central to almost every form of writing, learning how to write one is an important step in becoming a competent writer. Although a paragraph can be a complete piece of writing in itself—as it is in a short classroom exercise or an exam answer—most of the time a paragraph is part of a longer piece of writing.

A **paragraph** is a group of sentences that is unified by a single main idea. The **topic sentence** states the main idea, and the rest of the sentences in the paragraph provide **evidence** (details and examples) to support the main idea. The sentences in a paragraph are linked by **transitions**, words and phrases (such as *also* and *for example*) that show how they are related. At the end of the paragraph, a **summary statement** summarizes the main idea.

Teaching Tip
Detailed information on topic sentences, evidence, transitions, and summary statements is provided in Chapter 2.

Teaching Tip
Students will be concerned about how long their paragraphs should be. Tell them that a well-developed paragraph should be about eight to ten sentences long.

Paragraph

Topic Sentence

Evidence (details and examples)

Summary Statement

>   To write a paragraph, you need a main idea, support, transitions, and a summary statement. First, state the main idea of the paragraph in a topic sentence. This idea unifies the paragraph. Then, add sentences to provide support. In these sentences, you present evidence (details and examples) to help your readers understand your main idea. Next, link these sentences with transitions. Finally, write a summary statement, a sentence that sums up the paragraph's main idea. If you follow this general structure, you are on your way to writing an effective paragraph.

Transitions (boxed)

Note: The first sentence of a paragraph is **indented**, starting about half an inch from the left-hand margin. Every sentence begins with a capital letter and, in most cases, ends with a period. (Sometimes a sentence ends with a question mark or an exclamation point.)

Teaching Tip
Newspaper paragraphs
usually have fewer
sentences than other
paragraphs. Explain to
students that this length
is necessitated by the
width of the columns.

● **Practice 1-1**

Bring two paragraphs to class—one from a newspaper or magazine article and one from a textbook. Compare your paragraphs with those brought in by other students. What features do all your paragraphs share? How are the paragraphs different from one another?

Focusing on Your Assignment, Purpose, and Audience

Teaching Tip
Ask students to share
with the class the writing
tasks they have had in
the past month in school,
at work, and in the
community.

In college, the writing process usually begins with an assignment that tells you what to write about. Instead of jumping in headfirst and starting to write, take time to consider some questions about your **assignment** (*what* you are expected to write about), your **purpose** (*why* you are writing), and your **audience** (*for whom* you are writing). Finding out the answers to these questions at this point will save you time in the long run.

Questions about Assignment, Purpose, and Audience

Assignment

- What is your assignment?
- Do you have a word or page limit?
- When is your assignment due?
- Will you be expected to complete your assignment at home or in class?
- Will you be expected to work on your own or with others?
- Will you be allowed to revise before or after you hand in your assignment?

Purpose

- Are you expected to express your personal reactions—for example, to tell how you feel about a piece of music or a news event?
- Are you expected to present information—for example, to describe a process in a lab report or to summarize a story or essay you have read?
- Are you expected to take a position on a controversial issue?

Audience

- Who will read your paper—just your instructor or other students as well?
- How much will your readers know about your topic?
- Will your readers expect you to use formal or informal language?

● Practice 1-2

Each of the following writing tasks has a different audience and purpose. Think about how you would approach each task. (Use the Questions about Assignment, Purpose, and Audience on p. 5 and above to help you decide on the best strategy.) On a separate sheet of paper, make some notes about your approach. Discuss your responses with your class or in a small group.

1. For the other students in your writing class, describe your best or worst educational experience.

2. For the instructor of an introductory psychology course, discuss how early educational experiences can affect a student's performance throughout his or her schooling.

3. Write a short letter to your community's school board in which you try to convince members to make two or three specific changes that you believe would improve the schools you attended or those your children might attend.

4. Write a letter to a past or current work supervisor telling what you appreciate about his or her guidance and how it has helped you develop and grow as an employee.

1c   Finding Ideas

Once you know what, why, and for whom you are writing, you can begin to find ideas to write about. This process can be challenging, and it is different for every writer.

Stella Drew, a student in an introductory writing course, was given the following assignment.

Should community service—unpaid work in the community—be a required part of the college curriculum? Write a paragraph in which you answer this question.

Teaching Tip
If you like, you can
introduce students to
the term **invention**
(also called *prewriting* or
discovery) at this stage of
the writing process.

Teaching Tip
Be sure students
understand that they do
not have to use all four
strategies every time
they write.

Before she drafted her paragraph, Stella used a variety of strategies to help her find ideas to write about. The pages that follow illustrate the four strategies her instructor asked the class to try: *freewriting, brainstorming, clustering,* and *journal writing.*

Freewriting

When you **freewrite**, you write for a set period of time—perhaps five minutes—without stopping. Keep writing even if what you are writing doesn't seem to have a point or a direction. Your goal is to relax and let ideas flow without worrying about whether or not they are related. Sometimes you can freewrite without a topic in mind, but at other times you will focus your attention on a particular topic. This strategy is called **focused freewriting**.

When you finish freewriting, read what you have written. Then, underline any ideas you think you might be able to use. If you find an idea you want to explore further, freewrite again, using that idea as a starting point.

Here is Stella's focused freewriting on the topic of whether or not community service should be a required part of the college curriculum.

Community service. Community service. Sounds like what you do instead of going to jail. Service to the community—service in the community. Community center. College community—community college. Community service—I guess it's a good idea to do it—but when? In my spare time—spare time—that's pretty funny. So after school and work and all the reading and studying I also have to do <u>service</u>? Right. And what could I do anyway? Work with kids. Or homeless people. Old people? Sick people? Or not people—maybe animals. Or work for a political candidate. Does that count? But when would I do it? Maybe other people have time, but I don't. OK idea, could work—but not for me.

Freewriting

● Practice 1-3

Reread Stella's freewriting on the topic of community service for college students. If you were advising her, which of her ideas would you suggest she explore further? Underline these ideas in her freewriting.

● Practice 1-4

Teaching Tip
You may prefer to give students an alternate assignment or a choice of topics to write about.

Now, it is time for you to begin the work that will result in a finished paragraph. (You already have your assignment from the Focus on Writing box on p. 3: to write about whether the primary purpose of college is to give students a general education or to prepare them for specific careers.)

Your first step is to freewrite about this assignment. On a sheet of lined paper (or on your computer), write for at least five minutes without stopping. If you have trouble thinking of something to write, keep recopying the last word you have written until something else comes to mind.

● Practice 1-5

Reread the freewriting you did for Practice 1–4. Underline any ideas you think you might use in your paragraph. Then, choose one of these ideas, and use it as a starting point for another focused freewriting exercise.

Brainstorming

When you **brainstorm**, you write down or type all the ideas about your topic that you can think of. Unlike freewriting, brainstorming is often scattered all over the page. You don't have to use complete sentences; single words or phrases are fine. You can underline, star, or box important points. You can also ask questions, list points, draw arrows to connect ideas, and even draw pictures or diagrams.

Stella's brainstorming on the topic of community service appears on the next page.

Highlight: Collaborative Brainstorming	Usually, you brainstorm on your own. At times, however, you may find it helpful to do **collaborative brainstorming**, working with other students to find ideas. Sometimes your instructor may ask you and another student to brainstorm together. At other times, the class might brainstorm as a group while your instructor writes the ideas you think of on the board. Whichever method you use, your goal is the same: to come up with as much material about your topic as you can.

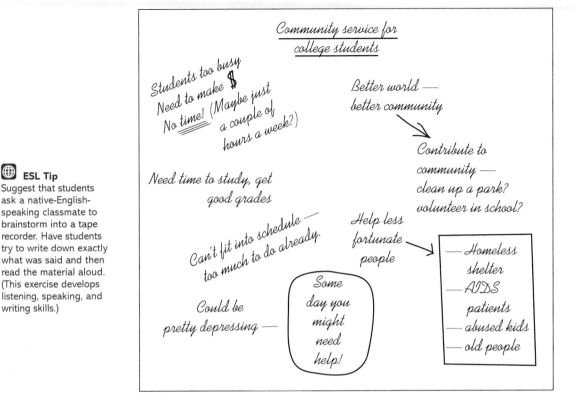

Brainstorming

ESL Tip
Suggest that students
ask a native-English-
speaking classmate to
brainstorm into a tape
recorder. Have students
try to write down exactly
what was said and then
read the material aloud.
(This exercise develops
listening, speaking, and
writing skills.)

● Practice 1-6

Reread Stella's brainstorming notes on community service (above). How is
her brainstorming similar to her freewriting on the same subject (p. 7)? How
is it different? If you were advising Stella, which ideas would you suggest
she write more about? Which ideas should she cross out? Write your suggestions on the lines below.

Write more on these ideas: <u>Answers will vary.</u>

_____

_____

Cross out these ideas: <u>Answers will vary.</u>

_____

_____

Teaching Tip
Some students may
be reluctant to write in
the book because they
are afraid of making
mistakes. (They will also
have been told in high
school never to write in
a textbook.) Encourage
them to write directly in
the text where it is
required.

● Practice 1-7

On a sheet of *unlined* paper, brainstorm about your assignment: What do you think is the primary purpose of college—to give students a general education or to prepare them for specific careers? (Begin by writing your topic, "The purpose of college," at the top of the page.) Write quickly, without worrying about using complete sentences. Try writing on different parts of the page, making lists, and drawing arrows to connect related ideas. When you have finished, look over what you have written. Which ideas are the most interesting? Did you come up with any new ideas as you brainstormed that you did not discover while freewriting?

● Practice 1-8

Working as a class or in a group of three or four students, practice collaborative brainstorming. First, decide as a group on a topic for brainstorming. (Your instructor may assign a topic.) Next, choose one person to write down ideas on a blank sheet of paper or on the board. (If your group is large enough, you might choose two people to write down ideas and have them compare notes at the end of the brainstorming session.) Then, discuss the topic informally, with each person contributing at least one idea. After fifteen minutes or so, review the ideas that have been written down. As a group, try to identify interesting connections among ideas and suggest ideas that might be explored further.

Clustering

Teaching Tip
Tell students that for a short paragraph, where they will not be expected to provide many details, they may select general ideas from the center of their cluster diagram. For longer, more complex writing assignments, however, they will need to use the more specific material they generated as they moved out from the center.

Clustering, sometimes called *mapping*, is another strategy that can help you find ideas to write about. When you cluster, you begin by writing your topic in the center of a sheet of paper. Then, you branch out, writing related ideas on the page in groups, or clusters, around the topic. As you add new ideas, you circle them and draw lines to connect the ideas to one another and to the topic at the center. (These lines will look like spokes of a wheel or branches of a tree.) As you move from the center to the corners of the page, your ideas will get more and more specific.

Stella's clustering on the topic of community service for college students appears on the next page.

Note: Sometimes one branch of your cluster exercise will give you all the material you need. At other times, you may decide to write about the ideas from several branches—or to choose one or two from each branch. If you find you need additional material after you finish your first cluster exercise, you can cluster again on a new sheet of paper, this time beginning with a topic from one of the branches.

Clustering

● Practice 1-9

Reread Stella's clustering on community service (above). How is it similar to her brainstorming on the same subject (p. 9)? How is it different? If you were advising Stella, which branches of the cluster diagram would you say seem most promising? Why? Can you add any branches? Can you extend any of her branches further? Write in your additions on Stella's cluster diagram. Then, discuss your suggestions with the class or in a small group.

● Practice 1-10

Try clustering on your Focus on Writing activity:

> What do you think is the primary purpose of college — to give students a general education or to prepare them for specific careers?

Begin by writing your topic in the center of a blank sheet of unlined paper. Circle the topic, and then branch out with specific ideas and examples, continuing to the edge of the page if you can. When you have finished, look over what you have written. What are the most interesting ideas in your cluster diagram? Which branches seem most promising as the basis for further writing? What new ideas have you come up with that you did not get from your freewriting or brainstorming?

Journal Writing

A **journal** is a notebook or a computer file in which you keep an informal record of your thoughts and ideas. In a journal, you can reflect, question, summarize, or even complain. Your journal is a place where you jot down ideas to write about and think about your assignments. Here, you can try to resolve a problem, restart a stalled project, argue with yourself about your topic, or comment on a draft of your paper. You can also try out different versions of sentences, keep track of details or examples, or keep a record of interesting things you read, see, or hear.

Journal writing works best when you write regularly, preferably at the same time each day, so that it becomes a habit. Once you have started making regular entries in your journal, take the time every week or so to go back and reread what you have written. You may find material you want to explore in further journal entries — or even an idea for a paper.

Here is Stella's journal entry on the topic of community service for college students.

> I'm not really sure what I think about community service. I guess I think it sounds like a good idea, but I still don't see why we should have to do it. I can't fit anything else into my life. I guess it would be possible if it was just an hour or two a week. And maybe we could get credit and a grade for it, like a course. Or maybe it should just be for people who have the time and want to do it. But if it's not required, will anyone do it?

Journal Entry

Highlight: Journals

Here are some subjects you can write about in your journal.

- *Your school work* You can use your journal to explore ideas for writing assignments. Your journal can also be a place where you think about what you have learned, ask questions about concepts you are having trouble understanding, and examine new ideas and new ways of seeing the world. Writing regularly in a journal about what you are studying in school can even help you become a better student.

- *Your job* In your journal, you can record job-related successes and frustrations, examine conflicts with coworkers, or review how you handled problems on the job. Reading over these entries can help you understand your strengths and weaknesses and become a more effective employee.

- *Your ideas about current events* Expressing your opinions in your journal can be a good way to explore your reactions to social or political issues in the news. Your entries may encourage you to write letters to your local or school newspaper or to public officials—and even to become involved in community projects or political activities.

- *Your impressions of what you see around you* Many writers carry their journals with them everywhere so they can record any interesting or unusual things they observe. If you get into the habit of recording what you see, you can later incorporate your observations into essays or other pieces of writing.

- *Aspects of your personal life* Although you may not want to record the intimate details of your life if your instructor plans to read your journal, such entries are very common in private journals. Writing about relationships with family and friends, personal problems, hopes and dreams—all the details of your life—can help you develop a better understanding of yourself and others.

Teaching Tip
If students are reluctant to write about personal details in their journals, you might give them the option of labeling some pages "Do not read."

● Practice 1-11

Buy a notebook to use as a journal. (Your instructor may require a specific size and format, particularly if journals are going to be collected at some point, or you may be permitted to keep your journal in a computer file.) Set a regular time to write for fifteen minutes or so in your journal—during your lunch break, for example, or when you check your email. Make entries daily or several times a week, depending on your schedule and your instructor's suggestions. For your first journal entry, write down your thoughts about the topic you have been working on in this chapter: the primary purpose of college.

1d   Identifying Your Main Idea and Writing a Topic Sentence

When you think you have enough material to write about, it is time for you to identify your **main idea**—the idea you will develop in your paragraph.

To find a main idea for your paragraph, begin by looking over what you have already written. As you read through your freewriting, brainstorming, clustering, or journal entries, look for the main idea that your material seems to support. The sentence that states this main idea and gives your writing its focus will be your paragraph's **topic sentence**.

The topic sentence is usually the first sentence of your paragraph. The topic sentence of your paragraph is important because it tells both you and your readers what the focus of your paragraph will be. An effective topic sentence has three characteristics.

Teaching Tip
Refer students to 2A for more on topic sentences.

Teaching Tip
You might want to mention that an effective topic sentence will help unify the ideas in a paragraph. The concept of **unity** is explained and illustrated in 2A.

1. **A topic sentence is a complete sentence.** There is a difference between a *topic* and a *topic sentence*. The **topic** is what the paragraph is about. A **topic sentence**, however, is a complete sentence that includes a subject and a verb and expresses a complete thought.

Topic	Community service
Topic sentence	Community service should be required for all students at our school.

2. **A topic sentence is more than just an announcement of what you plan to write about.** A topic sentence makes a point about the topic the paragraph discusses.

Announcement	In this paragraph, I will explain my ideas about community service.
Topic sentence	My ideas about community service changed after I started to volunteer at a homeless shelter.

3. **A topic sentence presents an idea that can be discussed in a single paragraph.** If your topic sentence is too broad, you will not be able to discuss it in just one paragraph. If your topic sentence is too narrow, you will not be able to say much about it.

Topic sentence too broad	Students all over the country participate in community service, making important contributions to their communities.

| **Topic sentence too narrow** | Our school has a community service requirement for graduation. |
| **Effective topic sentence** | Our school's community service requirement has had three positive results. |

When Stella Drew reviewed her notes, she saw that they included two kinds of ideas: ideas about the value of doing community service and ideas about the problems it presents. She thought she could write about how community service requires time and commitment but is still worthwhile. She stated this idea in a topic sentence.

Community service takes time, but it is so important that college students should be required to do it.

When Stella thought about how to express her topic sentence, she knew it had to be a complete sentence, not just a topic, and that it would have to make a point, not just announce what she planned to write about. When she reread the topic sentence she had written, she felt confident that it did these things. Her topic sentence was neither too broad nor too narrow, and it made a statement she could support in a paragraph.

● **Practice 1-12**

Read the following items. Put a check mark next to each one that has all three characteristics of an effective topic sentence.

Examples:

The common cold. _____

Many people are convinced that large doses of vitamin C will prevent the common cold. __✔__

1. Global warming, a crisis for our cities. _____
2. High school science courses should teach students about the dangers of global warming. __✔__
3. In this paragraph, I will discuss global warming. _____
4. Buying books online. _____
5. College students can save money by buying their textbooks online. __✔__

● **Practice 1-13**

Decide whether each of the following statements could be an effective topic sentence for a paragraph. If a sentence is too broad, write "too broad" in the blank following the sentence. If the sentence is too narrow, write "too narrow" in the blank. If the sentence is an effective topic sentence, write "OK" in the blank.

> **Example:** Thanksgiving always falls on the fourth Thursday in November. _too narrow_

1. Wireless computer networks are changing the world. _too broad_
2. There are five computer terminals in the campus library. _too narrow_
3. Our school should set up a wireless network on campus. _OK_
4. Soccer is not as popular in the United States as it is in Europe. _too broad_
5. Americans enjoy watching many types of sporting events on television. _too broad_
6. There is one quality that distinguishes a good coach from a bad one. _OK_
7. Vegetarianism is a healthy way of life. _too broad_
8. Uncooked spinach has fourteen times as much iron as steak does. _too narrow_
9. Fast-food restaurants are finally meeting the needs of vegetarians. _OK_
10. Medical schools in this country have high standards. _too broad_

● **Practice 1-14**

In Practices 1-4, 1-7, and 1-10, you practiced freewriting, brainstorming, and clustering. Now, you are ready to write a paragraph in response to the following assignment.

> Do you think the primary purpose of college is to give students a general education or to prepare them for specific careers?

Your first step is to find a main idea for your paragraph. Look over the work you have done so far, and try to decide what main idea your material can best support. Then, write a topic sentence that expresses this idea on the lines below.

Topic sentence: <u>*Answers will vary.*</u>

_____

STEP 2: ORGANIZING

1e

Choosing Supporting Points

Teaching Tip
You might want to explain that effective **support** (examples and details) for the topic sentence will make a paragraph more convincing. The concept of support is explained and illustrated in 2B.

After you have stated your paragraph's main idea in a topic sentence, review your notes again. This time, look for specific **evidence** (details and examples) to support your main idea. Write or type your topic sentence at the top of a blank page. As you review your notes, list all the points you think you might be able to use to support it.

Stella chose several points from her notes to write about. After she read through her list of points, she crossed out three that she thought would not support her topic sentence.

Main idea: Community service takes time, but it is so important that college students should be required to do it.

- ~~Community service helps people.~~
- ~~Some community service activities could be boring.~~
- Community service can help the world.
- Community service helps the community.
- College students are busy.
- Community service takes a lot of time.
- ~~Community service might not relate to students' majors.~~
- Community service can be upsetting or depressing.
- Community service can be part of a student's education.

● Practice 1-15

Now, continue your work on your own paragraph about the purpose of a college education. Reread your freewriting, brainstorming, and clustering, and list the points you believe can best support your topic sentence.

Topic sentence:

Answers will vary. _____

_____

_____

Supporting points:

• ____ *Answers will vary.* _____

• _____

• _____

• _____

• _____

Check carefully to make sure each point on your list supports your topic sentence. Cross out any points that do not.

Arranging Your Supporting Points

Your next step is to arrange your supporting points in the order in which you plan to discuss them in your paragraph.

When she read over her list of supporting points, Stella saw that she had two different kinds of points: some points dealt with the *problems* of doing community service, and other points dealt with the *advantages* of doing community service. When she arranged her points, she decided to group them in these two categories under the headings "problems" and "advantages."

Topic sentence: Community service takes time, but it is so important that college students should be required to do it.

Problems

• Community service takes a lot of time.
• College students are busy.
• Community service can be upsetting or depressing.

Advantages

• Community service helps the community.
• Community service can be part of a student's education.
• Community service can help the world.

Teaching Tip
Remind students that they will need specific examples to support their main ideas. Have two or three students who have done community service talk about their experiences.

● Practice 1-16

Look over the supporting points you listed in Practice 1–15. Decide which of your points are about going to college to get an education and which are about going to college to prepare for a career. Then, arrange your supporting points below in the order in which you plan to write about them.

Getting a general education:

- _Answers will vary._
- _____
- _____
- _____

Preparing for a career:

- _Answers will vary._
- _____
- _____
- _____

STEP 3: DRAFTING

 ## Drafting Your Paragraph

Once you have written a topic sentence for your paragraph, selected the points you will discuss, and arranged them in the order in which you plan to write about them, you are ready to write a first draft.

In a **first draft**, your goal is to get your ideas down on paper. Begin your paragraph with a topic sentence that states the paragraph's main idea. Then, following the list of points you plan to discuss, write or type without worrying about correct wording, spelling, or punctuation. If a new idea—one that is not on your list—occurs to you, write it down. Don't worry about whether it fits with your other ideas. Your goal is not to produce a perfect piece of writing but simply to create a draft. When you revise, you will have a chance to rethink ideas and rework sentences.

Because later on you will be making changes to this first draft—adding or crossing out words and phrases, reordering ideas and details, clarifying connections between ideas, and so on—you should leave wide margins, skip lines, and leave extra blank lines in places where you might need to add material. Feel free to be messy and to cross out; remember, the only person who will see this draft is you. (If you are typing your draft, you can use large type or leave extra space between lines to make the draft easier to revise.)

When you have finished your draft, don't make any changes right away. Take a break (overnight if possible), and think about something—anything—else. Then, return to your draft, and read it with a fresh eye.

Here is the first draft of Stella's paragraph on the topic of community service for college students.

Why Community Service Should Be Required

Community service takes time, but it is so important that college students should be required to do it. When college students do community service, they volunteer their time to do good for someone or for the community. Working in a soup kitchen, raking leaves for senior citizens, and reading to children are all examples of community service. Community service can require long hours and take time away from studying and jobs. It can force students to deal with unpleasant situations, but overall it is rewarding and helpful to others. Community service is good for the community and can be more fulfilling than playing sports or participating in clubs. Community service can be an important part of a college education. Students can even discover what they want to do with their lives. Community service can make the world a better place.

First Draft

● **Practice 1-17**

Reread Stella's draft paragraph. If you were advising her, what would you suggest that she change in her draft? What would you tell her to add? What do you think she should cross out? Discuss your ideas with your class or in a small group.

● **Practice 1-18**

Now, write a draft of your paragraph about the purpose of a college education, using the material you came up with for Practices 1-14 and 1-15. Be sure your paragraph states your main idea and supports it with specific points. If you handwrite your draft, leave wide margins and skip lines; if you type your draft, leave extra space between lines. When you are finished, give your paragraph a title.

TESTing Your Paragraph

When you have finished your draft, the first thing you should do is "test" what you have written to make sure it includes all the elements of an effective paragraph. You do this by asking yourself the following four **TEST** questions.

Highlight: TESTing Your Paragraph	• **Topic sentence** — Does your paragraph have a topic sentence that states its main idea?
Teaching Tip You might want to tell students that a summary statement will reinforce a paragraph's **unity** and that transitions will add **coherence**.	• **Evidence** — Does your paragraph include examples and details that support your topic sentence?
	• **Summary statement** — Does your paragraph end with a statement that summarizes and reinforces its main idea?
	• **Transitions** — Does your paragraph include transitional words and phrases that show readers how your ideas are related?

As you reread your paragraph, **TEST** it to identify the four elements of an effective paragraph. If your paragraph includes these four basic elements, you are off to a very good start. If it does not, you will need to add whatever is missing.

Teaching Tip
Refer students to
Chapter 2 for more on
TESTing paragraphs for
unity, support, and
coherence.

When Stella reread her draft paragraph, she used the **TEST** strategy to help her take a quick inventory of her paragraph.

- She decided that her topic sentence clearly stated her main idea.
- She thought she had enough evidence to support her topic sentence.
- She noticed that her paragraph had no summary statement.
- She realized she needed to add transitions to connect her ideas.

● Practice 1-19

TEST your draft paragraph for the four elements of an effective paragraph: **T**opic sentence, **E**vidence, **S**ummary statement, and **T**ransitions. (If any elements are missing, you will have to add them.)

STEP 4: REVISING AND EDITING

1i   ## Revising Your Paragraph

Once you have TESTed your paragraph to see if it is complete, you are ready to revise it.

Revision is the process of reseeing, rethinking, reevaluating, and rewriting your work. Revision usually involves more than substituting one word for another or correcting a comma here and there. Often, it means moving sentences, adding words and phrases, or even changing the direction or emphasis of your ideas. To get the most out of the revision process, begin by carefully rereading your draft. Then, use the checklist below to guide your revision.

Self-Assessment Checklist: Revising Your Paragraph

- ☐ Is your topic sentence clearly worded?
- ☐ Do you have enough evidence (details and examples) to support your paragraph's main idea, or do you need to look back at your notes or try another strategy to find additional supporting evidence?
- ☐ Should you cross out any examples and details?
- ☐ Do you need to explain anything more fully or more clearly?
- ☐ Do your transitional words and phrases show readers how your ideas are connected?
- ☐ Does every sentence say what you mean?

Self-Assessment Checklist: Revising Your Paragraph continued	☐ Can you combine any sentences to make your writing flow more smoothly?
	☐ Should you move any sentences?
	☐ Are all your words necessary, or can you cut some?
	☐ Should you change any words to make them more specific?
	☐ Does your summary statement clearly sum up the main idea of your paragraph?

Guided by the Self-Assessment Checklist above, Stella revised her paragraph, writing her changes in by hand on her typewritten draft.

Why Community Service Should Be Required

Community service takes time, but it is so impor-

tant that college students should be required to do

it. When college students do community service, they

~~volunteer their time to~~ do good for someone or for

For example, they work *rake*

the community. ~~Working~~ in a soup kitchen, ~~raking~~

^   *or read*   ^

leaves for senior citizens, ~~and reading~~ to children.

^   *These activities* ^

~~are all examples of community service. Community~~

^

~~service~~ can require long hours and take time away

important things like *However, community service is worth*

from ⋏ studying and jobs. ~~It can force students to~~

the time it takes.

~~deal with unpleasant situations, but overall it is~~

~~rewarding and helpful to others.~~ Community service

for students

~~is good for the community and~~ can be more fulfilling

other college activities, such as ^

than playing sports or participating in clubs. Commu-

^

also

nity service can ⋏ be an important part of a col-

learn about themselves, about their communities, and about their world,

lege education. Students can ⋏ even discover what they *and*

Finally, *they*

want to do with their lives. C̸ommunity service can *can*

^

make the world a better place. *For all these reasons,*

^

community service should be a required part of the college curriculum.

Revised Draft

When she revised, Stella did not worry about being neat. She crossed out words, added material, and made major changes in her words, sentences, and ideas. When she felt her revision was complete, she was ready to move on to edit her paragraph.

1j   Editing Your Paragraph

When you **edit**, you check for correct grammar, punctuation, mechanics, and spelling. You also proofread carefully for typographical errors that your computer spell checker may not identify. In addition, you check to make sure that you have indented the first sentence of your paragraph and that every sentence begins with a capital letter and ends with a period.

Remember, editing is a vital last step in the writing process. Many readers will not take your ideas seriously if your paragraph contains grammatical or mechanical errors. You can use the checklist below to guide your editing.

Self-Assessment Checklist: Editing Your Paragraph	☐ Are all your sentences complete and grammatically correct?
	☐ Do all your subjects and verbs agree?
	☐ Have you used the correct verb tenses?
	☐ Are commas used where they are required?
	☐ Have you used apostrophes correctly?
	☐ Have you used other punctuation marks correctly?
	☐ Have you used capital letters where they are required?
	☐ Are all words spelled correctly?
	For help with grammar, punctuation, mechanics, and spelling, see Units 6–7 of this text.

When Stella edited her paragraph, she checked her grammar, punctuation, mechanics, and spelling and looked carefully for typos. The final typed version of her paragraph appears on the next page.

Why Community Service Should Be Required

Topic Sentence —

Community service takes time, but it is so important that college students should be required to do it. When college students do community service, they do good for someone or for the community. For example, they work in a soup kitchen, rake leaves for senior citizens, or read to children. These activities can require long hours and take time away from important things like studying and jobs. However, community service is worth the time it takes. Community service can be more fulfilling for students than other college activities, such as playing sports or participating in clubs. Community service can also be an important part of a college education. Students can learn about themselves, about their communities, and about their world, and they can even discover what they want to do with their lives. Finally, community service can make the world a better place. For all these reasons, community service should be a required part of the college curriculum.

Evidence (details and examples) —

Summary Statement —

Transitions (boxed) —

● Practice 1-20

Reread the final draft of Stella's paragraph about community service for college students (above), and compare it with her first draft (p. 20). Then, answer the following questions about her revision.

1. Did Stella revise her paragraph's topic sentence? If so, why? If not, why not? Do you agree with her decision?

   She did not revise her topic sentence.

   _____

2. Did Stella add any new material to her paragraph? List any new points or examples on the lines below.

   Answers will vary.

   _____

   Can you think of any new points she *should* have added? List them below.

   Answers will vary.

   _____

3. What did Stella cross out? Why do you think she deleted this material? Do you think she should cross out any additional material?

   Answers will vary.

   _____

4. Why do you think Stella added "For example" (line 4), "However" (line 6), and "also" (line 9) to her final draft?

These words are transitions. They tell readers that she is giving

examples in line 4, introducing her discussion of the advantages of

community service in line 6, and adding another point in line 9.

5. Why do you think Stella added the word "Finally" in her next-to-last sentence?

She uses this word to introduce her last example in support of

community service for college students.

6. In her revision, Stella added a sentence at the end of the paragraph. Do you think this sentence is necessary?

Yes. This sentence sums up the point she is making in her

paragraph.

● Practice 1-21

Generally speaking, what kinds of changes did Stella make as she revised her paragraph? Which do you think are her most effective changes? Why? Do you think she needs to make any additional changes? Write your responses on a separate piece of paper. Then, with your class or in a small group, discuss your reactions to Stella's revised paragraph.

● Practice 1-22

Use the Self-Assessment Checklist on page 22 to evaluate the paragraph you drafted for Practice 1-18. What additions can you make to support your topic sentence more fully? Should anything be crossed out because it does not support your main idea? Can anything be stated more clearly? On a separate piece of paper, list some of the changes you might make in your draft.

Now, revise your draft. Cross out unnecessary material and material you want to rewrite, and add new and rewritten material between the lines and in the margins. After you finish your revision, edit your paragraph, checking grammar, punctuation, mechanics, and spelling—and look carefully for typos.

Review Checklist:
Writing a Paragraph

☐ Learning to write a paragraph is an important step in becoming a competent writer. (See 1A.)

☐ Before you start to write, consider your assignment, purpose, and audience. (See 1B.)

☐ Use freewriting, brainstorming, clustering, and journal writing to help you find ideas. (See 1C.)

☐ Identify your main idea, and write a topic sentence. (See 1D.)

☐ Choose points to support your topic sentence. (See 1E.)

☐ Arrange your supporting points in a logical order. (See 1F.)

☐ Write a first draft of your paragraph. (See 1G.)

☐ **TEST** your paragraph (see 1H.)

☐ Revise your paragraph. (See 1I.)

☐ Edit your paragraph. (See 1J.)

Chapter 2

TESTing Your Paragraphs

On average, the United States consumes six times more paper than the rest of the world and 25 percent more than Japan, the second-largest paper consumer.

As you learned in Chapter 1, it is a good idea to **TEST** every paragraph as soon as you finish drafting. Testing your paragraph will tell you whether or not it includes all the elements of an effective paragraph.

- Topic sentence
- Evidence
- Summary statement
- Transitions

When you **TEST** the following paragraph, you can see that it contains all four elements of an effective paragraph.

WORD POWER

pioneer to be the first to do something

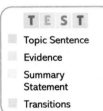

WORD POWER

innovation something newly invented; a new way of doing something

Although most people do not know it, the modern roller coaster got its start in Coney Island in Brooklyn, New York. First, in 1888, the Flip Flap Railway, which featured a circular loop, was built. The coaster was the first to go upside down, but it frequently injured people's necks. Next, in 1901, the Loop-the-Loop, which was safer than the Flip Flap Railway, was built. Then, from 1884 through the 1930s, over thirty roller coasters were constructed in Coney Island. Finally, in 1926, the most famous coaster in history, the Cyclone, was built at a cost of $100,000. Although it began operating over eighty years ago, it is still the standard by which all roller coasters are measured. It has steep drops, a lot of momentum, and only lap belts to hold riders in their seats. Still in operation, the Cyclone is the most successful ride in Coney Island history. It is the last survivor of the wooden roller coasters that once drew crowds to Coney Island. With their many innovations, Coney Island's roller coasters paved the way for the high-tech roller coasters in amusement parks today.

→ Focus on Writing

The picture on the opposite page shows a file cabinet. How do you organize the papers (schoolwork, bills, important records, notes and reminders, and so on) in your life? Does everything have its place, or do you place papers more randomly? Look at the picture, and write about how you organize the papers that are part of your life.

WORD POWER

pragmatic practical; active rather than passive

Using a Topic Sentence to Unify Your Paragraph

Teaching Tip
Remind students that a topic sentence is not a statement of fact or an announcement of what they plan to write about. It is a complete sentence whose idea can be discussed in a single paragraph. Refer them to 1D for more help with understanding topic sentences.

The first thing you do when you **TEST** a paragraph is look at the **topic sentence (T)**. An effective paragraph focuses on a single main idea, and the topic sentence states that main idea.

A paragraph is **unified** when its topic sentence states an idea that all the paragraph's sentences support. A paragraph is not unified when its sentences wander from the main idea stated in the topic sentence. When you revise, you can make your paragraphs unified by crossing out sentences that do not support your topic sentence.

The following paragraph is not unified because it contains sentences that do not support the paragraph's topic sentence. (These sentences have been crossed out.)

> The weak economy has led many people to move away from the rural Ohio community where I was raised. Over the years, farmland has become more and more expensive. Years ago, a family could buy each of its children twenty-five acres on which they could start farming. Today, the price of land is so high that the average farmer cannot afford to buy this amount of land, and those who choose not to farm have few alternatives. ~~After I graduate, I intend to return to my town and get a job there. Even though many factories have moved out of the area, I think I will be able to get a job. My uncle owns a hardware store, and he told me that after I graduate, he will teach me the business. I think I can contribute something to both the business and the community.~~ Young people just cannot get good jobs anymore. Factories have moved out of the area and taken with them the jobs that many young people used to get after high school. As a result, many eighteen-year-olds have no choice but to move away to find employment.

The following revised paragraph is unified. It discusses only the idea that is stated in the topic sentence.

> The weak economy has led many people to move away from the rural Ohio community where I was raised. Over the years, farmland has become more and more expensive. Years ago, a family could buy each of its children twenty-five acres on which they could start farming. Today, the price of land is so high that the average farmer cannot afford to buy this amount of land, and those who choose not to farm have few

T E S T
Topic Sentence
Evidence
Summary
Statement
Transitions

alternatives. Young people just cannot get good jobs anymore. Factories have moved out of the area and taken with them the jobs that many young people used to get after high school. As a result, many eighteen-year-olds have no choice but to move away to find employment.

● Practice 2-1

The following paragraphs are not unified because some sentences do not support the topic sentence. First, underline the topic sentence in each paragraph. Then, cross out any sentences in each paragraph that do not support the topic sentence.

1. <u>The one thing I could not live without is my car.</u> In addition to attending school full time, I hold down two part-time jobs that are many miles from each other, from where I live, and from school. Even though my car is almost twelve years old and has close to 120,000 miles on it, I couldn't manage without it. ~~I'm thinking about buying a new car, and I always check the classified ads, but I haven't found anything I want that I can afford. If my old car breaks down, I guess I'll have to, though. I couldn't live without my portable tape recorder because I use it to record all the class lectures I attend. Then I can play them back while I'm driving or during my breaks at work.~~ Three nights a week and on weekends, I work as a counselor at a home for teenagers with problems, and my other job is in the tire department at Sears. Without my car, I'd be lost.

2. <u>Studies conducted by Dr. Leonard Eron over a period of thirty years suggest that the more television violence children are exposed to, the more aggressive they are as teenagers and adults.</u> In 1960, Eron questioned parents about how they treated their children at home, including how much television their children watched. ~~There is more violence on television today than there was then.~~ Ten years later, he interviewed these families again and discovered that whether or not teenage sons were aggressive depended less on how they had been treated by their parents than on how much violent television programming they had watched as children. Returning in 1990, he found that these same young men, now in their thirties, were still more likely to be aggressive and to commit crimes. ~~Researchers estimate that a child today is likely to watch 100,000 violent acts on television before finishing elementary school.~~

3. <u>Libraries today hold a lot more than just books.</u> Of course, books still outnumber anything else on the shelves, but more and more libraries are

expanding to include other specialized services. For example, many libraries now offer extensive collections of tapes and compact discs, ranging from classical music to jazz to country to rock. Many have also increased their holdings of videotapes, both instructional programs and popular recent and vintage movies. Some libraries also stock DVDs. ~~However, most people probably still get more movies from video stores than from libraries.~~ In addition, the children's section often has games and toys that young patrons can play with in the library or even check out. Most important, libraries are offering more and more computerized data services, which can provide much more detailed and up-to-date information than printed sources. These expanding nonprint sources are the wave of the future for even the smallest libraries and will allow patrons access to much more information than books or magazines ever could. ~~People who don't know how to use a computer are going to be out of luck.~~

● **Practice 2-2**

The following paragraph has no topic sentence. Read it carefully, and then choose the most appropriate topic sentence from the list that follows the paragraph.

> Some people cannot bear to give away the books that they have read. They stack old paperbacks on tables, on the floor, and on their nightstands. Other people save magazines or newspapers. Who hasn't met someone who has a collection of old *National Geographic* magazines? Still others save movie-ticket stubs or postcards. Serious collectors hoard all sorts of things—including old toys, guns, knives, plates, figurines, maps, stamps, baseball cards, comic books, beer bottles, playbills, movie posters, dolls, clocks, old televisions, political campaign buttons, and even coffee mugs. Some things—such as matchbook covers or restaurant menus—may have value only to the people who collect them. Other items—such as stamps or coins—may be worth a lot of money. A very few collectors concentrate on items that are so large that housing a collection can present some real challenges. For example, people who collect automobiles or antique furniture may have to rent a garage or even a warehouse in which to store their possessions.

Put a check mark next to the topic sentence that best expresses the main idea of the paragraph above.

1. Everyone, regardless of age or occupation, seems to have the urge to collect. _____

2. Collecting things like matchbooks and restaurant menus can be fun, but collecting jewelry or coins can be very profitable. _____

3. The things people collect are as different as the people who collect them. ✔

4. In spite of the time and expense, collecting can be an interesting and fulfilling hobby. _____

5. Before you begin to collect things as a hobby, you should know what you are getting into. _____

● Practice 2-3

Teaching Tip
Tell students to work backwards from the supporting evidence and summary statement to determine what the paragraph's topic sentence should be.

The following paragraphs do not have topic sentences. Think of a topic sentence that expresses each paragraph's main idea, and write it on the lines above the paragraphs.

Example: _Possible answer: Early rock and roll was a creation of both_

black and white performers.

Early 1950s African-American musicians included performers such as Johnny Ace, Big Joe Turner, and Ruth Brown. Groups like the Drifters and the Clovers were also popular. By the mid-1950s, white performers such as Bill Haley and the Comets, Jerry Lee Lewis, and Elvis Presley imitated African-American music. Although their songs did not have the heavy back beat and explicit lyrics that most black music had, their music appealed to a white audience. Eventually, this combination of black and white musical styles became known as rock and roll.

1. _Possible answer: For most Americans, television is the major_

source of information, entertainment, and relaxation.

Most Americans own televisions. In fact, more people watch television than read magazines and newspapers. Television has even replaced the movies as the most popular form of entertainment. Not surprisingly, recent surveys have shown that most Americans get their news from television. Moreover, as anyone in the book industry knows, the best way for a book to become a best-seller is for it to be promoted on a popular television show. For example, a book that is endorsed by Oprah Winfrey is almost sure to become an instant best-seller. Finally, Americans spend many hours a day staring at their televisions, just trying to unwind.

2. *Possible answer: Applying for a job can be difficult, but the process can be made easier and more rewarding if you follow a few simple steps.*

First, you have to find a suitable job to apply for. Once you decide to apply, you have to type your résumé and send it to your potential employer. Then, when you are invited in for an interview, you need to decide what you are going to wear. At the interview, you need to speak slowly and clearly and answer all questions directly and honestly. After the interview, you need to send a note to the person who interviewed you, thanking him or her. Finally, if everything goes well, you will get a letter or a telephone call offering you the job.

3. *Possible answer: A lot of questions remain about Native Americans who were living in North America when the Europeans arrived.*

There are no written records left by the Native Americans themselves. Most of the early European settlers in North America were more interested in staying alive than in writing about the Native Americans. In addition, as the westward expansion took place, the Europeans met the Native Americans in stages, not all at once. Also, the Native Americans spoke at least fifty-eight different languages, which made it difficult for the Europeans to speak with them. Most important, by the time scholars decided to study Native American culture, many of the tribes no longer existed. Disease and war had wiped them out.

● Practice 2-4

Teaching Tip
Remind students to use TEST to check their paragraphs.

Read the following topic sentences. Then, write a paragraph that develops the main idea that is stated in each topic sentence. After you finish, check to make sure that all the sentences in your paragraph support your topic sentence.

1. On my first day as president, I would do three things.

2. My parents prepared me for life by teaching me a few important lessons.

3. Planning a successful party is easy if you follow a few simple steps.

Using Evidence to Support Your Paragraph's Main Idea

Teaching Tip
Have students discuss what makes support specific—facts, details, anecdotes with concrete evidence, for example.

The next thing you do when you **TEST** a paragraph is to make sure you have enough **evidence (E)** to support the main idea stated in your topic sentence.

The following paragraph does not include enough evidence to support the paragraph's main idea.

> Although pit bulls have a bad reputation, they actually make good pets. Part of their problem is that they can look frightening. Actually, however, pit bulls are no worse than other breeds of dogs. Even so, the bad publicity they get has given them a bad reputation. However, pit bulls do not deserve their bad reputation. Contrary to popular opinion, however, pit bulls can (and do) make friendly, affectionate, and loyal pets.

The following revised paragraph includes plenty of evidence (details and examples) to support the topic sentence.

T E S T
- Topic Sentence
- **Evidence**
- Summary Statement
- Transitions

> Although pit bulls have a bad reputation, they actually make good pets. Part of their problem is that they can look frightening. Their wide, powerful jaws, short muscular legs, and large teeth are ideally suited for fighting, and they were bred for this purpose. In addition, some pit bulls—especially males—can be very aggressive toward both people and other dogs. Actually, however, pit bulls are no worse than other breeds of dogs. As a recent newspaper article pointed out, the number of reported bites by pit bulls is no greater than the number of bites by other breeds. In fact, some breeds, such as cocker spaniels, bite more frequently than pit bulls. Even so, the bad publicity they get has given them a bad reputation. The problem is that whenever a pit bull attacks someone, the incident is reported on the evening news. Contrary to popular opinion, however, pit bulls can (and do) make friendly, affectionate, and loyal pets.

Note: Length alone is no guarantee that a paragraph has enough supporting evidence. A long paragraph that consists of one generalization after another may still not include enough support for the topic sentence.

● Practice 2-5

Underline the specific supporting evidence in each of the following paragraphs.

1. Hearing people have some mistaken ideas about the deaf community. First, some hearing adults think that all deaf people consider themselves disabled and would trade anything not to be "handicapped." Hearing people do not realize that many deaf people do not consider themselves handicapped and are proud to be part of the deaf community. They have their own language, customs, and culture. Second, many hearing people think that all deaf people read lips, so there is no need to learn sign language to communicate with them. Lip reading—or speech reading, as deaf people call the practice—is difficult. Not all hearing people say the same words in the same way, and facial expressions can also change the meaning of the words. If hearing people make more of an attempt to understand the deaf culture, communication between them will improve.

2. In 1996, the National Basketball Association (NBA) approved a women's professional basketball league. Within fifteen months, eight teams had been formed, four in the Eastern Conference and four in the Western Conference. Next, the teams began to draft players for these teams and to select a logo and uniforms. The final logo selected, a red, white, and blue shield, showed the silhouette of a woman player dribbling the ball, with the letters "WNBA" above her. The uniforms consisted of shorts and jerseys in the colors of the different teams. That first season, games were played in the summer when the television sports schedule was lighter so they could be televised during prime time. At the end of that season, the Houston Comets became the first WNBA champions. Today, the WNBA consists of sixteen teams that play 256 regular season games televised to audiences worldwide.

3. One of the largest celebrations of the passage of young girls into womanhood occurs in Latin American and Hispanic cultures. This event is called La Quinceañera, or the fifteenth year. It acknowledges that a young woman is now of marriageable age. The day usually begins with a Mass of Thanksgiving. The young woman wears a full-length white or pastel-colored dress and is attended by fourteen friends and relatives who serve as maids of honor and male escorts. Her parents and godparents surround her at the foot of the altar. When the Mass ends, other young relatives give small gifts to those who attended, while the Quinceañera places a bouquet of flowers on the altar of the Virgin. Following the Mass is an elaborate party, with dancing, cake, and toasts. Finally, to end the evening, the young woman dances a waltz with her favorite escort. For young Hispanic women, the Quinceañera is an important milestone.

● **Practice 2-6**

Provide two or three specific examples or details to support each of the following topic sentences. *Answers will vary.*

1. When it comes to feeding your family at the end of a hard day at work, there are several alternatives to fast food.

    ● _____

    ● _____

    ● _____

2. A romantic relationship with a coworker can create some serious problems.

    ● _____

    ● _____

    ● _____

3. When scheduling your classes, you need to keep several things in mind.

    ● _____

    ● _____

    ● _____

4. There are a number of steps you can take to protect yourself from identity theft.

    ● _____

    ● _____

    ● _____

5. Choosing the right computer was harder than I thought it would be.

    ● _____

    ● _____

    ● _____

● **Practice 2-7**

The two paragraphs that follow do not include enough supporting evidence. On a separate piece of paper, write three questions or suggestions that might help each writer develop his or her ideas more fully.

1. Computers can be a great help for students. Word processing can make writing assignments easier, and math drills can be fun when they are in the form of computer games. Also, when students have questions about almost anything, they can usually find the answer on the Internet. Even at a young age, children can do research by using computers. Computers are used so often by modern students that they cannot imagine what school was like before computers were invented.

2. Sometimes it is impossible to tell much about people from the clothes they wear. For example, athletic clothing is popular today, but almost everyone wears these clothes, not just athletes. Also, worn-out clothes do not necessarily show that people do not have enough money to buy new clothes. Faded, frayed, and ripped jeans are a popular style. In the past, black clothing was a symbol of mourning. Now, wearing black has nothing to do with being sad. Many times, clothing choices just indicate that people want to be in style.

Using a Summary Statement to Reinforce Your Paragraph's Unity

The third thing you do when you **TEST** a paragraph is to make sure it ends with a **summary statement (S)**—a sentence that restates your main idea in different words. By reminding readers what your paragraph is about, a summary statement helps to further **unify** your paragraph.

The following paragraph has no summary statement.

> The population problem is one of the biggest concerns for scientists. In 1900, there were 1.6 million people on earth, a quarter of today's population. At that time, life expectancy was also much shorter than it is now. By 2000, the world's population had grown to over 6 billion, and today, the average life expectancy worldwide is almost sixty-five years. The low death rate, combined with a high birth rate, is adding the equivalent of one new Germany to the world's population each year. According to a United Nations study, if present trends continue, by 2050 the world's population will be between 7.3 and 10.5 billion—so large that much of the world may be either malnourished or starving.

The summary statement in the following revised paragraph restates the paragraph's main idea.

The population problem is one of the biggest concerns for scientists. In 1900, there were 1.6 million people on earth, a quarter of today's population. At that time, life expectancy was also much shorter than it is now. By 2000, the world's population had grown to over 6 billion, and today, the average life expectancy worldwide is almost sixty-five years. The low death rate, combined with a high birth rate, is adding the equivalent of one new Germany to the world's population each year. According to a United Nations study, if present trends continue, by 2050 the world's population will be between 7.3 and 10.5 billion — so large that much of the world may be either malnourished or starving. Given these increases, it is no wonder that scientists who study population are worried.

● **Practice 2-8**

Read the following two paragraphs, which do not include summary statements. Then, on the lines below each paragraph, write a summary statement that adds unity to the paragraph by reinforcing the main idea stated in the topic sentence. Be careful not to use the same wording as the topic sentence.

1. Founded more than fifty years ago, NASCAR has become one of the most successful spectator sports in the world. In December 1947, Bill France formed the National Association for Stock Car Auto Racing (NASCAR). The first NASCAR race was held at Daytona Beach's auto racecourse in 1948. From this modest start, France turned NASCAR into a highly successful business. Attendance grew 8.2 percent during 1997, and 2,102,000 fans attended the thirty-one NASCAR events in 1998. This was the first time that NASCAR attendance topped the two million mark. Then, in 2001, NASCAR negotiated a multimillion-dollar television deal with Fox Sports/FX and NBC Sports/TNT. As a result, these networks began to televise the Winston Cup and Busch Series — two of NASCAR's most popular events.

Answers will vary.

_____

_____

2. The best way to deal with scrap tires that are worn out is to recycle them. Since the early 1990s, there has been an enormous growth in the demand for recycled tire rubber — "crumb rubber" — particularly in North America. The new products made from this material are often better than similar products made of conventional materials. For example, recycled tires are used to make mulch that serves as ground cover in playgrounds. This material is safer because it cushions falls, and it is cheaper than gravel or

woodchips. Material from recycled tires can also be mixed with asphalt to pave roads. The new surface is less expensive and more durable than surfaces made from conventional asphalt. Finally, recycled tires can be used to produce high-volume, low-tech products, such as livestock mats, railroad crossings, removable speed bumps, and athletic mats.

Answers will vary.

Using Transitions to Add Coherence to Your Paragraph

The final thing you do when you **TEST** a paragraph is make sure the paragraph includes **transitions (T)** that connect ideas in a clear, logical order.

   Transitional words and phrases create **coherence** by indicating how ideas are connected in a paragraph—for example, in *time order, spatial order,* or *logical order.* By signaling the order of ideas in a paragraph, these words and phrases make it easier for readers to follow your discussion.

● You use **time** signals to show readers the order in which events occurred.

> In 1883, my great-grandfather came to this country from Russia.

● You use **spatial** signals to show readers how people, places, and things stand in relation to one another. For example, you can move from top to bottom, from near to far, from right to left, and so on.

> In front of my bed is a bookcase that also serves as a room divider.

● You use **logical** signals to show readers how your ideas are connected. For example, you can move from the least important idea to the most important idea or from the least familiar idea to the most familiar idea.

> Certain strategies can help you do well in college. First, you should learn to manage your time effectively.

Because transitional words and phrases create coherence, a paragraph without them is difficult to understand. You can avoid this problem by checking to make sure you have included all the words and phrases that you need to link the ideas in your paragraph

Frequently Used Transitional Words and Phrases

Some Words and Phrases That Signal Time Order

after	finally	dates (for example,
afterward	later	"In June")
at first	next	dates (for example,
before	now	"In 1904")
during	soon	
earlier	then	
eventually	today	

Some Words and Phrases That Signal Spatial Order

above	in front	on the left
behind	inside	on the right
below	in the center	on top
beside	near	over
in back	next to	under
in between	on the bottom	

Some Words and Phrases That Signal Logical Order

also	last
although	moreover
as a result	next
consequently	not only . . .
first . . . second . . . third	but also
for example	one . . . another
for instance	similarly
furthermore	the least important
however	the most important
in fact	therefore

The following paragraph has no transitional words and phrases to link ideas.

During his lifetime, Jim Thorpe faced many obstacles. Thorpe was born in 1888, the son of an Irish father and a Native American mother. He was sent to the Carlisle Indian School in Pennsylvania. "Pop" Warner, the legendary coach at Carlisle, discovered Thorpe. Thorpe left Carlisle to play baseball for two seasons in the newly formed East Carolina minor league. He returned to Carlisle, played football, and was named to the All-American team. Thorpe went to the Olympic games in Stockholm, where he won two gold medals. Thorpe's career took a dramatic turn for the worse when a sportswriter who had seen him play baseball in North Carolina exposed him as a professional. The Amateur Athletic Union stripped him of his records and medals. Thorpe died in 1953. The International Olympic Committee returned Thorpe's Olympic medals to his family in 1982. Ironically, only in death was Thorpe able to overcome the difficulties that had frustrated him while he was alive.

The following revised paragraph includes transitional words and phrases that connect its ideas.

> During his lifetime, Jim Thorpe faced many obstacles. Thorpe was born in 1888, the son of an Irish father and a Native American mother. In 1904, he was sent to the Carlisle Indian School in Pennsylvania. The next year, "Pop" Warner, the legendary coach at Carlisle, discovered Thorpe. Thorpe left Carlisle in 1909 to play baseball for two seasons in the newly formed East Carolina minor league. In 1912, he returned to Carlisle, played football, and was named to the All-American team. Thorpe then went to the Olympic games in Stockholm, where he won two gold medals. The next year, however, Thorpe's career took a dramatic turn for the worse when a sportswriter who had seen him play baseball in North Carolina exposed him as a professional. As a result, the Amateur Athletic Union stripped him of his records and medals. Thorpe died in 1953. After years of appeals, the International Olympic Committee returned Thorpe's Olympic medals to his family in 1982. Ironically, only in death was Thorpe able to overcome the difficulties that had frustrated him while he was alive.

TEST
- Topic Sentence
- Evidence
- Summary Statement
- Transitions

● **Practice 2-9**

Read the following paragraph carefully. Then, select transitional words and phrases from the list below, and write them in the appropriate blanks. When you have finished, reread your paragraph to make sure that it is coherent.

Transitions

behind	inside
in front	next to
in the center	on top

The day I visited the Amish school, I knew it was unlike any other school I had ever seen before. A long tree-lined dirt road led to the small wooden schoolhouse. _____ of the school was a line of black bicycles and metal scooters. _____ the schoolhouse, a small baseball diamond had been carved into the dirt in the yard. _____ the school, two little outhouses stood next to each other. The schoolhouse itself was a small, one-story structure. White paint curled off its clapboard siding, and a short steeple, holding a brass bell, sat _____ of the roof. _____ the open door, a long line of identical black hats hung on wooden pegs. _____ of the small schoolhouse was an iron potbellied stove surrounded by the children's desks. From the moment I stepped into the room, I knew that this would be a day to remember.

● Practice 2-10

The following paragraph includes no transitions. Read the paragraph carefully. Then, after consulting the list of transitional words and phrases on page 41, add appropriate transitional words and phrases to connect the paragraph's ideas in **time order**.

In 1856, my great-great-great-grandparents, Anne and Charles McGinley, faced many hardships to come to the United States. _____ they left Ireland, their landlords, who lived in England, raised the rent on their land so much that my ancestors could not afford to pay it. _____ it took them three years to save the money for passage. _____ they had saved the money, they had to look for a ship that was willing to take them. _____, my great-great-great-grandparents were able to leave. They and their ten children spent four long months on a small ship. Storms, strong tides, and damaged sails made the trip longer than it should have been. _____, in November 1856, they saw land, and two days later they sailed into New York Harbor. _____ they took a train to Baltimore, Maryland, where their cousins lived and where we live today. At that time, they couldn't have known how thankful their descendants would be for their sacrifice.

● Practice 2-11

The following paragraph includes no transitions. Read the paragraph carefully. Then, after consulting the list of transitional words and phrases on page 41, add appropriate transitional words and phrases to connect the paragraph's ideas in **spatial order**.

The casinos in Atlantic City are designed to make sure you don't pay attention to anything except gambling. As soon as you walk in the door, you are steered toward the gaming room. _____ of you are the slot machines, blinking and making lots of noise. _____ of the slot machines are the table games—blackjack, roulette, and craps. _____ the gambling area, the ceiling is painted a dull, neutral color. _____ the floor is a carpet that has a complicated pattern that is hard to look at. Both the ceiling and the carpet are designed to make sure that gamblers look just at the games they are playing. All the way _____ of the casino are the bathrooms, and you have to walk through the entire slot machine area if you want to use one. The casino designers are betting that you will not be able to resist stopping to play. As you can see, the design of the casinos makes it difficult for the average person to come out ahead.

● Practice 2-12

The following paragraph includes no transitions. Read the paragraph carefully. Then, after consulting the list of transitional words and phrases on page 41, add appropriate transitional words and phrases to connect the paragraph's ideas in **logical order**.

My high school had three silly rules. The _____ silly rule was that only seniors could go outside the school building for lunch. In spite of this rule, many students went outside to eat because the cafeteria was not big enough to hold everyone. Understanding the problem, the teachers just looked the other way as long as we came back to school on time. The _____ silly rule was that we had to attend

95 percent of all the classes for each course. If we did not, we were supposed to fail. Of course, that rule was never enforced, because if it were, almost every student in the school would have failed everything. The _____ silly rule is that students were not supposed to throw their hats into the air at graduation. At one point in the past, a parent— no one can remember who—complained that a falling hat could poke someone in the eye. _____, graduating classes were told that under no circumstances could they throw their hats into the air. _____, on graduation day, we did what every graduating class has always done—ignored the silly rule and threw our hats into the air.

Focus on Writing: *Revising and Editing*

Review the work you did for the Focus on Writing activity on page 29. Then, revise your paragraph for unity, support, and coherence.

Chapter Review

Teaching Tip
Assign groups of three or four students to rewrite the Editing Practice paragraphs, adding details and examples.

Editing Practice

TEST each of the following paragraphs for unity, support, and coherence. Begin by underlining the topic sentence. Then, cross out any sentences that do not support the topic sentence. If necessary, add evidence (details and examples) to support the topic sentence. Next, add transitional words and phrases where they are needed. Finally, decide whether you need to make any changes to the paragraph's summary statement. *Answers will vary.*

1. In 1979, a series of mechanical and human errors in Unit 2 of the nuclear generating plant at Three Mile Island, near Harrisburg, Pennsylvania, caused an accident that changed the nuclear power industry. A combination of stuck valves, human error, and poor decisions caused a

partial meltdown of the reactor core. ~~Large~~ *As a result, large* amounts of radioactive gases were released into the atmosphere. ~~The~~ *Consequently, the* governor of Pennsylvania evacuated pregnant women from the area. Other residents *then* panicked and left their homes. The nuclear regulatory agency claimed that the situation was not really dangerous and that the released gases were not a health threat. ~~Activists~~ *However, activists* and local residents disagreed with this. ~~The reactor itself remained unusable for more than ten years.~~ Large demonstrations followed the accident, including a rally of more than 200,000 people in New York City. ~~Some people came because the day was nice.~~ By the mid-1980s, as a result of the accident, new construction of nuclear power plants in the United States had stopped.

2.   A survey of cigarette advertisements shows how tobacco companies have consistently encouraged people to smoke. One of the earliest television ads showed two boxes of cigarettes dancing to an advertising jingle. ~~Many people liked these ads.~~ ~~Other~~ *However, other* advertisements were more subtle. Some were aimed at specific audiences. Marlboro commercials, *for example,* with the rugged Marlboro man, targeted men. *In contrast,* Virginia Slims made an obvious pitch to women by saying, "You've come a long way, baby!" *Also,* Salem, a mentholated cigarette, showed rural scenes and targeted people who liked the freshness of the outdoors. *Similarly,* Kent, with its "micronite filter," appealed to those who were health conscious by claiming that Kent contained less tar and nicotine than any other brand. ~~This claim was not entirely true. Other brands had less tar and nicotine.~~ *Later,* Merit and other high-tar and high-nicotine cigarettes began to use advertisements that were aimed at minorities. ~~Cigarette~~ *Eventually, cigarette* companies responded to the national decline in smoking by directing advertising at young people. *For instance,* Camel introduced the cartoon character Joe Camel, which was aimed at teenagers and young adults. *As these examples show, cigarette companies have done whatever they could to keep people smoking, regardless of the health risks.*

3.　　Cities created police forces for a number of reasons. The first reason was status: after the Civil War, it became a status symbol for cities to have a uniformed police force. ~~A~~ *Second, a* police force provided jobs. This meant that politicians were able to reward people who worked to support them. ~~Police~~ *Third, police* forces made people feel safe. ~~Police~~ *for example, police* officers helped visitors find their way. ~~They~~ *In addition, they* took in lost children and sometimes fed the homeless. They *also* directed traffic, enforced health regulations, and provided other services. ~~Police~~ *Finally, police* officers kept order. Without a police force, criminals would have made life in nineteenth-century cities unbearable.

Collaborative Activities

1. Working in a group, list the reasons why you think students decide to attend your school. After working together to arrange these reasons in logical order—for example, from least to most important—write a topic sentence that states the main idea suggested by these reasons. Finally, on your own, draft a paragraph in which you discuss why students attend your school.

🌐 **ESL Tip**
Collaborative Activity 2 is an excellent exercise for bringing out students' creativity. Assign it as a group project, being sure to pair nonnative speakers with native speakers.

2. In a newspaper or magazine, find an illustration or photograph that includes a lot of details. Then, write a paragraph describing what you see. (Include enough supporting examples so that readers will be able to "see" it almost as clearly as you can.) Decide on a specific spatial order—from top to bottom or from left to right, for example—that makes sense to you. Use that spatial order to organize the details in your paragraph. Finally, trade paragraphs with another student, and offer suggestions that could improve his or her paragraph.

3. Bring to class a paragraph from a newspaper or a magazine article or from one of your textbooks. Working in a group, TEST each paragraph to see if it includes all the elements of an effective paragraph. If any paragraph does not follow the guidelines outlined in this chapter, work as a group to revise it.

Review Checklist: TESTing Your Paragraphs

☐ A topic sentence states a paragraph's main idea. (See 2A.)

☐ A paragraph should be unified, with all its sentences supporting the paragraph's main idea. (See 2A.)

☐ A paragraph should include enough evidence—examples or details—to support its main idea. (See 2B.)

☐ A paragraph should end with a summary statement that reinforces its main idea and helps to unify the paragraph. (See 2C.)

☐ A paragraph should be coherent, with all its sentences arranged in time order, spatial order, or logical order. (See 2D.)

☐ A paragraph should include transitional words and phrases that indicate how ideas are connected. (See 2D.)

Unit Two

Patterns of Paragraph Development

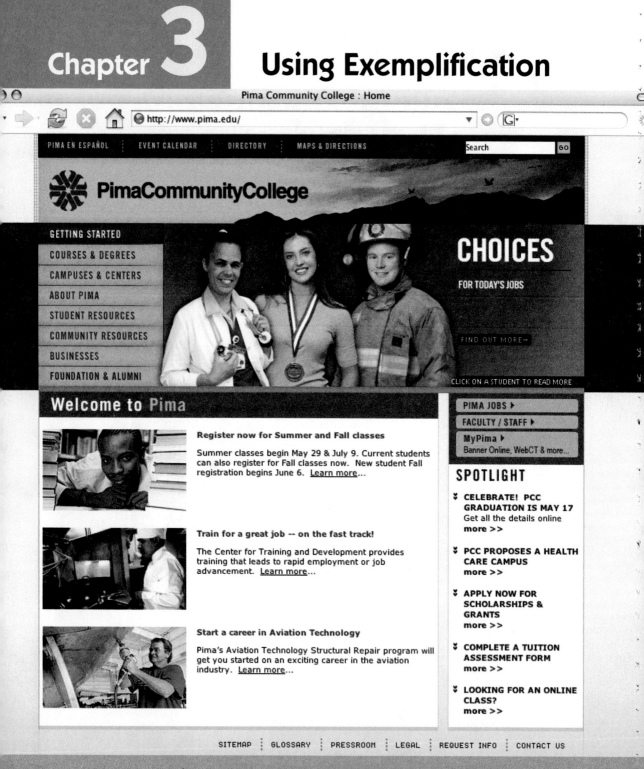

A university-level study found that women are more likely than men to go on to their second year of college when offered a combination of scholarships and student support services.

In Chapters 1 and 2, you learned how to write effective paragraphs. In Chapters 3 though 11, you will learn different ways of organizing your ideas within paragraphs. Understanding these patterns can help you organize ideas in your paragraphs and become a more effective, more confident writer.

Teaching Tip
You may want to tell students that the same patterns they use to shape paragraphs may also be used to shape essays.

What Is Exemplification?

Teaching Tip
Remind students that many everyday tasks call for exemplification. In a letter to a local newspaper, they might give examples of improvements that need to be made to a local neighborhood.

What do we mean when we tell a friend that an instructor is *good* or that a football team is *bad*? What do we mean when we say that a play is *boring* or that a particular war was *wrong*? To clarify general statements like these, we use **exemplification**—that is, we give **examples** to illustrate a general idea. In daily conversation and in school, you use examples to help explain your ideas.

General Statement	*Specific Examples*
Today is going to be a hard day.	Today is going to be a hard day because I have a history test in the morning and a lab quiz in the afternoon. I also have to go to work an hour earlier than usual.

➔ Focus on Writing

The picture on the opposite page shows the home page of the Pima Community College Web site. Many students go to this site for information about the school and the support services offered there. Look at the image of the home page, and then write a paragraph about what programs and services your school should offer to make it easier for students to adjust to college.

WORD POWER
adapt adjust to new surroundings
mentor a person who offers helpful guidance
facilitate to make easy

General Statement	*Specific Examples*
My car is giving me problems.	My car is burning oil and won't start on cold mornings. In addition, I need a new set of tires.

An **exemplification paragraph** explains or clarifies a general idea with specific examples. Personal experiences, class discussions, observations, conversations, and reading can all be good sources of examples.

An exemplification paragraph begins with a topic sentence that is followed by examples supporting the general statement made in the topic sentence. Examples should be arranged in **logical order**—for example, from least important to most important or from general to specific. How many examples you need depends on your topic sentence. A complicated statement might require many examples to support it. A simple, straightforward statement might require fewer examples. The paragraph closes with a summary statement that sums up its main idea.

An exemplification paragraph generally has the following structure.

Topic Sentence_____

Example #1_____

_____

Example #2_____

_____

Example #3_____

_____

Summary Statement_____

_____

The following paragraph uses examples to make the point that Philadelphia is an exciting city to visit.

Visiting Philadelphia

Topic Sentence —————

If you know where to go, Philadelphia can be an exciting city to visit. For example, Philadelphia is a city of museums. Within walking distance of each other are the Art Museum, the Rodin Museum, the Academy of Natural Sciences, and the Franklin Institute Science Museum. There are also less well-known museums, such as the Mutter Medical Museum, the Polish-American Cultural Center Museum, and the Please Touch Museum. In addition to museums, Philadelphia has a number of world-class sports teams. If you are lucky, you might be able to get tickets to see the Eagles play football at Lincoln Financial Field or the 76ers play basketball at The Wachovia Center. You can also see other professional sports teams, such as the Phillies, the Flyers, and the Wings, Philadelphia's professional lacrosse team. Finally, you can visit some of Philadelphia's historic sites, such as the Betsy Ross House, Independence Hall, the National Constitution Center, and the Liberty Bell. It is no wonder that many people who visit Philadelphia for the first time say that they can't wait to come back.

Examples —————

Summary Statement —————

Jeffrey Smith (student)

When you write an exemplification paragraph, be sure to include appropriate transitional words and phrases. These transitions will help readers follow your discussion by indicating how your examples are related and how each example supports the topic sentence.

Some Transitional Words and Phrases for Exemplification

also	furthermore	the most important
finally,	in addition	example
first . . . second . . .	moreover	the next example
(and so on)	one example . . .	
for example	another example . . .	
for instance	specifically	

Grammar in Context: Exemplification

When you write an exemplification paragraph, always use a comma after the introductory transitional word or phrase that introduces an example.

For example, Philadelphia is a city of museums.

In addition to museums, Philadelphia has a number of world-class sports teams.

Finally, you can visit some of Philadelphia's historic sites.

For information on using commas with introductory transitional words and phrases, see 30B.

● Practice 3-1

Read this exemplification paragraph; then, follow the instructions on page 55.

Teaching Tip
Before your students write exemplification paragraphs, you might want to explain the use of commas to set off introductory transitional elements (30B) and have them do Practice 30-2.

Jobs of the Future

Students should take courses that prepare them for the careers that will be in demand over the next ten years. For example, the health-care field will have the greatest growth. Hundreds of thousands of medical workers — such as home-care aides, physician assistants, and registered nurses — will be needed. Also, many new employees will be needed in the retail and customer-service areas. These are fields in which technology cannot completely replace human beings. In addition, certain computer fields will need many more workers. People who can work as database administrators or information systems managers will find many employment opportunities. Furthermore, education will be an attractive area for new job seekers. Many new teachers will be needed to replace the thousands who are expected to retire during the next ten years. Students who know what jobs will be available can prepare themselves for the future.

1. Underline the topic sentence of the paragraph.

2. List the specific examples the writer uses to support her topic sentence. The first example has been listed for you.

health-care jobs

retail and customer-service jobs

computer occupations

jobs in education

3. Circle the transitions that the writer uses to connect ideas in the paragraph.

4. Underline the paragraph's summary statement.

● **Practice 3-2**

Following are four possible topic sentences for exemplification paragraphs. Copy each topic sentence on a separate sheet of paper. Then, list three or four examples you could use to support each topic sentence. For example, if you were writing a paragraph about how difficult the first week of your new job was, you could mention waking up early, getting to know your coworkers, and learning new routines. *Answers will vary.*

1. I really like my neighborhood.

2. Internships give students valuable opportunities to develop job skills.

3. Good health care is sometimes difficult to get.

4. Some reality television shows insult the intelligence of their viewers.

3b **Writing an Exemplification Paragraph**

When Sarah Herman was asked to write a paragraph about work, she had little difficulty deciding on a topic. She had just finished a summer job waiting on tables in Sea Isle City, New Jersey. She knew, without a doubt, that this was the worst job she had ever had.

Once she had decided on her topic, Sarah brainstormed to find ideas to write about. After reviewing her brainstorming notes, she listed several examples that could support her topic sentence.

Restaurant too big

Boss disrespectful

No experience

Kitchen chaotic

Customers rude

Tips bad

After reading her list, Sarah wrote the following topic sentence to express the main idea of her paragraph.

Topic Sentence: Waiting on tables was the worst job I ever had.

After Sarah identified her main idea, she eliminated examples that she thought did not support her topic sentence. Then, she arranged the remaining examples in an order in which she could discuss them most effectively — in this case, from least important to most important example.

Topic Sentence: Waiting on tables was the worst job I ever had.
1. No experience
2. Customers rude
3. Tips bad
4. Boss disrespectful

Using her list of points as a guide, Sarah wrote the following draft of her paragraph.

> Waiting on tables was the worst job I ever had. I had little experience as a waitress. The first day of work was so bad that I almost quit. The customers were rude. All they wanted was to get their food as fast as possible so they could get back to the beach or the boardwalk. They were often impolite and demanding. The tips were bad. It was hard to be pleasant when you knew that the table you were waiting on was probably going to leave you a bad tip. Finally, the owner of the restaurant did not show us any respect. He often yelled at us, saying that if we didn't work harder, he would fire us. He never did, but his constant threats didn't do much to help our morale.

When she finished her draft, Sarah met with her instructor, who thought that her paragraph would be better if she made some of her examples more specific. For example, what experience did she have that made her want to quit? Exactly how were customers rude? Her instructor also reminded her that she needed to TEST her paragraph. As she applied the **TEST** strategy, Sarah assessed her paragraph and made some changes.

- She checked her **topic sentence** and decided that it was effective.
- She evaluated her **evidence**. Then, she added more examples and details and deleted irrelevant details.
- She noticed that she did not have a **summary statement**, so she added one at the end of her paragraph.
- She added more **transitions** to make it easier for readers to follow her discussion.

Teaching Tip
Refer students to 1J for information on revising and editing their paragraphs.

After making these changes, she went on to revise and edit her draft. Here is Sarah's final draft.

T E S T

Topic Sentence

Evidence

Summary Statement

Transitions

My Worst Job

Waiting on tables was the worst job I ever had. First, I had never worked in a restaurant before, so I made a lot of mistakes. Once, I forgot to bring salads to a table I waited on. A person at the table complained so loudly that the owner had to calm him down. I was so frustrated and upset that I almost quit. Second, the customers at the restaurant were often rude. All they wanted was to get their food as fast as possible so they could get back to the beach or the boardwalk. They were on vacation, and they wanted to be treated well. As a result, they were frequently very demanding. No one ever said, "excuse me," "please," or "thank you," no matter what I did for them. Third, the tips were usually bad. It was hard to be pleasant when you knew that the table you were waiting on was probably going to leave you a bad tip, if you were lucky. Finally, the owner of the restaurant never showed his workers any respect. He would yell at us, saying that if we didn't work harder, he would fire us. He never did, but his constant threats didn't do much to help our morale. Even though I survived the summer, I promised myself that I would never wait on tables again.

● **Practice 3-3**

Now, you are ready to write a draft of an exemplification paragraph. Choose one of the topics below (or choose your own topic) for an exemplification paragraph. Then, on a separate sheet of paper, use one or more of the strategies described in 1C to help you think of as many examples as you can for the topic you have chosen.

Effective (or ineffective) teachers	Things you can't do without
Qualities that make a great athlete	Terrible dates
Successful movies	Dangerous sports
Challenges that older students face	Role models
	Rude behavior
Traditions your family follows	Politicians
Unattractive clothing styles	Acts of bravery
Peer pressure	Lying
The benefits of iPods	Credit-card debt

● **Practice 3-4**

Review your notes from Practice 3-3, and list the examples that can best help you develop a paragraph on the topic you have chosen.

Answers will vary.

_____

_____

_____

_____

Teaching Tip
Walk around the room, checking topic sentences. Ask students to read particularly effective ones aloud.

● **Practice 3-5**

Teaching Tip
You may want to remind students that an effective topic sentence will help unify the ideas in a paragraph. Effective support for the topic sentence will make the paragraph more convincing. Transitions will add coherence.

Reread your list of examples from Practice 3-4. Then, draft a topic sentence that introduces your topic and communicates the main idea your paragraph will discuss.

Answers will vary.

_____

_____

_____

_____

Teaching Tip
Look at this exercise closely. Sometimes what students call logical order is not logical order at all.

⊕ **ESL Tip**
In addition to this exercise, give students a proof-reading exercise focusing on verb forms, verb endings, prepositions, and articles. Prepare this exercise ahead of time by keeping track of frequent errors in students' writing.

● Practice 3-6

Arrange the examples you listed in Practice 3-4 in a logical order—for example, from least important to most important.
Answers will vary.

1. _____

2. _____

3. _____

4. _____

● Practice 3-7

Draft your exemplification paragraph. Then, using the **TEST** checklist on page 61, check your paragraph for unity, support, and coherence.

● Practice 3-8

Now, revise your exemplification paragraph.

● Practice 3-9

Prepare a final draft of your exemplification paragraph.

Focus on Writing: *Revising and Editing*

Look back at your response to the Focus on Writing activity on page 51. Using the **TEST** checklist on page 61, evaluate the paragraph you wrote for unity, support, and coherence. Then, prepare a final draft of your paragraph.

Chapter Review

WORD POWER

ignorance the state of being uneducated, unaware, or uninformed

motivate to move to action

Focus on Writing

The billboard pictured below shows a public service advertisement promoting HIV/AIDS awareness. Study the picture carefully, and then write an exemplification paragraph explaining what is effective (or ineffective) about this ad. Begin with a topic sentence that states your opinion of the ad's strengths or weaknesses. Then, after briefly describing the ad, give specific examples to support the opinion you state in your topic sentence.

Real-World Writing

Write a one-paragraph memo to your employer suggesting improvements in your workplace environment, or write an email to your dean of students suggesting improvements to a campus service (the Writing Center, Student Health, or the Financial Aid Office, for example).

T E S T ing an Exemplification Paragraph

Topic Sentence Unifies Your Paragraph

☐ Do you have a clearly worded topic sentence that states your paragraph's main idea?

☐ Does your topic sentence state an idea that can be supported by examples?

Evidence Supports Your Paragraph's Topic Sentence

☐ Do all your examples support your main idea?

☐ Do you have enough examples, or do you need to include more?

Summary Statement Reinforces Your Paragraph's Unity

☐ Does your paragraph end with a statement that summarizes your main idea?

Transitions Add Coherence to Your Paragraph

☐ Do you use a transitional word or phrase to introduce each example your paragraph discusses?

☐ Do you need to add transitions to make your paragraph more coherent?

Chapter 4   Using Narration

The French actor who plays the part of the giant, Fezzik, in *The Princess Bride* was actually seven feet tall in real life. He was also a professional wrestler known as André the Giant.

4a

What Is Narration?

Teaching Tip
To help students understand the concept of narration, read aloud a tall tale or a fairy tale—or a plot summary from *Soap Opera Digest*.

Teaching Tip
Tell students that many everyday writing tasks require narration. In a complaint letter, they might summarize, in chronological order, the problems they had with a particular product.

Narration is writing that tells a story. A **narrative paragraph** begins with a topic sentence that tells readers why you are telling a particular story. For example, you could be telling how an experience you had as a child changed you, or that the Battle of Gettysburg was the turning point in the Civil War.

Effective narrative paragraphs include only those events that tell the story and avoid irrelevant information. The more specific the details you include, the better your narrative paragraph will be. Narrative paragraphs present events in **time order**, the order in which events actually occurred. A summary statement sums up the paragraph's main idea.

A narrative paragraph generally has the following structure.

Topic Sentence_____
Event #1_____
•_____
Event #2_____
_____
Event #3_____
_____
Summary Statement_____
_____

→ Focus on Writing

The picture on the opposite page shows a scene from the movie *The Princess Bride*, a fairy tale that includes giants, an evil prince, and a beautiful princess. Look at the picture, and then write a paragraph in which you retell a fairy tale, folk tale, or children's story that you know well. Make sure your topic sentence states the point of the story.

WORD POWER
fairy tale a story about make-believe people and magical deeds
folk tale an often-told story that includes a moral; it may or may not be true
memorable worth remembering
moral a lesson of a fable or story

The student writer of the following paragraph presents a series of events to support the idea that the fashion designer Chloe Dao had a difficult life.

Overnight Success

Topic Sentence ——————

<u>Chloe Dao traveled a difficult road to become a successful fashion designer.</u> When Dao was a baby, her parents decided to leave her native country, Laos, and come to the United States. Unfortunately, the Viet Cong captured her and her family as they tried to cross the border. They were sent to a refugee camp, where they stayed for four years. In 1979, when she was eight, Dao and her family were allowed to come to the United States. Then, they had to earn enough money to live on. Dao's mother worked three jobs. On the weekends, the entire family ran the snack bar at a flea market. Finally, they saved enough money to open a dry cleaning business. When she was twenty, Dao moved to New York to attend school. After she graduated, she got a challenging job as production manager for designer Melinda Eng. Eventually, she opened a boutique, where she featured clothes that she designed. Her big break came in 2006 when she was chosen as a finalist on the reality show *Project Runway*. <u>Although Chloe Dao may appear to be an "overnight success," she had to struggle to get where she is today.</u>

Events ——————

Summary Statement ——————

Christine Clark (student)

As you arrange your ideas in your narrative paragraphs, be sure to use clear transitional words and phrases, as the student writer does in the paragraph above. These signals help readers follow your narrative by indicating the order of the events you discuss.

Some Transitional Words and Phrases for Narration

after	immediately	specific times (for
as	in time	example, "two days,"
as soon as	later	"five minutes," "ten
before	later on	years")
by this time	meanwhile	suddenly
earlier	next	then
eventually	now	when
finally	soon	while
first . . . second . . . third . . .	specific dates (for example, "in 2006")	

**Grammar in
Context:
Narration**

When you write a narrative paragraph, you tell a story. As you become involved in your story, you might begin to string events together without proper punctuation. If you do, you will create a **run-on**.

Incorrect (run-on)	Dao's mother worked three jobs on the weekends, the entire family ran a snack bar at a flea market.
Correct	Dao's mother worked three jobs. On the weekends, the entire family ran the snack bar at a flea market.

For information on how to identify and correct run-ons, see Chapter 20.

Teaching Tip
Before your students
write narrative
paragraphs, you might
want to explain how to
identify and correct run-
ons and comma splices
(Chapter 20) and have
them do Practices 20-1
and 20-4.

Teaching Tip
Bring to class a
magazine photograph
that shows two people
talking. Ask students to
discuss what the people
might be saying and to
write out the conversa-
tion in dialogue format.
Then, have students
exchange papers and
check each other's work.
Explain how dialogue
enriches narrative writing.

● **Practice 4-1**

Read this narrative paragraph, and answer the questions that follow it.

⟨When⟩ I first came to live in a dormitory at college, I was home-sick. ⟨As soon as⟩ my parents left me at school, I felt sad. My room looked cramped and empty. I couldn't see how two people could live in such a tiny space, and I missed my room at home. My roommate hadn't arrived yet, so I picked out a bed on one side of the room and started to unpack my belongings. ⟨Then,⟩ my roommate burst through the door, smiling and joking. ⟨Immediately,⟩ I felt better. We talked about our high schools and our families. ⟨Later on,⟩ we made plans to fix up the room with some posters. ⟨When⟩ it was time to eat, we went to the cafeteria for dinner. I was used to meat and potatoes; however, the cafeteria was serving salads and veggie burgers. ⟨Suddenly,⟩ I wanted to be home, eating with my family. I even missed my little sister. ⟨When⟩ I went to bed that night, I thought about the changes that I would have to adapt to. ⟨Now,⟩ I realized that living away from home would be very challenging.

John Deni (student)

1. Underline the topic sentence of the paragraph.

2. List the major events of the narrative. The first event has been listed for you.

I felt sad.

I found my new dorm room to be cramped and empty.

I unpacked my belongings.

My roommate arrived.

I felt better.

We planned ways to fix up the room.

I didn't like the food in the cafeteria at dinner.

I missed my family.

3. Circle the transitional words and phrases that the writer uses to link events in time.

4. Underline the paragraph's summary statement.

● **Practice 4-2**

Below are four possible topic sentences for narrative paragraphs. Copy the topic sentences on a separate sheet of paper, and then list three or four events that could support each topic sentence. For example, if you were recalling a barbecue that turned into a disaster, you could tell about burning the hamburgers, spilling the soda, and forgetting to buy paper plates.
Answers will vary.

1. One experience made me realize that I was no longer as young as I thought.

2. The first time I _____, I got more than I bargained for.

3. I did not think I had the courage to _____, but when I did, I felt proud of myself.

4. I remember my reaction to one particular news story very clearly.

4b

Writing a Narrative Paragraph

Todd Kinzer's instructor asked the class to write a paragraph about an experience that had a great impact on them. Todd tried to narrow this topic by listing some experiences that he could possibly write about.

Accident at camp — Realized I wasn't as strong as I thought I was

Breaking up with Lindsay — That was painful

Shooting the winning basket in my last high school game — Sweet

The last Thanksgiving at my grandparents' house — Happy and sad

As Todd looked over the experiences on his list, he realized that he could write about all of them. He decided, however, to focus on the last Thanksgiving he spent at his grandparents' house. This occasion was especially meaningful to him because his grandfather died right after that Thanksgiving.

Todd began his writing process by freewriting on his topic. He wrote down whatever came into his mind about the dinner, without worrying about spelling, punctuation, or grammar. Here is Todd's freewriting paragraph.

Thanksgiving. Who knew? I remember the smells when I woke up. I can see Granddad at the stove. We were all happy. He told us stories about when he was a kid. I had heard some of them before, but so what? I loved to hear them. We ate so much I could hardly move. Turkey has something in it that puts you to sleep. We watched football all afternoon and evening. Too bad Granddad died. I still can't believe it. I guess I have the topic for my paragraph.

When he looked over his freewriting, Todd thought he had enough ideas for a first draft of his paragraph. His paragraph appears below.

Last Thanksgiving, my grandparents were up early. My grandfather stuffed the turkey, and my grandmother started cooking the other dishes. When I got up, I could smell the turkey in the oven. The table was already set for dinner, so we ate breakfast in the kitchen. My grandfather told us about the Thanksgivings he remembered from when he was a boy. When we sat down for dinner, a fire was burning in the fireplace. My grandmother said grace. My grandfather carved the turkey, and we all passed around dishes of food. For dessert, we had pecan pie and ice cream. After dinner, we watched football on TV. When I went to bed, I felt happy. This was my grandfather's last Thanksgiving.

Todd realized that his first draft needed work. Before he wrote his next draft, he tried to remember what other things had happened that Thanksgiving; he also tried to decide which idea was most important and what additional details could make his narrative more complete.

To help him plan his revision, he applied the **TEST** strategy to his paragraph; then, he made some changes.

- He added a **topic sentence** that stated his main idea.
- He added some more details and examples and crossed out sentences that did not belong in his paragraph; now, all his **evidence** supported his main idea.
- He wrote a stronger **summary statement**.
- He added **transitional words and phrases** to indicate the time order of the events in his paragraph.

Teaching Tip
Refer students to 1J for information on revising and editing their paragraphs.

After making these changes, Todd made some additional revisions; then, he edited his paragraph, checking his grammar, punctuation, mechanics, and spelling and looking carefully for typos. Here is his final draft.

Thanksgiving Memories

This past Thanksgiving was happy and sad because it was the last one I would spend with both my grandparents. The holiday began early. At 5 o'clock in the morning, my grandfather woke up and began to stuff the turkey. About an hour later, my grandmother began cooking corn pie and pineapple casserole. At 8 o'clock, when I got up, I could smell the turkey cooking. While we ate breakfast, my grandfather told us about Thanksgivings he remembered when he was a boy. Later, my grandfather made a fire in the fireplace, and we sat down for dinner. After my grandmother said grace, my grandfather carved and served the turkey. The rest of us passed around dishes of sweet potatoes, mashed potatoes, green beans, asparagus, cucumber salad, relish, cranberry sauce, apple butter, cabbage salad, stuffing, and, of course, corn pie and pineapple casserole. For dessert, my grandmother served pecan pie with scoops of ice cream. After dinner, we turned on the TV and the whole family watched football all evening. That night, I remember thinking that life couldn't get much better. Four months later, my grandfather died in his sleep. For my family and me, Thanksgiving would never be the same.

T E S T

Topic Sentence

Evidence

Summary Statement

Transitions

● Practice 4-3

Now, you are ready to write a draft of your narrative paragraph. Choose one of the topics below (or choose your own topic) for a narrative paragraph. On a separate sheet of paper, use one or more of the strategies described in 1C to help you recall events and details about the topic you have chosen.

A difficult choice	An embarrassing situation
A frightening situation	A surprise

A time of self-doubt	A sudden understanding or insight
A success	Something funny a friend did
An act of violence	Unexpected good luck
A lesson you learned	A conflict with authority
A happy moment	An event that changed your life
An instance of injustice	An important decision

● Practice 4-4

List the events you recalled in Practice 4-3 that can best help you develop a narrative paragraph on the topic you have chosen.

Answers will vary.

_____

_____

_____

_____

_____

● Practice 4-5

Reread your list of events from Practice 4-4. Then, draft a topic sentence that introduces your topic and communicates the main idea your paragraph will discuss.

Answers will vary.

_____

_____

● Practice 4-6

Write down the events you listed in Practice 4-4 in the order in which they occurred.

1. *Answers will vary.* _____

2. _____

3. _____

4. _____

5. _____

Teaching Tip
You may want to remind students that an effective topic sentence will help unify the ideas in a paragraph. Effective support for the topic sentence will make the paragraph more convincing. Transitions will add coherence.

● **Practice 4-7**

Draft your narrative paragraph. Then, using the **TEST** checklist on page 71, check your paragraph for unity, support, and coherence.

● **Practice 4-8**

Now, revise your narrative paragraph.

● **Practice 4-9**

Prepare a final draft of your narrative paragraph.

Focus on Writing: *Revising and Editing*

Look back at your response to the Focus on Writing activity on page 63. Using the **TEST** checklist on page 71, evaluate the paragraph you wrote for unity, support, and coherence. Then, prepare a final draft of your paragraph.

Chapter Review

Focus on Writing

The picture below shows a bride and groom at a Las Vegas wedding chapel. Study the picture carefully, and then write a narrative paragraph that tells the story behind it.

WORD POWER
impulsive acting without thought or without considering the results of one's actions
unique one of a kind

Real-World Writing

Assume that you are filling out a personality profile for an online dating service. One of the questions asks you to tell a story about yourself that illustrates your best character trait. Write a narrative paragraph that tells this story.

T E S Ting a Narrative Paragraph

Topic Sentence Unifies Your Paragraph

☐ Do you have a clearly worded topic sentence that states your paragraph's main idea?

☐ Does your topic sentence give readers an idea why you are telling the story?

Evidence Supports Your Paragraph's Topic Sentence

☐ Do all your examples and details support your paragraph's main idea?

☐ Do you include enough information about the events you discuss?

☐ Do you need to include more specific details to add interest to your narrative?

Summary Statement Reinforces Your Paragraph's Unity

☐ Does your paragraph end with a statement that summarizes your main idea?

Transitions Add Coherence to Your Paragraph

☐ Do your transitions indicate the time order of events in your paragraph?

☐ Do you need to add transitions to make your paragraph more coherent?

Chapter 5 Using Description

The restaurant industry employs about 12.5 million people, making it one of the largest employers in the United States.

What Is Description?

Teaching Tip
Before starting this chapter, write several "dead verbs" on the board, and ask students to give variations of each verb in "living verb" form. (For example, instead of *The snake* moved, they might say *slithered* or *wiggled*.)

Teaching Tip
Tell students that many everyday writing tasks require description. For example, in a job-application letter, they might describe equipment they have worked with.

In a personal email, you may describe a new boyfriend or girlfriend. In a biology lab paper, you may describe the structure of a cell. In a report for a nursing class, you may describe a patient you treated.

When you write a **description**, you choose words that paint a picture for your readers. You use language that creates a vivid impression of what you have seen, heard, smelled, tasted, or touched. The more details you include, the better your description will be.

The following description is flat because it includes no specific details.

Flat description   I saw a beautiful sunrise.

In contrast, the description below is full of details that convey the writer's experience to readers.

Rich description   Early this morning, as I walked along the sandy beach, I saw the sun rise slowly out of the ocean. At first, the ocean looked red. Then, it turned slowly to pink, to aqua, and finally to blue. As I stood watching the sun, I heard the waves hit the shore, and I felt the cold water swirl around my toes. For a moment, even the small grey and white birds that ran along the shore seemed to stop and watch the dazzling sight.

The revised description relies on sight (*looked red*; *turned slowly to pink, to aqua, and finally to blue*), touch (*the sandy beach*; *felt the cold water*), and sound (*heard the waves hit the shore*).

→ Focus on Writing

The picture on the opposite page shows a waitress serving food. Look at the picture, and then write a paragraph in which you describe a person you encounter every day—for example, a street vendor, a bus driver, or a worker in your school cafeteria.

WORD POWER
disregard to ignore; to neglect

Teaching Tip
To help students
understand the concept
of description, bring
some picture postcards
(or other images) to
class. Ask pairs of
students to write brief
descriptions of each
picture.

Teaching Tip
If you think your students
are ready for it, introduce
the idea of creating a
dominant impression in
their descriptive para-
graphs. Tell them that
this is the mood or
feeling they want to
communicate to readers.
The topic sentence of the
paragraph often conveys
this idea, and the rest of
the sentences in the
paragraph reinforce it.

A **descriptive paragraph** should have a topic sentence that states the paragraph's main idea. (*My sister's room is a pigpen*). This topic sentence should be followed by the details that support it. These details should be arranged in a definite **spatial order**, the order in which you observed the scene you are describing—for example, from near to far or from top to bottom. The paragraph ends with a summary statement that sums up the main idea stated in the topic sentence.

A descriptive paragraph generally has the following structure.

Topic Sentence_____

Detail #1_____

_____

Detail #2_____

_____

Detail #3_____

_____

Summary Statement_____

_____

Highlight:
Description

Vague, overused words—such as *good*, *nice*, *bad*, and *beautiful*—do not help readers see what you are describing. When you write a descriptive paragraph, try to use specific words and phrases that make your writing come alive.

The student writer of the following paragraph uses descriptive details to support the idea that the Lincoln Memorial is a monument to American democracy.

The Lincoln Memorial

Topic Sentence ———————— The Lincoln Memorial was built to celebrate American democracy. In front of the monument is a long marble staircase that leads from a reflecting pool to the memorial's entrance. Thirty-six columns surround the building. Inside the building are three rooms. The first room con-

Descriptive details ———————— tains the nineteen-foot statue of Lincoln. Seated in a chair, Lincoln

Descriptive details ——————

looks exhausted after the long Civil War. One of Lincoln's hands is a fist, showing his strength, and the other is open, showing his kindness. On either side of the first room are the two other rooms. Carved on the wall of the second room is the Gettysburg Address. On the wall of the third room is the Second Inaugural Address. Above the Gettysburg Address is a mural showing an angel freeing the slaves. Above the Second Inaugural Address is another mural, which shows the people of the North and the South coming back together.

Summary Statement ——————

As its design shows, the Lincoln Memorial was built to celebrate both the sixteenth president and the nation's struggle for democracy.

Nicole Lentz (student)

As you arrange your ideas in a descriptive paragraph, be sure to use appropriate transitional words and phrases. These signals will lead readers from one detail to another.

Some Transitional Words and Phrases for Description

above	in front of	on top of
behind	inside	outside
below	nearby	the first . . . the
between	next to	second . . .
beyond	on	the next
in	on one side . . .	under
in back of	on the other side . . .	

Grammar in Context: Description

When you write a descriptive paragraph, you sometimes use **modifiers**—words and phrases that describe another word in the sentence. A modifier should be placed as close as possible to the word it is supposed to modify. If you place a modifying word or phrase too far from the word it modifies, you create a **misplaced modifier** that will confuse readers.

Teaching Tip
Before your students write descriptive paragraphs, you might want to explain how to identify modification errors (Chapter 24) and have students do Practice 24-3.

Confusing   Seated in a chair, the long Civil War has clearly exhausted Lincoln. (Was the Civil War seated in a chair?)

Clear   Seated in a chair, Lincoln looks exhausted by the long Civil War.

For information on how to identify and correct misplaced modifiers, see Chapter 24.

● **Practice 5-1**

Read this descriptive paragraph; then, follow the instructions on the next page.

Teaching Tip
Remind students that most descriptive paragraphs mix objective description and subjective description. Although one kind of description may dominate, the other will probably be present as well.

⊕ **ESL Tip**
Have students copy the passage several times to help them strengthen their sentence structure before they work on their own descriptions.

Teaching Tip
Group students, and have them generate ideas to convey the dominant impression of college registration. Have one person in each group write down the ideas and read them to the class.

A House Left Behind

<u>Right in the middle of my block is a house that looks sad and deserted.</u> Black with mildew, the tan roof shingles curl in the hot sun. Two broken windows on the second floor have been patched with pieces of wood, and the other windows are grey with dirt. On the side of the house dangles a battered basketball hoop. The front door was once bright yellow; now, the paint is cracked and peeling, and underneath, bare wood is visible. In the past, evergreen shrubs were planted around the house, but no one has trimmed them for a long time. They are straggly, with long, thin branches blocking some of the first-floor windows. The front yard shows what happens when no one fertilizes the grass: it keeps growing but gets thinner and more yellow. In the back yard, tomato plants from an old garden have reseeded themselves. They grow tall and narrow but do not produce any tomatoes. <u>No one seems to care about this house anymore.</u>

1. Underline the topic sentence of the paragraph.

2. In a few words, summarize the main idea of the paragraph.
   A house in my neighborhood is very run down.

3. What are some of the details the writer uses to support this main idea? The first detail has been listed for you.
   roof black with mildew

   broken windows

   windows grey with dirt

   battered basketball hoop

   cracked and peeling front door

   straggly shrubs

4. Underline the paragraph's summary statement.

● **Practice 5-2**

Each of the four topic sentences below states a main idea for a descriptive paragraph. Copy each topic sentence on a separate sheet of paper, and then list three or four details that could support each one. For example, to support the idea that sitting in front of a fireplace is relaxing, you could describe the crackling of the fire, the pine scent of the smoke, and the changing colors of the flames. *Answers will vary.*

1. One look at the face of the traffic-court judge convinced me that I was in trouble.

2. The dog looked as if it had been living on the streets for a long time.

3. The woman behind the makeup counter was a walking advertisement for almost every product she sold.

4. One of the most interesting stores I know sells vintage clothing.

5b

Writing a Descriptive Paragraph

When Jared Lopez was asked to write a descriptive paragraph about someone he admired, he decided to write about his uncle Manuel, who had been a father figure for him.

Because he was familiar with his topic, Jared did not have to brainstorm or freewrite to find ideas. He decided to begin his paragraph by giving a general description of his uncle and then concentrate on his uncle's most noticeable feature: his hands. Here is the first draft of Jared's paragraph.

> My uncle's name is Manuel, but his friends call him Manny. He is over six feet tall, and he has long arms and legs. Although he is over fifty, he keeps in shape. Before he started his construction company, he used to be a stonemason. Uncle Manny's eyes are dark brown, almost black. They make him look very serious. When he laughs, however, he looks friendly. His nose is long and straight, and it makes Uncle Manny look very distinguished. Most interesting to me are Uncle Manny's hands. Even though he hasn't worked as a stonemason for years, his hands are still rough and scarred. They are large and strong, but they can be gentle too.

When Jared reread his draft, he felt it did not really focus on his uncle's most important qualities—his strength and gentleness. In addition, his sentences seemed choppy. To help him assess his paragraph's strengths and weaknesses, he applied the **TEST** strategy and then made some changes.

- He added a **topic sentence** that stated the main idea of his description.
- He added more details in his description to give readers more **evidence** of his uncle's strength and gentleness.
- He wrote a stronger **summary statement** to unify his paragraph.
- He included more **transitions** to move readers from one part of his description to the next.

Teaching Tip
Refer students to 1J for information on revising and editing their paragraphs.

After making these changes, Jared revised and edited his draft. Here is his final draft.

My Uncle Manny

My uncle Manuel is a strong but gentle person who took care of my mother and me when my father died. Manuel, or "Manny" as his friends and family call him, is over six feet tall. This is unusual for a Mexican of his generation. The first thing that most people notice about my uncle Manny is his eyes. They are large and dark brown, almost black. They make him look very serious. When he laughs, however, the sides of his eyes crinkle up and he looks warm and friendly. Another thing that stands out is his nose, which is long and straight. My mother says it makes Uncle Manny look strong and distinguished. The most interesting thing about Uncle Manny is his hands. Even though he hasn't worked as a stonemason since he opened his own construction company ten years ago, his hands are still rough and scarred from carrying stones. No matter how much he tries, he can't get rid of the dirt under the skin of his fingers. Uncle Manny's hands are big and rough, but they are also gentle and comforting. To me, they show what he really is: a strong and gentle man.

T E S T

Topic Sentence

Evidence

Summary Statement

Transitions

● **Practice 5-3**

Now, you are ready to write a draft of a descriptive paragraph. Choose one of the topics below (or choose your own topic) for a descriptive paragraph. On a separate sheet of paper, use one or more of the strategies described in 1C to help you come up with specific details about the topic you have chosen. If you can, observe your subject directly and write down your observations.

A favorite place	A favorite article of clothing
A place you felt trapped in	A useful object
A comfortable spot on campus	A pet
An unusual person	A building you think is ugly
Your dream house	Your car or truck

A family member or friend   The car you would like to have
A work of art   A statue or monument
A valued possession   Someone you admire
Your workplace   A cooking disaster

● Practice 5-4

List the details you came up with in Practice 5-3 that can best help you develop a descriptive paragraph on the topic you have chosen.

Answers will vary.

_____

_____

_____

_____

● Practice 5-5

Reread your list of details from Practice 5-4. Then, draft a topic sentence that summarizes the idea you want to convey in your paragraph.

Answers will vary.

_____

● Practice 5-6

Teaching Tip
Put a section of a descriptive piece of writing on an overhead transparency. Have students model their descriptions and sentence patterns on the sample.

Arrange the details you listed in Practice 5-4. You might arrange them in the order in which you are looking at them—for example, from left to right, near to far, or top to bottom.

1. *Answers will vary.*_____

2. _____

3. _____

4. _____

5. _____

6. _____

7. _____

● Practice 5-7

Draft your descriptive paragraph. Then, using the **TEST** checklist on page 81, check your paragraph for unity, support, and coherence.

Teaching Tip
You may want to remind students that an effective topic sentence will help unify the ideas in a paragraph. Effective support for the topic sentence will make the paragraph more convincing. Transitions will add coherence.

● **Practice 5-8**

Now, revise your descriptive paragraph.

● **Practice 5-9**

Prepare a final draft of your descriptive paragraph.

Focus on Writing: *Revising and Editing*

Look back at your response to the Focus on Writing activity on page 73. Using the **TEST** checklist on page 81, evaluate your paragraph for unity, support, and coherence. Then, prepare a final draft of your paragraph.

Chapter Review

Focus on Writing

The picture below shows a house surrounded by lush landscaping. Write a paragraph describing the house for a real estate brochure. Use your imagination to invent details that describe its setting, exterior, and interior. Your goal in this descriptive paragraph is to persuade a prospective buyer to purchase the house.

WORD POWER

mansion a large, stately house

lush characterized by luxuriant growth

Real-World Writing

Imagine that you have volunteered to read to the blind. At one point, the book you are reading mentions something that your listener has never seen—for example, a particular apparatus, artwork, or item of clothing. Write a one-paragraph description of this item that will help the sightless person "see" it.

T E S T ing a Descriptive Paragraph

Topic Sentence Unifies Your Paragraph

☐ Do you have a clearly stated topic sentence that states your paragraph's main idea?

☐ Does your topic sentence indicate what person, place, or thing you will describe in your paragraph?

Evidence Supports Your Paragraph's Topic Sentence

☐ Do all your examples and details help to support your paragraph's main idea?

☐ Do you have enough descriptive details, or do you need to include more details?

Summary Statement Reinforces Your Paragraph's Unity

☐ Does your paragraph end with a statement that summarizes your main idea?

Transitions Add Coherence to Your Paragraph

☐ Do your transitions lead readers from one detail to the next?

☐ Do you need to add transitions to make your paragraph more coherent?

Chapter 6

Using Process

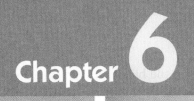

Breakdancing originated in New York in 1969. Dance-off-style "break battles" eventually replaced fights between rival street gangs.

What Is Process?

Teaching Tip
To help students understand the concept of process, photocopy the operating instructions for an appliance or electronic device. (Students could also be asked to bring instruction booklets or operating manuals to class.) Have students take turns reading steps aloud, and ask the class to supply any missing transitions.

Teaching Tip
Remind students that many everyday writing tasks might require them to explain a process. For example, they could write a set of instructions telling family members what to do in case of a fire.

When you describe a **process**, you tell readers how something works or how to do something. For example, you could explain how the optical scanner at the checkout counter of a food store works, how to hem a pair of pants, or how to send a text message.

A **process paragraph** should begin with a topic sentence that identifies the process and identifies the point you want to make about it (for example, "Parallel parking is easy once you know the secret," or "By following a few steps, you can design an effective résumé"). The rest of the paragraph should clearly describe the steps in the process, one at a time. These steps should be presented in strict **time order**—in the order in which they occur or are to be performed. The paragraph should end with a summary statement that sums up the process.

A process paragraph generally has the following structure.

Topic Sentence_____
Step #1_____
_____
Step #2_____
_____
Step #3_____
_____
Summary Statement_____
_____

→ Focus on Writing

The pictures on the opposite page show a man breakdancing. Look at the pictures, and then write a paragraph in which you explain how to dance to your favorite music or play your favorite game (it could be a board game, a video game, or an indoor game). Assume that your readers know nothing about your subject, and be sure to explain all the steps involved.

WORD POWER
compete to work against another person in pursuit of a goal
objective a purpose or goal
penalty a punishment

There are two types of process paragraphs: **process explanations** and **instructions**.

Process Explanations

In a **process explanation**, your purpose is to help readers understand how something works or how something happens—for example, how a cell phone operates or how to write a computer program. In this case, you do not expect readers to perform the process. The student writer of the following paragraph, a volunteer firefighter, explains how a fire extinguisher works.

How a Fire Extinguisher Works

Topic Sentence ———————

Even though many people have fire extinguishers in their homes, most people do not know how they work. A fire extinguisher is a metal cylinder filled with a material that will put out a fire. All extinguishers operate the same way. First, the material inside the cylinder is put under pressure. Next, when an operating lever on top of the metal cylinder is squeezed, a valve opens. The pressure inside the fire extin-

Step-by-step explanation ———

guisher is released. As the compressed gas in the cylinder rushes out, it carries the material in the fire extinguisher along with it. Then, a nozzle at the top of the cylinder concentrates the stream of liquid, gas, or powder coming from the fire extinguisher so it can be aimed at a fire. Finally, the material comes in contact with the fire and puts it out. Every home should have at least one fire extinguisher located

Summary Statement ———————

where it can be easily reached when it is needed.

David Turner (student)

Instructions

Teaching Tip
Remind students that they should generally not use the pronoun *you* in their writing. When they are giving instructions, however, the use of *you* is appropriate.

When you write instructions, your purpose is to give readers the information they need to actually perform a task or activity—for example, to fill out an application, to operate a piece of machinery, or to change a tire. Because you expect readers to follow your instructions, you address them directly, using **commands** to tell them what to do ("check the gauge" . . . "pull the valve"). In the following paragraph, the writer provides humorous instructions on how to get food out of a vending machine.

Man vs. Machine

Topic Sentence —————— <u>There is a foolproof method of outsmarting a vending machine that refuses to give up its food.</u>

1. First, approach the vending machine coolly. Make sure that you don't seem frightened or angry. The machine will sense these emotions and steal your money.

2. Second, be polite. Say hello, compliment the machine on its selection of goodies, and smile. Be careful. If the machine thinks you are trying to take advantage of it, it will steal your money.

Step-by-step instructions ——————

3. Third, if the machine steals your money, remain calm. Ask nicely to get the food you paid for.

4. Finally, it is time to get serious. Hit the side of the vending machine with your fist. If this doesn't work, lower your shoulder and throw yourself at the machine. (A good kick or two might also help.) When the machine has had enough, it will drop your snack, and you can grab it.

Summary Statement —————— <u>If you follow these few simple steps, you should have no trouble walking away from vending machines with the food you paid for.</u>

Adam Cooper (student)

Transitions are very important in process paragraphs like the two you have just read. Words like *first*, *second*, *third*, and so on enable readers to clearly identify each step. In addition, they establish a sequence that lets readers move easily though the process you are describing.

Some Transitional Words and Phrases for Process

after that	first	soon
as	immediately	the first (second, third) step
as soon as	later	the next step
at the same time	meanwhile	the last step
at this point	next	then
before	now	when
finally	once	while

When you write a process paragraph, you may find yourself making illogical shifts in tense, person, and voice. If you shift from one tense, person, or voice to another without good reason, you may confuse your reader.

Confusing	First, the vending machine should be approached coolly. Make sure that you don't seem frightened or angry. (illogical shift from passive to active voice)
Clear	First, approach the vending machine coolly. Make sure that you don't seem frightened or angry. (consistent use of active voice)

For information on how to avoid illogical shifts in tense, person, and voice, see Chapter 23.

● Practice 6-1

Read this process paragraph; then, follow the instructions below.

An Order of Fries

I never realized how much work goes into making French fries until I worked at a potato processing plant in Hermiston, Oregon. The process begins with freshly dug potatoes being shoveled from trucks onto conveyor belts leading into the plant. During this stage, workers must pick out any rocks that may have been dug up with the potatoes because these could damage the automated peelers. After the potatoes have gone through the peelers, they travel on a conveyor belt through the "trim line." Here, workers cut out any bad spots, being careful not to waste potatoes by trimming too much. Next, the potatoes are sliced in automated cutters and then fried for about a minute. After this, they continue along a conveyor belt to the "wet line." Here, workers again look for bad spots, and they throw away any rotten pieces. At this point, the potatoes go to a second set of fryers for three minutes before being moved to subzero freezers for ten minutes. Then, it's on to the "frozen line" for a final inspection. The inspected fries are weighed by machines and then sealed into five-pound plastic packages, which are weighed again by workers who also check that the packages are properly sealed. The bags are then packed into boxes and made ready for shipment to various restaurants across the western United States. <u>This complicated process goes on twenty-four hours a day to bring consumers the French fries they enjoy so much.</u>

Cheri Rodriguez (student)

1. Underline the topic sentence of the paragraph.
2. Is this a process explanation or instructions? <u>*process explanation*</u>
   How do you know? <u>*Verbs are not commands*</u>
3. List the steps in the process. The first step has been listed for you.

   The potatoes are unloaded, and the rocks are sorted out.

   They are peeled and carried to the "trim line."

   They are sliced and fried for a minute.

   They are carried to the "wet line."

   They are fried again and then frozen.

   They get a final inspection on the "frozen line."

   They are weighed, packaged, and boxed for shipment.

4. Underline the paragraph's summary statement.

● Practice 6-2

Following are four possible topic sentences for process paragraphs. Copy each topic sentence on a separate sheet of paper. Then, list three or four steps that explain the process each topic sentence identifies. For example, if you were explaining the process of getting a job, you could list preparing a résumé, looking at ads in newspapers or online, writing a job application letter, and going on an interview. Make sure each step follows logically from the one that precedes it. *Answers will vary.*

1. Downloading music from the Internet is a simple process.

2. Getting the most out of a student-teacher conference can take some preparation.

3. Breaking up with someone you are dating can be a tricky process.

4. Choosing the perfect outfit for a job interview can be a time-consuming task.

6b　Writing a Process Paragraph

When Manasvi Bari was assigned to write a paragraph in which she explained a process she performed every day, she decided to write about how to get a seat on a crowded subway car. To make sure she had enough to write about, she made the following list of possible steps she could include.

Don't pay attention to heat

Get into the train

Get the first seat

Look as if you need help

Get to a pole

Don't travel during rush hour

Choose your time

Be alert

Squeeze in

After looking over her list, Manasvi crossed out steps that she didn't think were essential to the process she wanted to describe.

~~Don't pay attention to heat~~

Get into the train

Get the first seat

Look as if you need help

~~Get to a pole~~

~~Don't travel during rush hour~~

~~Choose your time~~

Be alert

Squeeze in

Once she had decided on her list of steps, she rearranged them in the order in which they should be performed.

Get into the train

Be alert

Get the first seat

Squeeze in

Look as if you need help

At this point, Manasvi thought that she was ready to begin writing her paragraph. Here is her first draft.

> When the train arrives, get into the car as fast as possible. Be alert. If you see an empty seat, grab it, and sit down immediately. If there is no seat, ask people to move down, or squeeze into a space that seems too small. If none of this works, you'll have to use some imagination. Look helpless. Drop your books, and look as if the day can't get any worse. Sometimes a person will get up and give you a seat. If this strategy doesn't work, stand near someone who looks as if he or she is going to get up. When the person gets up, jump into the seat as fast as you can. Don't let the people who are getting on the train get the seat before you do.

Manasvi showed the draft of her paragraph to a writing center tutor. Together, they applied the **TEST** strategy and made the following decisions.

- They decided that her **evidence**—the details and examples that described the steps in her process—were clear and complete.

- They decided that she needed to add a **topic sentence** that identified the process and stated the point she wanted to make about it.
- They decided that she needed to add a **summary statement** that restated the point of the process.
- They decided that she needed to add **transitions** that helped readers follow the steps in the process.

Teaching Tip
Refer students to 1J for information on revising and editing their paragraphs.

After she made her changes, Manasvi revised and edited her paragraph. Here is her final draft.

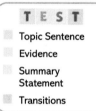

Surviving Rush Hour

Anyone who takes the subway to school in the morning knows how hard it is to find a seat, but by following a few simple steps, you should be able to get a seat almost every day. First, when the train arrives, get into the car as fast as possible. Be alert. As soon as you see an empty seat, grab it, and sit down immediately. Meanwhile, if there is no seat, ask people to move down, or try to squeeze into a space that seems too small. Next, if none of this works, you'll have to use some imagination. Look helpless. Drop your books, and look as if the day can't get any worse. Sometimes a person will get up and give you a seat. Don't be shy. Take it, and remember to say thank you. Finally, if this strategy doesn't work, stand near someone who looks as if he or she is going to get up. When the person gets up, jump into the seat as fast as you can. By following these steps, you should be able to get a seat on the subway and arrive at school rested and relaxed.

● **Practice 6-3**

Now, you are ready to write a draft of a process paragraph. Choose one of the topics below (or choose your own topic) for a process paragraph. Use one or more of the strategies described in 1C to help you come up with as many steps as you can for the topic you have chosen, and list these steps on a separate sheet of paper.

Making a major purchase
Strategies for winning
   arguments
How to save money

Buying a book or CD online
Your typical work or school day
How to discourage
   telemarketers

Your morning routine
How to use a digital camera
How to perform a particular
    household repair
How to apply for financial aid

A process involved in a hobby
    of yours
Painting a room
How to make your favorite dish
How to prepare for a storm

● Practice 6-4

Review your notes on the topic you chose in Practice 6-3, and decide whether to write a process explanation or a set of instructions. Then, on the lines below, choose the steps from the list you wrote in Practice 6-3 that can best help you develop a process paragraph on your topic.

Answers will vary.

_____   _____

_____   _____

_____   _____

_____   _____

● Practice 6-5

Reread your list of steps from Practice 6-4. Then, draft a topic sentence that identifies the process you will discuss and communicates the point you will make about it.

Answers will vary.

_____

_____

_____

● Practice 6-6

Review the steps you listed in Practice 6-4. Then, write them down in time order, moving from the first step to the last.

1. *Answers will vary.*   4. _____

2. _____   5. _____

3. _____   6. _____

Teaching Tip
You may want to remind students that an effective **topic sentence** will help unify the ideas in a paragraph. Effective **support** for the topic sentence will make the paragraph more convincing. Transitions will add **coherence**.

● Practice 6-7

Draft your process paragraph. Then, using the **TEST** checklist on page 93, check your paragraph for unity, support, and coherence.

● **Practice 6-8**

Now, revise your process paragraph.

● **Practice 6-9**

Prepare a final draft of your process paragraph.

Focus on Writing: *Revising and Editing*

Look back at your response to the Focus on Writing activity on page 83. Using the **TEST** checklist on page 93, evaluate your paragraph for unity, support, and coherence. Then, prepare a final draft of your paragraph.

Chapter Review

Focus on Writing

The picture below shows a scene of people moving. Study the picture carefully, and then list the steps involved in planning a move. Use this list to help you write a process paragraph that gives readers step-by-step instructions in the order in which the steps need to be done.

WORD POWER

priorities most important tasks

optimum the most favorable condition for a particular situation

Real-World Writing

Imagine that you will have to miss a day of work to keep an important appointment. Write a one-paragraph memo explaining your typical workday to the employee who will substitute for you. Your goal is to help that employee understand exactly how to do your job and in what order to perform various tasks.

**T E S T ing
a Process
Paragraph**

Topic Sentence Unifies Your Paragraph

- ☐ Do you have a clearly worded topic sentence that states your paragraph's main idea?
- ☐ Does your topic sentence identify the process you will discuss?
- ☐ Does your topic sentence indicate whether you will be explaining a process or giving instructions?

Evidence Supports Your Paragraph's Topic Sentence

- ☐ Have you included all the steps in the process?
- ☐ If your paragraph is a set of instructions, have you included all the information readers need to perform the process?

Summary Statement Reinforces Your Paragraph's Unity

- ☐ Does your paragraph end with a statement that summarizes your main idea?

Transitions Add Coherence to Your Paragraph

- ☐ Do your transitions indicate the order of steps in the process?
- ☐ Do you need to add transitions to make your paragraph more coherent?

Chapter 7

Using Cause and Effect

First available in the 1980s, cell phones originally weighed 2 pounds, and laptops originally weighed 24 pounds. Today, the average cell phone weighs about 4 ounces and a laptop weighs between 4 and 8 pounds.

What Is Cause and Effect?

Teaching Tip
To help students understand the concept of cause and effect, have them write a one-paragraph summary of a newspaper column or an editorial that deals with the causes or effects of a particular action or event.

What is causing global warming? Why is the cost of college so high? How does smoking affect a person's health? What would happen if the city increased its sales tax? How dangerous is bird flu? All these questions have one thing in common: they try to determine the causes or effects of an action, event, or situation. A **cause** is something or someone that makes something happen. An **effect** is a result of a particular cause.

Cause	Effect
Increased airport security ⟶	Long lines at airports
Weight gain ⟶	Health risks
Seatbelt laws passed ⟶	Increased use of seatbelts

Teaching Tip
Many everyday writing tasks may require students to identify causes and effects. For example, at work, they may be asked to write a memo that describes how a new procedure affects job performance.

   A **cause-and-effect paragraph** helps readers understand why something happened or is happening or shows readers how one thing affects something else. A cause-and-effect paragraph begins with a topic sentence that tells readers whether the paragraph is focusing on causes or on effects (for example, "There are several reasons why the cost of gas is so high" or "Going to the writing center has given me confidence as well as skills"). The rest of the paragraph should discuss the causes or the effects, one at a time. The causes or effects are arranged in some kind of **logical order**—for example, from least important to most important. The paragraph ends with a summary statement that restates the main idea.

Teaching Tip
You may want to point out to students that they should consider all possible causes, not just the obvious ones.

→ Focus on Writing

The picture on the opposite page shows someone talking on a cell phone while working on a laptop computer. Look at the picture, and then write a paragraph in which you describe the impact of a particular electronic appliance or gadget on your life or the life of your family—for example, the cell phone, the iPod, or the television remote control. Be sure that your topic sentence identifies the item that has an impact on you and your family and that the rest of the paragraph discusses how it affects you.

WORD POWER
gadget a small, specialized mechanical or electronic device

impact the effect of one thing on another

simplify to make easier

A cause-and-effect paragraph generally has the following structure.

Topic Sentence_____

_____

Cause (or effect) #1_____

_____

Cause (or effect) #2_____

_____

Cause (or effect) #3_____

_____

Summary Statement_____

_____

Causes

The following paragraph focuses on **causes**.

Health Alert

Topic Sentence ———

    For a number of reasons, Americans are gaining weight at a frightening rate. First, many Americans do not eat healthy foods. They eat a lot of food that is high in salt and that contains a lot of saturated fat. Also, many Americans eat on the run, grabbing a doughnut or muffin on the way to work and eating fast food for lunch or dinner. Another reason Americans are gaining weight is that they eat too much. They take too much food and think they must eat everything on their plates. They do not stop eating when they are full, and they often have second helpings and dessert. But the most important cause for this alarming weight gain is that many Americans do not exercise. They sit on the couch and watch hours of television or play video games and get up only to have a snack or a soda. The result of this unhealthy lifestyle is easy to predict — significant weight gain. Unless Americans begin eating better, many will develop severe health problems in the future.

Causes of weight gain ———

Summary Statement ———

Jen Toll (student)

Effects

The paragraph below focuses on **effects**.

Second Thoughts

Topic Sentence —————— When I dropped out of high school before my senior year, I had no idea how this action would affect my life. The first effect was that I became a social outcast. At the beginning, my friends called and asked me to go out with them. Gradually, school activities took up more and more of their time. Eventually, they had no time for me. Another effect was that I found myself stuck in a dead-end job. When I was in school, working part-time at a bookstore didn't seem bad. Once it became my full-time job, however, I knew that I was going nowhere. Without a diploma or some college education, I could not get a better job. The most important effect was that my girlfriend broke up with me. One day, she told me that she didn't like dating a drop-out. She said I had no goals and no future. I had to agree with her. When I heard that she had started dating a sophomore in college, something clicked. I went to school at night and got my GED and then applied to community college. Now, I realize how wrong I was to drop out of high school and

Effects of dropping out ——————

Summary Statement —————— how lucky I am to have a second chance.

Dan Tarr (student)

Transitions in cause-and-effect paragraphs, as illustrated in the two paragraphs above, introduce causes or effects. They may also show the connections between a cause and its effects or between an effect and its causes. In addition, they may tell which cause or effect is more important than another.

Some Transitional Words and Phrases for Cause and Effect

another cause	since	the most important
another effect	so	cause
as a result	the first (second,	the most important
because	third, final) cause	effect
consequently	the first (second,	the most important
finally	third, final)	reason
for (meaning	effect	therefore
because)	the first (second,	
for this reason	third, final)	
moreover	reason	

Grammar in Context: Cause and Effect

When you write a cause-and-effect paragraph, be careful not to confuse the words *affect* and *effect*. *Affect* is a verb meaning "to influence." *Effect* is a noun meaning "result."

When I dropped out of high school before my senior year, I had no
                                                                 affect
idea how this action would ~~effect~~ my life. (*affect* is a verb.)
               effect   ^
The first ~~affect~~ was that I became a social outcast. (*effect* is a noun)
          ^

For more information on *effect* and *affect*, see Chapter 34.

Teaching Tip
Before students write cause-and-effect paragraphs, you might want to review the use of *affect* and *effect*, pointing them to the examples in 34E and to the relevant items in Practice 34-6.

● **Practice 7-1**

Read this cause-and-effect paragraph; then, follow the instructions on page 99.

The Ultimate High

For me and for other experienced runners, the main effect of running is pure pleasure. As I begin my run, I breathe in the clean, cold air, and my lungs are immediately refreshed. As my muscles stretch and pump, all feelings of anger or frustration disappear. I mentally dive into my run and feel as though I am rising from the pavement and ascending into the air. My mind wanders, and I go wherever my thoughts take me. After I complete my run and cool down with long, deep breaths, I feel energized, as if I have just come off a roller coaster. I am more alert, my concentration is sharper, and I am relaxed and peaceful. Beginning runners initially experience soreness and fatigue rather than this kind of "high." They should be patient, however. As their bodies build up strength and tolerance, they will no longer associate running with pain but will feel alive, as I do.

Scott Weckerly (student)

1. Underline the topic sentence of the paragraph.

2. Does this paragraph deal mainly with the causes or the effects of running? ___effects___ How do you know? _The topic sentence says the paragraph will focus on the "main effect of running."_

3. List some of the effects the writer describes. The first effect has been listed for you.

   His lungs are refreshed with clean air.

   Tension and frustrations are released.

   He escapes into another world.

   He feels energized and alive afterward.

4. Underline the paragraph's summary statement.

● Practice 7-2

Following are four possible topic sentences for cause-and-effect paragraphs. Copy each topic sentence on a separate sheet of paper, and then list the effects that could result from the cause identified in each topic sentence. For example, if you were writing a paragraph about the effects of excessive drinking on campus, you could list low grades, health problems, and vandalism.   _Answers will vary._

1. Having a baby can change your life.
2. Learning a second language has many advantages.
3. MP3 players were a huge success for a number of reasons.
4. Impulse buying can have negative effects on a person's finances.

● Practice 7-3

On a separate sheet of paper, list three causes that could support each of the following topic sentences.
Answers will vary.

1. The causes of binge drinking are easy to identify.

2. Chronic unemployment can have many causes.

3. The high cost of college is not hard to explain.

4. There are several reasons why professional athletes' salaries are so high.

5. Eighteen- to twenty-nine-year-olds tend not to vote in national elections for a number of reasons.

7b   Writing a Cause-and-Effect Paragraph

When Sean Jin was asked to write a cause-and-effect essay for his composition class, he had no trouble thinking of a topic because of a debate that was going on in his hometown about building a Wal-Mart superstore there. He decided to write a paragraph that discussed the effects that such a store would have on the local economy.

His instructor told the class the main problem they could have in planning a cause-and-effect essay is making sure that a **causal relationship** exists—that one event actually causes another. In other words, just because one event follows another closely in time, students should not assume that the second event caused the first.

With this advice in mind, Sean listed the effects a Wal-Mart would have on his small town. Here is Sean's list of effects.

Provide new jobs

Offer low-cost items

Pay low wages

Push out small businesses

After reviewing his list of effects, Sean wrote the following first draft of his paragraph.

Wal-Mart can have good and bad effects on a small town. First, it provides jobs. A large store needs a lot of employees. So, many people from the area will be able to work. Also, Wal-Mart's prices are low. Families that don't have much money may be able to buy things they can't afford to buy at other stores. Not all of Wal-Mart's effects are positive. Wal-Mart pays employees less than other stores. Wal-Mart provides jobs, but those jobs don't pay very much. Also, when Wal-Mart comes into an area, many small businesses are forced to close. They just can't match Wal-Mart's prices or stock as much merchandise as Wal-Mart can.

When he finished his draft, Sean went to the writing center and met with a tutor. After going over his paragraph with the tutor and applying the **TEST** strategy, Sean decided to make several changes.

- He decided that he needed to sharpen his **topic sentence** to tie his discussion of Wal-Mart to the small town in which he lived.
- He decided to provide more **evidence** to support his topic sentence — for example, what exactly does Wal-Mart pay its salespeople?
- He decided to add a **summary statement** to reinforce his main idea.
- He decided to add **transitions** to identify positive and negative effects.

After making these changes, Sean revised and edited his paragraph. Here is his final paragraph.

Teaching Tip
Refer students to 1J for information on revising and editing their paragraphs.

T E S T

- Topic Sentence
- Evidence
- Summary Statement
- Transitions

Wal-Mart Comes to Town

When Wal-Mart comes to a small town, it can have good and bad effects. The first and most beneficial effect is that it provides jobs. A large Wal-Mart Superstore needs a lot of employees, so many people will be able to find work. In my rural town, almost 10 percent of the people are out of work. Wal-Mart could give these people a chance to improve their lives. Another positive effect that Wal-Mart can have is to keep prices low, so families that don't have much money will be able to buy things they couldn't afford to buy at other stores. My own observations show that items at a local Wal-Mart are about 20% cheaper than those at other stores. Not all of Wal-Mart's effects are positive, however. One negative effect Wal-Mart can have is that it can actually lower wages and benefits in an area. My aunt, a longtime employee, says that Wal-Mart pays beginning workers between $8 and $10 dollars an hour. This is less than they would get in stores that pay union wages. Another negative effect Wal-Mart can have is to drive other smaller businesses out. When Wal-Mart comes into an area, many small businesses are forced to close. They just can't match Wal-Mart's prices or selection of merchandise. It is clear that although Wal-Mart can have a number of positive effects, it can also have some negative ones.

● Practice 7-4

Now, you are ready to write a draft of a cause-and-effect paragraph. Choose one of the following topics (or choose your own topic) for a paragraph that examines causes or effects. Then, on a separate sheet of paper, use one or more of the strategies described in 1C to help you think of as many causes or effects as you can for the topic you have chosen.

> Why a current television show or movie is popular
>
> Some causes (or effects) of stress
>
> The negative effects of credit cards
>
> Why teenagers (or adults) drink
>
> The reasons you decided to attend college
>
> The effects of a particular government policy
>
> How becoming a vegetarian might change (or has changed) your life
>
> The benefits of home cooking
>
> Why a particular sport is popular
>
> How an important event in your life influenced you
>
> The effects of violent song lyrics on teenagers
>
> The problems of email (or instant messaging)
>
> Why some people find writing difficult
>
> The major reasons that high school or college students drop out of school
>
> How managers can get the best (or the worst) from their employees

● Practice 7-5

Review your notes on the topic you chose in Practice 7-4, and create a cluster diagram. Write the topic you have chosen in the center of the page, and draw arrows branching out to specific causes or effects.

● Practice 7-6

Teaching Tip
Refer students to 1C for more on creating a cluster diagram.

Choose a few of the most important causes or effects from the cluster diagram you made in Practice 7-5, and list them here.

Answers will vary.
_____

_____

_____

_____

_____

_____

_____

● Practice 7-7

Reread your list of causes or effects from Practice 7-6. Then, draft a topic sentence that introduces your topic and communicates the point you will make about it.

Answers will vary. _____

_____

_____

● Practice 7-8

List the causes or effects you will discuss in your paragraph, arranging them in an effective order—for example, from least to most important.

1. _Answers will vary._ _____

2. _____

3. _____

4. _____

● Practice 7-9

Draft your cause-and-effect paragraph. Then, using the **TEST** checklist on page 105, check your paragraph for unity, support, and coherence.

● Practice 7-10

Now, revise your cause-and-effect paragraph.

● Practice 7-11

Prepare a final draft of your cause-and-effect paragraph.

Teaching Tip
You may want to remind students that an effective topic sentence will help unify the ideas in a paragraph. Effective support for the topic sentence will make the paragraph more convincing. Transitions will add coherence.

Teaching Tip
When your students revise, they should consider the order in which they present their causes and effects.

Teaching Tip
Do not just mark students' errors. Write in corrections, and have students rewrite the material. Toward the end of the semester, depending on how often students receive graded assignments, you can start asking them to make corrections on their own.

Focus on Writing: *Revising and Editing*

Look back at your response to the Focus on Writing activity on page 95. Using the **TEST** checklist on page 105, evaluate the paragraph you wrote for unity, support, and coherence. Then, prepare a final draft of your paragraph.

Chapter Review

Focus on Writing

The picture below shows a happy couple, recent lottery winners, with a sign announcing their prize. Imagine you have won a multimillion-dollar lottery. How would your life change? Write a cause-and-effect paragraph that discusses specific ways in which your life would be different.

WORD POWER
annuity the annual payment of an allowance or income
windfall a sudden, unexpected piece of good luck

Real-World Writing

Imagine you have attended a community meeting. Some of your neighbors object to a proposal to build a new minimum-security prison nearby, and they appoint you to write a paragraph (to be sent to your city council representative) summarizing their objections. Write a paragraph outlining the negative effects you believe this new facility will have on your neighborhood.

T E S T ing a Cause-and-Effect Paragraph

Topic Sentence Unifies Your Paragraph

☐ Do you have a clearly worded topic sentence that states your paragraph's main idea?

☐ Does your topic sentence identify the cause or effect on which your paragraph will focus?

Evidence Supports Your Paragraph's Topic Sentence

☐ Do you need to add other important causes or effects?

☐ Do you need to explain your causes or effects in more detail?

☐ Do all your details and examples support your paragraph's main idea?

Summary Statement Reinforces Your Paragraph's Unity

☐ Does your paragraph end with a statement that summarizes your main idea?

Transitions Add Coherence to Your Paragraph

☐ Do your transitions show how your ideas are related?

☐ Do your transitions clearly introduce each cause or effect?

☐ Do you need to add transitions to make your paragraph more coherent?

Chapter 8 Using Comparison and Contrast

According to a survey on working-parent households, mothers spend an average of 25 hours per week on childcare and housework, while fathers spend 14.5 hours.

What Is Comparison and Contrast?

Teaching Tip
Remind students that many everyday writing tasks require comparison and contrast. For example, at work, they might be asked to write a paragraph comparing the qualifications of two people who are applying for the same job.

Teaching Tip
To help students understand the concept of comparison and contrast, have them go to the library and make copies of a few of the classified advertising pages of a newspaper printed on the day they were born. In class, discuss the differences and similarities between products and prices then and now.

When you buy something—for example, an air conditioner, a car, a hair dryer, or a computer—you often comparison-shop. You look at various models to determine how they are alike and how they are different. Eventually, you decide which one you want to buy. In other words, you *compare and contrast*. When you **compare**, you look at how two things are similar. When you **contrast**, you look at how they are different.

Comparison-and-contrast paragraphs can examine just similarities or just differences, or they can examine both. A comparison-and-contrast paragraph begins with a topic sentence that tells readers whether the paragraph is going to discuss similarities or differences. The topic sentence should also make clear the focus of the comparison (for example, "Toni Morrison and Maya Angelou have similar ideas about the effects of discrimination" or "My parents and I have different definitions of success"). The rest of the paragraph should discuss the same or similar points for both subjects. Points should be arranged in **logical order**—for example, from least important to most important. A comparison-and-contrast paragraph ends with a summary statement that reinforces the main point of the comparison.

There are two kinds of comparison-and-contrast paragraphs: *subject-by-subject comparisons* and *point-by-point comparisons*.

→ Focus on Writing

The picture on the opposite page shows a family at home. Look at the picture, and then write a comparison-and-contrast paragraph in which you explain how your family life is different from (or similar to) the life of the family shown here.

WORD POWER

diverge to go in different directions; to differ

generation a group of people born and living at about the same time

tradition a practice passed down from one generation to another

Subject-by-Subject Comparisons

In a **subject-by-subject comparison**, you divide your comparison into two parts and discuss one subject at a time. In the first part of the paragraph, you discuss all your points about one subject. Then, in the second part, you discuss all your points about the other subject. (In each part of the paragraph, you discuss the points in the same order.)

A subject-by-subject comparison is best for short paragraphs in which you do not discuss too many points. Readers will have little difficulty remembering the points you discuss for the first subject when you move on to discuss the second subject.

A subject-by-subject comparison generally has the following structure.

Topic Sentence_____
_____
Subject A_____
Point #1_____
_____
Point #2_____
_____
Point #3_____
_____
Subject B_____
Point #1_____
_____
Point #2_____
_____
Point #3_____
_____
Summary Statement_____
_____

The writer of the following paragraph uses a subject-by-subject comparison to compare two ways of traveling to Boston.

Getting to Boston

Topic Sentence

When I visited my sister in Boston last year, taking the train was better than traveling by car. Driving to Boston from Philadelphia takes about six-and-a-half hours. I often drive alone with only my car radio or iPod for company. By the third hour, I am bored and tired. Traffic is also a problem. The interstate roads are crowded and dangerous. Trucks often drive well above the speed limit, and cars weave in and out of lanes. If there is an accident, I might have to wait for over an hour until the police clear the highway. Going by train, however, is much better. When I went last year, I met other students and had some interesting conversations. In contrast to when I drove, on the train I took a nap when I got tired and snacked when I got hungry. I was even able to plug my laptop into an outlet on the train and work on some assignments. Best of all, unlike when I drove, I never got stuck in traffic. As a result, when I finally got to Boston, I was rested and ready for a visit with my sister. **This experience showed me that going to Boston by train is much better than driving.**

Subject A: Going to Boston by car

Subject B: Going to Boston by train

Summary Statement

Tad Curen (student)

Point-by-Point Comparisons

When you write a **point-by-point comparison**, you discuss a point about one subject and then discuss the same point for the second subject. You use this alternating pattern throughout the paragraph.

A point-by-point comparison is a better strategy for paragraphs in which you discuss many points. It is also a better choice if the points you are discussing are technical or complicated. Because you compare the two subjects one point at a time, readers will be able to see each point of comparison before moving on to the next point.

A point-by-point comparison generally has the following structure.

Topic Sentence _____

_____

Point 1_____

Subject A_____

_____

Subject B_____

_____

Point 2_____

Subject A_____

_____

Subject B_____

_____

Point 3_____

Subject A_____

_____

Subject B_____

_____

Summary Statement_____

_____

In the following paragraph, the writer uses a point-by-point-comparison to compare two characters in a short story.

Two Sisters

Topic Sentence ———

Point 1: Different personalities ———

Point 2: Different attitudes toward life ———

Although they grew up together, Maggie and Dee, the two sisters in Alice Walker's short story "Everyday Use," are very different. Maggie, who was burned in a fire, is shy and has low self-esteem. When she walks, she shuffles her feet and looks down at the ground. Her sister Dee, however, is confident and outgoing. She looks people in the eye when she talks to them and is very opinionated. Maggie never complains or asks for anything more than she has. She has remained at home with her mother in rural Georgia. In contrast, Dee has always wanted nicer things. She has gone away to school and hardly ever

Point 3: Different attitudes toward tradition

visits her mother and Dee. The biggest difference between Maggie and Dee is their attitude toward tradition. Although Maggie values her family's traditions, Dee values her African heritage. Maggie cherishes her family's handmade quilts and furniture, hoping to use them with her own family. In contrast, Dee sees the handmade objects as things to be displayed and shown off, not used every day. The many differ-

Summary Statement

ences between Maggie and Dee add conflict and tension to the story.

Margaret Caracappa (student)

Transitions are important in a comparison-and-contrast paragraph. Transitions tell readers when you are moving from one point (or one subject) to another. Transitions also make your paragraph more coherent by showing readers whether you are focusing on similarities (for example, *likewise* or *similarly*) or on differences (for example, *although* or *in contrast*).

Some Transitional Words and Phrases for Comparison and Contrast

although	one difference . . . another difference . . .
but	one similarity . . . another similarity . . .
even though	on the contrary
however	on the one hand . . . on the other hand . . .
in comparison	similarly
in contrast	though
like	unlike
likewise	whereas
nevertheless	

Grammar in Context:
Comparison and Contrast

Teaching Tip
Before your students write comparison-and-contrast paragraphs, you might want to explain the concept of parallelism (Chapter 18) and have them do Practices 18-1 and 18-2.

When you write a comparison-and-contrast paragraph, you should state the points you are comparing in **parallel** terms to highlight their similarities or differences.

Not parallel   Although Maggie values her family's traditions, the African heritage of their family is the thing that Dee values.

Parallel   Although Maggie values her family's traditions, Dee values their African heritage.

For more information on revising to make ideas parallel, see Chapter 18.

● **Practice 8-1**

Read this comparison-and-contrast paragraph; then, follow the instructions below.

Immigration: Past and Present

Immigration to the United States is quite different today from what it was a century ago. In the late nineteenth and early twentieth centuries, most immigrants to the United States came from southern and eastern Europe. In the last fifty years, however, about 80 percent of the immigrants have come from Latin America, the Caribbean, and Asia. A hundred years ago, most of the immigrants were uneducated, unskilled, and poor. Although some recent immigrants are in similar circumstances, many of the more recent arrivals are well-educated professionals who are not poor. Most immigrants a hundred years ago made a conscious effort to blend in. They saw the United States as a melting pot in which they could lose their immigrant identities and become like others in American society. More recent immigrants prefer to keep their distinctive identities while still taking part in American society. Regardless of these differences, most immigrants still come to the United States for the same reasons — to improve themselves economically and to find freedom.

George Hernandez (student)

Teaching Tip
Have students circle the transitions in this paragraph and explain why they are appropriate.

1. Underline the topic sentence of the paragraph.

2. Does this paragraph deal mainly with similarities or differences?
   differences   How do you know? _The topic sentence refers to differences._

3. Is this paragraph a subject-by-subject or point-by-point comparison?
   point-by-point   How do you know? _Discussion of points alternates between immigrants of a century ago and those of recent years._

4. List some of the contrasts the writer describes. The first contrast has been listed for you.

A century ago, most immigrants came from southern and eastern

Europe; more recently, most have come from Latin America, the

Caribbean, and Asia.

A century ago, most immigrants were uneducated, unskilled, and

had little money, while more recently many new arrivals are

well-educated professionals who are not poor.

Earlier immigrants wanted to blend in; more recent immigrants

want to keep their ethnic identities.

5. Underline the paragraph's summary statement.

● **Practice 8-2**

Following are three topic sentences. Copy each topic sentence on a separate sheet of paper. Then, list three or four similarities or differences between the two subjects in each topic sentence. For example, if you were writing a paragraph comparing health care provided by a local clinic with health care provided by a private physician, you could discuss the cost, the length of waiting time, the quality of care, and the frequency of follow-up visits. *Answers will vary.*

1. My mother (or father) and I are very much alike (or different).

2. My friends and I have similar views on _____.

3. Two of my college instructors have very different teaching styles.

Writing a Comparison-and-Contrast Paragraph

When Jermond Love was asked to write a comparison-and-contrast paragraph for his composition class, he began by brainstorming to find a topic that he could write about. When he reviewed his brainstorming notes, he came up with the following topics.

Football and soccer

Fast food and home cooking

The difference between my brother and me

Life in Saint Croix versus life in the United States

Jermond decided that he would write about the differences between life in New York City and life in Saint Croix, the Caribbean island on which he was raised. He listed a few subjects that he thought he could compare and contrast. Then, he crossed out the ones he didn't want to write about.

Size

Population

~~Economy~~

Friendliness

~~Businesses~~

Lifestyle

After brainstorming some more, Jermond listed the points he could discuss for each of his four subjects. He began with basic information and then moved on to the idea he wanted to emphasize: the different lifestyles.

Size
    Saint Croix
        Small size
        Small population
        Christiansted and Frederiksted
    New York
        Large size
        Large population
        Five boroughs
Lifestyle
    Saint Croix
        Laid back
        Friendly
    New York
        In a hurry
        Not always friendly

Because he would not discuss many points in this paragraph and because the points were not very complicated, Jermond decided to use a subject-by-subject organization for his paragraph. He did not think his readers would have much difficulty keeping track of his points between one section of his paragraph and the other.

Here is the first draft of Jermond's paragraph.

> Life in Saint Croix is very different from life in New York City. Saint Croix is much smaller than New York City. Saint Croix has a total population of about 60,000 people. The two main towns are Christiansted and Frederiksted. New York City is very large. Its residents are crowded into five boroughs. The lifestyle in Saint Croix is different from the lifestyle of New York City. In Saint Croix, people operate on "island time." Everyone is friendly. People don't see any point in getting anyone upset. In New York City, people are always in a hurry. They don't take the time to slow down and enjoy life. As a result, people can seem unfriendly. They don't take the time to get to know anyone. I hope when I graduate I can stay in New York City but visit my home in Saint Croix whenever I can.

Jermond put his paragraph aside for a day and then reread it. Although he was generally satisfied with what he had written, he thought that it could be better. To help students revise their paragraphs, his instructor paired students and asked them to read and discuss each other's paragraphs. After working with a classmate on his draft and applying the **TEST** strategy, Jermond made the following decisions.

- He decided that his **topic sentence** was clear and specific.
- He saw that he needed more **evidence**—details to help readers understand the differences between his two subjects. Would readers know the location of Saint Croix? Would they know the population of Christiansted and Frederiksted? Would they know what he meant by "island time"?
- He decided to change his **summary statement** because it didn't really restate the idea in his topic sentence.
- Finally, he decided that he needed to add **transitional words and phrases** that would show when he was moving from one idea to another.

After making these changes, Jermond revised and edited his paragraph, adding background about Saint Croix. (The classmate who read his draft pointed out that many people in the class would not know anything about it.)

The final draft below includes all the elements Jermond looked for when he applied the **TEST** strategy.

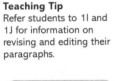

T E S T
☐ Topic Sentence
☐ Evidence
☐ Summary
   Statement
☐ Transitions

Saint Croix versus the United States

Life in Saint Croix is very different from life in New York City. One difference between Saint Croix and New York is that Saint Croix is much smaller than New York. Saint Croix, the largest of the United States Virgin Islands, has a population of about 60,000 people. The two main towns on the island are Christiansted, with a population of about 3,000 people, and Frederiksted, with a population of only about 830. Unlike Saint Croix, New York City is large. It has a population of over 8 million people crowded into the five boroughs of Manhattan, Brooklyn, the Bronx, Queens, and Staten Island. My neighborhood in Brooklyn is more than twice the size of Christiansted and Frederiksted combined. Another difference between Saint Croix and New York City is their lifestyles. Life in Saint Croix is slower than life in New York. In Saint Croix, people operate on "island time." Things get done, but people don't rush to do them. When a workman says "later," he can mean "this afternoon," "tomorrow," or even "next week." No one seems to mind, as long as the job gets done. Everyone is friendly. People don't see any point in getting anyone upset. In New York, however, people are always in a hurry. They don't take the time to slow down and enjoy life. Everything is fast — fast food, fast cars, and fast Internet access. As a result, people can seem unfriendly. Because Saint Croix and New York City are so different, moving from the small island to the big city requires a big adjustment.

● Practice 8-3

Now, you are ready to write a draft of a comparison-and-contrast paragraph. Choose one of the topics below (or choose your own topic) for a paragraph exploring similarities or differences. On a separate sheet of paper, use one or more of the strategies described in 1C to help you think of as many similarities and differences as you can for the topic you have chosen. (If you use clustering, create a separate cluster diagram for each of the two subjects you are comparing.)

Two popular television personalities or radio talk-show hosts

Dog owners versus cat owners

A common perception of something versus its reality

How you act in two different situations (home and work, for example) or with two different sets of people (such as your family and your friends)

Two ads for similar products directed at different audiences

Two Web sites

Men's and women's attitudes toward dating, shopping, or conversation

Your goals when you were in high school versus your goals today

Public school education versus home schooling

Two competing consumer items, such as two car models, two computer systems, or two cell phones

Two relatives who have very different personalities

Two different kinds of vacations

Two generations' attitudes toward a particular issue or subject (for example, how people in their forties and people in their teens view religion or politics)

● Practice 8-4

Review your notes on the topic you chose in Practice 8-3, and decide whether to focus on similarities or differences. On the following lines, list the similarities or differences that can best help you develop a comparison-and-contrast paragraph on the topic you have selected.

Answers will vary.

_____

_____

_____

_____

_____

● Practice 8-5

Reread your list of similarities or differences from Practice 8-4. Then, draft a topic sentence that introduces your two subjects and indicates whether your paragraph will focus on similarities or on differences.

Answers will vary.

_____

_____

_____

● Practice 8-6

Decide whether you will write a subject-by-subject or a point-by-point comparison. Then, use the appropriate outline below to help you plan your paragraph. Before you begin, decide on the order in which you will present your points— for example, from least important to most important. (For a subject-by-subject comparison, begin by deciding which subject you will discuss first.)

Subject-by-Subject Comparison

Subject A _____ *Answers will vary.* _____

    Point 1 _____

    Point 2 _____

    Point 3 _____

    Point 4 _____

Subject B _____ *Answers will vary.* _____

    Point 1 _____

    Point 2 _____

    Point 3 _____

    Point 4 _____

Point-by-Point Comparison

Point 1 _____ *Answers will vary.* _____

    Subject A _____

    Subject B _____

Point 2 _____ *Answers will vary.* _____

    Subject A _____

    Subject B _____

Point 3 _____ *Answers will vary.* _____

    Subject A _____

    Subject B _____

Point 4 _____ *Answers will vary.* _____

    Subject A _____

    Subject B _____

Teaching Tip
You may want to remind students that an effective **topic sentence** will help unify the ideas in a paragraph. Effective **support** for the topic sentence will make the paragraph more convincing. Transitions will add **coherence**.

● Practice 8-7

Draft your comparison-and-contrast paragraph. Then, using the **TEST** checklist on page 121, check your paragraph for unity, support, and coherence.

● Practice 8-8

Now, revise your comparison-and-contrast paragraph.

● Practice 8-9

Prepare a final draft of your comparison-and-contrast paragraph.

Focus on Writing: *Revising and Editing*

Look back at your response to the Focus on Writing activity on page 107. Using the **TEST** checklist on page 121, evaluate your paragraph for unity, support, and coherence. Then, prepare a final draft of your paragraph.

Chapter Review

Focus on Writing

The pictures below show two famous war memorials. Study the two photographs carefully, and then write a paragraph in which you compare them, considering both what the monuments look like and their emotional impact on you.

Iwo Jima memorial statue near Arlington National Cemetery

Vietnam Veterans Memorial in Washington, D.C.

Real-World Writing

Assume you ordered a product advertised in a TV infomercial. When it arrives, you are disappointed to discover that what you see is not exactly what you expected. Write a one-paragraph email to the manufacturer in which you compare the way the product was supposed to perform to the way it actually performed. (If you like, you may use information from an actual infomercial in your paragraph.)

T E S T ing a Comparison-and-Contrast Paragraph

Topic Sentence Unifies Your Paragraph

☐ Do you have a clearly worded topic sentence that states your paragraph's main idea?

☐ Does your topic sentence indicate whether you are focusing on similarities or on differences?

Evidence Supports Your Paragraph's Topic Sentence

☐ Do all your examples and details support your main idea?

☐ Do you need to include more similarities or differences?

Summary Statement Reinforces Your Paragraph's Unity

☐ Does your paragraph end with a statement that summarizes your main idea?

Transitions Add Coherence to Your Paragraph

☐ Do your transitions indicate whether you are focusing on similarities or on differences?

☐ Do transitional words and phrases lead readers from one subject or point to the next?

☐ Do you need to add transitions to make your paragraph more coherent?

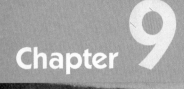

Chapter 9 Using Classification

Professional boxing was very popular from the 1920s to the 1940s, but attendance at all but the most heavily promoted matches declined in the 1950s when television became popular.

What Is Classification?

Classification is the act of sorting items (people, things, or ideas) into categories. You classify when you organize your bills into those you have to pay now and those you can pay later or when you sort the clothes in a dresser drawer into piles of socks, T-shirts, and underwear. College assignments often require you to classify. For example, a question on a history exam may ask you to discuss the kinds of people who fought in the American Revolution. To answer this question, you would have to sort these people into three groups: colonists, British soldiers, and British sympathizers (Tories).

In a **classification paragraph**, you tell readers how items can be sorted into categories or groups. The topic sentence introduces the subject of the paragraph and sometimes also identifies the categories you will discuss. (For example, "Animals can be classified as vertebrates or invertebrates" or "Before you go camping, you should sort the items you are thinking of packing into three categories: those that are absolutely necessary, those that could be helpful, and those that are not really necessary.")

The rest of the paragraph discusses each of the categories, one at a time. Your discussion of each category should include enough details and examples to show how it is different from the other categories. You should also treat each category in the same way. In other words, you should not discuss features of one category that you do not discuss for the others. The categories should be arranged in **logical order**—for example, from most important to least important or from smallest to largest.

Finally, each category should be *distinct*—that is, none of the items in one category should also fit into another category. For example, you would not classify novels into mysteries, romances, and paperbacks, because both mystery novels and romance novels could also be paperbacks. A classification

Teaching Tip
Remind students that many everyday writing tasks call for classification. For example, for a local library's book sale, they might have to write a flier classifying books according to subject or reading level.

Teaching Tip
To help students understand classification, give them lists of different musical groups, foods, sports figures, and so on, and ask them to classify the items on each list. (Each list should include at least twenty items.)

→ Focus on Writing

The picture on the opposite page shows boxers in the 1950s being classified according to their weight categories (heavyweight, middleweight, lightweight, featherweight, and so on). Look at the picture, and then write a paragraph that discusses the types of players in a sport that you follow. Why is each player placed within a particular category?

WORD POWER
qualifications standards that must be met

paragraph should end with a summary statement that reinforces the main point stated in the topic sentence.

A classification paragraph generally has the following structure.

Topic Sentence_____

_____

Category #1_____

_____

Category #2_____

_____

Category #3_____

_____

Summary Statement_____

_____

The writer of the following paragraph classifies items into three distinct groups.

Types of Bosses

Topic Sentence ——— Basically, I've had three kinds of bosses in my life: the uninterested boss, the supervisor, and the micromanager. The first type is an uninterested boss. This boss doesn't care what workers do as long as they do the job. When I was a counselor at summer camp, my boss fell into this category. As long as no campers (or worse yet, parents) complained, he left you alone. He never cared if you followed the activity plan for the day or gave the kids an extra snack to keep them quiet. The second type of boss is a supervisor. This kind of boss will check you once in a while and give you helpful advice. You'll have a certain amount of freedom but not too much. When I was a salesperson at the Gap, my boss fell into this category. She helped me through the first few weeks of the job and encouraged me to do my best. At the end of the summer, I had learned a lot about the retail business and had good feelings about the job. The last, and worst, type of boss is the micromanager. This kind of boss gets involved in everything. My boss at Taco Bell was this kind of person. No one could do anything right. There was always a better

First type of boss ———

Second type of boss ———

Last type of boss ———

Last type of boss ————

way to do anything you tried to do. If you rolled a burrito one way, he would tell you to do it another way. If you did it the other way, he would tell you to do it the first way. This boss never seemed to understand that people need praise every once in a while.

Summary
Statement ————

Even though the supervisor expects a lot and makes you work, it is clear to me that this boss is better than the other types.

Melissa Burrell (student)

Transitions are important in a classification paragraph. They introduce each new category and tell readers when you are moving from one category to another (for example, *the first type, the second type*). They can also indicate which categories you think are more important than others (for example, *the most important, the least important*).

Teaching Tip
Before students write classification paragraphs, you might want to explain the use of the colon to introduce a list (32B) and have students do the relevant items in Practice 32-2.

Some Transitional Phrases for Classification

one kind . . . another kind	the first group . . . the last group
one way . . . another way	the most (or least) important group
the first type . . . the second type	the next part
the first (second, third) category	

Grammar in Context: Classification

When you write a classification paragraph, you may list the categories you are going to discuss. If you use a colon to introduce your list, make sure that a complete sentence comes before the colon.

Incorrect	Basically, bosses can be divided into: the uninterested boss, the supervisor, and the micromanager.
Correct	Basically, I've had three kinds of bosses in my life: the uninterested boss, the supervisor, and the micromanager.

For more information on how to use a colon to introduce a list, see 32B.

● Practice 9-1

ESL Tip
As students do Practice 9-1, they can also circle articles and prepositions.

Read this classification paragraph; then, follow the instructions on page 126.

Three Kinds of Shoppers

Shoppers can be placed in three categories: practical, recreational, and professional. The first category is made up of practical shoppers, those who shop because they need something. You can recognize them because they go right to the item they are looking for in the store and then leave. They do not waste time browsing or walking aimlessly from store to store. For them, shopping is a means to an end. (The next category) is made up of recreational shoppers, those who shop for entertainment. For them, shopping is like going to the movies or out to dinner. They do it because it is fun. They will spend hours walking through stores looking at merchandise. More often than not, they will not buy anything. For recreational shoppers, it is the activity of shopping that counts, not the purchase itself. (The third category) is made up of professional shoppers, those who shop because they have to. For them, shopping is a serious business. You can see them in any mall, carrying four, five, or even six shopping bags. Whenever you walk through a mall, you will see all three types of shoppers.

Kimberly Toomer (student)

1. Underline the topic sentence of the paragraph.
2. What is the subject of the paragraph? *shoppers*
3. What three categories does the writer describe?

   practical shoppers

   recreational shoppers

   professional shoppers

4. Circle the transitional phrases the writer uses to introduce the three categories.

5. Underline the paragraph's summary statement.

● Practice 9-2

On a separate piece of paper, classify the following groups of items into categories.

1. All the items on your desk

2. Buildings on your college campus

3. Magazines or newspapers you read (or Web sites you consult regularly)

Writing a Classification Paragraph

Corey Levin had just completed a service-learning experience at a local Ronald McDonald House, a charity that houses families of seriously ill children receiving treatment at nearby hospitals. He had met several professional athletes there, and he was surprised to learn that many of them regularly donated their time and money to charity. After he finished his service-learning project, Corey was asked by his composition instructor to write a paragraph about something he had learned from his experience. Corey decided to write a paragraph that classified the ways in which professional athletes give back to their communities. To help him find ideas to write about, he jotted down the following list of categories.

> Starting foundations
>
> Guidance
>
> Responding to emergencies

Corey then listed examples under each of the three categories.

> Foundations
>> Michael Jordan
>>
>> Troy Aikman
>
> Guidance
>> Shaquille O'Neal
>>
>> The Philadelphia 76ers
>
> Responding to emergencies
>> Ike Reese
>>
>> Vince Carter

After completing this informal outline, Corey drafted a topic sentence for his paragraph: *High-profile athletes find many ways to give back to their communities.* Then, using his informal outline as a guide, Corey wrote the following draft of his paragraph.

> High-profile athletes find many ways to give back to their communities. Many athletes as well as teams do a lot to help people. For example, Michael Jordan built a Boys' and Girls' Club. Troy Aikman builds playgrounds for kids in hospitals. Shaquille O'Neal's Shaq's Paq helps inner-city children. The Philadelphia 76ers visit schools. They have donated over five thousand books. Ike Reese collects clothing and food for families that need help. Vince Carter founded

the Embassy of Hope Foundation. It distributes food to needy families at Thanksgiving and throws a Christmas party for disadvantaged families.

Following his instructor's suggestion, Corey emailed his draft to a classmate for feedback. In her email reply to Corey, she made the following suggestions based on the **TEST** strategy.

- Keep the **topic sentence** the way it is. "Many ways" shows you're writing a classification paragraph.
- Add more specific **evidence**. Give examples of each category of "giving back" to support the topic sentence. You also need to explain the athletes' contributions in more detail.
- Add a **summary statement** to sum up the paragraph's main idea.
- Add **transitions** to introduce the three specific categories you're discussing.

With these comments in mind, Corey revised and edited his paragraph. Here is his final draft.

Giving Back

High-profile athletes find many ways to give back to their communities. One way to give back is to start charitable foundations to help young fans. For example, Michael Jordan and the Chicago Bulls built a Boys' and Girls' Club on Chicago's West side. In addition, Troy Aikman set up a foundation that builds playgrounds for children's hospitals. Another way athletes give back to their communities is by mentoring, or giving guidance to young people. Many athletes work to encourage young people to stay in school. Shaquille O'Neal's Shaq's Paq, for example, provides guidance for inner-city children. The Philadelphia 76ers visit schools and have donated over five thousand books to local libraries. One more way athletes can contribute to their communities is to respond to emergencies. Football player Ike Reese collects clothing and food for families that need help. Basketball player Vince Carter founded the Embassy of Hope Foundation. It distributes food to needy families at Thanksgiving and hosts a Christmas party for disadvantaged families. These are just some of the ways that high-profile athletes give back to their communities.

T E S T
Topic Sentence
Evidence
Summary Statement
Transitions

● **Practice 9-3**

Now, you are ready to write a draft of a classification paragraph. Choose one of the topics below (or choose your own topic) for a classification paragraph.

On a separate sheet of paper, use one or more of the strategies described in 1C to help you classify the members of the group you have chosen into as many categories as necessary.

Your friends   Popular music
Drivers   Fitness routines
Commuters on public transportation   Popular Web sites
Television shows   Part-time jobs
Clothing styles   Teachers
Parents or children   Popular movies
Types of success   T-shirt slogans
Radio stations

● **Practice 9-4**

Review the information you came up with for the topic you chose in Practice 9-3. On the following lines, list three or four categories you can develop in your paragraph.

Category 1: *Answers will vary.* _____

Category 2: _____

Category 3: _____

Category 4: _____

● **Practice 9-5**

Reread the list you made in Practice 9-4. Then, draft a topic sentence that introduces your subject.

Answers will vary. _____

_____

● **Practice 9-6**

List below the categories you will discuss in your classification paragraph in the order in which you will discuss them.

1. *Answers will vary.* _____

2. _____

3. _____

4. _____

Teaching Tip
Divide the class into pairs, and have students use the TEST checklist to critique each other's paragraphs.

Teaching Tip
Refer students to 1 I-J for information on revising and editing their paragraphs.

● **Practice 9-7**

Draft your classification paragraph. Then, using the **TEST** checklist on page 131, check your paragraph for unity, support, and coherence.

● **Practice 9-8**

Now, revise your classification paragraph.

● **Practice 9-9**

Prepare a final draft of your classification paragraph.

Focus on Writing: *Revising and Editing*

Look back at your response to the Focus on Writing activity on page 123. Using the TEST checklist on page 131, evaluate the paragraph you wrote for unity, support, and coherence. Then, prepare a final draft of your paragraph.

Chapter Review

WORD POWER
finicky hard to please
glutton a person who eats without moderation

Focus on Writing

The picture below shows a person eating a hot dog. Look at the photo, and think about all the kinds of foods you eat in a typical week. Then, write a paragraph in which you classify the food you eat.

Real-World Writing

As part of a service-learning requirement for your English class, you spend several hours each week helping elementary school children improve their reading skills. As the semester goes along, you find yourself using a variety of materials—everything from comic books to Web sites—with your students. To guide future tutors, you decide to write a classification paragraph discussing the kinds of reading material—besides books—that can be used to help your students become better readers.

T E S Ting a Classification Paragraph

Topic Sentence Unifies Your Paragraph

☐ Do you have a clearly worded topic sentence that states your paragraph's main idea?

☐ Does your topic sentence identify the categories you will discuss?

Evidence Supports Your Paragraph's Topic Sentence

☐ Do all your examples and details support your paragraph's main idea?

☐ Do you need to include more examples or details?

Summary Statement Reinforces Your Paragraph's Unity

☐ Does your paragraph end with a statement that summarizes your main idea?

Transitions Add Coherence to Your Paragraph

☐ Do your transitions clearly indicate which categories are more important than others?

☐ Do your transitions tell readers when you are moving from one category to another?

☐ Do you need to add transitions to make your paragraph more coherent?

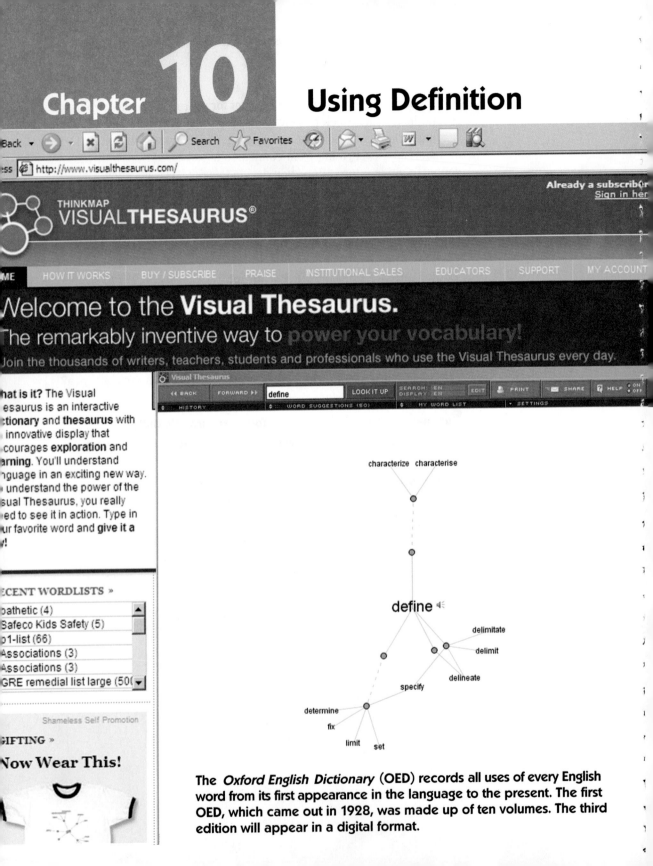

The *Oxford English Dictionary* (OED) records all uses of every English word from its first appearance in the language to the present. The first OED, which came out in 1928, was made up of ten volumes. The third edition will appear in a digital format.

What Is Definition?

During a conversation, you might say that a friend is *stubborn*, that a stream is *polluted*, or that a neighborhood is *dangerous*. Without some explanation, however, these terms mean very little. In order to make yourself clear, you have to define what you mean by *stubborn*, *polluted*, or *dangerous*. Like conversations, academic assignments also may involve definition. In a history paper, for example, you might have to define *imperialism*; on a biology exam, you might be asked to define *mitosis*.

A **definition** tells what a word means. When you want your readers to know exactly how you are using a specific term, you define it.

When most people think of definitions, they think of the **formal definitions** in a dictionary. Formal definitions have a three-part structure that includes the following parts.

- The term to be defined
- The general class to which the term belongs
- The things that make the term different from all other items in the general class to which the term belongs

A single-sentence formal definition is often not enough to define a specialized term (*point of view* or *premeditation*, for example), an abstract concept (*happiness* or *success*, for example), or a complicated subject (*global*

→ Focus on Writing

The picture on the opposite page shows the home page of an online dictionary. Look at the picture, and then write a one-paragraph definition of a new word you learned in one of your college courses. Assume that your readers are not familiar with the word you are defining.

WORD POWER
denote to indicate; to refer to specifically
signify to have meaning or importance

Term	Class	Differentiation
Ice hockey	is a game	played on ice by two teams on skates who use curved sticks to try to hit a puck into an opponent's goal.
Spaghetti	is a pasta	made in the shape of long, thin strings, usually served with a sauce.

warming or *autism*, for example). In these cases, you need to expand the basic formal definition by writing a definition paragraph.

A **definition paragraph** is an expanded formal definition. Definition paragraphs do not follow any one particular pattern of development. In fact, a definition paragraph may define a term by using any of the patterns discussed in this text. For example, a definition paragraph may explain a concept by *comparing* it to something else or by *giving examples*. Like other kinds of paragraphs, a definition paragraph ends with a summary statement that summarizes the main point of the paragraph.

Here is one possible structure for a definition paragraph. Notice that it uses a combination of **narration** and **exemplification** to make its point.

Topic Sentence_____
_____
Point #1_____
Narration_____
_____
Point #2_____
Example_____
Example_____
Point #3_____
Example_____
Example_____
Summary Statement_____
_____

The writer of the following paragraph uses several patterns of development—including classification and exemplification—to define the term *happiness*.

Happiness

Topic Sentence — Although people disagree about what brings happiness (a feeling of contentment or joy), I know exactly what happiness means to me. The

First kind of happiness — first kind of happiness is the result of money. It comes from unexpectedly finding a twenty-dollar bill in my pocket. It comes from hitting the jackpot on a slot machine after putting in just one quarter. The second kind

Second kind of happiness — of happiness is about success. It comes from getting an A on a test or being told that my financial aid has been renewed for another year.

Third kind of happiness — The most valuable kind of happiness comes from the small things in life that make me feel good. This kind of happiness is taking time to have a cup of coffee before class or eating lunch at an old-fashioned diner. It is watching kids play Little League ball in the summer or playing pick-up basketball with my friends. It is finding out that I can still run a couple of miles even though I haven't exercised in a while or that I can still remember all the state capitals that I had to memorize in school.

Summary Statement — For me, happiness is more than just money or success; it is the little things that bring joy to my life.

Edward Fernandez (student)

Transitions are important for definition paragraphs. In the paragraph above, the transitional words and phrases *The first kind*, *The second kind*, and *The most valuable kind* introduce the categories and tell readers when they are moving from one category to the next.

The following box lists some of the transitional words and phrases that are used in definition paragraphs. In addition to these transitions, you can use the transitional words and phrases for the specific pattern (or patterns) that you use to develop your paragraph.

Some Transitional Words and Phrases for Definition

also	like
first (second, third)	one characteristic . . . another characteristic
for example	one way . . . another way
in addition	specifically
in particular	the first kind . . . the second kind
	unlike

> **Grammar in Context: Definition**
>
> A definition paragraph often includes a formal definition of the term or idea you are going to discuss. When you write a formal definition, be careful not to use the phrase *is where* or *is when*.
>
> Happiness is ~~when you have~~ a feeling of contentment or joy.

● **Practice 10-1**

Read this definition paragraph; then, follow the instructions below.

Writer's Block

Writer's block is the inability to start writing. For nonprofessionals, writer's block almost always involves assigned writing, such as a paper for school or a report for work. Sometimes writer's block is caused by poor preparation: the writer has not allowed enough time to think and make notes. However, even prepared writers with many ideas already on paper can experience writer's block. It is like being tongue-tied, only writer's block is more like being brain-tied. All the ideas keep bouncing around but will not settle into any order, and the writer cannot decide what to say first. Often, the only cure for writer's block is to give up for a while, find something else to do, and try again later. By doing this, you give your mind a chance to clear and your ideas a chance to regroup and, eventually, to begin flowing.

Thaddeus Eddy (student)

1. Underline the topic sentence of the paragraph.
2. What is the subject of this definition? *writer's block*
3. What is the writer's one-sentence definition of the subject?
   Writer's block is the inability to start writing.

4. List some of the specific information the writer uses to define his subject. The first piece of information has been listed for you.

   It almost always involves assigned writing.

   It can be caused by poor preparation.

   It's like being "brain-tied."

5. What patterns of development does the writer use in his definition? List them here.

   uses description of writer's block

   uses examples of writer's block

   uses cause and effect to explain cause of writer's block

6. Underline the paragraph's summary statement.

● Practice 10-2

Following are four possible topic sentences for definition paragraphs. Each topic sentence includes an underlined word. In the space provided, list two possible patterns of development that you could use to expand a definition of the underlined word. For example, you could define the word *discrimination* by giving examples (exemplification) and by telling a story (narration).

1. During the interview, the job candidate made a <u>sexist</u> comment.

   Possible strategy: *Answers will vary.*

   Possible strategy: *Answers will vary.*

2. <u>Loyalty</u> is one of the chief characteristics of golden retrievers.

   Possible strategy: *Answers will vary.*

   Possible strategy: *Answers will vary.*

3. More than forty years after President Johnson's Great Society initiative, we have yet to eliminate <u>poverty</u> in the United States.

   Possible strategy: *Answers will vary.*

   Possible strategy: *Answers will vary.*

4. The problem with movies today is that they are just too <u>violent</u>.

   Possible strategy: *Answers will vary.*

   Possible strategy: *Answers will vary.*

10b Writing a Definition Paragraph

On a history exam, Lorraine Scipio was asked to write a one-paragraph definition of the term *imperialism*. Lorraine had studied for the exam, so she knew what *imperialism* was. Because she wanted to make sure that she did not leave anything out of her definition (and because she had a time limit), she quickly listed her points on the inside cover of her exam book. Then, she crossed out two items that did not seem relevant.

> A policy of control
> Military
> ~~Lenin~~
> Establish empires
> Cultural superiority
> Raw materials and cheap labor
> Africa, etc.
> ~~Cultural imperialism~~
> Nineteenth-century term

Next, Lorraine reorganized her points in the order in which she planned to write about them.

> Establish empires
> Nineteenth-century term
> Cultural superiority
> Africa, etc.
> Raw materials and cheap labor
> A policy of control
> Military

Consulting the points on her list, Lorraine wrote the following draft of her definition paragraph. Notice that she uses several patterns to develop her definition.

> The goal of imperialism is to set up an empire. The imperialist country thinks that it is better than the country it takes over. It says that it is helping the other country. But it isn't. Countries such as

Germany, Belgium, Spain, and England did this in Africa when they stole large areas of land. It happened in North and South America when Spain, Portugal, England, and France took territory there. The imperialist countries did not help these countries. The point of imperialism is to take as much out of the other countries as possible. In South America and Mexico, Spain stole tons of gold. It made slaves of the natives and forced them to work in mines. Then they sent troops to protect their interests. Imperialism kept the people in occupied countries in poverty. It broke down local governments and local traditions. Many people thought it was wrong.

After she finished writing her paragraph, Lorraine reread it quickly, using the **TEST** strategy to help her to make sure her paragraph answered the exam question. Then, she made the following changes.

- Because the question asked for a definition, she added a **topic sentence** that included a formal definition.
- She strengthened her **evidence**, explaining her supporting details more fully. She also deleted some vague statements.
- She added **transitional words and phrases** to make the connections between her ideas clearer.
- She added a **summary statement** to sum up the effects of imperialism.

Lorraine made her changes directly on the draft she had written, crossing out unnecessary information and adding missing information. She also edited her paragraph for grammar, punctuation, and mechanical errors. Then, because she had some extra time, she neatly copied over her revised and edited draft. The final draft of Lorraine's exam answer appears below. (This is an exam answer, so she does not include a title.)

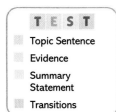

T E S T
- Topic Sentence
- Evidence
- Summary Statement
- Transitions

Imperialism is a nineteenth-century term that refers to the policy by which one country takes over the land or the government of another country. The object of imperialism is to establish an empire. The imperialist country thinks that it is superior to the country it takes over. It justifies its actions by saying that it is helping the other country. For instance, countries such as Germany, Belgium, Spain, and England followed their imperialist ambitions in Africa when they claimed large areas of land. The point of imperialism is to take as much out of the occupied countries as possible. For example, in South America and Mexico, Spain removed tons of gold from the areas it occupied. It made the natives slaves and forced them to work in mines. In order to protect their interests, imperialist countries sent troops to occupy the country and to keep order. As a result, imperialism kept the people in occupied countries in poverty and often broke down local governments and local traditions. Although European imperialism occasionally had benefits, at its worst it brought slavery, disease, and death.

Highlight: Writing Paragraph Answers on Exams

When you write paragraph answers on exams, you will not have much time to work, so you will need to be well prepared. Know your subject well, and memorize important definitions. You may have time to write an outline, a rough draft, and a final draft, but you will have to work quickly. Your final paragraph should include all the elements of a good paragraph: a topic sentence, evidence, transitions, and a summary statement.

● **Practice 10-3**

Teaching Tip
Encourage students to choose a topic from one of their other courses. By doing so, students can see how strategies they learn in this course can be helpful in other disciplines.

Now, you are ready to write a draft of a definition paragraph. Choose one of the topics below (or choose your own topic) for a definition paragraph. On a separate sheet of paper, use one or more of the strategies described in 1C to help you define the term you have chosen to discuss. Name the term, and then describe it, give examples of it, tell how it works, explain its purpose, consider its history or future, or compare it with other similar things. In short, do whatever works best for defining your specific subject.

A negative quality, such as envy, dishonesty, or jealousy

An ideal, such as the ideal friend or neighborhood

A type of person, such as a worrier or a show-off

A social concept, such as equality, opportunity, or discrimination

An important play or strategy in a particular sport or game

A hobby you pursue or an activity associated with that hobby

A technical term or specific piece of equipment that you use in your job

An object (such as an article of clothing) that is important to your culture or religion

A basic concept in a course you are taking

A particular style of music or dancing

A controversial subject whose definition not all people agree on, such as affirmative action, right to life, or gun control

A goal in life, such as success or happiness

● **Practice 10-4**

Review your notes for the topic you chose in Practice 10-3. On a separate sheet
of paper, list the details that can best help you to develop a definition paragraph.

● **Practice 10-5**

Reread your notes from Practice 10-4. Then, draft a topic sentence that summarizes the main point you want to make about the term you are going to define.

    Answers will vary.

● **Practice 10-6**

List the ideas you will discuss in your paragraph, arranging them in an effective order.

1. *Answers will vary.* _____

2. _____

3. _____

4. _____

5. _____

● **Practice 10-7**

Draft your definition paragraph. Then, using the **TEST** checklist on page
143, check your paragraph for unity, support, and coherence.

● **Practice 10-8**

Now, revise your definition paragraph.

● **Practice 10-9**

Prepare a final draft of your definition paragraph.

Focus on Writing: *Revising and Editing*

Look back at your response to the Focus on Writing activity on page 133.
Using the **TEST** checklist on page 143, evaluate the paragraph you wrote
for unity, support, and coherence. Then, prepare a final, edited draft of
your paragraph.

Chapter Review

Focus on Writing

The pictures below show Americans from several different backgrounds. Look at the pictures carefully, and then write a paragraph that defines the term *American*. In what way do the people in the pictures fit (or not fit) your definition? Begin your paragraph with a topic sentence that identifies the term you will define. Then, in the rest of the paragraph, use any of the patterns of development discussed in this text to help you define the term.

Real-World Writing

For a brochure designed to get people to buy homes in your neighborhood, write a one-paragraph definition of the word *community*. Develop your definition with examples that demonstrate that your neighborhood has the people, resources, and qualities that make up a community.

T E S Ting a Definition Paragraph

Topic Sentence Unifies Your Paragraph

☐ Do you have a clearly worded topic sentence that states your paragraph's main idea?

☐ Does your topic sentence identify the term you are defining?

Evidence Supports Your Paragraph's Topic Sentence

☐ Do all your examples and details support your paragraph's main idea?

☐ Do you need to add more examples or details to help you define your term?

Summary Statement Reinforces Your Paragraph's Unity

☐ Does your paragraph end with a statement that summarizes your main idea?

Transitions Add Coherence to Your Paragraph

☐ Are your transitions appropriate for the pattern (or patterns) of development you use?

☐ Do you need to add transitions to make your paragraph more coherent?

Chapter 11

Using Argument

After 1776, when America gained independence from Britain, individual states established the right to vote — but only for white, male landowners over the age of twenty-one.

11a

What Is Argument?

Teaching Tip
Remind students that many everyday writing tasks require argument. For example, in a letter to a local newspaper, they could argue for or against a law taxing motorists who drive into the city.

When most people hear the word *argument*, they think of heated exchanges on television interview programs. These discussions, however, are more like shouting matches than arguments. True **argument** involves taking a well-thought-out position on a **debatable topic**—a topic on which reasonable people may disagree (for example, "Should intelligent design be taught in high school classrooms?" or "Should teenagers who commit felonies be tried as adults?"). In an argument, you attempt to convince people of the strength of your ideas not by shouting but by presenting **evidence**. In the process, you also address opposing ideas. If they are strong, you acknowledge their strengths and try to **refute** (argue against) them. If your evidence is solid and your logic is sound, you will present a convincing argument.

When you write an **argument paragraph**, your purpose is to persuade readers that your position has merit. To write an effective argument paragraph, follow these guidelines.

→ Focus on Writing

The picture on the opposite page shows a person placing a vote in a ballot box. Look at the picture, and then write a paragraph in which you argue for or against one of the following policies:

- Requiring paper ballots that can be hand-counted.
- Requiring electronic ballots that can be registered on computer databases.
- Permitting people to vote in federal elections from their home computers.

Include examples from your own experience or from your reading to support your position.

WORD POWER
controversy a dispute
debate to discuss or argue about

● *Write a clear topic sentence that states your position.* Use words like *should, should not,* or *ought to* in your topic sentence to make your position clear to readers.

> The federal government <u>should</u> lower the tax on gasoline.

> The city <u>should not</u> build a new sports stadium.

● *Present points that support your topic sentence.* For example, if your purpose is to argue for placing warning labels on unhealthy snack foods, you should give several reasons why this would be a good idea.

● *Present convincing evidence.* Supporting each of your points with specific evidence will strengthen your position.

**Highlight:
Evidence for
Argument
Paragraph**

Two kinds of **evidence** can be used to support your arguments: *facts* and *examples.*

1. A **fact** is a piece of information that can be verified. If you make a point, you should be prepared to support it with facts — for example, statistics, observations, or statements that are accepted as true.

2. An **example** is a specific illustration of a general statement. To be convincing, an example should be clearly related to the point you are making.

● *Address opposing arguments.* Try to imagine what your opponent's arguments might be, and show how they are inaccurate or weak. By addressing these objections in your paragraph, you strengthen your position.

● *Write a summary statement.* A summary statement reinforces the main idea of your paragraph. In an argument paragraph, it is especially important to summarize the position you introduced in your topic sentence.

An argument paragraph generally has the following structure.

Topic Sentence_____

_____

Point #1_____

_____

Point #2_____

_____

Point #3_____

_____

Opposing Argument #1_____

_____

Opposing Argument #2_____

_____

Summary Statement_____

_____

The writer of the following paragraph argues against placing a tax on soda.

Taxing Soda

Topic Sentence —

<u>I am against taxing soda because it is unfair, it is unnecessary, and it will not work.</u> The first reason this kind of tax is bad is that it is not fair. The American Medical Association (AMA) thinks the tax will fight obesity in the United States. However, people should be allowed to decide for themselves whether they should drink soda. It is not right for a group of doctors or politicians to decide what is best for everybody. Another reason this kind of tax is bad is that it is unnecessary. It would be better to set up educational programs to help children make decisions about what they eat. In addition, the AMA should educate parents so they will stop buying soda for their children. Finally, this kind of tax is bad because it will not work. As long as soda is for sale, children will drink it. The only thing that will work is outlawing soda completely, and no one is suggesting this.

Arguments in support of the topic sentence —

Opposing arguments ——————

> Of course, some people say that soda should be taxed because it has no nutritional value. This is true, but many snack foods have little nutritional value, and no one is proposing a tax on snack food. In addition, not everyone who drinks soda is overweight, let alone obese. A tax on soda would hurt everyone, including healthy adults.

Summary Statement ——————

> The key to helping young people is not to tax them but to teach them what a healthy diet is.

Ashley Hale (student)

Transitions are important for argument paragraphs. In the paragraph above, the transitional words and phrases *The first reason, Another reason,* and *Finally* tell readers they are moving from one point to another. Later in the paragraph, the transitional phrases *Of course* and *In addition* consider and refute two opposing arguments.

Some Transitional Words and Phrases for Argument

accordingly	first . . . second . . .	on the one hand . . .
admittedly	however	on the other hand
although	in addition	since
because	in conclusion	the first reason . . .
but	in fact	another reason
certainly	in summary	therefore
consequently	meanwhile	thus
despite	moreover	to be sure
even so	nevertheless	truly
even though	nonetheless	
finally	of course	

Grammar in Context: Argument

For more information on how to create compound sentences, refer students to Chapter 15. For more information on how to create complex sentences, refer them to Chapter 16.

When you write an argument paragraph, you need to show the relationships among your ideas. You do this by creating compound and complex sentences.

Compound Sentence The only thing that will work is outlawing soda
                                          , and no
completely. ~~No~~ one is suggesting this.

Complex Sentence Recently, some people have suggested taxing
                                        , because they
soda. ~~They~~ think it is not healthy for young people.

● Practice 11-1

Read this argument paragraph; then, follow the instructions that follow.

Big Brother in the Workplace

<u>Employers should not routinely monitor the computer use of their employees.</u> First of all, monitoring computer use violates an employee's privacy. Every day, employees use their computers for work-related tasks, and in many companies every keystroke is recorded. In addition, some companies read employees' private email files as well as monitor the Internet sites they visit. This monitoring creates an unpleasant work environment because employees feel that someone is always watching them. In fact, at some companies, employees have even been fired for sending personal emails or humorous pictures. Of course, companies that believe computers should be used only for work-related tasks have a point. After all, the company pays for both the computers and the employees' time. The problem with this line of thinking, however, is that it ignores the fact that workers need some downtime in order to work effectively. For this reason, it makes sense to allow some use of computers for personal reasons (to send emails to friends, for example). <u>Unless a company has reason to suspect misuse of company computers, it should not routinely monitor all employees' computers.</u>

Scott Rathmill (student)

1. Underline the topic sentence of the paragraph.
2. What issue is the subject of the paragraph?
   personal computer use at work

   What is the writer's position?
   Employers should not routinely monitor the computer use of their employees.

3. What points does the writer use to support his topic sentence?

Monitoring computer use violates an employee's privacy.

Monitoring computer use creates an unpleasant work environment.

4. List some of the evidence that the writer uses to support his points. The first piece of evidence has been listed for you.

Every keystroke an employee makes is recorded.

Companies monitor personal emails and sites that employees visit.

Some companies have fired employees for sending personal emails or

humorous pictures.

5. What evidence does the writer use to support his points?

He uses facts and examples.

6. What other evidence could the writer have used?

He could have presented statements by experts about the effects of

monitoring employees' personal use of computers. He also could have

presented additional factual information in the form of statistics. Finally,

he could have given specific examples of workers who were fired.

7. What opposing argument does the writer address?

Computers should be used only for work-related tasks.

8. How does the writer refute this argument?

He shows how it ignores the fact that workers need downtime.

9. Underline the paragraph's summary statement.

● **Practice 11-2**

Following are four topic sentences for argument paragraphs. On a separate sheet of paper, list two or three points that could support each topic sentence. For example, if you were arguing in support of laws requiring motorcycle riders to wear safety helmets, you could say they cut down on medical costs and save lives.   *Answers will vary.*

1. Marijuana use for certain medical conditions should be legalized.

2. All student athletes should be paid a salary by their college or university.

3. College students caught cheating should be expelled.

4. The U.S. government should provide free health care for all citizens.

● Practice 11-3

Choose one of the topic sentences from Practice 11-2. Then, list two pieces of evidence that could support each point you listed. For example, if you said that wearing safety helmets saves lives, you could list "accident statistics" and "statements by emergency room physicians."

Answers will vary.

___

11b   Writing an Argument Paragraph

Phillip Zhu was asked to write an argument paragraph on a topic that interested him. Because he was taking a course in computer ethics, he decided to write about an issue that had been discussed in class: the way employers have recently begun searching social networking sites, such as MySpace, to find information about job applicants.

Phillip had already formed an opinion about this issue, and he knew something about the topic. For this reason, he was able to write a topic sentence right away.

> Employers should not use social networking sites to find information about job applicants.

Phillip then listed the following ideas that he could use to support his topic sentence.

> Social networking sites should be private
>
> People exaggerate on social networking sites
>
> Stuff meant to be funny
>
> No one warns applicant
>
> Need email address to register
>
> Expect limited audience
>
> Employers can misinterpret what they find

Employers going where they don't belong

Not fair

Not an accurate picture

Not meant to be seen by job recruiters

Phillip then arranged his ideas into an informal outline.

Social networking sites should be private

Need email address to register

Expect limited audience

Employers going where they don't belong

People exaggerate on social networking sites

Stuff meant to be funny

Not meant to be seen by job recruiters

No one warns applicant

Employers can misinterpret what they find

Not an accurate picture

Not fair

Once Phillip finished his informal outline, he tried to think of possible arguments against his position because he knew he would have to consider and refute these opposing arguments in his paragraph. He came up with two possible arguments against his positions:

1. Employers should be able to find out as much as they can.
2. Applicants have only themselves to blame.

Phillip then wrote the following draft of his paragraph.

Employers should not use social networking sites to find information about job applicants. For one thing, social networking sites should be private. By going on these sites, employers are going where they do not belong. People also exaggerate on social networking sites. They say things that are not true, and they put things on the sites they would not want job recruiters to see. No one ever tells applicants that recruiters search these sites, so they feel safe posting all kinds of material. Employers can misinterpret what they read. Employers and recruiters need to get as much information as they can. They should not use unfair ways to get this information. Also, it doesn't give them a good picture of the applicant. Applicants have only themselves to blame for their problems. They need to be more careful about what they put up online. This is true, but most applicants don't know that employers will search social networking sites. For this reason, it is not fair to judge applicants on the basis of what they post.

After finishing his draft, Phillip scheduled a conference with his instructor. Together, they went over his paragraph and applied the **TEST** strategy. They decided that Phillip needed to make the following changes.

- Make his **topic sentence** more specific and more forceful.
- Add more **evidence** (details and examples) to his discussion. For example, what social networking sites is he talking about? Which are restricted? How do employers gain access to these sites?
- Delete irrelevant discussion blaming job applicants for the problem.
- Add **transitional words and phrases** to clearly identify the points he is making in support of his argument and also to identify the two opposing arguments he discusses and refutes.
- Add a strong **summary statement** that sums up the argument.

After making these changes, Phillip revised and edited his paragraph. Here is his final draft.

Unfair Searching

T E S T
- Topic Sentence
- Evidence
- Summary Statement
- Transitions

Employers should not use social networking sites, such as MySpace and Facebook, to find information about job applicants. First, people who use social networking sites do not expect employers to access these sites. However, some employers routinely search these sites to find information about job applicants. Doing this is not right, and it is not fair. By visiting these sites, employers are going where they do not belong. Another reason why employers should not use information from social networking sites is that people frequently exaggerate on them or even say things that are not true. They may also put statements and pictures on the sites that they would not want job recruiters to see. Because no one ever tells applicants that recruiters search these sites, they feel safe posting embarrassing pictures or making exaggerated claims about drinking or sex. Finally, employers can misinterpret the material they see. As a result, they may reject a good applicant because they take seriously what is meant to be a joke. Of course, employers need to get as much information about a candidate as they can. They should not, however, use unfair tactics to get this information. In addition, prospective employers should realize that the profile they see on a social networking site does not accurately represent the job applicant. For this reason, they should not use these sites to do background checks.

● Practice 11-4

Now, you are ready to write a draft of an argument paragraph. Choose one of the topics below (or choose your own topic) for an argument paragraph. Then, on a separate sheet of paper, use one or more of the strategies described in 1C to help you focus on a specific issue to discuss in an argument paragraph.

An Issue Related to Your School

Grading policies   Financial aid
Required courses   Student activity fees
Attendance policies   Childcare facilities
Course offerings   Sexual harassment policies
Dining facilities   The physical condition of classrooms

An Issue Related to Your Community

The need for a traffic signal, a youth center, or something else you think would benefit your community

An action you think local officials should take, such as changing school hours, cleaning up a public space, or improving a specific service

A new law you would like to see enacted

A current law you would like to see repealed

A controversy you have been following in the news

● Practice 11-5

Once you have chosen an issue in Practice 11-4, write a journal entry about your position on the issue. Consider the following questions: Why do you feel the way you do? Do you think many people share your views, or do you think you are in the minority? What specific actions do you think should be taken? What objections are likely to be raised against your position? How might you respond to these objections?

● Practice 11-6

Teaching Tip
Divide students into pairs, and let each student take a turn arguing against the other's position on a particular topic (preferably the one the other student is writing about). Have students jot down their opponent's objections and later refute them in their own paragraphs.

Review your notes for the topic you chose in Practice 11-4, and select the points that best support your position. List these points below. (You may also want to list the strongest arguments against your position.)   *Answers will vary.*

Supporting points: _____

_____

Opposing arguments: _____

_____

● Practice 11-7

Draft a topic sentence that clearly expresses the position you will take in your paragraph.

Answers will vary. _____

_____

● Practice 11-8

In the space provided, arrange the points that support your position in an order that you think will be convincing to your audience.

1. *Answers will vary.* _____

2. _____

3. _____

4. _____

5. _____

● Practice 11-9

In the space provided, list the evidence (facts and examples) that you could use to support each of your points.   *Answers will vary.*

Evidence for point 1: _____

_____

Evidence for point 2: _____

_____

Evidence for point 3: _____

_____

● Practice 11-10

Draft your argument paragraph. Then, using the **TEST** checklist on page 158, check your paragraph for unity, support, and coherence.

● Practice 11-11

Now, revise your argument paragraph.

● Practice 11-12

Prepare a final draft of your argument paragraph.

Focus on Writing: *Revising and Editing*

Look back at your response to the Focus on Writing activity on page 145. Using the **TEST** checklist on page 158, evaluate the paragraph you wrote for unity, support, and coherence. Then, prepare a final, edited draft of your paragraph.

Chapter Review

Focus on Writing

The picture below shows a driver talking on a cell phone. Many states are considering (or have already adopted) a ban on cell phone use by drivers in moving vehicles. Look at the picture, and then write an argument paragraph in which you argue either that this ban is a good idea or that the convenience of cell phones outweighs the possible risk of accidents.

Real-World Writing

Your school has proposed banning trans fats at all food services on campus—including independently owned food stands and trucks that serve students. Write a one-paragraph editorial for your school newspaper in which you either support or argue against this idea.

T E S Ting an Argument Paragraph

Topic Sentence Unifies Your Paragraph

☐ Do you have a clearly worded topic sentence that states your paragraph's main idea?

☐ Does your topic sentence state your position on a debatable topic?

☐ Do you need to revise your topic sentence to include new ideas?

Evidence Supports Your Paragraph's Topic Sentence

☐ Does all your evidence support your paragraph's main idea?

☐ Have you included enough evidence to support your points, or do you need to add more?

Summary Statement Reinforces Your Paragraph's Unity

☐ Does your paragraph end with a statement that summarizes your main idea?

Transitions Add Coherence to Your Paragraph

☐ Do you use transitional words and phrases to let readers know when you are moving from one point to another?

☐ Do you use transitional words and phrases to indicate when you are addressing opposing arguments?

☐ Do you need to add transitions to make your paragraph more coherent?

Unit Three
Writing Essays

In 2005, the National Fire Protection Association reported that 87 percent of fire departments consist of volunteers. Only 13 percent consist of professional firefighters.

Most of the writing you do in school will be longer than a single paragraph. Often, you will be asked to write an **essay**—a group of paragraphs on a single subject. When you write an essay, you follow the same process you follow when you write a paragraph: you begin by planning your essay and then move on to organizing your ideas, drafting, revising, and editing.

STEP 1: PLANNING

12a Understanding Essay Structure

Teaching Tip
Remind students that most writing situations outside of school require more than a paragraph. The skills they learn in this chapter can also be helpful for these writing tasks.

Teaching Tip
Refer students to Chapter 1 for more on writing a paragraph.

An **essay** is a group of paragraphs about one subject. In this chapter, you will see how the strategies you learned for writing paragraphs can help you write essays.

In some ways, essays and paragraphs are similar. For example, both paragraphs and essays have a single **main idea**. In a paragraph, the main idea is stated in a **topic sentence**, and the rest of the paragraph supports this main idea with **evidence** (details and examples). **Transitional words and phrases** help readers follow the discussion. The paragraph ends with a **summary statement** that sums up the main idea.

→ Focus on Writing

The picture on the opposite page shows firefighters at the scene of a house fire. Look at the picture, and then think of the hardest job you ever had. This is the topic you will be writing about as you go through this chapter. (If you have never had a job, you may write about a specific task that you disliked or about a hard job that a friend or relative has had.)

WORD POWER
challenging demanding
arduous difficult; tiring

Paragraph

> The **topic sentence** states the main idea of the paragraph.
>
> **Evidence** supports the main idea.
>
> **Transitional words and phrases** show the connections between ideas.
>
> A **summary statement** ends the paragraph.

Teaching Tip
Explain to students that an essay includes more ideas, more discussion, and more support than a paragraph does. Even so, because of their similarities, the skills students developed for writing paragraphs will also help them to write essays.

Teaching Tip
Discuss how the concepts of unity, support, and coherence work in an essay. Ask students to compare a paragraph with the sample essay on pages 163–65.

In an essay, the main idea is presented in a **thesis statement**. The first paragraph—the **introduction**—presents the thesis statement. The main part of the essay consists of several **body paragraphs** that support the thesis statement. (Each of these body paragraphs begins with a topic sentence that states the paragraph's main idea, which is one point in support of the essay's thesis.) **Transitional words and phrases** help readers follow the discussion. The essay ends with a **conclusion**. The conclusion includes a **summary statement** that restates the thesis or sums up the main idea, and it ends with **concluding remarks**. This essay structure is called **thesis and support**.

Many of the essays you will write in college will have a thesis-and-support structure.

Essay

Introduction

> **Opening remarks** introduce the subject being discussed in the essay.
>
> The **thesis statement** presents the essay's main idea.

First body Paragraph

> The **topic sentence** states the essay's first point.
>
> **Examples and details** support the topic sentence.
>
> **Transitional words and phrases** connect the examples and details and show how they are related.

Second body Paragraph

> The **topic sentence** states the essay's second point.
>
> **Examples and details** support the topic sentence.
>
> **Transitional words and phrases** connect the examples and details and show how they are related.

Third body
Paragraph

> The **topic sentence** states the essay's third point.
>
> **Examples and details** support the topic sentence.
>
> **Transitional words and phrases** connect the examples and details and show how they are related.

Conclusion

> The **summary statement** restates the thesis, summarizing the essay's main idea.
>
> **Concluding remarks** present the writer's final thoughts on the subject.

The following student essay illustrates this thesis-and-support structure.

Becoming Chinese American

Introduction

Although I was born in Hong Kong, I have spent most of my life in the United States. However, my parents have always made sure that I did not forget my roots. They always tell stories of what it was like to live in Hong Kong. To make sure my brothers and sisters and I know what is happening in China, my parents subscribe to Chinese cable TV. When we were growing up, we would watch the celebration of the Chinese New Year, the news from Asia, and Chinese movies and music

Thesis statement

videos. As a result, I value Chinese culture even though I am an American.

First body paragraph

(Topic sentence states essay's first main point)

The Chinese language is an important part of my life as a Chinese American. Unlike some of my Chinese friends, I do not think Chinese is unimportant or embarrassing. First, I feel that it is my duty as a Chinese American to learn Chinese so that I can pass it on to my children. In addition, knowing Chinese enables me to communicate with my relatives. Because my parents and grandparents do not speak English well, Chinese is our main form of communication. Finally, Chinese helps me identify with my culture.

When I speak Chinese, I feel connected to a culture that is over five thousand years old. Without the Chinese language, I would not be who I am.

Chinese food is another important part of my life as a Chinese American. One reason is that everything we Chinese people eat has a history and a meaning. At a birthday meal, for example, we serve long noodles and buns in the shape of peaches. This is because we believe that long noodles represent long life and that peaches are served in heaven. Another reason is that to Chinese people, food is a way of reinforcing ties between family and friends. For instance, during a traditional Chinese wedding ceremony, the bride and the groom eat nine of everything. This is because the number nine stands for the Chinese words "together forever." By taking part in this ritual, the bride and groom start their marriage by making Chinese customs a part of their life together.

Religion is the most important part of my life as a Chinese American. At various times during the year, Chinese religious festivals bring together the people I care about the most. During Chinese New Year, my whole family goes to the temple. Along with hundreds of other families, we say prayers and welcome each other with traditional New Year's greetings. After leaving the temple, we all go to Chinatown and eat dim sum until the lion dance starts. As the colorful lion dances its way down the street, people beat drums and throw firecrackers to drive off any evil spirits that may be around. Later that night, parents give children gifts of money in red envelopes that symbolize joy and happiness in the coming year.

My family has taught me how important it is to hold on to my Chinese culture. When I was six, my parents sent me to a Chinese-American grade school. My teachers thrilled me with stories of Fa Mulan, the Shang Dynasty, and the Moon God. I will never forget how happy I was when I realized how special it is to be Chinese.

Second body paragraph

(Topic sentence states essay's second main point)

Third body paragraph

(Topic sentence states essay's third main point)

(Summary Statement sums up essay's main idea)

Conclusion

This is how I want my own children to feel. I want them to be proud of who they are and to pass their language, history, and culture on to the next generation.

● **Practice 12-1**

Following is an essay organized according to the diagram on pages 162–63. Read the essay, and then answer the questions that follow it.

Introduction

Maybe you have moved to a new city, so you need to find a new doctor for yourself and your family. Maybe your doctor has retired. Or maybe you need a specialist to deal with a difficult medical problem. In any case, your goal is clear—to find a doctor. Several strategies can help you in your search for a good doctor.

First body paragraph

First, you need to find a well-qualified doctor. One way to begin is to identify the best hospital in the area and find a doctor on the staff there. Good doctors are attracted to good hospitals, so this is a good place to start your search. Recommendations from friends and neighbors can also be useful. Once you have some names, find out whether the doctors are board certified in their specific fields. Board certification means that doctors have had extensive training in their specialties and take part in continuing education programs each year. You can easily find out whether a doctor is board certified by going to the American Board of Medical Specialties Web site at www.ABMS.org.

Second body paragraph

Next, you need to decide what things are important to you. For example, think about how far you are willing to travel to see the doctor. Do you need a doctor with a convenient location? This might be important if you expect to see the doctor frequently or if you have a physical disability. Also, consider when the doctor is available. Many doctors have office hours only on weekdays. Is this acceptable, or will you need evening or Saturday appointments? You should also find out the office policy concerning emergencies. Will you be able to see the doctor immediately, or will you have to go to a hospital emergency room? Finally, find out how you will pay for the medical care you receive. If you have medical insurance, find out if the doctor accepts your plan. Next, determine if someone at the doctor's office fills out insurance forms or if you have to do it yourself. If you do not have medical insurance, find out what payment options the doctor offers. Will you have to pay everything at once, or will you be able to arrange a payment plan?

If you are satisfied with the answers to all these questions, you should make an appointment to visit the office and meet the doctor. If

Third body
paragraph

the office seems crowded and disorganized, you should be on your guard. The doctor may be overscheduled, overworked, understaffed, or simply disorganized. Whatever the case, this situation does not make for good medical care. You should also see how long it takes for you to see the doctor. Unless the doctor is called away to an emergency, you should not have to sit in the waiting room for one or two hours. Finally, see if you feel comfortable talking to the doctor. If the doctor seems rushed or uninterested, you should take this as an indication of the type of medical care you will get. Finally, both the doctor and the office staff should treat you with respect. They should take the time to ask about your general health and to update your medical records.

Conclusion

Finding a good doctor requires careful planning and a lot of work. You may even have to take the time to see several doctors and assess each one. Remember, though, there are no short cuts. If the result of all your hard work is a qualified doctor who really cares about your well-being, then your time will have been well spent.

Teaching Tip
Have students form groups of three. Ask each student in each group to make up an additional example for each body paragraph. Each group should then evaluate all the new examples and agree on the best addition to each paragraph. If time permits, students can share their examples with the class.

1. Underline the essay's thesis statement.

2. Underline the topic sentence of each body paragraph.

3. What point does the first body paragraph make? What evidence supports this point?

4. What point does the second paragraph make? What evidence supports this point?

5. What point does the third body paragraph make? What evidence supports this point?

6. What transitions does the essay include? How do they connect the essay's ideas?

7. Where in the conclusion does the writer restate the essay's thesis? Underline this summary statement.

12b   Focusing on Your Assignment, Purpose, and Audience

An essay usually begins with an assignment given to you by your instructor. Before you focus on your assignment, however, you should think about your essay's **audience** and **purpose**. In other words, take the time to think about who will be reading your essay and what you hope to accomplish by writing it. After doing this, you will be ready to consider your assignment.

The following assignments are typical of those you might be given in your composition class:

- Discuss some things you would like to change about your school.
- What can college students do to improve the environment?
- Discuss an important decision you made during the past three years.

Teaching Tip
Refer students to 1B for more on audience and purpose.

Because these assignments are so general, they would be difficult to write about. What specific things would you change? Exactly what could you do to improve the environment? Which decision should you write about? Answering these questions will help you narrow these assignments into **topics** that you can write about.

Assignment	Topic
Discuss some things you would change about your school.	Three things I would change about Jackson County Community College
What can college students do to improve the environment?	A campus recycling project
Discuss an important decision you made during the past three years.	Deciding to go back to school

● Practice 12-2

Decide whether the following topics are suitable for an essay of four or five paragraphs. If a topic is suitable, write *OK* in the blank. If it is not, write in the blank a revised version of the same topic that is narrow enough for a brief essay.

Examples: Successful strategies for quitting smoking _____*OK*_____

Horror movies _____*1950s Japanese monster movies*_____

1. Violence in American public schools *Answers will vary.* _____
   Example: the need for metal detectors in a local high school

2. Ways to improve your study skills *OK* _____
   _____

3. Using pets as therapy for nursing-home patients *OK* _____
   _____

4. Teachers *Answers will vary.* _____

   Example: qualities of an effective teacher _____

5. Reasons children lie to their parents *OK* _____

_____

Focus on Writing: *Flashback*

Look back at the Focus on Writing activity on page 161. To narrow the topic to one you can write about, you need to decide which job to focus on. On a separate piece of paper, list a few jobs you could discuss.

Finding Ideas

Teaching Tip
Refer students to 1C for more on finding material to write about.

Before you start writing about a topic, you need to find out what you have to say about it. Sometimes ideas may come to you easily. More often, you will have to use one or more strategies, such as *freewriting* or *brainstorming*, to help you come up with ideas about your topic.

Freewriting

Teaching Tip
Refer students to Chapter 1 for more on finding something to say.

When you **freewrite**, you write for a fixed period of time without stopping. When you do **focused freewriting**, you write with a specific topic in mind. Then, you read what you have written and choose the ideas you think you can use. Following is an example of focused freewriting by a student, Jared White, on the topic "Deciding to go back to school."

> Deciding to go back to school. When I graduated high school, I swore I'd never go back to school. Hated it. Couldn't wait to get out. What was I thinking? How was I supposed to support myself? My dad's friend needed help. He taught me how to paint houses. I made good money, but it was boring. I couldn't picture myself doing it forever. Even though I knew I was going to have to go back to school, I kept putting off the decision. Maybe I was lazy. Maybe I was scared — probably both. I had this fear of being turned down.

How could someone who had bad grades all through high school go to college? Also, I'd been out of school for six years. And even if I did get in (a miracle!), how would I pay for it? How would I live? I met a guy while I was painting who told me that I could get into community college. Tuition was a lot lower than I thought. Then, I just had to push myself to go. Well, here I am — the first one in my family to go to college.

● **Practice 12-3**

Reread Jared White's freewriting. If you were advising Jared, which ideas would you suggest that he explore further? Why?

Focus on Writing: *Flashback*

Choose two of the jobs you listed for the Flashback activity on page 168. Freewrite about each of them on separate sheets of paper. Then, choose the job that suggested the most interesting material. Circle the ideas that you would like to develop further in an essay.

Brainstorming

When you **brainstorm** (either individually or in collaboration with others), you write down (or type) all the ideas you can think of about a particular topic. You can write a list or you can write notes scattered all over a sheet of paper. After you have recorded as much material as you can, you look over your notes to decide which ideas are useful and which ones are not. Here is Jared White's brainstorming about his decision to go back to school.

Deciding to Go Back to School

Money a problem

No confidence

Other students a lot younger

Paying tuition — how?

No one in family went to college

Friends not in college

Couldn't see myself in college

Relationship with Beth

Considered going to trade school

Computer programmer?

Grades bad in high school

Time for me to grow up

Wondered if I would get in

Found out about community college

Went to Web site

Admission requirements not bad

Afraid — too old, failing out, looking silly

Took time to get used to routine

Found other students like me

Liked studying

● **Practice 12-4**

Reread Jared White's brainstorming. Which ideas would you advise him to explore further?

Focus on Writing: *Flashback*

Review the freewriting you did in the Flashback activity on page 169. On a separate sheet of paper, brainstorm about the job for which you have the most interesting ideas. What ideas about the job did you get from brainstorming that you did not get from freewriting?

12d **Identifying Your Main Idea and Stating Your Thesis**

After you have gathered information about your topic, you need to decide what you want to say about it and what point you want to make. You can then express this point in a **thesis statement**: a single sentence that clearly expresses the main idea that you will discuss in the rest of your essay.

Topic	Thesis Statement
Three things I would change about Jackson County Community College	If I could change three things about Jackson County Community College, I would expand the food choices, decrease class size in first-year courses, and ship some of my classmates to the North Pole.
A campus recycling project	The recycling project recently begun on our campus should be promoted more actively.
Deciding to go back to school	I decided that if I really wanted to attend college full-time, I could.

Teaching Tip
Refer students to 2A for more on topic sentences.

Like a paragraph's topic sentence, an essay's thesis statement tells readers what to expect. An effective thesis statement has two important characteristics.

1. *An effective thesis statement makes a point about a topic. For this reason, it must do more than state a fact or announce what you plan to write about.*

Statement of fact	Many older students are returning to college.
Announcement	In this essay, I would like to discuss the difficulties many older students have going back to college.
Effective thesis statement	I decided that if I really wanted to attend college full-time, I could.
Statement of fact	My school has begun a campus-wide recycling project.
Announcement	I am going to discuss the campus-wide recycling project.
Effective thesis statement	The recycling project recently begun on campus should be promoted more actively.

Teaching Tip
Spend extra time on writing effective thesis statements and on their placement. Remind students not to make an announcement and not to state the thesis in their essay's first sentence.

A statement of fact is not an effective thesis statement because it takes no position and gives you nothing to develop in your essay. After all, how much can you say about the *fact* that many older students are returning to college or that your school has begun a recycling project? Likewise, an announcement of what you plan to discuss gives readers no idea what position you will take on your topic. An effective thesis statement makes a point.

2. *An effective thesis statement is clearly worded and specific.*

Vague thesis statement	Television commercials are not like real life.
Effective thesis statement	Television commercials do not accurately portray women or minorities.

The vague thesis statement above gives little indication of the ideas that the essay will discuss. It does not say, for example, *why* television commercials are not realistic. The effective thesis statement is more focused. It signals that the essay will probably give examples of television commercials that present unrealistic portrayals of women and minorities.

Highlight: Stating Your Thesis

You can sometimes revise a vague thesis statement by including in it a list of the specific points that you will discuss. Revised in this way, the thesis acts as a road map, telling readers what to expect as they read.

Vague thesis statement	Raising tropical fish is a good hobby.
Effective thesis statement	Raising tropical fish is a good hobby because it is inexpensive, interesting, and educational.

Teaching Tip
Tell students that at this stage of the process their thesis statements are not definite but tentative. They will probably change these tentative thesis statements as they write and revise their essays.

When Jared White looked over his notes, he saw that they included ideas about how difficult it would be to return to school. They also included information about how to overcome these difficulties. Jared decided that his essay could discuss the challenges he faced when he decided to return to college as an older student. He presented this idea in a thesis statement.

I decided that if I really wanted to attend college full-time, I could.

Jared knew that his thesis statement had to be a complete sentence. He also knew that it had to make a point about his topic. Finally, he knew that it had to be both clearly worded and specific. When Jared reviewed his thesis statement, he felt sure that it did these things and that it expressed an idea he could develop in his essay.

● Practice 12-5

In the space provided, indicate whether each of the following items is a statement of fact (*F*), an announcement (*A*), a vague statement (*VS*), or an effective thesis (*ET*).

Examples:

My commute between home and school takes more than an hour each way. __*F*__

I hate my commute between home and school. __*VS*__

1. Students who must commute a long distance to school are at a disadvantage compared to students who live close by. __*ET*__

2. In this paper, I will discuss cheating and why students shouldn't cheat. __*A*__

3. Schools should establish specific policies that will discourage students from cheating. __*ET*__

4. Cheating is a problem. __*VS*__

5. Television commercials are designed to sell products. __*F*__

6. I would like to explain why some television commercials are funny. __*A*__

7. Single parents have a rough time. __*VS*__

8. An article in the newspaper says that young people are starting to abuse alcohol and drugs at earlier ages than in the past. __*F*__

9. Alcohol and drug abuse are major problems in our society. __*VS*__

10. Families can use several strategies to help children avoid alcohol and drugs. __*ET*__

● Practice 12-6

Label each of the following thesis statements *VS* if it is a vague statement, *F* if it is a statement of fact, *A* if it is an announcement, or *ET* if it is an effective thesis. On a separate sheet of paper, revise those that are not effective thesis statements.

Answers to rewrites will vary.

1. Different types of amusement parks appeal to different types of people. <u>VS</u>

2. There are three reasons why Election Day should be a national holiday. <u>ET</u>

3. Every fourth year, the United States elects a new president. <u>F</u>

4. My paper will prove that DVDs are better than videotapes. <u>A</u>

5. The largest fish in the sea is the whale shark. <u>f</u>

6. Scientists once believed that the dinosaurs were killed off by the arrival of a new Ice Age. <u>F</u>

7. NASCAR drivers should take steps to make their sport safer than it is. <u>ET</u>

8. This paper will discuss the increase in the number of women in the military since the 1970s. <u>A</u>

9. Movies provide great entertainment. <u>VS</u>

10. Computers have made it easier for teachers and their students to communicate. <u>ET</u>

● **Practice 12-7**

Rewrite the following vague thesis statements.

Example: My relatives are funny.

Rewrite: <u>My relatives think they are funny, but sometimes their humor can be offensive.</u>

Answers will vary.

1. Email can save time.

2. Airport security could be better.

3. Athletes are paid too much.

4. Many people get their identities from their cars.

5. Being single has advantages.

Teaching Tip
Have students read their thesis statements aloud and let the class determine whether they are effective or not. Ask students to explain their decisions.

● Practice 12-8

A list of broad topics for essays follows. Select five of these topics, narrow them, and generate a thesis statement for each.   *Answers will vary.*

Terrorism	Required courses
Reality television	Computer games
U.S. immigration policies	Disciplining children
Music	Street sense
Dieting	Footwear

Focus on Writing: *Flashback*

Review your freewriting and brainstorming from the Flashback activities on page 169 and page 170. Then, draft a thesis statement for your essay on a separate piece of paper.

STEP 2: ORGANIZING

12e   Choosing Supporting Points

Once you have decided on a thesis statement, look over your freewriting and brainstorming again. List the points that best **support** your thesis, and cross out those that do not.

Jared White listed the following supporting points about his decision to go back to school. After he reviewed his list, he crossed out several points he thought would not support his thesis.

> *Thesis statement:* I decided that if I really wanted to attend college full-time, I could.

Deciding to Go Back to School

Money a problem

~~No confidence~~

Not a good student in high school

Paying tuition — how?

No one in family went to college

Friends not in college

Couldn't picture myself in college

~~Relationship with Beth~~

~~Considered going to trade school~~

~~Computer programmer?~~

Grades bad in high school

~~Time for me to grow up~~

Wondered if I would get in

Found out about community college

Went to Web site

Admission requirements not bad

Afraid — too old, failing out, looking silly

~~Took time to get used to routine~~

Found other students like me

Liked studying

● Practice 12-9

Look at Jared's list of supporting points above. Are there any points he crossed out that you think he should have kept? Are there any other points he should have crossed out?

12f   Arranging Your Supporting Points

After you have selected the points you think will best support your thesis, arrange them into groups. For example, after looking at the list of points above, Jared White saw that his points fell into three groups of excuses for not going back to school: not being able to pay tuition, not being a good student in high school, and not being able to picture himself in college.

After you have come up with your own groups, arrange them in the order in which you will discuss them (for example, from general to specific, or from least important to most important). Then, arrange the supporting points for each group in the same way. This orderly list can serve as a rough outline to guide you as you write.

Jared grouped and listed his points in the following order.

Excuse 1: Not being able to pay tuition
> Money a problem
>
> Found out about community college
>
> Went to Web site

Excuse 2: Not being a good student in high school
> Grades bad in high school
>
> Wondered if I would get in
>
> Admission requirements not bad

Excuse 3: Not being able to picture myself in college
> No one in family went to college
>
> Friends not in college
>
> Afraid — too old, failing out, looking silly
>
> Found other students like me
>
> Liked studying

● Practice 12-10

Look over Jared's list of points above. Do you think his arrangement is effective? Can you suggest any other ways he might have arranged his points? Write your response on the lines below.

Answers will vary.

Highlight: Preparing a Formal Outline

The rough outline illustrated above is usually all you need to plan a short essay. However, some writers — especially when they are planning longer, more detailed essays — like to use a more formal outline.

Formal outlines contain a combination of numbered and lettered headings and use roman numerals, capital letters, and Arabic numerals (and sometimes lower-case letters) to show the relationships among

→

**Highlight:
Preparing
a Formal
Outline**
continued

ideas. For example, the most important (and most general) ideas are assigned a roman numeral; the next most important ideas are assigned capital letters. Each level develops the idea above it, and each new level is indented. Here is a formal outline of the points that Jared planned to discuss in his essay.

Thesis statement: I decided that if I really wanted to attend college full-time, I could.

I.   Not being able to pay tuition
   A. Money a problem
   B. Community college
      1. Tuition low
      2. Expenses reasonable

II. Not being a good student in high school
   A. Grades bad
      1. Didn't care about high school
      2. Didn't do homework
   B. Anxiety about getting in
   C. Admissions requirements
      1. High school diploma
      2. County residence
      3. Placement tests

III. Not being able to picture myself in college
   A. Family no help
   B. Friends not in college
   C. Fear of going
      1. Too old
      2. Couldn't keep up
   D. Fears disappeared
      1. Found other students like me
      2. Liked studying

Teaching Tip
Take this opportunity to explain to students that all headings in a formal outline are stated in parallel terms. You might want to refer students to Chapter 18, Using Parallelism.

Focus on Writing: *Flashback*

Review your freewriting and brainstorming from the Flashback activities on pages 169 and 170. On a separate sheet of paper, list the points you plan to use to support your thesis statement. Cross out any points that do not support your thesis statement. Finally, group the remaining points, and arrange them in an order in which you could write about them.

STEP 3: DRAFTING

12g ● Drafting Your Essay

After you have decided on a thesis for your essay and arranged your points in the order in which you will discuss them, you are ready to draft your essay.

At this stage of the writing process, you should not worry about spelling or grammar or about composing a perfect introduction or conclusion. Your main goal is to get your ideas down so you can react to them. Remember that the draft you are writing will be revised, so leave room for your changes: write on every other line, and leave extra space between lines if you are typing. Follow your rough outline, but don't hesitate to depart from it if you think of new points or if your ideas take an interesting or unexpected turn as you write.

As you draft your essay, be sure that it has a **thesis-and-support** structure—that is, it should state a thesis and support it with details and examples. Jared White uses a thesis-and-support structure in the first draft of his essay.

Going Back to School

I have been out of school since I graduated from high school six years ago. The decision to return to school was one I had a lot of difficulty making. I had been around enough to know that without more education, I'd never get anywhere in life, but I always found reasons for not taking the plunge. However, after a lot of thinking, I realized that my reasons for not going to college were just excuses. I decided that if I really wanted to attend college full-time, I could.

My first excuse for not going to college was that I couldn't afford to go to school full-time. I had worked since I finished high school, but I hadn't put much money away. I kept wondering how I would pay for books and tuition. I needed to support myself and pay for rent, food, and car expenses. I was working as a house painter, and a house I was painting belonged to a college instructor. Painting wasn't hard work, but it was boring. I'd start in the morning and work without a break until lunch. We began talking. When I told him about my situation, he told me I should look at our local community college. I went online and looked at the college's Web site. I found out that tuition was forty dollars a credit, much less than I thought it would be.

Now that I had taken care of my first excuse, I had to deal with my second — that I hadn't been a good student in high school. When

I was a teenager, I didn't care much about school. School bored me to death. Now that I was considering going back to school, though, I wondered what price I would have to pay for my laziness and immaturity. The answer to this question was not as bad as I thought it would be. According to the community college's Web site, all I needed to be admitted was a high school diploma and county residence. I would have to take some placement tests, but I would be judged on my ability, not my high school grades. The Web site was easy to navigate, and I had no problem finding information.

I had a hard time picturing myself in college. No one in my family had ever gone to college. My friends were just like me; they all went to work right after high school. I had no role model or mentor who could give me advice. I thought I was just too old for college. After all, I was probably at least six years older than most of the students. How would I be able to keep up with the younger students in the class? I hadn't opened a textbook for years, and I'd never really learned how to study. Most of my fears disappeared during my first few weeks of classes. I saw a lot of students who were as old as I was, and some were even older. Studying didn't seem to be a problem either. I actually enjoyed learning. History, which had put me to sleep in high school, suddenly became interesting. So did math and English. It soon became clear to me that I was going to like being in college.

Going to college as a full-time student has changed my life, both personally and financially. I am no longer the same person I was in high school. I allowed laziness and insecurity to hold me back. Now, I have options that I didn't have before. When I graduate from community college, I plan to transfer to the state university and get a four-year degree.

● **Practice 12-11**

Reread Jared White's first draft. What changes would you suggest he make? What might he add? What might he delete?

Focus on Writing: *Flashback*

Draft an essay about the job you chose in the Flashback activity on page 169. Be sure to include the thesis statement you developed in the Flashback activity on page 175 as well as the points you listed in the Flashback activity on page 178.

12h TESTing Your Essay

Before you begin to revise the first draft of your essay, you should **TEST** it to make sure it contains the four elements that make it clear and effective.

Highlight: TESTing Your Essay

- **Thesis Statement**—Does your essay include a thesis statement that states your main idea?
- **Evidence**—Does your essay include examples and details that support your thesis statement?
- **Summary Statement**—Does your essay's conclusion include a summary statement that restates your thesis or sums up your main idea?
- **Transitions**—Does your essay include transitional words and phrases that show readers how your ideas are related?

As you reread your essay, use the **TEST** strategy to identify the four elements of an effective essay. If your essay includes these four elements, you can move on to revise and edit it. If not, you should supply whatever is missing.

When Jared reread the draft of his essay, he used the **TEST** strategy to help him quickly survey his essay.

- He thought his thesis statement clearly stated his main idea.
- He thought he could add some more support in his body paragraphs and delete some irrelevant details.
- He thought his summary statement summed up the idea expressed in his thesis statement.
- He realized he needed to add more transitions to connect ideas.

Focus on Writing: *Flashback*

Using the Highlight box above as a guide, evaluate the essay you drafted for the Flashback activity on page 180. (You may want to get feedback by exchanging essays with another student.)

STEP 4: REVISING AND EDITING

12i Revising Your Essay

Teaching Tip
Suggest that students revise and edit on hard copy before they type the changes into their documents.

When you **revise** your essay, you resee, rethink, reevaluate, and rewrite your work. Some of the changes you make—such as adding, deleting, or rearranging several sentences or even whole paragraphs—will be major. Other changes will be small—for example, adding or deleting words or phrases.

Before you begin revising, put your essay aside for a while. This "cooling-off" period allows you to see your draft more objectively when you return to it. (Keep in mind that revision is usually not a neat process. When you revise, feel free to write directly on your draft: draw arrows, underline, cross out, and write above lines and in the margins.)

Teaching Tip
Refer students to Chapter 2 for more on how to write paragraphs that are unified, well developed, and coherent.

Even when you write on a computer, it is a good idea to print out a hard copy and revise on it. With a hard copy, you are able to see a full page—or even two pages next to each other—as you revise. When you have finished, you can type your changes into your document. Do not delete sentences or paragraphs until you are certain you do not need them; instead, move unwanted material to the end of your draft.

To get the most out of revision, read your essay carefully, and use the following checklist as your guide.

Self-Assessment Checklist: Revising Your Essay

- [ ] Does your essay have an introduction, a body, and a conclusion?
- [ ] Does your introduction include a clearly worded thesis statement that states your essay's main idea?
- [ ] Does each body paragraph have a topic sentence?
- [ ] Does each topic sentence introduce a point that supports the thesis?
- [ ] Does each body paragraph include enough details and examples to support the topic sentence?
- [ ] Are the body paragraphs unified, well developed, and coherent?
- [ ] Does your conclusion include a summary statement that restates your thesis or sums up your main idea?

12j Editing Your Essay

When you **edit** your essay, you check grammar and sentence structure. Then, you look at punctuation, mechanics, and spelling.

As you edit, think carefully about the questions in the Self-Assessment Checklist that follows.

Self-Assessment Checklist: Editing Your Essay

Editing for Common Sentence Problems

☐ Have you avoided run-ons? (See Chapter 20.)

☐ Have you avoided sentence fragments? (See Chapter 21.)

☐ Do your subjects and verbs agree? (See Chapter 22.)

☐ Have you avoided illogical shifts? (See Chapter 23.)

☐ Have you avoided dangling and misplaced modifiers? (See Chapter 24.)

Editing for Grammar

☐ Are your verb forms and verb tenses correct? (See Chapters 25 and 26.)

☐ Have you used nouns and pronouns correctly? (See Chapter 27.)

☐ Have you used adjectives and adverbs correctly? (See Chapter 28.)

Editing for Punctuation, Mechanics, and Spelling

☐ Have you used commas correctly? (See Chapter 30.)

☐ Have you used apostrophes correctly? (See Chapter 31.)

☐ Have you used capital letters where they are required? (See 33A.)

☐ Have you used quotation marks correctly where they are needed? (See 33B.)

☐ Have you spelled every word correctly? (See Chapter 34.)

When Jared White typed the first draft of his essay about deciding to return to college, he left extra space so he could write more easily in the space between the lines. Here is his draft, with his handwritten revision and editing changes as well as the transitions he added after he finished **TEST**ing his essay.

Going Back to School *Starting Over*

I have been out of school since I graduated from high school six years ago. The decision to return to school was one I had a lot of difficulty making. I had been around enough to know that without more education, I'd never get anywhere in life, but I always found reasons for not taking the plunge. However, after a lot of thinking, I realized that my reasons for not going to college were just excuses. I decided that if I really wanted to attend college full-time, I could.

The other day, my sociology instructor mentioned that half the students enrolled in college programs across the country were twenty-five or older. His remarks caught my attention because I am one of those students.

My first excuse for not going to college was that I couldn't afford to go to school full-time. I had worked since I finished high school, but I hadn't put much money away. I kept wondering how I would pay for books and tuition. I also needed to support myself and pay for rent, food, and car expenses. *The solution to my problem came unexpectedly.* I was working as a house painter, and a house I was painting belonged to a college instructor. ~~Painting wasn't hard work, but it was boring. I'd start in the morning and work without a break until lunch.~~ *During my lunch break, we* We began talking. When I told him about my situation, he told me I should look at our local community college. I went online and looked at the college's Web site. I found out that tuition was forty dollars a credit, much less than I thought it would be. *The money I'd saved, along with what I could make painting houses on the weekends, could get me through.*

In class, I would stare out the window or watch the second hand of the clock move slowly around the dial. I never bothered with homework. School just didn't interest me.

Now that I had taken care of my first excuse, I had to deal with my second — that I hadn't been a good student in high school. When I was a teenager, I didn't care much about school. *In fact, school* ~~School~~ bored me ~~to death.~~ Now that I was considering going back to school, though, I wondered what price I would have to pay for my laziness and immaturity. The answer to this question was not as bad as I thought it would be. According to the community college's Web site, all I needed to be admitted was a high school diploma and county residence. I would have to take some placement tests, but I would be judged on my ability, not my high school grades.

~~The Web site was easy to navigate, and I had no problem finding information.~~

My biggest problem still bothered me:

I had a hard time picturing myself in college. No one in my family had ever gone to college. My friends were just like me; they all went to work right after high school. I had no role model or mentor who could give me advice. *Besides,* I thought I was just too old for college. After all, I was probably at least six years older than most of the students. How would I be able to keep up with the younger students in the class? I hadn't opened a textbook for years, and I'd never really learned how to study. *However, most* ~~Most~~ of my fears disappeared during my first few weeks of classes. I saw a lot of students who were as old as I was, and some were even older. Studying didn't seem to be a problem either. I actually enjoyed learning. History, which had put me to sleep in high school, suddenly became interesting. So did math and English. It soon became clear to me that I was going to like being in college.

Going to college as a full-time student has changed my life, both personally and financially. I am no longer the same person I was in high school. *In the past,* I allowed laziness and insecurity to hold me back. Now, I have options that I didn't have before. When I graduate from community college, I plan to transfer to the state university and get a four-year degree. *The other day, one of my instructors asked me if I had ever considered becoming a teacher. The truth is, I never had, but now I might. I'd like to be able to give kids like me the tough, realistic advice I wish someone had given me.*

● Practice 12-12

What kind of material did Jared White add to his draft? What did he delete? Why did he make these changes? Write your answers on a separate sheet of paper.

When his revisions and edits were complete, Jared proofread his essay to make sure he had not missed any errors. The final revised and edited version of his essay appears on pages 186–88. (Marginal annotations have been added to highlight key features of his paper.)

Jared White

Professor Wilkinson

English 120

7 Oct. 2007

Starting Over

Introduction

The other day, my sociology instructor mentioned that half the students enrolled in college programs across the country are twenty-five or older. His remarks caught my attention because I am one of those students. I have been out of school since I graduated from high school six years ago. The decision to return to school was one I had a lot of difficulty making. I had been around enough to know that without more education, I would never get anywhere in life, but I always found reasons for not taking the plunge. However, after a lot of thinking, I realized that my reasons for not going to college were just excuses.

Thesis statement

I decided that if I really wanted to attend college full-time, I could.

Topic Sentence (first main point)

My first excuse for not going to college was that I couldn't afford to go to school full-time. I had worked since I finished high school, but I hadn't put much money away. I kept wondering how I would pay for books and tuition. I also needed to support myself and pay for rent, food, and car expenses. The solution to my problem came unexpectedly.

Body paragraphs

I was working as a house painter, and a house I was painting belonged to a college instructor. During my lunch break, we began talking. When I told him about my situation, he told me I should look at our local community college. I went online and looked at the college's Web site. I found out that tuition was forty dollars a credit, much less than I thought it would be. The money I'd saved, along with what I could make painting houses on the weekends, could get me through.

Topic Sentence (second main point)

Now that I had taken care of my first excuse, I had to deal with my second — that I hadn't been a good student in high school. When I

was a teenager, I didn't care much about school. In fact, school bored me. In class, I would stare out the window or watch the second hand on the clock move slowly around the dial. I never bothered with homework. School just didn't interest me. Now that I was considering going back to school, though, I wondered what price I would have to pay for my laziness and immaturity. The answer to this question was not as bad as I thought it would be. According to the community college's Web site, all I needed to be admitted was a high school diploma and county residence. I would have to take some placement tests, but I would be judged on my ability, not my high school grades.

Topic Sentence (third main point)

My biggest problem still bothered me: I had a hard time picturing myself in college. No one in my family had ever gone to college. My friends were just like me; they all went to work right after high school. I had no role model or mentor who could give me advice. Besides, I thought I was just too old for college. After all, I was probably at least six years older than most of the students. How would I be able to keep up with the younger students in the class? I hadn't opened a textbook for years, and I'd never really learned how to study. However, most of my fears disappeared during my first few weeks of classes. I saw a lot of students who were as old as I was, and some were even older. Studying didn't seem to be a problem either. I actually enjoyed learning. History, which had put me to sleep in high school, suddenly became interesting. So did math and English. It soon became clear to me that I was going to like being in college.

Body paragraphs

(Summary Statement)

Going to college as a full-time student has changed my life, both personally and financially. I am no longer the same person I was in high school. In the past, I allowed laziness and insecurity to hold me back. Now, I have options that I didn't have before. When I graduate from community college, I plan to transfer to the state university and get a four-year degree. The other day, one of my instructors asked me

Conclusion

if I had ever considered becoming a teacher. The truth is, I never had, but now I might. I'd like to be able to give kids like me the tough, realistic advice that I wish someone had given me.

● Practice 12-13

Reread the final draft of Jared White's essay. Do you think this draft is an improvement over his first draft? What other changes could Jared have made? Write your ideas here.

Answers will vary.

_____

_____

_____

_____

_____

12k   Checking Your Essay's Format

The **format** of an essay is the way it looks on a page—for example, the size of the margins, the placement of page numbers, the space between lines. Most instructors expect you to follow a certain format when you type an essay. The essay format illustrated on the following page is commonly used in composition classes. Before you hand in an essay, you should make sure that it follows these guidelines.

Essay format: Sample first page

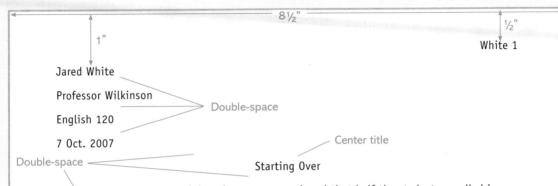

8½"

½"

White 1

1"

Jared White

Professor Wilkinson

English 120

7 Oct. 2007

Double-space

Center title

Starting Over

Double-space

Indent
½ inch

1"

1"

  The other day, my sociology instructor mentioned that half the students enrolled in college programs across the country are twenty-five or older. His remarks caught my attention because I am one of those students. I have been out of school since I graduated from high school six years ago. The decision to return to school was one I had a lot of difficulty making. I had been around enough to know that without more education, I would never get anywhere in life, but I always found reasons for not taking the plunge. However, after a lot of thinking, I realized my reasons for not going to college were just excuses. I decided that if I really wanted to attend college full-time, I could.

  My first excuse for not going to college was that I couldn't afford to go to school full-time. I had worked since I finished high school, but I hadn't put much money away. I kept wondering how I would pay for books and tuition. I also needed to support myself and pay for rent, food, and car expenses. The solution to my problem came unexpectedly. I was working as a house painter, and a house I was painting belonged to a college instructor. During my lunch break, we began talking. When I told him about my situation, he told me I should look at our local community college. I went online and looked at the college's Web site. I found out that tuition was forty dollars a credit, much less than I thought it would be. The money I'd saved, along with what I could make painting houses on weekends, could get me through.

  Now that I had taken care of my first excuse, I had to deal with my second — that I hadn't been a good student in high school. When I was a teenager, I didn't care much about school. In fact, school bored me. In class, I would stare out the window . . . .

1"

Focus on Writing: *Revising and Editing*

Now, revise and edit your draft, using the Self-Assessment Checklists on pages 182 and 183 to guide you. When you have finished, make sure your essay has the proper format. Then, prepare a final draft of your essay.

Chapter Review

Editing Practice

1. After reading the following student essay, write an appropriate thesis statement on the lines provided. (Make sure your thesis statement clearly communicates the essay's main idea.) Then, fill in the topic sentences for the second, third, and fourth paragraphs. Finally, add a summary statement in the conclusion.

Preparing for a Job Interview

I have looked at a lot of books and many Web sites that give advice on how to do well on a job interview. Some recommend practicing your handshake, and others suggest making eye contact. This advice is useful, but not many books tell how to get mentally prepared for an interview. [Thesis statement:] *Answers will vary.*

_____

_____

[Topic sentence for the second paragraph:] *Answers will vary.*

_____

_____

Feeling good about how I look is important, so I usually wear a jacket and tie to an interview. Even if you will not be dressing this formally on the job, try to make a good first impression. For this reason, you should never come to an interview dressed in jeans or shorts. Still, you should be careful not to overdress. For example, wearing a suit or a

dressy dress to an interview at a fast-food restaurant might make you feel good, but it could also make you look as if you do not really want to work there.

[Topic sentence for the third paragraph:] _Answers will vary._

_____

_____

Going on an interview is a little like getting ready to take part in a sporting event. You have to go in with the right attitude. If you think you are not going to be successful, chances are that you will not be. So, before I go on any interview, I spend some time building my confidence. I tell myself that I can do the job and that I will do well in the interview. By the time I get to the interview, I am sure I am the right person for the job.

[Topic sentence for the fourth paragraph:] _Answers will vary._

_____

_____

Most people go to an interview knowing little or nothing about the job. They expect the interviewer to tell them what they will have to do. Once, an interviewer told me that he likes a person who has taken the time to do his or her homework. Since that time, I have always done some research before I go on an interview — even for a part-time job. (Most of the time, my research is nothing more than a quick look at the company Web site.) This kind of research really pays off. At my last interview, for example, I was able to talk in detail about the job I would do. The interviewer must have been impressed because she offered me the job on the spot.

[Summary statement:] _Answers will vary._

_____

_____

Of course, following my suggestions will not guarantee that you get a job. You still have to do well at the interview itself. Even so, getting mentally prepared for the interview will give you an advantage over people who do almost nothing before they walk in the door.

2. Now, using the topic sentence below, write another body paragraph that you could add to the essay above. (This new paragraph will go right before the essay's conclusion.)

Another way to prepare yourself mentally is to anticipate and answer some typical questions interviewers ask. [New body paragraph:] _Answers will vary._

_____

_____

_____

_____

_____

_____

_____

Collaborative Activities

1. On your own, find a paragraph in a magazine or a newspaper about an issue that interests you. Working in a group, select one of the paragraphs. Choose three points about the issue discussed that you could develop in a short essay, and then brainstorm about these points. Finally, write a sentence that could serve as the thesis statement for an essay.

2. Working in a group, come up with thesis statements suitable for essays on three of the following topics.

Living on a budget	Gun safety
The Internet	Fitness
Safe driving	Patriotism
Parenthood	Bad habits
Honesty	How to prepare for a test

Teaching Tip
Refer students to 12D for information on stating a thesis.

3. Exchange your group's three thesis statements with those of another group. Choose the best one of the other group's thesis statements. A member of each group can then read the thesis statement to the class and explain why the group chose the thesis statement it did.

Review Checklist: Writing an Essay

- [ ] Most essays have a thesis-and-support structure. The thesis statement presents the main idea, and the body paragraphs support the thesis. (See 12A.)
- [ ] Begin by narrowing your assignment to a topic you can write about. (See 12B.)
- [ ] Find ideas to write about. (See 12C.)
- [ ] Identify your main idea, and develop an effective thesis statement. (See 12D.)
- [ ] List the points that best support your thesis, and arrange them in the order in which you plan to discuss them. (See 12E, 12F.)
- [ ] Write your first draft, making sure your essay has a thesis-and-support structure. (See 12G.)
- [ ] **TEST** your essay. (See 12H.)
- [ ] Revise your essay. (See 12I.)
- [ ] Edit your essay. (See 12J.)
- [ ] Make sure your essay's format is correct. (See 12K.)

In 2003, an estimated 35,000 women were employed as construction workers in the United States, making up 3 percent of the total number of construction jobs.

When you draft an essay, you usually focus on the **body** because it is the section in which you develop your ideas. A well-constructed essay, however, is more than a series of body paragraphs. It also includes an **introduction** and a **conclusion**, both of which contribute to the overall effectiveness of your writing.

13a   Introductions

Introductions

Teaching Tip
Remind students that the introduction should be a full paragraph.

Teaching Tip
Find two introductory paragraphs (one that is catchy and one that is dull), and read each one to the class. After you read each introduction, ask students whether they would like to hear the rest of the essay— and why or why not.

An **introduction** is the first thing people see when they read your essay. If your introduction is interesting, it will make readers want to read further. If it is not, readers may get bored and stop reading.

Your introduction, which should be a full paragraph, begins with some general introductory remarks to draw readers into your essay. The **thesis statement**, a sentence that presents the main idea of your essay, usually appears at the end of the introductory paragraph. (In each of the sample introductory paragraphs on pp. 196–97, the thesis statement is underlined and labeled.)

Here are some options you can experiment with when you write your introductions.

Beginning with a Narrative

You can begin an essay with a narrative drawn from your own experience or from a current news event.

→ Focus on Writing

The picture on the opposite page shows construction workers on their way to a job. Look at the picture, and then print out a copy of the essay about your hardest job that you wrote for Chapter 12. As you go through this chapter, you will be working on the introduction and conclusion of that essay.

WORD POWER
monotonous repetitious; lacking in variety
strenuous requiring great effort

On September 11, 2001, terrorists crashed two airplanes into the twin towers at the World Trade Center. Ignoring the danger to themselves, hundreds of firefighters rushed inside the buildings to try to save as many lives as possible. Their actions enabled thousands of people to get out, but half the firefighters — over three hundred — died when the twin towers collapsed. Although I have never faced a catastrophe like the one in New York, as a volunteer firefighter I am ready — day or night, whenever an alarm sounds — to deal with a dangerous situation.

Richard Pogue (student)

Thesis statement

Beginning with a Question (or a Series of Questions)

Asking one or more questions at the beginning of your essay is an effective strategy. Because readers expect you to answer the questions, they will want to read further.

Imagine this scene: A child is sitting under a Christmas tree opening her presents. She laughs and claps her hands as she gets a doll, a pair of shoes, and a sweater. What could spoil this picture? What information could cause the child's parents to feel guilt? The answer is that children from developing countries probably worked long hours in substandard conditions so this child could receive her gifts.

Megan Davia (student)

Thesis statement

Beginning with a Background Statement

A background statement can provide an overview of your subject and set the stage for the discussion to follow.

Teaching Tip
Students love to begin their introductions and conclusions with definitions. Encourage them to avoid introducing a definition with a tired opening phrase such as "According to *Webster's* . . ." or "The *American Heritage Dictionary* defines . . ."

English is the most widely spoken language in the history of our planet, used in some way by at least one out of every seven human beings around the globe. Half of the world's books are written in English, and the majority of international telephone calls are made in English. English is the language of over sixty percent of the world's radio programs, many of them beamed, ironically, by the Russians, who know that to win friends and influence nations, they're best off using

ESL Tip
Ask students why some-
one might think English is
"crazy."

English. More than 70 percent of international mail is written and addressed in English, and 80 percent of all computer text is stored in English. English has acquired the largest vocabulary of all the world's languages, perhaps as many as two million words, and has generated one of the noblest bodies of literature in the annals of the human race. Nonetheless, it is now time to face the fact that English is a crazy language.

Thesis statement

Richard Lederer, "English Is a Crazy Language"

Beginning with a Quotation

An appropriate saying or some interesting dialogue can draw readers into your essay.

According to the comedian Jerry Seinfeld, "When you're single, you are the dictator of your own life. . . . When you're married, you are part of a vast decision-making body." In other words, before you can do any-thing, you have to discuss it with someone else. These words kept going through my mind as I thought about asking my girlfriend to marry me. The more I thought about Seinfeld's words, the more I hesitated. I never suspected that I would pay a price for my indecision.

Thesis statement

Dan Brody (student)

Beginning with a Surprising Statement

You can begin your essay with a surprising or unexpected statement. Because your statement takes readers by surprise, it catches their attention.

Some of the smartest people I know never went to college. In fact, some of them never finished high school. They still know how to save 20 per-cent on the price of a dinner, fix their own faucets when they leak, get dis-counted prescriptions, get free rides on a bus to Atlantic City, use public transportation to get anywhere in the city, and live on about twenty-two dollars a day. These are my grandparents' friends. Some people would call them old and poor. I would call them survivors who have learned to make it through life on nothing but a Social Security check.

Thesis statement

Sean Ragas (student)

Highlight: What to Avoid in Introductions	• Do not begin your essay by announcing what you plan to write about. **Phrases to Avoid** This essay is about . . . In my essay, I will discuss . . . • Do not apologize for your ideas. **Phrases to Avoid** Although I don't know much about this subject . . . I might not be an expert, but . . .

● **Practice 13-1**

Look at the essays in Chapter 36, locating one introduction you think is particularly effective. Be prepared to explain the strengths of the introduction you chose.

Highlight: Choosing Titles	Every essay should have a **title** that suggests the subject of the essay and makes people want to read it.
	
	• Capitalize all words except for articles (*a, an, the*), prepositions (*at, to, of, around*, and so on), and coordinating conjunctions (*and, but*, and so on), unless they are the first or last word of the title.
	• Do not underline your title or enclose it in quotation marks.
	• Center the title at the top of the first page. Double-space between the title and the first line of your essay.
	
	As you consider a title for your paper, think about the following options.
	A title can highlight a key word or term.
	    A "Good" American Citizen
	    Orange Crush
	A title can be a straightforward announcement.
	    How to Stop a Car with No Brakes
	    Don't Hang Up, That's My Mom Calling
	A title can establish a personal connection with readers.
	    America, Stand Up for Justice and Democracy
	    Why We Need Animal Experimentation
	A title can be a familiar saying or a quotation from your essay itself.
	    The Dog Ate My Disk, and Other Tales of Woe

Teaching Tip
Refer students to 33C for more on setting off titles.

Focus on Writing: *Flashback*

Look back at the essay you reprinted for the Focus on Writing activity on page 195. Evaluate your introduction. Does it prepare readers for the essay to follow? Does it include a thesis statement? Is it likely to interest readers? On a separate sheet of paper, draft a different opening paragraph using one of the options presented in 13A. Be sure to include a clear thesis statement.

After you have finished drafting a new introduction, think of a new title that will attract your readers' attention. (Use one of the options listed in the Highlight box on p. 198.)

Conclusions

Teaching Tip
Read aloud several different types of conclusions, and have the class categorize them.

Because your **conclusion** is the last thing readers see, they often judge your entire essay by its effectiveness. For this reason, conclusions should be planned, drafted, and revised with care.

Like an introduction, a conclusion should be a full paragraph. Your conclusion should give readers a sense of completion. You can do this by including a summary statement and then making some general concluding remarks. If you can, try to end with a final thought or observation that readers will remember.

Here are some options you can use when you write your conclusions.

Concluding with a Narrative

Teaching Tip
Remind students that a conclusion should be a full paragraph.

A narrative conclusion can bring an event discussed in the essay to a logical, satisfying close.

> After twenty years, the tree began to bear. Although Grandfather complained about how much he lost because pollen never reached the poor part of town, because at the market he had to haggle over the price of avocados, he loved that tree. It grew, as did his family, and when he died, all his sons standing on each other's shoulders, oldest to youngest, could not reach the highest branches. The wind could move the branches, but the trunk, thicker than any waist, hugged the ground.
>
> Gary Soto, "The Grandfather"

Concluding with a Prediction

This type of conclusion not only sums up the thesis but also looks to the future.

> On that little street were the ghosts of the people who brought me into being and the flesh-and-blood kids who will be my children's companions in the twenty-first century. You could tell by their eyes that they couldn't figure out why I was there. They were accustomed to being ignored, even by the people who had once populated their rooms. And as long as that continues, our cities will burst and burn, burst and burn, over and over again.
>
> Anna Quindlen, "The Old Block"

Concluding with a Recommendation

Once you think you have convinced readers that a problem exists, you can make recommendations in your conclusion about how the problem should be solved. The following conclusion ends with a series of recommendations about a cancer drug made from the Pacific yew tree.

> Every effort should be made to ensure that the yew tree is made available for the continued research and development of taxol. Environmental groups, the timber industry, and the Forest Service must recognize that the most important value of the Pacific yew is as a treatment for cancer. At the same time, its harvest can be managed in a way that allows for the production of the cancer drug taxol without endangering the continual survival of the yew tree.
>
> Sally Thane Christensen, "Is a Tree Worth a Life?"

Concluding with a Quotation

Teaching Tip
Advise students to draft their body paragraphs before they spend much time writing introductions or conclusions. After they have developed the body of their essay, they can revise their introduction and conclusion so they fit in with the direction that their essay has taken.

A well-chosen quotation—even a brief one—can be an effective concluding strategy. In the following paragraph, the quotation reinforces the main idea of the essay.

> It was 4:25 a.m. when the ambulance arrived to take the body of Miss Genovese. It drove off. "Then," a solemn police detective said, "the people came out."
>
> Martin Gansberg, "Thirty-Eight Who Saw Murder Didn't Call the Police"

<table>
<tr><td>

Highlight: What to Avoid in Conclusions

</td><td>

● Do not introduce any new ideas. Your conclusion should sum up the ideas you discuss in your essay, not open up new lines of thought.

● Do not apologize for your opinions, ideas, or conclusions. Apologies will undercut your readers' confidence in you.

Phrases to Avoid

I may not be an expert . . .

At least that's my opinion . . .

I could be wrong, but . . .

</td></tr>
</table>

Highlight: What to Avoid in Conclusions	● Do not introduce any new ideas. Your conclusion should sum up the ideas you discuss in your essay, not open up new lines of thought. ● Do not apologize for your opinions, ideas, or conclusions. Apologies will undercut your readers' confidence in you. **Phrases to Avoid** I may not be an expert . . . At least that's my opinion . . . I could be wrong, but . . . ● Do not use overused phrases to announce your essay is coming to a close. **Phrases to Avoid** In summary, . . . In conclusion, . . .
Teaching Tip Explain that in essay exams, when time is limited, a one-sentence restatement of the thesis is often enough for a conclusion. Likewise, an essay exam may require just a one- or two-sentence introduction.	

● **Practice 13-2**

Look at the essays in Chapter 36, locating one conclusion you think is particularly effective. Be prepared to explain the strengths of the conclusion you chose.

Focus on Writing: *Flashback*

Look again at the essay you reprinted for the Focus on Writing activity on page 195. Evaluate your conclusion. Is it suitable for your topic and thesis? Does it bring your essay to a clear and satisfying close that will leave a strong impression on readers? On a separate sheet of paper, try drafting a different concluding paragraph using one of the options presented in 13B.

Focus on Writing: *Revising and Editing*

Reread your responses to the Flashback activity above and the one on page 199. Are the new paragraphs you wrote more effective than the introduction and conclusion of the essay you wrote in Chapter 12? If so, substitute them for the opening and closing paragraphs of that essay.

Chapter Review

Editing Practice

The following student essay has an undeveloped introduction and conclusion. Decide what introductory and concluding strategies would be most appropriate for the essay. Then, on a separate sheet of paper, rewrite both the introduction and the conclusion to make them more effective. Finally, think of an interesting title for the essay. *Answers will vary.*

Possible Title: Small but Dangerous

Although pocket bikes are fun to ride, they are dangerous for their riders and for other drivers.

Like many other American fads, the pocket-bike craze started in California and has spread eastward across the United States. Pocket bikes weigh about fifty pounds and are about eighteen inches high. Their tiny engines are similar to those used in leaf blowers. They buzz like chain saws as they speed down the street. Usually, pocket bikes can travel up to thirty-five miles per hour, but their engines can be modified to allow them to go faster. Owners of pocket bikes say that they are exciting to ride, burn very little gas, and cost a lot less than full-size motorcycles. They are so popular that dealers cannot keep them in stock.

However, police say that pocket bikes can be a hazard. They were originally developed to train professional motorcycle racers. Manufacturers say that they should be used only on closed tracks or in areas where there is no traffic. They are not meant to be driven on the street, and they do not meet federal safety standards. Many pocket bikers, though, ignore these restrictions and ride on residential streets. Unfortunately, pocket bikes are so low that other drivers cannot see them. If a car or truck hits a pocket bike, the bike's rider is likely to be severely injured or killed.

Another danger is that pocket bikes look like toys. Unsuspecting parents buy them for their children, who are not ready to drive a vehicle of any type. Recently, a number of fatalities have occurred when very young children lost control of their pocket bikes. Because of these dangers, several cities have banned pocket bikes. Other cities are starting to crack down on their use.

Although these bikes can be fun to ride, they are dangerous.

Collaborative Activities

1. Bring to class several copies of an essay you wrote for another class. Have each person in your group comment on your essay's introduction and conclusion. Revise the introduction and conclusion in response to your classmates' suggestions.

2. Find a magazine or newspaper article that interests you. Photocopy the article, and cut off the introduction and conclusion, and bring the body of the article to class. Ask your group to decide on the best strategy for introducing and concluding the article. Then, collaborate on writing new opening and closing paragraphs and an interesting title.

3. Working in a group, think of interesting and appropriate titles for essays on each of the topics listed below. Try to use as many of the different options outlined in the Highlight box on page 198 as you can.

   The difficulty of living with a roommate

   The joys of living in the city (or in the country)

   The responsibilities of having a pet

   The stress of job interviews

   The obligation to vote

   The uses of text messaging

   The problems of being in a long-term relationship

   The need for religious tolerance

**Review
Checklist:
Introductions
and Conclusions**

☐ The introduction of your essay should prepare readers for the ideas to follow and should include a thesis statement. It should also create interest. (See 13A.) You can begin an essay with any of the following strategies.

A narrative   A quotation
A question   A surprising statement
A background statement

☐ Your title should suggest the subject of your essay and make people want to read further. (See 13A.)

☐ The conclusion of your essay should include a summary statement and make some general concluding remarks. (See 13B.) You can conclude an essay with any of the following strategies.

A narrative   A recommendation
A prediction   A quotation

Unit Four

Writing Sentences

Chapter 14

Writing Simple Sentences

After the 2004 tsunami in Southeast Asia, Hideke Matsui (pictured here) donated 50 million yen ($481,000) to the Japanese Red Cross Society.

A **sentence** is a group of words that expresses a complete thought. Every sentence includes both a subject and a verb. A **simple sentence** consists of a single **independent clause**: one subject and one verb.

<u>Hideke Matsui</u> <u>is</u> a baseball player.

Subjects

Teaching Tip
Tell students that if a group of words does not include both a subject and a verb, it is a sentence fragment, not a sentence. Refer them to Chapter 21.

Every sentence includes a subject. The **subject** of a sentence tells who or what is being talked about in the sentence. Without a subject, a sentence is not complete. In each of the three sentences below, the subject is underlined.

<u>Derek Walcott</u> won the 1992 Nobel Prize in literature.

<u>He</u> was born in the Caribbean.

<u>St. Lucia</u> is an island in the Caribbean.

The subject of a sentence can be a noun or a pronoun. A **noun** names a person, place, or thing—*Derek Walcott, St. Lucia*. A **pronoun** takes the place of a noun—*I, you, he, she, it, we, they*, and so on.

The subject of a sentence can be *singular* or *plural*. A **singular subject** is one person, place, or thing (*Derek Walcott, St. Lucia, he*).

A **plural subject** is more than one person, place, or thing (*poems, people, they*).

Teaching Tip
Refer students to 22B for more on subject-verb agreement with compound subjects.

Walcott's <u>poems</u> have been collected in books.

→ Focus on Writing

The picture on the opposite page shows Japanese left-fielder Hideke Matsui, who signed with the New York Yankees in 2003. Look at the picture, and then write about a person you admire or with whom you would like to trade places. What appeals to you about this person's life?

WORD POWER

idol someone who is admired or adored

role model a person who serves as a model for other people to imitate

emulate to try to equal or excel

A plural subject that joins two subjects with *and* is called a **compound subject**.

St. Lucia and Trinidad are Caribbean islands.

● **Practice 14-1**

In the paragraph below, underline the subject of each sentence once.

Example: The poet's parents were both teachers.

(1) Derek Walcott was born in 1930. (2) His ancestors came from Africa, the Netherlands, and England. (3) Walcott's early years were spent on the Caribbean island of St. Lucia. (4) Poetry occupied much of his time. (5) His early poems were published in Trinidad. (6) He later studied in Jamaica and in New York. (7) Walcott eventually became a respected poet. (8) He was a visiting lecturer at Harvard in 1981. (9) In 1990, he published *Omeros*. (10) This long poem about classical Greek heroes is set in the West Indies. (11) In 1992, the sixty-two-year-old Caribbean poet won a Nobel Prize. (12) Walcott later worked with songwriter Paul Simon on *The Capeman*, a Broadway musical.

● **Practice 14-2**

Add a subject to each of the following sentences.

Example: ___Pets___ can reduce stress, high blood pressure, and depression.
Answers may vary.

1. For one thing, ___animals___ allow us to express affection openly.

2. ___We___ can stroke, cuddle, and talk baby talk to a kitten or puppy.

3. ___Pets___ also love us unconditionally, no matter what our faults.

4. Our ___animals___ do not care about our faults.

5. ___Employees___ sometimes bring animals into nursing homes and hospitals to visit patients.

6. For some patients, their only ___visitors___ are these animals.

7. These ___patients___ have better survival rates than those without animal visitors.

Teaching Tip
Point out to students that sometimes a two-word name (such as *Derek Walcott*) serves as a sentence's subject.

On the Web
For more practice, visit Exercise Central *at* <bedfordstmartins.com/focusonwriting>.

ESL Tip
Refer students to 29A for more on using subjects correctly and to 29B for more on distinguishing singular and plural nouns.

8. In prisons, _____*inmates*_____ sometimes train service dogs.

9. These _____*dogs*_____ help disabled people.

10. Their _____*trainers*_____ are making a contribution to society.

● Practice 14-3

Underline the subject in each sentence. Then, write *S* above singular subjects and *P* above plural subjects. Remember, compound subjects are plural.

> **Example:** *P*
> Engineers sometimes call the Channel Tunnel one of the seven wonders of the modern world.

1. A land <u>bridge</u> connected the island of Great Britain to the continent of Europe during the Ice Age. *(S above bridge)*

2. Now, <u>Great Britain and France</u> are joined by the Channel Tunnel. *(P above)*

3. The <u>Channel Tunnel</u> consists of three concrete tubes that run under the English Channel. *(S above)*

4. Each <u>tube</u> is five feet thick. *(S above)*

5. The <u>tubes</u> extend from Coquelles, France, to Folkestone, England. *(P above)*

6. Double-decker <u>trains</u> travel through two of the tubes at one hundred miles per hour. *(P above)*

7. The third <u>tube</u> is used only by maintenance and emergency vehicles. *(S above)*

8. <u>Passengers</u> board the cars of the train. *(P above)*

9. Cold-water <u>pipes</u> beside the tracks drain off the heat caused by the friction of the trains. *(P above)*

10. <u>Passengers</u> can now travel from London to Paris in about two and a half hours. *(P above)*

Focus on Writing: *Flashback*

Look back at your response to the Focus on Writing activity on page 207. Underline the subject of each of your sentences. Then, write *S* above each singular subject and *P* above each plural subject. (Remember that a compound subject is plural.)

14b Prepositional Phrases

A **prepositional phrase** consists of a **preposition** (a word such as *on, to, in,* or *with*) and its **object** (the noun or pronoun it introduces).

Preposition	+	Object	=	Prepositional Phrase
on		the stage		on the stage
to		Nia's house		to Nia's house
in		my new car		in my new car
with		them		with them

Because the object of a preposition is a noun or a pronoun, it may seem to be the subject of a sentence. However, the object of a preposition can never be the subject of a sentence. To identify a sentence's true subject, cross out each prepositional phrase. (Remember, every prepositional phrase is introduced by a preposition.)

       subject prep phrase
The cost of the repairs was astronomical.

   prep phrase   prep phrase   subject   prep phrase
At the end of the novel, after an exciting chase, the lovers flee to Mexico.

Frequently Used Prepositions

about	before	except	on	underneath
above	behind	for	onto	until
according to	below	from	out	up
across	beneath	in	outside	upon
after	beside	inside	over	with
against	between	into	through	within
along	beyond	like	throughout	without
among	by	near	to	
around	despite	of	toward	
at	during	off	under	

● Practice 14-4

Each of the following sentences includes at least one prepositional phrase. To identify each sentence's subject, begin by crossing out each prepositional phrase. Then, underline the subject of the sentence.

ESL Tip
Nonnative speakers need to do extra exercises on identifying prepositions. Give them a few paragraphs from which you have deleted all prepositions, and have them insert appropriate words.

Example: In presidential elections, third-party candidates have attracted many voters.

(1) With more than 27 percent of the vote, Theodore Roosevelt was the strongest third-party presidential candidate in history. (2) In the 1912 race with Democrat Woodrow Wilson and Republican William H. Taft, Roosevelt ran second to Wilson. (3) Before Roosevelt, no third-party candidate had won a significant number of votes. (4) After 1912, however, some candidates of other parties made strong showings. (5) For example, Robert M. LaFollette of the Progressive Party won 16 percent of the vote in the 1924 race. (6) In 1968, with more than 13 percent of the popular vote, American Independent Party candidate George C. Wallace placed third behind Republican Richard M. Nixon and Democrat Hubert H. Humphrey. (7) In 1980, John B. Anderson, an Independent, challenged Republican Ronald Reagan and Democrat Jimmy Carter and got 6.6 percent of the vote. (8) With nearly 19 percent of the popular vote, Independent Ross Perot ran a strong race against Democrat Bill Clinton and Republican George Bush in 1992. (9) In 2000, with the support of many environmentalists, Ralph Nader challenged Al Gore and George W. Bush for the presidency. (10) In 2004, Nader was also on the ballot in many states. (11) To this day, the two-party system of the United States has remained intact despite many challenges by third-party candidates.

Focus on Writing: *Flashback*

Look back at your response to the Focus on Writing activity on page 207. Have you used any prepositional phrases? Circle each one you find.

14c

Verbs

Teaching Tip
Refer students to Chapter 21 for information on how to recognize and correct sentence fragments.

In addition to its subject, every sentence includes a verb. This **verb** (also called a **predicate**) tells what the subject does or connects the subject to words that describe or rename it. Without a verb, a sentence is not complete.

Action Verbs

An **action verb** tells what the subject does, did, or will do.

> Nomar Garciaparra plays baseball.
>
> Renee will drive to Tampa on Friday.
>
> Amelia Earhart flew across the Atlantic.

Action verbs can also show mental and emotional actions.

> Travis always worries about his job.

Sometimes the subject of a sentence performs more than one action. In this case, the sentence includes two or more action verbs.

> He hit the ball, threw down his bat, and ran toward first base.

● Practice 14-5

In the following sentences, underline each action verb twice. Some sentences contain more than one action verb.

1. Many critics see one romance novel as just like another.
2. The plot usually involves a beautiful young woman, or heroine, in some kind of danger.
3. A handsome stranger offers his help.
4. At first, she distrusts him.
5. Then, another man enters the story and wins the heroine's trust.
6. Readers, however, see this man as an evil villain.
7. Almost too late, the heroine too realizes the truth.

8. Luckily, the handsome hero <u><u>returns</u></u> and <u><u>saves</u></u> her from a nasty fate.

9. Many readers <u><u>enjoy</u></u> the familiar plots of romance novels.

10. However, most critics <u><u>dislike</u></u> these books.

Linking Verbs

A **linking verb** does not show action. Instead, it connects the subject to a word or words that describe or rename it. The linking verb tells what the subject is (or what it was, will be, or seems to be).

A googolplex <u><u>is</u></u> an extremely large number.

Many linking verbs, like *is*, are forms of the verb *be*. Other linking verbs refer to the senses (*look, feel*, and so on).

The photocopy <u><u>looks</u></u> blurry.

Some students <u><u>feel</u></u> anxious about the future.

Frequently Used Linking Verbs

act	feel	seem
appear	get	smell
be (am, is, are, was, were)	grow	sound
	look	taste
become	remain	turn

● Practice 14-6

In the following sentences, underline each linking verb twice.

1. Urban legends <u><u>are</u></u> folktales created in our own time to teach a lesson.

2. One familiar urban legend <u><u>is</u></u> the story of Hookman.

3. According to this story, a young couple <u><u>is</u></u> alone in Lovers' Lane.

4. They <u><u>are</u></u> in a car, listening to a radio announcement.

5. An escaped murderer <u><u>is</u></u> nearby.

6. The murderer's left hand <u><u>is</u></u> a hook.

7. The young woman becomes hysterical.

8. Suddenly, Lovers' Lane seems very dangerous.

9. Later, they are shocked to see a hook hanging from the passenger door handle.

10. The purpose of this legend is to frighten young people into avoiding dangerous places.

● **Practice 14-7**

Underline every verb in each of the following sentences twice. Remember that a verb can be an action verb or a linking verb.

Example: Some books have a great impact on their readers.

(1) In 1948, Betty Smith wrote *A Tree Grows in Brooklyn*. (2) The novel tells the story of Francie Nolan. (3) Francie is very poor but seems determined to succeed. (4) She loves books and is an excellent student. (5) Francie lives with her parents and her younger brother, Neely. (6) She dreams of a better life for herself and her family. (7) Tragically, Francie's father dies. (8) Her mother supports her family and does her best for her children. (9) She works as a janitor in their apartment building. (10) Eventually, Francie graduates from high school, with a bright future ahead of her.

Helping Verbs

Teaching Tip
Remind students that every sentence must include a complete verb. Refer them to 21D for information on how to identify sentence fragments created by incomplete verbs.

Many verbs consist of more than one word. For example, the verb in the following sentence consists of two words.

Minh must make a decision about his future.

In this sentence, *make* is the **main verb**, and *must* is a **helping verb**.

Frequently Used Helping Verbs

does	will	must	should
did	was	can	would
do	were	could	
is	have	may	
are	has	might	
am	had		

In each of the following sentences, the complete verb is underlined twice, and the helping verbs are checkmarked.

Teaching Tip
Tell students that sometimes other words come between the parts of a complete verb.

Minh should have gone earlier.

Did Minh ask the right questions?

Minh will work hard.

Minh can really succeed.

Highlight: Helping Verbs with Participles

Teaching Tip
Refer students to Chapter 26 for information on past participles.

Present participles, such as *thinking,* and many irregular **past participles,** such as *gone,* cannot stand alone as main verbs in a sentence. They need a helping verb to make them complete.

Incorrect	Minh going to the library.
Correct	Minh is going to the library.
Incorrect	Minh gone to the library.
Correct	Minh has gone to the library.

● **Practice 14-8**

The verbs in the sentences that follow consist of a main verb and one or more helping verbs. In each sentence, underline the complete verb twice, and put a check mark above the helping verb(s).

Example: The Salk polio vaccine was ✓given to more than a million schoolchildren in 1954.

(1) By the 1950s, parents ✓had become terrified of polio. (2) For years, it ✓had puzzled doctors and researchers. (3) Thousands ✓had become ill each year in the United States alone. (4) Children ✓should ✓have ✓been playing happily. (5) Instead, they ✓would get very sick. (6) Polio ✓was sometimes called infantile paralysis. (7) In fact, it ✓did cause paralysis in children and in adults as well. (8) Some patients ✓could breathe only with the help of machines called iron lungs. (9) Others ✓would remain in wheelchairs for life. (10) By 1960, Jonas Salk's vaccine ✓had reduced the incidence of polio in the United States by more than 90 percent.

Focus on Writing: *Flashback*

Look back at your response to the Focus on Writing activity on page 207. In each sentence, underline the complete verb twice, and put a check mark above each helping verb.

Focus on Writing: *Revising and Editing*

Look back at your response to the Focus on Writing activity on page 207. Circle every action verb. Then, try to replace some of them with different action verbs that express more precisely what the subject of each sentence is, was, or will be doing. For example, you might replace *like* with *admire* or *respect*.

Chapter Review

Editing Practice

Read the following student essay. Underline the subject of each sentence once, and underline the complete verb of each sentence twice. If you have trouble locating the subject, try crossing out the prepositional phrases. The first sentence has been done for you.

The Origin of Baseball

Baseball is an American sport. In many people's minds, Abner Doubleday started baseball in 1839. He decided on the rules of the game. However, baseball games were played before then.

In fact, baseball was played in Pittsfield, Pennsylvania, in the late 1700s. According to historical records, Pittsfield had a new meeting house at that time. The building was damaged by baseballs. A new law banned baseballs within eighty yards of the meeting house.

Thousands of years earlier, baseball was played in ancient Egypt. Pharaohs played "batting the ball" with their priests in about 2400 B.C. Pictures of this game have been seen on the walls of Egyptian temples. The pictures resemble our game of stickball.

Today's game of baseball was actually derived from stickball. Stickball was usually played on city streets. Stickball players originally used broom handles for their bats. A section at the Museum of the City of New York honors great stickball players. It is called the Stickball Hall of Fame.

Abner Doubleday may have been a member of a stickball team. He did not really invent baseball. However, he changed stickball into our modern game of baseball.

Collaborative Activities

1. Fold a sheet of paper in half lengthwise. Working in a group of three or four students, spend two minutes listing as many nouns as you can in the column to the left of the fold. When your time is up, exchange papers with another group of students. Limiting yourselves to five minutes, write an appropriate action verb beside each noun. Each noun will now be the subject of a short sentence.

2. Choose five short sentences from those you wrote for Collaborative Activity 1. Working in the same group, collaborate to create more fully developed sentences. First, expand each subject by adding words or prepositional phrases that give more information about the subject. (For example, you could expand *boat* to *the small, leaky boat with the red sail.*) Then, expand each sentence further, adding ideas after the verb. (For example, the sentence *The boat bounced* could become *The small, leaky boat with the red sail bounced helplessly on the water.*)

3. Work in a group of three or four students to write one original sentence for each of the linking verbs listed on page 213. When you have finished, exchange papers with another group. Now, try to add words and phrases to the other group's sentences to make them more interesting.

Review Checklist: Writing Simple Sentences

☐ A sentence expresses a complete thought. The subject tells who or what is being talked about in the sentence. (See 14A.)

☐ A prepositional phrase consists of a preposition and its object (the noun or pronoun it introduces). The object of a preposition cannot be the subject of a sentence. (See 14B.)

☐ An action verb tells what the subject does, did, or will do. (See 14C.)

☐ A linking verb connects the subject to a word or words that describe or rename it. (See 14C.)

☐ Many verbs are made up of more than one word. The complete verb in a sentence includes the main verb plus any helping verbs. (See 14C.)

Chapter 15

Writing Compound Sentences

In 2001, college graduates made up 24 percent of all unplanned pregnancies, while teenagers who had not yet graduated from high school accounted for 50 percent.

Teaching Tip
Tell students that a **clause** is a group of words that contains a subject and a verb. Make sure they understand that an **independent clause** can stand alone as a sentence but a **dependent clause** cannot. Refer them to 16A.

The most basic kind of sentence, a **simple sentence**, consists of a single **independent clause**: one <u>subject</u> and one <u>verb</u>.

European <u>immigrants</u> <u>arrived</u> at Ellis Island.

A **compound sentence** is made up of two or more simple sentences (independent clauses).

Using Coordinating Conjunctions

Teaching Tip
Remind students that a comma alone cannot connect two independent clauses. Refer them to Chapter 20.

One way to form a compound sentence is by joining two independent clauses with a **coordinating conjunction** preceded by a comma.

European immigrants arrived at Ellis Island, <u>but</u> Asian immigrants arrived at Angel Island.

Teaching Tip
To help students remember the seven coordinating conjunctions, you might suggest that they use the acronym FANBOYS.

Coordinating Conjunctions

and	for	or	yet
but	nor	so	

WORD POWER
coordinate equal in importance, rank, or degree

Coordinating conjunctions join two ideas of equal importance. They describe the relationship between two ideas, showing how and why the ideas are related. Different coordinating conjunctions have different meanings.

→ Focus on Writing

The picture on the opposite page shows a high school graduation with two of the graduating students holding their children. Look at the picture, and then write a letter to the president of your college explaining why your campus needs a day-care center. (If your school already has a day-care center, explain why it deserves continued — or increased — funding.)

WORD POWER
stigmatize to characterize as disgraceful
controversial causing great differences of opinion

• To indicate addition, use *and.*

  He acts like a child, <u>and</u> people think he is cute.

• To indicate contrast or contradiction, use *but* or *yet.*

  He acts like a child, <u>but</u> he is an adult.

  He acts like a child, <u>yet</u> he longs to be taken seriously.

• To indicate a cause-and-effect relationship, use *so* or *for.*

  He acts like a child, <u>so</u> we treat him like one.

  He acts like a child, <u>for</u> he craves attention.

• To present alternatives, use *or.*

  He acts like a child, <u>or</u> he is ignored.

• To eliminate alternatives, use *nor.*

  He does not act like a child, <u>nor</u> does he look like one.

Teaching Tip
Remind students that when a compound sentence is formed with *nor,* the verb comes before the subject in the second independent clause.

Teaching Tip
Remind students that in a compound sentence, there is a complete independent clause on each side of the coordinating conjunction.

**Highlight:
Using
Commas with
Coordinating
Conjunctions**

When you use a coordinating conjunction to link two independent clauses into a single compound sentence, always put a comma before the coordinating conjunction.

  We can stand in line all night, or we can go home now.

● **Practice 15-1**

Fill in the coordinating conjunction—*and, but, for, nor, or, so,* or *yet*—that best links the two parts of each compound sentence. Remember to insert a comma before each coordinating conjunction.

Example: Fairy tales have been told by many people around the world
<u>, but</u> the stories by two German brothers may be the most famous.
Answers will vary.

(1) Jakob and Wilhelm Grimm lived in the nineteenth century
,<u>and</u> they wrote many well-known fairy tales. (2) Most people think
fondly of fairy tales ,<u>but/yet</u> the Brothers Grimm wrote many unpleasant and violent stories. (3) In their best-known works, children are
abused ,<u>and</u> endings are not always happy. (4) Either innocent chil-

 On the Web
For more practice, visit
Exercise Central *at*
<bedfordstmartins.com/
focusonwriting>.

dren are brutally punished for no reason , _____*or*_____ they are neglected.

(5) For example, in "Hansel and Gretel," the stepmother mistreats the children , _____*and*_____ their father abandons them in the woods. (6) In this story, the events are horrifying , _____*but/yet*_____ the ending is still happy. (7) The children outwit the evil adults , _____*so/and*_____ they escape unharmed. (8) Apparently, they are not injured physically , _____*nor*_____ are they harmed emotionally. (9) Nevertheless, their story can hardly be called pleasant , _____*for*_____ it remains a story of child abuse and neglect.

● Practice 15-2

Use a coordinating conjunction to join each of the following pairs of simple sentences into one compound sentence. Be sure to place a comma before the coordinating conjunction.

Example: A computer can make drafting essays easier. It also makes *, and it* ~~It~~

revision easier.

1. Training a dog to heel is difficult. ~~Dogs~~ naturally resist strict control. *, for dogs*

2. A bodhran is an Irish drum. ~~It~~ is played with a wooden stick. *, and it*

3. Students should spend two hours of study time for each hour of class time. ~~They~~ may not do well in the course. *, or they*

4. Years ago, students wrote their lessons on slates. ~~The~~ teacher could correct each student's work individually. *, so the*

5. Each state in the United States has two senators. ~~The~~ number of representatives depends on a state's population. *, but the*

6. In 1973, only 2.5 percent of those in the U.S. military were women. ~~By~~ 1999, that percentage had increased to 14.1 percent. *, but by*

7. A "small craft advisory" warns boaters of bad weather conditions. ~~These~~ conditions can be dangerous to small boats. *, for these*

8. A DVD looks like a compact disc. ~~It~~ can hold fifteen times as much information. *, but it*

9. Hip-hop fashions include sneakers and baggy pants. ~~These~~ styles are also very popular with young men. *, and these*

10. Multiple births have become more and more common/Even septuplets *, and even* have a reasonable chance of survival today.

● Practice 15-3

Add coordinating conjunctions to combine some of these simple sentences. Remember to put a comma before each coordinating conjunction you add.

Example: Years ago, few Americans lived to be one hundred/Today, *, but today,* there are over 32,000 centenarians.

Answers will vary.

(1) Diet, exercise, and family history may account for centenarians' long lives/(2) This is not the whole story. *, but this* (3) Recently, a study conducted in Georgia showed surprising common traits among centenarians. (4) They did not necessarily avoid tobacco and alcohol/(5) They *, nor* did not have low-fat diets. *they* (6) In fact, they ate relatively large amounts of fat, cholesterol, and sugar/(7) Diet could not explain their long lives. *, so diet* (8) They did, however, share four key survival characteristics. (9) First, all of the centenarians were optimistic about life/(10) All of them were positive thinkers. *, and all* (11) They were also involved in religious life and had deep religious faith. (12) In addition, all the centenarians had continued to lead physically active lives/(13) They remained mobile even as elderly people. *, and they* (14) Finally, all were able to adapt to loss. (15) They had all experienced the deaths of friends, spouses, or children/(16) They were *, but they* able to get on with their lives.

● Practice 15-4

Write another simple sentence to follow each of the simple sentences below. Then, connect the sentences with a coordinating conjunction. Be sure to insert a comma before each coordinating conjunction.

Example: Many patients need organ transplants/ *, but there is a* *serious shortage of organ donors.*

Answers will vary.

1. Smoking in bed is dangerous._____

_____

2. Many cars are equipped with navigation systems._____

_____

3. Diamonds are very expensive._____

_____

4. Kangaroos carry their young in pouches._____

_____

5. Dancing is good exercise._____

_____

6. Motorcycle helmet laws have been dropped in some states.___

_____

7. Some businesses sponsor bowling leagues for their employees.___

_____

8. Pretzels are a healthier snack than potato chips._____

_____

9. Many so-called juices actually contain very little real fruit juice.___

_____

10. Human beings tend to resist change._____

_____

Focus on Writing: *Flashback*

Look back at your response to the Focus on Writing activity on page 221. If you see any compound sentences, bracket them. If you see any pairs of simple sentences that could be combined into one compound sentence, try rewriting them on a separate sheet of paper, joining them with appropriate coordinating conjunctions.

Be sure each of your new compound sentences includes a comma before the coordinating conjunction.

15b Using Semicolons

Another way to create a compound sentence is by joining two simple sentences (independent clauses) with a **semicolon**. A semicolon is used to connect clauses whose ideas are closely linked.

> The AIDS quilt contains thousands of panels; each panel is rectangular.

Also use a semicolon to show a strong contrast between two ideas.

> With new drugs, people can live with AIDS for years; many people cannot get these drugs.

Highlight: Avoiding Sentence Fragments

Remember that a semicolon can join only two complete sentences (independent clauses). A semicolon cannot join a sentence and a fragment.

Teaching Tip
Refer students to Chapter 21 for information on identifying and correcting sentence fragments.

	───── FRAGMENT ─────
Incorrect	Because millions are dying of AIDS; more research is clearly needed.
	───── SENTENCE ─────
Correct	Millions are dying of AIDS; more research is clearly needed.

● **Practice 15-5**

Each of the following items consists of one simple sentence. Create a compound sentence for each item by changing the period to a semicolon and then adding another simple sentence.

Example: My brother is addicted to fast food*; he eats it every day.*
Answers will vary.

1. Fast-food restaurants are an American institution._____

_____

2. Families often eat at these restaurants._____

_____

3. Many teenagers work there._____

_____

4. McDonald's is known for its hamburgers._____

_____

5. KFC is famous for its fried chicken._____

_____

6. Taco Bell serves Mexican-style food._____

_____

7. Pizza Hut specializes in pizza._____

_____

8. Many fast-food restaurants offer some low-fat menu items._____

_____

9. Some offer recyclable packaging._____

_____

10. Some even have playgrounds._____

_____

Focus on Writing: *Flashback*

Look back at your response to the Focus on Writing activity on page 221. Do you see any pairs of simple sentences that you could connect with semicolons? On a separate piece of paper, try linking each pair with a semicolon.

15c Using Transitional Words and Phrases

Another way to create a compound sentence is by combining two simple sentences (independent clauses) with a **transitional word or phrase**. When a transitional word or phrase joins two sentences, a semicolon always comes *before* the transitional word or phrase, and a comma always comes *after* it.

> Some college students receive grants; <u>however</u>, others must take out loans.

> He had a miserable time at the party; <u>in addition</u>, he drank too much.

Frequently Used Transitional Words

also	instead	still
besides	later	subsequently
consequently	meanwhile	then
eventually	moreover	therefore
finally	nevertheless	thus
furthermore	now	
however	otherwise	

Frequently Used Transitional Phrases

after all	in comparison
as a result	in contrast
at the same time	in fact
for example	in other words
for instance	of course
in addition	on the contrary

Adding a transitional word or phrase makes the connection between ideas in a sentence clearer and more precise than it would be if the ideas were linked with just a semicolon. Different transitional words and phrases convey different meanings.

- Some signal addition (*also, besides, furthermore, in addition, moreover,* and so on).

  > I have a lot on my mind; <u>also</u>, I have a lot of things to do.

- Some make causal connections (*as a result, therefore, consequently, thus,* and so on).

  > I have a lot on my mind; <u>as a result</u>, it is hard to concentrate.

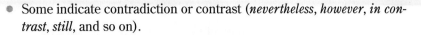

- Some indicate contradiction or contrast (*nevertheless, however, in contrast, still,* and so on).

  I have a lot on my mind; still, I must try to relax.

- Some present alternatives (*instead, on the contrary, otherwise,* and so on).

  I have a lot on my mind; otherwise, I could relax.

  I will try not to think; instead, I will relax.

- Some indicate time sequence (*at the same time, eventually, finally, later, meanwhile, now, subsequently, then,* and so on).

  I have a lot on my mind; meanwhile, I still have work to do.

● Practice 15-6

Add semicolons and commas where required to set off transitional words or phrases that join two simple sentences.

Example: Ketchup is a popular condiment ; therefore , it is available in almost every restaurant.

(1) Andrew F. Smith, a food historian, wrote a book about the tomato ; later , he wrote a book about ketchup. (2) This book, *Pure Ketchup*, was a big project ; in fact , Smith worked on it for five years. (3) The word *ketchup* may have come from a Chinese word ; however , Smith is not certain of the word's origins. (4) Ketchup has existed since ancient times ; in other words , it is a very old product. (5) Ketchup has changed a lot over the years ; for example , special dyes were developed in the nineteenth century to make it red. (6) Smith discusses many other changes ; for instance , preservative-free ketchup was invented in 1907. (7) Ketchup is now used by people in many cultures ; still , salsa is more popular than ketchup in the United States. (8) Today, designer ketchups are being developed ; meanwhile , Heinz has introduced green and purple ketchup in squeeze bottles. (9) Some of today's ketchups are

On the Web

For more practice, visit Exercise Central *at* <bedfordstmartins .com/focusonwriting>.

WORD POWER

condiment something used to add flavor to food

;   ,
chunky in addition some ketchups are spicy. (10) Ketchup continues to
      ;   ,
evolve however Smith is now working on a book about the history of
popcorn.

● Practice 15-7

Consulting the lists of transitional words and phrases on page 228, choose a word or phrase that logically connects each pair of simple sentences below into one compound sentence. Be sure to punctuate appropriately.

Example: Every year since 1927, *Time* has designated a Man of the
                                    ; however, the
Year. The Man of the Year has not always been a man.

Answers may vary.

(1) The Man of the Year has greatly influenced the previous year's
               ; consequently, the
events. The choice is often a prominent politician. (2) In the 1920s and
                                              ; for example,
1930s, world leaders were often chosen. Franklin Delano Roosevelt was
chosen twice. (3) During World War II, Hitler, Stalin, Churchill, and Roo-
                               ; in fact,
sevelt were all chosen. Stalin was featured twice. (4) Occasionally, the
                                          ; for instance, in
Man of the Year was not an individual. In 1950, it was The American
Fighting Man. (5) In 1956, The Hungarian Freedom Fighter was Man of
          ; then, in
the Year. In 1966, *Time* editors chose The Young Generation. (6) Only
                                    ; for example,
a few women have been selected. Queen Elizabeth II of England was
featured in 1952. (7) In 1975, American Women were honored as a
          ; nevertheless, the
group. The Man of the Year has nearly always been male. (8) Very few
                                              ; still,
people of color have been designated Man of the Year. Martin Luther
King Jr. was honored in 1963. (9) The Man of the Year has almost always
                                    ; however,
been one or more human beings. The Computer was selected in 1982
and Endangered Earth in 1988. (10) More recently, prominent politi-
                          ; for example, in
cians have once again been chosen. In 2001, New York City mayor Rudy
Giuliani was *Time*'s Man of the Year (now called Person of the Year).
                                              ; instead, it
(11) In 2003, *Time* did not choose a politician. It honored The American

; now, the
Soldier. (12) In 2004, *Time* selected President George W. Bush. ~~The~~ magazine was making a more traditional choice. (13) In 2005, *Time* wanted
; thus, the
to honor the contributions of philanthropists. ~~The~~ magazine named Bill Gates, Melinda Gates, and Bono its Persons of the Year. (14) In
; instead, its
2006, *Time* did not choose a specific person. ~~Its~~ person of the year was "you."

WORD POWER

philanthropist
someone who tries to improve human lives through charitable aid

● Practice 15-8

Add the suggested transitional word or phrase to each of the simple sentences below. Then, add a new independent clause to follow it. Be sure to punctuate correctly.

> **Example:** Commuting students do not really experience campus life.
> (however)
> *Commuting students do not really experience campus life; however,*
> *there are some benefits to being a commuter.*
> *Answers will vary.*

1. Campus residents may have a better college experience. (still)
   Campus residents may have a better college experience; still, being a
   commuter has its advantages.

2. Living at home gives students access to home-cooked meals. (in contrast)
   Living at home gives students access to home-cooked meals; in
   contrast, dorm residents eat dining hall food or takeout.

3. Commuters have a wide choice of jobs in the community. (on the other hand)
   Commuters have a wide choice of jobs in the community; on the other
   hand, students living on campus may have to take on-campus jobs.

4. Commuters get to live with their families. (however)
   Commuters get to live with their families; however, dorm students
   may live far from home.

5. There are also some disadvantages to being a commuter. (for example)

There are also some disadvantages to being a commuter; for example,

commuters may have trouble joining study groups.

6. Unlike dorm students, most commuters have family responsibilities. (in fact)

Unlike dorm students, most commuters have family responsibilities; in

fact, they may have children of their own.

7. Commuters might have to help take care of their parents or grand-parents. (in addition)

Commuters might have to help take care of their parents or grandparents;

in addition, they might have to babysit for younger siblings.

8. Commuters might need a car to get to school. (consequently)

Commuters might need a car to get to school; consequently, they

might have higher expenses than dorm students.

9. Younger commuters may be under the watchful eyes of their parents. (of course)

Younger commuters may be under the watchful eyes of their parents;

of course, parents are likely to be stricter than dorm counselors.

10. Commuting to college has pros and cons. (therefore)

Commuting to college has pros and cons; therefore, commuters are

not necessarily at a disadvantage.

● Practice 15-9

On a separate piece of paper, use the specified topics and transitional words or phrases to create five compound sentences. Be sure to punctuate appropriately.

Example:
Topic: fad diets
Transitional phrase: for example

People are always falling for fad diets; for example, some people eat

only pineapple to lose weight.

Answers will vary.

Teaching Tip
Have students write these
sentences on the board.
Get at least two versions
of each sentence.

1. *Topic:* laws to protect people with disabilities
   Transitional phrase: in addition

   _____

   _____

2. *Topic:* single men and women as adoptive parents
   Transitional word: however

   _____

   _____

3. *Topic:* prayer in public schools
   Transitional word: therefore

   _____

   _____

4. *Topic:* high school proms
   Transitional word: also

   _____

   _____

5. *Topic:* course requirements at your school
   Transitional phrase: for instance

   _____

   _____

Focus on Writing: *Flashback*

Look back at your response to the Focus on Writing activity on page 221.
Have you used any transitional words or phrases to link independent
clauses? If so, check to make sure that you have punctuated them
correctly. Then, check to see that you have used the transitional word or
phrase that best shows the relationship between the ideas in the two
independent clauses. Revise your work if necessary.

Focus on Writing: *Revising and Editing*

Look back at your response to the Focus on Writing activity on page 221. Now, try to add one of the new compound sentences you created in the Flashback activities on pages 225 and 227. Then, check each compound sentence to make sure you have used the coordinating conjunction or transitional word or phrase that best conveys your meaning and that you have punctuated these sentences correctly. When you have finished, look over a piece of writing you have done in response to another assignment, and try combining some pairs of simple sentences into compound sentences.

Chapter Review

Editing Practice

Read the following student essay. Then, create compound sentences by linking pairs of simple sentences where appropriate, joining them with a coordinating conjunction, a semicolon, or a semicolon followed by a transitional word or phrase. Remember to put commas before coordinating conjunctions and to use semicolons and commas correctly with transitional words and phrases. The first two sentences have been combined for you.

Answers may vary.

Teaching Tip
For a short writing assignment, ask students to write a similar passage about the life of one of their parents.

My Grandfather's Life

My great-grandparents were born in Ukraine. ˌ *, but they* They raised my grandfather in western Pennsylvania. The ninth of their ten children, he had a life I cannot begin to imagine. To me, he was my big, strong, powerful grandfather. ˌ *; however, he* He was also a child of poverty.

My great-grandfather worked for the American Car Foundry. The family lived in a company house. ˌ *, and they* They shopped at the company store. In 1934, my great-grandfather was laid off. ˌ *, so he* He went to work digging sewer lines for the government. At that time, the family was on welfare. Every week, they were entitled to get food rations. ˌ *, and my* My grandfather would go to pick up the food. They desperately needed the prunes, beans, flour, margarine, and other things.

For years, my grandfather wore his brothers' hand-me-down clothes/ *; in addition, he* ~~He~~ wore thrift-shop shoes with cardboard over the holes in the soles. He was often hungry/ *, so he* ~~He~~ would sometimes sit by the side of the railroad tracks, waiting for the engineer to throw him an orange. My grandfather would do any job to earn a quarter/ *; for example, once* ~~Once,~~ he weeded a mile-long row of tomato plants. For this work, he was paid twenty-five cents and a pack of Necco wafers.

My grandfather saved his pennies/ *; eventually,* ~~Eventually,~~ he was able to buy a used bicycle for two dollars. He dropped out of school at fourteen and got a job/ *, for the* ~~The~~ family badly needed his income. He woke up every day at 4 a.m. *, and he* ~~He~~ rode his bike to his job at a meatpacking plant. He worked for fifty cents a day.

In 1943, at the age of seventeen, my grandfather joined the U.S. Navy/ *; thus, he* ~~He~~ discovered a new world. For the first time in his life, he had enough to eat. He was always first in line at the mess hall/ *; in fact, he* ~~He~~ went back for seconds and thirds before anyone else. After the war ended in 1945, he was discharged from the Navy. He went to work in a meat market in New York City/ *; the* ~~The~~ only trade he knew was the meat business. Three years later, when he had saved enough to open his own store, Pete's Quality Meats, he knew his life of poverty was finally over.

Collaborative Activities

1. Working in a small group, pair each of the simple sentences in the left-hand column on the following page with a sentence in the right-hand column to create ten compound sentences. Use as many different coordinating conjunctions as you can to connect the independent clauses. Be sure each coordinating conjunction you choose conveys a logical relationship between ideas, and remember to put a comma before each one. You may use some of the listed sentences more than once. *Note:* Many different combinations—some serious and factually accurate, some humorous—are possible.

Some dogs wear little sweaters.

Pit bulls are raised to fight.

Bonobos are pygmy chimpanzees.

Many people fear Dobermans.

Leopards have spots.

Dalmatians can live in firehouses.

Horses can wear blankets.

All mules are sterile.

Great Danes are huge dogs.

Parrots can often speak.

Many are named Hamlet.

They live in groups.

One even sings Christmas carols.

They can wear bandanas.

They can play Frisbee.

Many live in equatorial Zaire.

Some people think they are gentle.

They don't get cold in winter.

They are half horse and half donkey.

They can be unpredictable.

2. Work in a group of three or four students to create a cast of five characters for a movie, a television pilot, or a music video. Working individually, write five descriptive short sentences—one about each character. Then, exchange papers with another student. Add a coordinating conjunction to each sentence on the list to create five new compound sentences.

Example:

Original sentence   Mark is a handsome heartthrob.

New sentence   Mark is a handsome heartthrob, but he has green dreadlocks.

Review Checklist: Writing Compound Sentences

☐ A compound sentence is made up of two simple sentences (independent clauses).

☐ A coordinating conjunction—*and, but, for, nor, or, so,* or *yet*—can join two independent clauses into one compound sentence. A comma always comes before the coordinating conjunction. (See 15A.)

☐ A semicolon can join two independent clauses into one compound sentence. (See 15B.)

☐ A transitional word or phrase can also join two independent clauses into one compound sentence. When it joins two independent clauses, a transitional word or phrase is always preceded by a semicolon and followed by a comma. (See 15C.)

The ban on smoking in bars and restaurants in the United States started in California in 1994. By 2006, eighteen other states had followed suit.

Identifying Complex Sentences

As you learned in Chapter 15, a simple sentence consists of a single independent clause. An **independent clause** can stand alone as a sentence.

> **Independent clause**   The <u>exhibit</u> <u>was</u> controversial.

However, a **dependent clause** cannot stand alone as a sentence. It needs an independent clause to complete its meaning.

> **Dependent clause**   Because the exhibit was controversial

What happened because the exhibit was controversial? To answer this question, you need to add an independent clause that completes the idea in the dependent clause. The result is a **complex sentence**—a sentence that consists of one independent clause and one or more dependent clauses.

> **Complex sentence**
>
> ┌──────── DEPENDENT CLAUSE ────────┐┌ INDEPENDENT CLAUSE ─
> Because the exhibit was controversial, many people came
> └────────────────────────────┘
> to see the paintings.

→ Focus on Writing

In March 2003, the state of New York passed a law that banned smoking in bars and restaurants. The picture opposite shows a person lighting a candle in 2004 to celebrate the one-year anniversary of this tough antismoking law. Look at the picture, and then describe something that you believe needs to be changed—for example, a rule, a law, a policy, a situation, or a custom. First, identify what you think needs to be changed; then, explain why you think a change is necessary.

WORD POWER
courtesy polite behavior
infringe to go beyond the limits of something
offend to cause anger or resentment

🌐 **ESL Tip**
Review the concept of
subordination. Discuss
how adding a subordinat-
ing conjunction can make
one idea depend on
another for completion.

● **Practice 16-1**

In the blank following each of the items below, indicate whether the group of words is an independent clause (*IC*) or a dependent clause (*DC*).

> **Example:** Gymnastics became popular in the United States in the
> twentieth century. __*IC*__

1. Gymnastics exercises help develop all parts of the body. __*IC*__
2. Gymnastics dates back to the athletes of ancient Greece. __*IC*__
3. Because a German named Frederick Jahn popularized gymnastics in the nineteenth century. __*DC*__
4. Although German immigrants to the United States participated in gymnastics. __*DC*__
5. Gymnastics later became an event in the Olympic games. __*IC*__
6. Even though women's gymnastics once stressed grace rather than strength. __*DC*__
7. In the 1970s, women Olympic gymnasts began to dominate the games. __*IC*__
8. When Mary Lou Retton became the first American woman to win a gold medal for gymnastics in 1984. __*DC*__
9. Who was only sixteen years old at the time of her gold-medal win. __*DC*__
10. The first U.S. women's gymnastics team to win a gold medal competed in the 1996 games. __*IC*__

● **Practice 16-2**

In the blank following each of the items below, indicate whether the group of words is an independent clause (*IC*) or a dependent clause (*DC*).

> **Example:** When novelist Toni Morrison was born in Ohio in 1931. __*DC*__

1. As a young reader, Toni Morrison liked the classic Russian novelists. __*IC*__
2. After she graduated from Howard University with a bachelor's degree in English. __*DC*__

3. Morrison based her novel *The Bluest Eye* on a childhood friend's prayers to God for blue eyes. __IC__

4. While she raised two sons as a single mother and worked as an editor at Random House. __DC__

5. As her reputation as a novelist grew with the publication of *Song of Solomon* and *Tar Baby*. __DC__

6. Her picture appeared on the cover of *Newsweek* in 1981. __IC__

7. Before her novel *Beloved* won the 1988 Pulitzer Prize for fiction. __DC__

8. *Beloved* was later made into a film starring Oprah Winfrey. __IC__

9. In 1993, Morrison became the first African-American woman to win the Nobel Prize in Literature. __IC__

10. Who published the novel *Paradise* in 1998. __DC__

Using Subordinating Conjunctions

WORD POWER
subordinate lower in rank or position; secondary in importance

One way to form a complex sentence is to use a **subordinating conjunction**—a dependent word such as *although* or *because*—to join two simple sentences (independent clauses).

Teaching Tip
Point out to students that a clause introduced by a subordinating conjunction does not express a complete thought. Used by itself, it is a sentence fragment. (See 21E.)

Two simple sentences	Muhammad Ali was stripped of his title for refusing to go into the army. Many people admired his antiwar position.
	DEPENDENT CLAUSE
Complex sentence	Although Muhammad Ali was stripped of his title for refusing to go into the army, many people admired his antiwar position.

Teaching Tip
Have students create sentences that start with the subordinating conjunctions listed here.

Frequently Used Subordinating Conjunctions

after	even though	since	whenever
although	if	so that	where
as	if only	than	whereas
as if	in order that	that	wherever
as though	now that	though	whether
because	once	unless	while
before	provided that	until	
even if	rather than	when	

Teaching Tip
Have students memorize the subordinating conjunctions and the relationships they express.

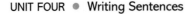 **ESL Tip**
Make sure students understand the subtle differences in meaning between different subordinating conjunctions.

Different subordinating conjunctions express different relationships between dependent and independent clauses.

Relationship between Clauses	Subordinating Conjunction	Example
Time	after, before, since, until, when, whenever, while	When the whale surfaced, Ahab threw his harpoon.
Reason or cause	as, because	Scientists abandoned the project because the government cut funds.
Result or effect	in order that, so that	So that students' math scores will improve, many schools have begun special tutoring.
Condition	even if, if, unless	The rain forest may disappear unless steps are taken immediately.
Contrast	although, even though, though, whereas	Although Thomas Edison had almost no formal education, he was a successful inventor.
Location	where, wherever	Pittsburgh was built where the Allegheny and Monongahela Rivers meet.

Highlight: Punctuating with Subordinating Conjunctions

Use a comma after the dependent clause in the sentence. Do not use a comma after the independent clause.

┌──────── DEPENDENT CLAUSE ────────┐┌─── INDEPENDENT CLAUSE ───┐
Although she wore the scarlet letter, Hester carried herself proudly.

┌──── INDEPENDENT CLAUSE ────┐┌──────── DEPENDENT CLAUSE ────────┐
Hester carried herself proudly although she wore the scarlet letter.

● **Practice 16-3**

In the blank in each of the sentences below, write an appropriate subordinating conjunction. Look at the list of subordinating conjunctions on page 241 to help you choose a conjunction that expresses the logical relationship between the two clauses it links. (The required punctuation has been provided.)

On the Web
For more practice, visit
Exercise Central *at*
<bedfordstmartins
.com/focusonwriting>.

Example: _____*When*_____ he was only six years old, Freddy Adu was playing informal soccer games with grown men. *Answers may vary.*

(1) His family moved from Ghana to the United States _____*when*_____ he was still a young boy. (2) Freddy did not play organized soccer _____*until*_____ he was in fourth grade. (3) _____*Although*_____ he is just out of his teens, Freddy is already one of America's most famous soccer players. (4) His remarkable talent excites even professional players and coaches _____*whenever*_____ they see him play. (5) _____*Since*_____ he was thirteen, he has been recruited by some of the greatest teams in the world. (6) One team offered his mother $750,000 _____*if*_____ Freddy would play for them. (7) _____*Although*_____ she needed the money, his mother turned down every offer. (8) The offers kept coming in _____*as*_____ Freddy continued to win major competitions for young players. (9) He and his mother finally agreed to a professional contract _____*that*_____ runs for six years. (10) _____*When*_____ Freddy joined DC United, he became the highest-paid player in American soccer.

● **Practice 16-4**

Form one complex sentence by combining each of the following pairs of sentences. Use a subordinating conjunction from the list on page 241 to clarify the relationship between the dependent and independent clauses in each sentence. Make sure you include a comma where one is required.

Example: Orville and Wilbur Wright built the first powered plane. ~~They~~ *although they* had no formal training as engineers. *Answers will vary.*

1. *Although professional* ~~Professional~~ midwives are used widely in Europe, ~~In~~ *in* the United States, they are less common.

     When

2. John Deere made the first steel plow in 1837,/ ˄A new era began in
   , *a*
   farming.

                                       even though he

3. Stephen Crane describes battles in *The Red Badge of Courage*,/ ~~He~~ never
   experienced a war.

     When   , *thousands*

4. Elvis Presley died suddenly in 1977,/ ~~Thousands~~ of his fans gathered in
   front of his mansion.

     After   , *the*

5. Jonas Salk developed the first polio vaccine in the 1950s,/ ~~The~~ number of
   polio cases in the United States declined.

     As the   , *some*

6. ~~The~~ salaries of baseball players rose in the 1980s,/ ~~Some~~ sportswriters
   predicted a drop in attendance at games.

     Before the

7. ~~The~~ Du Ponts arrived from France in 1800,/ American gunpowder was
   not as good as French gunpowder.

     After

8. Margaret Sanger opened her first birth-control clinic in America
             , *she*
   in 1916,/ ~~She~~ was arrested.

   Because ˄

9. Thaddeus Stevens thought plantation land should be given to freed
            , *he*
   slaves,/ ~~He~~ disagreed with Lincoln's peace plan for the South.

Even though ˄   , *he*

10. Steven Spielberg has directed some very popular movies,/ ~~He~~ did not
   win an Academy Award until *Schindler's List*.

Focus on Writing: *Flashback*

Look back at your response to the Focus on Writing activity on page 239. Identify two pairs of simple sentences that could be combined with subordinating conjunctions. On a separate sheet of paper, combine each pair into a complex sentence by making one sentence a dependent clause. Check to make sure you have punctuated your new sentences correctly.

16c Using Relative Pronouns

Another way to form a complex sentence is to use a **relative pronoun** (a dependent word such as *who, that, which,* and so on) to join two simple sentences (independent clauses).

Two simple sentences	Pit bulls were originally bred in England. They can be very aggressive.

—————— DEPENDENT CLAUSE ——————

Complex sentence	Pit bulls, which were originally bred in England, can be very aggressive.

Relative Pronouns

that	which	whoever	whomever
what	who	whom	whose

Different relative pronouns show different relationships between the ideas in the independent and dependent clauses that they link.

Two simple sentences	Nadine Gordimer comes from South Africa. She won the Nobel Prize in Literature in 1991.
Complex sentence	Nadine Gordimer, who won the Nobel Prize in Literature in 1991, comes from South Africa.
Two simple sentences	Last week I had a job interview. It went very well.
Complex sentence	Last week I had a job interview that went very well.
Two simple sentences	Transistors have replaced vacuum tubes in radios and televisions. They were invented in 1948.
Complex sentence	Transistors, which were invented in 1948, have replaced vacuum tubes in radios and televisions.

Note: The relative pronoun always refers to a word in the independent clause. *Who* and *whom* refer to people; *that* and *which* refer to animals or things.

● **Practice 16-5**

In each of the following complex sentences, underline the dependent clause once, and underline the relative pronoun twice. Then, draw an arrow from the relative pronoun to the word to which it refers.

On the Web
For more practice, visit
Exercise Central *at*
<bedfordstmartins
.com/focusonwriting>.

Example: MTV, which was the first TV show devoted to popular music videos, began in 1981.
Answers will vary.

1. MTV's very first music video, which was performed by a group called the Buggles, contained the lyric "Video killed the radio star."

2. MTV's early videos were simple productions that recorded live studio performances.

3. Recording executives, who had been suspicious of MTV at first, soon realized the power of music videos.

4. Music videos became elaborate productions that featured special effects and large casts of dancers.

5. The Cars' song "You Might Think" won the award for best video at the first MTV music awards, which aired in September 1984.

6. The game show *Remote Control*, which made fun of *Jeopardy*, began on MTV in 1987.

7. The fashion program *House of Style* became popular in 1989 because of supermodel Cindy Crawford, who was its first host.

8. *The Real World*, a reality series that featured a group of young people living together in New York City, also became popular then.

9. This same year, Bill Clinton, who would soon be elected president, met with young voters on MTV.

10. Today, MTV, which devotes less and less time to music videos, produces many hours of original programming.

● **Practice 16-6**

Combine each of the following pairs of simple sentences into one complex sentence, using the relative pronoun that follows each pair.

Example: Many college students perform community service. They are learning valuable skills. (who)

Many college students who perform community service are learning

valuable skills.

Answers will vary.

1. Their work is called service-learning. It benefits both the participants and the communities. (which)

   Their work, which benefits both the participants and the communities,

   is called service-learning.

2. A service-learning project meets a community need. It is sponsored either by a school or by the community. (which)

   A service-learning project, which is sponsored either by a school or

   by the community, meets a community need.

3. The young people work at projects such as designing neighborhood playgrounds. They are not paid. (who)

   The young people, who are not paid, work at projects such as

   designing neighborhood playgrounds.

4. It is challenging work. It gives young people satisfaction. (that)

   It is challenging work that gives young people satisfaction.

5. Designing a playground teaches them to cooperate. It requires teamwork. (which)

   Designing a playground, which requires teamwork, teaches them to

   cooperate.

6. Cooperation is an important skill. It is a skill they can use throughout their lives. (that)

   Cooperation is an important skill that they can use throughout their

   lives.

7. They also learn to solve problems. These are problems the community cannot solve by itself. (that)

   They also learn to solve problems that the community cannot solve by

   itself.

8. Being in charge of a project gives participants a sense of responsibility. It is a hard job. (which)

Being in charge of a project, which is a hard job, gives participants a

sense of responsibility.

9. The young participants gain satisfaction from performing a valuable service. They often lack self-confidence. (who)

The young participants, who often lack self-confidence, gain

satisfaction from performing a valuable service.

10. The community gets help solving its problems. It appreciates the young people's work. (which)

The community, which gets help solving its problems, appreciates the

young people's work.

Focus on Writing: *Flashback*

Look back at your response to the Focus on Writing activity on page 239. Identify two simple sentences that could be combined with a relative pronoun. (If you cannot find two appropriate sentences, write two new ones.) On a separate sheet of paper, write the new complex sentence.

Focus on Writing: *Revising and Editing*

Look back at your response to the Focus on Writing activity on page 239. Try adding at least one of the new complex sentences you created in the Flashback activities on page 244 and above. Then, check to make sure you have no errors in your use of subordinating conjunctions and relative pronouns. Finally, make sure that you have punctuated correctly.

Chapter Review

Editing Practice

Read the following student essay. Then, revise it by combining pairs of simple sentences with subordinating conjunctions or relative pronouns that indicate the relationship between them. Be sure to punctuate correctly. The first sentence has been revised for you.   *Answers may vary.*

Community Artist

When
I was in tenth grade at West Philadelphia High School in
Philadelphia, I took an art class. One day, my teacher started to talk
                                                    that we
about the free Philadelphia Mural Arts Program. We could sign up for
it. I needed something to do after school and during the summer.
Although
I didn't know much about the program, I signed up and was accepted.
It turned out to be a rewarding experience.

                                                            , which
   My teacher told us all about the Mural Arts Program. It had its
origins in the Philadelphia Anti-Graffiti Network in 1984. Philadelphia
                         , which
had a serious problem. The problem was graffiti. Graffiti artists had
painted their designs on buildings all over the city. A solution to the
                                                      , which
problem was the Philadelphia Anti-Graffiti Network. This offered
                                     If they   *, they*
graffiti artists an alternative. They would give up graffiti. They would
              Since they   *, they*
not be prosecuted. They enjoyed painting. They could paint murals on
public buildings instead. They could create scenic landscapes, portraits
                                      Although the
of local heroes, and abstract designs. The graffiti artists had once
                 , they
been lawbreakers. They could now help build community spirit.

   By 1996, the Philadelphia Anti-Graffiti Network was concentrating
on eliminating graffiti, and its Mural Arts Program worked to improve
                  While it   *, it*
the community. It no longer worked with graffiti offenders. It started
after-school and summer programs for students. The Mural Arts
Program got national recognition in 1997 when President Clinton
helped paint a mural. So far, the Mural Arts Program has completed
                 , which
more than 2,300 murals. This is more than any other public art
program in the country.

249

I joined the Mural Arts Program in 2001. My fellow students and
, *who came from all parts of the city,*
I visited some of the murals. ~~We came from all parts of the city.~~
^
The best part of the program was the summer when we learned to
When we
use computers to turn our ideas into works of art. ~~We~~ worked
, *we*
with an artist./~~We~~ actually got to paint parts of her mural on a build-
When people ^   , *they*
ing. ~~People~~ walk or drive by the building./~~They~~ can see our work.
^   *Although all* ^
I learned a lot in this program. ~~All~~ the students had to work
, *we*
together./~~We~~ also worked with artists and community residents. We
^   *Although at*
helped the community come together to create a mural. ~~At~~ first I
, *now*
didn't care about art./~~Now~~ I really appreciate it. I am grateful to my
^ , *who*
tenth-grade art teacher./~~He~~ got me interested in the program.
^

Collaborative Activities

1. Working in a group of four students, make a list of three or four of your favorite television shows. Divide into pairs, and with your partner, write two simple sentences describing each show. Next, use subordinating conjunctions or relative pronouns to combine each pair of sentences into one complex sentence. With your group, discuss how the ideas in each complex sentence are related, and make sure you have used the subordinating conjunction or relative pronoun that best conveys this relationship.

   Example: *The Brady Bunch* portrays a 1970s family. It still appeals to many viewers.

   Although *The Brady Bunch* portrays a 1970s family, it still appeals to many viewers.

2. Imagine that you and the members of your group live in a neighborhood where workers are repairing underground power lines. As they work, the workers talk loudly and use foul language. Write a letter of complaint to the power company in which you explain that the workers' behavior is offensive to you and to your children. Tell the company that you want the offensive behavior to end. Write the first draft of your letter in simple sentences. After you have written this draft, work as a group to combine as many sentences as you can with subordinating conjunctions and relative pronouns.

3. Assume you are in a competition to determine which collaborative group in your class is best at writing complex sentences. Working in a

group, prepare a letter to your instructor in which you present the strengths of your group. Be sure to use a subordinating conjunction or relative pronoun in each of the sentences in your letter. Finally, as a class, evaluate the letters, and choose the letter that is most convincing.

Review Checklist:
Writing Complex Sentences

☐ A complex sentence consists of one independent clause (simple sentence) combined with one or more dependent clauses. (See 16A.)

☐ Subordinating conjunctions—dependent words such as *although, after, when, while,* and *because*—can join two independent clauses into one complex sentence. (See 16B.)

☐ Relative pronouns—dependent words such as *who, which,* and *that*—can also join two independent clauses into one complex sentence. The relative pronoun shows the relationship between the ideas in the two independent clauses that it links. (See 16C.)

Chapter 17

Writing Varied Sentences

The first time capsule was probably created by Westinghouse for the company's exhibit at the 1939 World's Fair in New York. It is meant to be opened in the year 6939.

Varying Sentence Types

Teaching Tip
Explain that a statement ends with a period, a question ends with a question mark, and an exclamation ends with an exclamation point.

Most English sentences are **statements**. Others are **questions** or **exclamations**. One way to vary your sentences is to use an occasional question or exclamation where it is appropriate.

In the following paragraph, a question and an exclamation add variety.

Question

Teaching Tip
Remind students that exclamations are widely used in informal, personal writing and in dialogue, but they are not usually appropriate in college writing.

Exclamation

> Over a period of less than twenty years, the image of African Americans in television sitcoms seemed to change dramatically, reflecting the changing status of black men and women in American society. <u>But had anything really changed?</u> In *Beulah*, the 1950 sitcom that was the first to star an African-American woman, the title character was a maid. Her friends were portrayed as irresponsible and not very smart. *Amos 'n' Andy*, which also appeared in the 1950s, continued these negative stereotypes of black characters. In 1968, with the civil rights movement at its height, the NBC comedy hit *Julia* portrayed a black woman in a much more favorable light. A widowed nurse, raising a small boy on her own, Julia was a dedicated professional and a patient and devoted mother. The image of the African American was certainly more positive, but the character was no more balanced or three-dimensional than earlier black characters had been. <u>Julia was certainly not an object of ridicule; in fact, she was a saint!</u>

→ Focus on Writing

The picture on the opposite page shows items to be preserved in a time capsule at the History Center in Pittsburgh. Write about a time capsule that your children will open when they are adults. What items would you include? How would you expect each item to communicate to your children what you and your world were like? Look at the picture, and then explain your decisions.

WORD POWER
time capsule a sealed container that preserves contemporary items for future scientists and scholars.
memorabilia things worthy of remembering
nostalgia a longing for people or things that are no longer present

● **Practice 17-1**

Revise the following passage by changing one of the statements into a question and one of the statements into an exclamation.

Example: Some people pursue two different careers at the same time. (statement)

Why do some people pursue two different careers at the same time?
_____
(question)

Teaching Tip
Tell students that when
they write instructions,
they can also use
commands—statements
that address readers
directly: *Now, unplug the
appliance.*

   Answers will vary.

   (1) Many working people have more than one job. (2) For example, a police officer might moonlight as a security guard, an actor might also work as a waiter, and an artist or a writer might also teach. (3) These workers need their second jobs for survival. (4) In recent years, however, more and more successful professionals have decided to begin a second career without leaving the first one. (5) Often, the second career seems to be very different from the first one. (6) For example, a teacher might also work as a professional model. (7) Sometimes, however, the two careers really do have something in common. (8) After all, both teaching and modeling involve performing for an audience. (9) Similarly, a lawyer may be drawn to the ministry, another career that is dedicated to justice. (10) ~~Many things motivate~~ *What motivates* people to combine two seemingly different professions/ (11) Those who do so say they do it not for the money but for professional satisfaction. (12) Obviously, these workers are very lucky people/

Focus on Writing: *Flashback*

Look back at your response to the Focus on Writing activity on page 253. What questions does your writing answer? On a separate sheet of paper, try writing one of these questions. (You may need to substitute it for a sentence that is already there.)

   If you think an exclamation would be an appropriate addition to your writing, write one on a separate sheet of paper.

Varying Sentence Openings

When all the sentences in a paragraph begin in the same way, your writing is likely to seem dull and repetitive. In the following paragraph, for example, every sentence begins with the subject.

> Scientists have been observing a disturbing phenomenon. The population of frogs, toads, and salamanders has been declining. This decline was first noticed in the mid-1980s. Some reports blamed chemical pollution. Some biologists began to suspect that a fungal disease was killing these amphibians. The most reasonable explanation seems to be that the amphibians' eggs are threatened by solar radiation. This radiation penetrates the thinned ozone layer, which used to shield them from the sun's rays.

Beginning with Adverbs

Instead of opening every sentence with the subject, try beginning with one or more **adverbs**, as the following paragraph illustrates.

> Scientists have been observing a disturbing phenomenon. <u>Gradually but steadily</u>, the population of frogs, toads, and salamanders has been declining. This decline was first noticed in the mid-1980s. Some reports blamed chemical pollution. Some biologists began to suspect that a fungal disease was killing these amphibians. <u>However,</u> the most reasonable explanation seems to be that the amphibians' eggs are threatened by solar radiation. This radiation penetrates the thinned ozone layer, which used to shield them from the sun's rays.

● **Practice 17-2**

Underline the adverb in each of the following sentences, and then, on a separate sheet of paper, rewrite the sentence so that the adverb appears at the beginning. Be sure to punctuate correctly.

> **Example:** It is <u>often</u> difficult to buy a gift for someone in a distant city.
>
> *Often, it is difficult to buy a gift for someone in a distant city.*
>
> *Answers will vary.*

1. One way to deal with this problem, <u>however</u>, is to shop online.

2. Online shoppers must <u>first</u> use a search engine to find the category of product they want to purchase.

3. Customer reviews are often available to help shoppers make a choice.

4. Payment is generally by credit card.

5. Online shopping now brings the world to everyone with access to a computer.

● **Practice 17-3**

Teaching Tip
Refer students to Chapter 28 for more on adverbs.

In each of the following sentences, fill in the blank with an appropriate adverb. Be sure to punctuate correctly.

Example: _____Slowly,_____ the sun crept over the horizon.
Answers will vary.

1. _____ the speeding car appeared from out of nowhere.

2. _____ it crashed into the guard rail.

3. _____ someone used a cell phone to call 911.

4. _____ the ambulance arrived.

5. _____ emergency medical technicians went to work.

Beginning with Prepositional Phrases

Teaching Tip
Refer students to the list of frequently used prepositions in 14B.

You can also begin some sentences with prepositional phrases. A **prepositional phrase** (such as *along the river* or *near the diner*) is made up of a preposition and its object.

Teaching Tip
Remind students that an adverb or a prepositional phrase that opens a sentence is followed by a comma. However, if an introductory prepositional phrase has only one or two words, the comma is not required. Refer them to 30B.

In recent years, scientists have been observing a disturbing phenomenon. Gradually but steadily, the population of frogs, toads, and salamanders has been declining. This decline was first noticed in the mid-1980s. At first, some reports blamed chemical pollution. After a while, some biologists began to suspect that a fungal disease was killing these amphibians. However, the most reasonable explanation seems to be that the amphibians' eggs are threatened by solar radiation. This radiation penetrates the thinned ozone layer, which used to shield them from the sun's rays.

● **Practice 17-4**

Underline the prepositional phrase in each of the following sentences, and then rewrite the sentence so that the prepositional phrase appears at the beginning. Be sure to punctuate correctly.

Teaching Tip
Refer students to the
list of frequently used
prepositions in 14B.

Example: Very few American women worked in factories <u>before</u> the 1940s.

Before the 1940s, very few American women worked in factories.

Answers will vary.

1. Many male factory workers became soldiers <u>during World War II.</u>

_____

2. The U.S. government encouraged women to take factory jobs <u>in the war's early years.</u>

_____

3. Over six million women took factory jobs <u>between 1942 and 1945.</u>

_____

4. A new female image emerged <u>with this greater responsibility and independence.</u>

_____

5. Most women lost their factory jobs <u>after the war</u> and had to return to "women's work."

_____

● **Practice 17-5**

In each of the following sentences, fill in the blank with an appropriate prepositional phrase. Be sure to punctuate correctly.

Example: <u>*At the start of the New York marathon,*</u> I felt as if I could run forever.
Answers will vary.

Teaching Tip
Refer students to the list
of frequently used
prepositions in 14B.

1. _____ I warmed up by stretching and bending.

2. _____ it was hard to run because all the runners were crowded together.

3. _____ the route became more and more steep.

4. _____ my leg muscles started to ache, and I worried that I might get a bad cramp.

5. _____ I staggered across the finish line, happy and relieved that my first marathon was over.

● Practice 17-6

Several sentences in the following passage include phrases introduced by prepositions and adverbs. Revise the passage to vary the sentence openings, moving prepositional phrases to the beginnings of three sentences and adverbs to the beginnings of two other sentences. Be sure to place a comma after these introductory phrases.

Example: *In the Cuban–American community, people*
~~People in the Cuban-American community~~ often mention
José Julian Martí as one of their heroes.

Answers will vary.

(1) José Martí was born in Havana in 1853, at a time when Cuba was
By the time he was sixteen years old, he
a colony of Spain. (2) ~~He~~ had started a newspaper demanding Cuban
In 1870, the
freedom ~~by the time he was sixteen years old~~. (3) ~~The~~ Spanish authori-
. Openly continuing his fight, h
ties forced him to leave Cuba and go to Spain ~~in 1870~~. (4) ~~He~~ published
his first pamphlet calling for Cuban independence while in Spain, ~~openly~~
~~continuing his fight~~. (5) Working as a journalist and professor, he
returned to Cuba but was sent away again. (6) He then lived for fourteen
During his time in New York, he
years in New York City. (7) ~~He~~ started the journal of the Cuban Revolutionary Party ~~during his time in New York~~. (8) Martí's essays and
poems argued for Cuba's freedom and for the individual freedom of
Passionately following up his words with actions, he .
Cubans. (9) ~~He~~ died in battle against Spanish soldiers in Cuba, ~~passion-~~
~~ately following up his words with actions~~. (10) Today, his ideas are still
very much alive in the dreams of many Cubans.

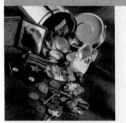

Focus on Writing: *Flashback*

Look back at your response to the Focus on Writing activity on page 253. Identify one sentence that you could begin with an adverb and one that could open with a prepositional phrase. (Note that the adverb or prepositional phrase may already be somewhere in the sentence.) On a separate piece of paper, try revising the openings of these two sentences.

17c Combining Sentences

You can also create sentence variety by experimenting with different ways of combining sentences.

Using Present Participles

The **present participle** is the *-ing* form of a verb: *carrying*, *using*. You can use a present participle to combine two sentences.

Two sentences	Duke Ellington composed more than a thousand songs. He worked hard to establish his reputation as a musician.
Combined (with present participle)	<u>Composing</u> more than a thousand songs, Duke Ellington worked hard to establish his reputation as a musician.

When the sentences are combined, the present participle (*composing*) introduces a phrase that describes the sentence's subject (*Duke Ellington*). Note that a comma follows the phrase introduced by the present participle.

● Practice 17-7

Use a present participle to combine each of the following pairs of sentences into a single sentence. Eliminate any unnecessary words, and place a comma after each phrase that is introduced by a present participle. When you are finished, underline the present participle in each new sentence.

> **Example:** The cost of operating America's prisons is rising steadily. It is getting higher as more people go to prison.
> *<u>Rising</u> steadily, the cost of operating America's prisons is getting*
> *higher as more people go to prison.*
> *Answers will vary.*

1. Some private businesses are taking advantage of this situation. They hire prisoners to work for them.
   <u>Taking</u> advantage of this situation, some private businesses hire
   prisoners to work for them.

Teaching Tip
Once they are introduced to present and past participles, students tend to overuse them. Caution students against starting too many sentences with participles.

Teaching Tip
Refer students to 24A for more on present participles.

Teaching Tip
In Practice 17-7, students may need to change a noun to a pronoun or vice versa when they combine sentences. Review the example sentences carefully.

Teaching Tip
Check students' work carefully to make sure they are not creating dangling modifiers. Refer them to 24B.

2. Prisoners are working for airlines. They are handling travel reservations over the phone.

Working for airlines, prisoners are handling travel reservations over the phone.

3. The prisoners learn new skills as they work. They are better prepared to find jobs after prison.

Learning new skills as they work, the prisoners are better prepared to find jobs after prison.

4. This arrangement helps prisoners stay out of prison. It works well for everyone.

Helping prisoners stay out of prison, this arrangement works well for everyone.

5. These prisons cost less to run. They benefit taxpayers.

Costing less to run, these prisons benefit taxpayers.

● **Practice 17-8**

On the Web
For more practice, visit Exercise Central *at* <bedfordstmartins .com/focusonwriting>.

In the sentences below, fill in the blank with a phrase that is introduced by an appropriate present participle. Be sure to punctuate correctly.

Example: ___*Selling candy door to door,*___ the team raised money for new uniforms.
Answers will vary.

1. _____ the judge called for order in the courtroom.

2. _____ the miners found silver instead.

3. _____ migrating birds often travel long distances in the early fall.

4. _____ fans waited patiently to buy tickets for the concert.

5. _____ the child seemed frightened.

Teaching Tip
Refer students to 24A for more on past participles and to 26B for a list of irregular past participles.

Using Past Participles

Past participles of verbs are usually formed with *-ed* (*carried*) or *-d* (*used*), but there are also many irregular past participle forms (*known, written*).

Two sentences can often be combined when one of them contains a past participle.

Two sentences	Nogales is located on the border between Arizona and Mexico. It is a bilingual city.
Combined (with past participle)	<u>Located</u> on the border between Arizona and Mexico, Nogales is a bilingual city.

When the sentences are combined, the past participle (*located*) introduces a phrase that describes the sentence's subject (*Nogales*). Note that a comma follows the phrase introduced by the past participle.

Teaching Tip
Make sure students understand that modifiers introduced by present or past participles must refer clearly to the words they describe. Refer them to 24A and 24B.

● Practice 17-9

Use a past participle to combine each of the pairs of sentences into a single sentence. Eliminate any unnecessary words, and place a comma after each phrase that is introduced by a past participle. When you are finished, underline the past participle in each new sentence.

Example: Sacajawea was born in about 1787. She lived among her Shoshone tribespeople until the age of eleven.
<u>Born</u> in about 1787, Sacajawea lived among her Shoshone tribespeople until the age of eleven.
Answers will vary.

Teaching Tip
This exercise asks students to combine sentences; it does *not* require that each revised sentence *begin* with a participle. If this is what you want students to do, tell them so.

1. She was captured as a young girl by a rival tribe. Sacajawea was later sold into slavery.
<u>Captured</u> as a young girl by a rival tribe, Sacajawea was later sold into slavery.

2. She was saved by a French Canadian fur trader named Charbonneau. Sacajawea became his wife.
<u>Saved</u> by a French Canadian fur trader named Charbonneau, Sacajawea became his wife.

3. The explorers Lewis and Clark hired Charbonneau in 1806. He brought his pregnant wife along on their westward expedition.
<u>Hired</u> by the explorers Lewis and Clark in 1806, Charbonneau brought his pregnant wife along on their westward expedition.

4. Sacajawea was skilled in several native languages. She helped Lewis and Clark on their journey.

Skilled in several native languages, Sacajawea helped Lewis and

Clark on their journey.

5. A U.S. dollar coin now shows her picture. It was created in 2000.

Created in 2000, a U.S. dollar coin now shows her picture.

● Practice 17-10

In the following sentences, fill in the blank with a phrase that is introduced by an appropriate past participle. Be sure to punctuate correctly.

Example: _____ *Buried for many years,* _____ the treasure was

discovered by accident.
Answers will vary.

1. _____ the child started crying

when the storm began.

2. _____ the hikers rested wearily

at the top of the mountain.

3. _____ the small boat almost capsized.

4. _____ the balloons in Macy's

Thanksgiving Day parade soared above the crowds.

5. _____ family stories help fami-

lies keep their traditions alive.

On the Web
For more practice, visit Exercise Central *at* <bedfordstmartins .com/focusonwriting>.

Using a Series of Words

Another way to vary your sentences is to combine a group of sentences into one sentence that includes a **series** of words (nouns, verbs, or adjectives). Notice how combining sentences in this way eliminates a boring string of similar sentences and repetitive phrases.

Teaching Tip
Remind students that a compound subject takes a plural verb. Refer them to 22B.

Group of sentences	College presidents want to improve athletes' academic performance. Coaches too want to improve athletes'

academic performance. The players themselves also want to improve their academic performance.

Combined (series of nouns)	College presidents, coaches, and the players themselves want to improve athletes' academic performance.
Group of sentences	In 1997, Arundhati Roy published her first novel, *The God of Small Things*. She won the Pulitzer Prize. She became a literary sensation.
Combined (series of verbs)	In 1997, Arundhati Roy <u>published</u> her first novel, *The God of Small Things*, <u>won</u> the Pulitzer Prize, and <u>became</u> a literary sensation.
Group of sentences	As the tornado approached, the sky grew dark. The sky grew quiet. The sky grew threatening.
Combined (series of adjectives)	As the tornado approached, the sky grew <u>dark</u>, <u>quiet</u>, and <u>threatening</u>.

Teaching Tip
Point out to students that the revised sentences are more concise as well as more varied. Refer them to 19B.

● **Practice 17-11**

Combine each of the following groups of sentences into one sentence that includes a series of nouns, verbs, or adjectives.

Example: Many years ago, Pacific Islanders from Samoa settled in Hawaii. Pacific Islanders from Fiji also settled in Hawaii. Pacific Islanders from Tahiti settled in Hawaii too.

Many years ago, Pacific Islanders from Samoa, Fiji, and Tahiti settled

in Hawaii. (three nouns)

1. In the eighteenth century, the British explorer Captain Cook came to Hawaii. Other explorers also came to Hawaii. European travelers came to Hawaii too.

   Answers will vary.

2. Explorers and traders brought commerce to Hawaii. They brought new ideas. They brought new cultures.

3. Missionaries introduced the Christian religion. They introduced a Hawaiian-language bible. Also, they introduced a Hawaiian alphabet.

4. In the mid-nineteenth century, pineapple plantations were established in Hawaii. Sugar plantations were established there too. Other industries were also established.

_____

5. By 1900, Japanese people were working in the plantations. Chinese people were also working in the plantations. Native Hawaiians were working there as well.

_____

6. People of many different races and religions now live in Hawaii. People of many different races and religions now go to school in Hawaii. People of many different races and religions now work in Hawaii.

_____

7. Schoolchildren still study the Hawaiian language. They learn about the Hawaiian kings and queens. They read about ancient traditions.

_____

8. Today, Hawaii is well known for its tourism. It is well known too for its weather. It is especially well known for its natural beauty.

_____

9. Tourists can swim. They can surf. They can play golf. They can ride in outrigger canoes.

_____

10. Today, the state of Hawaii remains lively. It remains culturally diverse. It remains very beautiful.

_____

Using Appositives

An **appositive** is a word or word group that identifies, renames, or describes a noun or pronoun. Creating an appositive is often a good way to combine two sentences about the same subject.

Two sentences	C. J. Walker was the first American woman to become a self-made millionaire. She marketed a line of hair-care products for black women.

Combined (with appositive)	C. J. Walker, the first American woman to become a self-made millionaire, marketed a line of hair-care products for black women.

In the example above, the appositive appears in the middle of the sentence. However, an appositive can also come at the beginning or at the end of a sentence.

The first American woman to become a self-made millionaire, C. J. Walker marketed a line of hair-care products for black women. (appositive at the beginning)

Several books have been written about C. J. Walker, the first American woman to become a self-made millionaire. (appositive at the end)

When you combine sentences with an appositive, always set off the appositive with commas. (See 30C.)

● Practice 17-12

On the Web
For more practice, visit Exercise Central at <bedfordstmartins .com/focusonwriting>.

Combine each of the following pairs of sentences into one sentence by creating appositives. Note that the appositive may appear at the beginning, in the middle, or at the end of the sentence. Be sure to use commas appropriately.

Example: Lorraine Hansberry's *A Raisin in the Sun* was one of the first American plays to focus on the experiences of African Americans, It was produced on Broadway in 1959. *Answers will vary.*

(1) Lorraine Hansberry was born in Chicago in 1930. She was a playwright who wrote the prize-winning *A Raisin in the Sun*. (2) Hansberry's father was a successful businessman, He moved the family from the south side of Chicago to a predominantly white neighborhood when Hansberry was eight. (3) Hostile neighbors there threw a brick through a window of their house, This was an act Hansberry never forgot.

(4) Such experiences inspired *A Raisin in the Sun.* ̷I̷t̷ ̷i̷s̷ the story of a family's struggle to escape a cramped apartment in a poor Chicago neighborhood.

Focus on Writing: *Flashback*

Look back at your response to the Focus on Writing activity on page 253. Find two or three pairs of sentences that you think could be combined. On a separate sheet of paper, combine each pair of sentences into a single sentence, using one of the methods discussed in 17C. Use a different method for each pair of sentences.

17d Varying Sentence Length

Teaching Tip
For information on creating compound and complex sentences, refer students to Chapters 15 and 16.

A paragraph of short, choppy sentences—or a paragraph of long, rambling sentences—can be monotonous. By mixing long and short sentences, perhaps combining some simple sentences to create compound and complex sentences, you can create a more interesting paragraph.

In the following paragraph, the sentences are all short, and the result is a dull passage.

> The world's first drive-in movie theater opened on June 6, 1933. This drive-in was in Camden, New Jersey. Automobiles became more popular. Drive-ins did too. By the 1950s, there were more than four thousand drive-ins in the United States. Over the years, the high cost of land led to a decline in the number of drive-ins. So did the rising popularity of television. Soon, the drive-in movie theater had almost disappeared. It was replaced by the multiplex. In 1967, there were forty-six drive-ins in New Jersey. Today, only one is still open. That one is the Delsea Drive-in in Vineland, New Jersey.

The revised paragraph that appears below is more interesting because it mixes long and short sentences.

The world's first drive-in movie theater opened on June 6, 1933, in Camden, New Jersey. As automobiles became more popular, drive-ins did too, and by the 1950s, there were more than four thousand drive-ins in the United States. Over the years, the high cost of land and the rising popularity of television led to a decline in the number of drive-ins. Soon, the drive-in movie theater had almost disappeared, replaced by the multiplex. In 1967, there were forty-six drive-ins in New Jersey, but today, only one is still open: the Delsea Drive-in in Vineland, New Jersey.

● **Practice 17-13**

The following passage contains a series of short, choppy sentences that can be combined. Revise it so that it mixes long and short sentences. Be sure to use commas and other punctuation appropriately.

Example: Kente cloth has special significance for many African

Americans,/Many other people do not understand this significance.
, but many

Answers will vary.

(1) Kente cloth is made in western Africa,/(2) It is produced primar-
and

ily by the Ashanti people. (3) It has been worn for hundreds of years by

African royalty,/(4) They consider it a sign of power and status. (5) Many
, who

African Americans wear kente cloth,/(6) They see it as a link to their her-
because they

itage. (7) Each pattern on the cloth has a name,/(8) Each color has a spe-
, and each

cial significance. (9) For example, red and yellow suggest a long and

healthy life,/(10) Green and white suggest a good harvest. (11) African
while green   *Although*

women may wear kente cloth as a dress or head wrap,/(12) African-

American women, like men, usually wear strips of cloth around their

shoulders. (13) Men and women of African descent wear kente cloth as

a sign of racial pride,/(14) It often decorates college students' gowns at
; in fact, it

graduation.

On the Web
For more practice, visit
Exercise Central *at*
<bedfordstmartins
.com/focusonwriting>.

Focus on Writing: *Flashback*

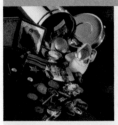

Look back at your response to the Focus on Writing activity on page 253. Count the number of words in each sentence, and write the results on the following lines.
Answers will vary.

Sentence 1 _____	Sentence 6 _____
Sentence 2 _____	Sentence 7 _____
Sentence 3 _____	Sentence 8 _____
Sentence 4 _____	Sentence 9 _____
Sentence 5 _____	Sentence 10 _____

Now, write a new short sentence to follow your longest sentence.

New sentence: _____

_____

Focus on Writing: *Revising and Editing*

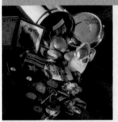

Look back at your response to the Focus on Writing activity on page 253. Using any strategies from this chapter that seem appropriate, revise your writing so that your sentences are varied, interesting, and smoothly connected. (You may want to incorporate sentences you wrote for the Flashback activities on pages 254, 258, 266, and above.) When you are finished, revise the sentences in an assignment you have completed for another course.

Editing Practice

The following student essay lacks sentence variety. All of its sentences are statements beginning with the subject, and it includes a number of short, choppy sentences. Using the strategies discussed in this chapter, revise the essay to achieve greater sentence variety. The first sentence has been edited for you.   *Answers will vary.*

Toys by Accident

Many popular toys and games are the result of accidents. ~~People~~ *when people* try to invent one thing but discover something else instead.
Sometimes, they are not trying to invent anything at all. ~~They~~ *and* are completely surprised to find a new product.

Play-Doh is one example of an accidental discovery. ~~Play-Doh is a~~ *, a popular preschool toy,* ~~popular preschool toy.~~ Play-Doh first appeared in Cincinnati. ~~A~~ company *, where a* made a compound to clean wallpaper. ~~They~~ *and* sold it as a cleaning product. The company then realized that this compound could be a toy. ~~Children could mold~~ *Molding* it like clay. ~~They~~ *, children* could use it again and again. The new toy was an immediate hit. Play-Doh was first sold in 1956. ~~Since then,~~ *Since* more than two billion cans ~~of Play-Doh~~ have been sold.

The Slinky was discovered by Richard James. ~~He was~~ an engineer. *, who* ~~He~~ was trying to invent a spring to keep ships' instruments steady at sea. ~~He~~ tested hundreds of springs of varying sizes, metals, and *Although he* tensions. ~~None~~ of them worked. One spring fell off the desk. ~~It~~ *, none* "walked" down a pile of books. ~~It~~ fell end over end onto the floor. ~~He thought~~ his children might enjoy playing with it. *, and* *Thinking* James took the spring home. They loved it. Every child in the neighborhood wanted one. ~~The~~ first Slinky was demonstrated at Gimbel's Department Store in *When the* Philadelphia in 1945. ~~All~~ four hundred Slinkys on hand were sold *, all* within ninety minutes. ~~The Slinky is simple~~ and inexpensive. ~~The~~ *Simple* *, the* Slinky is still popular with children.

The Frisbee was discovered by accident, too. According to one story, a group of Yale University students were eating pies from a local *frisbies* bakery. ~~The bakery was called Frisbies.~~ ~~They~~ *After they* finished eating the pies, ~~They~~ *, they* started throwing the empty pie tins around. A carpenter in California made a plastic version, ~~He~~ *, which he* called ~~it~~ the Pluto Platter. The Wham-O company bought the patent on the product, ~~Wham-o~~ renamed it the Frisbee after the bakery, ~~Wham-O~~ *, and* started selling it.

Some new toys are not developed by toy companies. Play-Doh, the Frisbee, and the Slinky are examples of very popular toys that resulted from accidental discoveries. Play-Doh started as a cleaning product, ~~The~~ *, the* Slinky was discovered by an engineer who was trying to invent something else, ~~The~~ *, and the* Frisbee was invented by students having fun. ~~The toys were discovered~~ *Discovered* unexpectedly, ~~All~~ *, all* three toys have become classics.

Collaborative Activities

1. Read the following list of sentences. Working in a small group, add to the list one related sentence that is a question or an exclamation. Then, add an appropriate adverb or prepositional phrase to one or more of the sentences on the list.

   Many well-known African-American writers left the United States in the years following World War II.

   Many went to Paris.

   Richard Wright was a novelist.

   He wrote *Native Son* and *Black Boy*.

   He wrote *Uncle Tom's Children*.

   He left the United States for Paris in 1947.

   James Baldwin wrote *Another Country*, *The Fire Next Time*, and *Giovanni's Room*.

   He also wrote essays.

   He came to Paris in 1948.

   Chester Himes was a detective story writer.

He arrived in Paris in 1953.

William Gardner Smith was a novelist and journalist.

He also left the United States for Paris.

These expatriates found Paris more hospitable than America.

They also found it less racist.

2. Continuing to work in your group, combine all the sentences on the list to create a varied and interesting paragraph. Use the strategies illustrated in 17C as a guide.

3. When your group's revisions are complete, trade paragraphs with another group and further edit the other group's paragraph to improve sentence variety.

Review Checklist: Achieving Sentence Variety

☐ Vary sentence types, using an occasional question or exclamation. (See 17A.)

☐ Vary sentence openings. (See 17B.)

☐ Combine sentences. (See 17C.)

☐ Vary sentence length. (See 17D.)

Chapter 18   Using Parallelism

The world's largest fountain, the Fountain of Wealth, is located in Singapore. Its base measures nearly one square mile.

Recognizing Parallel Structure

Parallelism means using matching words, phrases, clauses, and sentence structure to highlight similar items in a sentence. When you use parallelism, you are telling readers that certain items or ideas are related. By repeating similar grammatical structures to express similar ideas, you create balanced sentences that are clearer and easier to read.

In the following examples, the individual element in the parallel sentences are balanced; the elements in the other sentences are not.

Not Parallel	*Parallel*
Please leave your name, your number, and you should also leave a message.	Please leave your name, your number, and your message.
I plan to graduate from high school and then becoming a nurse would be a good idea.	I plan to graduate from high school and become a nurse.
The grass was soft, green, the smell was sweet.	The grass was soft, green, and sweet smelling.
Making the team was one thing; to stay on it was another.	Making the team was one thing; staying on it was another.
We can register for classes in person, or registering by email is another option.	We can register for classes in person, or we can register by email.

→ Focus on Writing

The picture on the opposite page shows children playing in a fountain in a public park in Portland, Oregon. Look at the picture and then write three positive things about your own neighborhood, school, or workplace. Support your statements with specific examples.

WORD POWER

enlighten to give insight to; to educate

enrich to make fuller or more rewarding

inspire to stimulate to action; to motivate

On the Web
For more practice, visit
Exercise Central *at*
<bedfordstmartins
.com/focusonwriting>.

● **Practice 18-1**

In the following sentences, decide whether the underlined words and phrases are parallel. If so, write *P* in the blank. If not, rewrite the sentences so that the ideas they express are presented in parallel terms.

Examples: Our letter carrier is <u>punctual</u>, <u>friendly</u>, and <u>dependable</u>. ___P___

When choosing a candidate, voters may think about whether the candi-
                   trustworthy,
dates are <u>likable</u>, <s>their trustworthiness,</s> and <s>if they are</s> <u>honest</u>. _____

           a head of   *, a pint of*
1. I just bought <s>some</s> <u>lettuce and mushrooms</u>, and <u>three pounds of toma-
         ^   ^
toes</u>. _____

2. Do you want it done <u>quickly</u>, or do you want it done <u>well</u>? ___P___

3. The plumber needs to <u>fix a leaky pipe</u>, <u>replace a missing faucet</u>, and
   fix a running toilet.
  <s>a toilet that is running should be fixed.</s> _____
  ^

                             played
4. When John was a college student, he <s>was on the</s> <u>football</u> <s>team and
                               ^
played</s> <u>baseball</u>, and <s>was on the</s> <u>basketball</u> <s>team.</s> _____

5. Our vacation turned out to be <u>relaxing</u> but <u>expensive</u>. ___P___

                                            my
6. On my refrigerator are magnets from my <u>accountant</u>, <s>one from the</s>
                                                ^
<u>doctor</u> <s>I went to see for the first time last week</s>, and my <u>dentist</u>. _____

7. Show me <u>a neat desk</u>, and I will show you <u>an empty mind</u>. ___P___

8. At my tenth class reunion, I was surprised to find that I enjoyed <u>meeting
my old classmates</u>, <u>walking around the school</u>, and <s>I had a surprisingly
good time</s> <u>talking with the principal</u>. _____

9. I just <u>washed the floor</u>. Can you <u>vacuum the rug</u>? ___P___

                              a leaky
10. Our old car <u>has poor gas mileage</u>, <s>its windshield</s> <u>leaks when it rains</u>, and
                                   ^   ^
  bad
  its <u>brakes</u> <s>don't work very well</s>. _____
  ^   ^

Focus on Writing: *Flashback*

Look back at your response to the Focus on Writing activity on
page 273, and underline the parallel words, phrases, and clauses.
Revise if necessary so that comparable ideas are presented in parallel
terms.

Using Parallel Structure

Teaching Tip
Remind students that
many everyday writing
tasks require parallelism.
For example, items listed
on a résumé should be in
parallel form.

Parallel structure is especially important for emphasizing the relationships in *paired items*, *comparisons*, and *items in a series*.

Paired Items

Use parallel structure when you connect ideas with a **coordinating conjunction**—*and*, *but*, *for*, *nor*, *or*, *so*, and *yet*.

> George believes in doing a good job and minding his own business.
> You can pay me now or pay me later.

Also use parallel structure for paired items joined by *both . . . and*, *not only . . . but also*, *either . . . or*, *neither . . . nor*, and *rather . . . than*.

> Jan is both artistically talented and mechanically inclined.
> The group's new recording not only has a dance beat but also has good lyrics.
> I'd rather eat one worm by itself than eat ten with ice cream.

Items in a Series

Teaching Tip
Refer students to 30A for
more on punctuating
items in a series.

Use parallel structure for items in a series—words, phrases, or clauses. (Be sure to use commas to separate three or more items in a series.)

> Every Wednesday I have English, math, and psychology. (Three words)
> Increased demand, high factory output, and a strong dollar all help the economy. (Three phrases)
> She is a champion because she stays in excellent physical condition, puts in long hours of practice, and has an intense desire to win. (Three clauses)

Items in a List or in an Outline

Use parallel structure for items in a numbered or bulleted list.

> There are three reasons to open an Individual Retirement Account (IRA):
> 1. To save money
> 2. To pay fewer taxes
> 3. To be able to retire

Use parallel structure for the elements in an outline.

    A. Basic types of rocks

        1. Igneous

        2. Sedimentary

        3. Metamorphic

● **Practice 18-2**

Fill in the blanks in the following sentences with parallel words, phrases, or clauses of your own that make sense in context.

    Example: At the lake, we can ___*go for a swim*___, ___*paddle a canoe*___,

    and ___*play volleyball*___.

    Answers will vary.

1. When I get too little sleep, I am _____, _____,

    and _____.

2. I am good at _____ but not at _____.

3. My ideal vacation would be _____ and _____.

4. I define success not only as _____ but also as

    _____.

5. I use my computer for both _____ and _____.

6. I like _____ and _____.

7. You need three qualities to succeed at college: _____,

    _____, and _____.

8. I enjoy not only _____ but also _____.

9. I would rather _____ than _____.

10. Classical music _____, but jazz _____.

Focus on Writing: *Flashback*

Look back at your response to the Focus on Writing activity on page 273. On a separate sheet of paper, write two new sentences that you could add to your response, and then revise them as follows: (1) In one sentence, use a coordinating conjunction, such as *and* or *but*; (2) in a second sentence, present items in a series. When you have finished, check to make sure that you have used parallel structure in each sentence and that you have punctuated correctly.

Focus on Writing: *Revising and Editing*

Look back at your response to the Focus on Writing activity on page 273, and try to add one or more of the sentences you wrote for the Flashback activity above. Then, revise your work, correcting faulty parallelism and adding parallel constructions to highlight relationships or increase clarity. When you are finished, do the same for another assignment you are currently working on.

Chapter Review

Editing Practice

Read the following student essay, which contains some elements that are not parallel. Identify the sentences you think need to be corrected, and make the changes required to achieve parallelism. Add punctuation as needed. The first error has been edited for you.   *Answers will vary.*

Questionable Heroes

The heroes we learn about in school are usually historical figures. We look up to them for their outstanding achievements／and their *for* personal qualities ~~are also admired.~~ Our heroes include our country's first leaders, American colonists, and soldiers ~~who were thought of as~~ *brave* ~~brave.~~ After the terrorist attacks on September 11, 2001, we realized that anyone who helps in a disaster can also be a hero. However,

some people confuse heroes with ~~people who are~~ celebrities. It is
much harder to be a hero than ~~becoming~~ [to be] famous. For example, many
entertainers and ~~people who play professional sports~~ [athletes] are famous, but
they ~~should~~ not ~~be thought of as~~ [are] heroes.

To be a real hero, a person should be a model for others. A
genuine hero like George Washington was brave and ~~showed~~ [determined]
~~determination~~ throughout his life. Soldiers often risk their lives to save [or even die]
other people~~, and sometimes death even results.~~ During the terrorist
attacks of September 11, 2001, heroic firefighters climbed up the
stairs of the burning World Trade Center buildings, and many lives ~~were~~ [saved]
~~able to be saved.~~ Even the thousands of Americans who pitched in to
help during the cleanup can be thought of as heroes. They brought
supplies to the rescue workers, ~~and in addition, food was brought.~~ [and food]

On the other hand, ~~to be~~ famous ~~does~~ [people are] not always ~~mean that~~
~~people are~~ heroes. Some athletes, for example, get a lot of attention for
their misbehavior. Sometimes they fight with their coaches, the media [curse at]
~~may be cursed at,~~ drug tests ~~may be failed,~~ [fail] and ~~they may~~ even get
arrested. Similarly, some entertainers get news coverage for their worst
behavior. Sometimes they get married many times, or very provocative [wear]
clothes ~~are worn by them.~~ Although sports superstars [and entertainment] can earn millions
of dollars, ~~and so can entertainers,~~ many parents do not want them to
be role models for their children.

Clearly, the image of the hero has changed over time. The heroes [and courageous]
of the past were dedicated leaders ~~and acted with courage.~~ Now, they
have often been replaced by superstars who are famous for all the
wrong reasons — for example, selfishness and ~~they cannot control their~~ [lack of self-control.]
~~own actions.~~ These people may be fascinating, but they are not
heroic.

Collaborative Activities

1. Working in a group, list three or four qualities that you associate with each word in the following pairs.

>Brothers/sisters
>
>Teachers/students
>
>Parents/children
>
>City/country
>
>Fast food/organic food
>
>Movies/TV shows
>
>Work/play

2. Write a compound sentence comparing each of the above pairs of words. Use a coordinating conjunction to join the clauses, and make sure each sentence uses clear parallel structure, mentions both words, and includes the qualities you listed for the words in Collaborative Activity 1.

3. Choose the three best sentences your group has written for Collaborative Activity 2. Assign one student from each group to write these sentences on the board so the entire class can read them. The class can then decide which sentences use parallelism most effectively.

Review Checklist: Using Parallelism

☐ Use matching words, phrases, clauses, and sentence structure to highlight similar items or ideas. (See 18A.)

☐ Use parallel structure with paired items. (See 18B.)

☐ Use parallel structure for items in a series. (See 18B.)

☐ Use parallel structure for items in a list and for the elements in an outline. (See 18B.)

Chapter 19

Using Words Effectively

On average, Americans read about five books per year; the French read seven, and Brazilians read less than two.

Using Specific Words

Specific words refer to particular people, places, things, ideas, or qualities; **general** words refer to entire classes or groups. Sentences that contain specific words are more precise and vivid—and often more memorable—than those that contain only general words. The following sentences use just general words.

Teaching Tip
Put a sentence on the board (for example, *The man was injured in an accident involving a shark*), and have students work as a team to make the sentence more specific and concrete. Asking students to write a news story about the sentence usually results in excellent paragraphs.

Sentences with General Words

While walking in the woods, I saw an <u>animal</u>.

<u>Someone</u> decided to run for Congress.

<u>Weapons</u> are responsible for many murders.

Denise bought new <u>clothes</u>.

I really enjoyed my <u>meal</u>.

Darrell had always wanted a <u>classic car</u>.

Specific words make the following revised sentences clearer and more precise.

Sentences with Specific Words

While walking in the woods, I saw a <u>baby skunk</u>.

<u>Rebecca</u> decided to run for Congress.

<u>Cheap imported handguns</u> are responsible for many murders.

Denise bought a new <u>blue dress</u>.

I really enjoyed my <u>pepperoni pizza with extra cheese</u>.

Darrell had always wanted a <u>black 1957 Chevy convertible</u>.

→ Focus on Writing

The picture on the opposite page shows a father reading to his children. Look at the picture, and then answer these questions. When you have children, how will you be involved in their education? If you already have children, what do you do now to help them? Discuss how your involvement could make a difference in their lives.

WORD POWER
aspire to strive toward an end
encourage to inspire with hope or confidence
nurture to nourish; to bring up

> **Highlight:
> Using Specific
> Words**
>
> One way to strengthen your writing is to avoid **utility words**—general words like *good*, *nice*, or *great*. Instead, take the time to think of more specific words. For example, when you say the ocean looked *pretty*, do you really mean that it *sparkled*, *glistened*, *rippled*, *foamed*, *surged*, or *billowed*?

Teaching Tip
Warn students that the synonyms they see listed in a thesaurus almost never have exactly the same meanings.

On the Web
For more practice, visit Exercise Central *at* <bedfordstmartins .com/focusonwriting>.

ESL Tip
Nonnative speakers often have trouble with adjective order. Explain why they should write *The tall, slender man drove away in a shiny new car.* Refer them to 29K.

● **Practice 19-1**

In the following passage, the writer describes a store in the town of Nameless, Tennessee. Underline the specific words in the passage that help you imagine the scene the writer describes. The first sentence has been done for you.

(1) The old store, lighted only by <u>three fifty-watt bulbs</u>, smelled of <u>coal oil</u> and <u>baking bread</u>. (2) In the middle of the <u>rectangular room</u>, where the <u>oak floor sagged a little</u>, stood an <u>iron stove</u>. (3) To the right was a <u>wooden table</u> with an <u>unfinished game of checkers</u> and a stool made from an <u>apple-tree stump</u>. (4) On shelves around the walls sat <u>earthen jugs</u> with <u>corncob stoppers</u>, a few <u>canned goods</u>, and some of the <u>two thousand old clocks and clockworks</u> Thurmond Watts owned. (5) Only one was ticking; the others he just looked at.

—William Least Heat-Moon, *Blue Highways*

● **Practice 19-2**

For each of the five general words below, write a more specific word. Then, on a separate sheet of paper, use the more specific word in a sentence.

Example: child *six-year-old*

All through dinner, my six-year-old chattered excitedly about his first

day of school.

Answers will vary.

1. emotion _____

2. building _____

3. said _____

4. animal _____

5. went _____

● **Practice 19-3**

The following job-application letter uses general words. On a separate sheet
of paper, rewrite the paragraph, substituting specific words for the general
words of the original and adding details where necessary. Start by making
the first sentence, which identifies the job, more specific (for example, "I
would like to apply for the sales position you advertised on March 15 in the
Post"). Then, add specific information about your background and qualifications, expanding the original paragraph into a three-paragraph letter.
Answers will vary.

I would like to apply for the position you advertised in today's paper.
I graduated from high school and am currently attending college. I have
taken several courses that have prepared me for the duties the position
requires. I also have several personal qualities that I think you would
find useful in a person holding this position. In addition, I have had certain experiences that qualify me for such a job. I would appreciate the
opportunity to meet with you to discuss your needs as an employer.
Thank you.

Focus on Writing: *Flashback*

Look back at your response to the Focus on Writing activity on page 281.
Find several general words, and write those words on a separate sheet of
paper. For each word, substitute another word that is more specific.

19b Using Concise Language

Concise writing says what it has to say in as few words as possible. Too often,
writers use words and phrases that add nothing to a sentence's meaning. A
good way to test a sentence for these words is to see if crossing them out
changes the sentence's meaning. If the sentence's meaning does not change,
you can assume that the words you crossed out are unnecessary.

~~It is clear that the~~ *The* United States was not ready to fight World War II.

~~In order to~~ *To* follow the plot, you must make an outline.

Sometimes, you can replace several unnecessary words with a single word.

                           Because
~~Due to the fact that~~ I was tired, I missed my first class.

Highlight: Using Concise Language

The following wordy phrases add nothing to a sentence. You can usually delete or condense them with no loss of meaning.

Wordy	Concise
It is clear that	(delete)
It is a fact that	(delete)
The reason is because	Because
The reason is that	Because
It is my opinion that	I think/I believe
Due to the fact that	Because
Despite the fact that	Although
At the present time	Today/Currently
At that time	Then
In most cases	Usually
In order to	To
In the final analysis	Finally
Subsequent to	After

Unnecessary repetition—saying the same thing twice for no reason—can also make your writing wordy. When you revise, delete repeated words and phrases that add nothing to your sentences.

My instructor told me the book was ~~old fashioned and~~ outdated. (An old-fashioned book *is* outdated.)

The ~~terrible~~ tragedy of the fire could have been avoided. (A tragedy is *always* terrible.)

● **Practice 19-4**

To make the following sentences more concise, delete or condense wordy expressions, and eliminate any unnecessary repetition.

                                              Although
Example: ~~Despite the fact that~~ people buy used cars whenever they

need ~~or have a requirement for~~ them, many do not know how to choose

a good car.   *Answers will vary.*

Teaching Tip
Encourage students to avoid flowery language and complicated sentences. Good writing is clear and concise.

(1) ~~In order to~~ ^{To} become an informed/~~knowledgeable~~ used-car buyer, the first thing a person should do is to look on the Internet and in the local newspapers ~~in the area~~ to get an idea of the prices. (2) ~~As a matter of fact, another~~ ^{Another} good source of information is a consumer magazine that may have a ~~consumer's~~ buyer's guide for used cars. (3) When first seeing ~~and inspecting~~ the car, carefully search ~~and inspect thoroughly~~ for new paint that looks different from the paint in the surrounding area. (4) ~~The reason is that this~~ ^{This} sign could mean ~~or suggest~~ that the car has ~~experienced or~~ been in an accident. (5) ~~Look at and check~~ ^{Check} the engine for problems like broken wires, cracked hoses, and leaks. (6) If, when you start the car, gray smoke keeps coming ~~and does not stop coming~~ from the exhaust pipe, do not buy the car. (7) Push down suddenly, ~~all at once,~~ on the accelerator while the car is running, and see ~~and observe~~ if the car hesitates. (8) While on a straight and level road, check the steering by letting go ~~and taking your hands off~~ of the steering wheel to see if the car keeps going straight ahead ~~without going from side to side.~~ (9) Even if there does not seem to be anything wrong with the car, take ~~and drive~~ it to a ~~car~~ mechanic you trust to inspect it ~~and give it a close look.~~ (10) If the owner refuses to allow you to ~~take~~ ^{do this,} ~~it to a mechanic, the very best thing to do at that time is to~~ leave and start looking for another car.

19c   Avoiding Slang

Slang is nonstandard language that calls attention to itself. It is usually associated with a particular social group—musicians, computer users, or teenagers, for example. Often, it is used for emphasis or to produce a surprising
or original effect. Because it is very informal, slang has no place in your
college writing.

> *easy*
> My psychology exam was really ~~sweet~~.
>
> *relax* ^
> On the weekends, I like to ~~chill~~ and watch old movies on TV.
>   ^

If you have any question about whether a term is slang or not, look it up
in a dictionary. If the term is identified as *slang* or *informal*, find a more suitable term.

● Practice 19-5

Edit the following sentences, replacing the slang expressions with clearer,
more precise words and phrases.

> *yelled at me*
> **Example:**   My father ~~lost it~~ when I told him I crashed the car.
>   ^

1. Whenever I get bummed, I go outside and jog.

2. Tonight I'll have to leave by 11 because I'm wiped out.

3. I'm not into movies or television.

4. Whenever we get into an argument, my boyfriend knows how to push
   my buttons.

5. I really lucked out when I got this job.

Focus on Writing: *Flashback*

Look back at your response to the Focus on Writing activity on page 281.
See if any sentences contain slang. If they do, replace the slang terms
with more suitable words or phrases.

19d

Avoiding Clichés

Clichés are expressions—such as "easier said than done" and "last but not least"—that have been used so often they have lost their meaning. These worn-out expressions do little to create interest; in fact, they may even get in the way of communication.

When you identify a cliché in your writing, replace it with a direct statement—or, if possible, a fresher expression.

Cliché   When school was over, she felt ~~free as a bird~~.

                                            seriously ill
Cliché   These days, you have to be ~~sick as a dog~~ before you are admitted to a hospital.

Highlight: Avoiding Clichés

Here are examples of some clichés you should avoid in your writing.

better late than never	hit the nail on the head
beyond a shadow of a doubt	pass the buck
break the ice	sadder but wiser
busy as a bee	sink or swim
cold, hard facts	the bottom line
face the music	tried and true
give 110 percent	wake up and smell the coffee
happy as a clam	water under the bridge
hard as a rock	what goes around comes around

 On the Web
For more practice, visit Exercise Central *at* <bedfordstmartins .com/focusonwriting>.

● Practice 19-6

Cross out any clichés in the following sentences, and either substitute a fresher expression or restate the idea more directly.

                                              free of financial worries
Example: Lottery winners often think they will be ~~on easy street~~ for the rest of their lives.
Answers will vary.

(1) Many people think that a million-dollar lottery jackpot allows the
                              long hours   *a comfortable life.*
winner to stop working ~~like a dog~~ and start living ~~high on the hog.~~

(2) ~~All things considered, however,~~ *In fact,* the reality for lottery winners is quite different. (3) For one thing, lottery winners who ~~hit the jackpot~~ *win big prizes* do not always receive their winnings all at once; instead, payments—for example, $50,000—can be spread out over twenty years. (4) Of that $50,000 a year, close to $20,000 goes to taxes and anything else the ~~lucky~~ *winner* ~~stiff~~ owes the government, such as student loans. (5) Next come relatives and friends ~~with their hands out,~~ *who ask for money,* leaving winners ~~between a rock and a hard place.~~ *with difficult choices to make.* (6) They can either ~~cough up~~ *give* gifts and loans or ~~wave bye-bye to~~ *lose the friendship of* many of their loved ones. (7) ~~Adding insult to injury,~~ *Even worse,* many lottery winners have lost their jobs because employers thought that once they were "millionaires," they no longer needed to draw a salary. (8) Many lottery winners wind up ~~way over their heads~~ *serious* in debt within a few years. (9) ~~In their hour of need,~~ *faced with financial difficulties,* many might like to sell their future payments to companies that offer lump-sum payments of forty to forty-five cents on the dollar. (10) This is ~~easier said than done,~~ *usually impossible,* however, because most state lotteries do not allow winners to sell their winnings.

Focus on Writing: *Flashback*

Look back at your response to the Focus on Writing activity on page 281. If you have used any clichés, circle them. Then, either replace each cliché with a more direct statement, or think of a more original way of expressing the idea.

19e

Using Similes and Metaphors

A **simile** is a comparison of two unlike things that uses *like* or *as.*

His arm hung at his side <u>like</u> a broken branch.

He was <u>as</u> content <u>as</u> a cat napping on a windowsill.

Teaching Tip
Point out that both
similes and metaphors
compare two *dissimilar*
things. If the items being
compared are *alike*, the
result is a statement of
fact (*Your boat is like my
boat*) and is not a simile
or a metaphor.

Teaching Tip
Warn students not to
use too many similes or
metaphors. Although a
few can enhance a piece
of writing, too many are
distracting.

Teaching Tip
Ask students to write
a paragraph about an
experience that was
important to them. Then,
have them exchange
papers with the person
next to them. Each
student should add at
least one simile and
one metaphor to the
other student's para-
graph. Discuss the
additions with the class.

A **metaphor** is a comparison of two unlike things that does *not* use *like* or *as*.

Invaders from another world, the dandelions conquered my garden.

He was a beast of burden, hauling cement from the mixer to the building site.

The force of similes and metaphors comes from the surprise of seeing two seemingly unlike things being compared and, as a result, seeing a hidden or unnoticed similarity between them. Used in moderation, similes and metaphors can make your writing more lively and more interesting.

● **Practice 19-7**

Use your imagination to complete each of the following items by creating three original similes.

Example: A boring class is like _toast without jam._

a four-hour movie.

a bedtime story.

Answers will vary.

1. A good friend is like _____

_____

_____

2. A thunderstorm is like _____

_____

_____

3. A workout at the gym is like _____

_____

_____

● **Practice 19-8**

Think of a person you know well. Using that person as your subject, fill in each of the following blanks to create metaphors. Try to complete each metaphor with more than a single word, as in the example.

Example: If _my baby sister_ were an animal, _she_ would be

a curious little kitten.

Answers will vary.

1. If _____ were a musical instrument, ____ would be _____

   _____

2. If _____ were a food, ____ would be _____

   _____

3. If _____ were a means of transportation, ____ would be _____

   _____

4. If _____ were a natural phenomenon, ____ would be _____

   _____

5. If _____ were a toy, ____ would be _____

   _____

Focus on Writing: *Flashback*

Look back at your response to the Focus on Writing activity on page 281. Find two sentences that could be enriched with a simile or a metaphor. Rewrite these two sentences, adding a simile to one sentence and a metaphor to the other.

19f   Avoiding Sexist Language

Sexist language refers to men and women in insulting terms. Sexist language is not just words like *stud* or *babe*, which many people find objectionable. It can also be words or phrases that unnecessarily call attention to gender or that suggest a job or profession is held only by a man (or only by a woman) when it actually is not.

You can avoid sexist language by being sensitive and using a little common sense. There is always an acceptable nonsexist alternative for a sexist term.

Sexist	*Nonsexist*
man, mankind	humanity, humankind, the human race
businessman	executive, business person
fireman, policeman, mailman	firefighter, police officer, letter carrier

Teaching Tip
Refer students to 27E
for more on subjects like
everyone (indefinite
pronoun antecedents).

Sexist	Nonsexist
male nurse, woman engineer	nurse, engineer
congressman	member of Congress, representative
stewardess, steward	flight attendant
man and wife	man and woman, husband and wife
manmade	synthetic
chairman	chair, chairperson
anchorwoman, anchorman	anchor
actor, actress	actor

Highlight: Avoiding Sexist Language

Do not use *he* when your subject could be either male or female.

Everyone should complete his assignment by next week.

You can correct this problem in three ways:

● *Use he or she or his or her.*

Everyone should complete his or her assignments by next week.

● *Use plural forms.*

Students should complete their assignments by next week.

● *Eliminate the pronoun.*

Everyone should complete the assignment by next week.

On the Web
For more practice, visit
Exercise Central *at*
<bedfordstmartins
.com/focusonwriting>.

● **Practice 19-9**

Edit the following sentences to eliminate sexist language. *Answers will vary.*

Example: A doctor should be honest with his patients. *or her (or omit "his")*

1. Many people today would like to see more ~~policemen~~ *police officers* patrolling the streets.

2. The attorneys representing the plaintiff are Geraldo Diaz and ~~Mrs.~~ Barbara Wilkerson.

3. ~~Every soldier~~ *All the soldiers* picked up ~~his~~ *their* weapons.

4. Chris Fox is the ~~female~~ mayor of Port London, Maine.

5. Travel to other planets will be a significant step for ~~man.~~ *humanity.*

Focus on Writing: *Flashback*

Look back at your response to the Focus on Writing activity on page 281. Have you used any words or phrases that unnecessarily call attention to gender? Have you used *he* when your subject could be either male or female? Cross out any sexist language, and substitute acceptable nonsexist alternatives.

Focus on Writing: *Revising and Editing*

Look back at your response to the Focus on Writing activity on page 281. Revise the paragraph, making sure your language is as specific as possible and that you have not used clichés or sexist expressions. Be sure to incorporate the revisions you made in this chapter's Flashback activities. When you have finished, revise another writing assignment you are currently working on.

Chapter Review

Editing Practice

Read the following student essay carefully, and then revise it. Make sure that your revision is concise, uses specific words, and includes no slang, sexist language, or clichés. Add an occasional simile or metaphor to increase interest. The first sentence has been edited for you.   *Answers will vary.*

Unexpected Discoveries

When we hear the word "accident," we think of bad things, *like dented fenders and broken glass.* But accidents can be ~~good~~, *lucky* too. Modern science has made important advances as a result of lucky accidents. ~~It is a fact that a~~ scientist *A* sometimes works ~~like a dog~~ *hard* for years in ~~his~~ *the* laboratory, only to make *an unexpected* ~~a weird~~ discovery ~~because of a mistake.~~ .

The most famous example of a ~~good,~~ beneficial accident is the discovery of penicillin. A scientist, Alexander Fleming, had seen many soldiers die of infections after they were wounded in World War I.

In fact,
~~All things considered,~~ many more soldiers died ~~due to the fact that~~ *from*
infections ~~occurred~~ than from wounds. Fleming wanted to find a drug
cure
that could ~~put an end to~~ these ~~terrible,~~ fatal infections. One day in
1928, Fleming went on vacation, leaving a pile of dishes in the lab
Luckily,
sink. ~~As luck would have it,~~ he had been growing bacteria in those
dishes. When he came back, he noticed that one of the dishes looked
Strangely,
moldy. ~~What was strange was that~~ near the mold, the bacteria were
realized
dead ~~as a doornail. It was crystal clear to~~ Fleming that the mold
had killed the bacteria. He had discovered penicillin, the first
antibiotic.

Everyone has heard the name "Goodyear." ~~It was~~ Charles Goodyear
~~who~~ made a discovery that ~~changed and~~ revolutionized the rubber
for years.
industry and made our modern tires last ~~so long.~~ In the early
melted
nineteenth century, rubber products ~~became thin and runny~~ in hot
weather and cracked in cold weather. One day in 1839, Goodyear
accidentally dropped some rubber mixed with sulfur on a hot stove.
It ~~changed color and~~ turned black, but after being cooled, it could be
, like a rubber band,
stretched/ and ~~it~~ would return to its original size and shape. This kind
of rubber is now used in tires and in many other products.
product
Another ~~thing~~ was discovered because of a lab accident involving
rubber. In 1953, Patsy Sherman, a ~~female~~ chemist for the 3M company,
was trying to find a new type of rubber. She created a batch of ~~man-made,~~
synthetic liquid rubber. Some of the liquid accidentally spilled onto a
lab assistant's new white canvas sneaker. According to one story, her
assistant used everything ~~but the kitchen sink~~ to clean the shoe, but
After a few weeks,
nothing worked. ~~Over time,~~ the rest of the shoe became dirty, but the
part where the spill had hit was still clean ~~as a whistle.~~ Sherman
a chemical
realized that she had found ~~something~~ that could actually keep fabrics
repelling
clean by ~~doing a number on~~ dirt. The 3M company named this new
product Scotchguard.

             Scientists   *their*

~~A scientist~~ can be clumsy and sloppy, but sometimes ~~his~~ mistakes

lead to ~~great and~~ significant discoveries. Penicillin, long-lasting tires,

and Scotchguard are examples of successful products that were the

result of scientific accidents.

Collaborative Activities

1. Photocopy two or three paragraphs of description from a romance novel, a western novel, or a mystery novel, and bring your paragraphs to class. Working in a group, choose one paragraph that seems to need clearer, more specific language.

2. As a group, revise the paragraph you chose for Collaborative Activity 1, making it as clear and specific as possible and eliminating any clichés or sexist language.

3. Exchange your revised paragraph from Collaborative Activity 2 with the paragraph revised by another group, and check the other group's work. Make any additional changes you think your paragraph needs.

Review Checklist:
Using Words Effectively

☐ Use specific words that convey your ideas clearly and precisely. (See 19A.)

☐ Use concise language that says what it has to say in the fewest possible words. (See 19B.)

☐ Avoid slang. (See 19C.)

☐ Avoid clichés. (See 19D.)

☐ Whenever possible, use similes and metaphors to make your writing more lively and more interesting. (See 19E.)

☐ Avoid sexist language. (See 19F.)

Editing Practice

Some of the following sentences have problems with parallelism and ineffective word use. Others are pairs of simple sentences that can be combined with coordinating conjunctions, semicolons, transitional words or phrases, subordinating conjunctions, or relative pronouns. Identify the problems, and correct them.   *Answers will vary.*

   Because many parents infants   *, they*

1. ~~Many women~~ of ~~infant children~~ work outside the home. ~~They~~ hire babysitters or bring their babies to day-care centers.

                                  realized what he had done

2. After Donald got out of jail, he ~~was sadder but wiser~~ and was determined never to break the law again.

                          , but

3. I left work at 5:00 p.m. I was late getting home because of a bad accident on I-70.

                                                      ; however, others

4. Some parents feel that their children should attend school. ~~Others~~ feel just as strongly that they should be taught at home.

   When volunteers   *, the*

5. ~~Volunteers~~ bring pets to hospitals and nursing homes. ~~The~~ patients benefit both physically and emotionally.

   Although it   *,*

6. ~~It~~ was very hot. Yosemite National Park was very crowded.

                                        until

7. Caroline lived in an apartment with her parents. ~~Then~~ she got married.

                             , which hit in October 2005,

8. Hurricane Wilma devastated some parts of Florida. ~~It hit in October 2005.~~

9. On the computer, it is possible to communicate by email, to do research, *to check* and spelling ~~can be checked.~~

   Usually,   *too much,*

10. ~~In most cases,~~ people gain weight because they eat ~~like horses,~~ even though they deny it.

Teaching Tip
You can use this exercise to warm students up for the multi-error editing practice that follows.

Editing Practice: Essay

Read the following student essay, which contains problems with sentence variety, parallelism, and word use. It also contains pairs of simple sentences that can be combined. Identify the sentences that need to be corrected, and edit them. The first editing change has been made for you.
Answers will vary.

Dangerous Animals

Lately, a number of people have been attacked and sometimes ~~they have been~~ killed by wild animals. Alligators, bears, and even *large* cats ~~that are large~~ have carried out these attacks. *Although there* ~~There~~ is no guarantee of safety~~/~~ ~~There are actions that~~ people can take *steps* to make these attacks less likely.

During the past fifty years, alligators have attacked more than 350 people in Florida~~/~~ *, and twenty-five* ~~Twenty-five~~ people have been killed. Three women were killed in the spring of 2006~~/~~ *, their* ~~Their~~ bodies ~~were~~ found near canals or ponds. Most alligator attacks happen in water, where these animals can move quickly. The most dangerous time is ~~when it is getting dark.~~ *dusk.* *Because this* ~~This~~ is when alligators are usually looking for food~~/~~ *, it* ~~It~~ is not the time to swim in alligator-infested waters. People take a big risk when they clean fish and then throw away the unwanted parts~~/~~ *because alligators* ~~Alligators~~ may be attracted by these remains. Golfers should not put their feet or hands into ponds to retrieve balls because alligators are attracted by motion~~/~~ *and* ~~They~~ can pull a golfer into the water. If an alligator attacks a golfer, the best thing he *or she* can do is make noise. *If the* ~~The~~ alligator believes that its victim is larger and more powerful than it expected~~/~~ *, it* ~~It~~ may let the victim go.

Bears ~~Wild bears~~ have also ~~been tough to deal with.~~ *caused problems.* Avoiding these animals is the best strategy. Sometimes, however, this is not ~~a piece of cake,~~ *easy,* because bears may live in *populated* ~~some~~ areas ~~that overlap neighborhoods where people live.~~ *In the wild, hikers* ~~Hikers~~ and campers sometimes encounter bears ~~in the wild.~~ To keep safe from bears, hikers should keep certain guidelines in mind. First, it is important not to surprise a bear or make it feel threatened. ~~It is also important not to~~ *Second, they should not* come between a mother bear and ~~its~~ *her* cubs ~~due to the fact that~~ *because* mother bears will attack someone who seems to threaten their ~~babies.~~ *cubs* Making a lot of noise while moving through bear country is a good way to avoid *surprising*

~~taking~~ this dangerous animal ~~by surprise.~~ Walking backwards slowly is

, which   *If the*

better than running away. ~~This~~ only encourages the bear to attack. ~~The~~

attacks, the

bear ~~may attack. The~~ best thing to do is to curl up on the ground,

and pretend

~~Pretending~~ to be dead ~~is good.~~

Large cats are sometimes reported in certain areas. They may be

, or they   *Usually*

escaped pets, ~~They~~ may be wild animals. ~~These cats are usually~~

, these cats

cougars, ~~They~~ can be dangerous to livestock and occasionally to

Also

humans. ~~Cougars are also~~ called mountain lions, panthers, or pumas,

cougars   *Like bears, they*

~~They~~ eat raccoons and deer. ~~Cougars, like bears,~~ chase whatever runs

, and joggers

away. In the West, mountain bikers ~~and~~ hikers are ~~endangered. Joggers~~

since

are also at risk. Hiking alone is especially dangerous. ~~Since~~ cougars

attack only hikers without companions. People who are attacked by a

cougar can shout and make themselves look bigger by putting up their

; as a result, the

hands or opening their coats. ~~The~~ cougar may be frightened and run

Because cougars   *, people*

away. ~~Cougars~~ are nocturnal. ~~People~~ should keep their pets and small

livestock protected at night.

beings   *their*

Wild animals can be a danger to ~~a~~ human ~~being~~ and to ~~his or her~~

pets. Alligators, bears, and cougars have injured and killed people in

recent years. However, people can protect themselves by knowing

about the habits of these animals.

Unit Five

Solving Common Sentence Problems

Chapter 20

Run-Ons

According to the Department of Health and Human Services, 16 percent of American young people (over nine million six- to nineteen-year-olds) are overweight.

Recognizing Run-Ons

A **sentence** consists of at least one independent clause—one subject and one verb.

> College costs are rising.

A **run-on** is an error that occurs when two sentences are joined incorrectly. There are two kinds of run-ons: *fused sentences* and *comma splices*.

A **fused sentence** occurs when two sentences are joined without any punctuation.

WORD POWER
fused melted together

Fused sentence   [College costs are rising] [many students are worried.]

A **comma splice** occurs when two sentences are joined with just a comma.

WORD POWER
splice to join together at the ends

Comma splice   [College costs are rising], [many students are worried.]

**Highlight:
Grammar
Checkers**

Computer grammar checkers sometimes identify a long sentence as a run-on. However, a long sentence can be correct. Before you make any changes, be sure you have actually made an error.

→ Focus on Writing

The picture on the opposite page shows chocolate-glazed donuts, a popular snack food. Many people believe such foods are to blame for our nation's overweight children. Why do you think so many American children are overweight? What do you think can be done about this problem? Look at the picture, and then try to answer these questions.

WORD POWER
trans-fats (trans fatty acids) unhealthy solid fats
obese extremely overweight
sedentary accustomed to sitting or getting little exercise

● **Practice 20-1**

Some of the sentences below are correct, but others are fused sentences or comma splices. In the blank after each sentence, write *C* if the sentence is correct, *CS* if it is a comma splice, and *FS* if it is a fused sentence.

> **Example:** Cynthia has new jeans, they look good on her. __CS__

1. My neighborhood is never quiet it is even noisy at midnight. __FS__

2. Some professional Italian soccer clubs have been accused of fixing games, the team that won the 2006 World Cup was not accused. __CS__

3. Many people in big cities ride the subway, it is a fast way to get to work. __CS__

4. Sonia hung the mirror in the hall, near the coats and shoes. __C__

5. I like to walk in the park, it is always full of people playing soccer and kick-ball. __CS__

6. The movie isn't rated yet maybe it isn't suitable for children. __FS__

7. In 2006, Merriam-Webster's dictionary added the word *google*. __C__

8. My favorite meal is fried chicken, black-eyed peas, and greens, both of my grandmothers are from the South. __CS__

9. Heather took a home repair course she wanted to learn basic carpentry. __FS__

10. I had to take my cat to the veterinarian, he was in a lot of pain. __CS__

● **Practice 20-2**

Teaching Tip
Tell students that a comma can join two sentences only when it is followed by a coordinating conjunction. (See 15A.)

Some of the sentences in the following passage are correct, but others are fused sentences or comma splices. In the blank after each sentence, write *C* if the sentence is correct, *CS* if it is a comma splice, and *FS* if it is a fused sentence.

Example: "Race movies" had all-black casts, they were intended for African-American audiences. _CS_

On the Web
For more practice, visit
Exercise Central at
<bedfordstmartins
.com/focusonwriting>.

(1) In 1919, African-American director Oscar Micheaux filmed *Within Our Gates* this movie examined black life in Chicago. _FS_ (2) The film included scenes of violence, it even depicted two lynchings. _CS_ (3) It also treated interracial relationships white censors banned it. _FS_ (4) Race riots had occurred in Chicago that year, the censors feared violence. _CS_ (5) Micheaux appealed to the censors they agreed to the film's release in Chicago. _FS_ (6) The movie was shown, twelve hundred feet of film were omitted. _CS_ (7) Micheaux later made many low-budget movies, but few survive today. _C_ (8) Some are musicals others are melodramas. _FS_ (9) Few are socially conscious films like *Within Our Gates*. _C_ (10) One, *Body and Soul*, was Paul Robeson's first film. _C_ (11) Micheaux died in 1951. _C_ (12) In 1990, an uncut version of *Within Our Gates* was discovered in Madrid, it was shown in Chicago for the first time in 1992. _CS_

Teaching Tip
Let students practice reading aloud passages from which you have deleted all end punctuation. Point out how their voices usually stop at the end of a sentence even when it contains no punctuation.

Focus on Writing: *Flashback*

Look back at your response to the Focus on Writing activity on page 301. Do you see any run-ons? If so, underline them.

20b   Correcting Run-Ons

You can correct run-ons in five ways.

1. *Use a period to create two separate sentences.*

   College costs are rising. Many students are worried.

2. *Use a coordinating conjunction (*and, but, or, nor, for, so, *or* yet*)*
   to connect ideas.

   College costs are rising, and many students are worried.

3. *Use a semicolon to connect ideas.*

   College costs are rising; many students are worried.

4. *Use a semicolon followed by a transitional word or phrase to*
   connect ideas.

   College costs are rising; as a result, many students are worried.

5. *Use a dependent word (*although, because, when, *and so on) to*
   connect ideas.

   Because college costs are rising, many students are worried.

---

1. **Use a period to create two separate sentences.** Be sure each sentence begins with a capital letter and ends with a period.

Incorrect **(fused sentence)**	Gas prices are very high some people are buying hybrid cars.
Incorrect **(comma splice)**	Gas prices are very high, some people are buying hybrid cars.
Correct	Gas prices are very high. Some people are buying hybrid cars. (two separate sentences)

● Practice 20-3

Correct each of the following run-ons by using a period to create two separate sentences. Be sure both of your sentences begin with a capital letter and end with a period.

Example: Hurricane Katrina hit the Gulf Coast hard, ~~many~~ *. Many* people lost everything.

1. Hurricane Katrina destroyed many homes in New Orleans *. It* ~~it~~ destroyed many businesses, too.

2. The city was flooded, ~~high~~ *. High* winds damaged the Mississippi and Alabama coasts.

3. Americans watched the terrible scenes, ~~hundreds~~ *. Hundreds* died waiting for rescuers.

4. Many police officers, soldiers, and firefighters acted heroically, ~~ordinary~~ *. Ordinary* citizens also took action.

5. Residents of flooded communities vowed to return ~~they~~ *. They* knew it would not be easy.

Teaching Tip
Refer students to 15A for more on connecting ideas with a coordinating conjunction.

2. **Use a coordinating conjunction to connect ideas.** If you want to indicate a particular relationship between ideas—for example, cause and effect or contrast—you can connect two independent clauses with a coordinating conjunction (*and, but, or, nor, for, so,* or *yet*) that makes this relationship clear. Always place a comma before the coordinating conjunction.

Incorrect (fused sentence)	Some schools require students to wear uniforms other schools do not.
Incorrect (comma splice)	Some schools require students to wear uniforms, other schools do not.
Correct	Some schools require students to wear uniforms, but other schools do not. (clauses connected with the coordinating conjunction *but,* preceded by a comma)

● **Practice 20-4**

Correct each of the following run-ons by using a coordinating conjunction (*and, but, or, nor, for, so,* or *yet*) to connect ideas. Be sure to put a comma before each coordinating conjunction.

Example: Many TV shows focus on war *, but* some are more realistic than others.

1. Right after World War II, some television programs showed actual
   and
   scenes of war, Victory at Sea and The Big Picture were two of those
   ^
   programs.

2. *Hogan's Heroes* was a 1960s comedy set in a German prisoner-of-war
   , so
   camp this show was bound to be very unrealistic.
   ^

3. In the 1970s, *MASH* depicted a Korean War medical unit, the show was
   yet
   ^
   really about the Vietnam War.

4. The 1980s drama *China Beach* was set in Vietnam, the main character
   and
   ^
   was an army nurse.

5. The Iraq War drama *Over There* was shown in 2005 it was cancelled after
   , but
   ^
   a few months.

3. **Use a semicolon to connect ideas.** If you want to indicate a particularly close connection — or a strong contrast — between two ideas, use a
semicolon.

Teaching Tip
Tell students that if
a period will not work
where the semicolon is,
then the semicolon is
probably incorrect. Refer
them to 15B for more on
connecting ideas with a
semicolon.

Incorrect (fused sentence)	Most professional basketball players go to college most professional baseball players do not.
Incorrect (comma splice)	Most professional basketball players go to college, most professional baseball players do not.
Correct	Most professional basketball players go to college; most professional baseball players do not. (clauses connected with a semicolon)

● **Practice 20-5**

Correct each of the following run-ons by using a semicolon to connect ideas.
Do not use a capital letter after the semicolon unless the word that follows it
is a proper noun.

Example: Many people in the United States have Hispanic back-
            ;
grounds/some of them have achieved great success.
         ^

1. New Mexico governor Bill Richardson has been a U.N. ambassador and
   ;
   a U.S. senator Nydia Velazquez is a U.S. representative.
   ^

2. Cesar Chavez was a leader of the United Farm Workers Union/Dolores
   ;
   ^
   Huerta also became known as a union leader.

3. Roberto Clemente was a professional baseball player;/Oscar de la Hoya achieved fame as a professional boxer.

4. Oscar Hijuelos wrote *The Mambo Kings Play Songs of Love*;/Julia Alvarez wrote *How the Garcia Girls Lost Their Accents*.

5. Luis Valdez is a noted playwright and film director; his plays include *Los Vendidos* and *The Zoot Suit*.

4. Use a semicolon followed by a transitional word or phrase to connect ideas. To indicate a specific relationship between two closely related ideas, add a transitional word or phrase after the semicolon.

Incorrect (fused sentence)	Finding a part-time job can be challenging sometimes it is even hard to find an unpaid internship.
Incorrect (comma splice)	Finding a part-time job can be challenging, sometimes it is even hard to find an unpaid internship.
Correct	Finding a part-time job can be challenging; in fact, sometimes it is even hard to find an unpaid internship. (clauses connected with a semicolon followed by the transitional phrase *in fact*)

Some Frequently Used Transitional Words and Phrases

as a result	moreover
finally	nevertheless
for example	now
for instance	still
however	therefore
in addition	thus
in fact	

For complete lists of transitional words and phrases, see 15C.

● Practice 20-6

Correct each of the following run-ons by using a semicolon, followed by the transitional word or phrase in parentheses, to connect ideas. Be sure to put a comma after the transitional word or phrase.

Example: High schools prepare students for college and jobs;/ *; in addition,* they can prepare students for life. (in addition)

1. High schools have always taught subjects like English and math many

   also teach personal finance and consumer education. (now)

   ; now, (margin annotation)

2. Personal-finance courses prepare students for life/students learn about

   money management, online banking, and identity theft. (for example)

   ; for example, (margin annotation)

3. Consumer-education courses can be very practical students can learn

   how to buy, finance, and insure a car. (for instance)

   ; for instance, (margin annotation)

4. Some high schools teach students how to avoid credit card debt/they

   teach students how to invest in stocks. (in addition)

   ; in addition, (margin annotation)

5. Academic subjects will always dominate the high school curriculum/

   courses focusing on practical life skills are becoming increasingly

   important. (however)

   ; however, (margin annotation)

Highlight: Connecting Ideas with Semicolons

Run-ons often occur when you use a transitional word or phrase to join two independent clauses *without also using a semicolon.*

Incorrect (fused sentence)	It is easy to download information from the Internet however it is not always easy to evaluate the information.
Incorrect (comma splice)	It is easy to download information from the Internet, however it is not always easy to evaluate the information.

To correct this kind of run-on, put a semicolon before the transitional word or phrase, and put a comma after it.

Correct	It is easy to download information from the Internet; however, it is not always easy to evaluate the information.

Teaching Tip
When covering this material, you may want to discuss independent and dependent clauses and explain the difference between coordination and subordination. If so, refer students to Chapters 15 and 16.

5. **Use a dependent word to connect ideas.** When one idea is dependent on another, you can connect the two ideas by adding a dependent word, such as *when, who, although,* or *because.*

Incorrect (fused sentence)	American union membership was high in the mid-twentieth century it has declined in recent years.

Incorrect (comma splice)	American union membership was high in the mid-twentieth century, it has declined in recent years.
Correct	<u>Although</u> American union membership was high in the mid-twentieth century, it has declined in recent years. (clauses connected with the dependent word *although*)
Correct	American union membership, <u>which</u> was high in the mid-twentieth century, has declined in recent years. (clauses connected with the dependent word *which*)

On the Web
For more practice, visit Exercise Central at <bedfordstmartins .com/focusonwriting>.

Some Frequently Used Dependent Words

after	if
although	instead
as	unless
because	until
before	when
even though	which
eventually	

For complete lists of dependent words, including **subordinating conjunctions** and **relative pronouns**, see 16B and 16C.

● Practice 20-7

Teaching Tip
You may also want to refer students to the lists of dependent words (subordinating conjunctions and relative pronouns) in Chapter 16.

Correct each of the following run-ons by adding a dependent word. Consult the list above to help you choose a logical dependent word. Be sure to add correct punctuation where necessary. *Answers may vary.*

Example: Harlem was a rural area until the nineteenth century *when* improved transportation linked it to lower Manhattan.

(1) *Although* Harlem was populated mostly by European immigrants at the turn of the last century, it saw an influx of African Americans beginning in 1910. (2) ~~This~~ *As this* migration from the South continued, Harlem became one of the largest African-American communities in the United States. (3) ~~Many~~ *After many* black artists and writers settled in Harlem during the

1920s/African-American art flowered. (4) This "Harlem Renaissance" was
an important era in American literary history it is not even mentioned
, although
in some textbooks. (5) ~~Scholars~~ recognize the great works of the Harlem
When scholars
Renaissance, they point to the writers Langston Hughes and Countee
Cullen and the artists Henry Tanner and Sargent Johnson. (6) Zora
After
Neale Hurston moved to Harlem from her native Florida in 1925, she
began work there on a book of African-American folklore. (7) Harlem
Because
was an exciting place in the 1920s people from all over the city went
there to listen to jazz and to dance. (8) ~~The~~ white playwright Eugene
When the
O'Neill went to Harlem to audition actors for his play *The Emperor Jones,*
he made an international star of the great Paul Robeson. (9) ~~Contemporary~~
Although contemporary
historians know about the Harlem Renaissance, its importance is still
not widely understood. (10) ~~The~~ Great Depression occurred in the
When the
1930s it led to the end of the Harlem Renaissance.

● **Practice 20-8**

Correct each of the run-ons below in one of the following four ways: by creating two separate sentences, by using a coordinating conjunction, by using
a semicolon, or by using a semicolon followed by a transitional word or phrase.
Be sure punctuation is correct. Remember to put a semicolon before, and a
comma after, each transitional word or phrase.

> **Example:** Some people believe chronic sex offenders should be given
>
> therapy; however, others believe they should be jailed indefinitely.
> *Answers will vary.*

1. Nursing offers job security and high pay; therefore, many people are
   choosing nursing as a career.

2. Anne Boleyn was the second wife of Henry VIII, her daughter was
   and
   Elizabeth I.

3. The Democratic Republic of the Congo was previously known as Zaire;
   before that it was the Belgian Congo.

4. Housewife Jean Nidetch started Weight Watchers in 1961 ^. She^ she sold the

company for $100 million in 1978.

5. Millions of Jews were killed during the Holocaust ^;^ in addition ^,^ Catholics,

Gypsies, homosexuals, and other "undesirables" were killed.

6. Sojourner Truth was born a slave ^, but^ she eventually became a leading abo-

litionist and feminist.

7. Japanese athletes now play various positions on American baseball

teams ^;^ at first ^,^ all the Japanese players were pitchers.

8. Oliver Wendell Holmes Jr. was a Supreme Court justice ^;^ his father was a

physician and writer.

9. Père Noël is the French name for Santa Claus ^;^ he is also known as

Father Christmas and St. Nicholas.

10. Latin is one classical language ^;^ Greek is another.

● Practice 20-9

Teaching Tip
Before students do
Practice 20-9, you may
want to review the five
ways of correcting
run-ons.

Correct each run-on in the following passage in the way that best indicates
the relationship between ideas. Be sure you use appropriate punctuation.

Example: Coney Island was once a bustling seaside resort ^, but^ it declined

considerably over the years.

Answers may vary.

(1) In the late nineteenth century, Coney Island was famous ^;^ in fact,
it was legendary. (2) It was always crowded, ^and^ people mailed hundreds of
thousands of postcards from the resort on some summer days. (3) Coney
Island was considered exotic and exciting ^; it^ ~~It~~ even had a hotel shaped
like an elephant. (4). ~~Some~~ *Although some* people saw Coney Island as seedy, others
thought it was a wonderful, magical place. (5) It had beaches, hotels,
racetracks, and a stadium ^;^ however ^,^ by the turn of the century, it was
best known for three amusement parks. (6) These parks were Luna
Park, Steeplechase, and Dreamland. (7) ~~Gaslight~~ *Even though gaslight* was still the norm in

New York, a million electric lights lit Luna Park. (8) *Although* Steeplechase offered many rides, its main attraction was a two-mile ride on mechanical horses. (9) At Dreamland, people could see a submarine; in addition, they could travel through an Eskimo village or visit Lilliputia, with its three hundred midgets. (10) Today, the old Coney Island no longer exists. (11) Fire destroyed Dreamland in 1911, *and* Luna Park burned down in 1946. (12) In 1964, Steeplechase closed. (13) The once-grand Coney Island is gone. *Still,* its beach and its boardwalk remain. (14) Its famous roller coaster, the Cyclone, still exists, *and* its giant Ferris wheel, the Wonder Wheel, keeps on turning. (15) Now, a ballpark has been built for a new minor league baseball team. *The* new team is called the Brooklyn Cyclones.

Focus on Writing: *Flashback*

Choose one run-on that you identified in the Flashback activity on page 303, and write two possible corrected versions.

Focus on Writing: *Revising and Editing*

Look back at your responses to the Focus on Writing activity on page 301 and the Flashback activities on page 303 and above. For each run-on you found, choose the revision that best conveys your meaning, and revise your Focus on Writing activity accordingly. If you do not find any run-ons in your own writing, work with a classmate to correct his or her writing, or edit the sentences you wrote for another assignment.

Chapter Review

Editing Practice: Paragraph

Read the following student paragraph, and revise it to eliminate run-ons. Correct each run-on in the way that best indicates the relationship between ideas. The first error has been corrected for you. *Answers may vary.*

Blood Sports

I used to play competitive sports, but I don't anymore. My parents
, *and*
encouraged my athletic career ^ they got me started in sports early on.
Between the ages of ten and seventeen, I was very active in martial
arts ⁄ I especially liked karate. As a young child, I competed in karate
^   , *and*
tournaments ^ I was injured frequently. I broke my nose three times ⁄
^
I also broke my hand twice and my foot once. As a competitor, I
;   ,
enjoyed the thrill of battle ⁄ however ^ I was always afraid of getting
^
;   ,
a serious injury. Eventually, I gave up karate ⁄ instead ^ I concentrated
^   ^
on football. Hard tackling and blocking were very important in
and
high school football, ^ I often hurt my opponents. I learned that
aggressiveness and pain are part of playing sports. I accept this as
.
part of the game ⁄ I just don't want to play anymore.
^

Editing Practice: Essay

Read the following student essay, and revise it by eliminating run-ons and correcting them to indicate the relationships between ideas. Be sure punctuation is correct. The first error has been corrected for you.

Answers may vary.

Dollars and Cents

but
Most of us handle money every day, ^ we rarely look closely at it or
think much about what goes into producing it. However, the U.S.
Treasury Department thinks a lot about our money. The Treasury
Department is always looking for ways to make money more interesting
. *It*
to consumers and collectors ⁄ ~~it~~ is also trying to make money harder for
^
counterfeiters to copy.

In the past few years, some major changes have been made to our

313

money. Between 1999 and 2008, the U.S. Mint will be issuing new
. The
quarters for every state ~~the~~ quarters are being issued in the order in
which the states ratified the Constitution. The design of each quarter
;
is different, each image represents a unique characteristic of the state
or its history. The coins are very popular, in fact, many people are
;
collecting sets for their children and grandchildren.

The Mint has also begun producing new nickels. The front of one
but
nickel still shows the head of Thomas Jefferson, our third president, it
;
is a new image. The back of the nickel features an American bison, the
bison is shown from the side. The new image of Jefferson also appears
. On
on another nickel, ~~on~~ the other side, this one shows the western
waters as first seen by the explorers Lewis and Clark. A third nickel
pictures a keelboat like the one that carried Lewis and Clark on their
;
expedition. The image on the other side of this nickel is not new it is
still the head of President Jefferson from the older coins.

The U.S. Treasury is always trying to stay ahead of counterfeiters.
In the spring of 2003, it printed the first colorful twenty-dollar
. These
bills ~~these~~ bills are printed in shades of blue, yellow, and peach
rather than the standard green and black. The picture of Andrew
Jackson is also larger and slightly off center. The type is bolder,
and
there is a blue eagle in the background. The Treasury plans to
change these bills every seven to ten years to make them harder to
. Eventually,
copy, ~~eventually~~ the fifty- and one hundred-dollar bills will also be
printed in color.
Although changes
~~Changes~~ in our money may be hard to get used to, they serve two
important purposes. They help to prevent counterfeiting and provide
us with attractive currency to collect — or to spend.

Collaborative Activities

1. Find an interesting paragraph in a newspaper or magazine article. Copy
it onto a separate sheet of paper, creating several run-ons.

ESL Tip
Nonnative speakers may
be no more likely to write
run-ons than the native
speakers in the class are.
For this reason, you can
feel comfortable calling
on nonnative students as
you review this unit.

Teaching Tip
Have students memorize
the five ways to correct
run-ons.

2. Exchange paragraphs with another student, and correct the run-ons in the paragraph you received. When you have finished, return the paragraph to the student who created it.

3. Evaluate the student's corrections to your paragraph, comparing it to the original newspaper or magazine paragraph. Pay particular attention to punctuation.

Review Checklist: Run-Ons

☐ A run-on is an error that occurs when two sentences are joined incorrectly. (See 20A.)

☐ A fused sentence occurs when two sentences are incorrectly joined without any punctuation. (See 20A.)

☐ A comma splice occurs when two sentences are incorrectly joined with just a comma. (See 20A.)

☐ Correct a run-on by using a period to create two separate sentences or by connecting ideas with a coordinating conjunction, a semicolon, a semicolon followed by a transitional word or phrase, or a dependent word. (See 20B.)

CLEAR CHANNEL

POM.
WONDERFUL
100% POMEGRANATE JUICE

It's been around for 5,000 year
Drink it and you might be too.

The antioxidant power of pomegranate juice.

In the produce department.

©2002 POM Wonderful, LLC. All rights

In ancient Egypt, the pomegranate
was believed to be a symbol of
fertility because of its many seeds.
Pharaohs would often request the
fruit to be buried with them after
their death.

Recognizing Fragments

A **sentence fragment** is an incomplete sentence. Every sentence must include at least one subject and one verb, and every sentence must express a complete thought. If a group of words does not do *all* these things, it is a fragment and not a sentence—even if it begins with a capital letter and ends with a period. The following is a complete sentence.

	s	v
Sentence	The <u>actors</u> in the play <u>were</u> very talented. (includes both a subject and a verb and expresses a complete thought)	

Because a sentence must have both a subject and a verb and express a complete thought, the following groups of words are not complete sentences; they are fragments.

Teaching Tip
Remind students that although they may see sentence fragments used in advertisements and other informal writing (*A full head of hair in just thirty minutes!*), fragments are not acceptable in college writing.

Fragment (no verb)	The actors in the play. (What point is being made about the actors?)
Fragment (no subject)	Were very talented. (Who were very talented?)
Fragment (no subject or verb)	Very talented. (Who was very talented?)
Fragment (does not express complete thought)	Because the actors in the play were very talented. (What happened because they were very talented?)

→ Focus on Writing

The picture on the opposite page shows a billboard advertising Pom pomegranate juice. Look at the picture, and then write several lines for a magazine ad for your favorite beverage, footwear, or health or beauty product.

WORD POWER
unique the only one
transform to change completely
empower to give strength or power to

**Highlight:
Identifying
Fragments**

Sentence fragments almost always appear next to complete sentences.

┌─ COMPLETE SENTENCE ─┐┌─────── FRAGMENT ───────┐
Celia took two electives. Physics 320 and Spanish 101.

The fragment above does not have a subject or a verb. The complete sentence that precedes it, however, has both a subject (*Celia*) and a verb (*took*).

Often, you can correct a sentence fragment by attaching it to a nearby sentence that supplies the missing words.

Celia took two electives, Physics 320 and Spanish 101.

Teaching Tip
Consider giving students a pretest to determine the types of problems they have. This will help you decide how much time you need to spend on fragments.

On the Web
For more practice, visit
Exercise Central *at*
<bedfordstmartins
.com/focusonwriting>.

● **Practice 21-1**

Some of the following items are fragments, and others are complete sentences. On the line following each item, write *F* if it is a fragment and *S* if it is a complete sentence.

Example: At the beginning of the test. __*f*__

1. The students in the classroom. __*f*__

2. Some students were very nervous about the test. __*S*__

3. With a number-two pencil. __*f*__

4. Opened their test booklets. __*f*__

5. After twenty-five minutes. __*f*__

6. The second part of the test was very hard. __*S*__

7. The last set of questions. __*f*__

8. It was finally over. __*S*__

9. Breathed a sigh of relief. __*f*__

10. The students ran out into the hallway. __*S*__

ESL Tip
Nonnative speakers may not have any more trouble with fragments than other students. If they aren't having problems in this area, work with them on problem areas such as count and noncount nouns (discussed in 29C).

● **Practice 21-2**

In the following passage, some of the numbered groups of words are missing a subject, a verb, or both. Identify each fragment by labeling it *F*. Then, attach each fragment to a nearby word group to create a complete new sentence. Finally, rewrite the entire passage, using complete sentences, on the lines provided.

Example:　Martha Grimes, Ruth Rendell, and Deborah Crombie write detective novels. _____ Set in England. _f_

Martha Grimes, Ruth Rendell, and Deborah Crombie write detective

novels set in England.

     (1) Sara Paretsky writes detective novels. _____ (2) Such as *Burn Marks* and *Guardian Angel*. _f_ (3) These novels are about V. I. Warshawski. _____ (4) A private detective. _f_ (5) V. I. lives and works in Chicago. _____ (6) The Windy City. _f_ (7) Every day as a detective. _f_ (8) V. I. takes risks. _____ (9) V. I. is tough. _____ (10) She is also a woman. _____

    Rewrite:

Sara Paretsky writes detective novels, such as <u>Burn Marks</u> *and*

<u>Guardian Angel</u>*. These novels are about V. I. Warshawski, a private*

detective. V. I. lives and works in Chicago, the Windy City. Every day

as a detective, V. I. takes risks. V. I. is tough. She is also a woman.

Focus on Writing: *Flashback*

Look back at your response to the Focus on Writing activity on page 317. Do all your sentences seem complete? Underline any that you think are not complete.

21b　Missing-Subject Fragments

Every sentence must include a subject and a verb. If the subject is left out, the sentence is incomplete. In the following example, the first word group is a sentence. It includes a subject (*He*) and a verb (*packed*). However, the second word group is a fragment. It includes a verb (*took*) but no subject.

          ————— SENTENCE —————　—————— FRAGMENT ——————

<u>He</u> <u>packed</u> his books and papers. And also took an umbrella.

One way to correct this kind of fragment is to attach it to the sentence that comes right before it. This sentence often contains the missing subject.

Correct   He packed his books and papers and also took an umbrella.

Another way to correct this kind of fragment is to add a new subject.

Correct   He packed his books and papers. He also took an umbrella.

● **Practice 21-3**

Each of the following items includes a missing-subject fragment. Using one of the two methods explained above, correct each fragment.

> **Example:**   Many schools give out summer reading lists. And also assign summer homework.
>
> _Many schools give out summer reading lists and also assign_
>
> _summer homework._
>
> _Many schools give out summer reading lists. They also assign_
>
> _summer homework._
>
> _Answers may vary._

1. Spelling bees help children learn to love words. And teach them to be good sports.

   _____

2. Some celebrities have their own charities. And give away millions of dollars.

   _____

3. The Peace Corps was a popular choice for college graduates in the 1960s. But is not a very popular choice today.

   _____

4. Johnny Depp starred in *Pirates of the Caribbean*. And also starred in its sequels.

   _____

5. People can get information from books. Or learn by observing and asking questions.

   _____

6. Some wealthy people retire to relax and play golf. But still help others by volunteering.

_____

7. Hybrid cars can save their owners money. And at the same time help the environment.

_____

8. Some credit cards earn miles. Or earn other rewards, such as hotel stays.

_____

9. In Madrid, people eat dinner at ten or eleven o'clock. But snack on tapas earlier in the evening.

_____

10. To protect your body from the sun, you should use sunscreen. And wear long-sleeved shirts.

_____

Focus on Writing: *Flashback*

Look back at your response to the Focus on Writing activity on page 317. Does every word group that is punctuated as a sentence include a subject? On a separate sheet of paper, correct any fragments you find.

21c   Phrase Fragments

Teaching Tip
Refer students to 17C for more on appositives. For information on punctuating appositives, refer them to 30C.

Every sentence must include a subject and a verb. A **phrase** is a group of words that is missing a subject or a verb or both. When you punctuate a phrase as if it is a sentence, you create a fragment.

Appositive Fragments

An **appositive** identifies, renames, or describes a noun or a pronoun. An appositive cannot stand alone as a sentence. To correct an appositive fragment,

Teaching Tip
Remind students that
they need to insert
a comma before the
appositive to connect
it to the rest of the
sentence.

attach it to the sentence that comes right before it. (This sentence usually includes the noun or pronoun that the appositive identifies.)

┌─ FRAGMENT ─┐

Incorrect   He decorated the room in his favorite colors. Brown and black.

Correct   He decorated the room in his favorite colors, brown and black.

Sometimes a word or expression like *especially*, *including*, *such as*, *for example*, or *for instance* introduces an appositive. Even if an appositive is introduced by one of these expressions, it is still a fragment.

┌─ FRAGMENT ─┐

Incorrect   A balanced diet should include high-fiber foods. Such as leafy

vegetables, fruits, beans, and whole-grain bread.

Correct   A balanced diet should include high-fiber foods, such as leafy vegetables, fruits, beans, and whole-grain bread.

● Practice 21-4

 On the Web
For more practice, visit
Exercise Central *at*
<bedfordstmartins
.com/focusonwriting>.

Each of the following items includes an appositive fragment. In each case, correct the fragment by attaching it to the sentence that comes before it.

> **Example:**   The Pledge of Allegiance was written in 1892 by Francis Bellamy. A Baptist minister.
>
> *The Pledge of Allegiance was written in 1892 by Francis Bellamy, a*
>
> *Baptist minister.*

1. The U.S. flag was designed by Francis Hopkinson. A New Jersey delegate to the Continental Congress.

   The U.S. flag was designed by Francis Hopkinson, a New Jersey

   delegate to the Continental Congress.

2. The first flag may have been sewn by Betsy Ross. A Philadelphia seamstress.

   The first flag may have been sewn by Betsy Ross, a Philadelphia

   seamstress.

3. Congress officially recognized the Pledge of Allegiance in 1942. The year the United States entered World War II.

   Congress officially recognized the Pledge of Allegiance in 1942, the

   year the United States entered World War II.

4. In 1814, Francis Scott Key composed "The Star-Spangled Banner." The U.S. national anthem.

In 1814, Francis Scott Key composed "The Star-Spangled Banner," the

U.S. national anthem.

5. Some people wanted a different national anthem. Such as "America" or "America the Beautiful."

Some people wanted a different national anthem, such as "America"

or "America the Beautiful."

Prepositional Phrase Fragments

A **prepositional phrase** consists of a preposition and its object. A prepositional phrase cannot stand alone as a sentence. To correct a prepositional phrase fragment, attach it to the sentence that comes right before it.

                                                    ┌──────── FRAGMENT ────────┐

Incorrect   She promised to stand by him. In sickness and in health.

Correct   She promised to stand by him in sickness and in health.

● Practice 21-5

Each of the following items includes a prepositional phrase fragment. In each case, correct the fragment by attaching it to the sentence that comes before it.

Example: A child's birth order has a strong influence. On his or her personality.

A child's birth order has a strong influence on his or her personality.

1. First-born children are reliable, serious, and goal-oriented. In most cases.

First-born children are reliable, serious, and goal-oriented in most cases.

2. More than half of U.S. presidents have been first-born or only children. In their families.

More than half of U.S. presidents have been first-born or only children

in their families.

3. In large families, middle children often form close relationships. Outside of the family.

In large families, middle children often form close relationships out-

side of the family.

4. The youngest child is always trying to get attention. From the older members of the family.

The youngest child is always trying to get attention from the older

members of the family.

5. Youngest children often take a while to settle down. Into careers and marriages.

Youngest children often take a while to settle down into careers and

marriages.

● Practice 21-6

Each of the following items is a phrase fragment, not a sentence. Correct each fragment by adding any words needed to turn the fragment into a complete sentence. (You may add words before or after the fragment.)

Example: During World War I. *During World War I, a flu epidemic*

killed millions of people. or A flu epidemic killed millions of people

during World War I.

Answers will vary.

1. The best player on the Yankees. _____

_____

2. From a developing nation in Africa. _____

_____

3. Such as tulips or roses. _____

_____

4. Behind door number 3. _____

_____

5. Including my parents and grandparents. _____

_____

6. With a new car in the driveway. _____

_____

7. A very small animal. _____

_____

8. For a long time. _____

_____

9. Turkey, stuffing, potatoes, and cranberry sauce. _____

_____

10. In less than a year. _____

_____

Focus on Writing: *Flashback*

Look back at your response to the Focus on Writing activity on page 317. Are any phrases incorrectly punctuated as sentences? On a separate sheet of paper, correct each fragment you find. (Hint: In many cases, you will be able to correct the fragment by attaching it to the sentence that comes right before it.)

21d Incomplete-Verb Fragments

Every sentence must include a subject and a verb. If the verb is missing or incomplete, a word group is a fragment, not a sentence.

Participle Fragments

Teaching Tip
Tell students that **helping verbs** include forms of *be, have,* and *do.* Refer them to 14C for a list of frequently used helping verbs.

Participles—verb forms that function as adjectives—are not complete verbs. They need **helping verbs** to complete them.

- **Present participles** always end in *-ing*. A present participle, such as *looking*, cannot stand alone in a sentence without a helping verb (*is looking, was looking, were looking,* and so on). When you use a present participle without a helping verb, you create a fragment.

	┌─── FRAGMENT ───┐

Incorrect   The twins are full of mischief. Always looking for trouble.

One way to correct the fragment is to attach it to the sentence that comes right before it.

Teaching Tip
Remind students to be careful not to create dangling modifiers with participles. Refer them to 24A.

Correct   The twins are full of mischief, always looking for trouble.

Another way to correct the fragment is to add a subject and a helping verb.

Correct	The twins are full of mischief. <u>They are</u> always looking for trouble.

Highlight: Incomplete-Verb Fragments with *Being*

The present participle *being* is often used incorrectly as if it were a complete verb.

Incorrect	I decided to take a nap. The outcome being that I slept through calculus class.

To correct this kind of fragment, substitute a form of the verb *be* that can stand alone in a sentence — for example, *is*, *was*, *are*, or *were*.

Correct	I decided to take a nap. The outcome <u>was</u> that I slept through calculus class.

Teaching Tip
Refer students to 26B for a list of irregular past participles.

- **Past participles** often end in *-ed*, but irregular past participles may have other endings. A past participle, such as *hidden*, cannot stand alone in a sentence without a helping verb (*is hidden*, *was hidden*, *had hidden*, and so on). When you use a past participle without a helping verb, you create a fragment.

	FRAGMENT
Incorrect	I found the letter. Hidden behind the sofa pillow.

One way to correct the fragment is to attach it to the sentence that comes right before it.

Correct	I found the letter, hidden behind the sofa pillow.

Another way to correct the fragment is to add a subject and a helping verb.

Correct	I found the letter. <u>It was</u> hidden behind the sofa pillow.

● Practice 21-7

Teaching Tip
You may want to refer students to 30D for information on punctuating restrictive and nonrestrictive clauses.

Each of the following items includes an incomplete-verb fragment. In each case, correct the fragment by attaching it to the sentence that comes before it.

Example: Keeping some buying tips in mind can help grocery shoppers. Saving them a lot of money.

Keeping some buying tips in mind can help grocery shoppers, saving

them a lot of money.

1. Always try to find a store brand. Costing less than the well-known and widely advertised brands.

   Always try to find a store brand costing less than the well-known and

   widely advertised brands.

2. Look for a product's cost per pound. Comparing it to the cost per pound of similar products.

   Look for a product's cost per pound, comparing it to the cost per

   pound of similar products.

3. Check supermarket flyers for sale items. Offered at a special low price.

   Check supermarket flyers for sale items offered at a special low

   price.

4. Buy different brands of the same product. Trying each one to see which brand you like best.

   Buy different brands of the same product, trying each one to see

   which brand you like best.

5. Finally, ask friends and neighbors for shopping suggestions. Based on their own experiences.

   Finally, ask friends and neighbors for shopping suggestions based on

   their own experiences.

● Practice 21-8

Teaching Tip
Remind students to be careful not to create dangling modifiers when they correct these fragments.

Each of the following items is a fragment because it does not include a complete verb. Correct each fragment either by adding a subject and a helping verb or by attaching the fragment to a new sentence that contains a subject and a complete verb.

Example: Hoping she would be lucky. *We were all hoping she*

would be lucky or Hoping she would be lucky, she bet her last few

dollars on the lottery.

Answers will vary.

1. Knowing that he was qualified for the job. _____

   _____

2. Leaving for an extended trip to Russia. _____

   _____

3. Worried about money for a long time. _____

_____

4. Trying to complete the loan application. _____

_____

5. Staying inside during the three-day snowstorm. _____

_____

6. Exhausted from a sleepless night. _____

_____

7. Really feeling optimistic about the future. _____

_____

8. Considered very good in math. _____

_____

9. Forbidden to see each other. _____

_____

10. Ignored by the waiter. _____

_____

Infinitive Fragments

An **infinitive**, which consists of *to* plus the base form of the verb (*to be, to go, to write*), is not a complete verb. An infinitive phrase (*to be free, to go home, to write a novel*) cannot stand alone as a sentence because it does not include a subject or a complete verb.

┌── FRAGMENT ──┐

Incorrect   Eric considered dropping out of school. To start his own

business.

Often, you can correct an infinitive fragment simply by attaching it to the sentence that comes right before it.

Correct   Eric considered dropping out of school to start his own
business.

Another way to correct an infinitive fragment is to add a subject and a complete verb.

Correct	Eric considered dropping out of school. <u>He wanted</u> to start his own business.

● Practice 21-9

Each of the following items includes an infinitive fragment. Correct each fragment by attaching it to the sentence that comes right before it.

Example: Many wetlands have been destroyed. To create new housing developments.

Many wetlands have been destroyed to create new housing developments.

Answers may vary.

1. Chimpanzees sometimes pick the leaves off twigs. To create a tool for scooping honey.

   Chimpanzees sometimes pick the leaves off twigs to create a tool for

   scooping honey.

2. My father didn't have enough health insurance. To pay for my sister's long hospitalization.

   My father didn't have enough health insurance to pay for my sister's

   long hospitalization.

3. You need to replace the bottle cap very tightly. To preserve the soda's carbonation.

   You need to replace the bottle cap very tightly to preserve the soda's

   carbonation.

4. Early telephone users said "Ahoy" instead of "Hello." To greet incoming callers.

   Early telephone users said "Ahoy" instead of "Hello" to greet callers.

5. With patience and skill, some hawks can be trained. To hunt small animals and birds for their human owners.

   With patience and skill, some hawks can be trained to hunt small

   animals and birds for their human owners.

● **Practice 21-10**

Each of the following items is an infinitive fragment. Correct each fragment, adding a subject and a complete verb.

> **Example:**   To say goodbye.
>
> *It was not easy to say goodbye.*
> _____
> *Answers will vary.*

1. To complete the loan application. _____

_____

2. To take the most scenic route through the mountains. _____

_____

3. To help his best friend. _____

_____

4. To use a digital camera. _____

_____

5. To eat a plate of nachos. _____

_____

Focus on Writing: *Flashback*

Look back at your response to the Focus on Writing activity on page 317. Underline any present or past participles or infinitives you find. Are the sentences in which they appear complete? On a separate sheet of paper, correct each fragment you find.

Dependent Clause Fragments

Teaching Tip
Refer students to 16A for more on identifying independent and dependent clauses.

Every sentence must include a subject and a verb. A sentence must also express a complete thought.

A **dependent** clause is a group of words that is introduced by a dependent word, such as *although, because, that,* or *after.* A dependent clause includes a subject and a verb, but it does not express a complete thought. Therefore, it cannot stand alone as a sentence. To correct a dependent clause fragment, you must complete the thought.

The following dependent clause is incorrectly punctuated as if it were a sentence.

Fragment <u>After</u> Simon won the lottery.

This sentence fragment includes both a subject (*Simon*) and a complete verb (*won*), but it does not express a complete thought. What happened after Simon won the lottery? To turn this fragment into a sentence, you need to complete the thought.

Sentence After Simon won the lottery, <u>he quit his night job.</u>

Some dependent clauses are introduced by dependent words called **subordinating conjunctions**.

Fragment <u>Although</u> Marisol had always dreamed of coming to America.

This sentence fragment includes a subject (*Marisol*) and a complete verb (*had dreamed*), but it is not a sentence; it is a dependent clause introduced by the subordinating conjunction *although*.

To correct this kind of fragment, attach it to an **independent clause** (a simple sentence) to complete the idea. (You can often find the independent clause you need right before or right after the fragment.)

Sentence Although Marisol had always dreamed of coming to America, <u>she did not have enough money for the trip until 1985.</u>

Highlight: Subordinating Conjunctions				
	after	even though	since	whenever
	although	if	so that	where
	as	if only	than	whereas
	as if	in order that	that	wherever
	as though	now that	though	whether
	because	once	unless	while
	before	provided that	until	
	even if	rather than	when	

For information on how to use subordinating conjunctions, see 16B.

> ### Highlight: Correcting Dependent Clause Fragments
>
> The simplest way to correct a dependent clause fragment is just to cross out the dependent word (the subordinating conjunction or relative pronoun) that makes the idea incomplete.
>
> ~~Although~~ Marisol had always dreamed of coming to America.
>
> However, when you delete the dependent word, readers may have trouble seeing the connection between the new sentence and the one before or after it. A better way to revise is to attach the dependent clause fragment to an independent clause.

Other dependent clauses are introduced by dependent words called **relative pronouns**.

Fragment	Novelist Richard Wright, who came to Paris in 1947.
Fragment	A quinceañera, which celebrates a Latina's fifteenth birthday.
Fragment	A key World War II battle that was fought on the Pacific island of Guadalcanal.

Each of the above sentence fragments includes a subject (*Richard Wright, quinceañera, battle*) and a complete verb (*came, celebrates, was fought*). However, they are not sentences because they do not express complete thoughts. In each case, a relative pronoun creates a dependent clause.

To correct each of these fragments, add the words needed to complete the thought.

Teaching Tip
You may want to refer students to 30D for information on punctuating restrictive and nonrestrictive clauses.

Sentence	Novelist Richard Wright, who came to Paris in 1947, spent the rest of his life there.
Sentence	A quinceañera, which celebrates a Latina's fifteenth birthday, signifies her entrance into womanhood.
Sentence	A key World War II battle that was fought on the Pacific island of Guadalcanal took place in 1943.

Highlight: Relative Pronouns		
that	whoever	
what	whom	
which	whomever	
who	whose	

For information on how to use relative pronouns, see 16C.

● **Practice 21-11**

Correct each of these dependent clause fragments by attaching it to the sentence before or after it. If the dependent clause comes at the beginning of a sentence, place a comma after it.

> **Example:** Before it became a state. West Virginia was part of Virginia.
>
> *Before it became a state, West Virginia was part of Virginia.*

On the Web
For more practice, visit Exercise Central *at* <bedfordstmartins .com/focusonwriting>.

1. Because many homeless people are mentally ill. It is hard to find places for them to live. *Answers will vary.*

2. People do not realize how dangerous raccoons can be. Even though they can be found in many parts of the United States. _____

3. I make plans to be a better student. Whenever a new semester begins. ____

4. Until something changes. We will just have to accept the situation. ____

Teaching Tip
Review punctuation with complex sentences. Refer students to 16B.

5. Because it is a very controversial issue. My parents and I have agreed not to discuss it. _____

● **Practice 21-12**

Correct each of these dependent clause fragments by adding the words needed to complete the idea.

Example: Many minor species of animals, which are rapidly disappearing.

Many minor species of animals, which are rapidly disappearing, need

to be protected.

1. The film that frightened me. *Answers will vary.*

_____

2. People who drink and drive. _____

_____

3. Some parents who are too strict with their children. _____

_____

4. The Vietnam War, which many Americans did not support. _____

_____

5. Animals that are used in medical research. _____

_____

● **Practice 21-13**

Each of the following is a fragment. Some are phrases incorrectly punctuated as sentences, others do not have a complete verb, and still others are
dependent clauses punctuated as sentences. Turn each fragment into a complete sentence, and write your revised sentence on the line below the fragment. Whenever possible, create two different correct sentences. Be sure to
punctuate correctly.

Example: Waiting in the dugout.

Revised: *Waiting in the dugout, the players chewed tobacco.*

Revised: *The players were waiting in the dugout.*

Answers will vary.

1. Because three-year-olds are still very attached to their parents.

Revised: _____

Revised: _____

2. Going around in circles.

Revised: _____

Revised: _____

3. To win the prize for the most unusual costume.

Revised: _____

Revised: _____

4. Students who thought they could not afford to go to college.

Revised: _____

Revised: _____

5. On an important secret mission.

Revised: _____

Revised: _____

6. Although many instructors see cheating as a serious problem.

Revised: _____

Revised: _____

7. Hoping to get another helping of chocolate fudge cake.

Revised: _____

Revised: _____

8. The rule that I always felt was the most unfair.

Revised: _____

Revised: _____

9. A really exceptional worker.

Revised: _____

Revised: _____

10. Finished in record time.

Revised: _____

Revised: _____

Focus on Writing: *Flashback*

Look back at your response to the Focus on Writing activity on page 317. Underline every subordinating conjunction you find, and underline *which*, *that*, and *who* wherever you find them. Do any of these words introduce a dependent clause that is punctuated as if it is a sentence? On a separate sheet of paper, correct each fragment you find either by deleting the subordinating conjunction or relative pronoun or by attaching the fragment to another word group to create a complete sentence.

Focus on Writing: *Revising and Editing*

Look back at your response to the Focus on Writing activity on page 317. Incorporating corrections from all the Flashback exercises in this chapter, revise your work. Then, check one more time to make sure every sentence is complete. If you do not find any fragments, work with a classmate to correct his or her writing, or edit the work you did for another assignment.

Chapter Review

Editing Practice: Paragraph

Read the following student paragraph, which includes incomplete sentences. Underline each fragment. Then, correct the fragment by attaching it to a nearby sentence that completes the idea. The first fragment has been underlined and corrected for you.

Answers will vary.

My First Job

When I was in high school, I had a terrible job. I worked as a

salesperson./~~In~~ a retail clothing store. I always seemed to be running./

~~Constantly~~ straightening the same racks over and over again. When the

store was busy, it was very hectic. Not all the customers were patient

or polite. Some lost their tempers./~~Because~~ they couldn't find a particular size or color. Then, they took their anger out on me. On slow nights, when the store was almost empty,/I was restless and bored. Eventually, I found a more rewarding position,/At a preschool for developmentally delayed children.

Editing Practice: Essay

Read the following student essay, which includes incomplete sentences. Underline each fragment. Then, correct it by attaching it to a nearby sentence that completes the idea. The first fragment has been underlined and corrected for you.

Answers will vary.

A Narrow Escape

Sometimes a dangerous experience can change the way people look at life. This is certainly true for me. One experience I had made me a different person,/*because* ~~Because~~ it made me realize how quickly my life could end.

It was the summer before my senior year of high school. I thought I was just going to spend a day at the beach,/*with* ~~With~~ two of my friends. We live near the beach in Florida, so we decided to drive over to Daytona Beach in the morning,/*to* ~~To~~ go swimming. Unfortunately, what happened that day landed me in the hospital,/*and* ~~And~~ really scared me.

My friends and I were swimming in about four feet of water,/*when* ~~When~~ I felt something grabbing my ankle,/*, trying* ~~Trying~~ to pull me straight down. I thought I was tangled up in something,/*, such* ~~Such~~ as some seaweed. Then one of my friends yelled, "Shark!" I kicked as hard as I could, and the shark let go. Although I was able to get out of the water on my own,/I had been badly bitten,/*on* ~~On~~ the back of my left foot.

My friends took me to Ocean County Hospital,/*where* ~~Where~~ I got eighty-two stitches. The doctors told me that I was lucky,/*because* ~~Because~~ my tendons hadn't been cut in two by the bite. I would probably make a full recovery. I never saw the shark, but my friends told me that it was about eight feet long,/*and* ~~And~~ looked like a bull shark.

because
This experience changed my life/~~Because~~ it made me afraid. I still go

to the beach, but I don't go swimming very often. I know that shark

to
attacks are rare, but I'm still a little scared/~~To~~ go back in the water.

Collaborative Activities

1. Exchange workbooks with another student, and read each other's responses to the Focus on Writing activity on page 317. On a separate sheet of paper, list five fragments that describe the product your partner has written about. When your own paper is returned to you, revise each fragment written by your partner, creating a complete sentence for each one. Finally, add one of these new sentences to your own Focus on Writing activity.

2. Working in a group of three or four students, add different subordinating conjunctions to sentences *a* through *d* below to create several different fragments. (See page 331 for a list of subordinating conjunctions.) Then, turn each of the resulting fragments into a complete sentence by adding words that complete the idea.

   Example:

Sentence	*Fragment*	*New Sentence*
I left the party.	As I left the party	As I left the party, I fell.
	After I left the party	After I left the party, the fun stopped.
	Until I left the party	Until I left the party, I had no idea it was so late.

   Sentences
   a. My mind wanders.
   b. She caught the ball.
   c. He made a wish.
   d. Disaster struck.

3. Working in a group of three or four students, build as many sentences as you can from the fragments listed below. Use your imagination to create as many creative sentences as you can.

   Example:

   Fragment   Known for his incredible memory

   Sentences   Zack, known for his incredible memory, has somehow managed to forget everything he learned about chemistry.

   Known for his incredible memory, Monty the Magnificent mesmerized audiences.

Teaching Tip
As a review, read some sentences (and some sentence fragments) to the class, and ask students to explain why each item is or is not a complete sentence

Fragments

a. wandering in the desert
b. stranded in the jungle
c. looking for his ideal mate
d. always using as much ketchup as possible
e. folded, stapled, and mutilated

Review Checklist: Sentence Fragments

☐ A sentence fragment is an incomplete sentence. Every sentence must include a subject and a verb and express a complete thought. (See 21A.)

☐ Every sentence must include a subject. (See 21B.)

☐ Phrases cannot stand alone as sentences. (See 21C.)

☐ Every sentence must include a complete verb. (See 21D.)

☐ Dependent clauses cannot stand alone as sentences. (See 21E.)

Chapter 22

Subject-Verb Agreement

The meaning of the word *strike* possibly comes from sailors
"striking" or lowering their sails to protest going to sea.

Understanding Subject-Verb Agreement

A sentence's subject (a noun or pronoun) and its verb must **agree**: singular subjects must have singular verbs, and plural subjects must have plural verbs.

        S   V

The museum opens at ten o'clock. (singular noun subject *museum* takes singular verb *opens*)

        S   V

The museums open at ten o'clock. (plural noun subject *museums* takes plural verb *open*)

  S   V

She always watches the eleven o'clock news. (singular pronoun subject *she* takes singular verb *watches*)

  S   V

They always watch the eleven o'clock news. (plural pronoun subject *they* takes plural verb *watch*)

Subject-Verb Agreement with Regular Verbs

	Singular	Plural
First person	I play	Molly and I/we play
Second person	you play	you play
Third person	he/she/it plays	they play
	the man plays	the men play
	Molly plays	Molly and Sam play

→ Focus on Writing

On October 25, 1990, after the *New York Daily News* demanded millions of dollars in concessions from its workers, the newspaper locked them out. Employees picketed for 148 days before returning to work after the unions agreed to salary reductions and major job cuts. The picture on the opposite page, by the artist Ralph Fasanella, depicts the *Daily News* strike. Look at the picture, and then describe what you think the artist is trying to convey. For example, do you think his sympathy is with the workers or with the *Daily News*? How do you know? Use the **present tense** in your response.

• Practice 22-1

Underline the correct form of the verb in each of the following sentences. Make sure the verb agrees with its subject.

Example: Radio stations (<u>broadcast</u>/broadcasts) many kinds of music.

(1) Most music fans (<u>know</u>/knows) about salsa, a popular style of Latin music. (2) However, they (<u>need</u>/needs) a little education when it comes to ranchera, a blend of several traditional forms of Mexican music. (3) These forms (<u>include</u>/includes) mariachi music as well as ballads and waltz-like tunes. (4) Ranchera (appeal/<u>appeals</u>) to a wide audience of Americans of Mexican descent. (5) Its performers (<u>sell</u>/sells) millions of records a year, and often they (<u>top</u>/tops) *Billboard*'s Latin charts. (6) In fact, Mexican recordings (<u>outsell</u>/outsells) any other form of Latin music in the United States. (7) This popularity (surprise/<u>surprises</u>) many people. (8) Older ranchera lovers (<u>tend</u>/tends) to be first-generation, working-class immigrants, but more and more young listeners (<u>seem</u>/seems) drawn to ranchera. (9) When one Los Angeles nightclub (host/<u>hosts</u>) a ranchera night, it (draw/<u>draws</u>) a large number of English-speaking fans in their twenties. (10) Clearly, ranchera musicians (<u>deserve</u>/deserves) more attention from the music industry.

On the Web
For more practice, visit
Exercise Central *at*
<bedfordstmartins
.com/focusonwriting>.

• Practice 22-2

Fill in the blank with the correct present tense form of the verb.

Example: At some point, most children ___*get*___ chewing gum in their hair. (get)

(1) To get the gum out, some parents ___*cut*___ their children's hair. (cut) (2) A less drastic solution ___*involves*___ ice cubes and a plastic bag. (involve) (3) First, the parent ___*puts*___ some ice cubes in a plastic bag. (put) (4) Next, the parent holds the plastic bag against the hair until the pieces of gum ___*freeze*___. (freeze) (5) If the ice cubes

_____ *grow* _____ too cold, the plastic bag can be wrapped in a washcloth. (grow) (6) When the gum is frozen, it _____ *becomes* _____ hard. (become) (7) Once the gum _____ *hardens* _____, it can be gently broken away from the hair. (harden) (8) If the ice cubes _____ *fail* _____, a parent can apply a small amount of olive oil to the gum and to the hair around it. (fail) (9) After massaging the oil into the hair and gum, the parent _____ *leaves* _____ it for twenty minutes. (leave) (10) Often, the gum _____ *slides* _____ out easily when it is gently combed out. (slide)

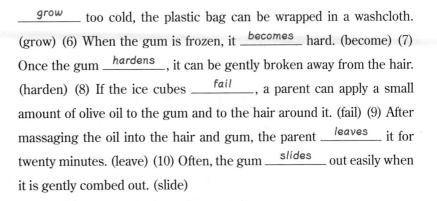

Focus on Writing: *Flashback*

Look back at your response to the Focus on Writing activity on page 341. Choose two sentences that contain present tense verbs, and rewrite them on a separate sheet of paper. Underline the subject of each sentence once and the verb twice. If the subject and verb of each sentence do not agree, correct them.

22b　Compound Subjects

Teaching Tip
Tell students that the rules governing compound subjects and *or* also govern compound subjects and *neither . . . nor.*

The subject of a sentence is not always a single word. It can also be a **compound subject**, consisting of two or more words. To avoid subject-verb agreement problems with compound subjects, follow these rules.

● When the parts of a compound subject are connected by *and*, the compound subject takes a plural verb.

　　　　　S　　　　V
　John and Marsha share an office.

Teaching Tip
Tell students that an *s* following a verb usually means the verb is singular. For example, in the sentence *He plays golf*, the verb needs an *s*, because *he* refers to just one person. (Point out the exception that occurs with *I* and *you*.)

● When the parts of a compound subject are connected by *or*, the verb agrees with the part of the subject that is closer to it.

　　　　　　　　S　　　　　　　V
　The mayor or the council members meet with community groups.

　　　　　　　　S　　　　　　　V
　The council members or the mayor meets with community groups.

● **Practice 22-3**

Underline the correct form of the verb in each of the following sentences. Make sure that the verb agrees with its compound subject.

Example: Gloves or a scarf (make/<u>makes</u>) a good wintertime gift.

1. Cars and trucks (<u>fill</u>/fills) the municipal parking lot each day.

2. Grapes or an apple (provide/<u>provides</u>) a nutritious addition to a lunch.

3. A security officer and a video monitoring system (<u>watch</u>/watches) the bank's lobby during business hours.

4. A vegetable or french fries (<u>come</u>/comes) with the steak dinner.

5. A pianist or a guitarist (play/<u>plays</u>) at the club every weekend.

6. Nurses or nurse practitioners (<u>offer</u>/offers) round-the-clock patient care.

7. According to an old saying, fish and houseguests (<u>smell</u>/smells) bad after three days.

8. Flowers or a get-well balloon (cheer/<u>cheers</u>) people up when they are ill.

9. The restaurant owner or her daughter always (greet/<u>greets</u>) customers.

10. A sliding glass door or French windows (<u>allow</u>/allows) light into a room.

Focus on Writing: *Flashback*

Look at the two sentences you wrote for the Flashback activity on page 343. Rewrite them with compound subjects. In each sentence, make sure the compound subjects agree with the verb.

22c   *Be, Have,* and *Do*

The verbs *be, have,* and *do* are irregular in the present tense. For this reason, they can present problems with subject-verb agreement. Memorizing their forms is the only sure way to avoid such problems.

Teaching Tip
Refer students to 25A
and 25B for more on
regular and irregular
verbs.

Subject-Verb Agreement with *Be*

	Singular	Plural
First person	I am	we are
Second person	you are	you are
Third person	he/she/it is	they are
	Tran is	Tran and Ryan are
	the boy is	the boys are

Teaching Tip
The dialect-related use of
be and *have* may be a
sensitive issue for some
students. You may want
to address it in individual
conferences outside of
class.

Subject-Verb Agreement with *Have*

	Singular	Plural
First person	I have	we have
Second person	you have	you have
Third person	he/she/it has	they have
	Shana has	Shana and Robert have
	the student has	the students have

Subject-Verb Agreement with *Do*

	Singular	Plural
First person	I do	we do
Second person	you do	you do
Third person	he/she/it does	they do
	Ken does	Ken and Mia do
	the book does	the books do

● Practice 22-4

Fill in the blank with the correct present tense form of the verb *be, have,* or *do.*

> **Example:** Sometimes, people __do__ damage without really meaning to. (do)

(1) Biologists __have__ serious worries about the damage that invading species of animals can cause. (have) (2) The English sparrow __is__ one example. (be) (3) It __has__ a role in the decline in the number of bluebirds. (have) (4) On the Galapagos Islands, cats __are__ another example. (be)

(5) Introduced by early explorers, they currently __do__ much damage to the eggs of the giant tortoises that live on the islands. (do) (6) Scientists today __are__ worried about a new problem. (be) (7) This __is__ a situation caused by wildlife agencies that put exotic fish into lakes and streams. (be) (8) They __do__ this to please those who enjoy fishing. (do) (9) Although popular with people who fish, this policy __has__ major drawbacks. (have) (10) It __has__ one drawback in particular: many species of fish have been pushed close to extinction. (have)

On the Web
For more practice, visit Exercise Central *at* <bedfordstmartins .com/focusonwriting>.

Focus on Writing: *Flashback*

Look back at your response to the Focus on Writing activity on page 341. Have you used a form of *be*, *have*, or *do* in any of your sentences? If so, copy these sentences on a separate sheet of paper. Have you used the correct forms of *be*, *have*, and *do*? Correct any agreement errors.

22d   Words between Subject and Verb

Teaching Tip
Refer students to 14B for more on prepositional phrases and for a list of prepositions.

Remember, a verb must always agree with its subject. Don't be confused when a group of words (for example, a prepositional phrase) comes between the subject and the verb. These words do not affect subject-verb agreement.

	S V
Correct	High <u>levels</u> of mercury <u>occur</u> in some fish.
	S V
Correct	<u>Water</u> in the fuel lines <u>causes</u> an engine to stall.
	S V
Correct	<u>Food</u> between the teeth <u>results</u> in decay.

An easy way to identify the subject of the sentence is to cross out the words that come between the subject and the verb.

> **Highlight: Words between Subject and Verb**
>
> Look out for words and phrases such as *in addition to*, *along with*, *together with*, *as well as*, *except*, and *including*. When they come between the subject and the verb, phrases introduced by these expressions do not affect subject-verb agreements.
>
>   s   v
> St. Thomas, ~~along with St. Croix and St. John~~, is part of the United States Virgin Islands.

On the Web
For more practice, visit Exercise Central at <bedfordstmartins .com/focusonwriting>.

High levels ~~of mercury~~ occur in some fish.

Water ~~in the fuel lines~~ causes an engine to stall.

Food ~~between the teeth~~ results in decay.

● **Practice 22-5**

In each of the following sentences, cross out the words that separate the subject and the verb. Then, underline the subject of the sentence once and the verb that agrees with the subject twice.

Example: The food ~~on the carpet~~ (suggest/suggests) that Hiro and Mika had a party.

1. The cupids ~~in the painting~~ (symbolize/symbolizes) lost innocence.
2. Fans ~~at a concert~~ (get/gets) angry if the band is late.
3. The appliances ~~in the kitchen~~ (make/makes) strange noises.
4. The United States, ~~along with Germany and Japan,~~ (produce/produces) most of the world's cars.
5. A good set ~~of skis and poles~~ (cost/costs) a lot.
6. Unfortunately, one ~~out of ten men~~ eventually (gets/get) prostate cancer.
7. Workers ~~in the city~~ (pays/pay) a high wage tax.
8. Each summer, fires ~~from lightning~~ (cause/causes) hundreds of millions of dollars in property damage.
9. Volunteers, ~~including people like my father,~~ (help/helps) paramedics in my community.
10. A doctor, ~~together with two nurses,~~ (staff/staffs) the clinic at the health center.

Focus on Writing: *Flashback*

Look back at your response to the Focus on Writing activity on page 341. Can you find any sentences in which a prepositional phrase comes between the subject and the verb? If so, cross out the prepositional phrase, and then correct any subject-verb agreement errors.

22e

Collective Noun Subjects

Collective nouns are words (like *family* and *audience*) that name a group of people or things but are singular. Because they are singular, they should be used with singular verbs.

The <u>team</u> <u>practices</u> five days a week in the gym.

Frequently Used Collective Nouns

army	club	family	jury
association	committee	gang	mob
band	company	government	team
class	corporation	group	union

● Practice 22-6

Fill in the blank with the correct present tense form of the verb.

Example: The club __is__ supposed to meet every Tuesday. (is)

1. The jury __reaches__ its verdict after much discussion. (reach)

2. Before the exam, the class __breaks__ into study groups. (break)

3. Each year the family __goes__ to the beach for a vacation. (go)

4. The corporation __establishes__ a pension plan for its employees. (establish)

5. A group of lions __is__ resting under the trees. (is)

Focus on Writing: *Flashback*

Look back at your response to the Focus on Writing activity on page 341. Can you find any sentences that have collective nouns as subjects? If so, check carefully to make sure the subjects and verbs agree. If they do not, revise each incorrect sentence.

22f Indefinite Pronoun Subjects

Teaching Tip
Remind students that many indefinite pronouns end in *-one*, *-body*, or *-thing*. These words are almost always singular.

Teaching Tip
Refer students to 27E for more on pronoun-antecedent agreement with indefinite pronouns.

Indefinite pronouns—*anybody, everyone*, and so on—do not refer to a particular person, place, or idea.

Most indefinite pronouns are singular and take singular verbs.

    S   V
No one likes getting up early.

    S   V
Everyone likes to sleep late.

    S   V
Somebody likes beets.

Singular Indefinite Pronouns

another	either	neither	one
anybody	everybody	nobody	somebody
anyone	everyone	no one	someone
anything	everything	nothing	something
each	much		

A few indefinite pronouns (*both, many, several, few, others*) are plural and take plural verbs.

    S   V
Many were left homeless by the storm.

**Highlight:
Indefinite
Pronouns as
Subjects**

If a prepositional phrase comes between the indefinite pronoun and the verb, cross out the prepositional phrase to help you identify the sentence's subject.

$$\overset{\text{S}}{\text{Each}} \text{ of the boys } \overset{\text{V}}{\text{has}} \text{ a bike.}$$

$$\overset{\text{S}}{\text{Many}} \text{ of the boys } \overset{\text{V}}{\text{have}} \text{ bikes.}$$

● Practice 22-7

 **On the Web**
For more practice, visit
Exercise Central *at*
<bedfordstmartins
.com/focusonwriting>.

Circle the correct verb in each sentence.

Example: Each of the three streams in our area ((is)/are) polluted.

1. One of the streams no longer (have/(has)) any fish.

2. Another (contain/(contains)) a lot of algae.

3. Everybody (want/(wants)) to improve the situation.

4. No one (are/(is)) willing to do anything.

5. Somebody always (take/(takes)) the lead.

6. Everyone (know/(knows)) that pollution is difficult to control.

7. Neither of the candidates (seem/(seems)) willing to act.

8. Whenever anyone (ask/(asks)) them for suggestions, neither (have, (has)) any.

9. According to the candidates, everything ((is)/are) being done that can be done.

10. One of my friends (say/(says)) that she will not vote for either candidate.

Focus on Writing: *Flashback*

Look back at your response to the Focus on Writing activity on page 341. Do any of the sentences contain indefinite pronoun subjects? Do the verbs in these sentences agree with the indefinite pronoun subjects? If you find any that do not, rewrite the sentences on a separate sheet of paper.

22g   Verbs before Subjects

A verb always agrees with its subject—even if the verb comes *before* the subject. In questions, for example, word order is reversed, with the verb coming before the subject or with the subject coming between two parts of the verb.

        V   S

Where is the bank?

    V   S   V

Are you going to the party?

ESL Tip
Point out that questions depart from conventional English word order. Write a series of statements on the board, and have students change them into questions.

If you have trouble identifying the subject of a question, answer the question with a statement.

        V   S   S   V

Where is the bank? The bank is on Walnut Street.

Highlight:
There Is* and *There Are

When a sentence begins with *there is* or *there are*, the word *there* can never be the subject of the sentence. The subject comes after the form of the verb *be*.

      V   S

There is one chief justice on the Court.

      V   S

There are nine justices on the Supreme Court.

● **Practice 22-8**

On the Web
For more practice, visit Exercise Central *at* <bedfordstmartins .com/focusonwriting>.

Underline the subject of each sentence, and circle the correct form of the verb.

Example: Who (is/are) the writer who won the 2007 Nobel Prize in Literature?

1. Where (is/are) the Bering Straits?
2. Why (do/does) the compound change color when it is exposed to light?
3. (Is/Are) the twins identical or fraternal?
4. How (do/does) Congress override a presidential veto?
5. What (have/has) this got to do with me?

6. There (is/are) ten <u>computers</u> in the writing center.

7. There (is/are) more than nine million <u>people</u> living in Mexico City.

8. There (is/are) several reference <u>books</u> in this library that can help you with your research.

9. There (is/are) four <u>reasons</u> why we should save the spotted owl from extinction.

10. There (is/are) more than one <u>way</u> to answer the question.

Focus on Writing: *Flashback*

Look back at your response to the Focus on Writing activity on page 341. Do you have any sentences in which the verb comes before the subject? If so, check carefully to make sure the subjects and verbs agree. If they do not, revise each incorrect sentence on a separate sheet of paper.

Focus on Writing: *Revising and Editing*

Look back at your response to the Focus on Writing activity on page 341. Incorporating changes and corrections from this chapter's Flashback activities, revise your work, making sure all your verbs agree with their subjects.

Chapter Review

Editing Practice: Paragraph

Read the following student paragraph, which includes errors in subject-verb agreement. Decide whether each of the underlined verbs agrees with its subject. If it does not, cross out the verb, and write in the correct form. If it does, write *C* above the verb. The first sentence has been done for you.

Watching Movies

C
I believe that to be appreciated fully, movies ~~has~~ *have* to be seen in
are
a theater on a big screen. There ~~is~~ many reasons why I and other
feel
movie-goers ~~feels~~ this way. In many cases, a blockbuster movie's
require
sound or its other special effects ~~requires~~ a theater screening if
C
the movie is to have its full impact on viewers. Even movies that
have *benefit*
~~has~~ no special effects ~~benefits~~ from being seen on a large screen.
C
There is something about sitting with other people in a darkened
respond
theater that audiences ~~responds~~ to in a special way. Although
does
it is true that a theater audience ~~do~~ sometimes cause disruptions,
C *have*
I see these as minor disturbances that ~~has~~ little effect on my
enjoyment.

Editing Practice: Essay

Read the following student essay, which includes errors in subject-verb agreement. Decide whether each of the underlined verbs agrees with its subject. If it does not, cross out the verb, and write in the correct form. If it does, write *C* above the verb. The first sentence has been done for you.

Party in the Parking Lot

is
Fun at football games ~~are~~ not limited to cheering for the home
arrive *set*
team. Many people ~~arrives~~ four or five hours early, ~~sets~~ up grills in the
C
parking lot, and start cooking. Typically, fans ~~drives~~ to the stadium in
drive
a pickup truck, a station wagon, or an SUV. They open up the tailgate,
C
lay *enjoy*
~~lays~~ out the food, and ~~enjoys~~ the atmosphere with their friends.
C
In fact, tailgating is so popular that, for some fans, it's more fun than
the game itself.

What ~~do~~ [does] it take to tailgate? First, most tailgaters plan [C] their menus in advance. To avoid forgetting anything, they ~~makes~~ [make] lists of what to bring. Disposable paper plates, along with a set of plastic glasses, make [C] it unnecessary to bring home dirty dishes. Jugs of water ~~is~~ [are] essential, and damp towels ~~helps~~ [help] clean up hands and faces. Also, lightweight chairs or another type of seating is [C] important.

At the game, parking near a grassy area or at the end of a parking row ~~are~~ [is] best. This strategy ~~give~~ [gives] tailgaters more space to cook and eat. If the food ~~are~~ [is] ready to eat by two hours before the game ~~start~~ [starts], there is [C] plenty of time to put out the fire in the grill and to clean up.

Some tailgaters ~~buys~~ [buy] expensive equipment. The simple charcoal grill ~~have~~ [has] turned into a combination grill, cooler, and fold-out table with a portable awning. There ~~is~~ [are] grills with their own storage space. Other grills ~~swings~~ [swing] out from the tailgate to provide access to the vehicle's storage area. Some deluxe grills even ~~has~~ [have] their own beer taps, stereo systems, and sinks.

Whatever equipment tailgaters ~~brings~~ [bring] to the game, the most important factors ~~is~~ [are] food and companionship. There is [C] a tradition of sharing food and swapping recipes with other tailgaters. Most tailgaters ~~loves~~ [love] to meet one another and ~~compares~~ [compare] notes on recipes. For many, the tailgating experience is [C] as important as the game itself.

Collaborative Activities

1. Working in a group of four students, list ten nouns (five singular and five plural) — people, places, or things — on the left-hand side of a sheet of paper. Beside each noun, write the present tense form of a verb that could logically be used with the noun. Exchange papers with another group, and check to see that singular nouns have singular verbs and plural nouns have plural verbs.

2. Working with your group, expand each noun-and-verb combination you listed in Collaborative Activity 1 into a complete sentence. Next, write a sentence that could logically follow each of these sentences, using a pro-

noun as the subject of the new sentence. Make sure the pronoun you choose refers to the noun in the previous sentence, as in this example: *Alan watches three movies a week. He is addicted to films.* Check to be certain the subjects in your sentences agree with the verbs.

3. Exchange the final version of your edited Focus on Writing activity with another student in your group. Answer the following questions about each sentence in your partner's work.

- Does the sentence contain a compound subject?
- Does the sentence contain words that come between the subject and the verb?
- Does the sentence contain an indefinite pronoun used as a subject?
- Does the sentence contain a verb that comes before the subject?

As you answer these questions, check to make sure all the verbs agree with their subjects. When your own work is returned to you, make any necessary corrections.

Review Checklist: Subject-Verb Agreement

- ☐ Singular subjects (nouns and pronouns) take singular verbs, and plural subjects take plural verbs. (See 22A.)
- ☐ Special rules govern subject-verb agreement with compound subjects. (See 22B.)
- ☐ The irregular verbs *be*, *have*, and *do* often present problems with subject-verb agreement in the present tense. (See 22C.)
- ☐ Words that come between the subject and the verb do not affect subject-verb agreement. (See 22D.)
- ☐ Collective nouns are singular and take singular verbs. (See 22E.)
- ☐ Most indefinite pronouns, such as *no one* and *everyone*, are singular and take a singular verb when they serve as the subject of a sentence. A few are plural and take plural verbs. (See 22F.)
- ☐ A sentence's subject and verb must always agree, even if the verb comes before the subject. (See 22G.)

Chapter 23

Illogical Shifts

Today, the average size of the U.S. home is 2,349 square feet. The Florida mansion above is much larger. Bill Gates's residence in Washington state is larger still at 66,000 square feet.

A **shift** occurs whenever a writer changes **tense**, **person**, or **voice**. As you write and revise, be sure that any shifts you make are **logical**—that is, they occur for a reason.

Shifts in Tense

Tense is the form a verb takes to show when an action takes place or when a situation occurs. Some shifts in tense (even within a single sentence) are necessary—for example, to indicate a change from past time to present time.

Teaching Tip
Refer students to
Chapters 25 and 26
for more on tense.

| **Logical shift** | When they first came out, cell phones <u>were</u> large and bulky, but now they <u>are</u> small and compact. |

An **illogical shift in tense** occurs when a writer shifts from one tense to another for no apparent reason.

Illogical shift in tense	The dog walked to the fireplace. Then, he circles twice and lies down in front of the fire. (shift from past tense to present tense)
Revised	The dog <u>walked</u> to the fireplace. Then, he <u>circled</u> twice and <u>lay</u> down in front of the fire. (consistent use of past tense)
Revised	The dog <u>walks</u> to the fireplace. Then, he <u>circles</u> twice and <u>lies</u> down in front of the fire. (consistent use of present tense)

→ Focus on Writing

The picture on the opposite page shows a mansion in Florida. Look at the picture, and then describe your dream house. Would it resemble the house in the picture, or would it be different? What would be inside the house? Be as specific as possible.

WORD POWER
appealing attractive or interesting
ideal a model of perfection; the best of its kind
practical useful

On the Web
For more practice, visit
Exercise Central *at*
<bedfordstmartins
.com/focusonwriting>.

● **Practice 23-1**

Edit the following sentences to correct illogical shifts in tense. If a sentence is correct, write *C* in the blank.

Examples:

During World War II, the 100th Battalion of the 442nd Combat Infantry
Regiment was made up of young Japanese Americans who ~~are~~ eager to
[*were* above *are*]
serve in the U.S. Army. _____

The 100th Battalion of the 442nd Infantry is the only remaining United
States Army Reserve ground combat unit that fought in World War II.
_*C*_

Teaching Tip
Have students assign a
year to each verb. For
instance, in the first
example sentence, both
actions occurred in the
past, so both should
use the past tense. In
the second example
sentence, the first action
occurs in the present, so
it requires the present
tense; the second action
occurred in the past,
so it requires the past
tense. Students enjoy this
activity, and it helps them
remember to watch for
illogical tense shifts.

(1) At the start of World War II, 120,000 Japanese Americans ~~are~~
[*were* above *are*]
sent to relocation camps because the government feared that they
might be disloyal to the United States. _____ (2) However, in 1943, the
[*sent* above *sends*]
United States needed more soldiers, so it ~~sends~~ recruiters to the camps
to ask for volunteers. _____ (3) The Japanese-American volunteers ~~are~~
[*were* above *are*]
organized into the 442nd Combat Infantry Regiment. _____ (4) The soldiers of the 442nd Infantry fought in some of the bloodiest battles of the
war, including the invasion of Italy at Anzio and a battle in Bruyeres,
[*captured* above *capture*]
France, where they ~~capture~~ over two hundred enemy soldiers. _____
[*were* above *are*]
(5) When other U.S. troops ~~are~~ cut off by the enemy, the 442nd Infantry
soldiers were sent to rescue them. _____ (6) The Japanese-American
[*received* above *receive*]
soldiers suffered the highest casualty rate of any U.S. unit and ~~receive~~
over eighteen thousand individual decorations. _____ (7) Former senator Daniel Inouye of Hawaii, a Japanese American, was awarded the Dis-
[*had* above *has*]
tinguished Service Cross for his bravery in Italy and ~~has~~ to have his
arm amputated. _____ (8) The 442nd Infantry was awarded more deco-
[*earned* above *earns*]
rations than any other combat unit of its size and ~~earns~~ eight Presidential Unit citations. _____ (9) The dedication and sacrifice of the 442nd
[*is* above *was*]
Infantry ~~was~~ now widely seen as evidence that Japanese Americans
were patriotic and committed to freedom and democracy. _____

(10) The bravery of the 442nd Infantry during World War II paved the way for today's desegregated American military. _C_

Focus on Writing: *Flashback*

Look back at your response to the Focus on Writing activity on page 357. Check each sentence to make sure it includes no illogical shifts from one tense to another. If you find an incorrect sentence, correct it on a separate sheet of paper.

23b   Shifts in Person

Person is the form a pronoun takes to show who is speaking, spoken about, or spoken to.

Person	Singular	Plural
First person	I	we
Second person	you	you
Third person	he, she, it	they

An **illogical shift in person** occurs when a writer shifts from one person to another for no apparent reason.

Illogical shift in person	The hikers were told that you had to stay on the trail. (shift from third person to second person)
Revised	The hikers were told that they had to stay on the trail. (consistent use of third person)
Illogical shift	Anyone can learn to cook if you practice. (shift from third person to second person)
Revised	You can learn to cook if you practice. (consistent use of second person)

Teaching Tip
Tell students to be careful not to use the pronoun *he* to refer to an indefinite pronoun antecedent, such as *anyone*, that could be either masculine or feminine. (See 27E.)

Revised Anyone can learn to cook if <u>he or she</u> practices. (consistent use of third person)

● **Practice 23-2**

The following sentences contain illogical shifts. Edit each sentence so that it uses pronouns consistently. Be sure to change any verbs that do not agree with the new subjects.

Example: Before a person finds a job in the fashion industry,
he or she has
~~you~~ have to have some experience.
^

(1) Young people who want careers in the fashion industry do not
they
always realize how hard ~~you~~ will have to work. (2) They think that work-
^
they
ing in the world of fashion will be glamorous and that ~~you~~ will quickly
he or she is, ^
make a fortune. (3) In reality, no matter how talented ~~you are~~, a recent
^
college graduate entering the industry is paid only about $22,000 a year.
them
(4) The manufacturers who employ new graduates expect ~~you~~ to work
they ^
for three years or more at this salary before ~~you~~ are promoted. (5) A
he or she is ^
young designer may receive a big raise if ~~you are~~ very talented, but this
^
they
is unusual. (6) New employees have to pay their dues, and ~~you~~ soon
their ^
realize that most of ~~your~~ duties are boring. (7) An employee may be
^
he or she has
excited to land a job as an assistant designer but then find that ~~you have~~
^
to color in designs that have already been drawn. (8) Other beginners
they *their*
discover that ~~you~~ spend most of ~~your~~ time sewing or typing up orders.
^ ^
he or she has
(9) If a person is serious about working in the fashion industry, ~~you have~~
^
to be realistic. (10) For most newcomers to the industry, the ability to do
they *their*
what ~~you~~ are told to do is more important than ~~your~~ artistic talent.
^ ^

Focus on Writing: *Flashback*

Look back at your response to the Focus on Writing activity on page 357. Check each sentence to make sure it includes no illogical shifts in person. If you find an incorrect sentence, correct it on a separate sheet of paper.

23c Shifts in Voice

Voice is the form a verb takes to indicate whether the subject is acting or is acted upon. When the subject of a sentence is acting, the sentence is in the **active voice**. When the subject of a sentence is acted upon, the sentence is in the **passive voice**.

Active voice	Nat Turner organized a slave rebellion in August 1831. (Subject *Nat Turner* is acting.)
Passive voice	A slave rebellion was organized by Nat Turner in 1831. (Subject *rebellion* is acted upon.)

An **illogical shift in voice** occurs when a writer shifts from active to passive voice or from passive to active voice for no apparent reason.

Illogical shift in voice	J. D. Salinger wrote *The Catcher in the Rye*, and *Franny and Zooey* was also written by him. (active to passive)
Revised	J. D. Salinger wrote *The Catcher in the Rye*, and he also wrote *Franny and Zooey*. (consistent use of active voice)
Illogical shift in voice	Radium was discovered by Marie Curie in 1910, and she won a Nobel Prize in chemistry in 1911. (passive to active)
Revised	Marie Curie discovered radium in 1910, and she won a Nobel Prize in chemistry in 1911. (consistent use of active voice)

Highlight: Changing from Passive to Active Voice

You should generally use the active voice in your college writing because it is stronger and more direct than the passive voice. To change a sentence from the passive to the active voice, determine who or what is acting, and make this noun the subject of the new active voice sentence.

Passive voice	The campus escort service is used by my friends. (*My friends* are acting.)
Active voice	My friends use the campus escort service.

● **Practice 23-3**

The following sentences contain illogical shifts in voice. Revise each sentence by changing the underlined passive-voice verb to the active voice.

Teaching Tip
Tell students that to convert the passive voice to the active voice, they should ask themselves, "Who carried out the action?" and make the answer the subject of the sentence.

 On the Web
For more practice, visit Exercise Central *at* <bedfordstmartins .com/focusonwriting>.

 ESL Tip
Have students label passive and active verbs before they make their corrections.

Example:

Several researchers are interested in leadership qualities, and a study of decision making <u>was conducted</u> by them.

Several researchers are interested in leadership qualities, *and they* *conducted a study of decision making.*

1. A local university funded the study, and the research team <u>was led</u> by Dr. Alicia Flynn.

   A local university funded the study, *and Dr. Alicia Flynn led the research team.*

2. The researchers developed a series of questions about decision making, and then one hundred subjects <u>were interviewed</u> by them.

   The researchers developed a series of questions about decision making, *and then they interviewed one hundred subjects.*

3. Intuition <u>was relied on</u> by two-thirds of the subjects, and only one-third used logic.

   Two-thirds of the subjects relied on intuition, and only one-third used logic.

4. After the researchers completed the study, a report <u>was written</u> about their findings.

   After the researchers completed the study, *they wrote a report about their findings.*

5. The report <u>was read</u> by many experts, and most of them found the results surprising.

   Many experts read the report, and most of them found the results surprising.

Focus on Writing: *Flashback*

Look back at your response to the Focus on Writing activity on page 357. Check each sentence to make sure it includes no illogical shifts in voice. If you find an incorrect sentence, correct it on a separate sheet of paper.

Focus on Writing: *Revising and Editing*

Look back at your response to the Focus on Writing activity on page 357. Revise any illogical shifts in tense, person, or voice by incorporating the changes and corrections you made in this chapter's Focus on Writing activities.

Chapter Review

Editing Practice: Paragraph

Read the following student paragraph, which includes illogical shifts in tense, person, and voice. Edit the passage to eliminate the unnecessary shifts, making sure subjects and verbs agree. The first error has been corrected for you.

The Origin of Baseball Cards

The first baseball cards appeared in the late 1800s. These
cardboard pictures ~~are~~ *were* inserted in packs of cigarettes. Some people
collected the cards, and the cigarette companies ~~use~~ *used* the cards to
encourage people to buy their products. By the early twentieth
century, ~~it was found by~~ candy makers *found* that they could use baseball
cards to sell candy to children, so they developed new marketing
plans. For example, each Cracker Jack box ~~contains~~ *contained* a baseball card. In
1933, gum manufacturers packaged bubblegum with baseball cards to
make "bubblegum cards." Children could trade these cards. Sometimes,
children would put cards in the spokes of their bike wheels. The cards
made noise when the wheels ~~turns~~ *turned*. Eventually, the bubblegum ~~is~~ *was*
dropped by the card manufacturers, and people collected the cards
themselves. Still, collecting baseball cards was seen as just a hobby
for children until the 1970s, when dealers began to sell their rarest
cards at high prices. Today, baseball-card collectors ~~were~~ *are* mainly adults
who are interested in investment, not baseball.

Editing Practice: Essay

Read the following student essay, which includes illogical shifts in tense, person, and voice. Edit the passage to eliminate the illogical shifts, making sure subjects and verbs agree. The first sentence has been edited for you.
Answers may vary.

The Mixing of Cultures

Because the United States is a land of opportunity, it ~~drew~~ *draws* thousands of immigrants from Europe, Asia, and Africa. Many of them come to the United States because they ~~wanted~~ *want* to become Americans. To me, this is the strength of the United States. As a Filipino American, I am able to be both Filipino and American. I know of no other country in the world where this ~~was~~ *is* true.

Many Filipino Americans want to keep parts of their original culture. This conflict confuses many Filipino immigrants. Some people think that to become American, ~~you~~ *they* have to give up ~~your~~ *their* ethnic identity. Others, however, realize that it is possible for a person to become an American without losing ~~your~~ *their* ethnic identity.

Many Filipino Americans are able to maintain their Filipino culture in the United States. For example, they ~~decorated~~ *decorate* their houses to look like houses in the Philippines. Filipinos also try to keep their native language. Although ~~every Filipino speaks~~ *all Filipinos speak* English, Tagalog ~~is also spoken by them~~ *they also speak* at home.

On holidays, Filipinos ~~followed~~ *follow* the traditions of the Philippines. They sing Filipino folk songs, do traditional dances, and cook Filipino foods. ~~Everyone tries~~ *They all try* to visit the Philippines as often as they can. In this way, a Filipino child can experience his or her ethnic culture firsthand.

A Filipino family that ~~wanted~~ *wants* to hold on to their ethnic background can enjoy life in America. Here, cultures mix and enrich one another. Each culture has something to offer America — ~~your~~ *its* food, language, and traditions. At the same time, America ~~had~~ *has*

Teaching Tip
Remind students that a collective noun such as *family* is usually singular and is used with a singular pronoun. Refer them to 27E.

something to offer each culture — economic opportunity, education, and freedom.

Collaborative Activities

1. On a separate sheet of paper, write five sentences that include shifts from present to past tense, some logical and some illogical. Exchange papers with another person in your group, and revise any incorrect sentences.

2. As a group, make up a test with five sentences containing illogical shifts in tense, person, and voice. Exchange tests with another group in the class. After you have taken their test, compare your answers with theirs.

Review Checklist: **Illogical Shifts**	☐ An illogical shift in tense occurs when a writer shifts from one tense to another for no apparent reason. (See 23A.)
	☐ An illogical shift in person occurs when a writer shifts from one person to another for no apparent reason. (See 23B.)
	☐ An illogical shift in voice occurs when a writer shifts from active to passive voice or from passive to active voice for no apparent reason. (See 23C.)

harriettstomato.com

http://www.harriettstomato.com/

Harriett's Tomato

...all food, all the time

APRIL 2007

Sun	Mon	Tue	Wed	Thu	Fri	Sat
1	2	3	4	5	6	7
8	9	10	11	12	13	14
15	16	17	18	19	20	21
22	23	24	25	26	27	28
29	30					

Subscribe to this blog's feed

Add me to your TypePad People list

FOOD VIDEOS

potato galette

stovetop espresso

RECENT POSTS

Martha and Alain in Outer Space

Of Cilantro and Stink Bugs

Chocolate Jesus

Food & Wine...and Tomato

Martyred Muffuletta

Mmmmmmmmm....

Strawberry Vice

Squirrel Salad Sandwich

Queen Elizabeth II on Food

Cheese Scrabble

CATEGORIES

Artisans and Purveyors

Cocktails

Eating In

Eating Out

Food Art

Food Books

Food Ephemera

Food News

Food Travel

Food Wit

Recipes

SUNDAY, APRIL 01, 2007

Simple Summer Food

Summer is here, and the wonderful thing about it is not the 102-degree weather, nor is it the fragrant, sizzling sidewalks. It is the fact that you can make an entire dish from about three ingredients.

The food in the above photo is almost cheating, it's so easy. Sunkissed chopped tomatoes, olive oil, garlic, thyme, salt & pepper on grilled olive bread. Grilled, as opposed to toasted -- if there is no real fire nearby, a cast-iron stovetop grill pan works quite well.

Tomato Bruschetta

2 ripe tomatoes, about 2/3 of a pound

1/4 cup extra virgin olive oil

1 clove fresh garlic, minced

2 teaspoons fresh thyme leaves

Fine seasalt & freshly ground black pepper

6 slices olive bread

Dice the tomatoes small and toss with the oil, thyme, salt and pepper. Let the mixture sit for a good 15 minutes. Grill the olive bread on both sides, no oil needed. Divide the tomatoes on top of the bread and eat immediately.

ABOUT

Email Me

FOOD SONGS

Abatoir Blues Nick Cave: Rogue's Gallery: Pirate Ballads, Sea Songs, and Chanteys

Almond Kisses Spacehog: Resident Alien

Ball and Biscuit White Stripes: Get Behind Me Satan

The tomato, native to the Americas, was not introduced in Europe until the sixteenth century. Many Europeans believed at first that tomatoes were poisonous.

Birthday Cake Cibo Matto: Viva! La Woman

Black Cherry Goldfrapp: Black Cherry

A **modifier** is a word or word group that **modifies** (identifies or describes) another word in a sentence. To avoid confusion, a modifier should be placed as close as possible to the word it modifies—ideally, directly before or directly after.

24a Correcting Dangling Modifiers

A **dangling modifier** "dangles" because the word it is supposed to modify does not appear in the sentence. Often, a dangling modifier comes at the beginning of a sentence and seems to modify the noun or pronoun that follows it.

Using my computer, the report was finished in two days.

In the sentence above, the modifier *Using my computer* seems to be modifying *the report*. But this makes no sense. (How can the report use a computer?) The word the modifier should logically modify is missing. To correct this sentence, you need to supply the missing word.

Using my computer, I finished the report in two days.

Teaching Tip
Spend extra time explaining why these examples are incorrect. This concept is difficult for many students to grasp.

To correct a dangling modifier, supply the noun or pronoun that the dangling modifier should actually modify.

→ Focus on Writing

On the opposite page is a recipe that appeared on a food blog. Read this recipe, and then write a recipe of your own. Begin by identifying the dish to be prepared; then, list the ingredients, and explain how to prepare the dish.

WORD POWER
assemble to put together into a whole
ingredient something required in a recipe

Incorrect	Moving the microscope's mirror, the light can be directed onto the slide. (Did the light move the mirror?)
Correct	Moving the microscope's mirror, you can direct the light onto the slide.
Incorrect	Paid in advance, the furniture was delivered. (Was the furniture paid in advance?)
Correct	Paid in advance, the movers delivered the furniture.

● Practice 24-1

Each of the following sentences contains a dangling modifier. To correct each sentence, add a noun or pronoun to which the modifier can logically refer.

Example: Waiting inside, my bus passed by.

Waiting inside, I missed my bus.

Answers will vary.

1. Paid by the school, the books were sorted in the library.

   _____

2. Pushing on the brakes, my car would not stop for the red light.

   _____

3. Lacking money, my trip was canceled.

   _____

4. Working overtime, his salary almost doubled.

   _____

5. Angered by the noise, the concert was called off.

   _____

6. Using the correct formula, the problem was easily solved.

   _____

7. Exhausted and hungry, the assignment was finished by midnight.

   _____

8. Jogging through the park, the pigeons were fed.

   _____

On the Web
For more practice, visit
Exercise Central *at*
<bedfordstmartins
.com/focusonwriting>.

Teaching Tip
Have students explain
the errors in these sen-
tences. Show them how
to correct dangling
modifiers by asking
questions (for example,
*Was the bus waiting
inside?*) to help them
identify the missing
subject.

9. Staying in bed on Sunday, the newspaper was read from beginning to end.

_____

10. Driving for a long time, my leg began to hurt.

_____

● **Practice 24-2**

Complete the following sentences, making sure to include a noun or pronoun to which each modifier can logically refer.

Example: Dancing with the man of her dreams, *she decided that it* _____ *was time to wake up.* _____

Answers will vary.

1. Begging for forgiveness, _____

2. Soaked by the rain, _____

3. Seeing a strange light in the sky, _____

4. Running down the steps at midnight, _____

5. Alerted by a sound from outside, _____

6. Sent to fight in a foreign land, _____

7. Grabbing the chandelier, _____

8. Disgusted by the horrible meal, _____

9. Wanting desperately to go to the concert, _____

10. Distrusting the advice he got from his friends, _____

Focus on Writing: *Flashback*

Look back at your response to the Focus on Writing activity on page 367. Do any of your sentences contain dangling modifiers? On a separate sheet of paper, rewrite any sentence that contains a dangling modifier, making sure to include a word to which the modifier can logically refer.

24b Correcting Misplaced Modifiers

Teaching Tip
To help students understand the difference between a dangling modifier and a misplaced modifier, point out that a misplaced modifier modifies a word that actually appears in the sentence.

A modifier should be placed as close as possible to the word it modifies. A **misplaced modifier** is a modifier that appears to modify the wrong word because it is placed incorrectly in the sentence. To correct this problem, move the modifier so it is as close as possible to the word it is supposed to modify (usually directly before or after it).

Incorrect   Sarah fed the dog wearing her pajamas. (Was the dog wearing Sarah's pajamas?)

Correct   Wearing her pajamas, Sarah fed the dog.

Incorrect   Dressed in a raincoat and boots, I thought my son was prepared for the storm. (Who was dressed in a raincoat and boots?)

Correct   I thought my son, dressed in a raincoat and boots, was prepared for the storm.

Incorrect   At the wedding, she danced with the groom in a beautiful white gown. (Was the groom wearing a white gown?)

Correct   At the wedding, she danced in a beautiful white gown with the groom.

On the Web
For more practice, visit
Exercise Central *at*
<bedfordstmartins
.com/focusonwriting>.

● Practice 24-3

Rewrite the following sentences, which contain misplaced modifiers, so that each modifier clearly refers to the word it is supposed to modify.

Example: Mark ate a pizza standing in front of the refrigerator.

Standing in front of the refrigerator, Mark ate a pizza.

1. The cat broke the vase frightened by a noise.
   Frightened by a noise, the cat broke the vase.

2. Running across my bathroom ceiling, I saw two large, hairy bugs.
   I saw two large, hairy bugs running across my bathroom ceiling.

3. The man was sitting in the chair with red hair.
   The man with red hair was sitting in the chair.

4. *ET* is a film about an alien directed by Steven Spielberg.

   ET is a film, directed by Steven Spielberg, about an alien.

5. With their deadly venom, people are sometimes killed by snakes.

   People are sometimes killed by snakes, with their deadly venom.

6. *Pudd'nhead Wilson* is a book about an exchange of identities by Mark Twain.

   Pudd'nhead Wilson, a book by Mark Twain, is about an exchange of identities.

7. I ran outside and saw eight tiny reindeer in my bathrobe.

   I ran outside in my bathrobe and saw eight tiny reindeer.

8. Barking all night, I listened to my neighbor's dog.

   I listened to my neighbor's dog barking all night.

9. The exterminator sprayed the insect wearing a mask.

   Wearing a mask, the exterminator sprayed the insect.

10. With a mysterious smile, Leonardo da Vinci painted the *Mona Lisa*.

    Leonardo da Vinci painted the Mona Lisa with a mysterious smile.

Focus on Writing: *Flashback*

Look back at your response to the Focus on Writing activity on page 367. Do any sentences contain misplaced modifiers? On a separate sheet of paper, rewrite any such sentences by placing the modifiers as close as possible to a word they can logically modify.

Focus on Writing: *Revising and Editing*

Look back at your response to the Focus on Writing activity on page 367. Then, add two sentences, one with an *-ing* modifier and one with an *-ed* modifier. Finally, check your work for any dangling or misplaced modifiers.

Editing Practice: Paragraph

Read the following paragraph. Rewrite sentences to correct dangling and misplaced modifiers. In some cases, you may have to supply a word or word group to which the modifier can logically refer. The first incorrect sentence has been corrected for you.   *Answers may vary.*

The Mystery of Stonehenge

Many tourists travel   to visit
~~Traveling~~ to England, Stonehenge ~~is visited by many tourists.~~

Everyone who has seen the large stone circle has wondered how

Stonehenge was built. Guessing that it was used for worshipping druid
some researchers thought
gods, Stonehenge was ~~thought to be~~ a temple. Others believed it was a

burial site. Now, however, some scientists think that Stonehenge may
people could have predicted
have been an observatory. Using the stones, eclipses and other solar

events ~~could have been predicted.~~ Taking a great deal of time and

effort, the people who created Stonehenge carried out an impressive
used tools made of antlers to dig
engineering feat. About five thousand years ago, they ~~dug~~ a ditch

~~with tools made of antlers.~~ The first stone circle was set up about

a thousand years later. Placed at the Stonehenge site~~, people~~
were dragged by people
~~dragged~~ these stones for hundreds of miles. ~~Weighing more than fifty~~
Six
~~tons each, six~~ hundred people would be needed to drag the stones
, weighing more than fifty tons each,
over the steepest part of the trip. Raising the stones to an upright
workers used
position, levers and ropes ~~were used by workers.~~ Probably finished in

about 1500 B.C., ~~the people who built it felt that~~ Stonehenge was very
to the people who built it.
important,

Editing Practice: Essay

Read the following student essay, which contains modification errors. Rewrite sentences to correct dangling and misplaced modifiers. In some cases, you may have to supply a word to which the modifier can logically refer. The first incorrect sentence has been corrected for you.   *Answers may vary.*

The ABCs of My Education

Born in New York City, I spent my early years in the Bronx. My parents worked hard but made just enough money to get by. Raised in this environment, *I saw* ~~there was~~ violence everywhere. I watched my friends get involved with gangs and drugs. Concerned about me, *one of my parents* ~~I~~ walked *me* to school every day ~~with one of my parents.~~ *Believing that school was a safe place for me, they* ~~They~~ took a lot of time out of their lives to see that I got an education, ~~believing that school was a safe place for me.~~ Agreeing with them, ~~school was the place where~~ I stayed longer and longer *at school*. One day, my guidance counselor suggested *, seeing my potential,* that I apply to A Better Chance (A.B.C.) ~~seeing my potential.~~

The A.B.C. program is nationally acclaimed. Participating in the program, ~~the extra classes are taken by~~ children with limited opportunities *take extra classes to* ~~to~~ improve their academic skills. *Based on my record,* I was able to transfer to a suburban high school, ~~based on my record.~~

Arriving at my new school, *I found* it ~~was~~ difficult ~~for me~~ to adjust. My teachers encouraged every student *in the program* to aim for college ~~in the program.~~ With the help of my teachers, my friends, and especially my parents, I began to excel. Graduating in the top 20 percent of my class, *I felt* my dreams had come true.

The A.B.C. program helped me get a good education. *Finished with my schooling,* I hope to return to the South Bronx, ~~finished with my schooling,~~ to become a teacher. Teaching in the Bronx, *I will show* my students ~~will be shown~~ the value of education. I will also tell them that only they themselves can ~~only~~ choose to make something positive of their lives.

Sometimes a teacher or school administrator can make a big difference in a person's life. A conversation or a remark can change a person's life forever. That is exactly what happened to me. Visiting my guidance counselor, *I had* a conversation *that* put me on a path that would eventually take me to college.

Collaborative Activities

1. Working in a group of five or six students, make a list of five *-ing* modifiers and five *-ed* modifiers. Exchange your list with another group, and complete one another's sentences.

    Example:

    Typing as fast as he could, <u>John could not wait to finish his</u>
    <u>screenplay.</u>

2. Working in a team of three students, compete with other teams to compose sentences that contain outrageous and confusing dangling or misplaced modifiers. As a class, correct the sentences. Then, vote on which group wrote the best sentences.

3. In a group of four or five students, find examples of confusing dangling and misplaced modifiers in magazines and newspapers. Rewrite the sentences, making sure each modifier is placed as close as possible to the word it describes.

Review Checklist: Dangling and Misplaced Modifiers

☐ A modifier is a word or word group that identifies or describes another word in a sentence. Modifiers should be placed near the words they modify.

☐ Correct a dangling modifier by supplying the word that the dangling modifier should actually modify. (See 24A.)

☐ Correct a misplaced modifier by moving the modifier as close as possible to the word it is supposed to modify. (See 24B.)

Editing Practice: Sentences

Read the following sentences, which contain run-ons, sentence fragments, errors in subject-verb agreement, illogical shifts, and dangling and misplaced modifiers. Identify the errors, and then correct them. Some sentences may have more than one error. *Answers will vary.*

Teaching Tip
You can use this exercise to warm students up for the multi-error editing practice that follows.

1. Driving up Mt. Washington in winter, ^*we saw that* the road was closed at 3,500 feet because of huge snowdrifts.

2. Each of the graduates ~~are~~ ^*is* planning to come to the event.

3. The floor plans for the new house ~~was~~ ^*were* not impressive/ ~~Because~~ ^*because* the rooms were very small.

4. *Although public* ~~Public~~ transportation can be cheap and fast, many people prefer to drive their cars to work.

5. There ~~was~~ ^*were* too many students in my biology class to fit in the room.

6. I couldn't get to class yesterday/ ~~The reason being that~~ ^*because* my car had a flat tire.

7. Anyone who visits a new city should take a bus tour so that ~~you~~ ^*he or she* can get a quick view of the most important sights.

8. *In China and Japan, it* ~~It~~ is traditional for the bride to wear red because it is considered a lucky color/ ~~In China and Japan.~~ ^.

9. After a series of questions were asked by the lawyers and the judge/ ~~The~~ ^*, the* jury ~~were~~ ^*was* chosen.

10. A chemistry book lay open on the desk ^*that Michael had read* ~~that Michael had read.~~ ^.

Editing Practice: Essay

Read the following student essay, which contains run-ons, sentence fragments, errors in subject-verb agreement, illogical shifts, and dangling and misplaced modifiers. Identify the errors, and then correct them. The first sentence has been edited for you. *Answers will vary.*

Photo Magic

More people now ~~buying~~ *buy* digital cameras than film cameras.

Small, light digital cameras are especially popular with amateur photographers*, who used* ~~Who used~~ these cameras to take snapshots. They may cost more*, but* digital cameras save money in the long run*, and* ~~And~~ give photographers control over their images. Also, ~~a family~~ *families* are able to share photos by posting them on a Web site.

It may cost more to buy a digital camera*; however,* the ongoing costs ~~is~~ *are* definitely lower. Everyone ~~have~~ *has* to buy film *with* ~~With~~ a film camera. The photographer must take the exposed film to be developed. *Although some* ~~Some~~ of the photos may not come out, it is still necessary to pay for them. With a digital camera, there is no film*, and* there is no cost to process the photos. The ~~photos~~ *photographer* can immediately ~~be seen by~~ *see* the ~~photographer.~~ *photos. If a* ~~A~~ photo does not seem worth keeping*,* it can be instantly deleted. *Although it* ~~It~~ is still possible to get prints, the photographer can choose only the best images for this process.

With a digital camera, *the photographer has* ~~you have~~ much more control over the picture. If there ~~is~~ *are* any problems with a photo, they can be corrected immediately*;* for example, there is no need to keep an out-of-focus photo. A photo can also be edited so that items in the background ~~is~~ *are* omitted. It's not necessary to wait for the processing lab to make the prints*;* an ordinary color printer or a special photo printer ~~allow~~ *allows* photographers to print their own photos.

Some features of digital cameras encourage sharing photos with others. Currently, most U.S. households ~~has~~ *have* access to email*;* this situation is good for digital photography. Digital photos are often sent to others by email*, and* ~~And~~ can even be posted online. Families and friends are able to see vacation photos *and* ~~sharing~~ *share* in birthday parties ~~can be done.~~ *.* Many digital cameras can be plugged into a television set*,* *making* ~~Making~~ it possible for everyone in the room to see and enjoy the photos. Sharing their images with viewers, a slide show. ~~can be~~ ^photographers can create^

~~created by photographers.~~ Digital photos can even be transferred to

other items~~,~~ ^, such^ ~~Such~~ as personal address labels, T-shirts, or coffee mugs.

For an amateur photographer, a digital camera is probably a better

choice than a film camera~~,~~ ^because^ there ~~is~~ ^are^ advantages in long-term costs and

in control over the images. In addition, digital photography ~~encourage~~ ^encourages^

people to share their photos. These cameras ~~has~~ ^have^ replaced film cameras

in many households.

Unit Six

Understanding Basic Grammar

James Brown, Legendary Musician, Dies at 73

When Martin Luther King Jr. was assassinated in 1968, riots occurred in many cities. When James Brown went ahead with his scheduled Boston concert, his performance helped to reduce tension in the city and bring people together.

On December 25, 2006, singer James Brown, 73, died of heart failure in Atlanta, Georgia. Nicknamed "The Godfather of Soul," Brown was a visionary musician who influenced the direction of soul, funk, and rap music in America.

Born in 1933, in Barnwell, South Carolina, Mr. Brown was raised in poverty. At the age of six, he was sent to live with an aunt who ran a house of prostitution. By seventh grade, he had dropped out of school, and at 16 he was arrested for attempting to steal a car. While in prison, he started a gospel quartet and performed for other prisoners. Once released, he founded the musical group The Flames.

In 1956, Brown's single "Please, Please, Please" sold over a million copies and launched his career. In spite of many hit singles, it was Brown's 1963 album "Live at the Apollo" that made him and his band a national success.

Known for his high-energy performances, strict work ethic, and deep passion for music, James Brown was one of the first African-American stars to own the rights to his own music. In 1992, after making over 40 albums, James Brown was presented with the lifetime achievement award at the 34th Grammy Awards.

At the time of his death, Brown was in the middle of his "Seven Decades Of Funk World Tour," performing for crowds up to 80,000 people. During his life, he inspired countless musicians, including The Jackson 5, Mick Jagger and Public Enemy. "Funky Drummer," Brown's 1969 hit, is the most sampled individual recording in the world.

Teaching Tip
Remind students that not all verbs ending in -ed or -d are in the past tense. Some are past participles. (See 26A.)

Tense is the form a verb takes to show when an action or situation takes place. The **past tense** indicates that an action occurred in the past.

Regular Verbs

Regular verbs form the past tense by adding either *-ed* or *-d* to the **base form** of the verb (the present tense form of the verb that is used with *I*).

ESL Tip
Verb tense is a challenge for nonnative speakers. Check everything they write, and have them write often.

Teaching Tip
Reinforce that all regular verbs use the same form for singular and plural in the past tense: *I cheered. They cheered.*

I registered for classes yesterday.

Walt Disney produced short cartoons in 1928.

Regular verbs that end in *-y* form the past tense by changing the *y* to *i* and adding *-ed*.

tr**y**	tr**ied**
appl**y**	appl**ied**

On the Web
For more practice, visit Exercise Central *at* <bedfordstmartins.com/focusonwriting>.

● Practice 25-1

Change the verbs in the following sentences to the past tense. Cross out the present tense form of each underlined verb, and write the past tense form above it.

→ Focus on Writing

The obituary on the opposite page tells about the life of singer James Brown. Read the obituary, and then write your own obituary. As you write, assume that you have led a long life and have achieved almost everything you hoped you would. Be sure to include the accomplishments for which you would most like to be remembered. Remember to use transitional words and phrases that clearly show how one event in your life relates to another. (Refer to yourself by name or by *he* or *she*.)

WORD POWER
accomplishment something completed successfully; an achievement
longevity long life
objective goal

Example: Every year, my mother ~~visits~~ *visited* her family in Bombay, India.

(1) She always ~~returns~~ *returned* with intricate designs on her hands and feet. (2) In India, women called henna artists ~~create~~ *created* these complex patterns. (3) Henna ~~originates~~ *originated* in a plant found in the Middle East, India, Indonesia, and northern Africa. (4) Many women in these areas ~~use~~ *used* henna to color their hands, nails, and parts of their feet. (5) Men ~~dye~~ *dyed* their beards, as well as the manes and hooves of their horses, with henna. (6) They also ~~color~~ *colored* animal skins with henna. (7) In India, my mother always ~~celebrates~~ *celebrated* the end of the Ramadan religious fast by going to a "henna party." (8) A professional henna artist ~~attends~~ *attended* the party to apply new henna decorations to the palms and feet of the women. (9) After a few weeks, the henna designs ~~wash~~ *washed* off. (10) In the United States, my mother's henna designs ~~attract~~ *attracted* the attention of many people.

Teaching Tip
This Flashback works well as a proofreading exercise. If students have omitted necessary endings, they usually recognize their errors.

Focus on Writing: *Flashback*

Look back at your response to the Focus on Writing activity on page 381. Underline the past tense verbs that end in *-ed* and *-d*.

25b Irregular Verbs

Unlike regular verbs, whose past tense forms end in *-ed* or *-d*, **irregular verbs** have irregular forms in the past tense. In fact, their past tense forms may look very different from their present tense forms.

The following chart lists the base form and past tense form of many of the most commonly used irregular verbs.

Irregular Verbs in the Past Tense

Base Form	Past	Base Form	Past
awake	awoke	hold	held
be	was, were	hurt	hurt
beat	beat	keep	kept
become	became	know	knew
begin	began	lay (to place)	laid
bet	bet	lead	led
bite	bit	leave	left
blow	blew	let	let
break	broke	lie (to recline)	lay
bring	brought	light	lit
build	built	lose	lost
buy	bought	make	made
catch	caught	meet	met
choose	chose	pay	paid
come	came	quit	quit
cost	cost	read	read
cut	cut	ride	rode
dive	dove (dived)	ring	rang
do	did	rise	rose
draw	drew	run	ran
drink	drank	say	said
drive	drove	see	saw
eat	ate	sell	sold
fall	fell	send	sent
feed	fed	set	set
feel	felt	shake	shook
fight	fought	shine	shone (shined)
find	found	sing	sang
fly	flew	sit	sat
forgive	forgave	sleep	slept
freeze	froze	speak	spoke
get	got	spend	spent
give	gave	spring	sprang
go (goes)	went	stand	stood
grow	grew	steal	stole
have	had	stick	stuck
hear	heard	sting	stung
hide	hid	swear	swore

(continued on the following page)

ESL Tip
Ask students to give examples of irregular verbs in their native languages.

🌐 **ESL Tip**
Irregular past tense verb forms are challenging for native speakers and even more so for nonnative ones. Have students write sentences using some of the verbs in the chart.

Irregular Verbs in the Past Tense

Base Form	Past	Base Form	Past
swim	swam	throw	threw
take	took	understand	understood
teach	taught	wake	woke
tear	tore	wear	wore
tell	told	win	won
think	thought	write	wrote

🖱 **On the Web**
For more practice, visit Exercise Central *at* <bedfordstmartins .com/focusonwriting>.

● **Practice 25-2**

In the following sentences, fill in the correct past tense form of the irregular verb in parentheses. Use the chart on pages 383–84 to help you find the correct irregular verb form. If you do not find a verb on the chart, look it up in the dictionary.

Example: Dr. David Ho and his research team ___found___ (find) ways to treat AIDS at a time when many patients were dying of the disease.

(1) Ho ___came___ (come) to the United States from Taiwan when he ___was___ (be) twelve years old. (2) He ___knew___ (know) no English at first, but he ___kept___ (keep) studying hard. (3) He ___went___ (go) to M.I.T. for one year. (4) Then, he ___got___ (get) a B.S. in physics from Caltech. (5) Soon, he ___became___ (become) interested in molecular biology and gene splicing. (6) While studying for his medical degree at the Harvard–M.I.T. School of Medicine, he ___saw___ (see) some of the first cases of AIDS. (7) Dr. Ho ___thought___ (think) that he could fight the disease by strengthening patients' immune systems. (8) He ___had___ (have) the idea of treating patients in the early stages of the disease with an AIDS "cocktail," which combined several AIDS medications. (9) Because of his work, deaths from AIDS ___began___ (begin) to decline. (10) In 1996, *Time* magazine ___gave___ (give) Dr. Ho the honor of being named its Man of the Year.

Focus on Writing: *Flashback*

Look back at your response to the Focus on Writing activity on page 381. Circle each irregular past tense verb you find. Then, list all the irregular past tense verbs on a separate sheet of paper. Beside each past tense verb, write its base form. (If necessary, consult the list of irregular verbs on pages 383–84 or a dictionary.)

25c   Problem Verbs: *Be*

The irregular verb *be* can cause problems for writers because it has two different past tense forms—*was* for singular subjects and *were* for plural subjects.

Carlo <u>was</u> interested in becoming a city planner. (singular)

They <u>were</u> happy to help out at the school. (plural)

Teaching Tip
Point out that *be* is the only verb in English with more than one past tense form. For information about subject-verb agreement with *be*, refer students to 22C.

Teaching Tip
Challenge students to try to identify another verb as irregular as *be*. Explain that *be* is the most irregular verb in the English language.

Past Tense Forms of the Verb *Be*

	Singular	Plural
First person	I <u>was</u> tired.	We <u>were</u> tired.
Second person	You <u>were</u> tired.	You <u>were</u> tired.
Third person	He <u>was</u> tired.	
	She <u>was</u> tired.	They <u>were</u> tired.
	It <u>was</u> tired.	
	The man <u>was</u> tired.	Frank and Billy <u>were</u> tired.

On the Web
For more practice, visit Exercise Central *at* <bedfordstmartins .com/focusonwriting>.

● Practice 25-3

Edit the following passage for errors in the use of the verb *be*. Cross out any underlined verbs that are incorrect, and write the correct forms above them. If a verb form is correct, label it *C*.

Example: Until the success of Margaret Cho, there <u>was</u> no well-known Korean-American comics.   *were*

$\overset{C}{}$
(1) When Cho <u>was</u> only sixteen, she started performing her comedy act in a San Francisco comedy club. (2) Many people said no Asians
$\overset{were}{\underset{\wedge}{\cancel{was}}}$ ever going to succeed in stand-up comedy, but Cho did not back
down. (3) She toured college campuses and $\overset{C}{\underline{was}}$ a big hit. (4) Cho $\overset{C}{\underline{was}}$
booked on television specials with Arsenio Hall and Bob Hope. (5) Then,
$\overset{was}{}$
she $\underset{\wedge}{\underline{\cancel{were}}}$ given her own ABC sitcom, *All-American Girl*. (6) Although
$\overset{was}{}$
the show $\underset{\wedge}{\cancel{were}}$ cancelled after only one season, Cho's fans $\overset{were}{\cancel{was}}$ still
eager to see her. (7) Her one-woman shows $\underline{were}$ all very successful.
$\overset{C}{}$
(8) One show, *State of Emergency*, $\underline{was}$ focused on political humor. (9) To
$\overset{was}{}$
Cho, this show $\underset{\wedge}{\underline{\cancel{were}}}$ a way to get out the vote in the 2004 presidential
$\overset{was}{}$
election. (10) Cho $\underset{\wedge}{\cancel{were}}$ honored by several organizations for her promotion of equal rights for all people.

Focus on Writing: *Flashback*

Look back at your response to the Focus on Writing activity on page 381. Find all the sentences in which you use the past tense of *be*. Then, identify the subject of each *be* verb. Make sure you have used the correct form of the verb in each case.

25d

Problem Verbs: *Can/Could* and *Will/Would*

The helping verbs *can/could* and *will/would* present problems because their past tense forms are sometimes confused with their present tense forms.

Can/Could

Can, a present tense verb, means "is able to" or "are able to."

First-year students <u>can</u> apply for financial aid.

Could, the past tense of *can*, means "was able to" or "were able to."

> Escape artist Harry Houdini claimed that he <u>could</u> escape from any prison.

Will/Would

Will, a present tense verb, talks about the future from a point in the present.

> A solar eclipse <u>will</u> occur in ten months.

Would, the past tense of *will*, talks about the future from a point in the past.

> I told him yesterday that I <u>would</u> think about it.

Would is also used to express a possibility or wish.

> If we stuck to our budget, we <u>would</u> be better off.
> Laurie <u>would</u> like a new stuffed animal.

**Highlight:
Will and Would**

Note that *will* is used with *can* and that *would* is used with *could*.

I will feed the cats if I can find their food.

I would feed the cats if I could find their food.

On the Web
For more practice, visit
Exercise Central *at*
<bedfordstmartins
.com/focusonwriting>.

● **Practice 25-4**

Circle the appropriate helping verb from the choices in parentheses.

Example: Grandparents and many parents ((can), could) still remember summers when children were kept indoors, even in hot weather.

(1) Every year, as summer approached, parents (will, (would)) worry that their children (will, (would)) become victims of polio, a terrible disease. (2) An infection of the brain and spinal cord, polio (will, (would)) spread wherever people gathered in large groups, such as in movie

theaters and swimming pools. (3) Polio epidemics (will, (would)) occur every summer. (4) Doctors (can,(could)) not predict when polio would strike a community. (5) Often, young and healthy people (will,(would)) develop the disease. (6) Some people (will, (would)) show symptoms, such as fever and headache, for only twenty-four hours, but others (can, (could)) become paralyzed. (7) Although no cure for polio existed, patients (can, (could)) be treated with bed rest, hot bandages, and physical therapy. (8) During the 1940s and 1950s, researchers tried to find a way in which they (can, (could)) prevent polio. (9) Two doctors, Jonas Salk and Albert S. Sabin, (will, (would)) eventually discover vaccines that would protect against polio. (10) Today, parents whose children have been vaccinated against polio ((can), could) be sure that this disease ((will), would) not affect them.

Focus on Writing: *Flashback*

Look back at your response to the Focus on Writing activity on page 381. On a separate sheet of paper, write a few sentences that describe what you would have accomplished in your lifetime if you had had the chance. Be sure to use *could* and *would* in your sentences.

Focus on Writing: *Revising and Editing*

Look back at your response to the Focus on Writing activity on page 381. Make sure you have used the correct past tense form for each of your verbs. If you have not, cross out the incorrect form, and write the proper past tense form of the verb above the line.

Chapter Review

Editing Practice

Read the following student essay, which includes errors in past tense verb forms. Decide whether each of the underlined past tense verbs is correct. If the verb is correct, write *C* above it. If it is not, cross out the verb, and write in the correct past tense form. The first sentence has been corrected for you. (If necessary, consult the list of irregular verbs on pages 383–84.)

Refer students to 34E for more on using *lie* and *lay*.

Teaching Tip

Healing

The window seat ~~were~~ *was* our favorite place to sit. I piled comfortable pillows on the ledge and ~~spended~~ *spent* several minutes rearranging them. Then, my friend and I ~~lied~~ *lay* on our backs and propped our feet on the wall. We sat *C* with our arms around our legs and ~~thinked~~ *thought* about the mysteries of life.

We stared at the people on the street below and ~~wonder~~ *wondered* who they ~~was~~ *were* and where they ~~was~~ *were* going. We imagined that they ~~can~~ *could* be millionaires, foreign spies, or ruthless drug smugglers. We believed that everyone except us ~~leaded~~ *led* wonderful and exciting lives.

I heard *C* a voice call my name. Reluctantly, I ~~standed~~ *stood* up, tearing myself away from my imaginary world. My oldest and dearest friend — my teddy bear — and I came back to the real world. I grabbed Teddy and ~~brung~~ *brought* him close to my chest. Together we ~~go~~ *went* into the cold sitting room, where twelve other girls ~~sit~~ *sat* around a table eating breakfast. None of them looked happy.

In the unit for eating disorders, meals ~~was~~ *were* always tense. Nobody ~~wants~~ *wanted* to eat, but the nurses watched us until we ~~eated~~ *ate* every crumb. I set *C* Teddy on the chair beside me and stared gloomily at the food on my plate. I closed my eyes and ~~taked~~ *took* the first bite. I ~~feeled~~ *felt* the calories adding inches of ugly fat. Each swallow ~~were~~ *was* like a nail being ripped from my finger. At last, it was *C* over. I had survived breakfast.

Days passed slowly; each passing minute was a victory. After a
while, I learned how to eat properly. I learned that other people
had problems too. I also learned that people loved me. Eventually,
even Teddy stopped feeling sorry for me. I begun to smile — and
laugh. Sometimes I even considered myself happy. My doctors
challenged me — and, surprisingly, I rised to the occasion.

Collaborative Activities

1. Working in a group of three or four students, choose a famous living figure — an actor, a sports star, or a musician, for example — and brainstorm together to list details about this person's life. Then, working on
   your own, use the details to write a profile of the famous person.

2. Working in a group, list several contemporary problems that you think
   will be solved within ten or fifteen years. Each member of the group
   should then select a problem from the list and write a paragraph or two
   describing how the problem could be solved. As a group, arrange the
   paragraphs so that they form the body of an essay. Develop a thesis
   statement, write an introduction and a conclusion, and then revise the
   body paragraphs of the essay.

Teaching Tip
Have students write a
paragraph using a
certain number of past
tense verbs from the
chart on pages 383–84.

3. Form a group with three other students. What national or world events
   do you remember most vividly? Take ten minutes to list news events
   that you think have defined the last five years. On your own, write a
   short essay in which you discuss the significance of the three or four
   events that the members of your group agree were the most important.

Review Checklist: Verbs: Past Tense

☐ The past tense is the form a verb takes to show that an action occurred in the past. (See 25A.)

☐ Regular verbs form the past tense by adding *-ed* or *-d* to the base form of the verb. (See 25A.)

☐ Irregular verbs have irregular forms in the past tense. (See 25B.)

☐ *Be* has two different past tense forms — *was* for singular subjects and *were* for plural subjects. (See 25C.)

☐ *Could* is the past tense of *can*. *Would* is the past tense of *will*. (See 25D.)

Chapter 26

Verbs: Past Participles

Salsa music, developed in the 1960s and '70s by Cuban immigrants and Puerto Rican migrants to New York City, can have lyrics with a political edge. Salsa stars Reuben Blades and Willie Colon, for example, have recorded songs about immigration and the environment.

Regular Past Participles

Every verb has a past participle form. The **past participle** form of a regular verb is identical to its past tense form. Both are formed by adding *-d* or *-ed* to the **base form** of the verb (the present tense form of the verb that is used with the pronoun *I*).

PAST TENSE

He <u>earned</u>.

PAST PARTICIPLE

He has <u>earned</u>.

● Practice 26-1

Fill in the correct past participle form of each verb in parentheses.

Example: Recently, vacationers have _____*discovered*_____ (discover) some new opportunities to get away from it all and to do good at the same time.

(1) Volunteer vacationers have _____*visited*_____ (visit) remote locations to help build footpaths, cabins, and shelters. (2) Groups such as Habitat for Humanity have _____*offered*_____ (offer) volunteers a chance to help build homes in low-income areas. (3) Habitat's Global Village

→ Focus on Writing

The picture on the opposite page shows a couple at a dance. Look at the picture, and then write about an activity—a hobby or a sport, for example—that you have been involved in for a relatively long time. Begin by identifying the activity and stating why it has been important to you. Then, describe the activity, paying particular attention to what you have gained from it over the years.

WORD POWER
benefit something that promotes well-being
diversion something that distracts or relaxes the mind

On the Web
For more practice, visit
Exercise Central *at*
<bedfordstmartins
.com/focusonwriting>.

trips have _____ *raised* _____ (raise) awareness about the lack of afford-able housing in many countries. (4) Participants in Sierra Club pro-grams have _____ *donated* _____ (donate) thousands of work hours to groups all over the United States. (5) Sometimes these volunteers have _____ *joined* _____ (join) forest service workers to help restore wilderness areas. (6) They have _____ *cleaned* _____ (clean) up trash and campsites. (7) They have also _____ *removed* _____ (remove) nonnative plants. (8) Some vacationers have _____ *traveled* _____ (travel) to countries such as Costa Rica, Russia, and Thailand to help with local projects. (9) Other vacationers have _____ *served* _____ (serve) as teachers of English. (10) Volunteering vacations have _____ *helped* _____ (help) to strengthen cross-cultural understanding.

Focus on Writing: *Flashback*

Look back at your response to the Focus on Writing activity on page 393, and identify each helping verb (a form of the verb *have*) that is followed by a regular past participle (ending in -*ed* or -*d*). Underline both the helping verb and the past participle.

26b Irregular Past Participles

Irregular verbs nearly always have irregular past participles. Irregular verbs do not form the past participle by adding -*ed* or -*d* to the base form of the verb.

Base Form	Past Tense	Past Participle
buy	bought	bought
choose	chose	chosen
ride	rode	ridden

The following chart lists the base form, the past tense, and the past par-ticiple of the most commonly used irregular verbs.

Irregular Past Participles

Base Form	Past Tense	Past Participle
awake	awoke	awoken
be (am, are)	was (were)	been
beat	beat	beaten
become	became	become
begin	began	begun
bet	bet	bet
bite	bit	bitten
blow	blew	blown
break	broke	broken
bring	brought	brought
build	built	built
buy	bought	bought
catch	caught	caught
choose	chose	chosen
come	came	come
cost	cost	cost
cut	cut	cut
dive	dove, dived	dived
do	did	done
draw	drew	drawn
drink	drank	drunk
drive	drove	driven
eat	ate	eaten
fall	fell	fallen
feed	fed	fed
feel	felt	felt
fight	fought	fought
find	found	found
fly	flew	flown
forgive	forgave	forgiven
freeze	froze	frozen
get	got	got, gotten
give	gave	given
go	went	gone
grow	grew	grown
have	had	had
hear	heard	heard
hide	hid	hidden
hold	held	held
hurt	hurt	hurt

(continued on the following page)

⊕ **ESL Tip**
Encourage students to keep a record of the irregular verbs that give them trouble.

Teaching Tip
Although such work may seem basic, students need to practice writing some of these challenging verb forms in sentences.

Irregular Past Participles

Base Form	Past Tense	Past Participle
keep	kept	kept
know	knew	known
lay (to place)	laid	laid
lead	led	led
leave	left	left
let	let	let
lie (to recline)	lay	lain
light	lit	lit
lose	lost	lost
make	made	made
meet	met	met
pay	paid	paid
quit	quit	quit
read	read	read
ride	rode	ridden
ring	rang	rung
rise	rose	risen
run	ran	run
say	said	said
see	saw	seen
sell	sold	sold
send	sent	sent
set	set	set
shake	shook	shaken
shine	shone, shined	shone, shined
sing	sang	sung
sit	sat	sat
sleep	slept	slept
speak	spoke	spoken
spend	spent	spent
spring	sprang	sprung
stand	stood	stood
steal	stole	stolen
stick	stuck	stuck
sting	stung	stung
swear	swore	sworn
swim	swam	swum
take	took	taken

(continued on the following page)

Irregular Past Participles

Base Form	Past Tense	Past Participle
teach	taught	taught
tear	tore	torn
tell	told	told
think	thought	thought
throw	threw	thrown
understand	understood	understood
wake	woke, waked	woken, waked
wear	wore	worn
win	won	won
write	wrote	written

● **Practice 26-2**

Fill in the correct past participle of each verb in parentheses. Refer to the chart on pages 395–97 as needed. If you cannot find a verb on the chart, look it up in the dictionary.

Example: Since 1836, the Alamo has _____*been*_____ (be) one of the most famous American historical sites.

On the Web
For more practice, visit
Exercise Central *at*
<bedfordstmartins
.com/focusonwriting>.

(1) American teachers have _____*taught*_____ (teach) their students about the defenders of the Alamo during Texas's battle for independence from Mexico. (2) Americans have _____*heard*_____ (hear) about how 189 Texans held off a Mexican army of thousands for thirteen days. (3) Many children have _____*built*_____ (build) models of the Alamo, which was once a home for Spanish missionaries. (4) Visitors have _____*come*_____ (come) to see the place where many American heroes, including Davy Crockett and Jim Bowie, died. (5) The slogan "Remember the Alamo" has _____*become*_____ (become) famous. (6) Now, however, one historian has _____*made*_____ (make) a startling claim. (7) Dr. Will Fowler, of St. Andrews University in Scotland, has _____*written*_____ (write) a book that suggests that we were wrong about the Alamo. (8) According to Fowler, the story that many people

have _____ *read* _____ (read) may not be accurate. (9) He has
_____ *said* _____ (say) that the Texans wanted to take land away from
Mexico and to preserve slavery in that territory. (10) Those who have
always _____ *seen* _____ (see) the defenders of the Alamo as heroes
strongly disagree with Fowler's position.

● Practice 26-3

Edit the following passage for errors in irregular past participles. Cross out
any underlined past participles that are incorrect, and write in the correct
form above them. If the verb form is correct, label it *C*.

Example: In recent years, some people have ~~standed~~ *stood* up against
overseas sweatshops.

    (1) Buying products from overseas sweatshops has ~~became~~ *become* contro-
versial over the last few decades. (2) American manufacturers have
~~sended~~ *sent* their materials to developing countries where employees work
under terrible conditions for very low wages. (3) Violations of basic U.S.
labor laws—such as getting extra pay for overtime and being paid
on time—have ~~lead~~ *led* to severe criticism. (4) Low-wage workers in developing countries have ~~finded~~ *found* themselves facing dangerous working
conditions as well as verbal and sexual abuse. (5) Even well-known
retailers—such as Sears, Tommy Hilfiger, and Target—have gotten *C*
in trouble with consumers for selling items made in sweatshops.
(6) Recently, colleges have ~~be~~ *been* criticized for using overseas sweatshops
to make clothing featuring school names. (7) Students have ~~spoke~~ *spoken* out
against such practices, and schools have had *C* to respond. (8) While
some manufacturers may have ~~losed~~ *lost* money by increasing wages for
overseas workers, they have ~~understanded~~ *understood* that this is the right thing to
do. (9) They have made *C* a promise to their customers that they will not
employ sweatshop labor. (10) Still, consumers have not always ~~forgave~~ *forgiven*
manufacturers who have a history of such practices.

ESL Tip
After students have com-
pleted Practice 26-3,
give them a correct
version of the exercise.
Have them copy the
paragraph and then
compare it with their
own version.

Teaching Tip
Point out that some
words (such as *not, also,
even,* and *hardly*) can
come between the help-
ing verb and the past
participle.

Focus on Writing: *Flashback*

Look back at your response to the Focus on Writing activity on page 393, and identify each form of the helping verb *have* that is followed by an irregular past participle. Then, underline both the helping verb and the irregular past participle.

The Present Perfect Tense

The past participle is used to form different verb tenses. For example, the past participle is combined with the present tense forms of *have* to form the **present perfect tense**.

> ### The Present Perfect Tense (*have* or *has* + past participle)
>
> | *Singular* | *Plural* |
> |---|---|
> | I have gained. | We have gained. |
> | You have gained. | You have gained. |
> | He has gained. | They have gained. |
> | She has gained. | |
> | It has gained. | |

- Use the present perfect tense to indicate an action that began in the past and continues into the present.

    Present perfect   The nurse has worked at the Welsh Mountain clinic for two years. (The working began in the past and continues into the present.)

Teaching Tip
Tell students that the words *just, now, already,* and *recently* indicate that an action has just occurred.

- Use the present perfect tense to indicate that an action has just occurred.

    Present perfect   I have just eaten. (The eating has just occurred.)

On the Web
For more practice, visit
Exercise Central *at*
<bedfordstmartins
.com/focusonwriting>.

● **Practice 26-4**

Circle the appropriate verb tense (past tense or present perfect) from the choices in parentheses.

Example: When I (visited, have visited) Montreal, I was surprised to discover a truly bilingual city.

(1) When I was in Montreal, I (heard, have heard) both English and French. (2) Montreal (kept, has kept) two languages as a result of its history. (3) Until 1763, Montreal (belonged, has belonged) to France. (4) Then, when France (lost, has lost) the Seven Years War, the city (became, has become) part of England. (5) When I was there last year, most people (spoke, have spoken) both French and English. (6) Although I (knew, have known) no French, I (found, have found) that I was able to get along quite well. (7) For example, all the museums (made, have made) their guided tours available in English. (8) Most restaurants (offered, have offered) bilingual menus. (9) There (were, have been) even English radio and television stations and English newspapers. (10) In Montreal, I (felt, have felt) both at home and in a foreign country.

● **Practice 26-5**

Fill in the appropriate tense (past tense or present perfect) of the verb in parentheses.

Example: Most Americans _____have had_____ (have) a special interest in the results of presidential election polls.

(1) During the 2004 presidential campaign, at least eight different polls ____measured____ (measure) people's views. (2) Until 1986, interviewers ____knocked____ (knock) on doors to determine people's opinions. (3) More recently, public opinion polls ____have used____ (use) random sampling, in which a computer ran-

domly dials phone numbers. (4) When they used this technique, pollsters _____*have had*_____ (have) to interview only about a thousand people to get an accurate cross-section of the American people. (5) It _____*has taken*_____ (take) great skill for pollsters to learn to ask unbiased questions. (6) Gallup Poll interviewers _____*have asked*_____ (ask) one particular question since the time when Franklin D. Roosevelt was president: "Do you approve or disapprove of the job the president is doing?" (7) Using the same wording _____*has ensured*_____ (ensure) an accurate view of people's feelings about the president over the years. (8) Despite the care that pollsters take, some people _____*have questioned*_____ (question) the accuracy of random sampling. (9) Also, some worry that the wide publicity that polls _____*have received*_____ (receive) encourages some people to support the candidate who is ahead in the polls. (10) Still, when Americans were asked recently to evaluate the accuracy of polls, most _____*said*_____ (say) that they forecast election results accurately.

Focus on Writing: *Flashback*

Look back at your response to the Focus on Writing activity on page 393. Choose three sentences with past tense verbs, and rewrite them on a separate sheet of paper, changing past tense to present perfect tense. How does your revision change the meaning of each sentence?

26d   The Past Perfect Tense

The past participle is also used to form the **past perfect tense**, which consists of the past tense of *have* plus the past participle.

The Past Perfect Tense (*had* + past participle)

Singular	*Plural*
I had returned.	We had returned.
You had returned.	You had returned.
He had returned.	They had returned.
She had returned.	
It had returned.	

Use the past perfect tense to show that one past action occurred before another past action.

PAST
PERFECT TENSE   PAST TENSE

Chief Sitting Bull had fought many battles before he defeated General Custer. (The fighting done by Sitting Bull occurred *before* he defeated Custer.)

● **Practice 26-6**

On the Web
For more practice, visit Exercise Central *at* <bedfordstmartins .com/focusonwriting>.

Circle the appropriate verb tense (present perfect or past perfect) from the choices in parentheses.

Example: Although the children (have eaten/had eaten) dinner, they still had room for ice cream.

1. Ren wondered where he (has left/had left) his keys.

2. He now believes he (has lost/had lost) them.

3. The receptionist told the interviewer that the applicant (has arrived/ had arrived).

4. The interviewer says that she (has waited/had waited) for an hour.

5. The jury decided that the defendant (has lied/had lied) on the witness stand.

6. The jury members are still discussing the case although they (have been/ had been) in the jury room for three days.

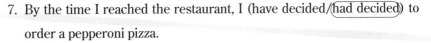

7. By the time I reached the restaurant, I (have decided/~~had decided~~) to order a pepperoni pizza.

8. By the time my pizza is ready, I usually (~~have finished~~/had finished) my pinball game.

9. The DVD (has been/~~had been~~) playing for only ten minutes when I ejected it.

10. This movie is excellent; I (~~have seen~~/had seen) it at least five times.

Focus on Writing: *Flashback*

Look back at your response to the Flashback activity on page 401. Rewrite your three present perfect tense sentences on a separate sheet of paper, this time changing them to the past perfect tense. How do your revisions change the meaning of each sentence?

26e   Past Participles as Adjectives

Teaching Tip
Refer students to 14C for more on linking verbs.

In addition to functioning as verbs, past participles can also function as adjectives modifying nouns that follow them.

I cleaned up the broken glass.

The exhausted runner finally crossed the finish line.

Past participles are also used as adjectives after **linking verbs**, such as *seemed* or *looked*.

Jason seemed surprised.

He looked shocked.

● **Practice 26-7**

Edit the following passage for errors in past participle forms used as adjectives. Cross out any underlined participles that are incorrect, and write the correct form above them. If the participle form is correct, label it *C*.

> *C*
> **Example:** College students are often <u>strapped</u> for cash.

(1) College students are ~~surprise~~ *surprised* when they find ~~preapprove~~ *preapproved* applications for credit cards in their mail. (2) Credit-card companies also recruit <u>targeted</u> *C* students through booths that are ~~locate~~ *located* on campus. (3) The booths are ~~design~~ *designed* to attract new customers with offers of gifts. (4) Why have companies gone to all this trouble to attract <u>qualified</u> *C* students? (5) Most older Americans already have at least five credit cards that are ~~stuff~~ *stuffed* in their wallets. (6) Banks and credit-card companies see younger college students as a major <u>untapped</u> *C* market. (7) According to experts, students are a good credit risk because ~~concern~~ *concerned* parents usually bail them out when they cannot pay a bill. (8) Finally, people tend to feel ~~tie~~ *tied* to their first credit card. (9) Companies want to be the first card that is ~~acquire~~ *acquired* by a customer. (10) For this reason, credit-card companies target ~~uninform~~ *uninformed* college students.

Focus on Writing: *Flashback*

Look back at your response to the Focus on Writing activity on page 393. Choose three nouns you used in your writing, and list them on a separate sheet of paper. Then, list a past participle that can modify each noun. Finally, use each noun and its past participle modifier in an original sentence.

Focus on Writing: *Revising and Editing*

Look back at your response to the Focus on Writing activity on page 393. Did you use incorrect present perfect or past perfect tense verb forms? If so, cross out the incorrect verb forms, and write your corrections above them. When you have finished, check the past participles and perfect tenses in another writing assignment on which you are currently working.

Chapter Review

Editing Practice

Read the following student essay, which includes errors in the use of past participles and in the use of the perfect tenses. Decide whether each of the underlined verbs or participles is correct. If it is correct, write *C* above it. If it is not, write in the correct verb form. The first error has been corrected for you.

Using the Internet to Get Out the Vote

The number of people who have <s>vote</s> *voted* in recent U.S. elections has <s>drop.</s> *dropped.* One reason is age. The younger a person is, the less likely it is that he or she will vote. Even though voting is very important, far too many young people have *C* not <s>took</s> *taken* part. Now, however, the Internet has *C* become an important way to reach voters, raise money for election campaigns, and motivate young people.

Many businesses have <s>turn</s> *turned* to the Internet to reach others, especially the young. Now, political campaigns have <s>find</s> *found* that they can attract voters and election workers by using the Internet. For example, both Democrats and Republicans <s>had</s> *have* used email to persuade voters to support candidates and to provide vote-by-mail ballots. At the same time, their Web sites and blogs have <s>stimulate</s> *stimulated* interest in politics and have <s>provide</s> *provided* ways for young people to meet each other and work for their candidates.

For example, in 2004, Democrats ~~have~~ _wanted_ to motivate young

people to work and vote for John Kerry in the presidential election.

As a result, the Moveon.org site ~~has organize~~ _organized_ and ~~promote~~ _promoted_ a tour

of some popular musicians, such as Bruce Springsteen and the Dixie

Chicks. It also _sold_ anti-Bush T-shirts and bumper stickers. Similarly,

GeorgeWBush.com ~~had~~ _offered_ young Republicans ways to use the

Internet to create a pro-Bush poster, download pro-Bush screensavers,

and order pro-Bush items. With such Web sites, the two main political

parties ~~have~~ _caught_ the interest of young people.

Recently, candidates who want to run for president in 2008 ~~have~~

~~turn~~ _turned_ to YouTube. This popular video-sharing site ~~has~~ _enabled_ candidates

to reach millions of young voters. Political candidates ~~had~~ _have_ recognized

the potential of this site. For example, Hillary Clinton has ~~post~~ _posted_

campaign ads and short talks on YouTube. Barack Obama has ~~post~~ _posted_

political advertisements. Some people have even ~~make~~ _made_ music videos

about political candidates. For political candidates, the best thing

about YouTube is that it is free.

In the recent past, many young Americans have not ~~express~~ _expressed_ much

interest in politics. However, their interest in the Internet has ~~teached~~ _taught_

them about government and politics and has ~~gave~~ _given_ them a new way to

participate in the democratic process.

Collaborative Activities

1. Exchange Focus on Writing activities with another student. Read each
   other's work, making sure that present perfect and past perfect tenses
   are used correctly.

Teaching Tip
Collaborative Activity 2
works well for getting
students involved in a
classroom discussion.

2. Assume that you are a restaurant employee who has been nominated for
   Employee of the Year. To win this award (along with a thousand-dollar
   prize), you have to explain in writing what you have done during the
   past year to deserve this honor. Write a letter to your supervisor and the
   awards committee. When you have finished, trade papers with another
   student, and edit his or her letter.

Review Checklist:
Verbs: Past Participles

☐ The past participle of regular verbs is formed by adding -ed or -d to the base form. (See 26A.)

☐ Irregular verbs usually have irregular past participles. (See 26B.)

☐ The past participle is combined with the present tense forms of *have* to form the present perfect tense. (See 26C.)

☐ The past participle is used to form the past perfect tense, which consists of the past tense of *have* plus the past participle. (See 26D.)

☐ The past participle can function as an adjective. (See 26E.)

Chapter 27

Nouns and Pronouns

Thought to be the earliest rock band still performing together, the Dutch group Golden Earring began performing in 1961 — one year before the Rolling Stones.

Identifying Nouns

Teaching Tip
Refer students to 33A for information on capitalizing proper nouns.

A **noun** is a word that names a person (*singer, Jennifer Lopez*), an animal (*dolphin, Flipper*), a place (*downtown, Houston*), an object (*game, Scrabble*), or an idea (*happiness, Darwinism*).

A **singular noun** names one thing. A **plural noun** names more than one thing.

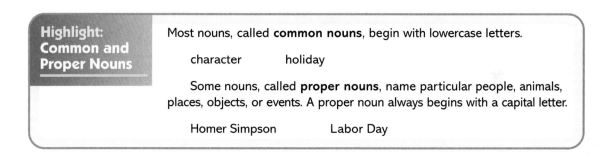

Highlight: Common and Proper Nouns

Most nouns, called **common nouns**, begin with lowercase letters.

character   holiday

Some nouns, called **proper nouns**, name particular people, animals, places, objects, or events. A proper noun always begins with a capital letter.

Homer Simpson   Labor Day

27b

Forming Plural Nouns

Most nouns that end in consonants add *-s* to form plurals. Other nouns form plurals with *-es*. For example, most nouns that end in *-o* add *-es* to form plurals. Other nouns, whose singular forms end in *-s*, *-ss*, *-sh*, *-ch*, *-x*, or *-z*, add *-es* to form plurals. Some nouns that end in *-s* or *-z* double the *s* or *z* before adding *-es*.

→ Focus on Writing

The picture on the opposite page shows a band giving a performance. Look at the picture, and then write about why you like a particular musician or group, TV show, or movie. Assume your readers are not familiar with the subject you are writing about.

WORD POWER
compelling extremely forceful
mesmerizing hypnotic

🌐 **ESL Tip**
Briefly review subject-verb agreement. Remind students that if the subject ends in -s, the verb usually does not. Refer students to Chapter 22.

Singular	Plural
street	streets
hero	heroes
gas	gases
class	classes
bush	bushes
church	churches
fox	foxes
quiz	quizzes

🌐 **ESL Tip**
Tell students that they can sometimes tell whether a word is singular or plural by the word that introduces it. For example, *each* always introduces a singular noun, and *many* always introduces a plural noun. Refer students to 29D.

Irregular Noun Plurals

Some nouns form plurals in unusual ways.

• Nouns whose plural forms are the same as their singular forms

Singular	Plural
a deer	a few deer
this species	these species
a television series	two television series

• Nouns ending in *-f* or *-fe*

Singular	Plural
each half	both halves
my life	our lives
a lone thief	a gang of thieves
one loaf	two loaves
the third shelf	several shelves

Exceptions: *roof* (plural *roofs*), *proof* (plural *proofs*), *belief* (plural *beliefs*)

• Nouns ending in *-y*

Singular	Plural
another baby	more babies
every worry	many worries

Note that when a vowel (*a, e, i, o, u*) comes before the *y*, the noun has a regular plural form: *monkey* (plural *monkeys*), *day* (plural *days*).

(continued on the following page)

Irregular Noun Plurals

- Hyphenated compound nouns

Singular	Plural
Lucia's sister-in-law	Lucia's two favorite sisters-in-law
a mother-to-be	twin mothers-to-be
the first runner-up	all the runners-up

- Miscellaneous irregular plurals

Singular	Plural
that child	all children
a good man	a few good men
the woman	lots of women
my left foot	both feet
a wisdom tooth	my two front teeth
this bacterium	some bacteria

● Practice 27-1

Next to each of the following singular nouns, write the plural form of the noun. Then, circle the irregular noun plurals.

Examples: bottle ___bottles___   child (children)

1. headache ___headaches___
2. life (lives)
3. foot (feet)
4. chain ___chains___
5. deer (deer)
6. honey ___honeys___
7. bride-to-be (brides-to-be)
8. woman (women)
9. loaf (loaves)
10. kiss ___kisses___

11. beach ___beaches___
12. duty (duties)
13. son-in-law (sons-in-law)
14. species (species)
15. wife (wives)
16. city (cities)
17. elf (elves)
18. tooth (teeth)
19. catalog ___catalogs___
20. patty (patties)

● **Practice 27-2**

Proofread the underlined nouns in the following paragraph, checking to make sure singular and plural forms are correct. If a correction needs to be made, cross out the noun, and write the correct form above it. If the noun is correct, write *C* above it.

Example: Getting through security lines at ~~airportes~~ *airports* has become difficult.

(1) Since September 11, 2001, ~~traveler-to-bes~~ *travelers-to-be* need to think carefully about what they pack in their carry-on luggage. (2) All airlines have to protect the ~~lifes~~ *lives* of the men *C* and ~~woman~~ *women* who fly on their planes. (3) On some days, *C* long ~~delayes~~ *delays* in the security lines occur as screeners carry out their ~~dutys~~ *duties*. (4) Most people *C* understand that they should never carry weapons and explosives onto a plane. (5) Hunters have to accept the fact that all firearms *C* must be unloaded and checked in at the gate, and that ~~boxs~~ *boxes* of ammunition should be packed separately. (6) Immediately after the ~~attackes~~ *attacks* on the World Trade Center, security ~~personnels~~ *personnel* began to take certain personal items, *C* like nail clippers and eyelash curlers, away from passengers. (7) Now, these things are allowed, but it is still forbidden to bring sharp ~~tooles~~ *tools* on board. (8) Vacationers who expect to go snorkeling can bring their ~~finz~~ *fins* and ~~maskes~~ *masks* into the cabin, but scuba divers must allow their dive ~~tankes~~ *tanks* to be placed in the baggage ~~compartmentes~~ *compartments*. (9) Compressed ~~gasses~~ *gases* in pressurized cylinders can be taken on board by scuba divers only if they are unsealed and can be inspected visually. (10) Most airlines allow two pieces *C* of carry-on luggage, including ~~pursess~~ *purses,* laptop ~~computeres~~ *computers,* and briefcases. *C*

Teaching Tip
Review the use of comparison and contrast as a strategy for paragraph development. Refer students to Chapter 8.

Focus on Writing: *Flashback*

Look back at your response to the Focus on Writing activity on page 409. Underline each noun. Write *P* above any plural nouns, and circle any irregular plurals.

Identifying Pronouns

A **pronoun** is a word that refers to and takes the place of a noun or another pronoun.

> Michelle was really excited because <u>she</u> had finally found a job that made <u>her</u> happy. (*She* refers to *Michelle*; *her* refers to *she*.)

In the sentence above, the pronouns *she* and *her* take the place of the noun *Michelle*.

Pronouns, like nouns, can be singular or plural.

Teaching Tip
Tell students that using too many pronouns can make a paragraph boring, especially when pronouns begin several sentences in a row. Remind them to try to vary their sentence openings. Refer them to 17B.

- Singular pronouns (*I, he, she, it, him, her,* and so on) are always singular and take the place of singular nouns or pronouns.

  > Geoff left his jacket at work, so <u>he</u> went back to get <u>it</u> before <u>it</u> could be stolen. (*He* refers to *Geoff*; *it* refers to *jacket*.)

Teaching Tip
Refer students to 27E, 27F, and 27H for lists of pronouns.

- Plural pronouns (*we, they, our, their,* and so on) are always plural and take the place of plural nouns or pronouns.

  > Jessie and Dan got up early, but <u>they</u> still missed <u>their</u> train. (*They* refers to *Jessie and Dan*; *their* refers to *they*.)

- The pronoun *you* can be either singular or plural.

  > When the volunteers met the mayor, they said, "We really admire <u>you</u>." The mayor replied, "I admire <u>you</u>, too." (In the first sentence, *you* refers to *the mayor*; in the second sentence, *you* refers to *the volunteers*.)

Highlight: Demonstrative Pronouns

Demonstrative pronouns—*this, that, these,* and *those*—point to one or more items.

- *This* and *that* point to one item: <u>This</u> is a work of fiction, and <u>that</u> is a nonfiction book.

- *These* and *those* point to more than one item: <u>These</u> are fruits, but <u>those</u> are vegetables.

● Practice 27-3

In the following sentences, fill in each blank with an appropriate pronoun.

Example: Whenever __*I*__ have hiccups, my parents have suggestions for how to get rid of them.

(1) First, my mother says that __*I*__ should relax. (2) __*I*__ answer that having hiccups is not exactly relaxing. (3) Next, my father tells me to stand on my head while __*he*__ pinches the back of my shoulders. (4) When that doesn't work, __*they*__ both offer to massage my eyeballs while __*I*__ keep my eyes closed. (5) Although __*I*__ have always turned down this offer, __*it*__ would be tempting to try __*it*__. (6) What harm could __*it*__ do? (7) My mother usually has another proposal; __*she*__ will help by blowing on my thumb while __*I*__ think of all the bald men that __*I*__ can. (8) Of course, after __*I*__ try this, __*I*__ am generally still hiccupping. (9) Finally, my father will say, "__*I*__ give up; __*you*__ are just going to have the hiccups forever." (10) Fortunately, __*he*__ is always wrong; as soon as __*I*__ stop thinking about my hiccups, __*they*__ stop.

Focus on Writing: *Flashback*

Look back at your response to the Focus on Writing activity on page 409. Draw a line down the middle of a sheet of paper, creating two columns. In the column on the left, list all the pronouns (*I, he, she, it, we, you, they*) you used. In the column on the right, list the noun or pronoun each pronoun takes the place of.

27d   Pronoun-Antecedent Agreement

The word that a pronoun refers to is called the pronoun's **antecedent**. In the following sentence, the noun *leaf* is the antecedent of the pronoun *it*.

The leaf turned yellow, but it did not fall.

A pronoun must always agree in **number** with its antecedent. If an antecedent is singular, as it is in the sentence above, the pronoun must be singular. If the antecedent is plural, as it is in the sentence below, the pronoun must also be plural.

The leaves turned yellow, but they did not fall.

Highlight:
Vague Pronoun
References

WORD POWER
inevitable something that cannot be avoided; unavoidable

A pronoun should always refer to a specific antecedent.

Vague   On the evening news, they said a baseball strike was inevitable. (Who said a strike was inevitable?)

Revised   On the evening news, the sportscaster said a baseball strike was inevitable. (noun replaces vague pronoun)

● Practice 27-4

In the following sentences, circle the antecedent of each underlined pronoun. Then, draw an arrow from the pronoun to the antecedent it refers to.

Example: College students today often fear they will be the victims of crime on campus.

On the Web
For more practice, visit
Exercise Central *at*
<bedfordstmartins
.com/focusonwriting>.

(1) Few campuses are as safe as they should be, experts say. (2) However, crime on most campuses is probably no worse than it is in any other community. (3) Still, students have a right to know how safe their campuses are. (4) My friend Joyce never sets foot on campus without her can of Mace. (5) Joyce believes she must be prepared for the worst. (6) Her boyfriend took a self-defense course that he said was very helpful. (7) My friends do not let fear of crime keep them from enjoying the college experience. (8) We know that our school is doing all it can to provide a safe environment.

Focus on Writing: *Flashback*

Look back at your response to the Focus on Writing activity on page 409. Underline each pronoun in your paragraph, circle its antecedent, and draw an arrow from each pronoun to its antecedent. Do all your pronouns agree with their antecedents? If not, correct your pronouns.

27e

Special Problems with Agreement

Certain kinds of antecedents can cause problems for writers because they cannot be easily identified as singular or plural.

Compound Antecedents

A **compound antecedent** consists of two or more words connected by *and* or *or*.

- Compound antecedents connected by *and* are plural, and they are used with plural pronouns.

> During World War II, Belgium and France tried to protect their borders.

Teaching Tip
Refer students to 22A for information about subject-verb agreement with compound subjects.

- Compound antecedents connected by *or* may take a singular or a plural pronoun. The pronoun always agrees with the word that is closer to it.

> Is it possible that European nations or Russia may send its [not *their*] troops?

> Is it possible that Russia or European nations may send their [not *its*] troops?

● Practice 27-5

In each of the following sentences, underline the compound antecedent, and circle the connecting word (*and* or *or*). Then, circle the appropriate pronoun in parentheses.

> **Example:** Groucho (and) Harpo were younger than (his/their) brother Chico.

1. Larry(and)Curly were younger than (his/their) partner Moe.
2. Either Chip(or)Dale has a stripe down (his/their) back.
3. Most critics believe Laurel(and)Hardy did (his/their) best work in silent comedies.
4. Lucy(and)Ethel never seem to learn (her/their) lesson.
5. Either *MASH*(or)*The Fugitive* had the highest ratings for (its/their) final episode.
6. Was it Francis Ford Coppola(or)Martin Scorcese who achieved the triumph of (his/their) career with *The Godfather*?
7. Either film(or)videotapes lose (its/their) clarity over time.
8. Either Tower(or)Blockbuster is having (its/their) grand opening today.
9. The popcorn(and)soft drinks here are expensive for (its/their) size.
10. Do comedies(or)dramas have a greater impact on (its/their) audiences?

Indefinite Pronoun Antecedents

Most pronouns refer to a specific person or thing. However, **indefinite pronouns** do not refer to any particular person or thing.

Most indefinite pronouns are singular.

Teaching Tip
You might want to tell students that some indefinite pronouns (such as *all, any, more, most, none,* and *some*) can be either singular or plural: *All is quiet; All were qualified.*)

Singular Indefinite Pronouns

another	everybody	no one
anybody	everyone	nothing
anyone	everything	one
anything	much	somebody
each	neither	someone
either	nobody	something

Teaching Tip
Refer students to 22F for information on subject-verb agreement with indefinite pronouns.

When an indefinite pronoun antecedent is singular, use a singular pronoun to refer to it.

Everything was in its place. (*Everything* is singular, so it is used with the singular pronoun *its*.)

Highlight: Indefinite Pronouns with *Of*

The singular indefinite pronouns *each*, *either*, *neither*, and *one* are often used in phrases with *of*—*each of*, *either of*, *neither of*, or *one of*—followed by a plural noun. Even in such phrases, these indefinite pronoun antecedents are always singular and take singular pronouns.

Each of the routes has <u>its</u> [not *their*] own special challenges.

ESL Tip
Remind students that singular indefinite pronouns do not have plural forms.

A few indefinite pronouns are plural.

Plural Indefinite Pronouns

both	others
few	several
many	

When an indefinite pronoun antecedent is plural, use a plural pronoun to refer to it.

They all wanted to graduate early, but few received <u>their</u> diplomas in January. (*Few* is plural, so it is used with the plural pronoun *their*.)

Highlight: Using *His or Her* with Indefinite Pronouns

Even though the indefinite pronouns *anybody*, *anyone*, *everybody*, *everyone*, *somebody*, *someone*, and so on are singular, many people use plural pronouns to refer to them.

Everyone must hand in <u>their</u> completed work before 2 p.m.

This usage is widely accepted in spoken English. Nevertheless, indefinite pronouns like *everyone* are singular, and written English requires a singular pronoun.

However, using the singular pronoun *his* to refer to *everyone* suggests that *everyone* refers to a male. Using *his or her* is more accurate because the indefinite pronoun may refer to either a male or a female.

Everyone must hand in <u>his or her</u> completed work before 2 p.m.

Highlight:
Using *His or Her*
with Indefinite
Pronouns
continued

When used over and over again, *he or she*, *him or her*, and *his or her* make sentences wordy and awkward. To avoid this problem, try to use plural forms.

All students must hand in <u>their</u> completed work before 2 p.m.

● Practice 27-6

In the following sentences, first circle the indefinite pronoun. Then, circle the pronoun in parentheses that refers to the indefinite pronoun antecedent.

Example: (Each) of the artists will have ((his or her)/their) own exhibit.

1. (Either) of those paintings will be sold with ((its)/their) frame.
2. (Each) of the artist's brushes has ((its)/their) own use.
3. (Everything) in the room made ((its)/their) contribution to the setting.
4. (Everyone) must remember to take ((his or her)/their) paint box.
5. (Neither) of my sisters wanted ((her)/their) picture displayed.
6. (Many) of the men brought (his/(their)) children to the exhibit.
7. (Several) of the colors must be mixed with (its/(their)) contrasting colors.
8. When (someone) compliments your work, be sure to tell ((him or her)/ them) that it is for sale.
9. (Anyone) can improve ((his or her)/their) skills as an artist.
10. (Both) of these workrooms have (its/(their)) own advantages.

● Practice 27-7

Edit the following sentences for errors in pronoun-antecedent agreement. When you edit, you have two options: either substitute *his or her* for *their* to refer to the singular antecedent, or replace the singular antecedent with a plural word.

Examples:

his or her
Everyone will be responsible for ~~their~~ own transportation.
                                                        ^

All
~~Each~~ of the children took their books out of their backpacks.
 ^
Answers may vary.

1. Everyone has the right to ~~their~~ *his or her* own opinion.
   All students ^
2. ~~Everyone~~ can eat their lunches in the cafeteria.
   ^
3. Somebody forgot ~~their~~ *his or her* backpack.
   All ^
4. ~~Each~~ of the patients had their own rooms, with their own televisions and
   ^

   their own private baths.
5. Someone in the store has left ~~their~~ *his or her* car's lights on.
   ^
6. Simone keeps everything in her kitchen in ~~their~~ *its* own little container.
7. Each of the applicants must have ~~their~~ *his or her* ^ driver's license.
   ^
8. Anybody who has ever juggled a job and children knows how valuable
   his or her
   ~~their~~ free time can be.
   ^
9. Either of the coffeemakers comes with ~~their~~ *its* own filter.
   Most people wait ^
10. ~~Almost everyone waits~~ until the last minute to file their income tax returns.
    ^

Collective Noun Antecedents

Collective nouns are words (like *band* and *team*) that name a group of people or things but are singular. Because they are singular, collective noun antecedents are used with singular pronouns.

The band played for hours, but it never played our song.

Frequently Used Collective Nouns

army	committee	government	orchestra
band	company	group	posse
class	family	jury	team
club	gang	mob	union

● Practice 27-8

Circle the collective noun antecedent in the following sentences. Then, circle the correct pronoun in parentheses.

Example: The (jury) returned with ((its)/their) verdict.

1. The (company) offers generous benefits to ((its)/their) employees.

2. All five study (groups) are supposed to hand in (its/(their)) projects by Tuesday.

3. Any (government) should care about the welfare of ((its)/their) citizens.

4. Every (family) has ((its)/their) share of problems.

5. To join the electricians' (union), applicants had to pass ((its)/their) test.

● Practice 27-9

Teaching Tip
Make sure students understand that an antecedent may be a compound, indefinite pronoun, or collective noun.

Edit the following passage for correct pronoun-antecedent agreement. First, circle the antecedent of each underlined pronoun. Then, cross out any pronoun that does not agree with its antecedent, and write the correct form above it. If the pronoun is correct, write *C* above it.

> **Example:**   The history of woman suffrage in the United States shows
>
> *their*
> that (women) were determined to achieve ~~her~~ equal rights.
> ^

　　(1) Before 1920, most American (women) were not allowed to vote
C
for the candidates <u>they</u> preferred. (2) Men ran the government, and
her
(a woman) could not express ~~their~~ views at the ballot box. (3) However, in
^
their
the mid-1800s, (women) began to demand ~~her~~ right to vote—or "woman
^
suffrage." (4) Supporters of woman suffrage believed (everyone), regard-
his or her
less of ~~their~~ gender, should be able to vote. (5) At the first woman suffrage
^
convention, (Elizabeth Cady Stanton and Lucretia Mott) gave speeches
their
explaining ~~his or her~~ views. (6) Susan B. Anthony started the National
^
Woman Suffrage Association, which opposed the (Fifteenth Amendment)
C
to the Constitution because <u>it</u> gave the vote to black men but not to
women. (7) The first state to permit (women) to vote was Wyoming, and
their
soon other states became more friendly to ~~her~~ cause. (8) Many (women)
^
they
called themselves "suffragettes" and participated in marches where <u>he</u>
C
~~or she~~ carried banners and posters for <u>their</u> cause. (9) During World
^
War I, (the U.S. government) found that the cooperation of women was

essential to ~~their~~ *its* military success. (10) Finally, in 1919, (the House of Representatives and the states) gave ~~its~~ *their* approval to the Nineteenth Amendment, which gave American women the right to vote.

Focus on Writing: *Flashback*

Look back at your response to the Focus on Writing activity on page 409. Does your paragraph include any antecedents that are compounds, indefinite pronouns, or collective nouns? Have you used the correct pronoun to refer to each of these antecedents? If not, correct your pronouns.

27f　Pronoun Case

A **personal pronoun** refers to a particular person or thing. Personal pronouns change form according to their function in a sentence. Personal pronouns can be *subjective, objective,* or *possessive.*

Personal Pronouns

Subjective Case	Objective Case	Possessive Case
I	me	my, mine
he	him	his
she	her	her, hers
it	it	its
we	us	our, ours
you	you	your, yours
they	them	their, theirs

Subjective Case

When a pronoun is a subject, it is in the **subjective case**.

Finally, <u>she</u> realized that dreams could come true.

Objective Case

When a pronoun is an object, it is in the **objective case**.

> If Joanna hurries, she can stop him. (The pronoun *him* is the direct object of the verb *can stop*.)
>
> Professor Miller sent us information about his research. (The pronoun *us* is the indirect object of the verb *sent*.)
>
> Marc threw the ball to them. (The pronoun *them* is the object of the preposition *to*.)

Possessive Case

When a pronoun shows ownership, it is in the **possessive case**.

> Hieu took his lunch to the meeting. (The pronoun *his* indicates that the lunch belongs to Hieu.)
>
> Debbie and Kim decided to take their lunches, too. (The pronoun *their* indicates that the lunches belong to Debbie and Kim.)

● **Practice 27-10**

Teaching Tip
Tell your students that they may find it helpful to consult the chart on page 422.

In the following passage, fill in the blank after each pronoun to indicate whether the pronoun is subjective (*S*), objective (*O*), or possessive (*P*).

Example: Famous criminals Bonnie Parker and Clyde Barrow committed their __*P*__ crimes during the Great Depression.

(1) With their __*P*__ gang, Bonnie and Clyde robbed a dozen banks, as well as many stores and gas stations, between 1932 and 1934. (2) In small towns, they __*S*__ terrorized the police; capturing them __*O*__ seemed impossible. (3) To many Americans, however, their __*P*__ crimes seemed exciting. (4) Many people resented the greed of big business, and they __*S*__ believed Bonnie and Clyde were striking back at it __*O*__. (5) Because Bonnie was a woman, she __*S*__ was especially fascinating to them __*O*__. (6) During their __*P*__ crimes, they __*S*__ would often carry a camera, take photographs of themselves, and send

them __O__ to the newspapers, which were happy to publish them
__O__. (7) Bonnie wrote a poem about their __P__ crimes, and it __S__
was also published in the newspapers. (8) Both Bonnie and Clyde knew
that, if caught, they __S__ would be executed. (9) By the time they __S__
were killed in an ambush by Texas and Louisiana law officers, Bonnie
and Clyde were famous all over the United States. (10) They __S__ were
the first celebrity criminals.

Focus on Writing: *Flashback*

Look back at your response to the Focus on Writing activity on page 409.
On a separate sheet of paper, draw vertical lines to create three columns.
Then, list all the personal pronouns you have used, classifying them as
subjective, objective, or possessive. Have you used correct pronoun case
in every sentence? Make any necessary corrections.

27g Special Problems with Case

When you are trying to determine which pronoun case to use, three kinds of
pronouns can cause problems: pronouns in compounds, pronouns in comparisons, and the pronouns *who* and *whom*.

Pronouns in Compounds

Sometimes, a pronoun is linked to a noun or to another pronoun with *and* or
or to form a **compound**.

> The teacher and I met for an hour.
>
> She and I had a good meeting.

To determine whether to use the subjective or objective case for a pronoun
in a compound, follow the same rules that apply for a pronoun that is not part
of a compound.

> **Highlight:
> Choosing
> Pronouns in
> Compounds**
>
> To determine which pronoun case to use in a compound that joins a noun and a pronoun, rewrite the sentence with just the pronoun.
>
> Toby and [*I* or *me*?] like jazz.
>
> I like jazz. (not *Me like jazz*)
>
> Toby and I like jazz.

Teaching Tip
Remind students that the first-person pronoun always comes last in compounds like *Toby and I* and *my father and me*.

Teaching Tip
Explain that the objective case is used with the contraction *let's*: *Let's (let us) you and me* (not *I*) *go swimming.* Remind students that *let's* includes the objective case pronoun *us*.

 On the Web
For more practice, visit Exercise Central *at* <bedfordstmartins .com/focusonwriting>.

- If the compound is a subject, use the subjective case.

  Toby and I [not *me*] like jazz.

  He and I [not *me*] went to the movies.

- If the compound is an object, use the objective case.

  The school sent my father and me [not *I*] the financial aid forms.

  This fight is between her and me [not *I*].

● **Practice 27-11**

In the following sentences, the underlined pronouns are part of compound constructions. Check them for correct subjective or objective case. If a correction needs to be made, cross out the pronoun, and write the correct form above it. If the pronoun is correct, write *C* above it.

Example: My sister and <u>~~me~~</u> heard a strange sound one night
last year.
(above *me*: *I*)

(1) Julia and <u>~~me~~</u> were about to go to sleep when we heard eerie howls. (2) At first, we thought that our parents had forgotten to turn off the television, but then we remembered that <u>they</u> had gone away for the weekend. (3) Alone in the house, Julia and <u>~~me~~</u> were in a panic. (4) Deciding what to do was up to <u>~~she~~</u> and <u>~~I~~</u>. (5) We considered calling 911, but we thought the police wouldn't believe us if we said that strange howls had been heard by my sister and <u>me</u>. (6) <u>~~Them~~</u> and the

911 operators might just think that Julia and ~~me~~ ^I were playing a trick on them. (7) Finally, we decided to wait until morning, when ~~her~~ ^{she} and ~~me~~ ^I would be able to figure out what had frightened us. (8) During the night, we remembered that our cat Annie and her kitten, Sam, were outside, and we began to worry about ~~she~~ ^{her} and ~~he.~~ ^{him.} (9) The next morning, we found traces of blood and scraps of fur in our backyard, but we never found ~~she~~ ^{her} and her kitten. (10) Now, we suspect that coyotes had been prowling around our neighborhood and that ~~them~~ ^{they} or other wild animals may have carried off our pets.

Pronouns in Comparisons

Sometimes, a pronoun appears after the word *than* or *as* in a **comparison**.

> John is luckier <u>than I</u>.
>
> The inheritance changed Raymond as much <u>as her</u>.

- If the pronoun is a subject, use the subjective case.

  > John is luckier <u>than I</u> [am].

- If the pronoun is an object, use the objective case.

  > The inheritance changed Raymond as much <u>as</u> [it changed] <u>her</u>.

Teaching Tip
Tell students that to decide whether to use the subjective or objective form of a pronoun, they should add in brackets the words needed to complete the comparison.

Highlight: Choosing Pronouns in Comparisons

Sometimes the pronoun you use can change your sentence's meaning. For example, if you say, "I like Cheerios more than he," you mean that you like Cheerios more than the other person likes them.

I like Cheerios more than he [does].

If, however, you say, "I like Cheerios more than *him*," you mean that you like Cheerios more than you like the other person.

I like Cheerios more than [I like] him.

● Practice 27-12

Each of the following sentences includes a comparison with a pronoun following the word *than* or *as*. Write in each blank the correct form (subjective or objective) of the pronoun in parentheses. In brackets, add the word or words needed to complete the comparison.

> **Example:** Many people are better poker players than _____*I [am]*_____ (I/me).

1. The survey showed that most people like the candidate's wife as much as _____*[they like] him*_____ (he/him).

2. No one enjoys shopping more than _____*she [does]*_____ (she/her).

3. My brother and Aunt Cecile were very close, so her death affected him more than _____*[it affected] me*_____ (I/me).

4. My neighbor drives better than _____*I [drive]*_____ (I/me).

5. That jacket fits you better than _____*[it fits] me*_____ (I/me).

Who and Whom

To determine whether to use *who* or *whom* (or *whoever* or *whomever*), you need to know how the pronoun functions within the clause in which it appears.

● When the pronoun is the subject of the clause, use *who*.

> I wonder <u>who</u> wrote that song. (*Who* is the subject of the clause *who wrote that song.*)

● When the pronoun is the object, use *whom*.

> <u>Whom</u> do the police suspect? (*Whom* is the direct object of the verb *suspect.*)

> I wonder <u>whom</u> the song is about. (*Whom* is the object of the preposition *about* in the clause *whom the song is about.*)

Highlight:
Who and Whom

To determine whether to use *who* or *whom*, try substituting another pronoun for *who* or *whom* in the clause. If you can substitute *he* or *she*, use *who*; if you can substitute *him* or *her*, use *whom*.

[Who/Whom] wrote a love song? <u>He</u> wrote a love song.

[Who/Whom] was the song about? The song was about <u>her</u>.

● **Practice 27-13**

Circle the correct form of *who* or *whom* in parentheses in each sentence.

Example: With (who/(whom)) did Rob collaborate?

1. For (who/(whom)) was the witness going to testify?

2. It will take time to decide ((who)/whom) the record holder is.

3. (Who/(Whom)) did Kobe take to the prom?

4. We saw the man ((who)/whom) fired the shots.

5. To (who/(whom)) am I speaking?

Focus on Writing: *Flashback*

Look back at your response to the Focus on Writing activity on page 409. Can you find any sentences that contain a pronoun used in a compound or in a comparison? If so, circle them. Then, circle any uses of *who* and *whom*. Have you used these pronouns correctly?

27h

Reflexive Pronouns

Reflexive pronouns always agree with their antecedents in person and number.

Reflexive pronouns always end in *-self* (singular) or *-selves* (plural). They indicate that people or things did something to themselves or for themselves.

Rosanna lost <u>herself</u> in the novel.

You need to watch <u>yourself</u> when you mix those solutions.

Mehul and Paul made <u>themselves</u> cold drinks.

Reflexive Pronouns

Singular Forms

Antecedent	Reflexive Pronoun
I	myself
you	yourself
he	himself
she	herself
it	itself

Plural Forms

Antecedent	Reflexive Pronoun
we	ourselves
you	yourselves
they	themselves

On the Web
For more practice, visit
Exercise Central *at*
<bedfordstmartins
.com/focusonwriting>.

● Practice 27-14

Fill in the correct reflexive pronoun in each of the following sentences.

Example: My aunt welcomed her visitors and told them to make
___*themselves*___ at home.

1. Mysteriously, migrating birds can direct ___*themselves*___ through clouds, storms, and moonless nights.

2. We all finished the marathon without injuring ___*ourselves*___.

3. Sometimes, he finds ___*himself*___ daydreaming in class.

4. The guide warned her to watch ___*herself*___ because the path was slippery.

5. You should give ___*yourself*___ a manicure.

Focus on Writing: *Flashback*

Look back at your response to the Focus on Writing activity on page 409. Have you used any reflexive pronouns? If so, circle them. If not, write a new sentence that includes a reflexive pronoun.

Focus on Writing: *Revising and Editing*

Look back at your response to the Focus on Writing activity on page 409. Recopy your work, incorporating the corrections you made for this chapter's Flashback activities. Then, change every singular noun to a plural noun and every plural noun to a singular noun, editing your pronouns so singular pronouns refer to singular nouns and plural pronouns refer to plural nouns.

Chapter Review

Editing Practice

Read the following student essay, which includes noun and pronoun errors. Check for errors in plural noun forms, pronoun case, and pronoun-antecedent agreement. Then, make any editing changes you think are necessary. The first sentence has been edited for you.

Cell Phone Misbehavior

Good ~~manneres~~ *manners* used to mean using the right fork and holding the door open for others. Today, however, people may find that good manners are more complicated than ~~it~~ *they* used to be. New inventions have led to new challenges. Cell phones, in particular, have created some problems.

One problem is the "cell yell," which is the tendency of ~~a person~~ *people*
to shout while they are using their cell phones. Why do we do this?
Maybe we do not realize how loud we are talking. Maybe we yell out of
frustration. Anyone can become angry when ~~they lose~~ *he or she loses* a call. Dead
~~batterys~~ *batteries* can be infuriating. Unfortunately, ~~the yeller annoys~~ *yellers annoy* everyone
around them.

Even if ~~the~~ cell-phone ~~user speaks~~ *users speak* normally, other people can hear
them. My friends and ~~me~~ *I* are always calling each other, and we do not
always pay attention to ~~whom~~ *who* can hear us. The result is that other people
are victims of "secondhand conversations." These conversations are
not as bad for people's health as secondhand smoke, but ~~it is~~ *they are* just
as annoying. ~~Whom~~ *Who* really wants to hear about the private ~~lifes~~ *lives* of
strangers? Restrooms used to be private; now, anyone in the next stall
can overhear a person's private conversation and learn ~~their~~ *his or her* secrets.

Also, some cell-phone ~~user~~ *users* seem to think that getting ~~his~~ *their* calls
is more important than anything else that might be going on. Phones
ring, chirp, or play silly tunes at ~~concertes,~~ *concerts,* in classrooms, at
weddings, in ~~churchs,~~ *churches,* and even at funerals. Can you picture a grieving
family at a cemetery having ~~their~~ *its* service interrupted by a ringing
phone? People should not have to be told to turn off ~~his or her~~ *their* cell
phones at times like these.

In the United States, there are more than 150 million cell phones.
Many people hate their cell phones, but they do not think they can live
without ~~it.~~ *them.* The problem is that cell phones became popular before there
were any rules for ~~its~~ *their* use. However, even if the government passed laws
about cell-phone behavior, ~~they~~ *it* would have a tough time enforcing ~~it.~~ *them.*
It seems obvious that ~~us~~ *we* cell-phone users should not need laws to make
us behave ~~ourself~~ *ourselves* and use ordinary courtesy.

Collaborative Activities

1. Working in a group, fill in the following chart, writing one noun on each line. If the noun is a proper noun, be sure to capitalize it.

Cars	Trees	Foods	Famous Couples	Cities
Answers will vary.				

Now, using as many of the nouns listed above as you can, write a one-paragraph news article that describes an imaginary event. Exchange your work with another group, and check the other group's article to be sure the correct pronoun refers to each noun. Return the articles to their original groups for editing.

2. Working in a group, write a silly story that uses each of these nouns at least once: *Martians, eggplant, MTV, toupee, kangaroo, Iceland, bat, herd,* and *kayak.* Then, exchange stories with another group. After you have read the other group's story, edit it so that it includes all of the following pronouns: *it, its, itself, they, their, them, themselves.* Return the edited story to its authors. Finally, reread your group's story, and check to make sure pronoun-antecedent agreement is clear and correct.

Review Checklist:
Nouns and Pronouns

☐ A noun is a word that names something. A singular noun names one thing; a plural noun names more than one thing. (See 27A.)

☐ Most nouns add -s or -es to form plurals. Some nouns have irregular plural forms. (See 27B.)

☐ A pronoun is a word that refers to and takes the place of a noun or another pronoun. (See 27C.)

☐ The word a pronoun refers to is called the pronoun's antecedent. A pronoun and its antecedent must always agree in number and gender. (See 27D.)

☐ Compound antecedents connected by *and* are plural and are used with plural pronouns. Compound antecedents connected by *or* may take singular or plural pronouns. (See 27E.)

☐ Most indefinite pronoun antecedents are singular and are used with singular pronouns; some are plural and are used with plural pronouns. (See 27E.)

☐ Collective noun antecedents are singular and are used with singular pronouns. (See 27E.)

☐ Personal pronouns can be in the subjective, objective, or possessive case. (See 27F.)

☐ Pronouns present special problems when they are used in compounds and comparisons. The pronouns *who* and *whom* can also cause problems. (See 27G.)

☐ Reflexive pronouns must agree with their antecedents in person and number. (See 27H.)

Chapter 28

Adjectives and Adverbs

According to the National Home Education Research Institute, home-schooled students do better on standardized tests than both public- and private-school students.

Identifying Adjectives and Adverbs

Adjectives and adverbs are words that **modify** (identify or describe) other words. They help make sentences clearer and more specific.

An **adjective** answers the question *What kind? Which one?* or *How many?* Adjectives modify nouns or pronouns.

Teaching Tip
Tell students that some adjectives, such as *Turkish*, are capitalized because they are formed from proper nouns. Refer them to 27A.

The Turkish city of Istanbul spans two continents. (*Turkish* modifies the noun *city*, and *two* modifies the noun *continents*.)

It is fascinating because of its location and history. (*Fascinating* modifies the pronoun *it*.)

Highlight: Demonstrative Adjectives

Demonstrative adjectives—*this, that, these,* and *those*—do not describe other words. They simply identify particular nouns.

This and *that* identify singular nouns and pronouns.

This Web site is much more up-to-date than that one.

These and *those* identify plural nouns.

These words and phrases are French, but those expressions are Creole.

→ Focus on Writing

The picture on the opposite page shows children being home schooled by their mother. Look at the picture, and then write about the advantages and disadvantages of being educated at home by parents instead of at school by professional teachers.

WORD POWER
tutor a private instructor
extracurricular outside the regular course of study
socialize to interact with others
cohort a group united by common experiences or characteristics

An **adverb** answers the question *How? Why? When? Where?* or *To what extent?* Adverbs modify verbs, adjectives, or other adverbs.

Traffic moved steadily. (*Steadily* modifies the verb *moved*.)

Still, we were quite impatient. (*Quite* modifies the adjective *impatient*.)

Very slowly, we moved into the center lane. (*Very* modifies the adverb *slowly*.)

Highlight:
Distinguishing
Adjectives from
Adverbs

Many adverbs are formed when *-ly* is added to an adjective.

Adjective	*Adverb*
slow	slowly
nice	nicely
quick	quickly
real	really

Adjective   Let me give you one quick reminder. (*Quick* modifies the noun *reminder*.)

Adverb   He quickly changed the subject. (*Quickly* modifies the verb *changed*.)

Note: Some adjectives—*lovely, friendly,* and *lively,* for example—end in *-ly.* Do not mistake these words for adverbs.

● Practice 28-1

On the Web
For more practice, visit
Exercise Central *at*
<bedfordstmartins
.com/focusonwriting>.

In the following sentences, circle the correct form (adjective or adverb) from the choices in parentheses.

Example: Women who are (serious/seriously) walkers or runners need to wear athletic shoes that fit.

(1) Doctors have found that many athletic shoes are (poor/poorly) designed for women. (2) Women's athletic shoes are actual/actually)

just smaller versions of men's shoes. (3) For this reason, they cannot provide a (true/truly) comfortable fit. (4) Studies have shown that to get a shoe that fits (comfortable/comfortably) in the heel, most women must buy one that is too (tight/tightly) for the front of the foot. (5) This can have a (real/really) negative impact on their athletic performance. (6) It can also cause (serious/seriously) pain. (7) Some manufacturers now market athletic shoes that are designed (specific/specifically) for women. (8) Experts say that women must become informed consumers and choose (careful/carefully) when they shop for athletic shoes. (9) One (important/importantly) piece of advice is to shop for shoes (immediate/immediately) after exercising or at the end of a work day, when the foot is at its largest. (10) Experts advise that athletic shoes should feel (comfortable/comfortably) from the moment they are tried on.

Teaching Tip
Explain that a linking verb such as *feel* is followed by an adjective, not an adverb. Refer students to 14C.

Highlight:
Good and Well

Be careful not to confuse *good* and *well*. Unlike regular adjectives, whose adverb forms add *-ly*, the adjective *good* is irregular. Its adverb form is *well*.

Adjective Fred Astaire was a good dancer. (*Good* modifies the noun *dancer*.)

Adverb He danced especially well with Ginger Rogers. (*Well* modifies the verb *danced*.)

Always use *well* when you are describing a person's health.

He really didn't feel well [not *good*] after eating the entire pizza.

● **Practice 28-2**

Circle the correct form (*good* or *well*) in the sentences below.

Example: It can be hard for some people to find a (good/well) job that they really like.

(1) Some people may not do (good/well) sitting in an office. (2) Instead, they may prefer to find jobs that take advantage of the (good/well) physical condition of their bodies. (3) Such people might consider becoming smoke jumpers—firefighters who are (good/well) at parachuting from small planes into remote areas to battle forest fires. (4) Smoke jumpers must be able to work (good/well) even without much sleep. (5) They must also handle danger (good/well). (6) They look forward to the (good/well) feeling of saving a forest or someone's home. (7) As they battle fires, surrounded by smoke and fumes, smoke jumpers may not feel very (good/well). (8) Sometimes, things go wrong; for example, when their parachutes fail to work (good/well), jumpers may be injured or even killed. (9) Smoke jumpers do not get paid (good/well). (10) However, they are proud of their strength and endurance and feel (good/well) about the excitement of their work.

Focus on Writing: *Flashback*

Look back at your response to the Focus on Writing activity on page 435. Underline each adjective and adverb, and draw an arrow from each to the word it describes or identifies. Do all adjectives modify nouns or pronouns? Do all adverbs modify verbs, adjectives, or other adverbs? Have you used *good* and *well* correctly? Revise any sentences that use adjectives or adverbs incorrectly.

28b   Comparatives and Superlatives

The **comparative** form of an adjective or adverb compares two people or things. Adjectives and adverbs form the comparative with *-er* or *more*. The **superlative** form of an adjective or adverb compares more than two things. Adjectives and adverbs form the superlative with *-est* or *most*.

Adjectives	This film is dull and predictable.
Comparative	The film I saw last week was even duller and more predictable than this one.

Superlative	The film I saw last night was the <u>dullest</u> and <u>most predictable</u> one I've ever seen.

Adverb	For a beginner, Jane did needlepoint <u>skillfully</u>.
Comparative	After she had watched the demonstration, Jane did needlepoint <u>more skillfully</u> than Rosie.
Superlative	Of the twelve beginners, Jane did needlepoint the <u>most skillfully</u>.

Forming Comparatives and Superlatives

Adjectives

● One-syllable adjectives generally form the comparative with *-er* and the superlative with *-est*.

    great   greater   greatest

● Adjectives with two or more syllables form the comparative with *more* and the superlative with *most*.

    wonderful   more wonderful   most wonderful

Exception: Two-syllable adjectives ending in *-y* add *-er* or *-est* after changing the *y* to an *i*.

    funny   funnier   funniest

Adverbs

● All adverbs ending in *-ly* form the comparative with *more* and the superlative with *most*.

    efficiently   more efficiently   most efficiently

● Some other adverbs form the comparative with *-er* and the superlative with *-est*.

    soon   sooner   soonest

Solving Special Problems with Comparatives and Superlatives

The following rules will help you avoid errors with comparatives and superlatives.

● Never use both *-er* and *more* to form the comparative or both *-est* and *most* to form the superlative.

Nothing could have been <u>more awful</u>. (not *more awfuller*)

Teaching Tip
Tell students that when
they form comparatives,
they should have only
one ending with an *r*
sound (not *more greater*
or *more better*, for
example).

Space Mountain is the <u>most frightening</u> (not *most frighteningest*) ride at Disney World.

- Never use the superlative when you are comparing only two things.

  This is the <u>more serious</u> (not *most serious*) of the two problems.

- Never use the comparative when you are comparing more than two things.

  This is the <u>worst</u> (not *worse*) day of my life.

● **Practice 28-3**

 On the Web
For more practice, visit
Exercise Central *at*
<bedfordstmartins
.com/focusonwriting>.

Fill in the correct comparative form of the word supplied in parentheses.

Example: Children tend to be _____ *noisier* _____ (noisy) than adults.

1. Traffic always moves _____ *more slowly* _____ (slow) during rush hour than late at night.

2. The weather report says temperatures will be _____ *colder* _____ (cold) tomorrow.

3. Some elderly people are _____ *healthier* _____ (healthy) than younger people.

4. It has been proven that pigs are _____ *more intelligent* _____ (intelligent) than dogs.

5. When someone asks you to repeat yourself, you usually answer _____ *more loudly* _____ (loud).

6. The _____ *taller* _____ (tall) of the two buildings was damaged by the fire.

7. They want to teach their son to be _____ *more respectiful* _____ (respectful) of women than many young men are.

8. Las Vegas is _____ *more famous* _____ (famous) for its casinos than for its natural resources.

9. The WaterDrop is _____*wilder*_____ (wild) than any other ride in the park.

10. You must move _____*more quickly*_____ (quick) if you expect to catch the ball.

● Practice 28-4

Fill in the correct superlative form of the word supplied in parentheses.

Example: Consumers now pay the _____*highest*_____ (high) surcharge ever when they buy tickets for arena events.

(1) Ticketmaster is the _____*largest*_____ (large) seller of sports and entertainment tickets in the country. (2) The company was the _____*earliest*_____ (early) to sell concert and sporting event tickets both by phone and through retail outlets. (3) It has also been the _____*most successful*_____ (successful). (4) Ticketmaster adds at least 20 percent to the cost of each ticket sold and has the _____*highest*_____ (high) markup in the business. (5) Because Ticketmaster is the _____*most powerful*_____ (powerful) ticket outlet in the country, fans have to pay the price. (6) Critics have argued that Ticketmaster's control of the market is the _____*strongest*_____ (strong) monopoly in the country. (7) Back in 1994, the rock group Pearl Jam launched what remains the _____*most serious*_____ (serious) offensive to date against the ticket giant. (8) Wanting its fans to be able to buy the _____*cheapest*_____ (cheap) tickets possible, Pearl Jam suggested lowering its own profits as well as Ticketmaster's for its summer tour; Ticketmaster refused. (9) Still one of the _____*most popular*_____ (popular) groups in the country, Pearl Jam tried to use arenas that were not controlled by Ticketmaster for its later tours. (10) Ticketmaster's president argues that his company has succeeded because it has worked the _____*hardest*_____ (hard) and is the _____*most aggressive*_____ (aggressive).

Highlight:
Good/Well and
Bad/Badly

Most adjectives and adverbs form the comparative with *-er* or *more* and the superlative with *-est* or *most*. The adjectives *good* and *bad* and their adverb forms *well* and *badly* are exceptions.

Adjective	Comparative Form	Superlative Form
good	better	best
bad	worse	worst

Adverb	Comparative Form	Superlative Form
well	better	best
badly	worse	worst

● **Practice 28-5**

Fill in the correct comparative or superlative form of *good, well, bad,* or *badly.*

Example: She is at her ____*best*____ (good) when she is under pressure.

1. Today in track practice, Luisa performed ____*better*____ (well) than she has in weeks.

2. In fact, she ran her ____*best*____ (good) time ever in the fifty meter.

3. When things are bad, we wonder whether they will get ____*better*____ (good) or ____*worse*____ (bad).

4. I've had some bad meals before, but this is the ____*worst*____ (bad).

5. The world always looks ____*better*____ (good) when you're in love than when you're not.

6. Athletes generally play the ____*worst*____ (badly) when their concentration is poorest.

7. The Sport Shop's prices may be good, but Athletic Attic's are the ____*best*____ (good) in town.

8. There are ____*better*____ (good) ways to solve conflicts than by fighting.

9. People seem to hear ____*better*____ (well) when they agree with what you're saying than when they don't agree with you.

10. Of all the children, Manda took the ____*best*____ (good) care of her toys.

Teaching Tip
Remind students that absolute adjectives such as *perfect, unique, dead, impossible,* and *infinite* do not have comparative or superlative forms.

Focus on Writing: *Flashback*

Look back at your response to the Focus on Writing activity on page 435. Divide a sheet of paper into three columns. Copy all the adjectives and adverbs from your writing activity in the column on the left. Then, write the comparative and superlative forms for each adjective or adverb in the other columns.

Focus on Writing: *Revising and Editing*

Look back at your response to the Focus on Writing activity on page 435. Have you used enough adjectives and adverbs to explain your ideas to readers? Add or substitute modifying words as needed to make your writing clearer and more interesting. Then, delete any unnecessary adjectives and adverbs.

Chapter Review

Teaching Tip
If you rewrite this Editing Practice to include other errors, such as fragments or subject-verb agreement errors, you can use it as a comprehensive editing exercise.

Editing Practice

Read the following student essay, which includes errors in the use of adjectives and adverbs. Make any changes necessary to correct adjectives incorrectly used for adverbs and adverbs incorrectly used for adjectives. Also, correct any errors in the use of comparatives and superlatives and in the use of demonstrative adjectives. Finally, try to add some adjectives and adverbs that you feel would make the writer's ideas clearer or more specific. The first sentence has been edited for you.   *Answers may vary.*

Starting Over

A wedding can be the ~~joyfullest~~ *most joyful* occasion in two people's lives, the beginning of a couple's ~~most~~ happiest years. For some unlucky women, however, a wedding can be the ~~worse~~ *worst* thing that ever happens; it is the beginning not of their happiness but of their battered lives. As I went through the joyful day of my wedding, I wanted ~~bad~~ *badly* to find happiness for the rest of my life, but what I hoped and wished for did not come true.

I was married in the savannah belt of the Sudan in the eastern part of Africa, where I grew up. I was barely twenty-two years old. The first two years of my marriage progressed ~~peaceful,~~ *peacefully,* but problems started as soon as our first child was born.

Many American women say, "If my husband gave me just one beating, that would be it. I'd leave." But ~~those~~ *this modern* attitude does not work in cultures where tradition has overshadowed women's rights and divorce is not accepted. All women can do is accept their ~~sadly~~ *sad* fate. Battered women give many reasons for staying in their ~~abusive~~ *abusive* marriages, but fear is the ~~commonest.~~ *most common.* Fear immobilizes these women, ruling their decisions, their actions, and their very lives. This is how it was for me. Of course, I was ~~real~~ *really* afraid whenever my husband hit me. I would run to my mother's house and cry, but she would always talk me into going back and being more ~~patiently~~ *patient* with my husband. Our tradition discourages divorce, and wife-beating is taken for granted. The situation is really quite ironic: the religion I practice sets harsh punishments for abusive husbands, but tradition has so overpowered religion that the laws do not work very ~~good.~~ *well.*

One night, after nine years of unhappiness, I asked myself whether life had treated me ~~fair.~~ *fairly.* True, I had a high school diploma and two of the ~~beautifullest~~ *most beautiful* children in the world, but it was not enough. I realized that to stand up to the husband who treated me so ~~bad,~~ *badly,* I would have to achieve a ~~more~~ better education than he had. That night, I decided to get a college education in the United States. My husband opposed *strongly* my decision, but with the support of my father and mother, I was able to change my life. My years as a student and single parent in the United States have been ~~real~~ *really* difficult for me, but I know I made the right choice.

Collaborative Activities

1. Working in a small group, write a one-paragraph plot summary for an imaginary film. Begin with one of the following three sentences.

   - Dirk and Clive were sworn enemies, but that night on Boulder Ridge they vowed to work together just this once, for the good of their country.
   - Genevieve entered the room in a cloud of perfume, and when she spoke, her voice was like velvet.
   - The desert sun beat down on her head, but Susanna was determined to protect what was hers, no matter what the cost.

2. Trade summaries with another group. Add as many adjectives and adverbs as you can to the other group's summary. Make sure each modifier is appropriate. Then, return the summary to the group that wrote it.

3. Reread your own group's plot summary, and edit it carefully, paying special attention to the way adjectives and adverbs are used.

**Review Checklist:
Adjectives and Adverbs**

☐ Adjectives modify nouns or pronouns. (See 28A.)

☐ Demonstrative adjectives — *this*, *that*, *these*, and *those* — identify particular nouns. (See 28A.)

☐ Adverbs modify verbs, adjectives, or other adverbs. (See 28A.)

☐ To compare two people or things, use the comparative form of an adjective or adverb. To compare more than two people or things, use the superlative form of an adjective or adverb. Adjectives and adverbs form the comparative with *-er* or *more* and the superlative with *-est* or *most*. (See 28B.)

☐ The adjectives *good* and *bad* and their adverb forms *well* and *badly* have irregular comparative and superlative forms. (See 28B.)

The Seattle Space Needle was built for the 1962 World's Fair. Every day, almost 20,000 people rode to the top.

Learning English as a second language involves more than just learning grammar. In fact, if you have been studying English as a second language, you may know more about English grammar than many native speakers do. However, you will still need to learn the conventions and rules that most native speakers already know.

29a Subjects in Sentences

English requires that every sentence state its subject. In addition, every dependent clause must also have a subject.

Incorrect	Elvis Presley was only forty-two years old when died. (When who died?)
Correct	Elvis Presley was only forty-two years old when he died.

When the real subject follows the verb and the normal subject position before the verb is empty, it must be filled by a "dummy" subject, such as *it* or *there*.

Incorrect	Is hot in this room.
Correct	It is hot in this room.
Incorrect	Are many rivers in my country.
Correct	There are many rivers in my country.

→ **Focus on Writing**

The image the opposite page shows fireworks at Seattle's Space Needle on the Fourth of July, Independence Day. Look at the picture, and then explain how you and your family celebrate a holiday that is important to you.

WORD POWER
commemorate to show respect for; celebrate
culture customs and behavior of a particular group

Standard English also does not permit a two-part subject in which the second part of the subject is a pronoun referring to the same person or thing as the first part.

Incorrect   The Caspian Sea it is the largest lake in the world.

Correct   The Caspian Sea <u>is</u> the largest lake in the world.

● Practice 29-1

On the Web
For more practice, visit
Exercise Central *at*
<bedfordstmartins
.com/focusonwriting>.

Each of the following sentences is missing the subject of a dependent or an independent clause. On the lines after each sentence, rewrite it, adding an appropriate subject. Then, underline the subject you have added.

Example: Reality TV programs are very popular, but some people believe are going too far.

Reality TV programs are very popular, but some people believe <u>they</u>

are going too far.

1. When the first season of the reality show *Survivor* aired, was an immediate hit.
   When the first season of the reality show Survivor aired, <u>it</u> was an

   immediate hit.

2. Millions of Americans planned their evening so that could be sure not to
   miss the next episode.
   Millions of Americans planned their evening so that <u>they</u> could be

   sure not to miss the next episode.

3. Was not surprising to see the many other reality shows that suddenly
   appeared on the air.
   <u>It</u> was not surprising to see the many other reality shows that

   suddenly appeared on the air.

4. A recent poll asked viewers: "Do enjoy reality TV, or has it gone too far?"
   A recent poll asked viewers: "Do <u>you</u> enjoy reality TV, or has it gone

   too far?"

5. Most viewers thought that reality TV had gone too far even though
   enjoyed shows like *Fear Factor* and *The Apprentice*.
   Most viewers thought that reality TV had gone too far even though

   <u>they</u> enjoyed shows like Fear Factor and The Apprentice.

● **Practice 29-2**

On the Web
For more practice, visit
Exercise Central *at*
<bedfordstmartins
.com/focusonwriting>.

The following sentences contain unnecessary two-part subjects. Rewrite each sentence correctly on the lines provided.

> **Example:** Travelers to China they often visit the Great Wall.
>
> *Travelers to China often visit the Great Wall.*

Answers will vary.

1. The first parts of the Great Wall they were built around A.D. 200.

   The first parts of the Great Wall were built around 200 A.D.

2. The purpose of the Great Wall it was built to keep out invading armies.

   The Great Wall was built to keep out invading armies.

3. The sides of the Great Wall they are made of stone, brick, and earth.

   The sides of the Great Wall are made of stone, brick, and earth.

4. The top of the Great Wall it is paved with bricks, forming a roadway for horses.

   The top of the Great Wall is paved with bricks, forming a roadway for

   horses.

5. The Great Wall it is the only man-made object that can be seen by astronauts in space.

   The Great Wall is the only man-made object that can be seen by

   astronauts in space.

Focus on Writing: *Flashback*

Look back at your response to the Focus on Writing activity on page 447. Does every sentence state its subject? Underline the subject of each sentence. If a sentence does not have a subject, add one. If any sentence has a two-part subject, cross out the unnecessary pronoun.

⟨29b⟩

Plural Nouns

Teaching Tip
Refer students to 27A and 27B for more on singular and plural nouns.

In English, most nouns add -*s* or -*es* to form plurals. Every time you use a noun, ask yourself whether you are talking about one item or more than one, and choose a singular or plural form accordingly. Consider this sentence.

Correct   The <u>books</u> in both <u>branches</u> of the <u>library</u> are deteriorating.

Teaching Tip
Tell students that many nouns—such as *child* and *goose*—have irregular plurals. Refer them to 27B.

The three nouns in this sentence are underlined: one is singular (*library*), and the other two are plural (*books, branches*). The word *both* is not enough to indicate that *branch* is plural even though it might be obvious that there are many books in any branch of a library. But even if a sentence includes information that tells you that a noun is plural, you must always use a form that shows that the noun is plural.

● Practice 29-3

On the Web
For more practice, visit Exercise Central *at* <bedfordstmartins .com/focusonwriting>.

Underline the plural nouns in the following sentences. (Not all the sentences contain plural nouns.)

Example: The shark is one of the earth's most feared <u>animals</u>.

Teaching Tip
Before students do this exercise, direct them to 27B, which deals with irregular noun plurals.

1. There are about 360 <u>species</u> of <u>sharks</u>.

2. These <u>fish</u> live in <u>oceans</u> and <u>seas</u> throughout the world but are most commonly found in warm water.

3. <u>Sharks</u> vary greatly in size and behavior.

4. Whale <u>sharks</u> are the largest, growing up to 40 <u>feet</u> long and weighing over 15 <u>tons</u>.

5. The smallest shark measures as little as half a foot and weighs less than an ounce.

6. Some <u>sharks</u> live in the deepest <u>areas</u> of the ocean, while other <u>sharks</u> stay near the water's surface.

7. Although all <u>sharks</u> are <u>meat-eaters</u>, only a few <u>species</u> are a danger to <u>people</u>.

8. Most <u>sharks</u> eat live <u>fish</u>, including other <u>sharks</u>.

9. <u>Sharks</u> are sometimes used in scientific research.

10. Few <u>sharks</u> have ever been found with cancer, and <u>scientists</u> hope to find out what protects these <u>creatures</u> from this disease.

Focus on Writing: *Flashback*

Look back at your response to the Focus on Writing activity on page 447. On a separate piece of paper, list all the plural nouns you used. Does each plural noun have a form that shows the noun is plural? Correct any errors you find.

29c Count and Noncount Nouns

A **count noun** names one particular thing or a group of particular things that can be counted: *a teacher, a panther, a bed, an ocean, a cloud, an ice cube; two teachers, many panthers, three beds, two oceans, several clouds, some ice cubes.* A **noncount noun**, however, names things that cannot be counted: *gold, cream, sand, blood, smoke, water.*

Count nouns usually have a singular form and a plural form: *cube, cubes.* Noncount nouns usually have only a singular form: *water.* Note how the nouns *cube* and *water* differ in the way they are used in sentences.

Teaching Tip
Tell students that sometimes a noncount noun, such as *smoke*, appears to have a plural form (*smokes*). Although such forms end in -*s*, they are verbs and not plural nouns: *The smoke is coming from his cigar. He smokes two cigars a day.*

Incorrect	The glass is full of waters.
Correct	The glass is full of ice cubes.
Correct	The glass is full of water.
Incorrect	The glass contains five waters.
Correct	The glass contains five ice cubes.
Correct	The glass contains some water.

Often, the same idea can be represented with either a count noun or a noncount noun.

Count	Noncount
people (plural of *person*)	humanity [*not* humanities]
tables, chairs, beds	furniture [*not* furnitures]
letters	mail [*not* mails]
supplies	equipment [*not* equipments]
facts	information [*not* informations]

Some words can be either count or noncount, depending on the meaning intended.

Count	He had many interesting <u>experiences</u> at his first job.
Noncount	It is often difficult to get a job if you do not have <u>experience</u>.

Highlight: Count and Noncount Nouns

Here are some guidelines for using count and noncount nouns.

● Use a count noun to refer to a living animal, but use a noncount noun to refer to the food that comes from that animal.

Count	There are three live <u>lobsters</u> in the tank.
Noncount	This restaurant specializes in <u>lobster</u>.

● If you use a noncount noun for a substance or class of things that can come in different varieties, you can often make that noun plural if you want to talk about those varieties.

Noncount	<u>Cheese</u> is a rich source of calcium.
Count	Many different <u>cheeses</u> come from Italy.

● If you want to shift attention from a concept in general to specific examples of it, you can often use a noncount noun as a count noun.

Noncount	You have a great deal of <u>talent</u>.
Count	My <u>talents</u> do not include singing.

On the Web
For more practice, visit Exercise Central *at* <bedfordstmartins.com/focusonwriting>.

● **Practice 29-4**

In each of the following sentences, identify the underlined word as a count or noncount noun. If it is a noncount noun, circle the *N* following the sentence, but do not write in the blank. If it is a count noun, circle the *C*, and then write the plural form of the noun in the blank.

Examples: Psychologists, sociologists, and anthropologists work in the field of behavioral <u>science</u>. Ⓝ C _____

They all have the same <u>goal</u>: to understand human behavior. N Ⓒ
_____*goals*_____

1. Each type of scientist has a different <u>approach</u> to solving a problem.
   N Ⓒ _____*approaches*_____

2. An <u>example</u> is the problem of homeless people on our cities' streets.
N Ⓒ _____*examples*_____

3. Sociologists concentrate on the social causes of <u>homelessness</u>. Ⓝ C

_____

4. They might study how <u>unemployment</u> contributes to a rise in the number of homeless people. Ⓝ C _____

5. A <u>shortage</u> of inexpensive housing can also cause someone to lose his or her home. N Ⓒ _____*shortages*_____

6. A sociologist's next question could be: How does <u>society</u> deal with homeless people? Ⓝ C _____

7. Psychologists, on the other hand, are interested in the <u>individual</u>. N Ⓒ
_____*individuals*_____

8. Their focus would be on how a homeless <u>person</u> feels and thinks. N Ⓒ
_____*people*_____

9. Anthropologists are interested in studying culture, a society's <u>system</u> of beliefs and its ways of doing things. N Ⓒ _____*systems*_____

10. An anthropologist might focus on how the <u>homeless</u> find food and shelter and on how they raise their children. Ⓝ C _____

29d

Determiners with Count and Noncount Nouns

Determiners are adjectives that *identify* rather than describe the nouns they modify. Determiners may also *quantify* nouns (that is, indicate an amount or a number).

Determiners include the following words.

● Articles: *a, an, the*
● Demonstrative pronouns: *this, these, that, those*
● Possessive pronouns: *my, our, your, his, her, its, their*
● Possessive nouns: *Sheila's, my friend's,* and so on
● *Whose, which, what*

- *All, both, each, every, some, any, either, no, neither, many, most, much, a few, a little, few, little, several, enough*
- All numerals: *one, two,* and so on

When a determiner is accompanied by one or more other adjectives, the determiner always comes first. For example, in the phrase *my expensive new gold watch, my* is a determiner; you cannot put *expensive, new, gold,* or any other adjective before *my.*

A singular count noun must always be accompanied by a determiner—for example, *my watch* or *the new gold watch,* not just *watch* or *new gold watch.* However, noncount nouns and plural count nouns sometimes have determiners but sometimes do not. *This honey is sweet* and *Honey is sweet* are both acceptable, as are *These berries are juicy* and *Berries are juicy.* (In each case, the meaning is different.) You cannot say, *Berry is juicy,* however; say instead, *This berry is juicy, Every berry is juicy,* or *A berry is juicy.*

**Highlight:
Determiners**

Teaching Tip
Students need to memorize the information in this box.

Teaching Tip
You might point out to students that *a few* and *a little* have positive connotations (*A few seats are left*), while *few* and *little* have negative connotations (*Few seats are left*).

Some determiners can be used only with certain types of nouns.

- *This* and *that* can be used only with singular nouns (count or non-count): *this berry, that honey.*

- *These, those, a few, few, many, both,* and *several* can be used only with plural count nouns: *these berries, those apples, a few ideas, few people, many students, both sides, several directions.*

- *Much, little,* and *a little* can be used only with noncount nouns: *much affection, little time, a little honey.*

- *Some, enough, all,* and *most* can be used only with noncount or plural count nouns: *some honey, some berries; enough trouble, enough problems; all traffic, all roads; most money, most coins.*

- *A, an, every, each, either,* and *neither* can be used only with singular count nouns: *a berry, an elephant, every possibility, each citizen, either option, neither candidate.*

On the Web
For more practice, visit Exercise Central *at* <bedfordstmartins .com/focusonwriting>.

● **Practice 29-5**

In each of the following sentences, circle the correct choice from each pair of words or phrases in parentheses.

Examples:

Volcanoes are among the most destructive of (all/every) natural forces on earth.

People have always been fascinated and terrified by (this/these) force of nature.

1. Not (all/every) volcano is considered a danger.

2. In (major some/some major) volcanic eruptions, huge clouds rise over the mountain.

3. (A few violent/Violent a few) eruptions are so dramatic that they blow the mountain apart.

4. (Most/Much) volcanic eruptions cannot be predicted.

5. Since the 1400s, (many/much) people—almost 200,000—have lost their lives in volcanic eruptions.

6. When a volcano erupts, (little/a little) can be done to prevent property damage.

7. (Many/Much) lives can be saved, however, if people in the area are evacuated in time.

8. Unfortunately, by the time people realize an eruption is about to take place, there rarely is (every/enough) time to escape.

9. Volcanoes can be dangerous, but they also produce (a little/some) benefits.

10. For example, (a few/a little) countries use energy from underground steam in volcanic areas to produce electric power.

Focus on Writing: *Flashback*

Look back at your response to the Focus on Writing activity on page 447. On a separate piece of paper, list all the count nouns in a column on the left and all the noncount nouns in a column on the right. Have you used count and noncount nouns correctly? Correct any errors you find.

29e Articles

Teaching Tip
Article use is difficult for most nonnative speakers. Go over 29E in class, encouraging students to give as many additional examples as they can.

The **definite article** *the* and the **indefinite articles** *a* and *an* are determiners that tell readers whether the noun that follows is one they can identify (*the book*) or one they cannot yet identify (*a book*).

The Definite Article

When the definite article *the* is used with a noun, the writer is saying to readers, "You can identify which particular thing or things I have in mind. The information you need to make that identification is available to you. Either you have it already, or I am about to give it to you."

Readers can find the necessary information in the following ways.

- By looking at other information in the sentence

    Meet me at the corner of Main Street and Lafayette Road.

    In this example, *the* is used with the noun *corner* because other words in the sentence tell readers which particular corner the writer has in mind: the one located at Main and Lafayette.

- By looking at information in other sentences

    Aisha ordered a slice of pie and a cup of coffee. The pie was delicious. She asked for a second slice.

    Here, *the* is used before the word *pie* in the second sentence to indicate that it is the same pie identified in the first sentence. Notice, however, that the noun *slice* in the third sentence is preceded by an indefinite article (*a*) because it is not the same slice referred to in the first sentence.

- By drawing on general knowledge

    The earth revolves around the sun.

    Here, *the* is used with the nouns *earth* and *sun* because readers are expected to know which particular things the writer is referring to.

Teaching Tip
Refer students to 28B for information on the superlative forms of adjectives and adverbs.

> **Highlight:**
> **Definite Articles**
>
> Always use *the* (rather than *a* or *an*) in the following situations.
>
> - Before the word *same*: the same *day*
> - Before the superlative form of an adjective: the youngest *son*
> - Before a number indicating order or sequence: the third *time*

Indefinite Articles

When an indefinite article is used with a noun, the writer is saying to readers, "I don't expect you to have enough information right now to identify a particular thing that I have in mind. I do, however, expect you to recognize that I'm referring to only one item."

Consider the following sentences.

> We need <u>a</u> table for our computer.
>
> I have <u>a</u> folding table; maybe you can use that.

In the first sentence, the writer is referring to a hypothetical table, not an actual one. Because the table is indefinite to the writer, it is clearly indefinite to the reader, so *a* is used, not *the*. The second sentence refers to an actual table, but because the writer does not expect the reader to be able to identify the table specifically, it is also used with *a* rather than *the*.

Teaching Tip
Refer students to the box on page 543 for a review of vowels and consonants.

Highlight: Indefinite Articles	Unlike the definite article (*the*), the indefinite articles *a* and *an* occur only with singular count nouns. *A* is used when the next sound is a consonant, and *an* is used when the next sound is a vowel. In choosing *a* or *an*, pay attention to sound rather than to spelling: *a house, a year, a union*, but *an hour, an uncle*.

No Article

Teaching Tip
Refer students to 29D for more on count and noncount nouns.

Only noncount and plural count nouns can stand without articles: *butter, chocolate, cookies, strawberries* (but *<u>a</u> cookie* or *<u>the</u> strawberry*).

Nouns without articles can be used to make generalizations.

> <u>Infants</u> need <u>affection</u> as well as <u>food</u>.

Teaching Tip
Sometimes (usually to suggest quantity), no article is used for particular (actual) things: *I can hear <u>dogs</u> barking.*

Here, the absence of articles before the nouns *infants, affection*, and *food* indicates that the statement is not about particular infants, affection, or food but about infants, affection, and food in general. Remember not to use *the* in such sentences; in English, a sentence like *The infants need affection as well as food* can only refer to particular, identifiable infants, not to infants in general.

Articles with Proper Nouns

Teaching Tip
Refer students to 27A and 33A for more on proper nouns.

Proper nouns can be divided into two classes: names that take *the* and names that take no article.

Teaching Tip
Remind students that
plurals of proper nouns
(such as *the Parkers*)
do not include apostro-
phes unless they are
possessive.

- Names of people usually take no article unless they are used in the plural to refer to members of a family, in which case they take *the*:
Napoleon, *Mahatma Gandhi*, but *the Parkers*.

- Names of places that are plural in form usually take *the*: *the Andes*, *the
United States*.

- The names of most places on land (cities, states, provinces, and countries) take no article: *Salt Lake City*, *Mississippi*, *Alberta*, *Japan*. The
names of most bodies of water (rivers, seas, and oceans, although not
lakes or bays) take *the*: *the Mississippi*, *the Mediterranean*, *the Pacific*
(but *Lake Erie*, *San Francisco Bay*).

- Names of streets take no article: *Main Street*. Names of unnumbered
highways take *the*: *the Belt Parkway*.

● Practice 29-6

In the following passage, decide whether each blank needs a definite article
(*the*), an indefinite article (*a* or *an*), or no article. If a definite or indefinite
article is needed, write it in the space provided. If no article is needed, leave
the space blank.

Example: Vicente Fox was born on _____ July 2, 1942, in _the_

Mexican capital of Mexico City.

(1) Vicente was _the_ second of nine children born to José Luis

Fox, _a_ wealthy farmer, and Mercedes Quesada. (2) When Vicente

was only four days old, _the_ Fox family went to live in San Francisco

del Rincón, in _the_ state of Guanajuato. (3) Vicente Fox studied _____

business administration at the Universidad Iberoamericana in Mexico

City. (4) He then moved to _the_ United States, where he received _a_

degree in management at _____ Harvard University. (5) When he

returned to Mexico, he went to work for Coca-Cola, and over _the_ next

fifteen years, he climbed _the_ corporate ladder and became _the_ com-

pany's youngest manager and eventually Coca-Cola's president for Mex-

ico and _____ Latin America. (6) Fox entered _____ politics by joining

the National Action Party during _the_ 1980s. (7) In 1988, he was

elected to _____ Congress. (8) _A_ few years later, in 1991, he ran for

the post of governor of Guanajuato but lost. (9) Four years later, how-

 On the Web
For more practice, visit
Exercise Central *at*
<bedfordstmartins
.com/focusonwriting>.

ever, he won by __a__ landslide. (10) In 1999, Fox took __a__ leave of absence as governor to run in __the__ presidential elections. (11) In one interview during his campaign, he said he wanted to rebuild Mexico into __a__ country "where _____ security and _____ justice prevail, where no one is above __the__ law." (12) After promoting himself as __a__ "down-to-earth man of __the__ people," on July 2, 2000, Vicente Fox became __the__ first opposition candidate to reach __the__ presidency of __the__ Republic of Mexico, and he served until 2006.

Focus on Writing: *Flashback*

Look back at your response to the Focus on Writing activity on page 447. Circle each definite article (*the*) and indefinite article (*a* or *an*) you have used. Have you used articles correctly? Correct any errors you find.

29f Negative Statements and Questions

Negative Statements

Teaching Tip
Refer students to 14C for more on helping verbs.

To form a negative statement, add the word *not* directly after the first help-ing verb of the complete verb.

> Global warming has been getting worse.
> Global warming has **not** been getting worse.

Teaching Tip
Tell students that if a sentence includes the word *some* (*I have some money*), when it is turned into a negative state-ment, *any* replaces *some* (*I don't have any money*).

When there is no helping verb, a form of the verb *do* must be inserted before *not*.

> Automobile traffic contributes to pollution.
> Automobile traffic **does not** contribute to pollution.

However, if the main verb is *am, is, are, was,* or *were*, do not insert a form of *do* before *not*: *Harry was late. Harry was **not** late.*

Remember that when *do* is used as a helping verb, the form of *do* used must match the tense and number of the original main verb. Note that in the negative statement on the preceding page, the main verb loses its tense and appears in the base form (*contribute*, not *contributes*).

Questions

To form a question, move the helping verb that follows the subject to the position directly before the subject.

> The governor <u>is</u> trying to compromise.
>
> <u>Is</u> the governor trying to compromise?
>
> The governor <u>is</u> working on the budget.
>
> <u>Is</u> the governor working on the budget?

The same rule applies even when the verb is in the past or future tense.

> The governor <u>was</u> trying to lower state taxes.
>
> <u>Was</u> the governor trying to lower state taxes?
>
> The governor <u>will</u> try to get reelected.
>
> <u>Will</u> the governor try to get reelected?

As with negatives, when the verb does not include a helping verb, you must supply a form of *do*. To form a question, put the correct form of *do* directly before the subject.

> The governor <u>works</u> hard.
>
> <u>Does</u> the governor <u>work</u> hard?
>
> The governor <u>improved</u> life in his state.
>
> <u>Did</u> the governor <u>improve</u> life in his state?

However, if the main verb is *am*, *is*, *are*, *was*, or *were*, do not insert a form of *do* before the verb. Instead, move the main verb so it comes before the subject (*Harry was late. <u>Was</u> Harry late?*)

Note: The helping verb never comes before the subject if the subject is a question word (such as *who* or *which*).

> <u>Who</u> is talking to the governor?
>
> <u>Which</u> bills have been vetoed by the governor?

● **Practice 29-7**

On the Web
For more practice, visit
Exercise Central *at*
<bedfordstmartins
.com/focusonwriting>.

Rewrite each of the following sentences in two ways: first, turn the sentence into a question; then, rewrite the original sentence as a negative statement.

> **Example:**   Her newest album is selling as well as her first one.
>
> *Question:* Is her newest album selling as well as her first one?
>
> *Negative statement:* Her newest album is not selling as well as her first one.

Teaching Tip
Students may need
help with past tense
sentences, where verbs
will change form in
questions and negative
statements.

1. Converting metric measurements to the system used in the United States is difficult.

   Question: Is converting metric measurements to the system used in the United States difficult?

   Negative statement: Converting metric measurements to the system used in the United States is not difficult.

2. The early frost damaged many crops.

   Question: Did the early frost damage many crops?

   Negative statement: The early frost did not damage many crops.

3. That family was very influential in the early 1900s.

   Question: Was the family very influential in the early 1900s?

   Negative statement: The family was not very influential in the early 1900s.

4. Most stores in malls are open on Sundays.

   Question: Are most stores in malls open on Sundays?

   Negative statement: Most stores in malls are not open on Sundays.

5. Choosing the right gift is a difficult task.

   Question: Is choosing the right gift a difficult task?

   Negative statement: Choosing the right gift is not a difficult task.

6. Many great artists are successful during their lifetimes.

   Question: Are many great artists successful during their lifetimes?

   Negative statement: Many great artists are not successful during their lifetimes.

7. The lawyer can verify the witness's story.

    Question: <u>Can the lawyer verify the witness's story?</u>

    Negative statement: <u>The lawyer cannot verify the witness's story.</u>

8. American cities are as dangerous as they were thirty years ago.

    Question: <u>Are American cities as dangerous as they were thirty years ago?</u>

    Negative statement: <u>American cities are not as dangerous as they were thirty years ago.</u>

9. The British royal family is loved by most of the British people.

    Question: <u>Is the British royal family loved by most British people?</u>

    Negative statement: <u>The British royal family is not loved by most British people.</u>

10. Segregation in the American South ended with the Civil War.

    Question: <u>Did segregation in the American South end with the Civil War?</u>

    Negative statement: <u>Segregation in the American South did not end with the Civil War.</u>

Focus on Writing: *Flashback*

Look back at your response to the Focus on Writing activity on page 447. Do you see any negative statements? If so, check to make sure you have formed them correctly. Then, on the line below, write a question that you could add to your Focus on Writing activity.

Question: <u>*Answers will vary.*</u>

Check carefully to make sure you have formed the question correctly.

29g   Verb Tense

Teaching Tip
Refer students to Chapters 25 and 26 for more on verb tense.

In English, a verb's form must indicate when an action took place (for instance, in the past or in the present). Use the appropriate tense of the verb, even if the time is obvious or if the sentence includes other indications of time (such as *two years ago* or *at present*).

| Incorrect | Albert Einstein emigrate from Germany in 1933. |
| Correct | Albert Einstein emigrated from Germany in 1933. |

Focus on Writing: *Flashback*

Look back at your response to the Focus on Writing activity on page 447. Are all your verbs in the present tense? Correct any errors you find.

⟨29h⟩ Stative Verbs

Stative verbs usually tell that someone or something is in a state that will not change, at least for a while.

> Hiro knows American history very well.

Most English verbs show action, and these action verbs can be used in the progressive tenses. The **present progressive** tense consists of the present tense of *be* plus the present participle (*I am going*). The **past progressive** tense consists of the past tense of *be* plus the present participle (*I was going*). Unlike other verbs, however, stative verbs are rarely used in the progressive tenses.

> **Incorrect** Hiro is knowing American history very well.

Highlight: Stative Verbs

Verbs that are stative—such as *know, understand, think, believe, want, like, love,* and *hate*—often refer to mental states. Other stative verbs include *be, have, need, own, belong, weigh, cost,* and *mean.* Certain verbs of sense perception, like *see* and *hear,* are also stative even though they can refer to momentary events as well as to unchanging states.

Many verbs have more than one meaning, and some of these verbs are active with one meaning but stative with another. An example is the verb *weigh.*

Active   The butcher <u>weighs</u> the meat.

Stative   The meat <u>weighs</u> three pounds.

In the first of these two sentences, the verb *weigh* means "to put on a scale"; it is active, not stative. In the second sentence, however, the same verb means "to have weight," so it is stative, not active. It would be unacceptable to say, "The meat is weighing three pounds," but "The butcher is weighing the meat" would be correct.

● Practice 29-8

On the Web
For more practice, visit Exercise Central at <bedfordstmartins .com/focusonwriting>.

In each of the following sentences, circle the verb or verbs. Then, correct any problems with stative verbs by crossing out the incorrect verb tense and writing the correct verb tense above the line. If the verb is correct, write *C* above it.

Example: Police officers (are knowing) [*know*] that fingerprint identification [*C*] (is) one of the best ways to catch criminals.

1. As early as 1750 B.C., ancient Babylonians (were signing) [*C*] their identities on clay tablets.

2. By A.D. 220, the Chinese (were becoming) [*C*] aware that ink fingerprints (could identify) [*C*] people.

3. However, it (was) [*C*] not until the late 1800s that anyone (was believing) [*believed*] that criminal identification (was) [*C*] possible with fingerprints.

4. Nowadays, we (know) [*C*] that each person (is having) [*has*] unique patterns on the tips of his or her fingers.

5. When police (study) [*C*] a crime scene, they (want) [*C*] to see whether the criminals (have left) [*C*] any fingerprint evidence.

6. There (is) [*C*] always a layer of oil on the skin, and police (are liking) [*like*] to use it to get fingerprints.

7. Crime scene experts (are often seeing) [*often see*] cases where the criminals (are touching) [*touch*] their hair and (pick up) [*C*] enough oil to leave a good fingerprint.

8. The police (are needing) [*need*] to judge whether the fingerprint evidence (has been damaged) [*C*] by sunlight, rain, or heat.

9. In the courtroom, juries often (weigh) fingerprint evidence before they
   ~~are deciding~~ on their verdict.
   decide
10. The FBI (is collecting) millions of fingerprints, which police departments
   (can compare) with the fingerprints they (find) at crime scenes.

Focus on Writing: *Flashback*

Look back at your response to the Focus on Writing activity on page 447.
Can you identify any stative verbs? If so, list them here on a separate
sheet of paper. Check carefully to be sure you have not used any of these
verbs in a progressive tense. Correct any errors you find.

Modal Auxiliaries

Teaching Tip
Refer students to 14C for
more on helping verbs.

A **modal auxiliary** (such as *can, may, might,* or *must*) is a helping verb that
is used with a sentence's main verb to express ability, possibility, necessity,
intent, obligation, and so on. In the following sentence, *can* is the modal auxiliary, and *imagine* is the main verb.

> I *can imagine* myself in Hawaii.

Modal auxiliaries usually intensify the main verb's meaning.

> I *must run* as fast as I can.
> You *ought to lose* some weight.

Modal Auxiliaries

can	ought to
could	shall
may	should
might	will
must	would

Highlight: Modal Auxiliaries

Modal auxiliaries can be used to do the following.

- Express physical ability

  I can walk faster than my brother.

- Express the possibility of something occurring

  He might get the job if his interview goes well.

- Express or request permission

  May I use the restroom in the hallway?

- Express necessity

  I must get to the train station on time.

- Express a suggestion or advice

  To be healthy, you should [or ought to] exercise and eat balanced meals.

- Express intent

  I will try to study harder next time.

- Express a desire

  Would you please answer the telephone?

● **Practice 29-9**

In the exercise below, circle the correct modal auxiliary.

Example: (May/Would) you help me complete the assignment?

1. It doesn't rain very often in Arizona, but today it looks like it (can/might).
2. I know I (will/ought to) call my aunt on her birthday, but I always find an excuse.
3. Sarah (should/must) study for her English exam, but she is happier spending time with her friends.
4. John (can/would) be the best person to represent our class.
5. Since the close presidential election of 2000, many people now believe they (could/should) vote in every election.

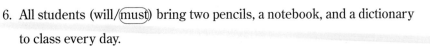

6. All students (will/must) bring two pencils, a notebook, and a dictionary to class every day.

7. (Would/May) you show me the way to the post office?

8. I (could/should) not ask for more than my health, my family, and my job.

9. Do you think they (could/can) come back tomorrow to finish the painting job?

10. A dog (should/might) be a helpful companion for your disabled father.

 29j

Gerunds

A **gerund** is a verb form ending in *-ing* that always acts as a noun.

> Reading the newspaper is one of my favorite things to do on Sundays.

Just like a noun, a gerund can be used as a subject, a direct object, a subject complement, or the object of a preposition.

Highlight: Gerunds	● A gerund can be the subject of a sentence.
	Playing tennis is one of my hobbies.
	● A gerund can be a direct object.
	My brother influenced my racing.
	● A gerund can be a subject complement.
	The most important thing is winning.
	● A gerund can be the object of a preposition.
	The teacher rewarded him for passing.

● Practice 29-10

To complete the sentences below, fill in the blanks with the gerund form of the verb provided in parentheses.

Example: _____*Typing*_____ (type) is a skill that every girl used to learn in high school.

1. _____*Eating*_____ (eat) five or six smaller meals throughout the day is healthier than eating two or three big meals.

2. In the winter, there is nothing better than _____*skating*_____ (skate) outdoors on a frozen pond.

3. The household task I dread the most is _____*cleaning*_____ (clean).

4. The fish avoided the net by _____*swimming*_____ (swim) faster.

5. _____*Quitting*_____ (quit) is easier than accomplishing a goal.

6. Her parents praised her for _____*remembering*_____ (remember) their anniversary.

7. Her favorite job is _____*organizing*_____ (organize) the files.

8. I did not like his _____*singing*_____ (sing).

9. For me, _____*cooking*_____ (cook) is relaxing.

10. The best way to prepare for the concert is by _____*practicing*_____ (practice).

Placing Modifiers in Order

Teaching Tip
Refer students to 29D for more on determiners.

Adjectives and other modifiers that come before a noun usually follow a set order.

Required Order

- Determiners always come first in a series of modifiers: *these fragile glasses*. The determiners *all* or *both* always precede any other determiners: *all these glasses*.

- If one of the modifiers is a noun, it must come directly before the noun it modifies: *these <u>wine</u> glasses*.

- Descriptive adjectives are placed between the determiners and the noun modifiers: *these fragile wine glasses*. If there are two or more descriptive adjectives, the following order is preferred.

Preferred Order

- Adjectives that show the writer's attitude generally precede adjectives that merely describe: *these lovely fragile wine glasses.*
- Adjectives that indicate size generally come early: *these lovely large fragile wine glasses.*

● Practice 29-11

Arrange each group of modifiers in the correct order, and rewrite the complete phrase in the blank.

On the Web
For more practice, visit Exercise Central *at* <bedfordstmartins .com/focusonwriting>.

Example: (annual, impressive, the, publisher's) report

the publisher's impressive annual report

1. (brand-new, a, apartment, high-rise) building
   a brand-new high-rise apartment building

2. (gifted, twenty-five-year-old, Venezuelan, this) author
   this gifted twenty-five-year-old Venezuelan author

3. (successful, short-story, numerous) collections
   numerous successful short-story collections

4. (her, all, intriguing, suspense) novels
   all her intriguing suspense novels

5. (publisher's, best-selling, the, three) works
   the publisher's three best-selling works

6. (main, story's, two, this) characters
   this story's two main characters

7. (young, a, strong-willed) woman
   a strong-willed young woman

8. (middle-aged, shy, the, British) poet
   the shy middle-aged British poet

9. (exquisite, wedding, an, white) gown
   an exquisite white wedding gown

10. (elaborate, wedding, an) reception
    an elaborate wedding reception

Focus on Writing: *Flashback*

Look back at your response to the Focus on Writing activity on page 447. Have you used several modifiers before a single noun? If so, list here all the modifiers you used and the noun that follows them.

Modifiers: <u>Answers will vary.</u>   _____   _____   Noun: _____

Modifiers: _____   _____   _____   Noun: _____

Have you arranged the modifiers in the correct order? Make any necessary corrections.

291

Choosing Prepositions

A **preposition** introduces a noun or pronoun and links it to other words in the sentence. The word the preposition introduces is called the object of the preposition.

A preposition and its object combine to form a **prepositional phrase**: *on the table, near the table, under the table.*

> I thought I had left the book <u>on</u> the table or somewhere <u>near</u> the table, but I found it <u>under</u> the table.

The prepositions *at, in,* and *on* sometimes cause problems for nonnative speakers of English. For example, to identify the location of a place or an event, you can use *at, in,* or *on.*

- The preposition *at* specifies an exact point in space or time.

  > The museum is <u>at</u> 1000 Fifth Avenue. Let's meet there <u>at</u> 10:00 tomorrow morning.

- Expanses of space or time are treated as containers and therefore require *in.*

  > Women used to wear long skirts <u>in</u> the early 1900s.

- *On* must be used in two cases: with names of streets (but not with exact addresses), and with days of the week or month.

  > We will move into our new office <u>on</u> 18th Street either <u>on</u> Monday or <u>on</u> March 12.

Prepositions in Familiar Expressions

Many familiar expressions end with prepositions. Learning to write clearly and **idiomatically**—following the conventions of written English—means learning which preposition is used in such expressions. Even native speakers of English sometimes have trouble choosing the correct preposition.

The sentences that follow illustrate idiomatic use of prepositions in various expressions. Note that sometimes different prepositions are used with the same word. For example, both *on* and *for* can be used with *wait* to form two different expressions with two different meanings (*He waited on their table*; *She waited for the bus*). Which preposition you choose depends on your meaning. (In the list that follows, pairs of similar expressions that end with different prepositions are bracketed.)

Expression with Preposition	Sample Sentence
acquainted with	During orientation, the university offers workshops to make sure that students are <u>acquainted with</u> its rules and regulations.
addicted to	I think Abby is becoming <u>addicted to</u> pretzels.
agree on (a plan or objective)	It is vital that all members of the school board <u>agree on</u> goals for the coming year.
agree to (a proposal)	Striking workers finally <u>agreed to</u> the terms of management's offer.
angry about or at (a situation)	Taxpayers are understandably <u>angry about</u> (or <u>at</u>) the deterioration of city recreation facilities.
angry with (a person)	When the mayor refused to hire more police officers, his constituents became <u>angry with</u> him.
approve of	Amy's adviser <u>approved of</u> her decision to study in Guatemala.
bored with	Salah got <u>bored with</u> economics, so he changed his major to psychology.
capable of	Hannah is a good talker, but she is not <u>capable of</u> acting as her own lawyer.
consist of	The deluxe fruit basket <u>consisted of</u> five pathetic pears, two tiny apples, a few limp bunches of grapes, and one lonely kiwi.
contrast with	Coach Headley's relaxed style <u>contrasts</u> sharply <u>with</u> Coach Morgan's more formal approach.

convenient for	The proposed location of the new day-care center is <u>convenient for</u> many families.
deal with	Many parents and educators believe it is possible to <u>deal with</u> the special needs of autistic children in a regular classroom.
depend on	Children <u>depend on</u> their parents for emotional as well as financial support.
differ from (something else)	A capitalist system <u>differs from</u> a socialist system in its view of private ownership.
differ with (someone else)	When Miles realized that he <u>differed with</u> his boss on most important issues, he handed in his resignation.
emigrate from	My grandfather and his brother <u>emigrated from</u> the part of Russia that is now Ukraine.
grateful for (a favor)	If you can arrange an interview next week, I will be very <u>grateful for</u> your time and trouble.
grateful to (someone)	Jerry Garcia was always <u>grateful to</u> his loyal fans.
immigrate to	Many Cubans want to leave their country and <u>immigrate to</u> the United States.
impatient with	Keshia often gets <u>impatient with</u> her four younger brothers.
interested in	Tomiko had always been <u>interested in</u> computers, so no one was surprised when she became a Web designer.
interfere with	College athletes often find that their dedication to sports <u>interferes with</u> their schoolwork.
meet with	I hope I can <u>meet with</u> you soon to discuss my research project.
object to	The defense attorney <u>objected to</u> the prosecutor's treatment of the witness.
pleased with	Most of the residents are <u>pleased with</u> the mayor's crackdown on crime.
protect against	Nobel Prize winner Linus Pauling believed that large doses of vitamin C could <u>protect</u> people <u>against</u> the common cold.
reason with	When two-year-olds have tantrums, it is nearly impossible to <u>reason with</u> them.

reply to	If no one <u>replies to</u> our ad within two weeks, we will advertise again.
responsible for	Should teachers be held <u>responsible for</u> their students' low test scores?
similar to	The blood sample found at the crime scene was remarkably <u>similar to</u> one found in the suspect's residence.
specialize in	Dr. Casullo is a dentist who <u>specializes in</u> periodontal surgery.
succeed in	Lisa hoped her M.B.A. would help her <u>succeed in</u> a business career.
take advantage of	Some consumer laws are designed to prevent door-to-door salespeople from <u>taking advantage of</u> buyers.
wait for (something to happen)	Many parents of teenagers experience tremendous anxiety while <u>waiting for</u> their children to come home at night.
wait on (in a restaurant)	We sat at the table for twenty minutes before someone <u>waited on</u> us.
worry about	Why <u>worry about</u> things you cannot change?

Teaching Tip
You may want to remind students that although *wait on* is often used for *wait for* in casual speech (*I'm waiting on my adviser, but he's late*), this usage is not acceptable in college writing.

Highlight: Using Prepositions in Familiar Expressions: Synonyms

Below is a list of familiar expressions that have similar meanings. They can often be used in the same contexts.

acquainted with, familiar with

addicted to, hooked on

angry with (a person), upset with

approve of, authorize

bored with, tired of

capable of, able to

consists of, has, contains, includes

deal with (a problem), address

depend on, rely on

differ from (something else), be different from

differ with (someone else), disagree

emigrate from, move from (another country)

grateful for (a favor), thankful for

immigrate to, move to (another country)

interested in, fascinated by

interfere with, disrupt

meet with, get together with

➡

Highlight: Using Prepositions in Familiar Expressions: Synonyms continued	object to, oppose	succeed in, attain success, reach a goal
	pleased with, happy with	take advantage of, use an opportunity
	protect against, guard against	
	reply to, answer	wait for (something to happen), expect
	responsible for, accountable for	
	similar to, almost the same as	wait on (in a restaurant), serve
	specialize in, devote oneself to (a special area of work)	

● **Practice 29-12**

On the Web
For more practice, visit Exercise Central at <bedfordstmartins .com/focusonwriting>.

In the following passage, fill in each blank with the correct preposition.

Example: Tony Bartoli is _____*in*_____ his second year _____*at*_____ a large state college.

(1) There have been many changes _____*in*_____ Tony's life _____*in*_____ the past few years. (2) _____*In*_____ 1997, Tony's family emigrated _____*from*_____ Argentina. (3) Although Tony had studied English _____*in*_____ Argentina, he was amazed _____*at*_____ how little he seemed to know when he got _____*to*_____ the States. (4) _____*On*_____ his first day _____*of*_____ high school, he met _____*with*_____ a guidance counselor who convinced him to take advantage _____*of*_____ the special English classes that were being offered _____*at*_____ the vocational-technical school. (5) Since Tony was very interested _____*in*_____ improving his English (and knew he would have to do that if he wanted to succeed _____*in*_____ his new world), he enrolled _____*in*_____ a class. (6) Now, Tony is grateful not only _____*to*_____ his guidance counselor but also _____*to*_____ all the teachers who supported him and showed him that he was capable _____*of*_____ succeeding. (7) Adjusting _____*to*_____ a new life _____*in*_____ a new country and getting acquainted _____*with*_____ a culture that differs greatly _____*from*_____ the one that he was used _____*to*_____ were challenges that he met _____*with*_____ enthusiasm and _____*with*_____ success.

(8) Last year, when he first arrived ___at___ Florida State, he was worried ___about___ taking regular college courses ___in___ his second language, English. (9) Some of the first-year classes were difficult, but he was pleased ___with___ his grades ___at___ the end ___of___ the year. (10) This year, Tony went back ___to___ school early so that he could look ___for___ a part-time job and a place to live. (11) When he found the apartment ___on___ College Avenue, he called his parents ___on___ the phone. (12) ___At___ first, they objected ___to___ his decision to live on his own, but they finally agreed ___to___ the idea. (13) It is going to be a great year, and Tony is looking forward ___to___ it.

Focus on Writing: *Flashback*

Look back at your response to the Focus on Writing activity on page 447. Have you used any of the idiomatic expressions listed on pages 471–73? If so, bracket each expression. Have you used the correct prepositions? Make any necessary corrections.

29n   Prepositions in Phrasal Verbs

Teaching Tip
You may want to mention that in some phrasal verbs, the second word is not a preposition but an adverb: *run across, speak up.*

A **phrasal verb** consists of two words, a verb and a preposition, that are joined to form an idiomatic expression. Many phrasal verbs are **separable**. This means that a direct object can come between the verb and the preposition. However, some phrasal verbs are **inseparable**; that is, the preposition must always come immediately after the verb.

Separable Phrasal Verbs

In many cases, phrasal verbs may be split, with the direct object coming between the two parts of the verb. When the direct object is a noun, the second word of the phrasal verb can come either before or after the object.

In the sentence below, *fill out* is a phrasal verb. Because the object of the verb *fill out* is a noun (*form*), the second word of the verb can come either before or after the verb's object.

Correct   Please fill out the form.

Correct   Please fill the form out.

When the object is a pronoun, however, these phrasal verbs must be split, and the pronoun must come between the two parts of the verb.

Incorrect   Please fill out it.

Correct   Please fill it out.

Some Common Separable Phrasal Verbs

ask out	give away	put back	throw away
bring up	hang up	put on	try out
call up	leave out	set aside	turn down
carry out	let out	shut off	turn off
drop off	make up	take down	wake up
fill out	put away	think over	

Remember, when the object of the verb is a pronoun, these phrasal verbs must be split, and the pronoun must come between the two parts (for example, *take (it) down*, *put (it) on*, *let (it) out*, and *make (it) up*).

Inseparable Phrasal Verbs

Some phrasal verbs, however, cannot be separated; that is, the preposition cannot be separated from the verb. This means that a direct object cannot come between the verb and the preposition.

Incorrect   Please go the manual over carefully.

Correct   Please go over the manual carefully.

Notice that in the correct sentence above, the direct object (*manual*) comes right after the preposition (*over*).

> ### Some Common Inseparable Phrasal Verbs
>
> | come across | run across | show up |
> | get along | run into | stand by |
> | go over | see to | |

● Practice 29-13

Consulting the lists of separable and inseparable phrasal verbs above, decide whether the preposition is placed correctly in each of the following sentences. If a sentence is correct, write *C* in the blank after the sentence. If it is not correct, edit the sentence.

On the Web
For more practice, visit
Exercise Central *at*
<bedfordstmartins
.com/focusonwriting>.

Example: People who live in American suburbs are often surprised to come across wild animals in their neighborhoods. __*C*__

1. In one case, a New Jersey woman found that a hungry bear woke ~~up~~ her
   up
   from a nap one afternoon. _____
   ^

2. She called the police, hung up the phone, and ran for her life. __*C*__
   into   ,
3. Actually, although it can be frightening to run bears ~~into~~, most wild
   ^   ^
   bears are timid. _____

4. When there is a drought, people are more likely to run into bears and
   other wild animals. __*C*__

5. The amount of blueberries and other wild fruit that bears eat usually
   off
   drops in dry weather ~~off~~. _____
   ^

6. Bears need to put on weight before the winter, so they may have to find
   food in suburban garbage cans. __*C*__
   over
7. It is a good idea for families to go their plans ~~over~~ to safeguard their
   ^
   property against bears. _____

8. People should not leave pet food out overnight, or else their dog might
   find that a hungry bear has eaten its dinner. __*C*__

9. If people have bird feeders in the yard, they should put ~~away~~ them
   away
   during the autumn. _____
   ^

10. As the human population grows, more and more houses are built in for-
merly wild areas, so bears and people have to learn to get along with
each other. _C_

Focus on Writing: *Flashback*

Look back at your response to the Focus on Writing activity on page 447.
Have you used any phrasal verbs? If so, list them on a separate piece of
paper. Have you placed the preposition correctly in each case? Make any
necessary corrections.

Focus on Writing: *Revising and Editing*

Look back at your response to the Focus on Writing activity on page 447.
Then, review all your Flashback activities, and be sure you have made
all necessary corrections in grammar and usage. When you have finished,
add any additional transitional words and phrases you need to make the
celebration you have described clear to your readers.

Editing Practice

Read the following student essay, which includes errors in the use of subjects, articles and determiners, and stative verbs, as well as errors with prepositions in idiomatic expressions. Check each underlined word or phrase. If it is not used correctly, cross it out, and write the correct word or phrase above the line. If the underlined word or phrase is correct, write *C* above it. The title of the essay has been edited for you.

in
How to <u>Succeed on</u> Multinational Business

on
Success in multinational business often <u>depends in</u> the ability

to understand other countries' cultures. Understanding how cultures
from   *this*
differ <u>to</u> our own, however, is only one key to <u>these</u> success.
it
Also, is crucial that businesses learn to adapt to different cultures.
Ethnocentrism   *the*
<u>The ethnocentrism</u> is the belief that one's own culture has <u>a</u> best way
it   *C*
of doing things. In international business, <u>is</u> necessary to <u>set aside</u>
use
this belief. A company cannot <u>uses</u> the same methods overseas as it

uses at home. If a company tries to sell exactly the same product in a
there
different country, <u>could be</u> problems.

To avoid problems, a company that wants to sell its product
some
internationally <u>it</u> should do <u>a few</u> market research. For example, when
in   *it*
McDonald's opened restaurants <u>on</u> India, <u>realized</u> that beef burgers

would not work in a country where many people believe that cows are
chicken.
sacred. Instead, burgers were created out of ground <u>chickens.</u> For

India's many vegetarians, McDonald's created several different
patties.
vegetable <u>patty.</u> McDonald's understood that both the religious and
characteristics
cultural <u>characteristic</u> of the country had to be considered if its new

restaurants were going to succeed.
an   *C*
Similarly, <u>American company</u> should always find out what the name
In
of the product means in the new language. <u>With</u> one famous example,

<u>the</u> General Motors tried to sell a car called the Chevy Nova in Spanish-

speaking countries. Then, the company discovered that although *nova*

means "bright star" in English, *no va* means "doesn't go" in Spanish,

                                                                    a
so it was not ~~good name~~ to use in Spanish-speaking countries. If
                                                                      of
General Motors' businesspeople had been capable ~~to~~ speaking and
                                              might
understanding the language, they ~~must~~ have avoided this embarassing
                                                              makes
situation. Communicating directly with customers ~~make~~ everyone more

comfortable and efficient.
There are
　~~It is~~ many aspects of a country that must be understood before
　　　　　　　C　　　　　　　　　　　　　　　*C*　　　*against*
successful international business can be carried out. To protect ~~from~~

legal errors, a company needs to understand the country's legal

system, which may be very different from its home country's legal
　　　　It may　　　　　　　　　　　　　　　　　　　　*into*
system. ~~May~~ be necessary to get licenses to export products ~~onto~~ other

countries. The role of women is also likely to be different; without

knowing this, businesspeople might unintentionally offend people.
　　　many
Also, ~~much~~ personal interactions in other countries may give the

wrong impression to someone who is inexperienced. For example, in
　　　　　　　　　　　　　　　　　　　stand
Latin American countries, people ~~are~~ often ~~standing~~ close together and

touch each other when they are talking. Americans may feel
　　　　　　　　　　　　　　　　　they
uncomfortable in such a situation unless understand it.
　　　　　　　　　　　　　　　　　　C　　　　　　　*this*
　　Over time, the marketplace is becoming more global. In ~~those~~

setting, individuals from numerous cultures come together. To perform

effectively, an international company must hire people with the right
experience.　　　　　*C*
~~experiences.~~ To deal with other cultures, multinational companies
in　　　　　　　　　　　　　*information*
~~inside~~ today's global market must have good ~~informations~~ and show
　　　　　　　　　　　　　　respect.
other cultures the highest ~~respects.~~

Collaborative Activities

1. Working in a small group, make a list of ten prepositional phrases that
   include the prepositions *above, around, at, between, from, in, on, over, under,*
   and *with.* Use specific nouns as objects of these prepositions, and use as
   many modifying words as you wish. (Try, for example, to write something
   like *above their hideous wedding portrait,* not just *above the picture.*)

2. Exchange lists with another group. Still working collaboratively, compose a list of ten sentences, each including one of the other group's

ten prepositional phrases. Give your list of ten sentences to another group.

3. Working with this new list of ten sentences, substitute a different prepositional phrase for each one that appears in a sentence. Make sure each sentence still makes sense.

Review Checklist:
Grammar and Usage for ESL Writers

- [ ] In almost all cases, English sentences must state their subjects. (See 29A.)

- [ ] In English, most nouns add -s or -es to form plurals. When a noun refers to more than one person or thing, always use a form that indicates that a noun is plural. (See 29B.)

- [ ] English nouns may be count nouns or noncount nouns. A count noun names one particular thing or a group of particular things (*a teacher*, *oceans*). A noncount noun names something that cannot be counted (*gold*, *sand*). (See 29C.)

- [ ] Determiners are adjectives that identify rather than describe the nouns they modify. Determiners may also indicate amount or number. (See 29D.)

- [ ] The definite article *the* and the indefinite articles *a* and *an* are determiners that indicate whether the noun that follows is one readers can identify (*the book*) or one they cannot yet identify (*a book*). (See 29E.)

- [ ] To form a negative statement, add the word *not* directly after the first helping verb of the complete verb. To form a question, move the helping verb that follows the subject to the position directly before the subject. (See 29F.)

- [ ] A verb's form must indicate when an action took place. (See 29G.)

- [ ] Stative verbs indicate that someone or something is in a state that will not change, at least for a while. Stative verbs are rarely used in the progressive tenses. (See 29H.)

- [ ] A modal auxiliary is a helping verb that expresses ability, possibility, necessity, intent, obligation, and so on. (See 29I.)

- [ ] A gerund is a verb form ending in -*ing* that is always used as a noun. (See 29J.)

- [ ] Adjectives and other modifiers that come before a noun usually follow a set order. (See 29K.)

- [ ] The prepositions *at*, *in*, and *on* sometimes cause problems for nonnative speakers of English. (See 29L.)

- [ ] Many familiar expressions end with prepositions. (See 29M.)

- [ ] A phrasal verb consists of two words, a verb and a preposition, that are joined to form an idiomatic expression. (See 29N.)

Editing Practice: Sentences

Read the following sentences, which contain errors in basic grammar. Identify errors in the use of past tenses, past participles, nouns, pronouns, adjectives, and adverbs, and edit the faulty sentences. Some sentences have more than one error.

Teaching Tip
You can use this exercise to warm students up for the multi-error editing practice that follows.

1. Whenever I went fishing with my brother, he ~~catched~~ *caught* fewer fish than ~~me~~ *I*.

2. Before Kylie typed her English essay, she ~~has~~ *had* never used a computer before; however, she ~~finded~~ *found* it ~~more~~ easier than she expected.

3. After the news conference, the soccer team (including the two ~~heros~~ *heroes* of the game) boarded ~~their~~ *its* bus and went home.

4. When I visited them last summer, neither my aunt nor her two ~~childs~~ *children* ~~can~~ *could* meet me at the train station.

5. After the power outage, everything in the freezer had to be ~~threw~~ *thrown* away because it was not ~~froze~~ *frozen* solid.

6. Airport security officers told everyone in line to remove ~~their~~ *his or her* shoes.

7. ~~Me and my~~ *My* roommate *and I* met for the first time during the summer.

8. The person ~~whom~~ *who* was working late last night ~~forgets~~ *forgot* to lock the office door.

9. As soon as I saw the first question, I knew I would do ~~bad~~ *badly* on the test.

10. When a person needs help, ~~you~~ *he or she* should ask for it.

Editing Practice: Essay

Read the following student essay, which contains errors in the use of the past tense, past participles, nouns, pronouns, and adjectives and adverbs. Identify the sentences that need to be corrected, and edit the faulty sentences. The first sentence has been edited for you.   *Answers will vary.*

Banning Soft Drinks and Snacks in School

Americans' weight problems ~~usual~~ *usually* start in childhood. Almost one-third of American ~~childrens~~ *children* are ~~more~~ heavier than children of past generations, and the number is increasing. Since ~~a child spent~~ *children spend* much of

their time in school, what they eat and drink there is important. As a
result, some ~~person~~ people have ~~sayed~~ said that soft drinks and snacks are ~~real~~
bad and should not be sold in schools. They say students would have
more healthier ~~lifes~~ lives as adults if they didn't eat so much snack food.
Banning such products would reduce the number of calories ~~consume~~ consumed
by students. However, those ~~whom opposed~~ who oppose such rules say that school
budgets would suffer ~~bad~~ badly from the loss of vending machine profits.

By the time they are adults, almost 65 percent of Americans are
either obese or overweight. In the past, adult-onset diabetes ~~are~~ was a
disease that ~~has~~ affected overweight ~~peoples~~ people over age forty-five; now,
it has ~~became~~ become common among the young. Also, obesity is related to
other diseases, such as some forms of cancer, high blood pressure, and
heart disease. Obesity leads to more than $100 billion in American
health-care costs every year. Obviously, anyone who cares about this
problem should do whatever ~~they~~ he or she can to make it better. We all want
each child to live the ~~most~~ longest, healthiest life possible.

One solution to the problem is to limit the amount of sugary soft
drinks and snacks that children consume every day. These ~~drink~~ drinks are a
major source of extra calories. Two out of three children consume
these drinks every day. Each can of soda ~~provide~~ provides about 50 grams of
sugar, and consumption is growing. More than 10 percent of a
~~children's~~ child's daily calories comes from soft drinks. For each can of sugar-
sweetened soda a child drinks each day, ~~their~~ his or her chance of becoming
obese grows by 60 percent. Sugary snacks, such as candy, ~~package~~ packaged
cakes, and cookies, also increase the number of calories. School
vending machines usually offer soda and sugary snacks, so students
buy them. If students ~~are~~ were offered ~~more~~ healthier drinks and snacks,
such as bottled water, orange juice, and popcorn, ~~him or her~~ they would
buy them instead.

Those who oppose a ban of sugary soft drinks and snacks in

schools are ~~concern~~ *concerned* about the ~~schools~~ *school's* finances. Many schools have
contracts with large ~~companyes~~ *companies* like Pepsi and Coke to place ~~its~~ *their*
vending machines in prominent locations. In fact, the schools earn a
percentage of the profits. When vending machines offer lower-calorie
drinks and healthier snacks, students don't buy them, so the schools'
profits are ~~reduce.~~ *reduced.* Because many schools depend on what they earn
from vending machines to pay for extras like field trips, SAT fees, and
band uniforms, ~~its~~ *their* budgets suffer.

Nevertheless, those who support the ban seem to be doing ~~good.~~ *well.*
Many school districts have started ~~its~~ *their* own programs to ban sugary soft
drinks and snacks. Also, in 2006, former president Bill Clinton and
Governor Mike Huckabee of Arkansas used ~~his~~ *their* fame to negotiate
~~agreementes~~ *agreements* with soft drink manufacturers like Coke and Pepsi. ~~This~~ *These*
agreements will ban the sale of high-calorie soft drinks in Arkansas
schools and limit the size of more healthful drinks. In addition,
manufacturers of sugary snacks ~~offered~~ *will offer* smaller portions.

Unit Seven

Understanding Punctuation, Mechanics, and Spelling

Chapter **30**

Using Commas

Habitat for Humanity is one of many nonprofit organizations that recruits volunteers to build houses in poor neighborhoods around the world.

A **comma** is a punctuation mark that separates words or groups of words within sentences. In this way, commas keep ideas distinct from one another.

Teaching Tip
Refer students to 15A for more on using commas in compound sentences.

In earlier chapters, you learned to use a comma between two simple sentences (independent clauses) linked by a coordinating conjunction to form a compound sentence.

> Some people are concerned about global warming, but others are not.

Teaching Tip
Refer students to 16B for more on using commas in complex sentences.

You also learned to use a comma after a dependent clause that comes before an independent clause in a complex sentence.

> Although bears in the wild can be dangerous, hikers can take steps to protect themselves.

Teaching Tip
Refer students to 33B for information on using commas with direct quotations.

In addition, commas are used to set off directly quoted speech or writing from the rest of the sentence.

> John F. Kennedy said, "Ask not what your country can do for you; ask what you can do for your country."

As you will learn in this chapter, commas have several other uses as well.

30a Commas in a Series

Use commas to separate all elements in a **series** of three or more words, phrases, or clauses.

> Leyla, Zack, and Kathleen campaigned for Representative Lewis.
> Leyla, Zack, or Kathleen will be elected president of Students for Lewis.

→ Focus on Writing

The picture on the opposite page shows volunteers building housing units in New Orleans. Look at the picture, and then write about an ideal public housing complex for families in need. Where should it be located? What kinds of buildings should be constructed? What facilities and services should be offered to residents?

WORD POWER
subsidized assisted or supported financially
low-density sparsely settled; not crowded

Leyla <u>made phone calls</u>, <u>stuffed envelopes</u>, and <u>ran errands</u> for the campaign.

Leyla <u>is president</u>, <u>Zack is vice president</u>, and <u>Kathleen is treasurer</u>.

| **Highlight: Using Commas in a Series** | Newspapers and magazines usually do not include a comma before the coordinating conjunction in a series. However, in college writing you should always use a comma before the coordinating conjunction.

Leyla, Zack, and Kathleen worked on the campaign. |

Teaching Tip
Students often use commas where they do not belong and omit them where they are needed. Begin this chapter by telling students to use commas only in the situations outlined in this chapter and referring them to the discussion of unnecessary commas in 30F.

Teaching Tip
Remind students not to use a comma before the first item in a series or after the last item in a series. (See 30F.)

On the Web
For more practice, visit Exercise Central *at* <bedfordstmartins .com/focusonwriting>.

● **Practice 30-1**

Edit the following sentences for the use of commas in a series. If the sentence is correct, write *C* in the blank.

Examples:

Costa Rica produces bananas, cocoa, and sugar cane. __*C*__

The pool rules state that there is no running‸ jumping‸ or diving. _____

1. The musician plays guitar‸ bass‸ and drums. _____

2. The organization's goals are feeding the hungry, housing the homeless‸ and helping the unemployed find work. _____

3. *The Price Is Right, Let's Make a Deal,* and *Jeopardy* are three of the longest-running game shows in television history. __*C*__

4. In native Hawaiian culture, yellow was worn by the royalty‸ red was worn by priests‸ and a mixture of the two colors was worn by others of high rank. _____

5. The diary Anne Frank kept while her family hid from the Nazis is insightful, touching‸ and sometimes humorous. _____

6. A standard bookcase is 60 inches tall‸ 48 inches wide‸ and 12 inches deep. _____

7. Most coffins manufactured in the United States are lined with bronze, copper, or lead. __C__

8. Young, handsome, and sensitive, Leonardo DiCaprio was the 1990s answer to the 1950s actor James Dean. _____

9. California's capital is Sacramento, its largest city is Los Angeles, and its oldest settlement is San Diego. _____

10. Watching television, playing video games, and riding a bicycle are the average ten-year-old boy's favorite pastimes. __C__

Focus on Writing: *Flashback*

Look back at your response to the Focus on Writing activity on page 487. Have you included a series of three or more words or word groups in any of your sentences? Did you use commas correctly to separate elements in the series? If not, correct your punctuation. If no sentence includes a series, write a new sentence that does on a separate sheet of paper.

 30b

Commas with Introductory Phrases and Transitional Words and Phrases

Teaching Tip
Tell students that when an introductory prepositional phrase has fewer than three words, a comma is not required (*In 1969 Neil Armstrong walked on the moon*) but that their sentences will be clearer if they include a comma after *every* introductory phrase.

 On the Web
For more practice, visit Exercise Central *at* <bedfordstmartins .com/focusonwriting>.

Introductory Phrases

Use a comma to set off an **introductory phrase** from the rest of the sentence.

In the event of a fire, proceed to the nearest exit.

Walking home, Nelida decided to change her major.

To keep fit, people should try to exercise regularly.

● **Practice 30-2**

Edit the following sentences for the use of commas with introductory phrases. If the sentence is correct, write *C* in the blank.

Teaching Tip
Review the use of commas in introductory phrases, asking students to read sentences aloud so they can hear where the natural pauses occur.

Examples:

From professional athletes to teenagers, people have begun to find alternatives to steroids.

Regulated by the Drug Enforcement Administration, steroids are a controlled substance and can be legally obtained only with a prescription. __C__

(1) In the past few years, many Olympic athletes have been disqualified because they tested positive for banned drugs. ___ (2) Only five days before the 2004 Athens Olympics, sixteen athletes were ejected from the games or stripped of their medals. ___ (3) In the past, banned steroids were the most common cause of positive drug tests. ___ (4) In recent years, other banned substances have also been used. ___ (5) For example, athletes have tested positive for male hormones and human growth hormones. __C__ (6) Among track and field athletes, doping has been especially common. ___ (7) Disappointing thousands of fans, two Greek sprinting stars refused to participate in a drug test at the Athens Olympics. ___ (8) Because of their failure to take the test, they were not allowed to run. __C__ (9) For using a banned stimulant in April 2004, American sprinter Torri Edwards was banned from competition for two years. ___ (10) Even in baseball, the records of home-run hitters like Barry Bonds and Sammy Sosa have been questioned because of the suspicion that they used banned substances. ___

Transitional Words and Phrases

Teaching Tip
Remind students that a transitional word or phrase that joins two complete sentences requires a semicolon and a comma: *Thoreau spent only one night in jail; however, he spent more than two years at Walden Pond.*

Use commas to set off **transitional words and phrases** whether they appear at the beginning, in the middle, or at the end of a sentence.

In fact, Thoreau spent only one night in jail.

He was, of course, bailed out by a friend.

He did spend more than two years at Walden Pond, however.

**Highlight:
Using Commas
in Direct
Address**

Always use commas to set off the name of someone whom you are **addressing** (speaking to) directly, whether the name appears at the beginning, in the middle, or at the end of a sentence.

Molly, come here and look at this.

Come here, Molly, and look at this.

Come here and look at this, Molly.

● **Practice 30-3**

Teaching Tip
Refer students to 15C for lists of frequently used transitional words and phrases.

Edit the following sentences for the use of commas with transitional words and phrases. If the sentence is correct, write *C* in the blank.

Example: Some holidays of course are fairly new.

(1) For example the African-American celebration of Kwanzaa was only introduced in the 1960s. _____ (2) This holiday celebrating important African traditions has, however attracted many people over its short life. _____ (3) By the way the word *Kwanzaa* means "first fruits" in Swahili. _____ (4) In other words, Kwanzaa stands for renewal. __C__ (5) This of course can be demonstrated in some of the seven principles of Kwanzaa. _____ (6) Kwanzaa is, in fact celebrated over seven days to focus on each of these seven principles. _____ (7) The focus first of all is on unity (*umoja*). _____ (8) Also Kwanzaa focuses on personal self-determination (*kujichagulia*). _____ (9) In addition Kwanzaa celebrations emphasize three kinds of community responsibility (*ujima, ujamaa,* and *nia*). _____ (10) The other principles of Kwanzaa are creativity (*kuumba*) and finally, faith (*imani*). _____

Focus on Writing: *Flashback*

Look back at your response to the Focus on Writing activity on page 487. Underline any introductory phrases or transitional words and phrases. Have you set off each of these with commas where appropriate? Revise any incorrect sentences, by adding commas where needed.

30c   Commas with Appositives

Use commas to set off an **appositive**—a word or word group that identifies, renames, or describes a noun or pronoun.

> I have visited only one country, Canada, outside the United States. (*Canada* is an appositive that identifies the noun *country*.)
>
> Carlos Santana, leader of the group Santana, played at Woodstock in 1969. (*Leader of the group Santana* is an appositive that identifies *Carlos Santana*.)
>
> A really gifted artist, he is also a wonderful father. (*A really gifted artist* is an appositive that describes the pronoun *he*.)

Highlight: Using Commas with Appositives	Appositives are set off by commas, whether they fall at the beginning, in the middle, or at the end of a sentence.
	A dreamer, he spent his life thinking about what he could not have.
	He always wanted to build a house, a big white one, overlooking the ocean.
	He finally built his dream house, a log cabin.

• Practice 30-4

Edit the following sentences for the correct use of commas to set off appositives. If the sentence is correct, write *C* in the blank.

Examples:

The Buccaneers have not joined the Cheese League, the group

of NFL teams that holds summer training in Wisconsin. _____

On the Web
For more practice, visit
Exercise Central *at*
<bedfordstmartins
.com/focusonwriting>.

William Filene, the Boston merchant who founded Filene's
department store, invented the concept of the "bargain
basement." _____

1. Traditional Chinese medicine is based on meridians, channels of energy
   believed to run in regular patterns through the body. _____
2. Acupuncture, the insertion of thin needles at precise points in the body,
   stimulates these meridians. _____
3. Herbal medicine, the basis of many Chinese healing techniques, requires
   twelve years of study. _____
4. Gary Larson, creator of the popular *Far Side* cartoons, ended the series
   in 1995. _____
5. A musician at heart, Larson said he wanted to spend more time practicing the guitar. __C__
6. *Far Side* calendars and other product tie-ins earned Larson over $500
   million, a lot of money for guitar lessons. _____
7. Nigeria, the most populous country in Africa, is also one of the fastest-
   growing nations in the world. _____
8. On the southwest coast of Nigeria lies Lagos, a major port. _____
9. The Yoruban people, the Nigerian settlers of Lagos, are unusual in Africa
   because they tend to form large urban communities. _____
10. A predominantly Christian people, the Yoruba have incorporated many
    native religious rituals into their practice of Christianity. _____

Focus on Writing: *Flashback*

Look back at your response to the Focus on Writing activity on page 487.
Have you used any appositives? Underline each one. Have you set off
appositives with commas? Revise any incorrect sentences by adding
commas where needed.

Commas with Nonrestrictive Clauses

WORD POWER
restrict to keep within limits
restrictive limiting

Teaching Tip
Have students read aloud sentences containing restrictive clauses, first with the clause and then without. Point out how the meaning changes when necessary information is omitted.

Clauses are often used to add information within a sentence. In some cases, you need to add commas to set off these clauses; in other cases, commas are not required. Use commas to set off **nonrestrictive clauses**, clauses that are not essential to a sentence's meaning. Do not use commas to set off **restrictive clauses**.

- A **nonrestrictive** clause does *not* contain essential information. Non-restrictive clauses are set off from the rest of the sentence by commas.

  Telephone calling-card fraud, which cost consumers and phone companies four billion dollars last year, is increasing.

Here, the clause between the commas (underlined) provides extra information to help readers understand the sentence, but the sentence would communicate the same idea without this information.

  Telephone calling-card fraud is increasing.

- A **restrictive** clause contains information that is essential to a sentence's meaning. Restrictive clauses are *not* set off from the rest of the sentence by commas.

  Many rock stars who recorded hits in the 1950s made little money from their songs.

In the sentence above, the clause *who recorded hits in the 1950s* supplies specific information that is essential to the idea the sentence is communicating: it tells readers which group of rock stars made little money. Without the clause, the sentence does not communicate the same idea because it does not tell which rock stars made little money.

  Many rock stars made little money from their songs.

> **Highlight:**
> **Which, That,**
> **and Who**
>
> ● *Which* always introduces a nonrestrictive clause.
>
>   The job, which had excellent benefits, did not pay well. (clause set off by commas)
>
> ● *That* always introduces a restrictive clause.
>
>   He accepted the job that had the best benefits. (no commas)
>
> ● *Who* can introduce either a restrictive or a nonrestrictive clause.
>
> **Restrictive** Many parents who work feel a lot of stress. (no commas)
>
> **Nonrestrictive** Both of my parents, who have always wanted the best for their children, have worked two jobs for years. (clause set off by commas)

Teaching Tip
Remind students not to use *that* to refer to people (as in *The girl that has on a red dress . . .*).

● Practice 30-5

On the Web
For more practice, visit Exercise Central at <bedfordstmartins .com/focusonwriting>.

Teaching Tip
Have students do Practice 30-5 in groups. (Fewer papers allow you more time for careful grading.) Students can also form groups to look over the graded assignment.

Edit the following sentences so that commas set off all nonrestrictive clauses. (Remember, commas are *not* used to set off restrictive clauses.) If a sentence is correct, write *C* in the blank.

Example: An Alaska museum exhibition that celebrates the Alaska highway tells the story of its construction. __*C*__

(1) During the 1940s, a group of African-American soldiers who defied the forces of nature and human prejudice were shipped to Alaska. __*C*__ (2) They built the Alaska highway, which stretches twelve hundred miles across Alaska. _____ (3) The troops who worked on the highway have received little attention in most historical accounts. __*C*__ (4) The highway, which cut through some of the roughest terrain in the world, was begun in 1942. _____ (5) The Japanese had just landed in the Aleutian Islands, which lie west of the tip of the Alaska Peninsula. _____ (6) Military officials, who oversaw the project, doubted the ability of the African-American troops. _____ (7) As a result, they made them work under conditions that made construction difficult. _____ (8) The troops who worked

on the road proved their commanders wrong by finishing the highway months ahead of schedule. __C__ (9) In one case, white engineers/who surveyed a river/said it would take two weeks to bridge. ____ (10) To the engineers' surprise, the soldiers who worked on the project beat the estimate by half a day. __C__ (11) A military report that was issued in 1945 praised them. __C__ (12) It said the goals that the African-American soldiers achieved would be remembered through the ages. __C__

Focus on Writing: *Flashback*

Look back at your response to the Focus on Writing activity on page 487. Make sure you have included commas to set off nonrestrictive clauses and have *not* set off restrictive elements with commas.

30e   Commas in Dates and Addresses

Teaching Tip
Ask each student to write his or her birth date and address on the board. Have the class check comma usage.

Dates

Use commas in dates to separate the day of the week from the month and the day of the month from the year.

Teaching Tip
Remind students not to use commas between a month and the number of the day (*May 5*) or between a month and a year (*May 1998*).

> The first Cinco de Mayo we celebrated in the United States was Tuesday, May 5, 1998.

When a date that includes commas falls in the middle of a sentence, place a comma after the date.

> Tuesday, May 5, 1998, was the first Cinco de Mayo we celebrated in the United States.

Addresses

Use commas in addresses to separate the street address from the city and the city from the state or country.

> The office of the famous fictional detective Sherlock Holmes was located at 221b Baker Street, London, England.

When an address that includes commas falls in the middle of a sentence, place a comma after the state or country.

> The office at 221b Baker Street, London, England, belonged to the famous fictional detective Sherlock Holmes.

On the Web
For more practice, visit
Exercise Central *at*
<bedfordstmartins
.com/focusonwriting>.

● **Practice 30-6**

Edit the following sentences for the correct use of commas in dates and addresses. Add any missing commas, and cross out any unnecessary commas. If the sentence is correct, write *C* in the blank.

Examples:

June 3, 1968, is the day my parents were married. _____

Their wedding took place in Santiago, Chile. _____

1. The American Declaration of Independence was approved on July 4, 1776. _____

2. The Pelican Man's Bird Sanctuary is located at 1705 Ken Thompson Parkway, Sarasota, Florida. _____

3. At 175 Carlton Avenue, Brooklyn, New York, is the house where Richard Wright began writing *Native Son*. _____

4. I found this information in the February 12, 1994, issue of the *New York Times*. _____

5. The Mexican hero Father Miguel Hidalgo y Costilla was shot by a firing squad on June 30, 1811. _*C*_

6. The Palacio de Gobierno at Plaza de Armas, Guadalajara, Mexico, houses a mural of the famous revolutionary. _____

7. The Pueblo Grande Museum is located at 1469 East Washington Street, Phoenix, Arizona. _____

8. Brigham Young led the first settlers into the valley that is now Salt Lake City, Utah, in July 1847. _____

9. St. Louis Missouri was the birthplace of writer Maya Angelou, but she spent most of her childhood in Stamps Arkansas. _____

10. Some records list the writer's birthday as May 19 1928 while others indicate she was born on April 4 1928. _____

30f   Unnecessary Commas

In addition to knowing where commas are required, it is also important to know when *not* to use commas.

- Do not use a comma before the first item in a series.

| Incorrect | *Duck Soup* starred, Groucho, Chico, and Harpo Marx. |
| Correct | *Duck Soup* starred Groucho, Chico, and Harpo Marx. |

- Do not use a comma after the last item in a series.

| Incorrect | Groucho, Chico, and Harpo Marx, starred in *Duck Soup*. |
| Correct | Groucho, Chico, and Harpo Marx starred in *Duck Soup*. |

- Do not use a comma between a subject and a verb.

| Incorrect | Students and their teachers, should try to respect one another. |
| Correct | Students and their teachers should try to respect one another. |

- Do not use a comma before the coordinating conjunction that separates the two parts of a compound predicate.

| Incorrect | The transit workers voted to strike, and walked off the job. |
| Correct | The transit workers voted to strike and walked off the job. |

- Do not use a comma before the coordinating conjunction that separates the two parts of a compound subject.

Incorrect	The transit workers, and the sanitation workers voted to strike.
Correct	The transit workers and the sanitation workers voted to strike.

Teaching Tip
Remind students that they *should* use commas to set off a nonrestrictive clause. Refer them to 30D.

● Do not use a comma to set off a restrictive clause.

Incorrect	People, who live in glass houses, should not throw stones.
Correct	People who live in glass houses should not throw stones.

Teaching Tip
Remind students that they *should* use a comma after a dependent clause when it comes *before* an independent clause: *Because he had driven all night, he was exhausted.*

● Finally, do not use a comma before a dependent clause that follows an independent clause.

Incorrect	He was exhausted, because he had driven all night.
Correct	He was exhausted because he had driven all night.

● Practice 30-7

Some of the following sentences contain unnecessary commas. Edit to elim-inate unnecessary commas. If the sentence is correct, write *C* in the blank following it.

Example: Both the Dominican Republic/ and the republic of Haiti occupy the West Indian island of Hispaniola. _____

1. The capital of the Dominican Republic/ is Santo Domingo. _____
2. The country's tropical climate, generous rainfall, and fertile soil/ make the Dominican Republic suitable for many kinds of crops. _____
3. Some of the most important crops are/ sugarcane, coffee, cocoa, and rice. _____
4. Mining is also important to the country's economy/ because the land is rich in many ores. _____
5. Spanish is the official language of the Dominican Republic, and Roman Catholicism is the state religion. __C__

6. In recent years, resort areas have opened/and brought many tourists to the country. ____

7. Tourists who visit the Dominican Republic/ remark on its tropical beauty. ____

8. Military attacks/and political unrest have marked much of the Dominican Republic's history. ____

9. Because the republic's economy has not always been strong, many Dominicans have immigrated to the United States. __C__

10. However, most Dominican immigrants maintain close ties to their home country/and return often to visit. ____

Focus on Writing: *Flashback*

Look back at your response to the Focus on Writing activity on page 487. Check your work carefully to make sure you have not used commas in any of the situations listed in 30F. Make any necessary corrections.

Focus on Writing: *Revising and Editing*

Look back at your response to the Focus on Writing activity on page 487. Then, make the following additions.

1. Add a sentence that includes a series of three or more words, phrases, or clauses.
2. Add introductory phrases to two of your sentences.
3. Add an appositive to one of your sentences.
4. Add a transitional word or phrase to one of your sentences (at the beginning, in the middle, or at the end).
5. Add a nonrestrictive clause to one of your sentences.

When you have made all the additions, reread your work and edit your use of commas with the new material.

Editing Practice

Read the following student essay, which includes errors in comma use. Add commas where necessary between items in a series and with introductory phrases, transitional words and phrases, appositives, and nonrestrictive clauses. Cross out any unnecessary commas. The first sentence has been edited for you. *Answers may vary.*

Brave Orchid

One of the most important characters in *The Woman Warrior*, Maxine Hong Kingston's autobiographical work is Brave Orchid, Kingston's mother. Brave Orchid was a strong woman but not a happy one. Through Kingston's stories about her mother, readers learn a lot about Kingston herself.

Readers are introduced to Brave Orchid, a complex character as an imaginative storyteller who tells vivid tales of China. A quiet young woman she nevertheless impresses her classmates with her intelligence. She is also a traditional woman. However she is determined to make her life exactly what she wants it to be. Brave Orchid strongly believes in herself; still, she considers herself a failure.

In her native China Brave Orchid trains to be a midwife. The other women in her class envy her independence brilliance and courage. One day Brave Orchid bravely confronts the Fox Spirit and tells him he will not win. First of all she tells him she can endure any pain that he inflicts on her. Next she gathers together the women in the dormitory to burn the ghost away. After this event the other women admire her even more.

Working hard Brave Orchid becomes a midwife in China. After coming to America however she cannot work as a midwife. Instead she works in a Chinese laundry and picks tomatoes. None of her classmates in China would have imagined this outcome. During her later years in America Brave Orchid becomes a woman who is overbearing and domineering. She bosses her children around, she tries to ruin her sister's life and she criticizes everyone and everything around her. Her daughter, a straight-A student is the object of her worst criticism.

Brave Orchid's intentions are good. Nevertheless she devotes her energy to the wrong things. She expects the people around her to be as strong as she is. Because she bullies them however she eventually loses them. In addition she is too busy criticizing her daughter's faults to see all her accomplishments. Brave Orchid an independent woman and a brilliant student never achieves her goals. She is hard on the people around her because she is disappointed in herself.

Collaborative Activities

1. Bring a homemaking, sports, or fashion magazine to class. Working in a small group, look at the people pictured in the ads. In what roles are men most often depicted? In what roles are women most often presented? Identify the three or four most common roles for each sex, and give each kind of character a descriptive name—*jock* or *mother*, for example.

2. Working on your own, choose one type of character from the list your group made in Collaborative Activity 1. Then, write a paragraph in which you describe this character's typical appearance and habits. Refer to the appropriate magazine pictures to support your characterization.

3. Collaborating with other members of your group, write two paragraphs, one discussing how men are portrayed in ads and one discussing how women are portrayed.

4. Circle every comma in the paragraph you wrote for Collaborative Activity 2. Then, work with your group to explain why each comma is used. If no one in your group can justify a particular comma's use, cross it out.

Review Checklist: Using Commas

- ☐ Use commas to separate all elements in a series of three or more words or word groups. (See 30A.)
- ☐ Use commas to set off introductory phrases and transitional words and phrases from the rest of the sentence. (See 30B.)
- ☐ Use commas to set off appositives from the rest of the sentence. (See 30C.)
- ☐ Use commas to set off nonrestrictive clauses. (See 30D.)
- ☐ Use commas to separate parts of dates and addresses. (See 30E.)
- ☐ Avoid unnecessary commas. (See 30F.)

Chapter 31

Using Apostrophes

Dr. Mae Jemison, a former NASA astronaut, was the first African-American woman to travel into space. She speaks six languages and has worked as a doctor in developing countries. In 1993, she appeared on the TV show *Star Trek: The Next Generation*.

An **apostrophe** is a punctuation mark that is used in two situations: to form a contraction and to form the possessive of a noun or an indefinite pronoun.

31a

Apostrophes in Contractions

Teaching Tip
Be sure your students understand that even though contractions are used in speech and informal writing, they are not acceptable in most business or college writing situations.

A **contraction** is a word that uses an apostrophe to combine two words. The apostrophe takes the place of the omitted letters.

I didn't (*did not*) realize how late it was.

It's (*it is*) not right for cheaters to go unpunished.

Teaching Tip
Remind students that this list does not include every contraction. For example, other personal pronouns (*he, she, they*) can also be combined with forms of *be* and *have*. (Students will need to know this to do Practice 31-1.)

Frequently Used Contractions

I + am = I'm	are + not = aren't
we + are = we're	can + not = can't
you + are = you're	do + not = don't
it + is = it's	will + not = won't
I + have = I've	should + not = shouldn't
I + will = I'll	let + us = let's
there + is = there's	that + is = that's
is + not = isn't	who + is = who's

→ Focus on Writing

The picture on the opposite page shows Dr. Mae Jemison at her job as a NASA astronaut. Certain jobs have traditionally been considered "men's work," and others have been viewed as "women's work." Although the workplace has changed considerably in recent years, some things have remained the same.

Look at the picture, and then write about the tasks that are considered "men's work" and "women's work" at your job or in your current household. Be sure to give examples of the responsibilities of the different people you are discussing. (Note: Contractions, such as *isn't* or *don't*, are acceptable in this informal response.)

WORD POWER

gender sexual identity (male or female)

stereotype (n) a conventional, usually oversimplified, opinion or belief; (v) to develop a fixed opinion

ESL Tip
Nonnative speakers
often misplace or omit
apostrophes in contrac-
tions. Spend extra time
checking their work.

● **Practice 31-1**

In the following sentences, add apostrophes to contractions if needed. If the
sentence is correct, write *C* in the blank.

Example: *What's*
Whats the deadliest creature on earth? _____

can't
(1) Bacteria and viruses, which we ~~cant~~ see without a microscope,
kill many people every year. _____ (2) When we speak about the dead-
we're
liest creatures, however, usually ~~were~~ talking about creatures that
cause illness or death from their poison, which is called venom. _____
you're
(3) After ~~your~~ bitten, stung, or stuck, how long does it take to die? _____
(4) The fastest killer is a creature called the sea wasp, but it isn't a wasp
at all. _C_ (5) The sea wasp is actually a fifteen-foot-long jellyfish, and
it's
although ~~its~~ not aggressive, it can be deadly. _____ (6) People who've
gone swimming off the coast of Australia may have encountered this
creature. _C_ (7) While jellyfish found off the Atlantic coast of the
aren't
United States can sting, they ~~arent~~ as dangerous as the sea wasp, whose
who's
venom is deadly enough to kill sixty adults. _____ (8) A person ~~whos~~
been stung by a sea wasp has anywhere from thirty seconds to four minutes to get help or die. _____ (9) Oddly, it's been found that something
as thin as pantyhose worn over the skin will prevent these stings. _C_
there's
(10) Also, ~~theres~~ an antidote to the poison in the stings that can save the
lives of victims. _____

Focus on Writing: *Flashback*

Look back at your response to the Focus on Writing activity on page 505,
and underline any contractions. Have you used apostrophes correctly to
replace the missing letters? On a separate sheet of paper, recopy all the
contractions correctly.

Apostrophes in Possessives

Teaching Tip
Tell students that pos-
sessive pronouns have
special forms, such as *its*
and *his*, and that these
forms never include
apostrophes. Refer
them to 27F.

Possessive forms indicate ownership. Nouns and indefinite pronouns do not have special possessive forms. Instead, they use apostrophes to indicate ownership.

Singular Nouns and Indefinite Pronouns

To form the possessive of singular nouns (including names) and indefinite pronouns, add an apostrophe plus an *s*.

Teaching Tip
Refer students to 22F
and 27E for more on
indefinite pronouns.

> Cesar Chavez's goal (*the goal of Cesar Chavez*) was justice for Ameri-
> can farm workers.
>
> The strike's outcome (*the outcome of the strike*) was uncertain.
>
> Whether it would succeed was anyone's guess (*the guess of anyone*).

Note: Even if a singular noun already ends in *-s*, add an apostrophe plus an *s* to form the possessive: *The class's next assignment was a research paper; Dr. Ramos's patients are participating in a clinical trial.*

Plural Nouns

Most plural nouns end in *-s*. To form the possessive of plural nouns ending in *-s* (including names), add just an apostrophe (not an apostrophe plus an *s*).

Teaching Tip
Tell students that most
nouns form the plural by
adding *-s*. Refer them
to the list of frequently
used irregular noun
plurals in 27B.

> The two drugs' side effects (*the side effects of the two drugs*) were quite
> different.
>
> The Johnsons' front door (*the front door of the Johnsons*) is red.

Some irregular noun plurals do not end in *-s*. If a plural noun does not end in *-s*, add an apostrophe plus an *s* to form the possessive.

> The men's room is right next to the women's room.

On the Web
For more practice, visit
Exercise Central *at*
<bedfordstmartins
.com/focusonwriting>.

● Practice 31-2

Rewrite the following phrases, changing the noun or indefinite pronoun that follows *of* to the possessive form. Be sure to distinguish between singular and plural nouns.

Examples:

the mayor of the city _the city's mayor_

the uniforms of the players _the players' uniforms_

1. the video of the singer _the singer's video_
2. the scores of the students _the students' scores_
3. the favorite band of everybody _everybody's favorite band_
4. the office of the boss _the boss's office_
5. the union of the players _the players' union_
6. the specialty of the restaurant _the restaurant's specialty_
7. the bedroom of the children _the children's bedroom_
8. the high cost of the tickets _the tickets' high cost_
9. the dreams of everyone _everyone's dreams_
10. the owner of the dogs _the dogs' owner_

Focus on Writing: *Flashback*

Look back at your response to the Focus on Writing activity on page 505. Circle any possessive forms of nouns or indefinite pronouns. Then, check to make sure you have used apostrophes correctly to form these possessives, and make any necessary corrections.

31c Incorrect Use of Apostrophes

Be careful not to confuse a plural noun (*boys*) with the singular possessive form of the noun (*boy's*). Never use an apostrophe with a plural noun unless the noun is possessive.

Termites can be dangerous pests [not *pest's*].

The Velezes [not *Velez's*] live on Maple Drive, right next door to the Browns [not *Brown's*].

Also be careful not to use apostrophes with possessive pronouns that end in -*s*: *theirs* (not *their's*), *hers* (not *her's*), *its* (not *it's*), *ours* (not *our's*), and *yours* (not *your's*).

Highlight: Possessive Pronouns	Be especially careful not to confuse possessive pronouns with sound-alike contractions. Possessive pronouns never include apostrophes.

Possessive Pronoun	*Contraction*
The dog bit its master.	It's (*it is*) time for breakfast.
The choice is theirs.	There's (*there is*) no place like home.
Whose house is this?	Who's (*who is*) on first?
Is this your house?	You're (*you are*) late again.

Teaching Tip
Be sure students understand that a computer's spell checker will not tell them when they have used a contraction for a possessive form — *it's* for *its*, for example.

On the Web
For more practice, visit Exercise Central *at* <bedfordstmartins .com/focusonwriting>.

Teaching Tip
Students often have trouble distinguishing plural nouns from singular possessive forms and using apostrophes correctly with possessive pronouns. You may want to review 31C and Practice 31-3 in class.

● Practice 31-3

Check the underlined nouns and pronouns in the following sentences for correct use of apostrophes. If a correction needs to be made, cross out the word, and write the correct version above it. If the noun or pronoun is correct, write *C* above it.

Example: The president's views were presented after several other
speakers   *theirs.*
~~speaker's~~ first presented ~~their's.~~

Parents
1. ~~Parent's~~ should realize that when it comes to disciplining children, the
   theirs.
   responsibility is ~~their's.~~

2. It's also important that parents offer praise for a child's good behavior.
   its   weeks
3. In ~~it's~~ first few ~~week's~~ of life, a dog is already developing a personality.
   hers   *couples,   C*
4. His and ~~her's~~ towels used to be popular with ~~couple's,~~ but it's not so
   common to see them today.
   Ryans   years
5. All the ~~Ryan's~~ spent four ~~year's~~ in college and then got good jobs.
                                      C   whose
6. From the radio came the lyrics "You're the one ~~who's~~ love I've been
   waiting for."
   classes,
7. If you expect to miss any ~~class's,~~ you will have to make arrangements
   C   your
   with someone who's willing to tell you ~~you're~~ assignment.

8. No other school's cheerleading squad ever tried as many tricky stunts as our's did.

9. Surprise test's are common in my economics class.

10. Jazz's influence on many mainstream musician's is one of the book's main subject's.

Focus on Writing: *Flashback*

Look back at your response to the Focus on Writing activity on page 505. Circle each plural noun. Then, circle each possessive pronoun that ends in *-s*. Have you incorrectly used an apostrophe with any of the circled words? If so, revise your work.

Focus on Writing: *Revising and Editing*

Look back at your response to the Focus on Writing activity on page 505. Because this is an informal exercise, contractions are acceptable; in fact, they may be preferable because they give your writing a conversational tone. Edit your writing so that you have used contractions in all possible situations.

Now, add two sentences—one that includes a singular possessive noun and one that includes a plural possessive noun. Make sure these two new sentences fit smoothly into your writing and that they, too, use contractions wherever possible.

Chapter Review

Editing Practice

Read the following student essay, which includes errors in the use of apostrophes. Edit it to eliminate errors by crossing out incorrect words and writing corrections above them. (Note that this is an informal response paper, so contractions are acceptable.) The first sentence has been edited for you.

The Women of Messina

In William ~~Shakespeares'~~ *Shakespeare's* play <u>Much Ado about Nothing</u>, the women of Messina, whether they are seen as love objects or as ~~shrew's,~~ *shrews,* have very few options. A ~~womans~~ *woman's* role is to please a man. She can try to resist, but she will probably wind up giving in.

The ~~plays~~ *play's* two women, Hero and Beatrice, are very different. Hero is the obedient one. ~~Heroes~~ *Hero's* cousin, Beatrice, tries to challenge the rules of the ~~mans~~ *man's* world in which she lives. However, in a place like Messina, even women like Beatrice find it hard to get the respect that should be ~~their's.~~ *theirs.*

Right from the start, we are drawn to Beatrice. ~~Shes~~ *She's* funny, she has a clever comment for most ~~situation's,~~ *situations,* and she always speaks her mind about other ~~peoples~~ *people's* behavior. Unlike Hero, she tries to stand up to the men in her life, as we see in her and ~~Benedicks~~ *Benedick's* conversations.

But even though Beatrice's intelligence is obvious, she often mocks herself. ~~Its~~ *It's* clear that she doesn't have much self-esteem. In fact, Beatrice ~~is'nt~~ *isn't* the strong woman she seems to be.

Ultimately, Beatrice does get her man, and she will be happy — but at what cost? ~~Benedicks'~~ *Benedick's* last ~~word's~~ *words* to her are "Peace! I will stop your mouth." Then, he kisses her. The kiss is a symbolic end to their bickering. It is also the mark of ~~Beatrices~~ *Beatrice's* defeat. She has lost. Benedick has silenced her. Now, she will be Benedick's wife and do what he wants her to do. Granted, she will have more say in her marriage than Hero will have in ~~her's,~~ *hers,* but she is still defeated.

Shakespeare's
~~Shakespeares~~ audience might have seen the ~~plays~~ *play's* ending as a
happy one. For contemporary ~~reader's~~ *readers*, however, the ending is
disappointing. Even Beatrice, the most rebellious of ~~Messinas~~ *Messina's* women,
finds it impossible to achieve anything of importance in this male-
dominated society.

Collaborative Activities

1. Working in a group of four and building on your individual responses to
   the Focus on Writing exercise at the beginning of the chapter, consider
   which specific occupational and professional roles are still associated
   largely with men and which are associated primarily with women. Make
   two lists, heading one "women's jobs" and one "men's jobs."

2. Now, work in pairs, with one pair of students in each group concentrating on men and the other pair on women. Write a paragraph that
   attempts to justify why the particular jobs you listed should or should
   not be restricted to one gender. In your discussion, list the various qualities men or women possess that qualify (or disqualify) them for particular jobs. Use possessive forms whenever possible—for example,
   women's energy (not *women have energy*).

3. Bring to class a book, magazine, or newspaper whose style is informal—
   for example, a romance novel, *TV Guide*, your school newspaper, or
   even a comic book. Working in a group, circle every contraction you can
   find on one page of each publication, and substitute for each contraction the words it combines. Are your substitutions an improvement?
   (You may want to read a few paragraphs aloud before you reach a
   conclusion.)

Review Checklist: Using Apostrophes

☐ Use apostrophes to form contractions. (See 31A.)

☐ Use an apostrophe plus an *s* to form the possessive of singular nouns and indefinite pronouns, even when a noun ends in -*s*. (See 31B.)

☐ Use an apostrophe alone to form the possessive of plural nouns ending in -*s*, including names. If a plural noun does not end in -*s*, add an apostrophe plus an *s*. (See 31B.)

☐ Do not use apostrophes with plural nouns unless they are possessive. Do not use apostrophes with possessive pronouns. (See 31C.)

Chapter 32

Using Other Punctuation Marks

In 1958, the year hula hoops were introduced, Americans bought one hundred million in the first four months.

Punctuation marks tell readers to slow down, to look ahead, or to pause. To write clear sentences, you need to use appropriate punctuation.

Every sentence ends with a punctuation mark.

- If a sentence is a statement, it ends with a **period**.

    Nine planets revolve around the sun.

- If a sentence is a question, it ends with a **question mark**.

    Is Venus the planet closest to the sun?

- If a sentence is an exclamation, it ends with an **exclamation point**.

    Look out! An asteroid is about to fall on Sioux Falls!

Other important punctuation marks are the **comma**, discussed in Chapter 30, and the **apostrophe**, discussed in Chapter 31. Four additional punctuation marks—*semicolons, colons, dashes,* and *parentheses*—are discussed and illustrated in this chapter.

→ Focus on Writing

The picture on the opposite page shows a child playing with a hula hoop, a popular toy of the 1960s. Look at the picture, and think about the games you used to play outdoors when you were a child. Write about some of your favorite outdoor toys and games.

WORD POWER

recreation activity that refreshes the mind or body; play

pastime pleasant activity that fills spare time

32a

Semicolons

Use a **semicolon** to join two simple sentences (independent clauses) into one compound sentence.

> Sandra Day O'Connor was the first woman to sit on the United States Supreme Court; Ruth Bader Ginsburg was the second.

Highlight: Semicolons

Never use a semicolon between a phrase and an independent clause. Use a comma instead.

Incorrect	I voted for the winning candidate; the Democrat.
Correct	I voted for the winning candidate, the Democrat.

Never use a semicolon between a dependent clause and an independent clause. Use a comma instead.

Incorrect	When Bob was in high school; he had shoulder-length hair.
Correct	When Bob was in high school, he had shoulder-length hair.

● Practice 32-1

Teaching Tip
You might tell students that semicolons are also used to separate items in a series — but only if one or more of the items includes a comma: *He dreamed of traveling to Cozumel, Mexico; Buenos Aires, Argentina; and Paris, France.*

Each of the following sentences includes errors in the use of semicolons. Correct any errors you find. If a sentence is correct, write *C* on the line after the sentence.

Example: A marsupial is a mammal ; many kinds of marsupials live in Australia today. _____

1. Marsupials have pouches ; mothers carry their young in these pouches. _____

2. Marsupials are covered with hair , and nursed by their mothers. _____

3. The opossum is the only marsupial now found in the United States; in prehistoric times, however, there were many others. __C__

4. Marsupials include the koala*,*/the kangaroo, and the wombat. _____

5. Many thousands of years ago, marsupials were common in South America *;* now, they are extinct. _____

Focus on Writing: *Flashback*

Look back at your response to the Focus on Writing activity on page 515. Have you used any semicolons in your writing? Have you used them correctly? Correct any errors you find.

32b

Colons

Colons are used to introduce quotations, explanations, clarifications, examples, and lists. A complete sentence always comes before the colon.

- Use a colon to introduce a quotation.

   Our family motto is simple: "accept no substitutes."

- Use a colon to introduce an explanation, a clarification, or an example.

   Only one thing kept him from climbing Mt. Everest: fear of heights.

- Use a colon to introduce a list. (Note that all items in a list are expressed in **parallel** terms.)

Teaching Tip
Refer students to Chapter 18 for information on parallelism.

   I left my job for four reasons: boring work, poor working conditions, low pay, and a terrible supervisor.

● Practice 32-2

The following sentences include errors in the use of colons to introduce quotations, examples, lists, and so on. Correct any errors you find. (Remember that every colon must be preceded by a complete sentence.) If a sentence is correct, write *C* on the line after the sentence.

> **Example:**   A new kind of amusement park is appearing the amuse-
>
> ment park with a religious theme. _____

1. Four parks with religious themes are/ the Holy Land Experience, Dinosaur Adventure Land, Ganga-Dham, and City of Revelation. _____

2. The Holy Land Experience is in Orlando/ Florida, near Disney World. _____

3. An advertisement for Dinosaur Adventure Land describes it in these words "where dinosaurs and the Bible meet!" _____

4. Ganga-Dham is scheduled to open soon/ in India. _____

5. In central Florida, another park is being planned: City of Revelation. __*C*__

Focus on Writing: *Flashback*

Look back at your response to the Focus on Writing activity on page 515. Do you see any places where you might add a quotation, an example, or a list to your writing? Write your possible new material on the lines below.

Quotation: _____

Example: _____

List: _____

32c

Dashes and Parentheses

Dashes and parentheses set words off from the rest of the sentence. In general, dashes call attention to the material that is set off, while parentheses do just the opposite.

Teaching Tip
Be sure students
understand that dashes
give writing an informal
tone and should therefore
be used sparingly in
college writing.

● Use **dashes** to set off important information.

> She parked her car — a red Firebird — in a towaway zone.

● Use **parentheses** to enclose information that is relatively unimportant.

> The weather in Portland (a city in Oregon) was overcast.

● Practice 32-3

Add dashes or parentheses to the following sentences where you think they are necessary to set off material from the rest of the sentence. Remember that dashes tend to emphasize the material they set off, while parentheses tend to de-emphasize the enclosed material.

Example: The National Basketball Association (NBA) was founded in the 1940s.

Answers may vary.

1. In the 1950s, Bob Cousy was a star player for the Boston Celtics. Cousy (an "old man" at age thirty-four) led his team to their fifth NBA championship in 1963.

2. During the 1960s, the legendary Wilt ("the Stilt") Chamberlain played for the Philadelphia Warriors.

3. Many people still consider game 5 of the 1976 NBA finals — which the Celtics won in triple overtime — the greatest basketball game ever played.

4. During the 1980s, five truly outstanding players — Magic Johnson, Kareem Abdul-Jabbar, Larry Bird, Julius ("Dr. J") Erving, and Michael Jordan — dominated the NBA.

5. Today, young players (some joining the NBA right out of high school) dream of making names for themselves as their heroes did.

Focus on Writing: *Flashback*

Look back at your response to the Focus on Writing activity on page 515. Try adding the quotation, example, or list from the Flashback activity on page 518 to your writing. Be sure to introduce this new material with a colon, and make sure the colon is preceded by a complete sentence.

Focus on Writing: *Revising and Editing*

Look back at your response to the Focus on Writing activity on page 515 and to the Flashback activities on pages 517, 518, and above. Check your work carefully to make sure all the punctuation marks discussed in this chapter are used correctly.

Chapter Review

Editing Practice

The following student essay includes errors in the use of semicolons, colons, dashes, and parentheses. (Some are used incorrectly; others have been omitted where they are needed.) Correct any errors you find. The first sentence has been corrected for you.   *Answers may vary.*

Just Right

In the fairy tale "Goldilocks and the Three Bears," a little girl called Goldilocks wanders away from home; and discovers an empty house in the forest. When she sees no one is home, she tries out different things in the house; bowls of cereal, chairs, and beds. When she tries the beds; one is too small, and one is too big. The third one is just right. As Goldilocks knew; finding the "just right" size is not easy.

In America today, many things are much too big. For example, food stores — and food portions — are often huge. The "mom and pop" grocery stores are gone; replaced by giant supermarkets. At McDonald's, you can "supersize" your meal; convenience stores sell

32-ounce cups of soda. At any diner, portion sizes are so big that food hangs off the edges of the plate.

Other things we encounter daily are also too big. Even with gas so expensive, some people still have to drive big vehicles, such as huge SUVs, vans, and pickups. Parents push baby strollers the size of Humvees, and some suburban houses are so big that they are called McMansions. Televisions have grown into "home theaters" with 60-inch screens; movie theaters are now multiplexes — that look like airport terminals.

At the same time so many things are getting bigger and bigger, many other things (particularly electronics) are getting smaller. Cameras are one example; cell phones are another. Some MP3 players are smaller than credit cards. Even M&Ms come in a mini version. And, of course, families have been getting smaller for years.

What is the right size? That is not an easy question to answer. As Goldilocks knew, sometimes you have to try out the "too big" and "too small" version before you find the "just right" one.

Collaborative Activities

1. Write five original compound sentences, each composed of two simple sentences connected with *and*. Then, exchange papers with another student, and edit each compound sentence so that it uses a semicolon instead of *and* to connect the independent clauses.

2. Compile three lists, each with three or four items (people, places, or things). Then, working in a group, compose a sentence that could introduce each of your lists. Use a colon after each introductory sentence.

Review Checklist: Using Other Punctuation Marks

☐ Use semicolons to separate two simple sentences (independent clauses). (See 32A.)

☐ Use colons to introduce quotations, explanations, clarifications, examples, and lists. (See 32B.)

☐ Use dashes and parentheses to set off material from the rest of the sentence. (See 32C.)

Chapter 33

Understanding Mechanics

The co-creator of Spider-Man, Stan Lee, makes a cameo appearance in all three Spider-Man movies.

Capitalizing Proper Nouns

A **proper noun** names a particular person, animal, place, object, or idea. Proper nouns are always capitalized. The list that follows explains and illustrates rules for capitalizing proper nouns.

- Always capitalize and names of **races, ethnic groups, tribes, nationalities, languages,** and **religions.**

Teaching Tip
Tell students that the words *black* and *white* are generally not capitalized when they name racial groups. However, *African American* and *Caucasian* are always capitalized.

> The census data revealed a diverse community of Caucasians, African Americans, and Asian Americans, with a few Latino and Navajo residents. Native languages included English, Korean, and Spanish. Most people identified themselves as Catholic, Protestant, or Muslim.

- Capitalize names of **specific people** and the **titles that accompany them.** In general, do not capitalize titles used without a name.

> In 1994, President Nelson Mandela was elected to lead South Africa.

> The newly elected fraternity president addressed the crowd.

- Capitalize names of **specific family members and their titles.** Do not capitalize words that identify family relationships, including those introduced by possessive pronouns.

→ Focus on Writing

The picture on the opposite page shows a scene from the 2007 film *Spider-Man 3.* Look at the picture, and then describe a memorable scene from your favorite movie. Begin by giving the film's title and listing the names of the major stars and the characters they play. Then, tell what happens in the scene, quoting a few words of dialogue if possible.

WORD POWER
empathize to identify with
plot a series of events in a story, play, or film
supernatural unexplainable; above and beyond what is natural

The twins, Aunt Edna and Aunt Evelyn, are Dad's sisters.

My aunts, my father's sisters, are twins.

- Capitalize names of **specific countries, cities, towns, bodies of water, streets,** and so on. Do not capitalize words that do not name specific places.

The Seine runs through Paris, France.

The river runs through the city.

- Capitalize names of **specific geographical regions**. Do not capitalize such words when they specify direction.

William Faulkner's novels are set in the South.

Turn right at the golf course, and go south for about a mile.

- Capitalize names of **specific buildings and monuments**. Do not capitalize general references to buildings and monuments.

He drove past the Liberty Bell and looked for a parking space near City Hall.

He drove past the monument and looked for a parking space near the government building.

- Capitalize names of **specific groups, clubs, teams,** and **associations**. Do not capitalize general references to such groups.

The Teamsters Union represents workers who were at the stadium for the Republican Party convention, the Rolling Stones concert, and the Phillies-Astros game.

The union represents workers who were at the stadium for the political party's convention, the rock group's concert, and the baseball teams' game.

- Capitalize names of **specific historical periods, events,** and **documents**. Do not capitalize nonspecific references to periods, events, or documents.

The Emancipation Proclamation was signed during the Civil War, not during Reconstruction.

The document was signed during the war, not during the postwar period.

- Capitalize names of **businesses, government agencies, schools,** and **other institutions.** Do not capitalize nonspecific references to such institutions.

  The Department of Education and Apple Computer have launched a partnership project with Central High School.

  A government agency and a computer company have launched a partnership project with a high school.

- Capitalize **brand names.** Do not capitalize general references to kinds of products.

  While Jeff waited for his turn at the Xerox machine, he drank a can of Coke.

  While Jeff waited for his turn at the copier, he drank a can of soda.

- Capitalize **titles of specific academic courses.** Do not capitalize names of general academic subject areas, except for proper nouns— for example, a language or a country.

  Are Introduction to American Government and Biology 200 closed yet?

  Are the introductory American government course and the biology course closed yet?

- Capitalize **days of the week, months of the year,** and **holidays.** Do not capitalize the names of seasons.

  The Jewish holiday of Passover usually falls in April.

  The Jewish holiday of Passover falls in the spring.

● Practice 33-1

On the Web
For more practice, visit Exercise Central *at* <bedfordstmartins .com/focusonwriting>.

Edit the following sentences, capitalizing letters or changing capitals to lowercase where necessary.

Example: The third largest City in the united states is chicago, Illinois.

Teaching Tip
Have students do
Practice 33-1 in pairs.

(1) Located in the midwest on lake Michigan, Chicago is an important port city, a rail and highway hub, and the site of O'Hare international airport, one of the Nation's busiest. (2) The financial center of the city is Lasalle street, and the lakefront is home to Grant park, where there are many Museums and monuments. (3) To the North of the city, soldier field is home to the chicago bears, the city's football team, and wrigley field is home to the chicago cubs, a national league Baseball Team. (4) In the mid-1600s, the site of what is now Chicago was visited by father jacques marquette, a catholic missionary to the ottawa and huron tribes, who were native to the area. (5) By the 1700s, the city was a trading post run by john kinzie. (6) The city grew rapidly in the 1800s, and immigrants included germans, irish, italians, poles, greeks, and chinese, along with african americans who migrated from the south. (7) In 1871, much of the city was destroyed in one of the worst fires in united states history; according to legend, the fire started when mrs. O'Leary's cow kicked over a burning lantern. (8) Today, Chicago's skyline has many skyscrapers, built by businesses like the john hancock company, sears, and amoco. (9) I know Chicago well because my Mother grew up there and my aunt jean and uncle amos still live there. (10) I also got information from the Chicago Chamber of Commerce when I wrote a paper for introductory research writing, a course I took at Graystone high school.

Focus on Writing: *Flashback*

Look back at your response to the Focus on Writing activity on page 523. Underline every proper noun. Check carefully to make sure each proper noun begins with a capital letter, and correct any that do not.

33b   Punctuating Quotations

A **direct quotation** reproduces the *exact* words of a speaker or writer. Direct quotations are always placed in quotation marks. A direct quotation is usually accompanied by an **identifying tag**, a phrase that names the person being quoted. In the following sentences, the identifying tag is underlined.

> <u>Lauren said</u>, "My brother and Tina have gotten engaged."
>
> <u>A famous advertiser wrote</u>, "Don't sell the steak; sell the sizzle."

When a quotation is a complete sentence, it begins with a capital letter and ends with a period, a question mark, or an exclamation point. When a quotation falls at the end of a sentence (as in the two examples above), the period is placed *inside* the quotation marks.

If the quotation is a question or an exclamation, the question mark or exclamation point is also placed *inside* the quotation marks.

> The instructor asked, "Has anyone read *Sula*?"
>
> Officer Warren shouted, "Hold it right there!"

If the quotation itself is not a question or an exclamation, the question mark or exclamation point goes *outside* the quotation marks.

> Did Joe really say, "I quit"?
>
> I can't believe he really said, "I quit"!

Highlight: Indirect Quotations

Be careful not to confuse direct and indirect quotations. A direct quotation reproduces someone's *exact* words, but an **indirect quotation** simply summarizes what was said or written.

Indirect quotations are not placed within quotation marks.

Teaching Tip
Tell students that an indirect quotation is usually introduced by the word *that* (*She told me that she was cold*).

Direct quotation	Martin Luther King Jr., said, "I have a dream."
Indirect quotation	Martin Luther King Jr., said that he had a dream.

The rules for punctuating direct quotations with identifying tags are summarized below.

Teaching Tip
You may need to explain
what an identifying tag is
by literally pointing it out.

- **Identifying tag at the beginning**   When the identifying tag comes *before* the quotation, it is followed by a comma.

  <u>Alexandre Dumas wrote</u>, "Nothing succeeds like success."

- **Identifying tag at the end**   When the identifying tag comes at the *end* of the sentence, it is followed by a period. A comma (or sometimes a question mark or exclamation point) inside the closing quotation marks separates the quotation from the identifying tag.

  "Life is like a box of chocolates," <u>stated Forrest Gump.</u>

  "Is that so?" <u>his friends wondered.</u>

- **Identifying tag in the middle**   When the identifying tag comes in the *middle* of the quoted sentence, it is followed by a comma. The first part of the quotation is also followed by a comma, placed inside the quotation marks. (Because the part of the quotation that follows the tag is not a new sentence, it does not begin with a capital letter.)

  "This is my life," <u>Bette insisted,</u> "and I'll live it as I please."

- **Identifying tag between two sentences**   When the identifying tag comes *between two* quoted sentences, it is preceded by a comma and followed by a period. (The second quoted sentence begins with a capital letter.)

  "Berry Gordy is an important figure in the history of music," <u>Tony explained.</u> "He was the creative force behind Motown records."

 On the Web
For more practice, visit
Exercise Central *at*
<bedfordstmartins
.com/focusonwriting>.

• Practice 33-2

The following sentences contain direct quotations. First, underline the identifying tag. Then, punctuate the quotation correctly, adding capital letters as necessary.

Example: Why Darryl asked are teachers so strict about deadlines?

1. The bigger they are said boxer John L. Sullivan the harder they fall.

2. Do you take Michael to be your lawfully wedded husband asked the minister.

3. Lisa Marie replied I do.

4. If you believe the *National Enquirer* my friend always says then you'll believe anything.

5. Yabba dabba doo Fred exclaimed this brontoburger looks great.

● Practice 33-3

The following quotations are followed in parentheses by the names of the people who wrote or spoke them. On the blank lines, write a sentence that includes the quotation and places the identifying tag in the position that the directions specify. Be sure to punctuate and capitalize correctly.

Example: Nothing endures but change. (written by the Greek philosopher Heraclitus)

Identifying tag in the middle *"Nothing endures," wrote the Greek philosopher Heraclitus, "but change."*

Answers will vary.

1. I want a kinder, gentler nation. (spoken by former president George Herbert Walker Bush)

   Identifying tag at the end *"I want a kinder, gentler nation," said former president George Herbert Walker Bush.*

2. When I'm good, I'm very good. When I'm bad, I'm better. (spoken by actress Mae West in the classic film *I'm No Angel*)

   Identifying tag in the middle *"When I'm good, I'm very good," said actress Mae West in the classic film I'm No Angel. "When I'm bad, I'm better."*

3. The rich rob the poor, and the poor rob one another. (spoken by abolitionist Sojourner Truth)

Identifying tag at the beginning <u>Abolitionist Sojourner Truth said,</u>

<u>"The rich rob the poor, and the poor rob one another."</u>

4. Heaven is like an egg, and the earth is like the yolk of the egg. (written by Chinese philosopher Chang Heng)

Identifying tag in the middle <u>"Heaven is like an egg," wrote Chinese</u>

<u>philosopher Chang Heng, "and the earth is like the yolk of the egg."</u>

5. If a man hasn't discovered something he will die for, then he isn't fit to live. (spoken by Martin Luther King Jr.)

Identifying tag at the end <u>"If a man hasn't discovered something he</u>

<u>will die for, then he isn't fit to live," said Martin Luther King Jr.</u>

Focus on Writing: *Flashback*

Look back at your response to the Focus on Writing activity on page 523. Make sure that you have enclosed any direct quotations in quotation marks, placed other punctuation correctly, and capitalized where necessary. Revise any incorrectly punctuated quotations.

33c ## Setting Off Titles

Teaching Tip
Remind students that they should underline to indicate italics in handwritten work. MLA style recommends underlining in typed work as well, but you may prefer that students use italics.

Some titles are typed in *italics* (or <u>underlined</u> to indicate italics). Others are enclosed in quotation marks. The following box shows how to set off different kinds of titles.

Italicized Titles	*Titles in Quotation Marks*
Books: *How the García Girls Lost Their Accents* Newspapers: *Miami Herald* Magazines: *People* Long poems: *John Brown's Body* Plays: *Death of a Salesman* Films: *The Rocky Horror Picture Show* Television or radio series: *Star Trek: The Next Generation*	Book chapters: "Understanding Mechanics" Short stories: "The Tell-Tale Heart" Essays and articles: "Delusions of Grandeur" Short poems: "Richard Cory" Songs and speeches: "America the Beautiful"; "The Gettysburg Address" Individual episodes of television or radio series: "The Montgomery Bus Boycott" (an episode of the PBS series *Eyes on the Prize*)

● **Practice 33-4**

In the following sentences, underline or insert quotation marks around titles. (Remember that titles of books and other long works are underlined, and titles of stories, essays, and other shorter works are enclosed in quotation marks.)

> **Example:**   An article in the <u>New York Times</u> called "It's Not Easy Being Green" is a profile of former Chicago Bulls player Dennis Rodman, who once had green hair.

1. Sui Sin Far's short story "The Wisdom of the New," from her book <u>Mrs. Spring Fragrance</u>, is about the clash between Chinese and American cultures in the early twentieth century.

2. Major league baseball games traditionally open with fans singing "The Star-Spangled Banner."

3. Interesting information about fighting skin cancer can be found in the article "Putting Sunscreens to the Test," which appeared in the magazine <u>Consumer Reports</u>.

4. One of the best-known poems of the twentieth century is Robert Frost's "The Road Not Taken."

5. Ang Lee has directed several well-received films, including <u>Crouching Tiger, Hidden Dragon.</u>

6. It is surprising how many people enjoy reruns of two 1960s television series: <u>Bewitched</u> and <u>I Dream of Jeannie.</u>

7. The title of Lorraine Hansberry's play <u>A Raisin in the Sun</u> comes from Langston Hughes's poem "Harlem."

8. In his autobiography, <u>Breaking the Surface,</u> Olympic diving champion Greg Louganis wrote about his struggle with AIDS.

ESL Tip

Students may forget to include articles in titles. Remind them to include articles—but not to capitalize an article unless it is the first word of the title.

Highlight:
Capital Letters
in Titles

Capitalize the first letters of all important words in a title. Do not capitalize an **article** (*a*, *an*, *the*), a **preposition** (*to*, *of*, *around*, and so on), or a **coordinating conjunction** (*and*, *but*, and so on)—unless it is the first or last word of the title or subtitle (*On the Road;* "To an Athlete Dying Young"; *No Way Out; And Quiet Flows the Don*).

● **Practice 33-5**

Edit the following sentences, capitalizing letters as necessary in titles.

Example: Eudora Welty's "ᴬ worn ᵂ path ᴾ" is a very moving short story.

1. The 1959 movie ᴾ*plan* ᴺ*nine from* ᴼ*outer* ˢ*space* has been called the worst picture of all time.

2. Gary Larson's cartoon collections include the books ᴬ*a* ᴾ*prehistory of the* ᶠ*far* ˢ*side* and ᵂ*weiner* ᴰ*dog* ᴬ*art.*

3. Everyone should read Martin Luther King Jr.'s "ᴵ*I* ᴴ*have a* ᴰ*dream*" speech and his essay "ᴸ*letter from* ᴮ*birmingham* ᴶ*jail.*"

4. Bruce Springsteen's album *the rising* includes the songs "Jonesome day," "Into the fire," and "my city of ruins."

5. CBS has had hits with *CSI, CSI: miami*, and *csi: new york*.

Focus on Writing: *Flashback*

Look back at your response to the Focus on Writing activity on page 523. Circle the film's title. Have you underlined it? Are capital letters used where necessary? Make any necessary corrections.

33d   Hyphens

A hyphen has two uses: to divide a word at the end of a line, and to join words in compounds.

Teaching Tip
Remind students that their computers will automatically carry a long word over to the next line.

● Use a hyphen to divide a word at the end of a line. If you need to divide a word, divide it between syllables. (Check your dictionary to see how a word is divided into syllables.) Never break a one-syllable word, no matter how long it is.

> When the speaker began his talk, all the people seated in the <u>audi-torium</u> grew very quiet.

● Use a hyphen in a **compound word**—a word that is made up of two or more words.

> The <u>over-excited</u> children finally calmed down.
>
> This theater shows <u>first-run</u> movies.

● Practice 33-6

Add hyphens to the following sentences where they are needed. Correct any hyphens that are used incorrectly.

Example: The course focused on nineteen̄ century American literature.

1. The ice skating rink finally froze over.

2. We should be kind to our four legged friends.

3. The first year students raised money for charity.

4. The under prepared soldiers were at a real disadvantage.

5. The hand carved sculpture looked like a pair of doves.

Abbreviations

An **abbreviation** is a shortened form of a word. Although abbreviations are generally not used in college writing, it is acceptable to abbreviate the following.

Teaching Tip
You may want to introduce students to the alternatives C.E. ("Common Era") and B.C.E. ("Before the Common Era").

- Titles—such as Mr., Ms., Dr., and Jr.—that are used along with names.
- a.m. and p.m. (also written A.M. and P.M.)
- B.C. and A.D. (in dates such as 43 B.C.)
- Names of organizations (NRA, CIA) and technical terms (DNA). Note that some abbreviations, called **acronyms**, are pronounced as words: AIDS, FEMA.

Teaching Tip
Remind students that the abbreviations they use in emails and text messages have no place in college writing.

Keep in mind that it is *not* acceptable to abbreviate days of the week, months, names of streets and places, names of academic subjects, or titles that are not used along with names.

● Practice 33-7

Edit the incorrect use of abbreviations in the following sentences.

Example:　In leap years, ~~Feb.~~ has twenty-nine days.
(*February*)

1. The ~~dr.~~ diagnosed a case of hypertension.
(*doctor*)

2. ~~Nov.~~ 11 is a federal holiday.
(*November*)

3. Derek registered for ~~Eng.~~ literature and a ~~psych~~ elective.
(*English*) (*psychology*)

4. The museum was located at the corner of Laurel ~~Ave.~~ *Avenue* and Neptune ~~St.~~ *Street*.

5. The clinic is only open ~~Tues.~~ *Tuesday* through ~~Thurs.~~ *Thursday* and every other ~~Sat.~~ *Saturday.*^

33f Numbers

In college writing, most numbers are spelled out (*forty-five*) rather than written as **numerals** (*45*). However, numbers more than two words long are always written as numerals (*4,530*, not *four thousand five hundred thirty*).

In addition, you should use numerals in the following situations.

Dates	January 20, 1976
Addresses	5023 Schuyler Street
Exact times	10:00 (If you use *o'clock*, spell out the number: *ten o'clock*)
Percentages and decimals	80% 8.2
Divisions of books	Chapter 3 Act 4 Page 102

Note: Never begin a sentence with a numeral. Either use a spelled-out number, or reword the sentence so the numeral does not come at the beginning.

● Practice 33-8

Edit the incorrect use of numbers in the following sentences.

Example: The population of the United States is over ~~three-hundred~~ *300* million.

1. Only ~~2~~ *two* students in the ~~8~~ *eight* o'clock lecture were late.

2. More than ~~seventy-five percent~~ *75%* of the class passed the exit exam.

3. Chapter ~~six~~ *6* begins on page 873.

4. The wedding took place on October ~~twelfth~~ *12* at 7:30.

5. Meet me at ~~Sixty-five~~ *65* Cadman Place.

Focus on Writing: *Flashback*

Look back at your response to the Focus on Writing activity on page 523. Have you used any hyphens, numbers, or abbreviations in your writing? If so, have you used them correctly? Make any necessary corrections.

Focus on Writing: *Revising and Editing*

Look back at your response to the Focus on Writing activity on page 523. If you have quoted dialogue from the film you discuss, check to be sure your punctuation is correct. If you did not use quotations, try adding one or two. Then, edit your work for proper use of capital letters, quotation marks, and underlining.

Chapter Review

Editing Practice

Read the following student essay, which includes errors in capitalization and punctuation and in the use of direct quotations, titles, abbreviations, and numbers. Edit the passage to correct any such errors. The first sentence has been edited for you.   *Answers may vary.*

The World of Gary Soto

My favorite A̶uthor is Gary Soto, a m̶exican-a̶merican poet and

fiction writer whose first book of poetry, "The Elements of San

Joaquin," was published in 1977. Soto was born in 1952 in f̶resno,

C̶alifornia, and grew up in a large s̶panish-speaking family. His F̶ather, who died when Soto was ~~3~~ *five*, worked in a factory, and his ~~Mother~~ *mother* picked grapes and other crops in the farms of the ~~s~~San ~~j~~Joaquin ~~v~~Valley. Much of Soto's writing is influenced by childhood memories. "These are the pictures I take with me when I write", he once said. "~~they~~ *They* stir the past, the memories that are so vivid."

Soto attended ~~f~~Fresno ~~c~~City ~~c~~College and later studied at the ~~U.~~ *University* of California at ~~f~~Fresno, where he originally majored in ~~Geol.~~ *geology.* There, according to Soto, "One day I came across a book of poetry on a shelf in the college library. I read it, liked it, and began to write poems of my own".

One of Soto's best poems is "Oranges," from his 1985 book *Black Hair.* In this poem, he describes the events of a cold ~~d~~December afternoon when a boy takes his ~~Girlfriend~~ *girlfriend* into a drugstore to buy her a treat. She wants a chocolate that costs a ~~Dime~~ *dime*, but he only has a ~~Nickel~~ *nickel*. He gives the ~~Saleslady~~ *saleslady* the coin plus an orange he has in his pocket, and she lets him pay for the candy this way.

This theme of money is picked up again in the ~~Title~~ *title* of one of Soto's books of stories, *Nickel ~~A~~and Dime.* The first story is called "We Ain't Asking Much" and is about Roberto, who loses his job, cannot pay his rent, and ends up on the ~~Street~~ *street*, trying to sell ~~C~~Christmas ornaments made of twigs to rich people. Silver, a ~~Character~~ *character* in another story, has something in common with Soto (he is a poet), but he also has trouble making enough money to live on.

Does Soto write from ~~Personal Experience~~ *personal experience*? He admits that this is partly true. He says, however, "Although the experiences in my stories, poems, and novels may seem autobiographical, much of what I write is the stuff of imagination".

Collaborative Activities

1. Work in a small group to list as many items in each of the following five categories as you can: planets, islands, musicians or bands, automobile models, sports teams. Be sure all your items are proper nouns, and use capital letters where necessary.

    On a separate sheet of paper, write five original sentences using one proper noun from each category in each sentence. When you are finished, exchange papers with another group, and check for the correct use of capital letters.

2. Imagine that you and the other members of your group are the nominations committee for this year's Emmy, Oscar, or Grammy Awards. Work together to compile a list of categories and several nominees for each category, deciding as a group when to use capital letters.

    Trade lists with another group. From each category, select the individual artist or work you believe deserves to win the award. Write a sentence about each winner, explaining why each is the best in its category.

    When you have finished, exchange papers with another group. Check one another's papers for correct use of capitals, quotation marks, and underlining.

Teaching Tip
Encourage students to
write at least five or six
sentences of dialogue.

3. Working in pairs, write a conversation between two characters, real or fictional, who have very different positions on a particular issue. Place all direct quotations within quotation marks, and include identifying tags that clearly indicate which character is speaking. (Begin a new paragraph each time a new person speaks.)

    Exchange your conversations with another pair of students, and check their work to see that all directly quoted speech is set within quotation marks and that capital letters and all other punctuation are used correctly.

Review Checklist:
Understanding Mechanics

- [ ] Capitalize proper nouns. (See 33A.)
- [ ] Always place direct quotations in quotation marks. (See 33B.)
- [ ] In titles, capitalize all important words. Use italics or quotation marks to set off titles. (See 33C.)
- [ ] Use hyphens to divide words at the end of a line and to join words in compounds. (See 33D.)
- [ ] Use abbreviations for titles used along with names, for names of organizations and technical terms, and in other conventional situations. (See 33E.)
- [ ] Use numerals for numbers that can be expressed in fewer than three words. Use numbers in most other cases. (See 33F.)

Chapter 34

Understanding Spelling

In 1987, Cherry Tree Elementary School in Baltimore was the first public school to require uniforms. Since then, uniforms have become a requirement in many public schools in New Orleans, Chicago, San Francisco, and elsewhere.

Becoming a Better Speller

Improving your spelling may take time, but the following steps can make this task a lot easier.

Teaching Tip
Suggest that students try proofreading for spelling by starting with the last sentence of their papers and reading backward to the beginning. This strategy allows them to focus on one word at a time without being distracted by the logic or order of their ideas.

Teaching Tip
Encourage students to keep a personal list of commonly misspelled words. Have students write words they often misspell on the board.

1. **Use a spell checker.** When you write on a computer, use your spell checker. It will correct most misspelled words and also identify many typos, such as transposed or omitted letters. Keep in mind, however, that spell checkers do not identify typos that create other words (*then/than, form/from,* or *big/beg,* for example). They also do not identify words that have been used incorrectly (*their/there* or *its/it's,* for example).

2. **Proofread carefully.** Even if you have used a spell checker, always proofread your papers for spelling before you hand them in.

3. **Use a dictionary.** As you proofread your papers, circle words whose spellings you are unsure of. After you have finished, look up these words in a dictionary, which will give you the spelling of a word and tell you how to pronounce it.

4. **Keep a personal spelling list.** Write down all the words you misspell. Whenever your instructor returns one of your papers, look for misspelled words—usually circled and marked *sp.* Add these to your personal spelling list.

5. **Look for patterns in your misspelling.** Do you consistently misspell words with *ei* combinations? Do you have trouble forming

→ Focus on Writing

In an effort to improve discipline and boost self-esteem, a number of schools across the country require students to wear uniforms. The picture on the opposite page shows two students at one such elementary school. Look at the picture, and then write about whether or not you think elementary school students should be required to wear uniforms such as the ones in the picture.

WORD POWER
conducive to leading to; contributing to
economical thrifty
individuality the quality of being distinct from others

plurals? Once you figure out which errors you make most frequently, you can take steps to eliminate them.

6. **Learn the basic spelling rules.** Memorize the spelling rules in this chapter, especially those that apply to areas in which you are weak. Remember that each rule can help you spell many words correctly.

7. **Review the list of commonly confused words in 34E.** If you have problems with any of these word pairs, add them to your personal spelling list.

8. **Use memory cues.** Memory cues help you remember how to spell certain words. For example, remembering that *definite* contains the word *finite* will help you remember that *definite* is spelled with an *i*, not an *a*.

9. **Learn to spell some of the most frequently misspelled words.** Identify those on the list below that give you trouble, and add them to your personal spelling list.

Frequently Misspelled Words

across	disappoint	loneliness	reference
all right	early	medicine	restaurant
a lot	embarrass	minute	roommate
already	entrance	necessary	secretary
argument	environment	noticeable	sentence
beautiful	everything	occasion	separate
becoming	exercise	occur	speech
beginning	experience	occurred	studying
believe	finally	occurrences	surprise
benefit	forty	occurring	tomato
calendar	fulfill	occurs	tomatoes
cannot	generally	personnel	truly
careful	government	possible	until
careless	grammar	potato	usually
cemetery	harass	potatoes	Wednesday
certain	height	prejudice	weird
conscience	holiday	prescription	window
definite	integration	privilege	withhold
definitely	intelligence	probably	woman
dependent	interest	professor	women
describe	interfere	receive	writing
develop	judgment	recognize	written

Teaching Tip
Discuss the fact that English spelling is complex and unpredictable. Mention that many languages have more regular spelling than English does.

Because English pronunciation is not always a reliable guide for spelling, most people find it useful to memorize some spelling rules.

Highlight: Vowels and Consonants	Knowing which letters are vowels and which are consonants will help you understand the spelling rules presented in this chapter.
	Vowels: *a, e, i, o, u*
	Consonants: *b, c, d, f, g, h, j, k, l, m, n, p, q, r, s, t, v, w, x, y, z*

34b   *ie* and *ei*

Memorize this rule: *i* comes before *e* except after *c*, or when the *ei* sound is pronounced *ay*.

Teaching Tip
Have students memorize spelling rules. Test them on these rules.

Teaching Tip
Tell students that when the *i* and *e* in a word are not pronounced as a unit (as in *science*), the "*i* before *e*" rule does not apply.

i *before* e	*except after* c	*or when* ei *is pronounced* ay
achieve	ceiling	eight
believe	conceive	freight
friend	deceive	neighbor
		weigh

Highlight: Exceptions to the "*i* before *e*" Rule	The exceptions to the "*i* before *e*" rule follow no pattern, so you must memorize them.			
	ancient	either	leisure	seize
	caffeine	foreign	neither	species
	conscience	height	science	weird

On the Web
For more practice, visit Exercise Central *at* <bedfordstmartins .com/focusonwriting>.

● Practice 34-1

Proofread the underlined words in the following sentences for correct spelling. If a correction needs to be made, cross out the incorrect word, and write the correct spelling above it. If the word is spelled correctly, write *C* above it.

Example: It was a <u>relief</u> to <u>recieve</u> the good news.
⟨above "relief": C⟩ ⟨above "recieve": receive⟩

1. Be sure to <u>wiegh</u> the pros and cons before making important decisions,
⟨above "wiegh": weigh⟩
particularly those involving <u>friends</u>.
⟨above "cons": C⟩ ⟨above "friends": C⟩

2. When your <u>beliefs</u> are tested, you may be able to <u>acheive</u> a better under-
⟨above "beliefs": C⟩ ⟨above "acheive": achieve⟩
standing of yourself.

3. In our <u>society</u>, many people <u>decieve</u> themselves into <u>beleiving</u> that they
⟨above "society": C⟩ ⟨above "decieve": deceive⟩ ⟨above "beleiving": believing⟩
are better than everyone else.

4. <u>Cheifly</u> because they have been lucky, they have reached a certain
⟨above "Cheifly": Chiefly⟩
<u>height</u> in the world.
⟨above "height": C⟩

5. They think that the blood running through <u>their</u> <u>viens</u> makes them
⟨above "their": C⟩ ⟨above "viens": veins⟩
belong to a higher <u>species</u> than the average person.
⟨above "species": C⟩

Focus on Writing: *Flashback*

Look back at your response to the Focus on Writing activity on page 541. Underline any words that have *ie* or *ei* combinations, and check a dictionary to make sure they are spelled correctly. Correct any spelling errors you find.

34c   Prefixes

A **prefix** is a group of letters added at the beginning of a word that changes the word's meaning. Adding a prefix to a word never affects the spelling of the original word.

dis + service = disservice	pre + heat = preheat
un + able = unable	un + natural = unnatural
co + operate = cooperate	over + rate = overrate

● Practice 34-2

Write in the blank the new word that results when the specified prefix is added to each of the following words.

Example: dis + respect = _disrespect_

On the Web
For more practice, visit
Exercise Central at
<bedfordstmartins
.com/focusonwriting>.

1. un + happy = _unhappy_   6. non + negotiable = _nonnegotiable_
2. tele + vision = _television_   7. im + patient = _impatient_
3. pre + existing = _preexisting_   8. out + think = _outthink_
4. dis + satisfied = _dissatisfied_   9. over + react = _overreact_
5. un + necessary = _unnecessary_   10. dis + solve = _dissolve_

Focus on Writing: *Flashback*

Look back at your response to the Focus on Writing activity on page 541. Underline any words that have prefixes, and check a dictionary to make sure each word is spelled correctly. Correct any spelling errors you find.

34d   Suffixes

A **suffix** is a group of letters added to the end of a word that changes the word's meaning or its part of speech. Adding a suffix to a word can change the spelling of the original word.

Words Ending in Silent *e*

If a word ends with a silent (unpronounced) *e*, drop the *e* if the suffix begins with a vowel.

Drop the *e*

hope + <u>i</u>ng = hoping   dance + <u>e</u>r = dancer
continue + <u>o</u>us = continuous   insure + <u>a</u>ble = insurable

Exceptions

change + able = changeable   courage + ous = courageous
notice + able = noticeable   replace + able = replaceable

Keep the *e* if the suffix begins with a consonant.

Keep the *e*

hope + <u>f</u>ul = hopeful   bore + <u>d</u>om = boredom

excite + <u>m</u>ent = excitement   same + <u>n</u>ess = sameness

Exceptions

argue + ment = argument   true + ly = truly

judge + ment = judgment   nine + th = ninth

• Practice 34-3

On the Web
For more practice, visit Exercise Central *at* <bedfordstmartins .com/focusonwriting>.

Write in the blank the new word that results from adding the specified suffix to each of the following words.

Examples:

insure + ance = _____*insurance*_____

love + ly = _____*lovely*_____

1. lone + ly = *lonely* _____   6. microscope + ic = *microscopic* _____

2. use + ful = *useful* _____   7. prepare + ation = *preparation* _____

3. revise + ing = *revising* _____   8. nine + th = *ninth* _____

4. base + ment = *basement* _____   9. indicate + ion = *indication* _____

5. desire + able = *desirable* _____   10. effective + ness = *effectiveness* _____

Words Ending in -y

When you add a suffix to a word that ends in *-y*, change the *y* to an *i* if the letter before the *y* is a consonant.

change *y* to *i*

beaut<u>y</u> + ful = beaut<u>i</u>ful   bus<u>y</u> + ly = bus<u>i</u>ly

tr<u>y</u> + ed = tr<u>i</u>ed   friendl<u>y</u> + er = friendl<u>i</u>er

exceptions

• Keep the *y* if the suffix starts with an *i*.

cry + <u>i</u>ng = crying   baby + <u>i</u>sh = babyish

- Keep the *y* when you add a suffix to certain one-syllable words.

     shy + er = shyer   dry + ness = dryness

- Keep the *y* if the letter before the *y* is a vowel.

keep the y

annoy + ance = annoyance   enjoy + ment = enjoyment
play + ful = playful   display + ed = displayed

exceptions

day + ly = daily   say + ed = said
gay + ly = gaily   pay + ed = paid

● Practice 34-4

Write in the blank the new word that results from adding the specified suffix to each of the following words.

Examples:

study + ed = ___studied___

employ + ment = ___employment___

1. happy + ness = _happiness_   6. annoy + ing = _annoying_
2. convey + or = _conveyor_   7. destroy + er = _destroyer_
3. deny + ing = _denying_   8. twenty + eth = _twentieth_
4. carry + ed = _carried_   9. lonely + ness = _loneliness_
5. ready + ness = _readiness_   10. spy + ing = _spying_

Doubling the Final Consonant

Teaching Tip
Refer students to the
Highlight box in 34A for
more on vowels and
consonants.

When you add a suffix that begins with a vowel—for example, *-ed*, *-er*, or *-ing*—sometimes you need to double the final consonant in the original word. Do this (1) if the last three letters of the word have a consonant-vowel-consonant (cvc) pattern and (2) if the word has one syllable (or if the last syllable is stressed).

final consonant doubled

drum   +   ing   =   drumming (cvc—one syllable)
bat   +   er   =   batter (cvc—one syllable)

pet	+	ed	=	petted (cvc—one syllable)
commit	+	ed	=	committed (cvc—stress is on last syllable)
occur	+	ing	=	occurring (cvc—stress is on last syllable)

Final consonant not doubled

answer	+	ed	=	answered (cvc—stress is not on last syllable)
happen	+	ing	=	happening (cvc—stress is not on last syllable)
act	+	ing	=	acting (no cvc)

● **Practice 34-5**

Teaching Tip
As a homework assignment, have students think of other examples to add to the suffix lists in 34D.

Write in the blank the new word that results from adding the specified suffix to each of the following words.

Examples:

rot + ing = _____rotting_____

narrow + er = _____narrower_____

1. hope + ed = _hoped_____
2. shop + er = _shopper_____
3. rest + ing = _resting_____
4. combat + ed = _combatted_____
5. reveal + ing = _revealing_____

6. open + er = _opener_____
7. unzip + ed = _unzipped_____
8. trap + ed = _trapped_____
9. cram + ing = _cramming_____
10. omit + ed = _omitted_____

Focus on Writing: *Flashback*

Look back at your response to the Focus on Writing activity on page 541. Underline any words that have suffixes, and check a dictionary to make sure each word is spelled correctly. Correct any spelling errors you find.

34e   Commonly Confused Words

Accept/Except   *Accept* means "to receive something." *Except* means "with the exception of" or "to leave out or exclude."

> "I accept your challenge," said Alexander Hamilton to Aaron Burr.
>
> Everyone except Darryl visited the museum.

Affect/Effect   *Affect* is a verb meaning "to influence." *Effect* is a noun meaning "result."

> Carmen's job could affect her grades.
>
> Overexposure to sun can have a long-term effect on skin.

All ready/Already   *All ready* means "completely prepared." *Already* means "previously, before."

> Serge was all ready to take the history test.
>
> Gina had already been to Italy.

Brake/Break   *Brake* is a noun that means "a device to slow or stop a vehicle." *Break* is a verb meaning "to smash" or "to detach" and sometimes a noun meaning either "a gap or an interruption" or "a stroke of luck."

> Peter got into an accident because his foot slipped off the brake.
>
> Babe Ruth thought no one would ever break his home run record.
>
> The baseball game was postponed until there was a break in the bad weather.

Buy/By   *Buy* means "to purchase." *By* is a preposition meaning "close to" or "next to" or "by means of."

> The Stamp Act forced colonists to buy stamps for many public documents.
>
> He drove by but did not stop.
>
> He stayed by her side all the way to the hospital.
>
> Malcolm X wanted "freedom by any means necessary."

Teaching Tip
Teach students how to use mnemonic devices to remember spellings. (For example, *their* refers to ownership, and so does *heir*; *there* refers to location, and so does *here*.)

On the Web
For more practice, visit
Exercise Central *at*
<bedfordstmartins
.com/focusonwriting>.

● **Practice 34-6**

Proofread the underlined words in the following sentences for correct spelling. If a correction needs to be made, cross out the incorrect word, and write the correct spelling above it. If the word is spelled correctly, write *C* above it.

                     accept   *C*

Example:　We must ~~except~~ the fact that the human heart can <u>break</u>.

1. The ~~affects~~ (*effects*) of several new AIDS drugs have ~~all ready~~ (*already*) been reported.

2. *Consumer Reports* gave high ratings to the ~~breaks~~ (*brakes*) on all the new cars tested ~~accept~~ (*except*) one.

3. Advertisements urge us to ~~by~~ (*buy*) a new product even if we <u>already</u> (*C*) own a similar item.

4. If you ~~except~~ (*accept*) the charges for a collect telephone call, you will probably have to ~~brake~~ (*break*) your piggy bank to pay their bill.

5. Cigarette smoking <u>affects</u> (*C*) the lungs <u>by</u> (*C*) creating deposits of tar that make breathing difficult.

Conscience / Conscious　*Conscience is a noun that refers to the part of the mind that urges a person to choose right over wrong. Conscious is an adjective that means "aware" or "deliberate."*

> After he cheated at cards, his <u>conscience</u> started to bother him.
>
> As she walked through the woods, she became <u>conscious</u> of the hum of insects.
>
> Elliott made a <u>conscious</u> decision to stop smoking.

Everyday / Every day　*Everyday is a single word that means "ordinary" or "common." Every day is two words that mean "occurring daily."*

> *I Love Lucy* was a successful comedy show because it appealed to <u>everyday</u> people.
>
> <u>Every day</u>, Lucy and Ethel would find a new way to get into trouble.

Fine / Find　*Fine means "superior quality" or "a sum of money paid as a penalty." Find means "to locate."*

He sang a <u>fine</u> solo at church last Sunday.

Demi had to pay a <u>fine</u> for speeding.

Some people still use a willow rod to <u>find</u> water.

Hear / Here   *Hear* means "to perceive sound by ear." *Here* means "at or in this place."

I moved to the front so I could <u>hear</u> the speaker.

My great-grandfather came <u>here</u> in 1883.

Its / It's   *Its* is the possessive form of *it*. *It's* is the contraction of *it is* or *it has*.

The airline canceled <u>its</u> flights because of the snow.

<u>It's</u> twelve o'clock, and we are late.

Ever since <u>it's</u> been in the accident, the car has rattled.

● **Practice 34-7**

Teaching Tip
Students often use *it's* instead of *its*. Read aloud a sentence containing this error, replacing the contraction with the two words it stands for (for example, *The baby climbed out of it is high chair*). The error should be immediately apparent.

Proofread the underlined words in the following sentences for correct spelling. If a correction needs to be made, cross out the incorrect word, and write the correct spelling above it. If the word is spelled correctly, write *C* above it.

Example: <u>It's</u> *(C)* often difficult for celebrities to adjust to <u>every day</u> *(everyday)* life.

1. <u>Hear</u> *(Here)* at Simonson's Fashions, we try to make our customers feel that <u>everyday</u> *(every day)* is a sale day.

2. My uncle was a <u>find</u> *(fine)* person, and <u>its</u> *(it's)* a shame that he died so young.

3. That inner voice you <u>hear</u> *(C)* is your <u>conscious</u> *(conscience)* telling you how you should behave.

4. In the <u>every day</u> *(everyday)* world of work and school, it can be hard to <u>fine</u> *(find)* the time to relax and enjoy life.

5. By the time I became <u>conscience</u> *(conscious)* of the leaking pipe, <u>it's</u> *(its)* damage had run to more than a hundred dollars.

Know / No / Knew / New   *Know* means "to have an understanding of " or "to have fixed in the mind." *No* means "not any," "not at all," or "not one." *Knew* is the past tense form of the verb *know*. *New* means "recent or never used."

I <u>know</u> there will be a lunar eclipse tonight.

You have <u>no</u> right to say that.

He <u>knew</u> how to install a <u>new</u> light switch.

Lie / Lay   *Lie* means "to rest or recline." The past tense of *lie* is *lay. Lay* means "to put or place something down." The past tense of *lay* is *laid.*

Every Sunday, I <u>lie</u> in bed until noon.

They <u>lay</u> on the grass until it began to rain, and then they went home.

Tammy told Carl to <u>lay</u> his cards on the table.

Brooke and Cassia finally <u>laid</u> down their hockey sticks.

Loose / Lose   *Loose* means "not fixed or rigid" or "not attached securely." *Lose* means "to mislay" or "to misplace."

In the 1940s, many women wore <u>loose</u>-fitting pants.

I don't gamble because I hate to <u>lose</u>.

Passed / Past   *Passed* is the past tense of the verb *pass.* It means "moved by" or "succeeded in." *Past* is a noun meaning time "earlier than the present time."

The car that <u>passed</u> me was doing more than eighty miles an hour.

David finally <u>passed</u> his driving test.

The novel was set in the <u>past</u>.

Peace / Piece   *Peace* means "the absence of war" or "calm." *Piece* means "a part of something."

The British prime minister thought he had achieved <u>peace</u> with honor.

My <u>peace</u> of mind was destroyed when the flying saucer landed.

"Have a <u>piece</u> of cake," said Marie.

● **Practice 34-8**

Proofread the underlined words in the following sentences for correct spelling. If a correction needs to be made, cross out the incorrect word, and write the correct spelling above it. If the word is spelled correctly, write *C* above it.

Example: Although the soldiers stopped fighting, a <u>piece</u> treaty was *(peace)* never signed.

1. Because he was late for the job interview, he was afraid he would ~~loose~~ *lose* his chance to work for the company.

2. While she ~~laid~~ *lay* down to rest, her children cooked dinner and cleaned the house.

3. There will be ~~know~~ *no* wool sweaters on sale before the holidays.

4. The ~~passed~~ *past* chair of the committee left a lot of unfinished business.

5. The broken knife found in the trash turned out to be a ~~peace~~ *piece* of the murder weapon.

Principal / Principle   *Principal* means "first" or "highest" or "the head of a school." *Principle* means "a law or basic assumption."

> She had the principal role in the movie.
>
> I'll never forget the day the principal called me into his office.
>
> It was against his principles to lie.

Quiet / Quite   *Quiet* means "free of noise" or "still." *Quite* means "actually" or "very."

> Jane looked forward to the quiet evenings at the lake.
>
> "You haven't quite got the hang of it yet," she said.
>
> After practicing all summer, Tamika got quite good at tennis.

Raise / Rise   *Raise* means "to elevate" or "to increase in size, quantity, or worth." The past tense of *raise* is *raised*. *Rise* means "to stand up" or "to move from a lower position to a higher position." The past tense of *rise* is *rose*.

> Carlos raises his hand whenever the teacher asks for volunteers.
>
> They finally raised the money for the down payment.
>
> The crowd rises every time their team scores a touchdown.
>
> Aurea rose before dawn so she could see the eclipse.

Sit / Set   *Sit* means "to assume a sitting position." The past tense of *sit* is *sat*. *Set* means "to put down or place" or "to adjust something to a desired position." The past tense of *set* is *set*.

> I usually sit in the front row at the movies.
>
> They sat at the clinic waiting for their names to be called.

Elizabeth <u>set</u> the mail on the kitchen table and left for work.

Every semester I <u>set</u> goals for myself.

Teaching Tip
Remind students not to drop the *d* of *supposed* before *to: He is supposed to study* (not *He is suppose to study.*)

Suppose / Supposed   *Suppose* means "to consider" or "to assume." *Supposed* is both the past tense and the past participle of *suppose*. *Supposed* also means "expected" or "required." (Note that when *supposed* has this meaning, it is followed by *to*.)

<u>Suppose</u> researchers were to find a cure for cancer.

We <u>supposed</u> the movie would be over by ten o'clock.

You were <u>supposed</u> to finish a draft of the report by today.

● **Practice 34-9**

Proofread the underlined words in the following sentences for correct spelling. If a correction needs to be made, cross out the incorrect word, and write the correct spelling above it. If the word is spelled correctly, write *C* above it.

Example: Boarding took <u>quite</u> ^C^ a long time because of the security

process.

1. Jackie was <u>~~suppose~~</u> ^supposed^ to mow the lawn and trim the bushes last weekend.

2. It is important to <u>~~sit~~</u> ^set^ the computer in a place where the on-off switch can be reached.

3. If you <u>raise</u> ^C^ the window, a pleasant breeze will blow into the bedroom.

4. The <u>~~principle~~</u> ^principal^ reason for her <u>~~raise~~</u> ^rise^ to the position of <u>principal</u> ^C^ of the school was hard work.

5. We were all told to <u>sit</u> ^C^ and wait for the crowd to become <u>~~quite.~~</u> ^quiet.^

Their / There / They're   *Their* is the possessive form of the pronoun *they*. *There* means "at or in that place." *There* is also used in the phrases *there is* and *there are*. *They're* is the contraction of "they are."

They wanted to improve <u>their</u> living conditions.

I put the book over <u>there</u>.

<u>There</u> are three reasons I will not eat meat.

<u>They're</u> the best volunteer firefighters I've ever seen.

Then / Than   *Then* means "at that time" or "next in time." *Than* is used in comparisons.

> He was young and naive <u>then</u>.
>
> I went to the job interview and <u>then</u> stopped off for a chocolate shake.
>
> My dog is smarter <u>than</u> your dog.

Threw / Through   *Threw* is the past tense of *throw*. *Through* means "in one side and out the opposite side" or "finished."

Teaching Tip
Remind students not to use the informal spelling *thru* for *through*.

> Satchel Paige <u>threw</u> a baseball more than ninety-five miles an hour.
>
> It takes almost thirty minutes to go <u>through</u> the tunnel.
>
> "I'm <u>through</u>," said Clark Kent, storming out of Perry White's office.

To / Too / Two   *To* means "in the direction of." *Too* means "also" or "more than enough." *Two* denotes the numeral 2.

> During spring break, I am going <u>to</u> Disney World.
>
> My roommates are coming <u>too</u>.
>
> The microwave popcorn is <u>too</u> hot to eat.
>
> "If we get rid of the Tin Man and the Cowardly Lion, the <u>two</u> of us can go to Oz," said the Scarecrow to Dorothy.

Use / Used   *Use* means "to put into service" or "to consume." *Used* is both the past tense and past participle of *use*. *Used* also means "accustomed." (Note that when *used* has this meaning, it is followed by *to*.)

> I <u>use</u> a soft cloth to clean my glasses.
>
> "Hey! Who <u>used</u> all the hot water?" he yelled from the shower.
>
> Marisol had <u>used</u> all the firewood during the storm.
>
> After two years in Alaska, they got <u>used</u> to the short winter days.

● **Practice 34-10**

Proofread the underlined words in the following sentences for correct spelling. If a correction needs to be made, cross out the incorrect word, and write the correct spelling above it. If the word is spelled correctly, write *C* above it.

> **Example:**   Because of good nutrition, people are taller <u>then</u> they <u>use</u> to be in the past.
>
> *than*   *used*

1. After the power went out in the dorms, many students then went ~~too~~ the library to study. [*C* above "then"; *to* above "too"]

2. Whenever he ~~through~~ out the trash, he walked ~~threw~~ the backyard on his way ~~two~~ the alley. [*threw* above "through"; *through* above "threw"; *to* above "two"]

3. Get your tickets before ~~their~~ all gone. [*they're* above "their"]

4. I ~~use~~ to think that my ancestors all came from northern Europe, but I recently learned that one of my great-grandparents used to live in South Africa. [*used* above "use"; *C* above "used"]

5. The countries that signed the peace treaty have not lived up to ~~they're~~ responsibilities. [*their* above "they're"]

Weather / Whether *Weather* refers to temperature, humidity, precipitation, and so on. *Whether* is used to introduce alternative possibilities.

> The *Farmer's Almanac* says that the <u>weather</u> this winter will be severe.
>
> <u>Whether</u> or not this prediction will be correct is anyone's guess.

Where / Were / We're *Where* means "at or in what place." *Were* is the past tense of *are*. *We're* is the contraction of "we are."

> <u>Where</u> are you going, and <u>where</u> have you been?
>
> Charlie Chaplin and Mary Pickford <u>were</u> popular stars of silent movies.
>
> <u>We're</u> doing our back-to-school shopping early this year.

Whose / Who's *Whose* is the possessive form of *who*. *Who's* is the contraction of either "who is" or "who has."

> My roommate asked, "<u>Whose</u> book is this?"
>
> "<u>Who's</u> there?" squealed the second little pig as he leaned against the door.
>
> <u>Who's</u> left a yellow 1957 Chevrolet blocking the driveway?

Your / You're *Your* is the possessive form of *you*. *You're* is the contraction of "you are."

> "You should have worn <u>your</u> running shoes," said the hare as he passed the tortoise.
>
> "<u>You're</u> too kind," said the tortoise sarcastically.

● Practice 34-11

Proofread the underlined words in the following sentences for correct spelling. If a correction needs to be made, cross out the incorrect word, and write the correct spelling above it. If the word is spelled correctly, write *C* above it.

Example: As citizens, ~~were~~ all concerned with where our country is
going.
we're   *C*

1. Authorities are attempting to discover ~~who's~~ fingerprints were left at the
whose   *C*
scene of the crime.

2. Cancer does not care ~~weather~~ ~~your~~ rich or poor, young or old; it can
whether *you're*
strike anyone.

3. Santa Fe, ~~were~~ I lived for many years, has better weather than New Jer-
where   *C*
sey has.

4. Whenever we listen to politicians debate, ~~were~~ likely to be wondering
we're
~~whose~~ telling the truth.
who's

5. You should take your time before deciding ~~weather~~ to focus your energy
C   *whether*   *C*
on school or on work.

Focus on Writing: *Flashback*

Look back at your response to the Focus on Writing activity on page 541. Identify any words that appear on the lists of commonly confused words (on the preceding pages), and check to make sure you have spelled them correctly.

Focus on Writing: *Revising and Editing*

Type your response to the Focus on Writing activity on page 541 if you have not already done so. Now, run a spell check. Did the computer pick up all the errors? Which did it identify? Which did it miss? Correct the spelling errors the computer identified as well as the ones that you found while proofreading. (You can also check spelling in this way in a longer writing assignment you are currently working on.)

Chapter Review

Editing Practice

Read the following student essay, which includes spelling errors. Identify the words you think are misspelled; then, look them up in a dictionary. Finally, cross out each incorrectly spelled word, and write the correct spelling above the line. The first sentence has been edited for you. *Answers may vary.*

Coming Home

When my Uncle Joe, a soldier in the Marines, ~~returnned~~ *returned* from Iraq, I was glad he was home. He had ~~fullfilled~~ *fulfilled* his responsibility and was safe. My family welcomed him at the airport with flags and flowers. He ~~huged~~ *hugged* us all and looked ~~thriled~~ *thrilled* to be home. However, returning to civilian life turned out to be more difficult for him than any of us had expected.

Being in the military is very different from any other ~~expereince.~~ *experience.* ~~Soldeirs~~ *Soldiers.* are trained to kill. To do this, they have to forget what they have been taught in the ~~passed~~ *past* about not harming others. They have to get ~~use~~ *used* to ignoring what their ~~conscious~~ *conscience* tells them to do and become less sensitive to others' feelings. Also, to survive, they have to be ~~suspitious~~ *suspicious* of everything around them. They must be alert at all times. Most important, ~~thier~~ *their* emotions must be ~~controled.~~ *controlled.* In combat, they have to function like a machine: when given an order, they must follow it. ~~They're~~ *Their* own lives and those of ~~there~~ *their* fellow soldiers depend on ~~obedeince.~~ *obedience.*

War changed Uncle Joe, and I learned that this was true of many veterans. Although insensitivity and suspicion are ~~necesary~~ *necessary* for a soldier, ~~niether~~ *neither* is of much use in civilian life. For example, when my uncle ~~overreacted~~ *overreacted* about a dirty dish left on the kitchen counter, his wife became confused and angry. Similarly, when his family asked him about the war, he became ~~annoied~~ *annoyed* and ~~refussed~~ *refused* to talk about it. His family did not understand. As a result, he felt isolated from his ~~freinds~~ *friends* and family. When he slept, he had nightmares of being back in combat. He also missed his fellow Marines.

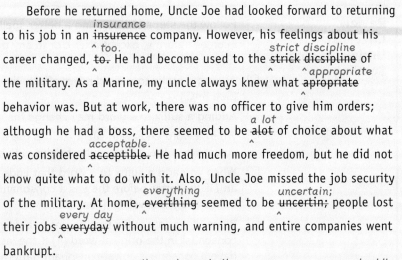

Before he returned home, Uncle Joe had looked forward to returning

insurance

to his job in an ~~insurence~~ company. However, his feelings about his

^ *too.* *strict discipline*

career changed, ~~to.~~ He had become used to the ~~strick dicsipline~~ of

^ ^ ^ *appropriate*

the military. As a Marine, my uncle always knew what ~~apropriate~~

^

behavior was. But at work, there was no officer to give him orders;

a lot

although he had a boss, there seemed to be ~~alot~~ of choice about what

acceptable. ^

was considered ~~acceptible.~~ He had much more freedom, but he did not

^

know quite what to do with it. Also, Uncle Joe missed the job security

everything *uncertain;*

of the military. At home, ~~everthing~~ seemed to be ~~uncertin;~~ people lost

every day ^ ^

their jobs ~~everyday~~ without much warning, and entire companies went

^

bankrupt.

through similar *buddies*

What my uncle went ~~threw~~ was ~~similiar~~ to what many of his ~~buddys~~

^ ^ ^

experienced. Even with counseling, it took him a long time to be able

to trust the people around him. Eventually, he was able to become

tried

more sensitive to the feelings of others, and he ~~tryed~~ to rely on his

^

civilian friends and family the way he had relied on his fellow Marines.

Occasionally, *occur*

~~Ocasionaly,~~ he still has nightmares about the war, but they ~~ocurr~~

^ ^

less often. For Uncle Joe, the war did not end when he came home.

beginning

Returning home was just the ~~begining~~ of his own personal struggle.

^

Collaborative Activities

1. Working in pairs, compare responses to the Focus on Writing activity on page 541. How many misspelled words did each of you find? How many errors did you and your partner have in common?

2. Are there any patterns of misspelling in your Flashback activities? What types of spelling errors seem most common?

3. Collaborate with your partner to make a spelling list for the two of you, and then work with other groups to create a spelling list for the whole class. When you have finished, determine which types of errors are most common.

Review Checklist: Understanding Spelling

☐ Follow the steps to becoming a better speller. (See 34A.)

☐ *I* comes before *e*, except after *c* or in any *ay* sound, as in *neighbor*. (See 34B.)

☐ Adding a prefix to a word never affects the word's spelling. (See 34C.)

☐ Adding a suffix to a word may change the word's spelling. (See 34D.)

☐ When a word ends with silent *e*, drop the *e* if the suffix begins with a vowel. Keep the *e* if the suffix begins with a consonant. (See 34D.)

☐ When you add a suffix to a word that ends with a *y*, change the *y* to an *i* if the letter before the *y* is a consonant. Keep the *y* if the letter before the *y* is a vowel. (See 34D.)

☐ When you add a suffix that begins in a vowel, double the final consonant in the original word (1) if the last three letters of the word have a consonant-vowel-consonant pattern (cvc) and the word has one syllable or (2) if the last three letters have a cvc pattern and the last syllable is stressed. (See 34D.)

☐ Memorize the spellings of the most commonly confused words. (See 34E.)

Editing Practice: Sentences

Read the following sentences, which contain errors in punctuation, mechanics, and spelling. Identify the sentences that need to be corrected, and edit the faulty sentences. Some sentences have more than one error.

1. There are ~~fourty~~ *forty* restuarants within ~~5~~ *five* miles of my house *,* but the most popular place to eat is *,* Golden Crown *,* a Chinese buffet.

2. Mr *.* Glass *,* my middle school ~~principle,~~ *principal,* retired last year *,* after he turned ~~65~~ *sixty-five* .

3. Mike has lived in Chicago *,* Illinois *,* since he was born on ~~Aug. eleventh~~ *August 11,* 1986.

4. When we moved into our new apartment *,* Tony said, *"* ~~their~~ *there* were ~~alot~~ *a lot* of ants in the kitchen *,* and the front door lock ~~didnt~~ *didn't* work. *"*

5. There are several ways to~~o~~ keep a computer secure *:* install spam blocking software *,* change your email ~~adress~~ *address* frequently *,* and keep ~~your're~~ *your* real name a secret.

6. What kind of ~~vaccum~~ *vacuum* cleaner is ~~Jins~~ *Jin's* grandmother using ~~/~~ *?*

7. ~~Its~~ *It's* clear that the clerk at the registration desk *,* one of the first people guests see when they check in *,* needs better ~~comunication~~ *communication* skills.

8. Stan and his wife spent part of their ~~S~~ *s* ummer vacation in Philadelphia, visiting Constitution ~~center~~ *Center* and ~~independance hall.~~ *Independence Hall.*

9. At first, readers thought that in his book <u>The Painted Bird</u>, ~~writter~~ *writer* Jerzy Kosinski was ~~discribeing~~ *describing* his own ~~dificult~~ *difficult* life as a young boy in Nazi occupied ~~poland~~ *P*oland, but now ~~they're~~ *there* are real doubts about ~~weather~~ *whether* he ever had those ~~experiances~~ *experiences* (or even wrote the book himself) .

10. Lenders say that a family should spend no more ~~then~~ *than* 35% of ~~there~~ *their* total income on housing, but many ~~familyies~~ *families* are spending almost 50%.

Teaching Tip
You can use this exercise to get students ready for the multi-error editing practice that follows.

Editing Practice: Essay

Read the following student essay, which contains errors in the use of punctuation, mechanics, and spelling. Identify the sentences that need to be corrected, and edit the faulty sentences. The first sentence has been edited for you. *Answers will vary.*

Telenovelas

What is the most-watched kind of television program in Spanish speaking countries. It's the telenovela, a Spanish language soap opera. Televised in the prime ~~evenning~~ *evening* hours telenovelas started in the early 1950s ~~nineteen hundred fifties~~ and are still popular today. In fact more telenovelas are shown in *C*entral America and South *A*merica than any other type of TV drama. In a 1998 study, more than half the population of Latin American countries said that they watch these shows. Telenovelas are different from *A*merican soap operas in the way they are ~~planed~~ *planned* and scheduled. Also they dont have the same kind of plot. ~~Telenovela's~~ *Telenovelas'* popularity can be seen in ~~there~~ *their* Web sites and ~~buy~~ *by* their growth in countries that do not speak *S*panish.

Telenovelas are ~~quiet~~ *quite* different from American *S*oap *O*peras. In the United States, there have been some evening soap opera dramas (*D*allas and *D*ynasty are good examples but they have usually been televised once a week; however telenovelas usually appear ~~Mon.~~ *Monday* through ~~Fri.~~ *Friday*. In the United States soap operas; ~~genneraly~~ *generally* continue for months and years, until viewers stop watching and the ratings fall. The ~~writters~~ *writers* of an *A*merican soap opera do not ~~no~~ *know* how the plot will ~~develope~~ *develop* or when it will end. In contrast ~~telenovela's~~ *telenovelas* are usually completely planned at the ~~beggining~~ *beginning*. In general a telenovela continues for about ~~8~~ *eight* months and then it is finished. A new telenovela takes ~~it's~~ *its* place.

The plots may seem ~~wierd~~ *weird* to *A*merican viewers. In a typical telenovela the beautiful heroine is a girl who has no money but has a good heart. The hero — a rich handsome man, rejects his rich but evil

562

girlfriend
~~girlfreind~~ in favor of the heroine. ~~Eventualy~~ *Eventually,* the heroine may turn out
to~~o~~ be the secret child of a wealthy family. The ~~unnhappy~~ *unhappy* villains may
wind up in the ~~cemetary~~ *cemetery ,* and the heroine and her hero will live happily
ever after. Other telenovelas ~~occurr~~ *occur* in the ~~passed~~ *past* or may deal with
modern social problems such as drug abuse , or ~~predjudice~~ *prejudice*. Some
telenovelas are really ~~cereal~~ *serial* comedies and are more like American
sitcoms.

Telenovelas are ~~becomeing~~ *becoming* more and more popular. There are even
Web sites dedicated to popular telenovelas and ~~there~~ *their* actors. For
example , viewers can go to the Web site called *T*opnovelas to access
plot summaries , lists of the most popular shows , and downloads of
episodes. Although telenovelas started in Spanish-speaking countries ,
they have spread to other countries. The first telenovela to be
translated into another language was "The Rich Cry *T*oo" (Los Ricos
También Lloran) , which was first produced in Mexico in ~~nineteen~~ *1979*
~~seventy-nine~~ and was brought to , China, the Soviet Union , and the
United States. Other places where telenovelas are popular include the
following countries : *F*rance , *I*srael , *J*apan, *M*alaysia , Singapore , and
*I*ndonesia.

The popularity of the telenovela in the United *S*tates is only partly
a reflection of ~~its'~~ *its* millions of *S*panish - speaking people. While it is true
that networks want *H*ispanic viewers , it is also true that the format
and subject matter ~~truely~~ *truly* ~~interrest~~ *interest* English-speaking viewers. ~~Its~~ *It's* quite
~~possable~~ *possible* that the once - a - week format of most *A*merican TV shows may
be a thing of the past and that telenovelas in English will soon appear
every night.

Unit Eight
Reading Essays

Chapter 35

Reading for College

The largest library in the
United States, the Library of
Congress, contains about
thirty million books.

Reading is essential to all your college courses. To get the most out of your reading, you should approach the books and articles you read in a practical way, always asking yourself what information they can offer you. You should also approach assigned readings critically, just as you approach your own writing when you revise.

Reading critically does not mean challenging or arguing with every idea, but it does mean wondering, commenting, questioning, and judging. Most of all, it means being an active rather than a passive reader. Being an **active reader** means participating in the reading process: approaching a reading assignment with a clear understanding of your purpose, previewing a selection, highlighting and annotating it, and perhaps outlining it—all *before* you begin to respond in writing to what you have read.

To gain an understanding of your **purpose**—your reason for reading— you should start by answering some questions.

Teaching Tip
Encourage students to read any end-of-chapter or end-of-essay questions before reading a chapter or essay. Then, when they find the answer to a question, they can underline the answer and write the question number in the margin.

Questions about Your Purpose

- Why are you reading?
- Will you be expected to discuss what you are reading? If so, will you discuss it in class or in a conference with your instructor?
- Will you have to write about what you are reading? If so, will you be expected to write an informal response (for example, a journal entry) or a more formal one (for example, an essay)?
- Will you be tested on the material?

Once you understand your purpose, you are ready to begin reading.

35a   Previewing

Your first step is to preview the material you have been assigned to read. When you **preview**, you skim to get a sense of the writer's main idea and key supporting points as well as his or her general emphasis. You can begin by focusing on the title, the first paragraph (which often contains a thesis statement or overview), and the last paragraph (which often contains a summary of the writer's points). You should also look for clues to the writer's message in other **visual signals** (headings, boxes, and so on) as well as in

567

verbal signals (the words and phrases the writer uses to convey order and emphasis).

Teaching Tip
Remind students that much of the material they read will have only a few of these visual signals.

Using Visual Signals

- Look at the title.
- Look at the opening and closing paragraphs.
- Look at each paragraph's first sentence.
- Look at headings.
- Look at *italicized* and **boldfaced** words.
- Look at numbered lists.
- Look at bulleted lists (like this one).
- Look at graphs, charts, tables, photographs, and so on.
- Look at any information that is boxed.
- Look at any information that is in color.

Using Verbal Signals

- Look for phrases that signal emphasis ("The *primary* reason"; "The *most important* idea").
- Look for repeated words and phrases.
- Look for words that signal addition (*also, in addition, furthermore*).
- Look for words that signal time sequence (*first, after, then, next, finally*).
- Look for words that identify causes and effects (*because, as a result, for this reason*).
- Look for words that introduce examples (*for example, for instance*).
- Look for words that signal comparison (*likewise, similarly*).
- Look for words that signal contrast (*unlike, although, in contrast*).
- Look for words that signal contradiction (*however, on the contrary*).
- Look for words that signal a narrowing of the writer's focus (*in fact, specifically, in other words*).
- Look for words that signal summaries or conclusions (*to sum up, in conclusion*).

When you have finished previewing the material, you should have a general sense of what the writer wants to communicate.

WORD POWER
bilingual able to communicate in two languages

● Practice 35-1

"No Comprendo" ("I Don't Understand") is a newspaper article by Barbara Mujica, a professor of Spanish at Georgetown University in Washington,

D.C. In this article, which was published in the *New York Times*, Mujica argues against bilingual education (teaching students in their native language as well as in English).

In preparation for class discussion and for other activities that will be assigned later in this chapter, preview the article. As you read, try to identify the writer's main idea and key supporting points, and then write them on the lines that follow the article, on page 570.

No Comprendo

Teaching Tip
Direct students' attention to this essay's title, thesis statement, topic sentences, and opening and closing paragraphs.

Last spring, my niece phoned me in tears. She was graduating from high 1 school and had to make a decision. An outstanding soccer player, she was offered athletic scholarships by several colleges. So why was she crying?

My niece came to the United States from South America as a child. 2 Although she had received good grades in her schools in Miami, she spoke English with a heavy accent, and her comprehension and writing skills were deficient. She was afraid that once she left the Miami environment, she would feel uncomfortable and, worse still, have difficulty keeping up with class work.

Programs that keep foreign-born children in Spanish-language class- 3 rooms for years are only part of the problem. During a visit to my niece's former school, I observed that all business, not just teaching, was conducted in Spanish. In the office, secretaries spoke to the administrators and the children in Spanish. Announcements over the public-address system were made in an English so fractured that it was almost incomprehensible.

WORD POWER
Spanglish a mixture of Spanish and English

I asked my niece's mother why, after years in public schools, her daugh- 4 ter had poor English skills. "It's the whole environment," she replied. "All kinds of services are available in Spanish or Spanglish. Sports and after-school activities are conducted in Spanglish. That's what the kids hear on the radio and in the street."

Until recently, immigrants made learning English a priority. But even 5 when they didn't learn English themselves, their children grew up speaking it. Thousands of first-generation Americans still strive to learn English, but others face reduced educational and career opportunities because they have not mastered this basic skill they need to get ahead.

Teaching Tip
You may want to discuss the use of the terms *Hispanic* (a term coined by the U.S. Census Bureau) and *Latino/Latina* and the issue of referring to groups by the terms they prefer.

According to the 1990 census, 40 percent of the Hispanics born in the 6 United States do not graduate from high school, and the Department of Education says that a lack of proficiency in English is an important factor in the drop-out rate.

People and agencies that favor providing services only in foreign lan- 7 guages want to help people who do not speak English, but they may be doing these people a disservice by condemning them to a linguistic ghetto from which they cannot easily escape.

And my niece? She turned down all of her scholarship opportunities, [8] deciding instead to attend a small college in Miami, where she will never have to put her English to the test.

Writer's main idea

Because Hispanics are not being encouraged to learn English, their

opportunities are limited.

Key supporting points

1. *Writer's niece is afraid to go to college away from Miami.*

2. *foreign-born students are kept in Spanish-language classes.*

3. *Many services are provided in Spanish.*

4. *Many Hispanics do not graduate from high school.*

35b Highlighting

After you have previewed the assigned material, read through it carefully, highlighting as you read. **Highlighting** means using underlining and symbols to identify key ideas. This active reading strategy will help you understand the writer's ideas and make connections among these ideas when you reread. Be selective; don't highlight too much. Remember, you will eventually be rereading every highlighted word, phrase, and sentence—so highlight only the most important, most useful information.

Using Highlighting Symbols

- <u>Underline</u> key ideas—for example, topic sentences.
- words or phrases you want to remember.
- Place a check mark (✔) or star (✱) next to an important idea.
- Place a double check mark (✔✔) or double star (✱✱) next to an especially significant idea.
- Draw lines or arrows to connect related ideas.
- Put a question mark (?) beside a word or idea that you need to look up.
- Number the writer's key supporting points or examples.

Highlight: Knowing What to Highlight

You want to highlight what's important — but how do you *know* what's important? As a general rule, you should look for the same **visual signals** you looked for when you did your previewing. Many of the ideas you will need to highlight will probably be found in material that is visually set off from the rest of the text — opening and closing paragraphs, lists, and so on. Also, continue to look for **verbal signals** — words and phrases like *however, therefore, another reason, the most important point,* and so on — that often introduce key points. Together, these visual and verbal signals will give you clues to the writer's meaning and emphasis.

Here is how a student highlighted an excerpt from a newspaper column, "Barbie at Thirty-Five" by Anna Quindlen.

But consider the recent study at the University of Arizona investigating the attitudes of white and black teenage girls toward body image. The attitudes of the white girls were a nightmare. Ninety percent expressed dissatisfaction with their own bodies, and many said they saw dieting as a kind of all-purpose panacea. "I think the reason I would diet would be to gain self-confidence," said one. "I'd feel like it was a way of getting control," said another. And they were curiously united in their description of the perfect girl. She's 5 feet 7 inches, weighs just over 100 pounds, has long legs and flowing hair. The researchers concluded, "The ideal girl was a living manifestation of the Barbie doll."

While white girls described an impossible ideal, black teenagers talked about appearance in terms of style, attitude, pride, and personality. White respondents talked "thin," black ones "shapely." Seventy percent of the black teenagers said they were satisfied with their weight, and there was little emphasis on dieting. "We're all brought up and taught to be realistic about life," said one, "and we don't look at things the way you want them to be. You look at them the way they are."

The student who highlighted this passage was preparing to write an essay about eating disorders. She began her highlighting by underlining and starring the writer's main idea. She then boxed the names of the two key groups the passage compares — *white girls* and *black teenagers* — and underlined two phrases that illustrate how the attitudes of the two groups differ (*dissatisfaction with their own bodies* and *satisfied with their weight*). Check marks in the margin remind the student of the importance of these two phrases, and arrows connect each phrase to the appropriate group of girls.

The student also circled three related terms that characterize white girls' attitudes—*perfect girl, Barbie doll,* and *impossible ideal*—drawing lines to connect them. Finally, she circled the unfamiliar word *panacea* and put a question mark above it to remind herself to look the word up in a dictionary.

● Practice 35-2

Review the highlighted passage on page 571. How would your own highlighting of this passage be similar to or different from the sample student highlighting?

● Practice 35-3

Reread "No Comprendo" (pp. 569–70). As you reread, highlight the article by underlining and starring main ideas, boxing and circling key words, check-marking important points, and, if you wish, drawing lines and arrows to connect related ideas. Be sure to circle each unfamiliar word and put a question mark above it.

35c   Annotating

As you highlight, you should also *annotate* what you are reading. **Annotating** a passage means making notes—of questions, reactions, reminders, and ideas for writing or discussion—in the margins or between the lines. Keeping an informal record of ideas as they occur to you will prepare you for class discussion and provide a useful source of material for writing.

As you read a passage, asking the following questions will help you make useful annotations.

Teaching Tip
Encourage students to write notes in the margin as they read, even if a thought seems irrelevant. Such notes are often useful for class discussion.

> **Questions for Annotating**
> • What is the writer saying? What do you think the writer is suggesting or implying?
> • What is the writer's purpose (his or her reason for writing)?
> • What kind of audience is the writer addressing?
>
> *(continued on the following page)*

- Is the writer discussing another writer's ideas?
- What is the writer's main idea?
- What examples and explanations does the writer use to support his or her points?
- Does the writer include enough examples and explanations?
- Do you understand the writer's vocabulary?
- Do you understand the writer's ideas?
- Do you agree with the points the writer is making?
- How are the ideas presented here like (or unlike) those presented in other things you have read?

The following passage, which reproduces the student's highlighting from page 571, also illustrates her annotations.

But consider the recent study at the University of Arizona investigating the attitudes of white and black teenage girls toward body image. The attitudes of the white girls were a nightmare. Ninety percent expressed dissatisfaction with their own bodies, and many said they saw dieting as a kind of all-purpose panacea. "I think the reason I would diet would be to gain self-confidence," said one. "I'd feel like it was a way of getting control," said another. And they were curiously united in their description of the perfect girl. She's 5 feet 7 inches, weighs just over 100 pounds, has long legs and flowing hair. The researchers concluded, "The ideal girl was a living manifestation of the Barbie doll."

While white girls described an impossible ideal, black teenagers talked about appearance in terms of style, attitude, pride, and personality. White respondents talked "thin," black ones "shapely." Seventy percent of the black teenagers said they were satisfied with their weight, and there was little emphasis on dieting. "We're all brought up and taught to be realistic about life," said one, "and we don't look at things the way you want them to be. You look at them the way they are."

Margin annotations:

= cure-all

Need for control, perfection. Why? Media? Parents?

Barbie doll = plastic, unreal

"Thin" vs. "shapely"

Only 30% dissatisfied — but 90% of white girls

vs. Barbie doll (= unrealistic)   overgeneralization?

With her annotations, this student wrote down the meaning of the word *panacea*, put the study's conclusions and the contrasting statistics into her own words, and recorded questions she intended to explore further.

● Practice 35-4

Teaching Tip
Ask students to consider whether they believe "No Comprendo" includes any biased assumptions about Hispanics or about bilingual education. You might also ask them what they think has changed in the years since the article was written.

Reread "No Comprendo" (pp. 569–70). As you reread, refer to the Questions for Annotating (pp. 572–73), and use them as a guide while you write down your own thoughts and questions in the margins of the article. Note where you agree or disagree with the writer, and briefly explain why. Quickly summarize any points you think are particularly important. Take time to look up any unfamiliar words you have circled and to write brief definitions. Think of these annotations as your preparation for discussing the article in class and eventually writing about it.

● Practice 35-5

Trade workbooks with another student, and read over his or her highlighting and annotating of "No Comprendo." How are your written responses similar to the other student's? How are they different? Do your classmate's responses help you see anything new about the article?

35d Outlining

Teaching Tip
Tell students that formal outlines can help them keep track of ideas in long essays or research papers. Refer them to 12F and Appendix B, section 7, for examples of formal outlines.

Outlining is another technique you can use to help you understand a reading assignment. Unlike a **formal outline**, which follows strict conventions, an **informal outline** enables you to record a writer's ideas in the order in which they are presented. After you have finished an informal outline, you should be able to see the writer's emphasis (which ideas are more important than others) as well as how the ideas are related.

**Highlight:
Making an
Informal
Outline**

1. Write or type the writer's main idea at the top of a sheet of paper. (This will remind you of the writer's focus and help keep your outline on track.)
2. At the left margin, write down the most important idea of the first body paragraph or first part of the reading.

→

Highlight:
Making an
Informal
Outline
continued

3. Indent the next line a few spaces, and list the examples or details that support this idea. (You can use your computer's Tab key to help you set up your outline.)

4. As ideas become more specific, indent further. (Ideas that have the same degree of importance are indented the same distance from the left margin.)

5. Repeat the process with each body paragraph or part of the passage.

The student who highlighted and annotated the excerpt from Anna Quindlen's "Barbie at Thirty-Five" (p. 573) made the following informal outline to help her understand the writer's ideas.

Main idea: Black and white teenage girls have very different attitudes about their body images.

White girls dissatisfied
       90% dissatisfied with appearance
       Dieting = cure-all
          — self-confidence
          — control
     Ideal = unrealistic
         — tall and thin
         — Barbie doll
Black girls satisfied
       70% satisfied with weight
       Dieting not important
       Ideal = realistic
         — shapely
         — not thin

● **Practice 35-6**

Working on your own or in a small group, make an informal outline of "No Comprendo" (pp. 569–70). Refer to your highlighting and annotations as you construct your outline. When you have finished, check to make certain your outline accurately represents the writer's emphasis and the relationships among her ideas.

35e Summarizing

Once you have highlighted, annotated, and outlined a passage, you may want to try summarizing it to help you understand it better. A **summary** retells, *in your own words*, what a passage is about. A summary condenses a passage, so it leaves out all but the main idea and perhaps the key supporting points. A summary omits examples and details, and it does *not* include your own ideas or opinions.

Highlight: Writing a Summary

Teaching Tip
Refer students to Appendix B, section B4, for more on writing a summary.

1. Review your outline.
2. Consulting your outline, restate the passage's main idea *in your own words*.
3. Consulting your outline, restate the passage's key supporting points. Add transitional words and phrases between sentences where necessary.
4. Reread the original passage to make sure you haven't left out anything significant.

Note: To avoid accidentally using the exact language of the original, do not look at the passage while you are writing your summary. If you want to use a distinctive word or phrase from the original passage, put it in quotation marks.

The student who highlighted, annotated, and outlined the excerpt from "Barbie at Thirty-Five" (p. 571) wrote the following summary.

> As Anna Quindlen reports in "Barbie at Thirty-Five," a University of Arizona study found that black and white teenage girls have very different attitudes about their body images. Almost all white girls said they were dissatisfied with their appearance. To them, the "perfect girl" would look like a Barbie doll (tall and very thin). Quindlen sees this attitude as unrealistic. Black girls in the study, however, were generally satisfied with their appearance. In fact, most said that they were happy with their weight. They did not say they wanted to be thin; they said they wanted to be "shapely."

● Practice 35-7

Write a brief summary of "No Comprendo" (pp. 569–70). Use your outline to guide you, and keep your summary short and to the point. Your summary should be about one-quarter to one-third the length of the original article.

35f   Writing a Response Paragraph

Once you have highlighted and annotated a reading selection, you are ready to write about it—perhaps in a **response paragraph** in which you record your informal reactions to the writer's ideas.

Because a response paragraph is informal, no special guidelines or rules govern its format or structure. As in any paragraph, however, you should include a topic sentence, examples and details to support the topic sentence, appropriate transitions, and a summary statement. In a response paragraph, informal style and personal opinions are acceptable.

The student who highlighted, annotated, outlined, and summarized the Quindlen passage wrote this response paragraph.

Teaching Tip
Remind students that contractions are acceptable here only because this is an informal paragraph.

> Why are white and black girls' body images so different? Why do black girls think it's okay to be "shapely" while white girls want to be thin? Maybe it's because music videos and movies and fashion magazines show so many more white models, all half-starved, with perfect hair and legs. Or maybe white girls get different messages from their parents or from the people they date. Do white and black girls' attitudes about their bodies stay the same when they get older? And what about <u>male</u> teenagers' self-images? Do white and black <u>guys</u> have different body images too? These are questions that really need to be answered.

The process of writing this paragraph was very helpful to the student. The questions she asked suggested some interesting ideas that she could explore in class discussion or in a more fully developed piece of writing.

● Practice 35-8

On a separate sheet of paper, write an informal response paragraph expressing your reactions to "No Comprendo" (pp. 569–70) and to the issue of bilingual education.

Review Checklist: Reading for College	☐ Preview the material. (See 35A.)
	☐ Highlight the material. (See 35B.)
	☐ Annotate the material. (See 35C.)
	☐ Outline the material. (See 35D.)
	☐ Summarize the material. (See 35E.)
	☐ Write a response paragraph. (See 35F.)

Teaching Tip
Tailor your reading
assignments to your
students. If the class is
still struggling with the
basics, do not assign a
difficult essay.

ESL Tip
In choosing essays to
assign, consider the non-
native students in your
class. For example, an
essay by a Hispanic
writer may interest stu-
dents whose first lan-
guage is Spanish.

Teaching Tip
You may want to
introduce or review the
material on active read-
ing strategies in Chap-
ter 35 before you assign
the essays in this chapter.

Teaching Tip
You might want to remind
students that newspaper
and magazine articles
often omit the comma
before *and* in a series
and after introductory
elements. Tell them,
however, that their
writing will be clearer if
they include these
commas.

The following eighteen essays by student and professional writers offer interesting material to read, react to, think critically about, discuss, and write about. The essays are grouped in three thematic categories: Working and Learning, Culture and Custom, and Life and Times. Each essay is accompanied by a short introduction that tells you something about the reading and its author. Definitions of some of the words used in the essay appear in **Word Power** boxes in the margins.

Following each essay are four **Thinking about the Reading** discussion questions, some of which can be done collaboratively. (These are marked in the text with a star.) With your instructor's permission, you can discuss your responses to these questions with other students and then share them with the class. Three **Writing Practice** activities also follow each essay.

As you read these essays, you should **highlight** and **annotate** them to help you understand what you are reading. (Highlighting and annotating are discussed in Chapter 35.) Then, reread them more carefully in preparation for class discussion and for writing.

Working and Learning

Culture and Custom

Teaching Tip
Students may notice that some of the essays in this chapter do not follow the rules outlined in 33F. Explain that journalism and scientific and technical writing have different conventions for the use of numbers and numerals.

WORKING AND LEARNING

Don't Hang Up, That's My Mom Calling

Bobbi Buchanan

Teaching Tip
This is an argument essay.

Telemarketers' sales calls often interrupt our already hectic lives. Bobbi Buchanan's article reminds us that there is a real, and sometimes familiar, person on the other end of every telemarketing call. Buchanan, whose writing has appeared in the *New York Times* and the *Louisville Review*, is the editor of the online journal *New Southerner*.

Teaching Tip
Remind students to familiarize themselves with the end-of-essay questions before reading the essay.

The next time an annoying sales call interrupts your dinner, think of my 71-year-old mother, LaVerne, who works as a part-time telemarketer to supplement her Social Security income. To those Americans who have signed up for the new national do-not-call list, my mother is a pest, a nuisance, an invader of privacy. To others, she's just another anonymous voice on the other end of the line. But to those who know her, she's someone struggling to make a buck, to feed herself and pay her utilities — someone who personifies the great American way.

In our family, we think of my mother as a pillar of strength. She's survived two heart surgeries and lung cancer. She stayed at home her whole life to raise the seven of us kids. She entered the job market unskilled and physically limited after my father's death in 1998, which ended his pension benefits.

Telemarketing is a viable option for my mother and the more than six mil- 3

WORD POWER
viable capable of success or effectiveness
exempt to free from an obligation
impervious impossible to affect

lion other Americans who work in the industry. According to the American Teleservices Association, the telemarketing work force is mostly women; 26 percent are single mothers. More than 60 percent are minorities; about 5 percent are disabled; 95 percent are not college graduates; more than 30 percent have been on welfare or public assistance. This is clearly a job for those used to hardship.

Interestingly enough, the federal list exempts calls from politicians, 4 pollsters, and charities, and companies that have existing business relationships with customers can keep calling. Put this in perspective. Are they not the bulk of your annoying calls? Telemarketing giants won't be as affected by the list but smaller businesses that rely on this less costly means of sales will. The giants will resort to other, more expensive forms of advertisement and pass those costs along to you, the consumer.

My mother doesn't blame people for wanting to be placed on the do- 5 not-call list. She doesn't argue the fairness of its existence or take offense when potential clients cut her off in mid-sentence. All her parenting experience has made her impervious to rude behavior and snide remarks, and she is not discouraged by hang-ups or busy signals. What worries my mother is that she doesn't know whether she can do anything else at her age. As it is, sales are down and her paycheck is shrinking.

So when the phone rings at your house during dinnertime and you can't 6 resist picking it up, relax, breathe deeply and take a silent oath to be polite. Try these three painless words: "No, thank you."

Think of the caller this way: a hard-working, first-generation American; 7 the daughter of a Pittsburgh steelworker; a survivor of the Great Depression; the widow of a World War II veteran; a mother of seven, grandmother of eight, great-grandmother of three. It's my mother calling.

Thinking about the Reading

Teaching Tip
Remind students to answer all questions in complete sentences.

1. What does Buchanan want readers to know about her mother?

2. In paragraph 3, Buchanan says that telemarketing is "clearly a job for those used to hardship." What does she mean?

3. What is Buchanan's objection to the national "do-not-call list"? Do you agree with her?

*4. What was your opinion of telemarketers before you read this essay? Did the essay change your mind in any way?

Writing Practice

Teaching Tip
If your students are writing essays, these prompts will work as essay topics. Otherwise, you can have students write paragraphs.

1. Write a letter to Buchanan arguing that although telemarketers may be nice people who need the income, they are still annoying invaders of your privacy.

2. What do you think can be done to achieve a compromise between telemarketers' need for employment and our desire not to be bothered by their calls? Suggest some ways to make such calls less annoying.

3. Imagine you have just accepted a job as a telemarketer, and that your friends disagree with your decision. Respond to their criticisms, explaining why you took the job and what you hope to get out of it.

Delusions of Grandeur

Henry Louis Gates Jr.

Award-winning writer and critic Henry Louis Gates Jr. is currently the W. E. B. DuBois Professor of the Humanities at Harvard. In the following essay, first published in *Sports Illustrated* in 1991, he attempts to awaken black youth from their dreams of basketball stardom. He encourages them, instead, to focus on education, where a more realistic chance of success awaits them.

Standing at the bar of an all-black VFW post in my hometown of Pied- 1 mont, West Virginia, I offered five dollars to anyone who could tell me how many African-American professional athletes were at work today. There are 35 million African-Americans, I said.

"Ten million!" yelled one intrepid soul, too far into his cups. 2

"No way . . . more like 500,000," said another. 3

"You mean *all* professional sports," someone interjected, "including golf 4 and tennis, but not counting the brothers from Puerto Rico?" Everyone laughed.

"Fifty thousand, minimum," was another guess. 5

Here are the facts: 6

There are 1,200 black professional athletes in the U.S.

There are 12 times more black lawyers than black athletes.

There are 2½ times more black dentists than black athletes.

There are 15 times more black doctors than black athletes.

Nobody in my local VFW believed these statistics; in fact, few people 7 would believe them if they weren't reading them in the pages of *Sports Illustrated*. In spite of these statistics, too many African-American youngsters still believe that they have a much better chance of becoming another Magic Johnson or Michael Jordan than they do of matching the achievements of Baltimore Mayor Kurt Schmoke or neurosurgeon Dr. Benjamin Carson, both of whom, like Johnson and Jordan, are black.

In reality, an African-American youngster has about as much chance of 8 becoming a professional athlete as he or she does of winning the lottery. The tragedy for our people, however, is that few of us accept that truth.

Let me confess that I love sports. Like most black people of my 9 generation—I'm 40—I was raised to revere the great black athletic heroes,

WORD POWER

revere to regard with
awe and respect

epic a long poem
celebrating heroic acts

imbued thoroughly
influenced

and I never tired of listening to the stories of triumph and defeat that, for blacks, amount to a collective epic much like those of the ancient Greeks: Joe Louis's demolition of Max Schmeling; Satchel Paige's dazzling repertoire of pitches; Jesse Owens's in-your-face performance in Hitler's 1936 Olympics; Willie Mays's over-the-shoulder basket catch; Jackie Robinson's quiet strength when assaulted by racist taunts; and a thousand other grand tales.

Nevertheless, the blind pursuit of attainment in sports is having a dev- 10 astating effect on our people. Imbued with a belief that our principal avenue to fame and profit is through sport, and seduced by a win-at-any-cost system that corrupts even elementary school students, far too many black kids treat basketball courts and football fields as if they were classrooms in an alternative school system. "O.K., I flunked English," a young athlete will say. "But I got an A plus in slam-dunking."

The failure of our public schools to educate athletes is part and parcel of 11 the schools' failure to educate almost everyone. A recent survey of the Philadelphia school system, for example, stated that "more than half of all students in the third, fifth and eighth grades cannot perform minimum math and language tasks." One in four middle school students in that city fails to pass to the next grade each year. It is a sad truth that such statistics are repeated in cities throughout the nation. Young athletes—particularly young black athletes—are especially ill-served. Many of them are functionally illiterate, yet they are passed along from year to year for the greater glory of good old Hometown High. We should not be surprised to learn, then, that only 26.6% of black athletes at the collegiate level earn their degrees. For every successful educated black professional athlete, there are thousands of dead and wounded. Yet young blacks continue to aspire to careers as athletes, and it's no wonder why; when the University of North Carolina recently commissioned a sculptor to create archetypes of its student body, guess which ethnic group was selected to represent athletes?

WORD POWER

archetypes models

prevailed upon
persuaded

shirked avoided
responsibility

earmark to set aside
for a particular purpose

Those relatively few black athletes who do make it in the professional 12 ranks must be prevailed upon to play a significant role in the education of all of our young people, athlete and nonathlete alike. While some have done so, many others have shirked their social obligations: to earmark small percentages of their incomes for the United Negro College Fund; to appear on television for educational purposes rather than merely to sell sneakers; to let children know the message that becoming a lawyer, a teacher or a doctor does more good for our people than winning the Super Bowl; and to form productive liaisons with educators to help forge solutions to the many ills that beset the black community. These are merely a few modest proposals.

WORD POWER

emulate to imitate

A similar burden falls upon successful blacks in all walks of life. Each of 13 us must strive to make our young people understand the realities. Tell them to cheer Bo Jackson but to emulate novelist Toni Morrison or businessman

Reginald Lewis or historian John Hope Franklin or Spelman College president Johnetta Cole—the list is long.

Of course, society as a whole bears responsibility as well. Until colleges 14 stop using young blacks as cannon fodder in the big-business wars of so-called nonprofessional sports, until training a young black's mind becomes as important as training his or her body, we will continue to perpetuate a system akin to that of the Roman gladiators, sacrificing a class of people for the entertainment of the mob.

Thinking about the Reading

Teaching Tip
Remind students to answer all questions in complete sentences.

1. What do you think this essay's title means? According to Gates, what "delusions" do many young African Americans have?

2. Reread paragraph 10, where Gates explains why he sees African Americans' drive to succeed in sports as a problem. In your own words, summarize his argument.

*3. What does Gates think the schools should do to solve the problem he identifies? What does he think black athletes should do? What does he think other successful African Americans must do?

*4. *Cannon fodder* is a term that refers to soldiers sent into battle by superiors who know they are very likely to be injured or killed in combat. What do you think Gates means when he says that colleges use young African-American men as "cannon fodder" (paragraph 14)?

Writing Practice

Teaching Tip
If your students are writing essays, these prompts will work as essay topics. Otherwise, you can have students write paragraphs.

1. Imagine you are making a speech to a group of teenage boys. Try to explain the information in paragraph 6 in terms they can understand, and use this information to convince your audience how important it is for them to stay in school.

2. When you were a child, what did you want to be when you grew up? How did your goals change as you grew up? Why?

3. Young people's heroes are often celebrities in sports and the arts. What do young people admire about such celebrities? What do they envy? Do you think having such individuals as role models helps or hurts young people?

At the Heart of a Historic Movement

John Hartmire

Teaching Tip
This is a cause-and-effect essay.

Teaching Tip
Remind students to familiarize themselves with the end-of-essay questions before reading the essay.

As executive director of the National Farmworker Ministry, John Hartmire's father worked closely with Cesar Chavez to fight for social justice for farmworkers. However, his father's dedication to the cause meant that he was absent for most of Hartmire's childhood. In this essay, Hartmire discusses what it is like to make a personal sacrifice for a social cause.

When my friend's daughter asked me if I knew anything about the man 1 her school was named after, I had to admit that I did. I told her that in California there are at least twenty-six other schools, seventeen streets, seven parks, and ten scholarships named after Cesar Chavez. Not only that, I said, I once hit a ground ball through his legs during a softball game, and I watched his two dogs corner my sister's rabbit and, quite literally, scare it to death. I used to curse his name to the sun gods while I marched through one sweltering valley or another knowing my friends were at the beach staring at Carrie Carbajal and her newest bikini.

During those years I wasn't always sure of how I felt about the man, but 2 I did believe Cesar Chavez was larger than life. The impact he had on my family was at once enriching and debilitating. He was everywhere. Like smoke and cobwebs, he filled the corners of my family's life. We moved to California from New York in 1961 when my father was named executive director of the National Farmworker Ministry, and for the next thirty-plus years our lives were defined by Cesar and the United Farm Workers.

During those years my father was gone a lot, traveling with, or for, 3 Cesar. I "understood" because the struggle to organize farmworkers into a viable union was the work of a lifetime, and people would constantly tell me how much they admired what Dad was doing. Hearing it made me proud. It also made me lonely. He organized the clergy to stand up for the union, went to jail defying court injunctions, and was gone from our house for days on end, coming home, my mother likes to say, only for clean underwear. It was my father who fed the small piece of bread to Cesar ending his historic twenty-five-day fast in 1968. It's no wonder Dad missed my first Little League home run.

The experience of growing up in the heart of a historic movement has 4 long been the stuff of great discussions around our dinner table. The memories are both vibrant and difficult. There were times when Cesar and the union seemed to be more important to my father than I was, or my mother was, or my brothers and sister were. It is not an easy suspicion to grow up with, or to reconcile as an adult.

While my friends surfed, I was dragged to marches in the Coachella and 5 San Joaquin valleys. I was taken out of school to attend union meetings and rallies that interested me even less than geometry class. I spent time in supermarket parking lots reluctantly passing out leaflets and urging shoppers not to buy nonunion grapes and lettuce. I used to miss Sunday-afternoon NFL telecasts to canvass neighborhoods with my father. Since my dad wanted his family to be a part of his life, I marched and slept and ate and played with Cesar Chavez's kids. When we grew older his son, Paul, and I would drink beer together and wonder out loud how our lives would have been different had our fathers been plumbers or bus drivers.

But our fathers were fighting to do something that had never been done 6 before. Their battle to secure basic rights for migrant workers evolved into a moral struggle that captured the nation's attention. I saw it all, from the

WORD POWER
debilitate to take away strength

WORD POWER
viable able to survive

WORD POWER
orchestrate to arrange

WORD POWER
transcend to be
greater than; to go
beyond

union's grape strike in 1965, to the signing of the first contracts five years later, to the political power gained then lost because, for Cesar, running a union was never as natural as orchestrating a social movement.

My father and Cesar parted company four years before Chavez died in 7 1993. Chavez, sixty-six at the time of his death, father of eight, grandfather of twenty-seven, leader of thousands, a Hispanic icon who transcended race, left the world a better place than he found it. He did it with the help of a great many good people, and the sacrifice of their families, many of whom believed in his cause but didn't always understand what he was asking of, or taking from, them.

So as students here attend Cesar Chavez Elementary School, as families 8 picnic in a Sacramento park named after him and public employees opt to take off March 31 in honor of his birthday, I try to remember Cesar Chavez for what he was—a quiet man, the father of friends, a man intricately bound with my family—and not what he took from my childhood. Namely, my father. I still wrestle with the cost of my father's commitment, understanding that social change does not come without sacrifice. I just wonder if the price has to be so damn high.

Do I truly know Cesar Chavez? I suppose not. He was like a boat being 9 driven by some internal squall, a disturbance he himself didn't always understand, and that carried millions right along with him, some of us kicking and screaming.

Thinking about the Reading

Teaching Tip
Remind students to
answer all questions in
complete sentences.

1. When he was a child, why did Hartmire "curse [Cesar Chavez's] name to the sun gods" (paragraph 1)? Do you think he still feels bitterness about his childhood? If so, at whom is this bitterness directed?

2. In paragraph 2, Hartmire says that Chavez was "larger than life. The impact he had on my family was at once enriching and debilitating. He was everywhere." What does he mean?

*3. In paragraph 5, Hartmire says that he and Paul Chavez used to try to imagine how their lives might have been different if their fathers had been "plumbers or bus drivers." How do you think their lives would have been different?

4. How has Hartmire's opinion of Chavez changed over the years? Has his opinion of his father also changed?

Writing Practice

Teaching Tip
If your students are
writing essays, these
prompts will work as
essay topics. Otherwise,
you can have students
write paragraphs.

1. What historical or political figure was "larger than life" for your family? Write an essay explaining the impact that this person had on you.

2. Who is your greatest living hero? Write an essay about your hero's personal qualities and contributions to society. (If you like, you may write a recommendation for an award, addressing your remarks to the awards committee.)

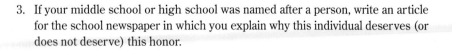

3. If your middle school or high school was named after a person, write an article for the school newspaper in which you explain why this individual deserves (or does not deserve) this honor.

The Little Pretzel Lady

Sara Price

For some children, adult responsibility comes early in life. Student writer Sara Price recounts her experience as a ten-year-old working a Saturday job with her brother. For three years, to help their financially strapped family, Sara and her brother sold pretzels in a local shopping center.

Teaching Tip
This is a narrative essay.

Teaching Tip
Remind students to familiarize themselves with the end-of-essay questions before reading the essay.

WORD POWER

persist to continue to do something despite setbacks

When I was ten years old, selling pretzels at the corner of a shopping 1 center was not my favorite weekend activity. Unfortunately, however, I had no alternative. My father had recently been injured on the job, and we had been experiencing severe financial difficulties. His disability payments and my mother's salary were not enough to support four children and my grandparents. When my parents could not pay our monthly mortgage, the bank threatened to take our house.

Knowing we had to find jobs to help, my older brother and I asked the 2 local soft pretzel dealer to give us work on Saturdays. At first he refused, saying we were too young. But we simply would not take no for an answer because our parents desperately needed financial help. When we persisted, the pretzel dealer agreed to let us start the next week. In return for his kindness, my brother and I agreed to work faithfully for the next three years.

On the first Saturday morning, my brother and I reported promptly to 3 our positions in front of the Cool-Rite appliance shop at the Academy Plaza shopping center. When Tom, our dealer, arrived with three hundred pretzels, he set up the stand and gave us instructions to sell each pretzel for a quarter, and five for a dollar. Then, Tom wished us luck and said he would be back later to pick up the table and the money. The arrangement with him was that we would get one-third of the total sales.

On that first Saturday, after selling our three hundred pretzels, my brother 4 and I earned ten dollars each. (We also received a two-dollar tip from a friendly man who bought fifteen pretzels.) Our first day was considered a good one because we sold out by 4 p.m. However, the days that followed were not always as smooth as the first. When the weather was bad, meaning rain or snow, sales decreased; there were times when we had to stay as late as 7 p.m. until the last pretzel was sold.

To my regular customers, I was the little pretzel lady. But to my class- 5 mates, I was the target of humiliation. My worst nightmare came true when they found out that I ran a pretzel stand. Many of the boys made fun of me by calling out nasty names and harassing me for free pretzels. It was extremely embarrassing to see them walk by and stare while I stood like a helpless beggar on the street. I came to dread weekends and hate the sight of pretzels. But I was determined not to give up because I had a family that needed support and a three-year promise to fulfill. With that in mind, I continued to work.

Although winter was the best season for sales, I especially disliked 6 standing in the teeth-chattering cold. I still remember that stinging feeling when the harsh wind blew against my cheeks. In order to survive the hours of shivering, I usually wore two or three pairs of socks and extra-thick clothing. Many times, I felt like a lonesome, leafless tree rooted to one spot and unable to escape from the bitter cold of winter.

The worst incident of my pretzel career occurred when I was selling 7 alone because my brother was sick. A pair of teenage boys came up to the stand, called me offensive names, and squirted mustard all over the pretzels. My instant reaction was total shock, and before I could do anything else, they quickly ran away. A few minutes later, I discarded the pretzels, desperately fighting back the tears. I felt helpless and angry because I could not understand their actions.

The three years seemed like forever, but finally they were over. Even 8 though selling pretzels on the street was the worst job I ever had, I was grateful for it. The money I earned each Saturday accumulated over the three years and helped my family. Selling pretzels also taught me many important values, such as responsibility, teamwork, independence, and appreciation for hard-earned money. Today, as I pass the pretzel vendors on my way to school, I think of a time not too long ago when I was the little pretzel lady.

Thinking about the Reading

1. What emotions did you experience as you read "The Little Pretzel Lady"? Which parts of the essay caused these emotions?

2. Children are often cruel to one another. What do you think caused the cruelty that Sara Price experienced?

3. Sara says that she sometimes felt like "a lonesome, leafless tree rooted to one spot and unable to escape from the bitter cold of winter" (paragraph 6). Explain how this image suits Sara's situation.

*4. Do you think that Sara's experience as a "pretzel lady" was more hurtful than beneficial to her? Give reasons to support your answer.

Writing Practice

1. Write about a time in your childhood when you felt different from others and vulnerable to teasing or cruelty by other children.

WORD POWER
offensive hurtful; disagreeable; unpleasant
accumulate to gather or pile up little by little

Teaching Tip
Remind students to answer all questions in complete sentences.

Teaching Tip
If your students are writing essays, these prompts will work as essay topics. Otherwise, you can have students write paragraphs.

2. Write about the "little pretzel lady" and her experiences from the point of view of a clerk in the Cool-Rite appliance shop who watches the two children sell pretzels every Saturday.

3. Write about an experience you had at work that made you like or dislike your job. Be sure to include details about the workplace, your job responsibilities, the other people involved in the situation, and any conversations you remember.

WORD POWER
woe sadness

The Dog Ate My Disk, and Other Tales of Woe

Carolyn Foster Segal

Teaching Tip
This is a classification essay.

Carolyn Foster Segal, assistant professor of English at Cedar Crest College in Pennsylvania, has heard practically every student excuse for handing in late papers. In this humorous essay, she divides student excuses into categories. This article appeared in *The Chronicle of Higher Education*, a periodical for college teachers.

WORD POWER
feline (noun) a member of the cat family; (adjective) catlike

Taped to the door of my office is a cartoon that features a cat explaining 1
to his feline teacher, "The dog ate my homework." It is intended as a gently humorous reminder to my students that I will not accept excuses for late work, and it, like the lengthy warning on my syllabus, has had absolutely no effect. With a show of energy and creativity that would be admirable if applied to the (missing) assignments in question, my students persist, week after week, semester after semester, year after year, in offering excuses about why their work is not ready. Those reasons fall into several broad categories: the family, the best friend, the evils of dorm life, the evils of technology, and the totally bizarre.

Teaching Tip
Remind students to familiarize themselves with the end-of-essay questions before reading the essay.

The Family The death of the grandfather/grandmother is, of course, 2
the grandmother of all excuses. What heartless teacher would dare to question a student's grief or veracity? What heartless student would lie, wishing death on a revered family member, just to avoid a deadline? Creative students may win extra extensions (and days off) with a little careful planning and fuller plot development, as in the sequence of "My grandfather/grandmother is sick"; "Now my grandfather/grandmother is in the hospital"; and finally, "We could all see it coming—my grandfather/grandmother is dead."

WORD POWER
veracity truthfulness

WORD POWER
conjure up to bring to mind

Another favorite excuse is "the family emergency," which (always) goes 3
like this: "There was an emergency at home, and I had to help my family." It's a lovely sentiment, one that conjures up images of Louisa May Alcott's little women rushing off with baskets of food and copies of *Pilgrim's Progress*, but I do not understand why anyone would turn to my most irresponsible students in times of trouble.

WORD POWER

adjunct an instructor at a college or university who is not a permanent staff member; any temporary employee

The Best Friend   This heartwarming concern for others extends   4
beyond the family to friends, as in, "My best friend was up all night and I had to (a) stay up with her in the dorm, (b) drive her to the hospital, or (c) drive to her college because (1) her boyfriend broke up with her, (2) she was throwing up blood [no one catches a cold anymore; everyone throws up blood], or (3) her grandfather/grandmother died."

At one private university where I worked as an adjunct, I heard an inter-   5
esting spin that incorporated the motifs of both best friend and dead relative: "My best friend's mother killed herself." One has to admire the cleverness here: A mysterious woman in the prime of her life has allegedly committed suicide, and no professor can prove otherwise! And I admit I was moved, until finally I had to point out to my students that it was amazing how the simple act of my assigning a topic for a paper seemed to drive large numbers of otherwise happy and healthy middle-aged women to their deaths. I was careful to make that point during an off week, during which no deaths were reported.

The Evils of Dorm Life   These stories are usually fairly predictable;   6
almost always feature the evil roommate or hallmate, with my student in the role of the innocent victim; and can be summed up as follows: My roommate, who is a horrible person, likes to party, and I, who am a good person, cannot concentrate on my work when he or she is partying. Variations include stories about the two people next door who were running around and crying loudly last night because (a) one of them had boyfriend/girlfriend problems; (b) one of them was throwing up blood; or (c) someone, somewhere, died. A friend of mine in graduate school had a student who claimed that his roommate attacked him with a hammer. That, in fact, was a true story; it came out in court when the bad roommate was tried for killing his grandfather.

The Evils of Technology   The computer age has revolutionized the   7
student story, inspiring almost as many new excuses as it has Internet businesses. Here are just a few electronically enhanced explanations:

● The computer wouldn't let me save my work.

● The printer wouldn't print.

● The printer wouldn't print this disk.

● The printer wouldn't give me time to proofread.

● The printer made a black line run through all my words, and I know you can't read this, but do you still want it, or wait, here, take my disk. File name? I don't know what you mean.

● I swear I attached it.

- It's my roommate's computer, and she usually helps me, but she had to go to the hospital because she was throwing up blood.

- I did write to the newsgroup, but all my messages came back to me.

- I just found out that all my other newsgroup messages came up under a different name. I just want you to know that its really me who wrote all those messages, you can tel which ones our mine because I didnt use the spelcheck! But it was yours truely :) Anyway, just in case you missed those messages or dont belief its my writting. I'll repeat what I sad: I thought the last movie we watched in clas was borring.

The Totally Bizarre   I call the first story "The Pennsylvania Chain 8 Saw Episode." A commuter student called to explain why she had missed my morning class. She had gotten up early so that she would be wide awake for class. Having a bit of extra time, she walked outside to see her neighbor, who was cutting some wood. She called out to him, and he waved back to her with the saw. Wouldn't you know it, the safety catch wasn't on or was broken, and the blade flew right out of the saw and across his lawn and over her fence and across her yard and severed a tendon in her right hand. So she was calling me from the hospital, where she was waiting for surgery. Luckily, she reassured me, she had remembered to bring her paper and a stamped envelope (in a plastic bag, to avoid bloodstains) along with her in the ambulance, and a nurse was mailing everything to me even as we spoke.

That wasn't her first absence. In fact, this student had missed most of 9 the class meetings, and I had already recommended that she withdraw from the course. Now I suggested again that it might be best if she dropped the class. I didn't harp on the absences (what if even some of this story were true?). I did mention that she would need time to recuperate and that making up so much missed work might be difficult. "Oh, no," she said, "I can't drop this course. I had been planning to go on to medical school and become a surgeon, but since I won't be able to operate because of my accident, I'll have to major in English, and this course is more important than ever to me." She did come to the next class, wearing—as evidence of her recent trauma—a bedraggled Ace bandage on her left hand.

You may be thinking that nothing could top that excuse, but in fact I 10 have one more story, provided by the same student, who sent me a letter to explain why her final assignment would be late. While recuperating from her surgery, she had begun corresponding on the Internet with a man who lived in Germany. After a one-week, whirlwind Web romance, they had agreed to meet in Rome, to rendezvous (her phrase) at the papal Easter Mass. Regrettably, the time of her flight made it impossible for her to attend

WORD POWER

harp on to repeat over and over again

WORD POWER

rendezvous (verb) to meet at a prearranged place and time; (noun) a prearranged meeting

class, but she trusted that I—just this once—would accept late work if the pope wrote a note.

Thinking about the Reading

Teaching Tip
Remind students to answer all questions in complete sentences.

1. What categories of excuses does Segal identify? Can you think of others she does not mention?

*2. **Sarcastic** remarks mean the opposite of what they say and are usually meant to mock or poke fun at someone or something. Where does Segal use sarcasm?

*3. Do you think this essay is funny? Do you find it offensive in any way? Explain.

4. Would you be interested in reading a serious essay on Segal's topic? Why or why not?

Writing Practice

Teaching Tip
If your students are writing essays, these prompts will work as essay topics. Otherwise, you can have students write paragraphs.

1. Write about the strangest excuse you have ever been given by someone for not doing something he or she was supposed to do. Explain the circumstances of this excuse in a humorous manner.

2. Discuss one of the following topics (or a similar topic of your own choice).

    ● Ways to turn down a date

    ● Types of unacceptable behavior by a child or pet

    ● Types of students at your school

3. Write a letter to Carolyn Foster Segal explaining why your English paper will be late. Admit that you have read her essay about various categories of student excuses, but insist that *your* excuse is true.

Take-Out Restaurant

Kimsohn Tang

In this essay, student writer Kimsohn Tang examines the life of her Uncle Meng, the owner of a Chinese take-out restaurant. As Kim describes the stresses and risks of this demanding job, she asks whether the money he makes is worth the problems that Uncle Meng faces.

Teaching Tip
This is an exemplification essay.

WORD POWER
profanity vulgar, abusive language

My Uncle Meng owns the New Phoenix Take-Out Restaurant at the corner of Main Street and Landfair Avenue in North Philadelphia, a dangerous place. Words of profanity and various kinds of graffiti are written on the wall outside his restaurant. On his windows are black bars just like those on the windows of prisons. Inside his take-out, bulletproof glass separates the customers' area from the workers' area. Every day, Uncle Meng works in his restaurant with his wife and a cook. He must prepare the food, carry it

WORD POWER

wholesaler a person
who sells large amounts
of merchandise to
stores or individuals,
who then resell it

marinate to let meat,
fish, or vegetables soak
in a sauce to make
them more flavorful or
tender

to the cooking area, take orders, run back and forth to get things, cook the food, and satisfy his customers. Although he earns a decent salary, his job not only takes him away from his family but is also stressful, hard, and dangerous.

Uncle Meng works long hours, from 11 a.m. to midnight. He is constantly working. Even before he opens the restaurant, he has to prepare the food by getting the raw food from the wholesaler, marinating and putting bread crumbs on fifty pounds of chicken, coloring rice, making soup, and carrying heavy pots and pans of food to the cooking area. After he opens the take-out, the customers come in, and now Uncle Meng has to take orders; cook the food; put the food in containers, place sodas, drinks, and food in bags; and hand the customers the bags through the little hole in the bullet-proof glass. Throughout the day and into the night, Uncle Meng continues to work. Even at midnight, after the take-out is closed, his work is not finished because he has to clean up the place.

Because of his long working hours, Uncle Meng has little time to spend with his family, especially his two children, a sixteen-year-old daughter and a thirteen-year-old son. Most of his time is spent in his restaurant. The only time he is free is on Sunday, when the restaurant is closed; this is the only time he and his family actually spend together. On regular school days, if he has time, Uncle Meng brings his children to and from school; otherwise, his sister or one of his other relatives takes them. When his children get home, they stay in their apartment above the take-out and only come down once in a while. Because Uncle Meng is so busy, he does not even have time to help his children with their homework.

Having little time to spend with his family is not the worst thing about his job; the stress from customers is even worse. Customers will yell out, "Man, where's my food? Why is it taking so long? I can't wait all day, you know!" Uncle Meng must have a lot of patience with the customers and not yell back at them. If the customers complain about getting different food from what they have ordered, Uncle Meng has to calm them down and make another dish for them. In addition, the customers are always asking for various things, such as more forks, spoons, or napkins, which is hard for Uncle Meng to handle. When a customer has a question pertaining to a dish on the menu, Uncle Meng also has to explain what ingredients are in the dish. He has to satisfy the customers and give them what they want, or else they will give him more trouble.

Uncle Meng's working conditions are the worst aspect of his job. Because the cooking area is always hot, Uncle Meng is never comfortable. The working area is also a dangerous place to be in; if he is not cautious while frying, he can get burns from the splattering oil. Lifting heavy pans while stir-frying, which requires a great amount of strength, causes Uncle Meng a lot of pain in his arms and wrists. In addition, because he has to stand on his feet

WORD POWER

pertaining to relating
to or having to do with

all day and run all over the take-out to get food, he often gets pains in his legs. By the time the take-out is closed, Uncle Meng is always exhausted.

Uncle Meng works long hard hours at difficult, physical labor. Although the take-out brings in a lot of money, it is a stressful and risky environment. Money is worthless compared to family and health. Even though money can buy many things, it cannot buy strong family relationships or good health. Working in a take-out, therefore, is not a desirable job. 6

Thinking about the Reading

Teaching Tip
Remind students to answer all questions in complete sentences.

1. According to Kimsohn Tang, how do job stresses harm Uncle Meng's health? Give examples.

2. In what ways is Uncle Meng's job dangerous? Consider how both the working conditions at the restaurant and the neighborhood in which it is located are dangerous.

3. How does Uncle Meng's job affect his family life? Give examples.

*4. Why do you think Kimsohn chose to write about her Uncle Meng? What does she think of her uncle's way of life?

Writing Practice

Teaching Tip
If your students are writing essays, these prompts will work as essay topics. Otherwise, you can have students write paragraphs.

1. Suppose that you are Uncle Meng's teenage son or daughter. Write a letter to your father telling him how you feel about the sacrifices he is making by working at the restaurant.

2. Have you ever worked at a job that was stressful or dangerous? Give examples of the stresses and dangers and the effect they had on you. If you have never held a job that fits this description, write about a friend's or relative's job.

3. Kimsohn states, "Money is worthless compared to family and health" (paragraph 6). Explain why you agree or disagree with this statement. Give examples from your own experience and observation of the world to support your position.

The Online Alternative
Marc Williams

As more and more schools offer online courses, students must think carefully about the advantages and disadvantages of enrolling in them. In the following essay, student writer Marc Williams compares and contrasts an online class and a traditional class.

Teaching Tip
This is a comparison-and-contrast essay.

1

Last semester, my friend Jason and I decided to sign up for a course called Twentieth-Century African-American Literature. We were both interested in the course's subject, and we thought we could study for exams together, share our notes, and maybe even buy just one set of books. When the course schedule came out, I realized I had a problem. The course was

Teaching Tip
Remind students to
familiarize themselves
with the end-of-essay
questions before reading
the essay.

WORD POWER
online connected to
the Internet
posted entered
electronically
log on to identify
oneself on a computer
by entering a username
and password

scheduled for Monday, Wednesday, and Friday at noon—a convenient time for Jason but impossible for me because I was working the lunch shift in the cafeteria. When I told my advisor my problem, she had an idea: she suggested that I take the course online. This seemed like a good idea, so I signed up. However, when Jason and I compared notes at the end of the semester, I realized that online learning was not for me.

In some ways, the two courses were a lot alike. For example, Jason and 2 I had the same teacher and the same writing assignments. We had to read the same short stories, plays, poems, and articles, as well as *Invisible Man*, a novel by Ralph Ellison. The course materials were posted on the course's Web site for both traditional and online students. And, of course, we would both take proctored exams (although mine would be scheduled in the campus testing center, not given in class). According to the course syllabus (also the same), our final grades would depend on the same thing: papers, exams, and class participation. Also, we both got three credits for the course. Despite these similarities, the two courses were very different from day one.

On the first day of his class, Jason met the instructor and the other stu- 3 dents taking the course. The students talked about other literature classes they had taken, works by African-American writers they had read, and their experiences with writing papers about literature. They also asked questions about the syllabus and the course materials. My introduction to the course was different. The instructor emailed me information about how the online course would work. She set up a bulletin board on Blackboard, and students in the class could introduce themselves there and tell why they were taking the course. (This bulletin board would stay up all term so we could talk informally about the class if we wanted to.) So, the first thing I did was log on and write a little bit about myself. Then, I read what other students had written. Although it was possible to chat with other students, I didn't want to take the time, and only a few students participated regularly.

As the semester continued, I realized that the two courses were run 4 very differently. In Jason's class, the instructor gave short lectures about various writers and works and provided historical background when necessary. She also answered questions as they came up and helped move the class discussion along. In my course, the instructor posted a lecture every week, along with a set of questions. Our assignment was to read the lecture material and email her our answers to the questions. Class "discussion" was also different. In Jason's class, students exchanged ideas orally. In my class, everything happened online. The teacher posted questions for online discussion, and then the students in the class would all log on at a prearranged time and have a discussion about the posted questions. We could also ask questions about the assigned readings during this time.

Contact with the instructor was also different. For Jason, contact was 5 whatever he wanted it to be. He could email the instructor, drop in or call during her office hours, or schedule an appointment. For online students, contact was more limited. Although we could request face-to-face conferences, this wasn't encouraged. So, I was limited to emailing and to phone calls during the two hours a week that were set aside for online students. When I needed face-to-face help with my papers, I went to the writing center.

The hardest thing for me to get used to was the lack of real interaction 6 with other students. Jason set up study groups with other students. In class, they watched and discussed a DVD of Alice Walker's short story "Everyday Use," acted out scenes from *A Raisin in the Sun*, read Yusef Komunyakaa's poetry out loud, and critiqued drafts of other students' papers. Some of these things were also possible in my online class, but it just wasn't the same. Arranging an online discussion with other students in real time was hard because of our different school and work schedules. We could watch films on our own, but we couldn't all discuss the film together right after we saw it. And I missed the chance to see other students' physical reactions and expressions and hear their voices.

At the end of the semester, when Jason and I talked about our classes, it 7 was easy for me to see the positive side of my online course. The most important advantage was convenience. Instead of having to attend classes during specific hours each week, I was able to log on whenever I had time. Still, I didn't feel I got as much out of my course as Jason got out of his. In regular classes, when I have something to say, I raise my hand and say it, and I get instant feedback from other students and from the instructor. In the online class, I usually had to wait to get an email reply to a posting. I also missed being able to drop by the instructor's office to talk about a problem. Most of all, I missed the chance to get to know other students in the class by working with them in study groups, collaborating with them on projects, or talking to them informally outside of class. For me, taking the online class was definitely worth it because this was the only way I could take the class at all. Even so, I don't think I'll do it again.

Thinking about the Reading

Teaching Tip
Remind students to answer all questions in complete sentences.

1. Where does Marc Williams discuss the *similarities* between online and traditional courses?

2. List the differences Marc identifies between online and traditional courses.

3. What advantages does Marc's online course have over Jason's more traditional course? What disadvantages does Marc identify?

*4. Can you think of advantages of online courses that Marc doesn't mention? Can you think of additional disadvantages?

Teaching Tip
If your students are writing essays, these prompts will work as essay topics. Otherwise, you can have students write paragraphs.

Writing Practice

1. Write an email to Marc's instructor suggesting ways to improve her online course.

2. Imagine that the writing course you are now taking were to be conducted online. How would it be different?

3. Interview a few students who have taken online courses, and write a summary of their views on the advantages and disadvantages of this kind of learning.

WORD POWER

transaction an exchange or transfer of goods, services, or money; an exchange of thoughts and feelings

The Transaction

William Zinsser

William Zinsser has written many articles and books on improving writing and study skills. He has also had a long career as a professional newspaper and magazine writer, drama and film critic, and author of nonfiction books on subjects ranging from jazz to baseball. This excerpt is from his book *On Writing Well: An Informal Guide to Writing Nonfiction.*

Teaching Tip
This is a comparison-and-contrast essay.

Teaching Tip
Remind students to familiarize themselves with the end-of-essay questions before reading the essay.

WORD POWER

vocation an occupation; regular employment

avocation a hobby or interest pursued for enjoyment rather than for money

arduous difficult and tiring

A school in Connecticut once held "a day devoted to the arts," and I was 1 asked if I would come and talk about writing as a vocation. When I arrived, I found that a second speaker had been invited—Dr. Brock (as I'll call him), a surgeon who had recently begun to write and had sold some stories to magazines. He was going to talk about writing as an avocation. That made us a panel, and we sat down to face a crowd of students, teachers, and parents, all eager to learn the secrets of our glamorous work.

Dr. Brock was dressed in a bright red jacket, looking vaguely bohemian, 2 as authors are supposed to look, and the first question went to him. What was it like to be a writer?

He said it was tremendous fun. Coming home from an arduous day at 3 the hospital, he would go straight to his yellow pad and write his tensions away. The words just flowed. It was easy. I then said that writing wasn't easy and it wasn't fun. It was hard and lonely, and the words seldom just flowed.

Next, Dr. Brock was asked if it was important to rewrite. Absolutely not, 4 he said. "Let it all hang out," he told us, and whatever form the sentences take will reflect the writer at his most natural. I then said that rewriting is the essence of writing. I pointed out that professional writers rewrite their sentences over and over and then rewrite what they have rewritten.

"What do you do on days when it isn't going well?" Dr. Brock was asked. 5 He said he just stopped writing and put the work aside for a day when it would go better. I then said that the professional writer must establish a daily schedule and stick to it. I said that writing is a craft, not an art, and that the man who runs away from his craft because he lacks inspiration is fooling himself. He is also going broke.

"What if you're feeling depressed or unhappy?" a student asked. "Won't 6 that affect your writing?"

Probably it will, Dr. Brock replied. Go fishing. Take a walk. Probably it 7 won't, I said. If your job is to write every day, you learn to do it like any other job.

A student asked if we found it useful to circulate in the literary world. 8 Dr. Brock said he was greatly enjoying his new life as a man of letters, and he told several stories of being taken to lunch by his publisher and his agent at Manhattan restaurants where writers and editors gather. I said that professional writers are solitary drudges who seldom see other writers.

"Do you put symbolism in your writing?" a student asked me. 9

"Not if I can help it," I replied. I have an unbroken record of missing the 10 deeper meaning in any story, play, or movie, and as for dance and mime, I have never had any idea of what is being conveyed.

"I *love* symbols!" Dr. Brock exclaimed, and he described with gusto the 11 joys of weaving them through his work.

So the morning went, and it was a revelation to all of us. At the end 12 Dr. Brock told me he was enormously interested in my answers—it had never occurred to him that writing could be hard. I told him I was just as interested in *his* answers—it had never occurred to me that writing could be easy. Maybe I should take up surgery on the side.

As for the students, anyone might think we left them bewildered. But in 13 fact we probably gave them a broader glimpse of the writing process than if only one of us had talked. For there isn't any "right" way to do such personal work. There are all kinds of writers and all kinds of methods, and any method that helps you to say what you want to say is the right method for you. Some people write by day, others by night. Some people need silence, others turn on the radio. Some write by hand, some by word processor, some by talking into a tape recorder. Some people write their first draft in one long burst and then revise; others can't write the second paragraph until they have fiddled endlessly with the first.

But all of them are vulnerable and all of them are tense. They are driven 14 by a compulsion to put some part of themselves on paper, and yet they don't just write what comes naturally. They sit down to commit an act of literature, and the self who emerges on paper is far stiffer than the person who sat down to write. The problem is to find the real man or woman behind all the tension.

Ultimately, the product that any writer has to sell is not the subject being 15 written about, but who he or she is. I often find myself reading with interest

WORD POWER

symbolism the use of a symbol (something that stands for something else) in a work of art or literature

gusto an enthusiasm; a lively enjoyment

about a topic I never thought would interest me—some scientific quest, perhaps. What holds me is the enthusiasm of the writer for his field. How was he drawn into it? What emotional baggage did he bring along? How did it change his life? It's not necessary to want to spend a year alone at Walden Pond[1] to become deeply involved with a writer who did.

This is the personal transaction that's at the heart of good nonfiction 16 writing. Out of it come two of the most important qualities that this book will go in search of: humanity and warmth. Good writing has an aliveness that keeps the reader reading from one paragraph to the next, and it's not a question of gimmicks to "personalize" the author. It's a question of using the English language in a way that will achieve the greatest strength and the least clutter.

Can such principles be taught? Maybe not. But most of them can be 17 learned.

Thinking about the Reading

Teaching Tip
Remind students to answer all questions in complete sentences.

1. Why do you think Zinsser chose to use an interview format to compare and contrast his own writing methods and experiences with those of Dr. Brock?

2. What is Zinsser's purpose in comparing his views on the writing process with those of Dr. Brock? In what ways does he suggest that his work and methods are superior to those of the doctor?

3. Zinsser claims that "rewriting is the essence of writing" (paragraph 4). Use your own experience to support or challenge this statement.

*4. Zinsser says that the writer's ability to draw the reader into his subject is the "personal transaction" (paragraph 16) or exchange between two people that makes writing come alive. Consider the essays in this chapter that you have read. Which of the topics did not really interest you until you were drawn in by the writer's personal view of the topic?

Writing Practice

Teaching Tip
If your students are writing essays, these prompts will work as essay topics. Otherwise, you can have students write paragraphs.

1. Suppose that you have been asked some of the same questions as Zinsser and Dr. Brock—but about your own experience as a college student. How would you respond? Be sure to include answers to the following questions: What is it like to be a student? What do you do when schoolwork or classes are not going well? Does being depressed or unhappy affect your performance in the classroom? How?

---

1. The place where Henry David Thoreau (1817–1862), an American writer, naturalist, and political activist, lived for two years in a cabin he built himself. He wrote about the experience in his most famous book, *Walden*.

2. In paragraph 13, Zinsser writes, "There are all kinds of writers and all kinds of methods." Describe the kind of writer you are. Do you find writing easy, as Dr. Brock does, or difficult, as Zinsser does? What methods do you use to come up with ideas or to get through a particularly difficult assignment? Do you use any of the methods that Zinsser describes in paragraph 13?

3. Zinsser claims that the most successful pieces of writing are produced when the writer really cares about his or her subject. Try to identify three or four topics that interest you—for example, a book, a sport, a famous person, a political opinion, or a religious belief. Try to explain why each of these topics interests you.

CULTURE AND CUSTOM

Tortillas

José Antonio Burciaga

José Antonio Burciaga was born in El Paso, Texas, in 1940. His Chicano identity is the main subject of his widely published poems, stories, and essays. In this essay, Burciaga explores his childhood memories—as well as the cultural significance—of tortillas. The thin, round griddle-cakes made of cornmeal are a staple of Mexican cooking.

Teaching Tip
This is a definition essay.

My earliest memory of *tortillas* is my *Mamá* telling me not to play with 1 them. I had bitten eyeholes in one and was wearing it as a mask at the dinner table.

Teaching Tip
Remind students to familiarize themselves with the end-of-essay questions before reading the essay.

As a child, I also used *tortillas* as hand warmers on cold days, and my 2 family claims that I owe my career as an artist to my early experiments with *tortillas*. According to them, my clowning around helped me develop a strong artistic foundation. I'm not so sure, though. Sometimes I wore a *tortilla* on my head, like a *yarmulke*, and yet I never had any great urge to convert from Catholicism to Judaism. But who knows? They may be right.

WORD POWER
maize corn
abscond to leave quickly and hide

For Mexicans over the centuries, the *tortilla* has served as the spoon 3 and the fork, the plate and the napkin. *Tortillas* originated before the Mayan civilizations, perhaps predating Europe's wheat bread. According to Mayan mythology, the great god Quetzalcoatl, realizing that the red ants knew the secret of using maize as food, transformed himself into a black ant, infiltrated the colony of red ants, and absconded with a grain of corn. (Is it any wonder that to this day, black ants and red ants do not get along?) Quetzalcoatl then put maize on the lips of the first man and woman, Oxomoco and

Cipactonal, so that they would become strong. Maize festivals are still celebrated by many Indian cultures of the Americas.

When I was growing up in El Paso, *tortillas* were part of my daily life. I used to visit a *tortilla* factory in an ancient adobe building near the open *mercado* in Ciudad Juárez. As I approached, I could hear the rhythmic slapping of the *masa* as the skilled vendors outside the factory formed it into balls and patted them into perfectly round corn cakes between the palms of their hands. The wonderful aroma and the speed with which the women counted so many dozens of *tortillas* out of warm wicker baskets still linger in my mind. Watching them at work convinced me that the most handsome and *deliciosas tortillas* are handmade. Although machines are faster, they can never adequately replace generation-to-generation experience. There's no place in the factory assembly line for the tender slaps that give each *tortilla* character. The best thing that can be said about mass-producing *tortillas* is that it makes it possible for many people to enjoy them.

In the *mercado* where my mother shopped, we frequently bought *taquitos de nopalitos*, small tacos filled with diced cactus, onions, tomatoes, and *jalapeños*. Our friend Don Toribio showed us how to make delicious, crunchy *taquitos* with dried, salted pumpkin seeds. When you had no money for the filling, a poor man's *taco* could be made by placing a warm *tortilla* on the left palm, applying a sprinkle of salt, then rolling the *tortilla* up quickly with the fingertips of the right hand. My own kids put peanut butter and jelly on *tortillas*, which I think is truly bicultural. And speaking of fast foods for kids, nothing beats a *quesadilla*, a *tortilla* grilled-cheese sandwich.

Depending on what you intend to use them for, *tortillas* may be made in various ways. Even a run-of-the-mill *tortilla* is more than a flat corn cake. A skillfully cooked homemade *tortilla* has a bottom and a top; the top skin forms a pocket in which you put the filling that folds your *tortilla* into a taco. Paper-thin *tortillas* are used specifically for *flautas*, a type of taco that is filled, rolled, and then fried until crisp. The name *flauta* means *flute*, which probably refers to the Mayan bamboo flute; however, the only sound that comes from an edible *flauta* is a delicious crunch that is music to the palate. In México *flautas* are sometimes made as long as two feet and then cut into manageable segments. The opposite of *flautas* is *gorditas*, meaning *little fat ones*. These are very thick small *tortillas*.

The versatility of *tortillas* and corn does not end here. Besides being tasty and nourishing, they have spiritual and artistic qualities as well. The Tarahumara Indians of Chihuahua, for example, concocted a corn-based beer called *tesgüino*, which their descendants still make today. And everyone has read about the woman in New Mexico who was cooking her husband a *tortilla* one morning when the image of Jesus Christ miraculously appeared on it. Before they knew what was happening, the man's breakfast had become a local shrine.

WORD POWER
versatility ability to serve many purposes well
concocted mixed ingredients together to create something new

Then there is *tortilla* art. Various Chicano artists throughout the South- 8
west have, when short of materials or just in a whimsical mood, used a dry
tortilla as a small, round canvas. And a few years back, at the height of the
Chicano movement, a priest in Arizona got into trouble with the Church
after he was discovered celebrating mass using a *tortilla* as the host. All of
which only goes to show that while the *tortilla* may be a lowly corn cake,
when the necessity arises, it can reach unexpected distinction.

Thinking about the Reading

Teaching Tip
Remind students to
answer all questions in
complete sentences.

1. In one sentence, define *tortilla*.

2. List some of the uses for tortillas that Burciaga identifies.

3. What exactly does the tortilla mean to Burciaga? Why are tortillas so important
   to him?

*4. What food in your culture represents for you what the tortilla represents for
   Burciaga?

Writing Practice

Teaching Tip
If your students are
writing essays, these
prompts will work as
essay topics. Otherwise,
you can have students
write paragraphs.

1. Write about another food that you think is as useful as tortillas are. Use your
   imagination to identify as many unusual uses for this food as you can.

2. Write about the foods that you consider to be typically American. Define each
   food, and explain what makes it "American."

3. Imagine you have met someone who knows nothing about your family's culture.
   Explain the different ethnic foods eaten in your household. Include information
   about when and where these foods are eaten and why they are important to your
   family.

Emil's Big Chance
Leaves Me Uneasy

Tricia Capistrano

In this essay Tricia Capistrano tells about taking her son to the Philippines
to audition for commercials. Although she hopes that her light-skinned son's
media success might help to pay for his college tuition later on, she is critical
of the commercials. Capistrano believes that the commercials' exclusive use
of light-skinned actors reinforces racism and self-hatred.

Teaching Tip
This is a narrative essay.

Brad Pitt and Angelina Jolie may have the most popular baby in the 1
world right now, but I do not envy them. I had my taste of celebrity when I
took my infant son on a trip to the Philippines two years ago. I walked away
from him for a moment at a baby-goods store in Manila and when I returned,

WORD POWER
ogling staring at

Teaching Tip
Remind students to familiarize themselves with the end-of-essay questions before reading the essay.

he was surrounded by four women in their 20s who were ogling him. "He is so cute!" they said. "So fair-skinned!" Whether we were in the mall or at church, people would gather around to look at his face.

My son is mestizo, of mixed race. My husband is Caucasian with ancestors from Sweden and Slovakia. I am a brown-skinned woman from the Philippines, where many people I know have a fascination with the lighter skinned—probably because our islands were invaded so many times by whites who tried to convince us that they were better and more beautiful than us. We were under Spain's rule for nearly 400 years, the United States' for almost 50. As a result, skin-whitening products fly off the pharmacy shelves.

"Any plans to move back here?" my relatives ask when I visit.

"I'll send Emil when he is a teenager so he can become a matinee idol and fund our retirement," I joke. Most of the country's famous actors are of mixed race, and the teen actors who are on their way up don't have to be talented, just fair-skinned and preferably of Spanish, American or Chinese descent.

I started to reconsider my response several months ago after my husband and I read that by the time our son goes to college in 16 years, his education will cost about $500,000. When we visited my parents last January, I asked my friends in the advertising industry if I could bring my son by their offices to take some test shots. I wondered if he could land a commercial for diapers, cereal or maybe ice cream.

By the time I got the number of an agent, I had started to second-guess my idea. I realized that I was going to be part of the system that can sometimes make us dark-skinned people believe that we are inferior. I do not want Filipino children who look like me to feel bad about themselves. When I was a kid, my grandmother would get upset whenever I told her that I'd be spending the afternoon swimming in my cousin's pool, because it meant that my skin would get darker than it already was. My mom, whose nose I acquired, has one of the widest among her brothers and sisters. She taught me to pinch the bridge daily so that the arch would be higher, like my cousins. Most of her girlfriends got blond highlights and nose jobs as soon as they received their first paychecks, almost as a rite of passage.

As a teenager, I tried to hang out with the mestizas, because I wanted to be popular like them. It was only when I was 22 years old and moved to New York, where people of different colors, beliefs and sexual orientations are embraced, that I learned to appreciate my brown skin, wide nose, straight, black hair and five-foot stature. Because of the self-confidence I saw in the people I met, I found everyone—in the subway, on the street, in restaurants— beautiful.

WORD POWER
second-guess to reconsider a decision

When some of my friends in Manila express disappointment that their   8
children are not as light-skinned as Emil, I tell them it doesn't matter. And
for a long time, I've been content with my decision to scrap my plans for Emil
to be on the airwaves. I felt I was doing my share for my brown brothers and
sisters.

Then, on one of the first warm days this spring, Emil and I went to the   9
playground with our half-Irish, half-Polish neighbor, Julia, and her son.
While we were watching the kids play, I joked that I was going to send Emil
to the Philippines to be on TV. "Oh, that would be great!" she said earnestly.
She told me that as a little girl she had been in a series of Kodak commercials in the 1970s, ads I remember seeing during episodes of "Three's Company." Julia's parents were working class, so it was the only way they could
afford to pay for her college education.

Once again, I'm tempted to call that agent. After all, I am sure other fair-   10
skinned children are being chosen to appear in Philippine commercials even
as I write this. I know my boycott is just an anecdote in the world's bigger
drama. The real stage is in my decolonized mind. If my son ever lands a part
on TV because of his color, do I want to be the one who has cast him?

Thinking about the Reading

1. Capistrano faces a **dilemma**, a choice between equally undesirable options. What
   does she see as her options? What arguments does she offer for each option?

2. Why does Capistrano's son attract so much attention in Manila? How does she
   account for his appeal?

3. In paragraphs 6 and 7, Capistrano remembers some of her own childhood experiences. How do you think these experiences might explain the decision she
   finally makes about auditioning her son?

*4. What do you think Capistrano should do? Why?

Writing Practice

1. Write an editorial for a college newspaper in the Philippines. In your editorial,
   argue that Capistrano owes it to her fellow Filipinos not to let her son appear on
   TV commercials.

2. Write about a time when you faced a dilemma. What two options did you have?
   Which did you choose, and why? Do you regard this decision as the right one?

3. Do you think the people you see in television commercials look like the people
   you see every day? How are they like your relatives, friends, and neighbors?
   How are they different? Do you think advertisers should select actors who look
   more like "real people"? Why or why not?

Orange Crush
Yiyun Li

At age twenty-four, Yiyun Li moved from Beijing, China, to the United States to study biology. Before long, however, she enrolled in the Iowa Writers' Workshop, where she wrote a collection of stories, *A Thousand Years of Good Prayers*. In the following article, she recalls her childhood desire for a trendy Western drink that her family in China could not afford.

Teaching Tip
This is a narrative essay.

Teaching Tip
Remind students to familiarize themselves with the end-of-essay questions before reading the essay.

WORD POWER
provision something that is supplied
assess to measure
induce to cause, bring about

During the winter in Beijing, where I grew up, we always had orange and tangerine peels drying on our heater. Oranges were not cheap. My father, who believed that thrift was one of the best virtues, saved the dried peels in a jar; when we had a cough or cold, he would boil them until the water took on a bitter taste and a pale yellow cast, like the color of water drizzling out of a rusty faucet. It was the best cure for colds, he insisted.

I did not know then that I would do the same for my own children, preferring nature's provision over those orange- and pink- and purple-colored medicines. I just felt ashamed, especially when he packed it in my lunch for the annual field trip, where other children brought colorful flavored fruit drinks—made with "chemicals," my father insisted.

The year I turned 16, a new product caught my eye. Fruit Treasure, as Tang was named for the Chinese market, instantly won everyone's heart. Imagine real oranges condensed into a fine powder! Equally seductive was the TV commercial, which gave us a glimpse of a life that most families, including mine, could hardly afford. The kitchen was spacious and brightly lighted, whereas ours was a small cube—but at least we had one; half the people we knew cooked in the hallways of their apartment buildings, where every family's dinner was on display and their financial status assessed by the number of meals with meat they ate every week. The family on TV was beautiful, all three of them with healthy complexions and toothy, carefree smiles (the young parents I saw on my bus ride to school were those who had to leave at 6 or even earlier in the morning for the two-hour commute and who had to carry their children, half-asleep and often screaming, with them because the only child care they could afford was that provided by their employers).

The drink itself, steaming hot in an expensive-looking mug that was held between the child's mittened hands, was a vivid orange. The mother talked to the audience as if she were our best friend: "During the cold winter, we need to pay more attention to the health of our family," she said. "That's why I give my husband and my child hot Fruit Treasure for extra warmth and vitamins." The drink's temperature was the only Chinese aspect of the commercial; iced drinks were considered unhealthful and believed to induce stomach disease.

As if the images were not persuasive enough, near the end of the ad an 5 authoritative voice informed us that Tang was the only fruit drink used by NASA for its astronauts—the exact information my father needed to prove his theory that all orange-flavored drinks other than our orange-peel water were made of suspicious chemicals.

Until this point, all commercials were short and boring, with catchy 6 phrases like "Our Product Is Loved by People Around the World" flashing on screen. The Tang ad was a revolution in itself: the lifestyle it repre-sented—a more healthful and richer one, a Western luxury—was just start-ing to become legitimate in China as it was beginning to embrace the West and its capitalism.

Even though Tang was the most expensive fruit drink available, its sales 7 soared. A simple bottle cost 17 yuan, a month's worth of lunch money. A boxed set of two became a status hostess gift. Even the sturdy glass con-tainers that the powder came in were coveted. People used them as tea mugs, the orange label still on, a sign that you could afford the modern American drink. Even my mother had an empty Tang bottle with a snug orange nylon net over it, a present from one of her fellow schoolteachers. She carried it from the office to the classroom and back again as if our fam-ily had also consumed a full bottle.

The truth was, our family had never tasted Tang. Just think of how many 8 oranges we could buy with the money spent on a bottle, my father reasoned. His resistance sent me into a long adolescent melancholy. I was ashamed by our lack of style and our life, with its taste of orange-peel water. I could not wait until I grew up and could have my own Tang-filled life.

To add to my agony, our neighbor's son brought over his first girlfriend, 9 for whom he had just bought a bottle of Tang. He was five years older and a college sophomore; we had nothing in common and had not spoken more than 10 sentences. But this didn't stop me from having a painful crush on him. The beautiful girlfriend opened the Tang in our flat and insisted that we all try it. When it was my turn to scoop some into a glass of water, the fine orange powder almost choked me to tears. It was the first time I had drunk Tang, and the taste was not like real oranges but stronger, as if it were made of the essence of all the oranges I had ever eaten. This would be the love I would seek, a boy unlike my father, a boy who would not blink to buy a bottle of Tang for me. I looked at the beautiful girlfriend and wished to replace her.

My agony and jealousy did not last long, however. Two months later the 10 beautiful girlfriend left the boy for an older and richer man. Soon after, the boy's mother came to visit and was still outraged about the Tang. "What a waste of money on someone who didn't become his wife!" she said.

WORD POWER

covet to desire something that belongs to someone else

melancholy sadness, depression

"That's how it goes with young people," my mother said. "Once he has a 11 wife, he'll have a better brain and won't throw his money away."

"True. He's just like his father. When he courted me, he once invited me 12 to an expensive restaurant and ordered two fish for me. After we were married, he wouldn't even allow two fish for the whole family for one meal!"

That was the end of my desire for a Tangy life. I realized that every 13 dream ended with this bland, ordinary existence, where a prince would one day become a man who boiled orange peels for his family. I had not thought about the boy much until I moved to America 10 years later and discovered Tang in a grocery store. It was just how I remembered it—fine powder in a sturdy bottle—but its glamour had lost its gloss because, alas, it was neither expensive nor trendy. To think that all the dreams of my youth were once contained in this commercial drink! I picked up a bottle and then returned it to the shelf.

Thinking about the Reading

Teaching Tip
Remind students to answer all questions in complete sentences.

1. What does Tang represent for Li and for her family and friends? Why do you think they find it so appealing?

2. The drink Li discusses, called Tang in the United States, is called Fruit Treasure in China. Why? What might these two different names suggest to consumers?

*3. What products do you think hold the same fascination for children today that Tang held for Li? Why?

4. What does Li learn from her family's experiences with Tang?

Writing Practice

Teaching Tip
If your students are writing essays, these prompts will work as essay topics. Otherwise, you can have students write paragraphs.

1. Write about a food that was considered a luxury in your family when you were growing up. Tell about some of the occasions on which your family ate this special food.

2. In paragraphs 3 through 6, Li discusses the TV commercials for Tang that were shown in China. Think about commercials you have seen that make ordinary products seem desirable, and write about how these commercials persuade consumers to buy the products.

3. Part of the appeal of Tang to Li was the fact that it was "exotic" and foreign. What products from other countries have this kind of appeal for you? Why do you think these products are more appealing than familiar American products?

Boris Kosachev, Russian Pianist

Danielle McLarin

Growing up in a musical family in St. Paul, Minnesota, student writer Danielle McLarin learned to play the piano at a young age. In the following essay, she describes her Russian piano teacher, whose appearance and manners made a strong impression on her.

Teaching Tip
This is a descriptive essay.

Teaching Tip
Remind students to familiarize themselves with the end-of-essay questions before reading the essay.

WORD POWER
intricately elaborately

WORD POWER
torso the human body without the head, arms, and legs

1   As a daughter of professional musicians, I was encouraged by my parents at an early age to develop my musical talents. After learning the basics with my mother, I began taking lessons with a professional: Boris Kosachev, Russian pianist. While taking lessons with him, I always found Mr. Kosachev unfairly strict and rigid, but now I understand what it was that motivated him.

2   At first glance, Mr. Kosachev looked like an ordinary little old man: he was nearly eighty years old when I took lessons with him, and he was very small even from the perspective of a nine-year-old. He was probably about five foot four, but his miniature features made him appear almost childlike. His small black eyes were almost hidden by his eyelids, and small spectacles were mounted on his sharply lined nose. His ears, which stuck out slightly from the sides of his head, were equally small and as intricately shaped as the petal lines of a budding rose. His teeth were almost always hidden — except for the rare occasions when he would smile a broad, genuine smile and the top row of tiny teeth, pointed and rigid, appeared stretched in a small row and divided in the center. I always knew he was truly pleased when I could see the bottom row of teeth, lined up like old gravestones falling in front of one another.

3   His mustache was thick and white, carefully trimmed to the corners of his mouth. In contrast, his eyebrows were unusually thin, with only a few fine white hairs. The hair on his head, however, was as thick as his mustache, and it flowed from his head in thick waves that stood outward from his scalp as if electronically charged. His hair, like his mustache, was white, with a few black strands serving as reminders of his long-ago youth.

4   By the time I knew Mr. Kosachev, the skin on his cheeks and under his chin drooped from his face in pale wrinkled layers. The skin on his hands and fingers, however, was tight and thin, making every bone and vein visible as he maneuvered his hands all over the keyboard. Though they were not large, his hands seemed big because of his unusually long, thin fingers.

5   In the summer, when he wore short sleeves, I noticed how strong and muscular his arms seemed. His torso was thin, but over the years he began to develop a slight belly, possibly because of his strict pianist diet: "You must eat more Stroganoff. The mushrooms and the meat; they are what good pianists eat. Good physique is good playing." His legs were short and thin,

WORD POWER

hover to hang
suspended above
something

***forte, crescendo,
rubato*** musical terms
meaning loud and
forceful; a gradual
increase in volume or
intensity; and flexible
rhythm

but that did not stop him from leaping quickly to the piano when he heard
something he didn't like.

During our lessons, he would stand over my shoulder, hovering over me   6
as I played each note, yelling commands in broken English (and sometimes
resorting to Russian curses). Often, however, after I had polished a piece, he
would sit behind me in a state of deep meditation with his hands pressed
together, his fingers pointing upward to support his chin, his right leg
crossed over his left. His eyes remained closed, and they wrinkled slightly
only when I would arrive at the *forte* at the end of a *crescendo* a beat too soon
or overdramatize the *rubato* of a phrase. Sometimes he would compliment
me on my work—"Ah, you have done much work on this section!"—but
most of these compliments were inevitably followed by criticism: "This is
falling apart, what is these notes, you play them wrong."

For most of my time with Mr. Kosachev, I knew little of his life and   7
career. It was not until my last year of study with him, when I was in high
school, that I learned more about his experiences as a pianist. Until his early
twenties, he lived in Russia, where he studied piano at the Moscow Conser-
vatory, but he was less successful than most Russian pianists of his age.
After winning some small prizes in Russian competitions, as well as some in
Europe, he gave up his performing career and moved to the United States in
hopes of having a more successful career. Unfortunately, although on a few
occasions he was able to play with famous orchestras, he found little success. Eventually, he decided it would be best to earn his living as a piano
teacher.

WORD POWER

rigorous harsh; precise

As I learned more about the rigorous training of the Russian school and   8
the competitiveness of piano performance, I began to understand Mr. Kosachev's harshness and his high expectations for me. Many times he would
say to me, "I only ask you to practice two hours a day. In Russia, I was six
years old, and I practice two hours a day. When I was your age, I practice all
day after school. Ah, the American life is no good for pianist." Still, it was not
until years afterward that I understood his goals for me and for his other students: he wanted us to live up to our potential as artists, and maybe one day
to become better pianists than he was and enjoy the prestige that he had
dreamed of for himself. For this reason, he held true to the Russian music
tradition and work ethic—even in America.

Thinking about the Reading

Teaching Tip
Remind students to
answer all questions in
complete sentences.

1. What are Mr. Kosachev's most obvious physical characteristics? In one sentence, describe what he looks like.

2. Apart from his physical appearance, what are Mr. Kosachev's most striking traits?

*3. Do you think Danielle should have described herself? The piano? The room in
   which she had her lessons with Mr. Kosachev? Why or why not?

Teaching Tip
If your students are
writing essays, these
prompts will work as
essay topics. Otherwise,
you can have students
write paragraphs.

*4. Do you think Danielle liked Mr. Kosachev? Admired him? Feared him? What is *your* opinion of the man as she describes him?

Writing Practice

1. Write a description of someone you consider to be eccentric. Include specific details that show readers what the person looks like as well as examples of his or her words and actions.

2. Describe a place where you learned something important: a skill, a lesson, or an idea.

3. Describe the setting of a song that has special meaning for you.

WORD POWER
eccentric behaving in
an odd or unusual way

LIFE AND TIMES

America, Stand Up for Justice and Decency

Macarena Hernández

Born in Texas to migrant Mexican workers, Macarena Hernández is an editorial columnist for the *Dallas Morning News*. In this article, she reports on the dangers that undocumented immigrants often face. She also suggests changes to help reduce this kind of violence and suffering.

Teaching Tip
This is an argument
essay.

On the last night of September, while they slept after a long day of work 1 in the fields, six men were beaten to death with aluminum bats. One was shot in the head. Among the victims, a father and son killed in the same battered trailer.

The killers demanded money as they broke their bones. 2

Teaching Tip
Remind students to
familiarize themselves
with the end-of-essay
questions before reading
the essay.

The victims were all Mexican farm workers living in rundown trailer 3 parks spread across two counties in southern Georgia. They had earned the money the killers were after by sweating their days on cotton and peanut farms or building chicken coops—the kind of jobs you couldn't pay Americans enough to do.

In a few hours, the killers hit four trailers. In one, they raped a woman 4 and shot her husband in the head, traumatizing their three small children, who were present. In others, they left at least a half-dozen men wounded. Some are still in the hospital with shattered bones, including broken wrists from trying to protect their faces from the bats.

WORD POWER
reverberated had a
prolonged or continuing
effect

The news of the killings in Georgia reverberated outside Tift and Colquitt 5 counties, but it didn't cling to national headlines like you would expect with such a bloodbath. Two weeks later, residents are still afraid the attackers will come back, even though the Georgia Bureau of Investigation has arrested six suspects and charged them with the slayings.

Across the country, assaults on immigrants are common and happen at a much higher rate than reported. Two years ago in Grand Prairie, a pushcart ice cream vendor was shot to death and robbed. Seven months later, another one met the same fate in West Oak Cliff. In March, at a far north Dallas apartment complex, two thieves raped and killed a 20-year-old woman. They slit her husband's throat. 6

In Dallas, attacks against immigrants are one reason individual robberies have gone up in the last five years. Authorities call undocumented immigrants "ready-made victims." Without proper documentation to open bank accounts, many resort to stashing their sweat-soaked earnings under mattresses, in kitchen cabinets, in their socks or boots. If they are robbed, many don't call police for fear of deportation or because, back home, cops aren't trusted, anyway. 7

Some solutions are simple and concrete, such as making it easier for immigrants to establish bank accounts. Wells Fargo and Bank of America are among the banks that require only a Mexican consulate–issued ID card to open an account; others require documentation many immigrants lack. If there was ever a reason for adopting the more lenient policy, this is it. 8

More globally, horrors like these demand that a nation descended from immigrants take a hard look at the ways we think and speak about these most recent arrivals. 9

When Paul Johnson, the mayor of Tifton, where three of the four attacks took place, responded by flying the Mexican flag at City Hall, some residents complained. "I did that as an expression of sorrow for the Hispanic community," he told reporters. "For those who were offended, I apologize, but I think it was the right thing to do." 10

Were the complainers angrier about the red, white, and green Mexican flag fluttering in the Georgia air than they were about the horrific murders? Do they watch Fox's *The O'Reilly Factor*, where the anchor and the callers constantly point to the southern border as the birth of all America's ills? (Sample comment: "Each one of those people is a biological weapon.") 11

It is one thing to want to secure the borders and another to preach hate, to talk of human beings as ailments. Taken literally, such rhetoric gives criminals like those in southern Georgia license to kill; it gives others permission to look the other way. In this heightened anti-immigrant climate, what Mr. Johnson did was not only a welcome gesture, but a brave one, too. 12

There are those who will want to gloss over the deaths of these six men because they are "criminals" and "lawbreakers," in this country illegally. But regardless of where you stand on the immigration reform debate, you can't stand for the senseless death of the vulnerable. 13

WORD POWER
pushcart a light cart pushed by hand

WORD POWER
lenient not harsh or strict

WORD POWER
ailment an illness
rhetoric elaborate, insincere, or pretentious language
gloss over to hide the true nature of something
vulnerable susceptible to physical or emotional injury

We should all be outraged. We must demand justice. Or else the real 14 criminals here will win.

Thinking about the Reading

Teaching Tip
Remind students to answer all questions in complete sentences.

1. What specific events inspired Hernández to write this article? Why do you think she wrote it?

*2. What other events does Hernández mention? How are they like the events that occurred in the trailer parks in Georgia?

3. According to Hernández, "Authorities call undocumented immigrants 'ready-made victims'" (paragraph 7). Why? What solution does she suggest for this problem?

4. How does Hernández believe the nation should respond to the incidents she discusses?

Writing Practice

Teaching Tip
If your students are writing essays, these prompts will work as essay topics. Otherwise, you can have students write paragraphs.

1. Write a letter to Paul Johnson, the mayor of Tifton, telling him why you agree or disagree with his decision to fly the Mexican flag at City Hall.

2. What more, if anything, do you think needs to be done to "secure the border" between the United States and Mexico?

3. In addition to Hernández's suggestion in paragraph 8, what do you think can be done to protect undocumented immigrants from crimes like the ones she describes?

Before Air Conditioning

Arthur Miller

Teaching Tip
This is a descriptive essay.

The late Pulitzer Prize–winner Arthur Miller is considered one of America's greatest playwrights. His dramas *Death of a Salesman*, *All My Sons*, and *The Crucible* are classics of the modern theater. In the following essay, Miller recalls his life in New York City in the days before air conditioning became common.

Teaching Tip
Remind students to familiarize themselves with the end-of-essay questions before reading the essay.

Exactly what year it was I can no longer recall—probably 1927 or '28— 1 there was an extraordinarily hot September, which hung on even after school had started and we were back from our Rockaway Beach bungalow. Every window in New York was open, and on the streets venders manning little carts chopped ice and sprinkled colored sugar over mounds of it for a couple of pennies. We kids would jump onto the back steps of the slow-moving, horse-drawn ice wagons and steal a chip or two; the ice smelled vaguely of manure but cooled palm and tongue.

WORD POWER
bourgeois middle-class

People on West 110th Street, where I lived, were a little too bourgeois to 2 sit out on their fire escapes, but around the corner on 111th and farther uptown mattresses were put out as night fell, and whole families lay on those iron balconies in their underwear.

Even through the nights, the pall of heat never broke. With a couple of other kids, I would go across 110th to the park and walk among the hundreds of people, singles and families, who slept on the grass, next to their big alarm clocks, which set up a mild cacophony of the seconds passing, one clock's ticks syncopating with another's. Babies cried in the darkness, men's deep voices murmured, and a woman let out an occasional high laugh beside the lake. I can recall only white people spread out on the grass; Harlem began above 116th Street then. 3

Later on, in the Depression thirties, the summers seemed even hotter. Out West, it was the time of the red sun and the dust storms, when whole desiccated farms blew away and sent the Okies,[1] whom Steinbeck immortalized, out on their desperate treks toward the Pacific. My father had a small coat factory on Thirty-ninth Street then, with about a dozen men working sewing machines. Just to watch them handling thick woolen winter coats in that heat was, for me, a torture. The cutters were on piecework, paid by the number of seams they finished, so their lunch break was short—fifteen or twenty minutes. They brought their own food: bunches of radishes, a tomato perhaps, cucumbers, and a jar of thick sour cream, which went into a bowl they kept under the machines. A small loaf of pumpernickel also materialized, which they tore apart and used as a spoon to scoop up the cream and vegetables. 4

The men sweated a lot in those lofts, and I remember one worker who had a peculiar way of dripping. He was a tiny fellow, who disdained scissors, and, at the end of a seam, always bit off the thread instead of cutting it, so that inch-long strands stuck to his lower lip, and by the end of the day he had a multicolored beard. His sweat poured onto those thread ends and dripped down onto the cloth, which he was constantly blotting with a rag. 5

Given the heat, people smelled, of course, but some smelled a lot worse than others. One cutter in my father's shop was a horse in this respect, and my father, who normally had no sense of smell—no one understood why—claimed that he could smell this man and would address him only from a distance. In order to make as much money as possible, this fellow would start work at half past five in the morning and continue until midnight. He owned Bronx apartment houses and land in Florida and Jersey, and seemed half mad with greed. He had a powerful physique, a very straight spine, a tangle of hair, and a black shadow on his cheeks. He snorted like a horse as he pushed through the cutting machine, following his patterns through some 6

WORD POWER
desiccated dried-up
immortalize to make famous forever
trek a difficult journey

WORD POWER
disdained looked down on; despised

WORD POWER
physique the structure or form of a person's body

---

1. Oklahoma farmers forced to abandon their farms during the dust storms of the 1930s; subject of the 1939 Pulitzer Prize–winning novel *The Grapes of Wrath* by John Steinbeck.

eighteen layers of winter-coat material. One late afternoon, he blinked his eyes hard against the burning sweat as he held down the material with his left hand and pressed the vertical, razor-sharp reciprocating blade with his right. The blade sliced through his index finger at the second joint. Angrily refusing to go to the hospital, he ran tap water over the stump, wrapped his hand in a towel, and went right on cutting, snorting, and stinking. When the blood began to show through the towel's bunched layers, my father pulled the plug on the machine and ordered him to the hospital. But he was back at work the next morning, and worked right through the day and into the evening, as usual, piling up his apartment houses.

There were still elevated trains then, along Second, Third, Sixth, and Ninth   7
Avenues, and many of the cars were wooden, with windows that opened. Broadway had open trolleys with no side walls, in which you at least caught the breeze, hot though it was, so that desperate people, unable to endure their apartments, would simply pay a nickel and ride around aimlessly for a couple of hours to cool off. As for Coney Island on weekends, block after block of beach was so jammed with people that it was barely possible to find a space to sit or to put down your book or your hot dog.

My first direct contact with an air conditioner came only in the sixties,   8
when I was living in the Chelsea Hotel. The so-called management sent up a machine on casters, which rather aimlessly cooled and sometimes heated the air, relying, as it did, on pitchers of water that one had to pour into it. On the initial filling, it would spray water all over the room, so one had to face it toward the bathroom rather than the bed.

A South African gentleman once told me that New York in August was   9
hotter than any place he knew in Africa, yet people here dressed for a northern city. He had wanted to wear shorts but feared that he would be arrested for indecent exposure.

High heat created irrational solutions: linen suits that collapsed into   10
deep wrinkles when one bent an arm or a knee, and men's straw hats as stiff as matzohs,[2] which, like some kind of hard yellow flower, bloomed annually all over the city on a certain sacred date—June 1 or so. Those hats dug deep pink creases around men's foreheads, and the wrinkled suits, which were supposedly cooler, had to be pulled down and up and sideways to make room for the body within.

The city in summer floated in a daze that moved otherwise sensible   11
people to repeat endlessly the brainless greeting "Hot enough for ya? Ha-ha!" It was like the final joke before the meltdown of the world in a pool of sweat.

---

2. Large, crisp flatbread eaten during the Jewish holiday of Passover.

Thinking about the Reading

Teaching Tip
Remind students to
answer all questions in
complete sentences.

1. The opening paragraphs describe how poor people coped with extreme heat in the 1920s. Was Miller's family poor? Which details in the essay supply the answer to this question?

*2. Why do you suppose New York businessmen in the 1920s wore suits instead of cooler, more comfortable clothes? How has men's summer business wear changed since the days Miller writes about?

3. Why do you think Miller focuses on the man in his father's factory who smelled like a horse? How does Miller feel about this man? Which details reveal his attitude?

4. Why do you think Miller decided to write about life before air conditioning? Does he accomplish his purpose?

Writing Practice

Teaching Tip
If your students are
writing essays, these
prompts will work as
essay topics. Otherwise,
you can have students
write paragraphs.

1. Write a description of a day when you had to live without a modern convenience, such as a refrigerator, a computer, or electricity. How did you cope? As an alternative, imagine a day in your life without one of these conveniences, and write about how your life would be affected.

2. Write a description of your workplace. Include descriptions of one or two particular coworkers, if you like.

3. Write about a time when you were physically uncomfortable—hot, cold, exhausted, or in pain or discomfort. What caused this situation? What ended it?

The Last Generation to Live on the Edge

Robb Moretti

Teaching Tip
This is an exemplification
essay.

Is our culture becoming obsessed with protecting children from everyday life? Robb Moretti reminds us that there was a time when children had more fun even though they lived more dangerous lives than they do today.

WORD POWER

malign to make harmful statements about

My parents are part of what has been labeled the Greatest Generation. I 1 hail from a great generation as well. That's because my peers and I, the oft-maligned baby boomers,[1] came before seat belts, bike helmets, and all things plastic protected children from the hazards of everyday life. We were the last Americans to grow up without a childproof safety net.

I know that many of today's protective gadgets prevent kids from get-2 ting seriously injured. Looking back, I sometimes wonder how my friends

---

1. The generation born between 1946 and 1964.

Teaching Tip
Remind students to
familiarize themselves
with the end-of-essay
questions before reading
the essay.

WORD POWER
diligence attentive care

and I survived childhood at all. But I believe that we experienced a kind of freedom that children who came after us have not.

I was born in November 1954 and whisked from the hospital during a 3 violent California rainstorm, not in a car seat but in my mother's arms. Since our car didn't have seat belts, we drove commando.

As a baby, I was tucked into my crib without a padded bumper guard 4 or a machine that soothed me to sleep with amplified sounds of the ocean. Baby pictures show me smiling while I stuck my big head through the wooden bars. At night my mother swaddled me in warm pajamas—the non-flame-retardant kind.

Once I could walk, I was free to roam around the house under the watch- 5 ful eye of my parents. Unfortunately, their diligence couldn't prevent every mishap. My mom still tells the story of how I learned not to play with electricity by sticking my toy into an open light socket. When my parents needed peace and quiet, they didn't put me in front of the television to watch a "Baby Einstein" video; they plopped me in a chair to watch my mom do housework or cook.

My dad drove a monstrous Chrysler that had a rear window ledge large 6 enough to provide a comfortable sleeping area during long drives. As a five-year-old, I loved lying on that ledge, staring at the sky or the stars while we roared down the new California freeways. I was a projectile object waiting to happen! Riding in the front didn't improve my odds much: whenever the car came to an abrupt stop, my mother or father would fling an arm across my chest to keep me from going airborne.

During my grade-school years, my mother would often leave my younger 7 sister and me in the car, keys in the ignition and doors unlocked, while she went shopping. When we got home, I would run out to join my friends, with the only rule being to get home by dark. My parents weren't terrified if I was out of their sight. In fact, they enjoyed the silence.

Playing at the park was a high-risk adventure for my friends and me. The 8 jungle gym was a heavy gray apparatus with metal bars, screws, and hooks. On a hot day the metallic surface of the sliding board would burn our behinds. A great afternoon at the park usually meant coming home with blisters on our hands, a bump or two on the melon, and the obligatory skinned knee.

I rode my red Schwinn Stingray without wearing a bike helmet; my 9 Davy Crockett cap protected me from serious head injury. Although I did not have the benefit of a crossing guard at the blind intersection I had to traverse to get to school, I was sure the snapping sound made by the baseball cards stuck in my spokes alerted the oncoming traffic to my presence.

Every school day my mother packed my Jetsons lunchbox with a tuna- 10 fish sandwich, which we found out later often contained high levels of mercury and a dolphin or two. Also stuffed in my lunchbox was a pint of whole chocolate milk and a package of Hostess Twinkies or cupcakes.

Despite our high-fat, high-sugar diets, my friends and I were not out of shape. Maybe that was because we worked so hard in phys-ed class every day. Occasionally our teacher pushed us so far that some poor kid would throw up his lunch. 11

In the afternoons we all played in a school-sponsored baseball league. We didn't wear plastic batting helmets or cups, and we hit pitched balls instead of hitting off a plastic tee. Worst of all, we received trophies or medals only if our team won the championship. 12

Last February, Americans were captivated by the skeleton event at the 2002 Winter Olympics. But thirty-five years earlier, my junior-high friends and I had invented our own version of the sport. We'd roar down steep Bay Area streets on a flexible sled with wheels instead of runners. Like the Olympians, we held our chins just inches above the ground. You don't see kids today with two false front teeth nearly as often as you did in 1967. 13

We baby boomers may not have weathered the Depression or stormed the beaches at Normandy. But we were the last generation to live on the edge and, I believe, to have fun! 14

Thinking about the Reading

Teaching Tip
Remind students to answer all questions in complete sentences.

1. What examples does Moretti give to support his claim that his generation lived "on the edge" (paragraph 14)?

2. How were Moretti's childhood experiences different from those of today's children? How do you explain the differences?

3. Do you agree with Moretti that his life "on the edge" was worth the risk, or do you believe that the dangers of his generation's behavior outweighed the benefits?

*4. How were Moretti's childhood experiences like and unlike your own? Do you think he is correct in saying that his generation was "the last generation to live on the edge" (paragraph 14)?

Writing Practice

Teaching Tip
If your students are writing essays, these prompts will work as essay topics. Otherwise, you can have students write paragraphs.

1. Explain in what sense you "lived on the edge" when you were a child—and in what sense you did not.

2. What risks do you experience as part of your adult life? Do you see these risks as necessary? Do you seek them out? Do you think you "live on the edge"?

3. Do you believe today's parents are overprotective? Do you think children should be given fewer rules? Write a letter to the editor of a parenting magazine in which you support your position with examples from your own experience.

Why We Need Animal Experimentation

Thuy Nguyen

Student writer Thuy Nguyen argues that animal experimentation is necessary to improve medical technology and thus to save human lives. As you read her essay, note the specific examples she supplies to support her points.

Teaching Tip
This is an argument essay.

Teaching Tip
Remind students to familiarize themselves with the end-of-essay questions before reading the essay.

WORD POWER
sterilization the process of making something free of germs
microbe a germ

WORD POWER
hypertensive having high blood pressure

With our advanced medical technology today, medicine has helped save 1 many lives. The advances in medical technology that have saved these lives, for the most part, have been developed from animal experimentation. However, some people have claimed that animal experimentation is cruel and should not be continued. In my opinion, because medical research is so dependent on it, animal experimentation should be continued. It provides preventive measures to protect humans against getting diseases, helps discover cures and treatments for diseases, and helps surgeons to perfect the surgical techniques that are needed to save human lives.

First of all, animal experimentation provides preventive measures to 2 protect humans from getting diseases. With the help of medical research on animals, scientists have found useful applications of vaccines to prevent many diseases. For example, the vaccines for polio, typhoid, diphtheria, tetanus, tuberculosis, measles, mumps, and rubella were all developed through animal experimentation. In addition, the principle of sterilization came out of Pasteur's[1] discovery, through animal experimentation, that microbes cause diseases. As a result, nowadays, medical professionals know that it is extremely important to sterilize medical tools such as gloves and syringes in order to keep them bacteria-free and to prevent patients from getting infections. Also, from experiments on rats, the connection between smoking and lung cancer was conclusively proved. This led many people to quit smoking and avoid getting cancer.

Besides leading to preventive measures, animal experimentation also 3 leads to the discovery of cures and treatments for many diseases. For instance, it has helped with the treatment of diabetic patients who are in need of insulin. Through experiments on cows and pigs, researchers have found the usefulness of cows' and pigs' insulin for treating diabetes. In addition, many drugs discovered through animal tests have been proven to cure ill patients. For example, a number of antibiotics, such as penicillin and sulfonamides, which were found from animal experimentation, help cure many infections. Also, many antihypertension medicines, which were developed in experiments on cats, help control blood pressure in hypertensive

---

1. Louis Pasteur (1822–1895) was a French chemist.

patients. Similarly, anticancer drugs were developed from tests on rats and dogs.

Besides providing preventive measures to protect humans from getting 4 diseases and helping discover cures and treatments for many diseases, animal experimentation also helps surgeons to perfect the surgical techniques needed to save human lives. Surgeons have always been searching for better techniques to make surgery safer and more effective for their patients. One good way to perfect these techniques is to practice them on animals. From experiments on cats, researchers have found new techniques for human transplants. Similarly, techniques for open heart surgery were perfected through many years of animal experimentation. Animal research programs have also helped surgeons to refine their techniques for kidney dialysis needed by patients with kidney failure.

Animal experimentation should be continued because it provides pre- 5 ventive measures to protect humans against diseases, helps to discover cures and treatments for diseases, and helps surgeons to perfect their surgical techniques. Therefore, animal experimentation is vital for the medical research that saves human lives.

Thinking about the Reading

Teaching Tip
Remind students to answer all questions in complete sentences.

1. What are the three points Thuy Nguyen makes to develop her argument that animal experimentation is essential to medical research?

2. What does the first paragraph of this essay accomplish? Where does Thuy first state each of her reasons for continuing animal experimentation? Where does she support each of these points? What does the last paragraph achieve?

*3. Are the examples Thuy presents convincing? Does she present enough support? Do any of the following elements appear in this essay?

   ● An explanation of what animal experimentation means

   ● Expert opinions on the subject of animal experimentation

   ● A refutation of possible arguments *against* Thuy's point of view

   If not, how would the addition of these elements improve the essay?

*4. Do you agree with Thuy's position on animal experimentation? What objections do you have? Try to support your position with facts and examples from your reading and experience.

Teaching Tip
If your students are writing essays, these prompts will work as essay topics. Otherwise, you can have students write paragraphs.

Writing Practice

1. Revise Thuy's essay to give it more personal appeal for readers. For example, try adding one or two paragraphs about specific people who could be helped by animal experimentation.

2. Write an editorial that takes a position *against* the use of animal experimentation. Consider some of the following points made by opponents of animal experimentation.

- The same medical results could be obtained by means other than animal experimentation.
- Some animal experimentation is not necessary and could be eliminated.
- Animal experimentation is not humane.

3. Choose an issue that is important to you, and write an essay supporting your position on that issue. Use evidence from your reading and experience to support your point of view.

How to Stop a Car with No Brakes

Joshua Piven and David Borgenicht

In this instructional essay from *The Worst-Case Scenario Handbook*, Joshua Piven and David Borgenicht explain how to avoid catastrophe in a car with no brakes. Piven and Borgenicht are the authors of the best-selling book *The Worst-Case Scenario Handbook* (1999), whose success sparked a series of *Worst-Case Scenario* books as well as a reality television show.

1. Begin pumping the brake pedal and keep pumping it. You may be able to build up enough pressure in the braking system to slow down a bit, or even stop completely. If you have anti-lock brakes, you do not normally pump them—but if your brakes have failed, this may work.

2. Do not panic—relax and steer the car smoothly. Cars will often safely corner at speeds much higher than you realize or are used to driving. The rear of the car may slip; steer evenly, being careful not to over-correct.

3. Shift the car into the lowest gear possible and let the engine and transmission slow you down.

4. Pull the emergency brake—but not too hard. Pulling too hard on the emergency brake will cause the rear wheels to lock, and the car to spin around. Use even, constant pressure. In most cars, the emergency brake (also known as the hand brake or parking brake) is cable operated and serves as a fail-safe brake that should still work even when the rest of the braking system has failed. The car should slow down and, in combination with the lower gear, will eventually stop.

5. If you are running out of room, try a "bootlegger's turn." Yank the emergency brake hard while turning the wheel a quarter turn in either

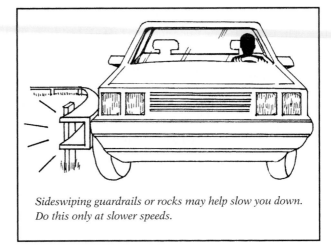

Sideswiping guardrails or rocks may help slow you down. Do this only at slower speeds.

direction—whichever is safer. This will make the car spin 180 degrees. If you were heading downhill, this spin will head you back uphill, allowing you to slow down.

6. If you have room, swerve the car back and forth across the road. Making hard turns at each side of the road will decrease your speed even more.

7. If you come up behind another car, use it to help you stop. Blow your horn, flash your lights, and try to get the driver's attention. If you hit the car, be sure to hit it square, bumper to bumper, so you do not knock the other car off the road. This is an extremely dangerous maneuver: It works best if the vehicle in front of you is larger than yours—a bus or truck is ideal—and if both vehicles are traveling at similar speeds. You do not want to crash into a much slower-moving or stopped vehicle, however.

8. Look for something to help stop you. A flat or uphill road that intersects with the road you are on, a field, or a fence will slow you further but not stop you suddenly. Scraping the side of your car against a guardrail is another option. Avoid trees and wooden telephone poles: They do not yield as readily.

9. Do not attempt to sideswipe oncoming cars.

10. If none of the above steps has enabled you to stop and you are about to go over a cliff, try to hit something that will slow you down before you go over. This strategy will also leave a clue to others that someone has gone over the edge. But since very few cliffs are sheer drops, you may fall just several feet and then stop.

WORD POWER

readily easily

WORD POWER

sheer very steep; almost perpendicular

Thinking about the Reading

Teaching Tip
Remind students to answer all questions in complete sentences.

*1. Because the steps in the process are numbered, they do not include transitions to indicate the order of the steps or the relationship between one step and the next. Can you suggest some transitional words and phrases that could be added?

2. What warnings and reminders do the writers include? Do you think they need additional cautions to guide readers?

3. Do you think the picture on page 621 is necessary? Can you suggest other visuals that might be more effective?

*4. Do you think the writers should have omitted the last paragraph? Why or why not?

Writing Practice

Teaching Tip
If your students are writing essays, these prompts will work as essay topics. Otherwise, you can have students write paragraphs.

1. Write an introduction and a conclusion for "How to Stop a Car with No Brakes." Then, select the most useful information in the essay, and use it to help you write a short article *in your own words* for a driver education manual.

2. List ten steps that would help readers survive a different difficult or dangerous situation. Then, expand the items on your list into several paragraphs.

3. Write a paragraph directed at an urban audience in which you explain a process that is familiar to residents of rural areas. Or, write a paragraph for a rural audience in which you explain a process that is familiar to city dwellers.

A "Good" American Citizen

Linda S. Wallace

Teaching Tip
This is a definition essay.

What is patriotism, and how should we demonstrate it? In this article, media consultant and former journalist Linda Wallace uses the controversy surrounding the war in Iraq to explore the role of dissent in the American system of government.

Teaching Tip
Remind students to familiarize themselves with the end-of-essay questions before reading the essay.

Recently, I passed an antiwar protest in Center City Philadelphia, a mix 1 of young and old, office workers and students, patting drums to the rhythm of their rap. A moment later, a pickup truck filled with guys clad in bluejeans drove by, waving the American flag and yelling, "Go, America!" Passers-by cringed as they tensely viewed the scene and caught a glimpse of the hundred police officers monitoring the drama from across the street.

This "we versus we" conflict is uncomfortable. Even U.S. leaders seem 2 more focused on middle ground rather than finding ways to disagree more productively. But there is a critical conversation America has yet to have with itself. And with the ongoing dissension over the war with Iraq, it appears that now is the perfect time.

Definitions of what qualifies as national loyalty have always shifted as 3 American society has diversified and matured. A person who is viewed by many as a troublemaker, such as Dr. Martin Luther King Jr., just might end up an honored U.S. hero.

So what defines a patriot, exactly? Is it a person who supports the government through right and wrong in a war or a crisis or the person who disagrees loudly and engages in lawful protest? Are those who push us all to conform and unite as one country the folks who most love this nation, or is it those who embrace differences and challenge fellow citizens' assumptions in order to reorder society and find hidden flaws? 4

There is no national handbook—at least not yet—that details how to be a good American. Some would prefer a manual filled with "dos" and "don'ts" to point to and say, "I'm the real deal, and you are the pretender." 5

So it seems for the moment, each person is left to follow his or her own set of personal rules regarding patriotism, even though those lists are bound to disagree. The first few rules on my own list are simple: 6

1. Vote in every federal, state, and local election even when you can't find one candidate you like.
2. Learn the names of elected officials, and email them periodically to offer insight. (Most of mine are white, and I am African American.)
3. Attend community or council meetings, and stay abreast of public policy and key issues by reading newspapers, listening to the radio, or watching the evening TV news.
4. Model the behavior you want to see in others: Put democratic principles into practice by challenging bias and discrimination in everyday life.

The next rules, which came with wisdom and experience, require a bit more effort and resolve:

5. Respect the rights of other Americans to disagree with you.
6. Accept that your point of view is not the only legitimate perspective.
7. Tolerate dissent.

As I watch American commentators condemn fellow citizens for expressing views contrary to the government, it saddens me. Some people see conformity and unity as building blocks of strength, but I tend to view them as indicators that fear or intimidation is stifling helpful dissent. I am like the CEO who prefers to identify the drawbacks before launching a new product rather than wait until after it hits the stores. The country that is able to identify the weakness of its own arguments, and make strategic adjustments, is more likely to win over its opponents. 7

Some Americans will look at these scenes of antiwar protesters standing off against those who support the war effort and shake their heads. They may see a nation in turmoil, but I see a country with the will and savvy to tolerate 8

WORD POWER

patriot someone who loves and supports his or her country

WORD POWER

dissent a difference of opinion; a disagreement

WORD POWER

savvy practical knowledge

dissent. Those who think that the opinion of the majority is somehow sacred might wish to revisit history. Our Founding Fathers decided to create a republic instead of a democracy because many feared the majority would not, could not, rule without eventually becoming oppressive and unfair.

Wisely, they opted for a republic, once described by John Adams as "an empire of laws, not of men." Therefore, the protection of the laws that safeguard liberty and free expression is more critical to us than any national consensus ever will be. 9

The law protects free speech, and those who seek to silence protesters in the name of patriotism might remember these words that Thomas Jefferson wrote in 1815: 10

> Difference of opinion leads to enquiry, and enquiry to truth; and that, I am sure, is the ultimate and sincere object of us both. We both value too much the freedom of opinion sanctioned by our Constitution, not to cherish its exercise even where in opposition to ourselves.

If we decide that sincere patriots are those who rally behind the government, then we have suppressed the law and sidestepped principles in order to gain a temporary accord. That's not only unpatriotic; it's downright dangerous. 11

Thinking about the Reading

1. What is the "critical conversation" that Wallace believes "America has yet to have with itself" (paragraph 2)?

*2. In paragraph 4, Wallace asks a series of questions. Answer those questions.

*3. How does Wallace define a patriot? Do you agree with her definition? Do you agree with all seven of her rules?

4. Why does Wallace begin her essay by describing an antiwar protest? How does she use this protest to support her position?

Writing Practice

1. Using the seven rules that Wallace lists in paragraph 6 as a starting point, write a pamphlet *in your own words* for middle-school students (or for new American citizens). Call your pamphlet "How to Be a Good American Citizen." (If you like, you may add rules of your own to Wallace's list.)

2. Choose one of Wallace's seven rules, and write an essay about an incident you witnessed or experienced that illustrates the importance of the rule.

3. Choose an issue on which you and a friend, parent, or coworker strongly disagree. Interview the person whose position differs from yours, and then express your support for his or her position.

Appendix  Strategies for College Success

Orientation Strategies

Some strategies come in handy even before school begins, as you orient yourself to life as a college student. Here are some things you need to do.

1. ***Make sure you have everything you need:*** a college catalog, a photo ID, a student handbook, a parking permit, and any other items that entering students at your school are expected to have.

2. ***Read your school's orientation materials*** (distributed as handouts or posted on the school Web site) carefully. These materials will help you familiarize yourself with campus buildings and offices, course offerings, faculty members, extracurricular activities, and so on.

3. ***Be sure you know your academic adviser's name*** (and how to spell it), email address, office location, and office hours. Copy this information into your personal address book.

4. ***Get a copy of the library's orientation materials.*** These will tell you about the library's hours and services and explain procedures such as how to use the online catalog.

5. ***Be sure you know where things are***—not just how to find the library and the parking lot, but also where you can do photocopying or buy a newspaper.

First-Week Strategies

College can seem like a confusing place at first, but from your first day as a college student, there are steps you can take to help you get your bearings.

Teaching Tip
Tell students not to email
their instructors asking
them to fill them in on
work they missed. It is
the student's responsi-
bility to get this infor-
mation from a classmate.

WORD POWER

networking interacting
with others to share
information

1. ***Make yourself at home****.* Find places on campus where you can get something to eat or drink, and find a good place to study or relax before or between classes. As you explore the campus, try to locate all the things you need to feel comfortable—for example, ATMs, rest rooms, and vending machines.

2. ***Know where you are going and when you need to be there****.* Check the building and room number for each of your classes and the days and hours the class meets. Copy this information onto the front cover of the appropriate notebook. Pay particular attention to classes with irregular schedules (for example, a class that meets from 9 a.m. to 10 a.m. on Tuesdays but from 11 a.m. to noon on Thursdays).

3. ***Get to know your fellow students****.* Networking with other students is an important part of the college experience. Get the name, phone number, and email address of at least one student in each of your classes. If you miss class, you will need to get in touch with someone to find out what material you missed.

4. ***Familiarize yourself with each course's syllabus****.* At the first meeting of every course, your instructor will hand out a **syllabus**, an outline or summary of course requirements, policies, and procedures. (The syllabus may also be posted on the course's Web page.) A syllabus gives you three kinds of useful information.

   ● Practical information, such as the instructor's office number and email address and what books and supplies to buy

   ● Information that can help you plan a study schedule—for example, when assignments are due and when exams are scheduled

   ● Information about the instructor's policies on absences, grading, class participation, and so on

   Read each syllabus carefully, ask questions about anything you do not understand, refer to all your course syllabi regularly—and do not lose them.

5. ***Buy books and supplies****.* When you buy your books and supplies, be sure to keep the receipts, and do not write your name in your books until you are certain that you are not going to drop a course. (If you write in a book, you will not be able to return it.) If your schedule of courses is not definite, wait a few days to buy your texts. You should, however, buy some items right away: a separate notebook and folder for each course you are taking, a college dictionary, and a pocket organizer (see A4). In

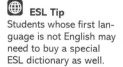

ESL Tip
Students whose first lan-
guage is not English may
need to buy a special
ESL dictionary as well.

**Highlight:
Using a
Dictionary**

Even though your computer has a spell checker, you still need to buy a dictionary. A college dictionary tells you not only how to spell words but also what words mean and how to use them.

addition to the books and other items required for a particular course (for example, a lab notebook, a programmable calculator, art supplies), you should buy pens and pencils in different colors, paper clips or a stapler, self-stick notes, highlighter pens, and so on. Finally, you will need to buy a backpack or bookbag in which to keep all these items.

6. ***Set up your notebooks.*** Establish a separate notebook (or a separate section of a divided notebook) for each of your classes. Write your instructor's name, email address, phone number, and office hours and location on the inside front cover of the notebook; write your own name, address, and phone number on the outside, along with the class location and meeting times. (Notebooks with pocket folders can help you keep graded papers, handouts, and the class syllabus all in one place, near your notes.)

Day-to-Day Strategies

As you get busier and busier, you may find that it is hard to keep everything under control. Here are some strategies to help you as you move through the semester.

1. ***Find a place to study.*** As a college student, you will need your own private place to work and study. This space should include everything you will need to make your work easier—quiet, good lighting, a comfortable chair, a clean work surface, storage for supplies, and so on.

2. ***Set up a bookshelf.*** Keep your textbooks, dictionary, calculator, supplies, and everything else you use regularly for your coursework in one place—ideally, in your own workspace. That way, when you need something, you will know exactly where it is.

3. ***Set up a study schedule***. Identify thirty- to forty-five-minute blocks of free time before, between, and after classes. Set this time aside for review. Remember, studying should be part of your regular routine, not something you do only the night before an exam.

<table>
<tr>
<td>Highlight:
Skills Check</td>
<td>Don't wait until you have a paper to write to discover that your computer skills need improvement. Be sure your basic word-processing skills are at the level you need for your work. If you need help, get it right away. Your school's computer lab should be the first place you turn for help with word processing, but writing center and library staff members may also be able to help you.</td>
</tr>
</table>

4. ***Establish priorities***. It is very important to understand what your priorities are. Before you can establish priorities, however, you have to know which assignments are due first, which ones can be done in steps, and which tasks or steps will be most time consuming. Then, you must decide which tasks are most pressing. For example, studying for a test to be given the next day is more pressing than reviewing notes for a test scheduled for the following week. Finally, you have to decide which tasks are more important than others. For example, studying for a midterm is more important than studying for a quiz, and the midterm for a course you are in danger of failing is more important than the midterm for a course in which you are doing well. Remember, you cannot do everything at once; you need to decide what must be done immediately and what can wait.

5. ***Check your mail***. Check your campus mailbox and email account regularly—if possible, several times a day. If you miss a message, you may miss important information about changes in assignments, canceled classes, or rescheduled quizzes.

6. ***Schedule conferences***. Try to meet with each of your instructors during the semester even if you are not required to do so. You might schedule one conference during the second or third week of the semester and another a week or two before a major exam or paper is due. Your instructors will appreciate and respect your initiative.

7. ***Become familiar with the student services available on your campus.*** There is nothing wrong with getting help from your school's writing center or tutoring center or from the center for disabled students (which serves students with learning disabilities as well as physical challenges), the office of international students, or the counseling center, as well as from your adviser or course instructors. Think of yourself as a consumer. You are paying for your education, and you are entitled to—and should take advantage of—all the available services you need.

Highlight: Asking for Help

Despite all your careful planning, you may still run into trouble. For example, you may miss an exam and have to make it up; you may miss several days of classes in a row and fall behind in your work; you may have trouble understanding the material in one of your courses; or a family member may get sick. Do not wait until you are overwhelmed to ask for help. If you have an ongoing personal problem or a family emergency, let your instructors and the dean of students know immediately.

A4 Time-Management Strategies

Learning to manage your time is very important for success in college. Here are some strategies you can adopt to make this task easier.

1. ***Use an organizer.*** Whether you prefer a print organizer or an electronic one, you should certainly use one—and use it consistently. If you are most comfortable with paper and pencil, purchase a "week-on-two-pages" academic year organizer (one that begins in September, not January); the "week-on-two-pages" format (see pp. 630 and 631) gives you more writing room for Monday through Friday than for the weekend, and it also lets you view an entire week at once.

   Carry your organizer with you at all times. At the beginning of the semester, copy down key pieces of information from each course syllabus—for example, the date of every quiz and exam and the due date of every paper. As the semester progresses, continue to write in assignments and deadlines. In addition, enter information such as days when a class will be canceled or will meet in the computer lab or in the library, reminders to bring a particular book or piece of equipment to class, and appointments with instructors or other college personnel.

If you like, you can also jot down reminders and schedule appointments that are not related to school—for example, changes in your work hours, a dental appointment, or lunch with a friend. (In addition to writing notes on the pages for each date, some students like to keep a separate month-by-month "to do" list. Crossing out completed items can give you a feeling of accomplishment—and make the road ahead look shorter.)

The sample organizer pages below show how you can use an organizer to keep track of deadlines, appointments, and reminders. The sample organizer pages on page 631 include not only this information but also a study schedule, with notes about particular tasks to be done each day.

2. *Use a calendar.* Buy a large calendar, and post it where you will see it every morning—on your desk, on the refrigerator, or wherever you keep your keys and your ID. At the beginning of the semester, fill in

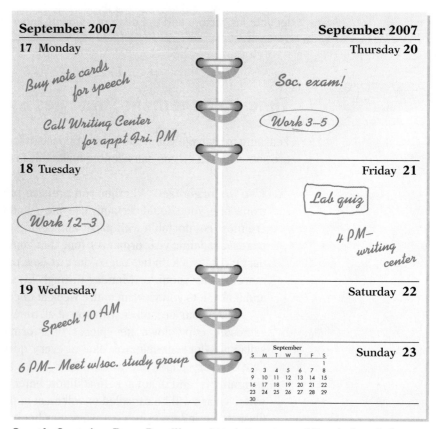

September 2007

17 Monday

Buy note cards for speech

Call Writing Center for appt Fri. PM

18 Tuesday

Work 12–3

19 Wednesday

Speech 10 AM

6 PM— Meet w/soc. study group

September 2007

Thursday **20**

Soc. exam!

Work 3–5

Friday **21**

Lab quiz

4 PM— writing center

Saturday **22**

Sunday **23**

	September					
S	M	T	W	T	F	S
						1
2	3	4	5	6	7	8
9	10	11	12	13	14	15
16	17	18	19	20	21	22
23	24	25	26	27	28	29
30						

Sample Organizer Page: Deadlines, Appointments, and Reminders Only

important dates such as school holidays, work commitments, exam dates, and due dates for papers and projects. When you return from school each day, update the calendar with any new information you have entered into your organizer.

Teaching Tip
Have students compare the notes they have taken up to this point with the advice given in section A5 of this appendix. Encourage them to go back to highlight important points and add examples.

3. **Plan ahead.** If you think you will need help from a writing center tutor to revise a paper that is due in two weeks, don't wait until day thirteen to make an appointment; all the time slots may be filled by then. To be safe, make an appointment for help about a week in advance.

4. **Learn to enjoy downtime.** One final—and important—point to remember is that you are entitled to "waste" a little time. When you have a free minute, take time for yourself—and don't feel guilty about it.

Sample Organizer Page: Deadlines, Appointments, Reminders, and Study Schedule

Note-Taking Strategies

Learning to take notes in a college class takes practice, but taking good notes is essential for success in college. Here are some basic guidelines that will help you develop and improve your note-taking skills.

During Class

1. **Come to class**. If you miss class, you miss notes—so come to class, and come on time. Sit where you can see the board or screen and hear the instructor. Do not feel you have to keep sitting in the same place in each class every day; change your seat until you find a spot that is comfortable for you.

2. **Date your notes**. Begin each class by writing the date at the top of the page. Instructors frequently identify material that will be on a test by dates. If you do not date your notes, you may not know what to study.

Teaching Tip
Suggest that students try dividing their notebook page into two sections by drawing a vertical line down the middle. One side can be for notes on lectures or readings; the other side can be for their responses to and questions about the material.

3. **Know what to write down**. You cannot possibly write down everything an instructor says. If you try, you will miss a lot of important information. Listen carefully *before* you write, and listen for cues to what is important. For example, sometimes the instructor will tell you that something is important, or that a particular piece of information will be on a test. If the instructor emphasizes an idea or underlines it on the board, you should do the same in your notes. (Of course, if you have done the assigned reading before class, you will recognize important topics and know to take especially careful notes when these topics are introduced in class.)

4. **Include examples**. Try to write down an example for each important concept introduced in class—something that will help you remember what the instructor was talking about. (If you do not have time to include examples as you take notes during class, add them when you review your notes.) For instance, if your world history instructor is explaining *nationalism,* you should write down not only a definition but also an example, such as "Germany in 1848."

5. **Write legibly, and use helpful signals**. Use dark (blue or black) ink for your note-taking, but keep a red or green pen handy to highlight important information, jot down announcements (such as a change in a test date), note gaps in your notes, or question confusing points. Do not take notes in pencil, which is hard to read and not as permanent as ink.

6. **Ask questions**. If you do not hear (or do not understand) something your instructor said, or if you need an example to help you understand

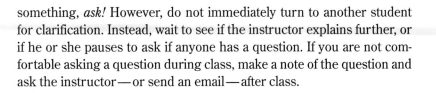

something, *ask!* However, do not immediately turn to another student for clarification. Instead, wait to see if the instructor explains further, or if he or she pauses to ask if anyone has a question. If you are not comfortable asking a question during class, make a note of the question and ask the instructor—or send an email—after class.

After Class

1. ***Review your notes***. After every class, try to spend ten or fifteen minutes rereading your notes, filling in gaps and examples while the material is still fresh in your mind.

2. ***Recopy information***. When you have a break between classes, or when you get home, recopy important pieces of information from your notes. (Some students even find it helpful to recopy their notes after every class to reinforce what they have learned.)

   - Copy announcements (such as quiz dates) onto your calendar.
   - Copy reminders (for example, a note to schedule a conference before your next paper is due) into your organizer.
   - Copy questions you want to ask the instructor onto the top of the next blank page in your class notebook.

Teaching Tip
Refer students to section A4 of this appendix for information on calendars and organizers.

Before the Next Class

1. ***Reread your notes***. Leave time to skim the previous class's notes just before each class. This strategy will get you oriented for the class to come and will remind you of anything that needs clarification or further explanation. (You might want to give each day's notes a title so you can remember the topic of each class. This can also help you find information when you study.)

2. ***Ask for help***. Call or email a classmate if you need to fill in missing information; if you still need help, see the instructor during his or her office hours, or come to class early to ask your question before class begins.

A6 Homework Strategies

Doing homework is an important part of your education. Homework gives you a chance to practice your skills and measure your progress. If you are having trouble with the homework, chances are you are having trouble with the course. Ask the instructor or teaching assistant for help *now;* do not wait until the day before the exam. Here are some tips for getting the most out of your homework.

1. *Write down the assignment.* Do not expect to remember an assignment; copy it down. If you are not sure exactly what you are supposed to do, check with your instructor or with another student.

2. *Do your homework, and do it on time.* Teachers assign homework to reinforce classwork, and they expect homework to be done on a regular basis. It is easy to fall behind in college, but trying to do three—or five—nights' worth of homework in one night is not a good idea. If you do several assignments at once, you not only overload yourself, you also miss important day-to-day connections with classwork.

3. *Be an active reader.* Get into the habit of highlighting your textbooks and other material as you read.

4. *Join study groups.* A study group of three or four students can be a valuable support system for homework as well as for exams. If your schedule permits, do some homework assignments—or at least review your homework—with other students on a regular basis. In addition to learning information, you will learn different strategies for doing assignments.

A7

Exam-Taking Strategies

Preparation for an exam should begin well before the exam is announced. In a sense, you begin this preparation on the first day of class.

Before the Exam

1. *Attend every class.* Regular attendance in class—where you can listen, ask questions, and take notes—is the best possible preparation for exams. If you do have to miss a class, arrange to copy (and read) another student's notes *before the next class* so you will be able to follow the discussion.

2. *Keep up with the reading.* Read every assignment, and read it before the class in which it will be discussed. If you do not, you may have trouble understanding what is going on in class.

3. *Take careful notes.* Take careful, thorough notes, but be selective. If you can, compare your notes on a regular basis with those of other stu-

dents in the class; working together, you can fill in gaps or correct errors. Establishing a buddy system will also force you to review your notes regularly instead of just on the night before the exam.

Teaching Tip
If you give exams in your course, be sure to give students specific information about the kinds of questions you will be asking. You might even consider giving a practice exam.

4. ***Study on your own.*** When an exam is announced, adjust your study schedule—and your priorities—so you have time to review everything. (This is especially important if you have more than one exam in a short period of time.) Over a period of several days, review all your material (class notes, readings, and so on), and then review it again. Make a note of anything you do not understand, and keep track of topics you need to review. Try to predict the most likely questions, and—if you have time—practice answering them.

5. ***Study with a group.*** If you can set up a study group. Studying with others can help you understand the material better. However, do not come to group sessions unprepared and expect to get everything from the other students. You must first study on your own.

6. ***Make an appointment with your instructor.*** Make a conference appointment with the instructor or with the course's teaching assistant a few days before the exam. Bring to this meeting any specific questions you have about course content and about the format of the upcoming exam. (Be sure to review all your study material before the conference.)

7. ***Review the material one last time.*** The night before the exam is not the time to begin your studying; it is the time to review. When you have finished your review, get a good night's sleep.

**Highlight:
Writing Essay
Exams**

If you are asked to write an essay on an exam, remember that what you are really being asked to do is write a **thesis-and-support essay**. Chapter 12 tells you how to do this.

During the Exam

By the time you walk into the exam room, you will already have done all you could to get ready for the test. Your goal now is to keep the momentum going and not do anything to undermine all your hard work.

Teaching Tip
Encourage students to practice timing themselves at home, or have them do practice timed tests in class.

1. ***Read through the entire exam***. Be sure you understand how much time you have, how many points each question is worth, and exactly what each question is asking you to do. Many exam questions call for just a short answer—*yes* or *no, true* or *false*. Others ask you to fill in a blank with a few words, and still others require you to select the best answer from among several choices. If you are not absolutely certain what kind of answer a particular question calls for, ask the instructor or the proctor *before* you begin to write.

2. ***Budget your time***. Once you understand how much each section of the exam and each question are worth, plan your time and set your priorities, devoting the most time to the most important questions. If you know you tend to rush through exams, or if you find you often run out of time before you get to the end of a test, you might try putting a mark on your paper when about one-third of the allotted time has passed (for a one-hour exam, put a mark on your paper after twenty minutes) to make sure you are pacing yourself appropriately.

3. ***Reread each question***. Carefully reread each question *before* you start to answer it. Underline the **key words**—the words that give specific information about how to approach the question and how to phrase your answer.

   Remember, even if everything you write is correct, your response is not acceptable if you do not answer the question. If a question asks you to *compare* two novels, writing a *summary* of one of them will not be acceptable.

Teaching Tip
Refer students to 1C and 12C for more on brainstorming.

4. ***Brainstorm to help yourself recall the material***. If you are writing a paragraph or an essay, look frequently at the question as you brain-

---

Highlight: Key Words

Here are some helpful key words to look for on exams.

analyze	explain	suggest results, effects, outcomes
argue	give examples	
compare	identify	summarize
contrast	illustrate	support
define	recount	take a stand
demonstrate	suggest causes, origins, contributing factors	trace
describe		
evaluate		

Teaching Tip
Refer students to 2A and
2C for more on topic
sentences and to 12D
for more on thesis
statements.

 ESL Tip
Brainstorming may be an
unfamiliar term for non-
native speakers. Make
sure all students under-
stand this concept.

Teaching Tip
Suggest that students
use the TEST strategy to
test their essay exams.
Refer them to 12H.

storm. (You can write your brainstorming notes on the inside cover of the exam book.) Quickly write down all the relevant points you can think of—what the textbook had to say, your instructor's comments, and so on. The more information you can think of now, the more you will have to choose from when you write your answer.

5. *Write down the main idea.* Looking closely at the way the question is worded and at your brainstorming notes, write a sentence that states the main idea of your answer. If you are writing a paragraph, this sentence will be your **topic sentence**; if you are writing an essay, it will be your **thesis statement**.

6. *List your main points.* You do not want to waste your limited (and valuable) time making a detailed outline, but an informal outline that lists just your key points is worth the little time it takes. An informal outline will help you plan a clear direction for your paragraph or essay.

7. *Draft your answer.* You will spend most of your time actually writing the answers to the questions on the exam. Follow your outline, keep track of time, and consult your brainstorming notes when you need to—but stay focused on your writing.

8. *Reread, revise, and edit.* When you have finished drafting your answer, reread it carefully to make sure it says everything you want it to say—and that it answers the question.

Teaching Tip
Refer students to
Appendix B, section B5,
for more on avoiding
plagiarism.

Highlight: Academic Honesty

Academic honesty—the standard for truth and fairness in work and behavior—is very important in college. Understanding academic honesty goes beyond simply knowing that it is dishonest to cheat on a test. To be sure you are conforming to the rules of academic honesty, you need to pay attention to the following situations:

● Don't reuse papers you wrote in high school. The written work you are assigned in college is designed to help you learn, and your instructors expect you to do the work for the course when it is assigned.

● Don't copy information from a book or article or paste material from a Web site directly into your papers. Using someone else's words or ideas without proper acknowledgment constitutes **plagiarism**, a very serious offense.

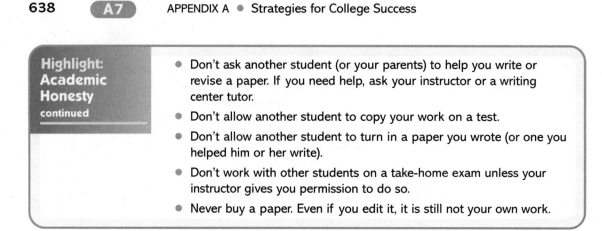

**Highlight:
Academic
Honesty**
continued

- Don't ask another student (or your parents) to help you write or revise a paper. If you need help, ask your instructor or a writing center tutor.
- Don't allow another student to copy your work on a test.
- Don't allow another student to turn in a paper you wrote (or one you helped him or her write).
- Don't work with other students on a take-home exam unless your instructor gives you permission to do so.
- Never buy a paper. Even if you edit it, it is still not your own work.

Appendix B

Using Research in Your Writing

In many essays, you use your own ideas to support your points. In other essays, you may need to supplement your own ideas with **research**: information from outside sources, such as books, periodicals (journals, magazines, and newspapers), and Internet sites.

When you write an essay that calls for research, you will have an easier time if you follow the steps discussed below.

Choosing a Topic

The first step in writing an essay that calls for research is finding a topic to write about. Before you choose a topic, try to answer the following questions:

- What is your page limit?
- When is your paper due?
- How many sources are you expected to use?
- What kind of sources are you expected to use?

The answers to these questions will help you tell if your topic is too broad or too narrow.

When Allison Rogers, a student in a composition course, was asked to write a three- to four-page essay that was due in five weeks, she decided that she wanted to write about the violence she saw in society. She knew, however, that the general topic "violence" would be too broad for her essay.

In her film class, she had just seen the movie *Natural Born Killers* and was shocked by its graphic violence. She remembered her instructor saying that the movie had caused a great deal of controversy and that two teenagers who committed murder had actually used it as a defense in their trial. This led Allison to narrow her focus to the link between film violence and behavior. Because she was majoring in early childhood education, she decided to concentrate on the effects of violent movies on the behavior of children.

Allison thought this topic would work well because she could discuss it in the required number of pages and because she would be able to finish her paper within the five-week time limit.

B2   Exploring Your Topic

Before you choose a topic for an essay that calls for research, you should make sure you will be able to find enough material. You can begin exploring your topic by looking at the resources of your college library.

Begin by searching your library's catalog by subject to see what books it lists on your topic. For example, under the general subject of *violence*, Allison saw the related headings *movie violence* and *media violence*. Under each of these headings, she saw a variety of books and government publications on her topic.

In addition to books, look for articles. To do this, consult a general index such as *Readers' Guide to Periodical Literature*, which lists articles in newspapers and magazines, or *InfoTrac*, a computer database that contains the texts of many articles. A quick look at *Readers' Guide* showed Allison that many articles had been written about violence in the media. A few focused specifically on children, examining the effect of violent movies and television on their behavior.

The Internet can also help you get an overview of your topic. Begin by carrying out an Internet search. When Allison did an Internet search using the key words *movie violence* and *Natural Born Killers*, she saw many articles that related to her topic.

B3   Doing Research

Once you are satisfied that you can find material on your topic, you can begin the job of doing research—of gathering the sources that you will need to write your essay.

Finding Information in the Library

The best place to start your research is in your college library, which contains resources that you cannot find anywhere else—including on the Internet. For the best results, you should do your library research systematically: begin by looking at reference works; then, search the library's card catalog and periodical indexes; and finally, look for any additional facts or statistics that you need to support your ideas.

Remember, once you find information in the library, you still have to **evaluate** it—that is, to determine its usefulness and reliability. For example, an article in a respected periodical such as the *New York Times* or the *Wall Street Journal* is more trustworthy and believable than one in a tabloid such as the *National Enquirer* or the *Sun*. You should also look at the date of publication to decide if the book or article is up to date. Finally, look at the author's biographical information. Is he or she an expert? Does the author's background suggest that he or she has a particular point of view to advance? Your instructor or reference librarian can help you select sources that are both appropriate and reliable.

WORD POWER

periodical a magazine or newspaper published at regular intervals, such as daily or weekly.

tabloid a newspaper that emphasizes stories with sensational content.

Finding Information on the Internet

Teaching Tip
At the start of the semester, assess your students' levels of computer and Internet expertise.

The Internet can give you access to a great deal of information that can help you develop your essay. To use the Internet, you need an Internet **browser**, a tool that enables you to display Web pages. The most popular browsers are Netscape Navigator and Microsoft Internet Explorer. Most new computers come with one of these browsers already installed.

Before you can access the Internet, you need to connect to a **search engine**, a program that helps you find information by sorting through the millions of documents that are available on the Internet. Among the most popular search engines are Google (**google.com**), AltaVista (**altavista.com**), Infoseek (**infoseek.com**), and Yahoo (**yahoo.com**).

There are three ways to use a search engine to find information.

1. *You can enter a Web site's URL.* All search engines have a box in which you can enter a Web site's electronic address, or **uniform resource locator (URL)**. When you click on the URL or hit your computer's Enter or Return key, the search engine connects you to the Web site.

2. *You can do a keyword search.* To do a **keyword search**, you type a term into a box, and the search engine looks for documents that contain the term, listing all the **hits** (documents containing one or both of these words) that it found.

Teaching Tip
Encourage students to **bookmark** useful sites by selecting the Bookmark or Favorites option at the top of the browser's screen. Once they bookmark a site, they can easily return to it.

3. *You can do a subject search.* Some search engines, such as Yahoo, let you do a **subject search**. First, you choose a broad subject from a list: *The Humanities, The Arts, Entertainment, Business*, and so on. Each of these

general subjects leads you to more specific subjects, until eventually you get to the topic that you want.

Not every site you access is a valuable source of information. In fact, anyone can put information on the Internet. For this reason, it is a good idea to approach Internet sites with skepticism. Just as you would with a print source, you should evaluate information you find on the Internet to see if it is believable and useful.

Highlight: Avoiding Plagiarism

When you transfer information from Web sites into your notes, you may be tempted to "cut and paste" text without noting where the text came from. If you then copy this text into a draft of your paper, you are committing **plagiarism** — and plagiarism is the theft of ideas. Every college has rules that students must follow when using words, ideas, and visuals from books, articles, and Internet sources. Consult your school's Web site or student handbook for information on the appropriate use of such information.

Teaching Tip
Point out that a Web site's URL can give you information about the site's purpose. For example, the abbreviation *.edu* indicates that the site is sponsored by an educational institution, *.gov* indicates a government agency, *.org* indicates a nonprofit organization, and *.com* indicates a business.

When Allison searched a periodical database in her college library for the term *media violence*, she found the National Institute of Mental Health (NIMH) Web site, which contained an article titled "Child and Adolescent Violence Research at the NIMH." Using the terms *Natural Born Killers* and *movie violence*, Allison also found an article by John Grisham attacking the violence in *Natural Born Killers* and an article by Oliver Stone, the movie's director, in which he responds to Grisham's criticism.

B4

Taking Notes

Teaching Tip
Encourage students to record full publication information (including page numbers) for all material they photocopy or download. They will need this information when they document their sources.

Once you have gathered the material you will need, read it carefully, recording any information you think you can use in your essay. You can record your notes on 3- by 5-inch cards, on separate sheets of paper, or in a computer file you have created for this purpose. As you take notes, keep your topic in mind; this will help you decide what material is useful.

Summarizing

A **summary** is a general restatement, in your own words, of the main ideas of a passage. A summary is always much shorter than the original, but it can be one sentence, several sentences, or several paragraphs long, depending on how long and how complex the original passage is.

Before you begin to write, make sure you understand the material you are going to summarize. Read it several times, identifying the writer's main idea and key supporting points. As you write, be sure to use your own words, not those of your source. When you revise, make sure that your summary includes just the ideas expressed in your source, not your own opinions or conclusions. Finally, because a summary represents someone else's original ideas, not your own, you must always include appropriate **documentation**.

Here is a passage from the article "Child and Adolescent Violence Research at the NIMH," followed by Allison's summary.

Original

Many studies indicate that a single factor or a single defining situation does not cause child and adolescent antisocial behavior. Rather, multiple factors contribute to and shape antisocial behavior over the course of development. Some factors relate to characteristics within the child, but many others relate to factors within the social environment (e.g., family, peers, school, neighborhood, and community contexts) that enable, shape, and maintain aggression, antisocial behavior, and related behavioral problems.

Summary

A study conducted by the National Institute of Mental Health (NIMH) indicates that many factors—some within the child and some in his or her environment—can work together to create antisocial behavior ("Child and Adolescent Violence Research").

Quoting

When you quote, you use the author's exact words as they appear in the source, including all punctuation and capitalization. Enclose all words from your source in quotation marks—*followed by documentation*. Because quotations distract readers, use them only when you think that the author's exact words will add something important to your discussion.

Teaching Tip
Refer students to
section B9 for more on
documenting sources.

Quotation

According to NIMH researchers, "multiple factors contribute to and shape antisocial behavior over the course of development" ("Child and Adolescent Violence Research").

**Highlight:
When to Quote**

1. Quote when the words of a source are so memorable that to put them into your own words would lessen their impact.
2. Quote when the words of a source are so concise that a paraphrase or summary would change the meaning of the original.
3. Quote when the words of a source add authority to your discussion. The words of a recognized expert can help you make your point convincingly.

B5

Watching Out for Plagiarism

🌐 ESL Tip
Ask students whether any culture they are familiar with defines plagiarism differently. Use this as a springboard to a discussion of the conventions of plagiarism. Make sure students understand that in American culture, plagiarism is not acceptable.

As a rule, you must **document** (give source information for) all words, ideas, or statistics from an outside source. (It is not necessary, however, to document **common knowledge**, factual information widely available in reference works.) When you present information from another source as if it is your own (whether you do it intentionally or unintentionally), you commit **plagiarism**—and plagiarism is theft. You can avoid plagiarism by understanding what you must document and what you do not have to document.

**Highlight:
Avoiding
Plagiarism**

Teaching Tip
Explain how to paraphrase without accidentally plagiarizing, giving students lots of practice material.

You should document

- All word-for-word quotations from a source
- All summaries of material from a source
- All ideas—opinions, judgments, and insights—of others
- All tables, graphs, charts, and statistics that you get from a source

You do not need to document

- Your own ideas
- Common knowledge
- Familiar quotations

Read the following paragraph from "Frankenstein Must Be Destroyed: Chasing the Monster of TV Violence," an essay by Brian Siano, and the four rules that follow. This material will help you understand the most common causes of plagiarism and show you how to avoid it.

Original

Of course, there are a few crazies out there who will be unfavorably influenced by what they see on TV. But even assuming that somehow the TV show (or movie or record) shares some of the blame, how does one predict what future crazies will take for inspiration? What guidelines would ensure that people write, act, or produce something that *will not upset a psychotic*? Not only is this a ridiculous demand, it's insulting to the public as well. We would all be treated as potential murderers in order to gain a hypothetical 5 percent reduction in violence.

1. Document Ideas from Your Sources

Plagiarism

Even if we were to control the programs that are shown on television, we would decrease violence in society by only perhaps 5 percent.

Even though the student writer does not quote Siano directly, she must still identify him as the source of this material because it expresses his ideas, not her own.

Correct

According to Brian Siano, even if we were to control the programs that are shown on television, we would decrease violence in society by only perhaps 5 percent (24).

2. Place Borrowed Words in Quotation Marks

Plagiarism

According to Brian Siano, there will always be a few crazies out there who will be unfavorably influenced by what they see on television (24).

Although the student writer cites Siano as the source, the passage incorrectly uses Siano's exact words without quoting them. The writer must quote the borrowed words.

Correct (borrowed words in quotation marks)

According to Brian Siano, there will always be "a few crazies out there who will be unfavorably influenced by what they see on TV" (24).

3. Use Your Own Phrasing

Plagiarism

Naturally, there will always be people who are affected by what they view on television. But even if we agree that television programs can influence people, how can we really know what will make people commit crimes? How can we be absolutely sure that a show will not disturb someone who is insane? The answer is that we cannot. To pretend that we can is insulting to law-abiding citizens. We cannot treat everyone as if they were criminals just to reduce violence by a small number of people (Siano 24).

Even though the student writer acknowledges Siano as her source, and even though she does not use Siano's exact words, her passage closely follows the order, emphasis, sentence structure, and phrasing of the original. In the following passage, the writer uses her own wording, quoting (and documenting) one distinctive phrase from Siano's essay.

Correct

According to Brian Siano, we should not censor a television program just because "a few crazies" may be incited to violence (24). Not only would such censorship deprive the majority of people of the right to watch what they want, but it will not significantly lessen the violence in society (24).

Note: Even though the paragraph ends with documentation, the quotation requires its own citation.

B6   Drafting a Thesis Statement

After you have taken notes, review the information you have gathered, and draft a thesis statement. Your **thesis statement** is a single sentence that states the main idea of your paper and tells readers what to expect. (Keep in mind that at this stage, your thesis statement is tentative. You will probably change it as you write your paper.) After reviewing her notes, Allison Rogers came up with the following thesis statement for her paper on media violence.

Thesis Statement

Only for young children do violent movies present a real danger.

Making an Outline

Once you have drafted a thesis statement, you are ready to make an outline. Your outline, which covers just the body paragraphs of your paper, can be either a **topic outline** (in which each idea is expressed in a word or a short phrase) or a **sentence outline** (in which each idea is expressed in a complete sentence).

After reviewing her notes, Allison Rogers wrote the following sentence outline for her paper. (Note that the outline uses roman numerals for first-level headings, capital letters for second-level headings, and numbers for third-level headings. All the outline's points are stated in parallel terms.)

I. Teenagers claim the movie <u>Natural Born Killers</u> made them commit murder.
    A. According to John Grisham, the movie inspired the teenagers to commit their crimes.
    B. Grisham says that several murders have been committed by teenagers who say they were influenced by the movie.

II. The idea that movie violence causes violent behavior is not supported.
    A. Other factors could have influenced the teenagers.
    B. No clear link between media violence and aggressive behavior has been discovered.

III. The link between "copycat crimes" and media violence is not clear.
    A. Movies are seldom directly linked to crimes.
    B. Crimes caused by movies are very rare.

IV. Young children are easily influenced by what they see but parents (not the media) should protect them.
    A. Parents should monitor what children see on TV and in the movies.
    B. Parents should limit their children's TV viewing and discuss the content of movies and TV shows with their children.

V. The right of the majority to watch movies and television shows of their choice should not be limited because some unbalanced people may commit crimes.
    A. Movie theaters should enforce rating systems.
    B. Violent programs should not be shown on stations whose audience is primarily children.

Teaching Tip
Refer students to Chapter 18 for more on parallelism.

Writing Your Paper

Teaching Tip
Take this opportunity
to review thesis-
and-support structure
(see 12A).

Teaching Tip
Refer students to 13A
and 13B for more on
introductions and
conclusions.

Once you have decided on a thesis and written an outline, you are ready to write a draft of your essay.

Begin with an **introduction** that includes your thesis statement. Usually, your introduction will be a single paragraph, but sometimes it will be longer.

In the **body** of your essay, support your thesis statement, with each body paragraph developing a single point. These paragraphs should have clear topic sentences so that your readers will know exactly what points you are making. Use transitional words and phrases to help readers follow your ideas.

Finally, write a **conclusion** that gives readers a sense of completion. Like your introduction, your conclusion will usually be a single paragraph, but it could be longer. It should include a summary statement that reinforces your thesis statement and should end with a memorable sentence.

Remember, you will probably write several drafts of your essay before you hand it in. You can use the Self-Assessment Checklists on pages 182 and 183 to help you revise and edit your paper.

Allison Rogers's completed essay on media violence begins on page 654.

Documenting Your Sources

When you **document** your sources, you tell readers where you found the ideas you used in your essay. The Modern Language Association (MLA) recommends the *parenthetical references* in the body of the paper that refer to a *works-cited list* at the end of the paper.

Parenthetical References in the Text

A parenthetical reference should include just enough information to lead readers to a specific entry in your works-cited list. A typical parenthetical reference consists of the author's last name and the page number (Grisham 2). If you use more than one work by the same author, include a shortened form of the title in the parenthetical reference (Grisham, "Killers" 4). Notice that there is no comma and no *p* or *p.* before the page number.

Whenever possible, introduce information from a source with a phrase that includes the author's name. (If you do this, include only the page number in parentheses.) Place documentation so that it does not interrupt the flow of your ideas, preferably at the end of a sentence.

> As John Grisham observes in "Unnatural Killers," Oliver Stone celebrates gratuitous violence (4).

In the four special situations listed below, the format for parenthetical references departs from these guidelines.

1. When You Are Citing a Work by Two Authors

> Film violence has been increasing during the past ten years (Williams and Yorst 34).

2. When You Are Citing a Work without a Listed Author

> Ever since cable television came on the scene, shows with graphically violent content have been common ("Cable Wars" 76).

3. When You Are Citing a Statement by One Author That Is Quoted in a Work by Another Author

> When speaking of television drama, Leonard Eron, of the University of Illinois, says "perpetrators of violence should not be rewarded for violent acts" (qtd. in Siano 23).

4. When You Are Citing an Electronic Source

> While observing participants, researchers saw "real differences between the children who watched the violent shows and those who watch nonviolent ones" ("Childhood Exposure to Media Violence").

Teaching Tip
Point out that Internet sources often do not contain page numbers. For this reason, parenthetical documentation of Internet sources may consist of just the author's last name (or a shortened title of an article).

The Works-Cited List

The works-cited list includes all the works you **cite** (refer to) in your essay. Use the guidelines in the box on page 653 to prepare your list.

The following sample works-cited entries cover the situations you will encounter most often. Follow the formats exactly as they appear here.

Books

Books by One Author

List the author with last name first. Underline the title. Include the city of publication and a shortened form of the publisher's name—for example,

Bedford for *Bedford/St. Martin's*. Use the abbreviation *UP* for *University Press*, as in *Princeton UP* and *U of Chicago P*. End with the date of publication.

> Ono, Yoko. Memories of John Lennon. New York: Harper Entertainment, 2005.

Note: MLA recommends that you underline book titles, not put them in italics.

Books by Two or Three Authors

List second and subsequent authors with first name first, in the order in which they are listed on the book's title page.

> Halioua, Bruno, and Bernard Ziskind. Medicine in the Days of the Pharoahs. Cambridge, MA: Harvard UP, 2005.

Book by More Than Three Authors

List only the first author, followed by the abbreviation *et al.* ("and others").

> Ordeman, John T., et al. Artists of the North American Wilderness: George and Belmore Browne. New York: Warwick, 2004.

Two or More Books by the Same Author

List two or more books by the same author in alphabetical order according to title. In each entry after the first, use three unspaced hyphens (followed by a period) instead of the author's name.

> Angelou, Maya. Mother: A Cradle to Hold Me. New York: Random House, 2006.
>
> ---. Hallelujah! The Welcome Table: A Lifetime of Memories with Recipes. New York: Random House, 2004.

Edited Book

Teaching Tip
Explain that when the abbreviation *ed.* follows a name, it means "editor" (*eds.* means "editors"). When the abbreviation *Ed.* comes before one or more names, it means "edited by."

> Whitman, Walt. The Portable Walt Whitman. Ed. Michael Warner. New York: Penguin, 2004.

Anthology

> Kirszner, Laurie G., and Stephen R. Mandell, eds. Patterns for College Writing. 8th ed. New York: Bedford, 2001.

Essay in an Anthology

Grisham, John. "Unnatural Killers." Patterns for College Writing. Ed.
Laurie G. Kirszner and Stephen R. Mandell. 8th ed. New York:
Bedford, 2001. 566–75.

Periodicals

Journals

A **journal** is a publication aimed at readers who know a lot about a particular subject—literature or history, for example. The articles they contain can sometimes be challenging.

Article in a Journal with Continuous Pagination throughout Annual Volume

Some scholarly journals have continuous pagination; that is, one issue might end on page 234, and the next would then begin with page 235. In this case, the volume number is followed by the date of publication in parentheses.

Rubenstein, Rachel. "Going Native, Becoming Modern: American Indians, Walt Whitman, and the Yiddish Poet." American Quarterly 58
(2006): 431–53.

Article in a Journal with Separate Pagination in Each Issue

For a journal in which each issue begins with page 1, the volume number is followed by a period and the issue number and then by the date. Leave no space after the period.

Chu, Patricia E. "Dog and Dinosaur: The Modern Animal Story." Mosaic
40.1 (2007): 110–23.

Magazines

A **magazine** is a publication aimed at general readers. For this reason, it contains articles that are easier to understand than those in scholarly journals. Frequently, an article in a magazine does not appear on consecutive pages. For example, it may begin on page 40, skip to page 47, and continue on page 49. If this is the case, include only the first page, followed by a plus sign.

Article in a Monthly or Bimonthly Magazine

Royte, Elizabeth. "Corn Plastic to the Rescue?" Smithsonian Aug.
2006: 84+.

Newspapers

Article in a Newspaper

Friedman, Thomas. "Big Talk, Little Will." <u>New York Times</u> 16 Aug.
   2006: A17.

Editorial or Letter to the Editor

"The London Plot." Editorial. <u>New York Times</u> 11 Aug. 2006: A14.

Internet Sources

Full source information is not always available for Internet sources. When citing Internet sources, include whatever information you can find—ideally, the title of the Internet site (underlined), the date of electronic publication (if available), and the date you accessed the source. Always include the electronic address (URL) enclosed in angle brackets.

Document within a Web Site

"Food Borne Diseases." <u>National Institutes of Health Web Site</u>. Feb.
   2005. 16 Aug. 2007 <http://www.niaid.nih.gov/factsheets/
   foodbornedis.htm>.

Personal Site

Lynch, Jack. Home page. 14 Aug. 2007
   <http://andromeda.rutgers.edu/~jlynch>.

Article in an Online Reference Book or Encyclopedia

"Afghanistan." <u>The World Factbook</u>. 2006. Central Intelligence Agency.
   8 Aug. 2007 <http://www.cia.gov/cia/publications/factbook/
   geos/af.html>.

Article in a Newspaper

Meller, Paul. "European Court Reviews Two Cases Central to Issue of
   Competition." <u>New York Times on the Web</u> 27 Sept. 2004. 4 Oct.
   2007 <http://query.nytimes.com>.

Editorial

"Clarifying What Mr. Rumsfeld Meant." Editorial. <u>Washington Post</u> 27
   Sept. 2004. 4 Oct. 2007 <http://proquest.umi.com>.

Teaching Tip
Refer students to a hand-
book for additional
models.

Article in a Magazine

Greenberg, Randi. "Crop Cul-de-Sac." <u>Metropolis Magazine</u> Aug. 2006.
   17 July 2007 <http://www.metropolismag.com/cdd/
   story.php?artid=2241>.

Highlight: Preparing the Works-Cited List	• Begin the works-cited list on a new page after the last page of your essay.
	• Number the works-cited page as the next page of your essay.
	• Center the heading *Works Cited* one inch from the top of the page; do not underline the heading or place it in quotation marks.
	• Double-space the list.
	• List entries alphabetically according to the author's last name.
	• Alphabetize unsigned articles according to the first major word of the title.
	• Begin typing each entry at the left-hand margin.
	• Indent second and subsequent lines five spaces (or one-half inch).

Sample Essay (MLA Style)

Teaching Tip
Refer students to 12K for
format guidelines for their
papers.

Teaching Tip
Tell students that MLA
does not recommend a
separate title page.

Following is Allison Rogers's completed essay on the topic of media violence. The essay follows the MLA documentation style. Note that it has been
reproduced in a narrower format than a standard (8½- by 11-inch) sheet of
paper.

Rogers 1

Allison Rogers

Professor Sullivan

English 122

8 April 2007

Violence in the Media

Mickey and Mallory, two characters in Oliver Stone's film Natural Born Killers, travel across the Southwest, killing fifty-two people. After watching this movie, two teenagers went on a crime spree and killed one person and wounded another, paralyzing her for life. At their trial, their defense was that watching Natural Born Killers had made them commit their crimes and that Hollywood, along with the director of the movie, Oliver Stone, was to blame. As interesting as this defense is, it is no excuse for violent behavior. Only for young children do violent movies present a real danger.

According to John Grisham, Oliver Stone's Natural Born Killers "inspired two teenagers to commit murder" (5). Grisham goes on to say that several murders were committed by troubled adolescents who claimed they were influenced by Mickey and Mallory (5). This type of defense keeps reappearing as the violence in our everyday lives increases: "I am not to blame," says the perpetrator. "That movie (or television show) made me do it" (5).

The idea that media violence causes violent behavior is not supported by the facts. When we look at Ben and Sarah, the two teenagers who supposedly imitated Mickey and Mallory, it is

Introduction

Thesis statement

Paragraph combines quotation and summary from Grisham article with Allison's observations

Paragraph combines Allison's own conclusions with summaries of Stone's article and article from NIMH Web site

clear that factors other than Natural Born Killers influenced their decision to commit murder. Both young adults had long histories of drug and alcohol abuse as well as psychiatric treatment (Stone 39). In addition, no clear link between violent movies and television shows and aggressive behavior was established. In fact, recent studies suggest that no single factor causes antisocial behavior. Rather, such behavior develops over time and is influenced by the personality of the individual as well as his or her social environment ("Child and Adolescent Violence Research at the NIMH").

What are we supposed to make of crimes that seem to be inspired by the media? In most cases the movie or television show is never directly linked to the crime. For example, a Kentucky high school student fired an automatic weapon into a crowd of students in the school lobby. He killed three and wounded five, claiming he had seen this done by Leonardo DiCaprio's character in the movie Basketball Diaries. Naturally, it appeared as if the movie had inspired the crime. However, similar crimes had occurred throughout the country before the movie's release. So the question remains: Did the movie really cause the violence, or did it simply reflect a violent mood that was already present in society? The truth is that we cannot answer this question.

Paragraph contains Allison's own ideas so no documentation needed

Crimes that are actually caused by violent movies are extremely rare. Only a few people have had such extreme reactions to such movies, and because these people were mentally

Rogers 3

unbalanced, no one could have predicted what would set them off. It could have been a movie like <u>Natural Born Killers</u>, but it could also have been a Bugs Bunny cartoon or a Three Stooges movie.

Even though no direct link between media violence and violent behavior has been found, however, most people agree that young children are easily influenced by what they see. According to the American Academy of Pediatrics, the level of violence in children's cartoons is five times that of prime time television ("Some Things"). One study showed that children who watch violent shows "identify with aggressive same-sex TV characters" and believe that TV violence is real. These children tend to show aggressive behavior as young adults ("Childhood Exposure to Media Violence").

Clearly, young children should be protected from media violence. However, the responsibility for this protection lies with parents, not with the media. First, parents need to understand the need for monitoring what their children see on television and in the movies. Second, as the American Academy of Pediatrics suggests, parents should limit their children's TV viewing and discuss the content of the movies and shows children see ("Some Things").

There is no doubt that violence is learned and that violent media images encourage violent behavior in young children. It is not clear, however, that violent movies and television shows will actually cause a normal adult to commit a crime. For this reason, society should not limit the right of adults to watch

Paragraph combines Allison's own ideas with quotation from APA article and summary of article from American Academy of Pediatrics Web site

Conclusion

Rogers 4

movies and television shows just because a few unbalanced individuals might commit crimes. Placing blame on the media is just an easy way to sidestep the hard questions, such as what is causing so much violence in our society and what can be done about it. If we prohibit violent programs, we will deprive many adults of their right to view the programs of their choice, and we will prevent artists from expressing themselves freely. In the process, these restrictions will deprive society of a good deal of worthwhile entertainment.

Conclusion needs no documentation because it contains Allison's own ideas

Rogers 5

Works Cited

"Child and Adolescent Violence Research at the NIMH." <u>National Institute of
Mental Health Web Site</u>. 2000. 2 Mar. 2007 <http://www.nimh.nih.gov/
publicat/violenceresfact.cfm>.

"Childhood Exposure to Media Violence Predicts Young Adult Aggressive
Behavior." <u>American Psychological Association Web Site</u>. 9 Mar. 2003.
27 Feb. 2007 <http://www.uncg.edu/edu/ericcass/violence/index/htm>.

Grisham, John. "Unnatural Killers." <u>The Oxford American</u> Spring, 1996: 2–5.

"Some Things You Should Know about Media Violence and Media Literacy."
<u>American Academy of Pediatrics Web Site</u>. June 1995. 2 Mar. 2007
<http://www.aap.org/advocacy/childhealthmonth/media.htm>.

Stone, Oliver. "Memo to John Grisham: What's Next — A Movie Made Me
Do It?" <u>LA Weekly</u> 29 Mar. 1996: 39.

Articles from Web sites are listed by title because authors' names are not posted.

During your time as a student, you have probably taken a standardized test. In fact, you've probably taken several. (For example, a student in New York City takes an average of twenty-one standardized tests before graduating from high school.)

The most common standardized tests are exit exams and placement tests. **Exit exams** (like the Georgia Regents' Testing Program) determine whether you should graduate from college. They can also assess whether you are ready to move higher up in a program. **Placement tests** (like the COMPASS and ASSET tests) are designed to place you in classes that are right for your skill level.

Whether you're taking an exit exam or a placement test, there are several things you can do to prepare for them. Adequate preparation will help decrease your anxiety and increase your score.

Dealing with Anxiety

Not knowing what to expect from a standardized test can make you anxious. Some amount of test anxiety is natural and can actually help you to work harder and faster. However, if you are too worried, your judgment may be impaired, or you may freeze at the first question, wasting valuable time. The best way to beat test anxiety is to know your test before you take it and then practice as much as you can.

Preparing for Standardized Tests

1. *Read.* Learn about your test in advance so you know what it looks like and what kinds of questions it usually asks. In other words, look at examples of previous tests.

2. *Practice.* Go to the test's Web site to look for practice tests and other materials that can help you prepare. If your test is specific to your school, ask your instructor or librarian if a practice test is available. To review specific writing, grammar, and mechanics skills, refer to material covered in *Focus on Writing*. For extra practice questions, go to Exercise Central at **bedfordstmartins.com/focusonwriting.**

3. *Plan your time.* While you take the practice tests, figure out how much time you will need to complete each section, and develop a **time-plan** that tells you how much time to spend on each part of the test and how much time to spend planning and reviewing. Give yourself extra time for challenging sections, but don't spend all your time there. Then, on test day, write your time-plan in the test's margins, and refer back to it as you work (be sure to ask the exam proctor if you are allowed to write on the exam). Remember to reserve time to review your work at the end.

4. **Be rested and ready.** On the night before the exam, relax. Don't stay up too late, and avoid cramming. Instead, prepare a few days in advance so that you are not stressed out. In the morning, eat a good breakfast and review your time-plan. If you've done your research and taken a few practice tests, you should be ready.

Highlight: Common Exit Exams and Placement Tests

The following is a list of common exit exams and placement tests. Use the resources listed below to help you prepare for your test.

Accuplacer

To read more about how to prepare for the test, visit **collegeboard.com /student/testing/accuplacer/index.html** for tips, general information, and sample questions.

COMPASS/ASSET

To get more information about the COMPASS and ASSET tests, and to view student guides and samples, visit these Web sites: **act.org/compass** and **act.org/asset.**

CUNY/ACT

For sample student essays and practice tests for the CUNY/ACT test, visit the Skills Assessment Program's Web site at **rwc.hunter.cuny.edu/act /index.html**.

**Highlight:
Common Exit
Exams and
Placement Tests**
continued

THEA

For more information on the THEA and for access to a practice test, visit the THEA Web site at **thea.nesinc.com**.

CLAST

For general information on the CLAST, visit the CLAST Web site at **firn.edu/doe/sas/clsthome.htm**.

Georgia Regents' Tests

For more information on this test, including a sample reading skills test and a list of approved essay topics, go to **www2.gsu.edu/~wwwrtp**.

Tips for Multiple-Choice Questions

Multiple-choice questions measure both your ability to remember facts and your critical-thinking skills. These questions often have several answers that seem right. You are expected to find the *best* answer.

1. *Use your time-plan.* Before the test, find out what kind of time-keeping device (for example, a watch or a cellphone) you are allowed to bring into the exam. During the test, use the time-plan you developed to help you pace your work.

2. *Read the directions carefully.* The directions will tell you how to answer the questions, how much time you have for each question, and how questions will be graded. Keep these directions in mind as you work.

3. *Answer what is asked.* Be sure you know exactly what the question is asking. Read the question carefully, and be sure to highlight the question's key words. Think about how to answer the question before you answer it.

4. *Answer questions in order.* If you are taking a paper test, stay organized. Answer the questions in order, do not linger too long on any one question, and keep track of answers you have doubts about. After you have answered all the questions, recheck the ones you were uncertain of.

5. *Try to anticipate the answer.* Try to answer the question before you read through the answer choices (A, B, C, and D). Then, compare each of the possible choices to the answer you thought of. Be sure to read every word of each possible answer; often, the choices are similar.

6. ***Divide and conquer.*** If you cannot anticipate the answer, check each answer choice against the question. Eliminate any answers you know are incorrect. Of the remaining statements, pick the one that most precisely answers the question. If you are having trouble determining which one is most correct, try focusing on the differences between the remaining answers.

7. ***Consider "All of the above."*** If there is an "All of the above" answer choice and you have determined that at least two answer choices are correct, select "All of the above."

8. ***Identify negatives and absolutes.*** Underline negative words like *not*, *but*, *never*, and *except*. Negative words can change a question in important ways. For example, "Choose the answer that is correct" is very different from "Choose the answer that is *not* correct." Be especially alert for double (and even triple) negatives within a sentence. Work out each question's true meaning before you attempt to answer it. (For example, "He was *not* unfriendly" means that he was friendly.) Also underline absolutes such as *always*, *never*, and *only*. Answers containing absolutes are often incorrect because exceptions can be found to almost every absolute statement.

9. ***Make an educated guess.*** If you're still not sure which answer to select, make an educated guess. Before guessing, eliminate as many answers as possible. Then, select an answer that uses a qualifying term, like *usually*, *often*, or *most*. If all else fails, choose the answer that you first thought seemed right. Your first instinct is often correct.

10. ***Computer-adaptive tests.*** If you are taking a computer-adaptive test, keep in mind that the questions get harder as you answer them correctly. Do not get discouraged if the final questions of each section are very difficult (the final questions affect your score much less than earlier questions). Also remember that computer-adaptive tests prevent you from returning to difficult questions. Even so, you should not spend too much time on one question; if you aren't sure, make an educated guess. Finally, be sure to use scratch paper. You will not be able to use the computer to work out answers.

Tips for Essay Questions

The essays you write on standardized tests are similar to the essays that you write in class. However, test essays are often scored differently. In addition, some tests might call for more than one essay—for example, one essay will assess grammar and mechanics while another will assess critical-thinking skills. Pay close attention to the instructions on your test. Review the points that follow to help you prepare.

1. ***Know how to score points.*** Before the test, find out how your essay will be scored. Ask your teacher or librarian, look at a practice test, or visit the test's Web site to find out what the test emphasizes. If this information is not available, assume that large issues (like ideas, logic, and organization) will be more important than small ones (like spelling and grammar) — although all of these elements count.

2. ***Know what's being asked.*** When you take the test, read through each essay question and all of the directions. Make sure you understand them before continuing. Some standardized tests require you to write multiple essays in a limited amount of time; find out in advance if that is the case with your test.

3. ***Tackle easy questions first.*** Read all the questions, and begin with the one that seems the easiest. Starting strong will help ease your anxiety and give you momentum. In addition, you will score higher if you finish your best work before time runs out.

4. ***Make a plan.*** Quickly jot down your initial essay ideas. Then, develop a thesis, and make a rough outline of your essay. The few minutes you spend planning will improve your essay's organization and keep you on track as you work.

5. ***Get down to business.*** On standardized essay tests, keep your writing lean and efficient. Avoid long, complicated introductions. Instead, begin your first paragraph with a sentence that directly answers the essay question and states your thesis. After you've stated your thesis, keep it in mind for the rest of your essay. Look back at the question as you write, and make sure your essay is answering it.

6. ***Manage your time.*** If you run out of time before you finish writing, quickly jot down an outline of your remaining ideas. If you have time, use the **TEST** strategy to check your essay, looking for a clear thesis, supporting evidence, a summary statement, and transitions. Finally, quickly proofread your work and correct any grammatical or mechanical errors.

Teaching Tip
Refer students to 12H for information on **TEST**ing an essay.

7. ***Use in-class essays as practice.*** As you write essays for your classes, ask yourself how effective your essay would be if you were writing it on a standardized test. How would you change the essay to achieve a higher score? Over time, this kind of practice will help you to be more confident and accurate in test situations.

Word Power: Your Personal Vocabulary List

On the pages that follow, keep a list of new words you come across in your reading. Write down a brief definition of each word, and then use it in a sentence.

Example:

Word: _____memento_____ **Definition:** _____a reminder of the past_____

_____

Sentence: _____I kept a seashell as a memento of our vacation at the beach._____

_____

Word: _____ **Definition:** _____

_____

Sentence: _____

_____

Word: _____ **Definition:** _____

_____

Sentence: _____

_____

Word: _____ **Definition:** _____

_____

Sentence: _____

_____

Word: _____ **Definition:** _____

_____

Sentence: _____

_____

Word: _____ Definition: _____

_____

Sentence: _____

_____

Word: _____ Definition: _____

_____

Sentence: _____

_____

Word: _____ Definition: _____

_____

Sentence: _____

_____

Word: _____ Definition: _____

_____

Sentence: _____

_____

Word: _____ Definition: _____

_____

Sentence: _____

_____

Word: _____ Definition: _____

_____

Sentence: _____

_____

Word: _____ Definition: _____

_____

Sentence: _____

_____

Word: _____ Definition: _____

_____

Sentence: _____

_____

Word: _____ Definition: _____

_____

Sentence: _____

_____

Word: _____ Definition: _____

_____

Sentence: _____

_____

Word: _____ Definition: _____

_____

Sentence: _____

_____

Word: _____ Definition: _____

_____

Sentence: _____

_____

Word: _____ Definition: _____

_____

Sentence: _____

_____

Word: _____ Definition: _____

_____

Sentence: _____

_____

Word: _____ Definition: _____

_____

Sentence: _____

_____

Word: _____ Definition: _____

_____

Sentence: _____

_____

Word: _____ Definition: _____

_____

Sentence: _____

_____

Word: _____ Definition: _____

_____

Sentence: _____

_____

Word: _____ Definition: _____

_____

Sentence: _____

_____

Answers to Odd-Numbered Exercise Items

Chapter 14

● Practice 14-1, page 208

Answers: **1.** Derek Walcott **3.** years **5.** poems **7.** Walcott **9.** he **11.** poet

● Practice 14-2, page 208

Possible answers: **1.** animals **3.** Pets **5.** Employees **7.** patients **9.** dogs

● Practice 14-3, page 209

Answers: **1.** bridge; singular **3.** Channel Tunnel; singular **5.** tubes; plural **7.** tube; singular **9.** pipes; plural

● Practice 14-4, page 210

Answers: **1.** ~~With more than 27 percent of the vote~~, Theodore Roosevelt was the strongest third-party candidate ~~in history~~. **3.** ~~Until Roosevelt~~, no third-party candidate had won a significant number ~~of votes~~. **5.** ~~For example~~, Robert M. LaFollette ~~of the Progressive Party~~ won about 16 percent ~~of the vote in the 1924 race~~. **7.** ~~In 1980~~, John B. Anderson, an Independent, challenged Republican Ronald Reagan and Democrat Jimmy Carter and got 6.6 percent ~~of the vote~~. **9.** ~~In 2000~~, ~~with the support of many environmentalists~~, Ralph Nader challenged Al Gore and George W. Bush ~~for the presidency~~. **11.** ~~To this day~~, the two-party system ~~of the United States~~ has remained intact ~~despite many challenges by third-party candidates~~.

● Practice 14-5, page 212

Answers: **1.** see **3.** offers **5.** enters; wins **7.** realizes **9.** enjoy

● Practice 14-6, page 213

Answers: **1.** are **3.** is **5.** is **7.** becomes **9.** are

● Practice 14-7, page 214

Answers: **1.** wrote **3.** is; seems **5.** lives **7.** dies **9.** works

● Practice 14-8, page 215

Answers: **1.** Complete verb: had become; helping verb: had **3.** Complete verb: had become; helping verb: had **5.** Complete verb: would get; helping verb: would **7.** Complete verb: did cause; helping verb: did **9.** Complete verb: would remain; helping verb: would

Chapter 15

● Practice 15-1, page 222

Possible answers: **1.** and **3.** and **5.** and **7.** so/and **9.** for

● Practice 15-2, page 223

Possible answers: **1.** Training a dog to heel is difficult, for dogs naturally resist strict control. **3.** Students should spend two hours of study time for each hour of class time, or they may not do well in the course. **5.** Each state in the United States has two senators, but the number of representatives depends on the state's population. **7.** A "small craft advisory" warns boaters of bad weather conditions, for these conditions can be dangerous to small boats. **9.** Hip-hop fashions include sneakers and baggy pants, and these styles are also very popular with young men.

● Practice 15-3, page 224

Possible edits: Diet, exercise, and family history may account for centenarians' long lives, but this is not the whole story. Recently, a study conducted in Georgia showed surprising common traits among centenarians. They did not necessarily avoid tobacco and alcohol, nor did they have low-fat diets. In fact, they ate relatively large amounts of fat, cholesterol, and sugar, so diet could not explain their long lives. They did, however, share four key survival characteristics. First, all of the centenarians were optimistic about life, and all of them were positive thinkers. They were also involved in religious life and had deep religious faith. In addition, all the centenarians had continued to lead physically active lives, and they remained mobile even as elderly people. Finally, all were able to adapt to loss. They had all experienced the deaths of friends, spouses, or children, but they were able to get on with their lives.

● Practice 15-4, page 224

Answers will vary.

● Practice 15-5, page 226

Answers will vary.

● Practice 15-6, page 229

Answers: 1. Andrew F. Smith, a food historian, wrote a book about the tomato; later, he wrote a book about ketchup.   **3.** The word *ketchup* may have come from a Chinese word; however, Smith is not certain of the word's origins.   **5.** Ketchup has changed a lot over the years; for example, special dyes were developed in the nineteenth century to make it red.   **7.** Ketchup is now used by people in many cultures; still, salsa is more popular than ketchup in the United States.   **9.** Some of today's ketchups are chunky; in addition, some ketchups are spicy.

● Practice 15-7, page 230

Possible answers: 1. The Man of the Year has greatly influenced the previous year's events; consequently, the choice is often a prominent politician. **3.** During World War II, Hitler, Stalin, Churchill, and Roosevelt were all chosen; in fact, Stalin was featured twice.   **5.** In 1956, The Hungarian Freedom Fighter was Man of the Year; then, in 1966, *Time* editors chose The Young Generation.   **7.** In 1975, American Women were honored as a group; nevertheless, the Man of the Year has nearly always been male. **9.** The Man of the Year has almost always been one or more human beings; however, The Computer was selected in 1982 and Endangered Earth in 1988.   **11.** In 2003, *Time* did not choose a politician; instead, it honored The American Soldier. **13.** In 2005, *Time* wanted to honor the contributions of philanthropists; thus, the magazine named Bill Gates, Melinda Gates, and Bono its Persons of the Year.

● Practice 15-8, page 231

Possible answers: 1. Campus residents may have a better college experience; still, being a commuter

has its advantages.   **3.** Commuters have a wide choice of jobs in the community; on the other hand, students living on campus may have to take on-campus jobs.   **5.** There are also some disadvantages to being a commuter; for example, commuters may have trouble joining study groups.   **7.** Commuters might have to help take care of their parents or grandparents; in addition, they might have to babysit for younger siblings.   **9.** Younger commuters may be under the watchful eyes of their parents; of course, parents are likely to be stricter than dorm counselors.

● Practice 15-9, page 232

Answers will vary.

Chapter 16

● Practice 16-1, page 240

Answers: 1. IC   **3.** DC   **5.** IC   **7.** IC   **9.** DC

● Practice 16-2, page 240

Answers: 1. IC   **3.** IC   **5.** DC   **7.** DC   **9.** IC

● Practice 16-3, page 242

Possible answers: 1. when   **3.** Although **5.** Since   **7.** Although   **9.** that

● Practice 16-4, page 243

Possible answers: 1. Although professional midwives are used widely in Europe, in the United States, they are less common.   **3.** Stephen Crane describes battles in *The Red Badge of Courage* even though he never experienced a war.   **5.** After Jonas Salk developed the first polio vaccine in the 1950s, the number of polio cases in the United States declined.   **7.** Before the Du Ponts arrived from France in 1800, American gunpowder was not as good as French gunpowder.   **9.** Because Thaddeus Stevens thought plantation land should be given to free slaves, he disagreed with Lincoln's peace plan for the South.

● Practice 16-5, page 246

Possible answers: 1. Dependent clause: which was performed by a group called the Buggles; relative pronoun: which; noun: video   **3.** Dependent clause: who had been suspicious of MTV at first; relative pronoun: who; noun: executives   **5.** Dependent clause: which aired in September 1984; relative pronoun: which; noun: awards   **7.** Dependent clause: who was its first host; relative pronoun: who; noun: Cindy Crawford   **9.** Dependent clause: who would soon be elected president; relative pronoun: who; noun: Bill Clinton

● Practice 16-6, page 246

Possible answers: 1. Their work, which benefits both the participants and the communities, is called service-learning.   **3.** The young people, who are not paid, work at projects such as designing neighborhood playgrounds.   **5.** Designing a playground, which requires teamwork, teaches them to cooperate.   **7.** They also learn to solve problems that the community cannot solve by itself. **9.** The young participants, who often lack self-confidence, gain satisfaction from performing a valuable service.

Chapter 17

● Practice 17-1, page 254

Answers will vary.

● Practice 17-2, page 255

Revised sentences will vary. Adverbs: 1. however **3.** often   **5.** now

● Practice 17-3, page 256

Answers will vary.

● Practice 17-4, page 256

Revised sentences will vary. Prepositional phrases: 1. during World War II   **3.** between 1942 and 1945 **5.** after the war

● Practice 17-5, page 257

Answers will vary.

● Practice 17-6, page 258

Possible answers: 1. José Martí was born in Havana in 1853, at a time when Cuba was a colony of Spain.   **3.** In 1870, the Spanish authorities forced him to leave Cuba and go to Spain.   **5.** Working as a journalist and professor, he returned to Cuba but was sent away again.   **7.** During his time in New York, he started the journal of the Cuban Revolutionary party.   **9.** Passionately following up his words with actions, he died in battle against Spanish soldiers in Cuba.

● Practice 17-7, page 259

Possible answers: 1. Taking advantage of this situation, some private businesses hire prisoners to work for them.   **3.** Learning new skills as they work, the prisoners are better prepared to find jobs after prison.   **5.** Costing less to run, these prisons benefit taxpayers.

● Practice 17-8, page 260

Answers will vary.

● Practice 17-9, page 261

Possible answers: 1. Captured as a young girl by a rival tribe, Sacajawea was later sold into slavery. **3.** Hired by the explorers Lewis and Clark in 1806, Charbonneau brought his pregnant wife along on their westward expedition.   **5.** Created in 2000, a U.S. dollar coin now shows her picture.

● Practice 17-10, page 262

Answers will vary.

● Practice 17-11, page 263

Answers will vary.

● Practice 17-12, page 265

Possible answers: 1. A playwright who wrote the prize-winning *A Raisin in the Sun*, Lorraine Hansberry was born in Chicago in 1930. **3.** Hostile neighbors there threw a brick through a window of their house, an act Hansberry never forgot.

● Practice 17-13, page 267

Possible edits: Kente cloth is made in western Africa and produced primarily by the Ashanti people. It has been worn for hundreds of years by African royalty, who consider it a sign of power and status. Many African Americans wear kente cloth because they see it as a link to their heritage. Each pattern on the cloth has a name, and each color has a special significance. For example, red and yellow suggest a long and healthy life while green and white suggest a good harvest. Although African women may wear kente cloth as a dress or a head wrap, African-American women, like men, usually wear strips of cloth around their shoulders. Men and women of African descent wear kente cloth as a sign of racial pride; in fact, it often decorates college students' gowns at graduation.

Chapter 18

● Practice 18-1, page 274

Answers: **1.** I just bought a head of lettuce, a pint of mushrooms, and three pounds of tomatoes.
3. The plumber needs to fix a leaky pipe, replace a missing faucet, and fix a running toilet.   **5.** P
7. P   **9.** P

● Practice 18-2, page 276
Answers will vary.

Chapter 19

● Practice 19-1, page 282

Answers: **1.** three fifty-watt bulbs; coal oil; baking bread   **3.** wooden table; unfinished game of checkers; apple-tree stump   **5.** none

● Practice 19-2, page 282
Answers will vary.

● Practice 19-3, page 283
Answers will vary.

● Practice 19-4, page 284

Possible edits: **1.** To become an informed used-car buyer, the first thing a person should do is to look on the Internet and in the local newspapers to get an idea of the prices.   **3.** When first seeing the car, carefully search for new paint that looks different from the paint in the surrounding area.   **5.** Check the engine for problems like broken wires, cracked hoses, and leaks.   **7.** Push down suddenly on the accelerator while the car is running, and see if the car hesitates.   **9.** Even if there does not seem to be anything wrong with the car, take it to a mechanic you trust to inspect it.

● Practice 19-5, page 286
Answers will vary.

● Practice 19-6, page 287

Possible answers: **1.** Many people think that a million-dollar lottery jackpot allows the winner to stop working long hours and start living a comfortable life.   **3.** For one thing, lottery winners who win big prizes do not always receive their winnings all at once; instead, payments—for example, $50,000—can be spread out over twenty years.   **5.** Next come relatives and friends who ask for money, leaving winners with difficult choices to make.   **7.** Even worse, many lottery winners have lost their jobs because employers thought that once they were "millionaires," they no longer needed to draw a salary.
9. Faced with financial difficulties, many might like to sell their future payments to companies that offer lump-sum payments of forty or forty-five cents on the dollar.

● Practice 19-7, page 289
Answers will vary.

● Practice 19-8, page 289
Answers will vary.

● Practice 19-9, page 291

Possible edits: **1.** Many people today would like to see more police officers patrolling the streets.
3. All the soldiers picked up their weapons.
5. Travel to other planets will be a significant step for humanity.

Chapter 20

● Practice 20-1, page 302

Answers: **1.** FS   **3.** CS   **5.** CS   **7.** C   **9.** FS

● Practice 20-2, page 302

Answers: **1.** FS   **3.** FS   **5.** FS   **7.** C   **9.** C
11. C

● Practice 20-3, page 304

Answers: **1.** Hurricane Katrina destroyed many homes in New Orleans. It destroyed many businesses, too.   **3.** Americans watched the terrible scenes. Hundreds died waiting for rescuers.
5. Residents of flooded communities vowed to return. They knew it would not be easy.

● Practice 20-4, page 305

Answers: **1.** Right after World War II, some television programs showed actual scenes of war, and *Victory at Sea* and *The Big Picture* were two of those programs.   **3.** In the 1970s, *MASH* depicted a Korean War medical unit, yet the show was really about the Vietnam War.   **5.** The Iraq War drama *Over There* was shown in 2005, but it was cancelled after a few months.

● Practice 20-5, page 306

Answers: **1.** New Mexico governor Bill Richardson has been a U.N. ambassador and a U.S. senator; Nydia Velazquez is a U.S. representative. **3.** Roberto Clemente was a professional baseball player; Oscar de la Hoya achieved fame as a professional boxer. **5.** Luis Valdez is a noted playwright and film director; his plays include *Los Vendidos* and *The Zoot Suit*.

● Practice 20-6, page 307

Answers: **1.** High schools have always taught subjects like English and math; now, many also teach personal finance and consumer education. **3.** Consumer-education courses can be very practical; for instance, students can learn how to buy, finance, and insure a car. **5.** Academic subjects will always dominate the high school curriculum; however, courses focusing on practical life skills are becoming increasingly important.

● Practice 20-7, page 309

Possible answers: **1.** Although Harlem was populated mostly by European immigrants at the turn of the last century, it saw an influx of African Americans beginning in 1910. **3.** After many black artists and writers settled in Harlem during the 1920s, African-American art flowered. **5.** When scholars recognize the great works of the Harlem Renaissance, they point to the writers Langston Hughes and Countee Cullen and the artists Henry Tanner and Sargent Johnson. **7.** Because Harlem was an exciting place in the 1920s, people from all over the city went there to listen to jazz and to dance. **9.** Although contemporary historians know about the Harlem Renaissance, its importance is still not widely understood.

● Practice 20-8, page 310

Possible answers: **1.** Nursing offers job security and high pay; therefore, many people are choosing nursing as a career. **3.** The Democratic Republic of the Congo was previously known as Zaire; before that, it was the Belgian Congo. **5.** Millions of Jews were killed during the Holocaust; in addition, Catholics, Gypsies, homosexuals, and other "undesirables" were killed. **7.** Japanese athletes now play various positions on American baseball teams; at first, all the Japanese players were pitchers.

9. Père Nöel is the French name for Santa Claus; he is also known as Father Christmas and St. Nicholas.

● Practice 20-9, page 311

Possible answers: **1.** In the late nineteenth century, Coney Island was famous; in fact, it was legendary. **3.** Coney Island was considered exotic and exciting; it even had a hotel shaped like an elephant. **5.** It had beaches, hotels, racetracks, and a stadium; however, by the turn of the century, it was best known for three amusement parks. **7.** Even though gaslight was still the norm in New York, a million electric lights lit Luna Park. **9.** At Dreamland, people could see a submarine; in addition, they could travel through an Eskimo village or visit Lilliputia, with its three hundred midgets. **11.** Fire destroyed Dreamland in 1911, and Luna Park burned down in 1946. **13.** The once-grand Coney Island is gone. Still, its beach and its boardwalk remain. **15.** Now, a ballpark has been built for a new minor league baseball team. The new team is called the Brooklyn Cyclones.

Chapter 21

● Practice 21-1, page 318

Answers: **1.** F **3.** F **5.** F **7.** F **9.** F

● Practice 21-2, page 318

Answers: Items 2, 4, 6, and 7 are fragments. *Rewrite:* Sara Paretsky writes detective novels, such as *Burn Marks* and *Guardian Angel*. These novels are about V. I. Warshawski, a private detective. V. I. lives and works in Chicago, the Windy City. Every day as a detective, V. I. takes risks. V. I. is tough. She is also a woman.

● Practice 21-3, page 320

Answers will vary.

● Practice 21-4, page 322

Answers: **1.** The U.S. flag was designed by Francis Hopkinson, a New Jersey delegate to the Continental Congress. **3.** Congress officially recognized the Pledge of Allegiance in 1942, the year the United States entered World War II. **5.** Some people wanted a different national anthem, such as "America" or "America the Beautiful."

● Practice 21-5, page 323

Answers: **1.** First-born children are reliable, serious, and goal-oriented in most cases. **3.** In large families, middle children often form close relationships outside of the family. **5.** Youngest children often take a while to settle down into careers and marriages.

● Practice 21-6, page 324

Answers will vary.

● Practice 21-7, page 326

Answers: **1.** Always try to find a store brand costing less than the well-known and widely advertised brands. **3.** Check supermarket flyers for sale items offered at a special low price. **5.** Finally, ask friends and neighbors for shopping suggestions based on their own experiences.

● Practice 21-8, page 327

Answers will vary.

● Practice 21-9, page 329

Possible answers: **1.** Chimpanzees sometimes pick the leaves off twigs to create a tool for scooping honey. **3.** You need to replace the bottle cap very tightly to preserve the soda's carbonation. **5.** With patience and skill, some hawks can be trained to hunt small animals and birds for their human owners.

● Practice 21-10, page 330

Answers will vary.

● Practice 21-11, page 333

Answers will vary.

● Practice 21-12, page 333

Answers will vary.

● Practice 21-13, page 334

Answers will vary.

Chapter 22

● Practice 22-1, page 342

Answers: **1.** know **3.** include **5.** sell; top **7.** surprises **9.** hosts; draws

● Practice 22-2, page 342

Answers: **1.** cut **3.** puts **5.** grow **7.** hardens **9.** leaves

● Practice 22-3, page 344

Answers: **1.** fill **3.** watch **5.** plays **7.** smell **9.** greets

● Practice 22-4, page 345

Answers: **1.** have **3.** has **5.** do **7.** is **9.** has

● Practice 22-5, page 347

Answers: **1.** The cupids in the painting symbolize lost innocence. **3.** The appliances in the kitchen make strange noises. **5.** A good set of skis and poles costs a lot. **7.** Workers in the city pay a high wage tax. **9.** Volunteers, including people like my father, help paramedics in my community.

● Practice 22-6, page 348

Answers: **1.** reaches **3.** goes **5.** is

● Practice 22-7, page 350

Answers: **1.** has **3.** wants **5.** takes **7.** seems **9.** is

● Practice 22-8, page 351

Answers: **1.** Subject: Bering Straits; verb: are **3.** Subject: twins; verb: Are **5.** Subject: this; verb: has **7.** Subject: people; verb: are **9.** Subject: reasons; verb: are

Chapter 23

● Practice 23-1, page 358

Answers: **1.** At the start of World War II, 120,000 Japanese Americans were sent to relocation camps because the government feared that they might be disloyal to the United States. **3.** The Japanese-American volunteers were organized into the 442nd Combat Infantry Regiment. **5.** When other U.S. troops were cut off by the enemy, the 442nd Infantry soldiers were sent to rescue them. **7.** Former senator Daniel Inouye of Hawaii, a Japanese American, was awarded the Distinguished Service Cross for his bravery in Italy and had to have his arm amputated. **9.** The dedication and sacrifice of the 442nd Infantry is now widely seen as evidence that Japanese Americans were patriotic and committed to freedom and democracy.

● Practice 23-2, page 360

Answers: **1.** Young people who want careers in the fashion industry do not always realize how hard they will have to work. **3.** In reality, no matter how talented he or she is, a recent college graduate entering the industry is paid only about $22,000 a year. **5.** A young designer may receive a big raise if he or she is very talented, but this is unusual. **7.** An employee may be excited to land a job as an assistant designer but then find that he or she has to color in designs that have already been drawn. **9.** If a person is serious about working in the fashion industry, he or she has to be realistic.

● Practice 23-3, page 361

Answers: **1.** A local university funded the study, and Dr. Alicia Flynn led the research team. **3.** Two-thirds of the subjects relied on intuition, and only one-third used logic. **5.** Many experts read the report, and most of them found the results surprising.

Chapter 24

● Practice 24-1, page 368

Answers will vary.

● Practice 24-2, page 369

Answers will vary.

● Practice 24-3, page 370

Possible answers: **1.** Frightened by a noise, the cat broke the vase. **3.** The man with red hair was sitting in the chair. **5.** People are sometimes killed by snakes, with their deadly venom. **7.** I ran outside in my bathrobe and saw eight tiny reindeer. **9.** Wearing a mask, the exterminator sprayed the insect.

Chapter 25

● Practice 25-1, page 381

Answers: **1.** She always returned with intricate designs on her hands and feet. **3.** Henna originated in a plant found in the Middle East, India, Indonesia, and northern Africa. **5.** Men dyed their beards, as well as the manes and hooves of their horses, with henna. **7.** In India, my mother always celebrated the end of the Ramadan religious fast by going to a "henna party." **9.** After a few weeks, the henna designs washed off.

● Practice 25-2, page 384

Answers: **1.** came; was **3.** went **5.** became **7.** thought **9.** began

● Practice 25-3, page 385

Answers: **1.** Correct **3.** Correct **5.** was **7.** Correct **9.** was

● Practice 25-4, page 387

Answers: **1.** would; would **3.** would **5.** would **7.** could **9.** would

Chapter 26

● Practice 26-1, page 393

Answers: **1.** visited **3.** raised **5.** joined **7.** removed **9.** served

● Practice 26-2, page 397

Answers: **1.** taught **3.** built **5.** become **7.** written **9.** said

● Practice 26-3, page 398

Answers: **1.** become **3.** led **5.** Correct **7.** spoken; Correct **9.** Correct

● Practice 26-4, page 400

Answers: **1.** heard **3.** belonged **5.** spoke **7.** made **9.** were

● Practice 26-5, page 400

Answers: **1.** measured **3.** have used **5.** has taken **7.** has ensured **9.** have received

● Practice 26-6, page 402

Answers: **1.** had left **3.** had arrived **5.** had lied **7.** had decided **9.** had been

● Practice 26-7, page 404

Answers: **1.** surprised; preapproved **3.** designed **5.** stuffed **7.** concerned **9.** acquired

Chapter 27

● Practice 27-1, page 411

Answers: **1.** headaches (regular) **3.** feet (irregular) **5.** deer (irregular) **7.** brides-to-be (irregular)

9. loaves (irregular)   **11.** beaches (regular)
13. sons-in-law (irregular)   **15.** wives (irregular)
17. elves (irregular)   **19.** catalogs (regular)

● Practice 27-2, page 412

Answers: 1. travelers-to-be   **3.** Correct; delays;
duties   **5.** Correct; boxes   **7.** tools   **9.** gases

● Practice 27-3, page 414

Answers: 1. I   **3.** he   **5.** I; it; it   **7.** she; I; I
9. I; you

● Practice 27-4, page 415

Answers: 1. Antecedent: campuses; pronoun:
they   **3.** Antecedent: students; pronoun: their
5. Antecedent: Joyce; pronoun: she   **7.** Antecedent:
friends; pronoun: them

● Practice 27-5, page 416

Answers: 1. Compound antecedent: Larry and
Curly; connecting word: and; pronoun: their
3. Compound antecedent: Laurel and Hardy; connecting word: and; pronoun: their   **5.** Compound
antecedent: *MASH* or *The Fugitive*; connecting word:
or; pronoun: its   **7.** Compound antecedent: film or
videotapes; connecting word: or; pronoun: their
9. Compound antecedent: popcorn and soft drinks;
connecting word: and; pronoun: their

● Practice 27-6, page 419

Answers: 1. Indefinite pronoun: either; pronoun:
its   **3.** Indefinite pronoun: Everything; pronoun:
its   **5.** Indefinite pronoun: Neither; pronoun: her
7. Indefinite pronoun: Several; pronoun: their
9. Indefinite pronoun: Anyone; pronoun: his or her

● Practice 27-7, page 419

Possible answers: 1. Everyone has the right to his
or her own opinion.   **3.** Somebody forgot his or her
backpack.   **5.** Someone in the store has left his or
her car's lights on.   **7.** Each of the applicants must
have his or her driver's license.   **9.** Either of the
coffeemakers comes with its own filter.

● Practice 27-8, page 420

Answers: 1. Collective noun antecedent: company;
pronoun: its   **3.** Collective noun antecedent: government; pronoun: its   **5.** Collective noun antecedent:
union; pronoun: its

● Practice 27-9, page 421

Answers: 1. Antecedent: women; pronoun:
Correct   **3.** Antecedent: women; pronoun: their
5. Antecedent: Elizabeth Cady Stanton and Lucretia
Mott; pronoun: their   **7.** Antecedent: women; pronoun: their   **9.** Antecedent: the U.S. government;
pronoun: its

● Practice 27-10, page 423

Answers: 1. Possessive   **3.** Possessive
5. Subjective   **7.** Possessive; Subjective
9. Subjective

● Practice 27-11, page 425

Answers: 1. I   **3.** I   **5.** Correct   **7.** she; I
9. her

● Practice 27-12, page 426

Answers: 1. [they like] him   **3.** [it affected] me
5. [it fits] me

● Practice 27-13, page 428

Answers: 1. whom   **3.** Whom   **5.** whom

● Practice 27-14, page 429

Answers: 1. themselves   **3.** himself   **5.** yourself

Chapter 28

● Practice 28-1, page 436

Answers: 1. poorly   **3.** truly   **5.** really   **7.** specifically   **9.** important; immediately

● Practice 28-2, page 437

Answers: 1. well   **3.** good   **5.** well   **7.** well
9. well

● Practice 28-3, page 440

Answers: 1. more slowly   **3.** healthier   **5.** more
loudly   **7.** more respectful   **9.** wilder

● Practice 28-4, page 441

Answers: 1. largest   **3.** most successful   **5.** most
powerful   **7.** most serious   **9.** most popular

● Practice 28-5, page 442

Answers: 1. better   **3.** worse   **5.** better   **7.** best
9. better

Chapter 29

● Practice 29-1, page 448

Answers: **1.** When the first season of the reality show *Survivor* aired, it was an immediate hit. **3.** It was not surprising to see the many other reality shows that suddenly appeared on the air. **5.** Most viewers thought that reality TV had gone too far even though they enjoyed shows like *Fear Factor* and *The Apprentice*.

● Practice 29-2, page 449

Possible answers: **1.** The first parts of the Great Wall were built around 200 A.D. **3.** The sides of the Great Wall are made of stone, brick, and earth. **5.** The Great Wall is the only man-made object that can be seen by astronauts in space.

● Practice 29-3, page 450

Answers: **1.** species; sharks **3.** Sharks **5.** No plural nouns **7.** sharks; meat-eaters; species; people **9.** Sharks

● Practice 29-4, page 452

Answers: **1.** Count: approaches **3.** Noncount **5.** Count: shortages **7.** Count: individuals **9.** Count: systems

● Practice 29-5, page 454

Answers: **1.** every **3.** A few violent **5.** many **7.** Many **9.** some

● Practice 29-6, page 458

Answers: **1.** the; a **3.** No article needed **5.** the; the; the; No article needed **7.** No article needed **9.** a **11.** a; No article needed; No article needed; the

● Practice 29-7, page 461

Answers will vary.

● Practice 29-8, page 464

Answers: **1.** were signing: Correct **3.** was: Correct; was believing: believed; was: Correct **5.** study: Correct; want: Correct; have left: Correct **7.** are often seeing: often see; are touching: touch; pick up: Correct **9.** weigh: Correct; are deciding: decide

● Practice 29-9, page 466

Answers: **1.** might **3.** should **5.** should **7.** Would **9.** can

● Practice 29-10, page 467

Answers: **1.** Eating **3.** cleaning **5.** Quitting **7.** organizing **9.** cooking

● Practice 29-11, page 469

Answers: **1.** a brand-new high-rise apartment building **3.** numerous successful short-story collections **5.** the publisher's three best-selling works **7.** a strong-willed young woman **9.** an exquisite white wedding gown

● Practice 29-12, page 474

Answers: **1.** in; in **3.** in; at; to **5.** in; in; in **7.** to; in; with; from; to; with; with **9.** with; at; of **11.** on; on **13.** to

● Practice 29-13, page 477

Answers: **1.** In one case, a New Jersey woman found that a hungry bear woke her up from a nap one afternoon. **3.** Actually, although it can be frightening to run into bears, most wild bears are timid. **5.** The amount of blueberries and other wild fruit that bears eat usually drops off in dry weather. **7.** It is a good idea for families to go over their plans to safeguard their property against bears. **9.** If people have bird feeders in the yard, they should put them away during the autumn.

Chapter 30

● Practice 30-1, page 488

Answers: **1.** The musician plays guitar, bass, and drums. **3.** Correct **5.** The diary Anne Frank kept while her family hid from the Nazis is insightful, touching, and sometimes humorous. **7.** Correct **9.** California's capital is Sacramento, its largest city is Los Angeles, and its oldest settlement is San Diego.

● Practice 30-2, page 489

Answers: **1.** In the past few years, many Olympic athletes have been disqualified because they tested positive for banned drugs. **3.** In the past, banned steroids were the most common cause of positive

drug tests.   **5.** Correct   **7.** Disappointing thousands of fans, two Greek sprinting stars refused to participate in a drug test at the Athens Olympics.
9. For using a banned stimulant in April 2004, American sprinter Torri Edwards was banned from competition for two years.

● Practice 30-3, page 491

Answers: **1.** For example, the African-American celebration of Kwanzaa was introduced in the 1960s.
3. By the way, the word *Kwanzaa* means "first fruits" in Swahili.   **5.** This, of course, can be demonstrated in some of the seven principles of Kwanzaa.   **7.** The focus, first of all, is on unity (*umoja*).
9. In addition, Kwanzaa celebrations emphasize three kinds of community responsibility (*ujima*, *ujamaa*, and *nia*).

● Practice 30-4, page 492

Answers: **1.** Traditional Chinese medicine is based on meridians, channels of energy believed to run in regular patterns through the body.   **3.** Herbal medicine, the basis of many Chinese healing techniques, requires twelve years of study.   **5.** Correct
7. Nigeria, the most populous country in Africa, is also one of the fastest-growing nations in the world.
9. The Yoruban people, the Nigerian settlers of Lagos, are unusual in Africa because they tend to form large urban communities.

● Practice 30-5, page 495

Answers: **1.** Correct   **3.** Correct   **5.** The Japanese had just landed in the Aleutian Islands, which lie west of the tip of the Alaska Peninsula.   **7.** As a result, they made them work under conditions that made construction difficult.   **9.** In one case, white engineers who surveyed a river said it would take two weeks to bridge.   **11.** Correct

● Practice 30-6, page 497

Answers: **1.** The American Declaration of Independence was approved on July 4, 1776.   **3.** At 175 Carlton Avenue, Brooklyn, New York, is the house where Richard Wright began writing *Native Son*.   **5.** Correct   **7.** The Pueblo Grande Museum is located at 1469 East Washington Street, Phoenix, Arizona.
9. St. Louis, Missouri, was the birthplace of writer Maya Angelou, but she spent most of her childhood in Stamps, Arkansas.

● Practice 30-7, page 499

Answers: **1.** The capital of the Dominican Republic is Santo Domingo.   **3.** Some of the most important crops are sugarcane, coffee, cocoa, and rice.
5. Correct   **7.** Tourists who visit the Dominican Republic remark on its tropical beauty.   **9.** Correct

Chapter 31

● Practice 31-1, page 506

Answers: **1.** Bacteria and viruses, which we can't see without a microscope, kill many people every year.   **3.** After you're bitten, stung, or stuck, how long does it take to die?   **5.** The sea wasp is actually a fifteen-foot-long jellyfish, and although it's not aggressive, it can be deadly.   **7.** While jellyfish found off the Atlantic coast of the United States can sting, they aren't as dangerous as the sea wasp, whose venom is deadly enough to kill sixty adults.
9. Correct

● Practice 31-2, page 507

Answers: **1.** the singer's video   **3.** everybody's favorite band   **5.** the players' union   **7.** the children's bedroom   **9.** everyone's dreams

● Practice 31-3, page 509

Answers: **1.** Parents; theirs   **3.** its; weeks
5. Ryans; years   **7.** classes; Correct; your   **9.** tests

Chapter 32

● Practice 32-1, page 516

Answers: **1.** Marsupials have pouches; mothers carry their young in these pouches.   **3.** Correct
5. Many thousands of years ago, marsupials were common in South America; now, they are extinct.

● Practice 32-2, page 518

Answers: **1.** Four parks with religious themes are the Holy Land Experience, Dinosaur Adventure Land, Ganga-Dham, and City of Revelation.
3. An advertisement for Dinosaur Adventure Land describes it in these words: "where dinosaurs and the Bible meet!"   **5.** Correct

● Practice 32-3, page 519

Possible answers: **1.** In the 1950s, Bob Cousy was a star player for the Boston Celtics. Cousy (an "old man" at age thirty-four) led his team to their fifth

NBA championship in 1963. **3.** Many people still consider game 5 of the 1976 NBA finals—which the Celtics won in triple overtime—the greatest basketball game ever played. **5.** Today, young players (some joining the NBA right out of high school) dream of making names for themselves as their heroes did.

Chapter 33

● Practice 33-1, page 525

Answers: **1.** Midwest; Lake; Chicago; O'Hare International Airport; nation's **3.** north; Soldier Field; Chicago Bears; Wrigley Field; Chicago Cubs; National League baseball team **5.** John Kinzie **7.** United States; Mrs.; cow **9.** mother; Aunt Jean; Uncle Amos

● Practice 33-2, page 528

Answers: **1.** "The bigger they are," said boxer John L. Sullivan, "The harder they fall." **3.** Lisa Marie replied, "I do." **5.** "Yabba dabba doo," Fred exclaimed. "This brontoburger looks great."

● Practice 33-3, page 529

Possible answers: **1.** "I want a kinder, gentler nation," said former president George Herbert Walker Bush. **3.** Abolitionist Sojourner Truth said, "The rich rob the poor, and the poor rob one another." **5.** "If a man hasn't discovered something he will die for, then he isn't fit to live," said Martin Luther King Jr.

● Practice 33-4, page 531

Answers: **1.** Sui Sin Far's short story "The Wisdom of the New," from her book Mrs. Spring Fragrance, is about the clash between Chinese and American cultures in the early twentieth century. **3.** Interesting information about fighting skin cancer can be found in the article "Putting Sunscreens to the Test," which appeared in the magazine Consumer Reports. **5.** Ang Lee has directed several well-received films, including Crouching Tiger, Hidden Dragon. **7.** The title of Lorraine Hansberry's play A Raisin in the Sun comes from Langston Hughes's poem "Harlem."

● Practice 33-5, page 532

Answers: **1.** *Plan Nine from Outer Space* **3.** "I Have a Dream"; "Letter from Birmingham Jail" **5.** *CSI*; *CSI: Miami*; *CSI: New York*

● Practice 33-6, page 533

Answers: **1.** The ice-skating rink finally froze over. **3.** The first-year students raised money for charity. **5.** The hand-carved sculpture looked like a pair of doves.

● Practice 33-7, page 534

Answers: **1.** The doctor diagnosed a case of hypertension. **3.** Derek registered for English literature and a psychology elective. **5.** The clinic is only open Tuesday through Thursday and every other Saturday.

● Practice 33-8, page 535

Answers: **1.** Only two students in the eight o'clock lecture were late. **3.** Chapter 6 begins on page 873. **5.** Meet me at 65 Cadman Place.

Chapter 34

● Practice 34-1, page 543

Answers: **1.** weigh; Correct **3.** Correct; deceive; believing **5.** Correct; veins; Correct

● Practice 34-2, page 544

Answers: **1.** unhappy **3.** preexisting **5.** unnecessary **7.** impatient **9.** overreact

● Practice 34-3, page 546

Answers: **1.** lonely **3.** revising **5.** desirable **7.** preparation **9.** indication

● Practice 34-4, page 547

Answers: **1.** happiness **3.** denying **5.** readiness **7.** destroyer **9.** loneliness

● Practice 34-5, page 548

Answers: **1.** hoped **3.** resting **5.** revealing **7.** unzipped **9.** cramming

● Practice 34-6, page 550

Answers: **1.** effects; already **3.** buy; Correct **5.** Correct; Correct

● Practice 34-7, page 551

Answers: **1.** Here; every day **3.** Correct; conscience **5.** conscious; its

● Practice 34-8, page 552

Answers: **1.** lose **3.** no **5.** piece

● Practice 34-9, page 554

Answers: **1.** supposed **3.** Correct **5.** Correct; quiet

● Practice 34-10, page 555

Answers: **1.** Correct; to **3.** they're **5.** their

● Practice 34-11, page 557

Answers: **1.** whose; Correct **3.** where; Correct **5.** Correct; whether; Correct

Acknowledgments

Picture acknowledgments

2TL Bill Aron/PhotoEdit Inc.; **2TR** Chung Sung-Jun/Getty Images; **2BL** Tiffany Schoepp/Getty Images; **2BR** Rene Sheret/Getty Images; **28** George Doyle/Getty Images; **50** PimaCommunityCollege Website homepage. www.pima.edu/ Reprinted courtesy of Web Systems, Pima College Community; **60** Bill Aron/PhotoEdit Inc.; **62** Princess Bride 1987/Courtesy of Photofest; **70** pnc/Brand X Pictures/Jupiter Images; **72** Wolf/Laif/Aurora Photos; **80** Frank Siteman; **82** Juan Capistran, The Breaks, 2001; **92** © C. Devan/zefa/Corbis; **94** Henry Georgi/Aurora Photos; **104** Darren McCollester/Getty Images; **106** John Kraus; **120T** © Dennis MacDonald/Index Stock Imagery Inc.; **120B** © richardpasley.com; **122** Neal Boenzi/Getty Images; **130** Michael Nichols/National Geographic Image Collection; **132** Image from the Visual Thesaurus (http://www.visualthesaurus.com), Copyright ©1998–2007 Thinkmap, Inc. All rights reserved.; **142TL** Alistair Berg/Getty Images; **142TR** David Young-Wolff/Getty Images; **142BL** Ken Chernus/Photodisc Red/Getty Images; **142BR** Jeff Greenberg/PhotoEdit Inc.; **144** H. Armstrong Roberts/Robertstock; **157** Bob Daemmrich/Stock Boston, LLC; **160** Kevin Taylor; **194** Phil Schermeister/National Geographic Image Collection; **206** Elsa/Getty Images; **220** Stephen Ferry/Getty Images; **238** David Duprey/AP Images; **252** Michael Ray/Senator John Heinz History Center; **272** Peter Essick/Aurora Photos; **280** Katja Heinemann/Aurora Photos; **300** Westend61/Getty Images; **316** Bill Aron/PhotoEdit Inc.; **340** Courtesy of ACA Galleries, New York; **356** Matthew Wakem/Aurora Photos; **366** Courtesy of Michèle Gentille from www.harriettstomato.com; **380** Scott Barbour/Getty Images; **392** Scott Warren/Aurora Photos; **408** © Lisa Kahane, NYC; **434** Bridget Besaw/Aurora Photos; **446** Paul Souders; **486** Justin Sullivan/Getty Images; **504** NASA Astronaut Mae C. Jemison Space Shuttle Endeavor 1992; **514** © Bonnie Jacobs; **522** Courtesy Columbia Pictures © 2006 Columbia Pictures Industries, Inc. All Rights Reserved.; **540** Melissa Farlow/Aurora Photos; **566** Frank Herholdt/Getty Images.

Text acknowledgments

Kiku Adatto. "Trigger-Happy Birthday." From *The New York Times*. Copyright © The New York Times Company. Reprinted by permission.

Bobbi Buchanan. "Don't Hang Up, That's My Mom Calling." From *The New York Times*, December 8, 2003. Copyright © 2003 by The New York Times Company. Reprinted by permission.

José Antonio Burciaga. "Tortillas." Reprinted by permission of Cecilia P. Burciaga.

Tricia Capistrano. "Emil's Big Chance Leaves Me Uneasy." Originally published in *Newsweek*, June 19, 2006. Copyright © 2006 Tricia Capistrano. Reprinted with permission of the author.

Henry Louis Gates Jr. "Delusions of Grandeur." Originally published in *Sports Illustrated*. Copyright © 1991 by Dr. Henry Louis Gates Jr. Reprinted with the permission of the author.

Ray Hanania. "One of the Bad Guys?" Originally published in *Newsweek*, November 2, 1998. Copyright © 1998 Ray Hanania. Reprinted with permission of the author.

John Hartmire. "At the Heart of a Historic Movement." From *Newsweek*, July 24, 2000, p. 12. Copyright © 2000 Newsweek, Inc. Reprinted with permission. All rights reserved.

Macarena Hernández. "America, Stand Up for Justice and Decency." From the *Dallas Morning News*, October 15, 2005. Copyright © 2005 Dallas Morning News. Reprinted with permission of the Dallas Morning News.

Yiyun Li. "Orange Crush." From *The New York Times Magazine*, January 22, 2006. Copyright © 2006 by The New York Times Company. Reprinted by permission.

Arthur Miller. "Before Air Conditioning." Copyright © Arthur Miller. Reprinted with permission of International Creative Management, Inc.

Robb Moretti. "The Last Generation to Live on the Edge." From *Newsweek*, August 5, 2002. Copyright © 2002 Newsweek, Inc. Reprinted with permission. All rights reserved.

Pima Community College Web site homepage. www.pima.edu/ Reprinted courtesy of Web Systems, Pima College Community.

Joshua Piven and David Borgenicht. "How to Stop a Car with No Brakes (including line art)." From *Worst Case Scenario Survival Handbook: Travel* by Joshua Piven and David Borgenicht. Copyright © 2001 by book soup publishing, inc. Used with permission of Chronicle Books LLC, San Francisco. Visit www.chroniclebooks .com.

Lucie Prinz. "Say Something." Originally published in *Atlantic Monthly*, October 1996. Copyright © 1996 Lucie Prinz. Reprinted with permission of the author.

Carolyn Foster Segal. "The Dog Ate My Disk, and Other Tales of Woe." Originally published in *The Chronicle of Higher Education*. Copyright © Carolyn Foster Segal. Reprinted with permission of the author.

Thinkmap. *The Visual Thesaurus* homepage screen shot. From The Visual Thesaurus © Thinkmap, Inc. Copyright © 1998–2007 Thinkmap, Inc. Reprinted with permission. All rights reserved. www.visualthesaurus.com.

Linda S. Wallace. "A 'Good' American Citizen." Originally published in *The Christian Science Monitor*, April 1, 2003, p. 11. Copyright © 2003 by Linda S. Wallace. Reprinted with permission of the author.

William Zinsser. "The Transaction." From *On Writing Well*, Seventh (30th Anniversary) edition by William Zinsser. Copyright © 1976, 1980, 1985, 1988, 1990, 1994, 1998, 2001, 2006 by William K. Zinsser. Reprinted by permission of the author.

Index

Note: Page numbers in **bold** type indicate pages where terms are defined.

Index of Rhetorical Patterns

Correction Symbols

This chart lists symbols that many instructors use to point out writing problems in student papers. Next to each problem is the chapter or section of *Focus on Writing* where you can find help with that problem. If your instructor uses different symbols from those shown here, write them in the space provided.

YOUR INSTRUCTOR'S SYMBOL	STANDARD SYMBOL	PROBLEM
_____	adj	problem with use of adjective 28A
_____	adv	problem with use of adverb 28A
_____	agr	agreement problem (subject-verb) 22
		agreement problem (pronoun-antecedent) 27D–E
_____	apos	apostrophe missing or used incorrectly 31
_____	awk	awkward sentence structure 23, 24
_____	cap	capital letter needed 33A
_____	case	problem with pronoun case 27F–G
_____	cliché	cliché 19D
_____	coh	lack of paragraph coherence 1I; 2D
_____	combine	combine sentences 15, 17C
_____	cs	comma splice 20
_____	d	diction (poor word choice) 19
_____	dev	lack of paragraph development 1B; 2B
_____	frag	sentence fragment 21
_____	fs	fused sentence 20
_____	ital	italics or underlining needed 33C
_____	lc	lower case; capital letter not needed 33A
_____	para or ¶	indent new paragraph 1A
_____	pass	overuse of passive voice 23C
_____	prep	nonstandard use of preposition 29L–N
_____	ref	pronoun reference not specific 27E
_____	ro	run-on 20
_____	shift	illogical shift 23
_____	sp	incorrect spelling 34
_____	tense	problem with verb tense 25, 26
_____	thesis	thesis unclear or not stated 12D
_____	trans	transition needed 2D
_____	unity	paragraph not unified 2A
_____	w	wordy, not concise 19B
_____	//	problem with parallelism 18
_____	⌣	problem with comma use 30
_____	⌣	problem with semicolon use 32A
_____	" "	problem with quotation marks 33B
_____	⌒	close up space
_____	^	insert
_____	ℓ	delete
_____	∼	reversed letters or words
_____	X	obvious error
_____	✓	good point, well put